Macromedia® Studio MX 2004 All-in-One Desk Reference For Dummies®

Document-related view buttons in Dreamweaver MX 2004

Button/Tool	Name	What You Can Do
Code	Show Code View button	Enables you to view the HTML page code full-screen
Split	Show Code and Design View button	Allows you to view the HTML page code and the Document window at the same time
Design	Show Design View button	Enables you to view the Document window full-screen
	Server Debug	Runs the page through the server in the workspace window rather than in the browser
	Live Data View	Allows you to test your dynamic content in the workspace window rather than in the browser
	File Management button	Enables you to select Get to retrieve files from the Web site host or to select Put to send files to the host
	Preview/Debug in Browser button	Enables you to select to preview or debug in IE or Navigator
	Refresh	Reloads your page
	Browser Check button	Gives you access to a window that warns you of any potential anomalies that would prevent the page from displaying properly in a Web browser
	Tag Chooser button	Opens a dialog box from which you can select standard HTML, CFML and other tags to insert in your document
	View Options button	Enables you to select tools (such as Visual Aids and the Ruler) to assist you in viewing your site

Macromedia® Studio MX 2004 All-in-One Desk Reference For Dummies®

Keyboard shortcuts for opening and closing panels in Fireworks MX 2004

Panel	Keyboard Shortcut
Tools	Ctrl+F2
Properties	Ctrl+F3
Answers	Alt+F1
Optimize	F6
Layers	F2
Frames	Shift+F2
History	Shift+F10
Styles	Shift+F11
Library	F11
URL	Alt+Shift+F10
Color Mixer	Shift+F9
Swatches	Ctrl+F9
Info	Alt+Shift+F12
Behaviors	Shift+F3

Copyright © 2004 Wiley Publishing, Inc.
All rights reserved.

Item 4407-1.

For more information about Wiley Publishing,
call 1-800-762-2974.

For Dummies: Bestselling Book Series for Beginners

Macromedia® Studio MX 2004

ALL-IN-ONE DESK REFERENCE

FOR

DUMMIES®

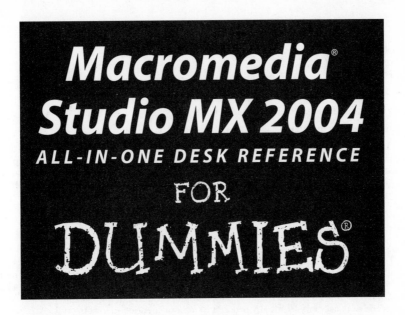

Macromedia® Studio MX 2004
ALL-IN-ONE DESK REFERENCE
FOR DUMMIES®

by Damon Dean, Andy Cowitt, Ellen Finkelstein, Doug Sahlin, and Camille McCue

WILEY

Wiley Publishing, Inc.

Macromedia® Studio MX 2004 All-in-One Desk Reference For Dummies®
Published by
Wiley Publishing, Inc.
111 River Street
Hoboken, NJ 07030-5774

Copyright © 2004 by Wiley Publishing, Inc., Indianapolis, Indiana

Published by Wiley Publishing, Inc., Indianapolis, Indiana

Published simultaneously in Canada

For general information on our other products and services or to obtain technical support, please contact our Customer Care Department within the U.S. at 800-762-2974, outside the U.S. at 317-572-3993, or fax 317-572-4002.

Wiley also publishes its books in a variety of electronic formats. Some content that appears in print may not be available in electronic books.

ISBN: 0764544071

Manufactured in the United States of America

10 9 8 7 6 5 4 3 2 1

1O/RZ/RR/QT/IN

About the Authors

Damon Dean has been working in Internet technologies and development for nearly a decade as an Editor, Producer, and Developer. As a Development Editor for Sybex, Damon was responsible for developing both the multimedia and computer game book lines. After developing those properties into profitable units, he moved on to Postlinear Entertainment, where he produced and designed online multiplayer computer games for publishers such as Sega and MGM. Three years later, Damon took his software development skills and moved into Web development. As a founding member of 415 Productions, Damon worked with several large companies, including Credit Suisse, Robert Mondavi, HP, and BART. His application design and development resume includes architecting and building Content Management Systems, Extranets, corporate Intranets, and enterprise CRMs. After four years at 415, Damon moved on in the summer of 2001 to be the Internet Services Director at a private foundation in Oakland, CA.

Damon has written several books dating back to 1996. His first book, *A Pocket Tour of Multimedia on the Internet* (Sybex), was eventually translated into five languages. In 1997, Damon began a relationship with Wiley Publishing (formerly IDG Books), and has written several books for them, including *Web Channel Development For Dummies, FrontPage 2000 For Dummies Quick Reference, Act! 2000 For Dummies Quick Reference* (Co-Author), and most recently, *Cascading Style Sheets For Dummies*.

Andy Cowitt is a freelance Web developer who spent five years learning the trade at the award-winning firm, 415, Inc. While at 415, Andy worked on multimedia presentations and Web sites for Apple, Oracle, Macromedia, the San Francisco Symphony, KQED, and Stag's Leap Wine Cellars. He's been using Macromedia's products since each of them arrived on the scene. In his spare time, Andy plays guitar and ukulele and makes videos. He lives in Oakland with illustrator Michael Wertz and their dog, Olive.

Dedication

Damon Dean: For Chris, Gatsby, and China

Andy Cowitt: For Michael Wertz and Olive

Acknowledgments

Damon Dean and Andy Cowitt: As with any book, there's a big cast of characters that help to bring it all together. First and foremost, we'd like to acknowledge the patient, thoughtful work of editors: Project Editor Paul Levesque, Copy Editor Jean Rogers, and Technical Editors, Danilo Celic, Jim Kelly, Ron Rockwell and Sheldon Sargent. Additionally, we'd like to thank Acquisitions Editor Steve Hayes, who for some reason, keeps asking us to come back and write books. I guess we miss our deadlines better than the other guys.

Damon would like to thank Craig Ziegler, Vincent James, Eric Schmidt, and Daniel Hai, all of whom work at the California HealthCare Foundation, for their support while writing this book. In addition, Damon would like to thank his friends and family, who consistently put up with his crankiness as this book got closer and closer to being completed, specifically Chris Jennings, Ryan Clifford, Matthew Allington, and of course, his parents, John Dean and Kathy Dean. He'd also like to thank his grandmother . . . just because.

Andy wishes to thank his parents, Ben and Adria Cowitt, and his extended family, with special nods to Michael Wertz, Phil Benson, and especially Damon Dean, for all their encouragement and support.

Publisher's Acknowledgments

We're proud of this book; please send us your comments through our online registration form located at www.dummies.com/register/.

Some of the people who helped bring this book to market include the following:

Acquisitions, Editorial, and Media Development

Project Editor: Paul Levesque

(Previous Edition: Kala Schrager)

Acquisitions Editor: Steven Hayes

Copy Editor: Jean Rogers

Technical Editors: Danilo Celic, Jim Kelly, Ron Rockwell, Sheldon Sargent

Editorial Manager: Kevin Kirschner

Permissions Editor: Carmen Kirkorian

Media Development Manager: Laura VanWinkle

Media Development Supervisor: Richard Graves

Editorial Assistant: Amanda Foxworth

Cartoons: Rich Tennant (www.the5thwave.com)

Production

Project Coordinator: Kristie Rees

Layout and Graphics: Seth Conley, LeAndra Hosier, Michael Kruzil, Lynsey Osborn, Julie Trippetti, Shae Lynn Wilson

Proofreaders: Carl Pierce, Evelyn Still, Brian H. Walls

Indexer: Sherry Massey

Special Help: *Teresa Artman; John Edwards*

Publishing and Editorial for Technology Dummies

Richard Swadley, Vice President and Executive Group Publisher

Andy Cummings, Vice President and Publisher

Mary C. Corder, Editorial Director

Publishing for Consumer Dummies

Diane Graves Steele, Vice President and Publisher

Joyce Pepple, Acquisitions Director

Composition Services

Gerry Fahey, Vice President of Production Services

Debbie Stailey, Director of Composition Services

Contents at a Glance

Table of Contents

Introduction

Macromedia has always been known as a leading-edge design company. Since it introduced Director more than a decade ago, Macromedia has shrewdly developed products (like Fireworks and Dreamweaver) and acquired products (such as Flash and FreeHand) geared toward turning artists into developers. With its acquisition of Allaire, Macromedia added a powerful technology platform to its suite of design-oriented products. Macromedia Studio MX 2004 represents the natural evolution and integration of the Macromedia products into a single set of Web development tools. The result? We've worked in Web development since its inception, and we can honestly say that there's never been a product that is as user friendly, powerful, and complete as Macromedia Studio MX 2004.

About This Book

Macromedia Studio MX 2004 All-in-One Desk Reference For Dummies (we know, it's a mouthful) is designed to be a hands-on, easy-to-understand guide to the features in all the Macromedia Studio products. The no-nonsense approach is designed to help you begin to build Web sites by covering the basics in a clear and concise fashion. The way we see it, you've got things to do, and reading a book, even a clever one, takes up valuable time. The faster we can help you do something or answer a question, the better.

How to Use This Book

You can use this book in a few different ways:

✦ **As a reference:** If you already have a Web site and use Macromedia Studio, this book can be a handy refresher for that thing you couldn't quite remember how to do. Whether it's exporting graphics to Macromedia Flash from FreeHand, or the right syntax for a query in ColdFusion, use this book to fill in those gaps that we all have . . . especially as we get older.

✦ **To guide you through building a Web site:** Several authors contributed to the creation of this book. All of us have a wealth of experience in the process of building Web sites. In this book, we've tried to impart as much of our collective knowledge about the processes and pitfalls of building Web sites using these tools as we can.

✦ **To learn about the tools:** In this All-in-One Desk Reference, each mini-book has at most 150 pages to cover a product or topic, which means that we get right to the point and make the topics covered easy to understand. We believe that this approach makes figuring out these products easier.

Three Presumptuous Assumptions

Before you dive in to the book, we thought we should give you some advance warning of our expectations. We know, you're the audience, so we shouldn't be presuming anything! But, just so you know where we're coming from, here are our three basic assumptions about you, the reader:

✦ **You're in a hurry.** Frankly, if you wanted a more in-depth book, you'd have picked up a regular *For Dummies* book on one or all of these products. Hence the no-nonsense, get it done, and keep on moving approach you're gonna see inside this book.

✦ **You know something about Web development.** This isn't a book where we're going to spend a lot of time talking about HTML and how it works. So you won't find a chapter anywhere in this book titled, "What the Internet Is and How It Works."

✦ **You'll experiment on your own.** The approach here is to give you quick, useful examples of how things work across all these products. In some cases, the examples can be fairly sophisticated. In most cases, though, it's the basics. Our hope is that you'll take those basic examples and build your own, more complex ones on top of that, according to the complexity of your site.

Macintosh versus Windows

Macromedia Studio is both a Windows and a Macintosh product. In this book, you see us use the Windows commands, and the figures are all showing Windows XP. The reason we chose to use the Windows version is because the ColdFusion MX 6.1 Developer Edition is included on the Windows version, but not the Macintosh version of the product. If you are using Macromedia Studio on the Mac, you can still do everything in Book VI if you're using ColdFusion at your place of business or if your Internet Service Provider (ISP) supports ColdFusion.

In general, you can convert between Windows (PC) and Macintosh key commands by using the following equivalencies:

✦ The Ctrl key on a PC is equivalent to the Cmd (⌘) key on a Mac.

✦ The Alt key on a PC is equivalent to the Option key on a Mac.

✦ The Enter key on a PC is equivalent to the Return key on a Mac.

How This Book Is Organized

Like all the All-in-One Desk References, this book's chapters are organized into minibooks. Most of the minibooks revolve around products, but one is geared toward the Web development process. The following sections describe each minibook in more detail.

Book 1: An Introduction to Building Web Sites

Before we jump into the products in the Macromedia Studio suite, we want to frame the conversation around how Web sites get built: things to consider, organizing yourself, and so on. This minibook walks you through how to figure out what it is you're really building, and how you should go about preparing to build it.

Book II: Dreamweaver MX 2004

Dreamweaver MX 2004 is the crux of any Web development effort with Macromedia Studio, so naturally, this is a good place to start. In this minibook, you get a hands-on look at how you can use Dreamweaver to create and manage your Web sites, whether they're more design-oriented (with Macromedia Flash) or technology-driven (with ColdFusion).

Book III: Fireworks MX 2004

Whereas Dreamweaver is the tool that helps you manage your Web site, Fireworks MX 2004 is designed to spur your creative vision. This minibook shows you how to use the variety of tools in this impressive program to bring the look and feel of your site to life. It also shows you how to use Fireworks in conjunction with the other Macromedia Studio products (such as Macromedia Flash) effectively.

Book IV: FreeHand MX

This is the minibook for the true illustrators. Whether the final product is a Flash-based or a traditional HTML-based site, FreeHand MX gives designers the tools they need to create compelling imagery. In this minibook, you find out how to turn your ideas into working graphical art to be used in a variety of Web applications.

Book V: Macromedia Flash MX 2004

Macromedia Flash MX 2004 is probably the most exciting of the Macromedia products. Macromedia Flash delivers animation, sound, and interactivity to the Web like no other product ever has. If you've ever wanted to find out how to use this tool to add some new zeal to your Web site, then this is the minibook for you!

Book VI: ColdFusion MX 6.1 Developer Edition

ColdFusion, once left for dead by many in the industry, now appears well poised to lead mainstream Web development into the dynamic content arena. In this minibook, you too can find out just how easy it is to use ColdFusion to create dynamic Web sites.

Book VII: Contribute 2

In this minibook, we introduce you to the newest member of the Macromedia family, Contribute 2. Designed as a collaborative tool that turns your hard development work into an easy interface for non-techies to update and publish content to the Web, Contribute puts the power of building Web sites in the hands of the people you work with. In this minibook, you find everything you need to know to get you and your collaborators up and running with Contribute in no time flat.

Icons Used in This Book

Along the way, when there's something of interest to point out, we toss in one of the icons you see in the left margins. When you see one, slow down for a moment to check it out to see what's up!

If there's a way to make something easier, or a more commonly accepted way of doing something, we tell you about it. This is the icon to look for!

When we really want to reinforce something, we throw in a Remember icon.

Pitfall ahead! That's what this icon is all about. If something could cause trouble, we let you know.

Because we love technology, you have to forgive us for geeking out every now and then. When we do, though, we let you know with this icon.

This icon highlights new features in the Macromedia Studio MX 2004 suite of products.

Where to Go from Here

If you've read this far, then you may actually be a candidate for reading this book cover to cover! From here, we suggest you dive right in to whatever section you're most interested in. Remember, all these minibooks are self-contained and don't require you to read the others. So have at it. It's buffet time, and your plate needs fillin' up!

Book I

An Introduction to Building Web Sites

The 5th Wave   By Rich Tennant

Tarzan - Lord of the Web

"...and then one day it hit Tarzan, Lord of Jungle - where future in that?"

Contents at a Glance

Chapter 1: Why Build a Web Site?

In This Chapter

✔ **Exploring the reasons that Web sites get built**

✔ **Finding your place on the Web**

✔ **Understanding what drives people to the Web**

✔ **Investigating common types of Web sites**

✔ **Getting ready to build a Web site**

So you want to build a Web site? Well, congratulations! If you're reading this book, then you've probably already purchased a copy of Macromedia Studio MX 2004, and you're ready to dive right in. Macromedia Studio is a fantastic tool that enables you to create a wide array of content and graphics to deploy on a Web site that is dynamic and easy to maintain.

But software isn't all you need in order to create a wonderful Web site. It also takes creativity, a good eye, a well-thought-out plan, and some serious soul searching about why you want to undertake this endeavor in the first place. This chapter offers some insight into how sites get built, why they are created, and who they are aimed at. So grab your pen and paper and get ready to jot down your own ideas about the great site that you want to build.

Understanding Why People Build Web Sites

In the early days of the Internet, all Web sites generally looked the same and served similar functions. Back then, an average Web site could be described as a big online book with linked pages. In short, in its infancy, the Internet was not all that interesting graphically and was severely lacking in interactive sophistication.

All that has changed. Today's Internet is a dynamic amalgam of text, graphics, interactive tools, commerce, and communication. If you are part of a business, an association, the government, or an academic institution, chances are a Web site supports some or all of the mission of the group. But not every venture requires a Web site, which naturally leads to the question, "Why build a Web site?" Most organizations and individuals establish a presence on the Internet for one or more of the following reasons:

✦ To sell a product or service directly online, as shown in Figure 1-1

✦ To provide information or tools

✦ To provide an extension of — or support for — products and services

✦ To find other organizations or people to work in a particular area of interest

✦ To introduce and promote an organization and its mission

✦ To remain competitive with other organizations that are already on the Internet

✦ To promote community development by bringing groups of people together around ideas, people, or causes, either online or in person

✦ To share artwork, writing, or photographs

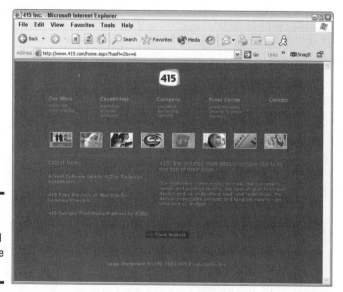

Figure 1-1:
A common product and service style Web site.

Finding Your Place on the Web

Before you begin to think about the kind of site you're going to build (either for yourself or for your organization), you should consider each of the following questions carefully. Doing so can help you target your site to an appropriate audience and prepare yourself for the work ahead.

✦ **Consider your content:**

- What is the content going to be on your site? Is it unique?

- How often will you be updating this content?

- Are there any other sites that already do what you want to do? If so, how will you differentiate your site?

Consider the early explosion of sites during the dot-com boom. At one point, more than five pet sites were all trying to hawk their wares to users. Only one survived, and that was because it was a traditional retailer first. Market saturation is a sure way to spell doom for your venture, so be sure to check out the competition first!

✦ **Select a format and interface:**

- In what formats will your content be delivered? Will you just use text and graphics, or will you also need animation and/or forms that respond to user input?

- What are the technical requirements needed to view your content? Will users need a video or audio player or plug-in? For example, to view a Flash animation, users need the Macromedia Flash Player plug-in.

✦ **Know your audience:**

- What audience or audiences are you trying to reach with this content?

- Do they need or want it?

- Is there any other place they can get this content already?

- What are the demographics and technical capabilities of this audience?

- If your site has more than one audience, are there differences between them and do they need the content delivered differently? If so, you will want to take advantage of ColdFusion's dynamic scripting language to deliver different content to different audiences.

✦ **Manage your workload:**

- How much time and effort are you willing to give in order to support this site?

- Are other people working on the site with you?

- Who's going to create the graphical design for the site? Of course, if it's you, you've got powerful tools at your disposal with Macromedia Studio MX 2004.

- Are there any deadlines you need to keep in mind when developing your site?

These questions have no right or wrong answers. Instead, they're designed to help you formulate an idea of where you're going when you're building a site. Frankly, if you're building a personal site, then these questions are moot to some degree because you can build whatever you want and it may not matter whether someone else can read it or see it. Of course, if you're thinking about selling your new products on the Web, then these questions can be critical to your overall business success, not just your Web site's success. For example, if you find that a number of other sites have similar products or a similar focus to what you had in mind for your site, you may consider not building a site at all or changing the focus of the products you are selling.

What Drives People to the Web

What kinds of services, you may be wondering, are people looking for on the Internet? Six years ago, the Internet was largely a research medium, meaning that people would hit the Internet to try to find information about something fairly academic or obscure. This is not surprising, given that universities were the first groups to start putting their content online.

Today, the number of reasons people head to the Internet has grown dramatically, and includes the following:

+ To research, compare, and purchase products

+ To find and interact with other people (business colleagues, friends, romantic interests)

+ To get daily news and information delivered in real time

+ To search for and find information about any topic or organization of interest

+ To deliver and promote their own messages and products to others on the Web

+ To watch or listen to events, online and otherwise, delivered in a variety of audio and video formats

+ To educate themselves via online classes and enrollment in universities

+ To play games and entertain themselves

+ To complete all sorts of personal and professional tasks that can now be done securely online, such as online banking, personal finance, investing, tax submission, travel, donating, and procurement

These items run the gamut of professional and personal, and they cross demographic lines. What is common among most online users, though, is that they begin their online usage with a focused purpose, and that focus then bleeds over into surfing for things that interest them throughout the Web.

Choosing the Right Type of Web Site

For all its diversity in content, the Internet really doesn't have that many different types of Web sites. Why do so many Web sites look alike? The main reason is that people want their sites to be easy to use, free (or close to it), and similar to other sites they've seen or experienced. This has resulted in the emergence of some standard types of Web sites. A number of components for these sites can be found in ColdFusion. Where applicable, we've noted it in the following list. The most common types of sites include:

✦ **The Product Site:** The most common type of site. Generally, the site offers some basic information about a company, its products, staff members, perhaps a product demo, and a way to contact the organization to get more information. Examples of this kind of site would be www.symantec.com, www.amf.com, and www.nadelectronics.com.

✦ **The Commerce Site:** A storefront on the Internet. Whether it's a single company that carries just their own specialized products or a retailer that sells a wide array of products, these sites are geared towards purchasing products and offering accessories to complement those products. An example of this kind of site would be www.macys.com. ColdFusion offers tools that can help you to add a shopping cart, a search function, and more to your site easily.

✦ **The Portal Site:** A site that aggregates content from a wide variety of sources. Portal sites tend to be rich in content and links but short on graphics. The idea is to provide users with a launching pad to other destinations on the Internet, though in recent years, many of these portals are adding features to try to keep their users on their own site. An example of this kind of site is www.yahoo.com. ColdFusion includes robust search capabilities that enable you to have more content-rich sites that are easily indexed and searched.

✦ **The News Site:** A site that, in general, mirrors an offline counterpart, such as ABC News. These sites provide a lot of the same information as their offline counterparts through the use of text, video, audio, and graphics, and also provide services geared towards the online audience, such as chat sessions, newsletters, and personalized content. An example of this kind of site would be www.cnn.com. ColdFusion includes tools for adding chat to your site as well.

✦ **The Application Site:** A type of site that offers perhaps the greatest diversity of all the sites. Application sites are geared towards a specific purpose, such as banking, investing, automobile purchasing, travel planning, photo galleries, event planning, or online greetings. Some of the commonalities among these sites include user accounts, password protection, and the widespread use of e-mail campaigns to try to keep users coming back. Examples of this kind of site include www.egreetings.com, www.imotors.com, and www.bankofamerica.com.

✦ **The Personal Site:** Personal sites also offer a great deal of variety in their design and function. Personal sites usually include some of the designer's work, opinions, and rants; links to other sites; and pictures. Examples of this kind of site would be www.loungeboy.com and www.katswindow.net.

Macromedia Studio MX 2004: Your Ally in Development

After you've answered a number of the questions in the "Finding Your Place on the Web" section, you may be wondering how you're going to build your grand Web site. Well, don't fret. With Macromedia Studio, you have the most complete, user-friendly, and popular development suite on the market. Even though professionals use these products all the time, the programs in the Macromedia Studio suite are truly designed for the first-time Web developer. With an array of tutorials, wizards, and interfaces that keep you as distant from the code as you want to be, Macromedia Studio makes the Herculean task of building powerful Web applications seem like just another project.

The goal with Macromedia Studio is to help you, the developer, build compelling and powerful Web sites in the shortest amount of time, while simultaneously helping you alleviate cost and resource issues common to Web development. Macromedia Studio includes several tools to help make this happen:

✦ **Dreamweaver MX 2004:** The premier tool for easily building Web pages. In recent versions, it has been combined with ColdFusion to make developing dynamic Web applications much easier.

✦ **Fireworks MX 2004:** A leading tool for the graphical development of a site. Fireworks helps you design the look and feel of your site, as well as prepare the graphics for inclusion in an HTML or CFML file.

✦ **Macromedia Flash MX 2004:** The world's most popular tool for adding animation and sound to Web sites. Macromedia Flash will truly change the way any site works.

✦ **FreeHand MX:** The Web developer's best friend for creating illustrations for Fireworks and Macromedia Flash.

✦ **ColdFusion MX 6.1 Developer Edition:** Give yourself the powerful tools to add databases, e-mail servers, and other dynamic elements to your site. ColdFusion allows you to take control of one of the most powerful — but also easy to learn — scripting languages for the development of compelling Web applications.

✦ **Contribute 2:** Collaborate with others and take all the development hassle out of building (and maintaining) Web sites with Contribute. Using this tool in combination with Dreamweaver will help you design Web sites in such a way that just about anyone in your organization who can use a word processing program will be able to add and modify content on the site.

Before You Start: Things to Know

Hopefully, all this information hasn't scared you into dropping this book and deciding to open a lemonade stand instead. This last section is just a quick check of some things you should be aware of before you jump into this venture called Web development:

✦ **Plan ahead.** Building a Web site always takes longer than you think, so give yourself more time than you originally planned for!

✦ **Get organized.** Remember to categorize your content and use those categories as the initial architecture for your site when you're doing the user interface design.

✦ **Always do the user interface design before the graphics design.** The user interface design specifies how your site will work, while the graphical design is the look and feel. If you do the graphics before the architecture is done, you'll likely end up redoing a lot of your design after you've figured out how your site is going to work.

✦ **Not all browsers are the same.** Internet Explorer and Netscape Navigator are the two most common browsers, and in recent versions, they've adopted the same standards. But there are still quirky differences between the two browsers, and you have to check your work on both browsers.

✦ **Not all platforms are the same.** If only they were! Explorer and Navigator work slightly differently on the Mac, in Windows, and in Unix. If you're developing on the PC, find a friend or a graphic designer with a Mac and check your work on her system as well. Dreamweaver also includes some tools to help you verify whether your site will work the way you hope it does on a variety of platforms.

✦ **Learn from sites you like.** If you like the way a page looks — but can't imagine how such a design could have been translated to the Web — you can view the source code in your browser to see how the page was constructed. Seeing how other people have coded their pages can spur you on to create your own unique designs.

✦ **Lots of stuff can be had for free.** The Web is filled with geeks like us who have made all sorts of crazy applications, like chat engines, bulletin boards, and even wholesale applications. A lot of them can be had for free or something close to it. This is where sites like `www.google.com` and `www.download.com` can be your friends.

✦ **Old content equals a dead site.** You have to be prepared to update your site on a semi-regular basis. When content is stale, people will notice, and they will stop coming.

✦ **If you build it, tell someone.** It's one thing to build a site. Site-search spiders will eventually find you, but if you really want to be seen, then you really need to promote yourself. When you're done building, remember, it's time to start promoting.

✦ **Don't be afraid to ask.** Building sites can be fun, but it can be especially frustrating if you can't figure out how to do something. Well, here's a secret: Developers like to talk about what they do. So if you're stuck, try finding a user group or searching the Web for an answer to your question. Someone may have come across the problem before, and if they haven't, then there are plenty of resources for the asking. Macromedia is also very good about supporting these kinds of groups, so you can always check out its Web site at `www.macromedia.com` for listings of developer resources.

Chapter 2: Developing Web Content

In This Chapter

✔ **Developing content: An overview**

✔ **Categorizing Web content**

✔ **Organizing your content**

✔ **Creating your content**

✔ **Prepping your content for the Web**

*O*ne of the things you find out when you do Web development for a living is that the Internet is all about repetition. No matter how many sites you build, the discussion always begins with "So, what's the content gonna be for this site?" Usually, the response is a blank stare. Companies, organizations, and individuals usually come to the conclusion that they need a Web site long before they've thought about what should be on that site.

Some basic rules of content development are common to all Web sites. This chapter gives you the basics to consider as you're doing perhaps the most important part of building your Web site: contemplating, designing, and creating your content.

Developing Content: A Four-Step Process

Developing your content strategy can be the best part of building a Web site because it's the one time you can sit around a table with your fellow colleagues (or your trusty pet, if you're building a personal site) and truly be creative about the kinds of things you want on your Web site. When you're in the throes of development, you may find yourself uttering: "Remember when we thought this was a good idea!"

Content development follows a fairly structured course in the modern world of Web design. It usually includes the following four basic steps:

1. Brainstorm the types of information that you want to include on your Web site.

2. Put that information into categories that make sense for the type of Web site you're building and the way you want users to interact with the site.

3. Gather and create the content for the site.

4. Prepare your content for the Web.

A great temptation is to just start building a site the moment something cool comes along, be it an idea, a graphic, or even words. The reason to do all this planning before even cracking any HTML code in Dreamweaver or generating any graphics in Fireworks is to make sure that you don't get too far down the path of development and suddenly find yourself backed into a corner, trying to put content where it doesn't really belong.

Choosing and Organizing Content

You may be wondering just what, exactly, is considered content. Here's a little content quiz consisting of three simple yes or no questions:

1. Is a mailing list sign-up form, as shown in Figure 2-1, considered content?

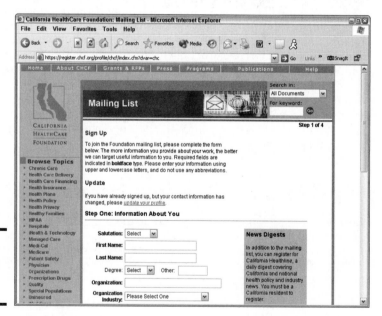

Figure 2-1:
Hmm . . .
is this
content?

2. Is a downloadable file considered content?

3. Is a picture of a product, or even of your pet ferret, considered content?

The answer to all these questions is yes. In practical terms, every single thing you put on a Web site is considered content.

Classifying common types of Web content

The fact that everything is content doesn't really help you get your site organized. Thankfully, while anything can be content, things tend to show up on Web sites in some pretty common formats.

As you begin to think about what you want to put on your Web site, you should also consider the different forms that you want that content to take. To give you a kick-start, Table 2-1 includes the most common forms of content and the data that makes up that content.

Table 2-1	Common Types of Web Site Content
Content Type	*Data Commonly Associated with This Type of Content*
Graphics	GIF and JPEG files
Documents	Word, Excel, PowerPoint, and Adobe Acrobat (PDF) files
Text	HTML text
Audio	WAV, AIFF, MP3, Real Audio, and Windows Media files
Video	QuickTime, Real Video, and Windows Video
Plug-Ins	Flash animations, QuickTime VR, IPIX, and other tools that allow users to view video and graphic content beyond what basic HTML can support
Forms	Elements within HTML designed either to submit information or to return targeted content back to a user's browser

Categorizing your content

In addition to organizing your content by its file type, assigning meaningful categories to your content makes developing your site infinitely easier. You can organize your content in any way that makes logical sense for the site you're building. Most of the time, a single piece of content can be categorized in more than one way, so don't worry about limiting yourself to just one classification method.

The following list includes some of the most common ways to categorize content:

✦ **Organizing by concept:** This varies from site to site, but this method entails organizing your site by the major thematic elements, as defined by the content that you're going to be putting up. An example of this is organizing a company site around the various products it offers.

✦ **Classifying by function:** *Functions* are things you can do on a site and can serve as organizing principles for your site. For example, a financial services company may categorize its content around a series of investing and banking tools. In fact, that financial services company may choose to categorize its content not only by the tools on the site (functions) *but also* by the various products it offers (concepts), which demonstrates that there's more than one way to slice content.

✦ **Categorizing by logical steps:** Some sites dispense with the notion of concepts or functions altogether and focus on tasks that get something done. Online auto sites, for example, like to walk visitors through a series of steps to find the car they're looking for, offering related content at appropriate points along the way.

✦ **Sorting by topics or keywords:** Sites with a diverse array of content tend to offer users a couple of ways of getting at information. Keywords (topics) are a common way to associate content with more than one area of interest. For example, a music store may organize its site by concepts such as instruments, sheet music, and accessories, *and* sort the content by topics such as pianos, drums, guitars, amplifiers, and flutes, to name just a few.

✦ **Arranging hierarchically:** This method of categorization assumes that some content elements are more important than others, which is reflected in how the content is displayed on the site. Hierarchy is often used in conjunction with another categorization scheme. To go back to the banking example for a moment, imagine that you've got your portfolio online. Usually, your portfolio is organized by concept or function, as well as by hierarchy. The portfolio is given more prominence than the other products the bank sells, because the folks at the bank know that the content in the portfolio is more important to the user.

✦ **Grouping by type:** As noted in the previous section, content type is the other major way to categorize content. On a number of media sites, such as the ABC News site (www.abcnews.com), you can easily find all the video content in a single location, in addition to being able to get your news by feature area.

Creating Content for the Web

If you've got the right tools, creating content for the Web is a breeze. And because you've got a copy of Macromedia Studio MX 2004, you've already got a host of tools that can help you create all sorts of content for your site. To recap, here is a list of some of the content you can create with the products in the Macromedia Studio suite:

✦ **Fireworks MX 2004:** Create quality photorealistic graphics that can be used in Dreamweaver or Macromedia Flash.

✦ **Dreamweaver MX 2004:** Create pages from basic HTML to complete database driven applications, as well as use the publishing tools to help you maintain your site.

✦ **FreeHand MX:** Make illustrations that can be used to create the look and feel of your Web site or your Flash movie.

✦ **Macromedia Flash MX 2004:** Create animations that bring your site to life.

✦ **ColdFusion MX 6.1 Developer Edition:** Create dynamic, database-driven applications.

✦ **Contribute 2:** Have non-technical colleagues add and modify content on the site in both the development and maintenance phases of the Web site's life.

In addition to these tools, you'll find that other non-Macromedia software tools can be essential to generating and managing content:

✦ **Microsoft Word:** Word is the most common word processor in the world for a reason. When you're creating text for Web sites, there's still no better tool out there than Word for quickly and easily creating text.

✦ **Adobe Acrobat:** The Acrobat PDF format has become the downloadable document format of choice in the Web world. If you're going to develop large, professionally-designed text- and image-heavy documents for the Web, then investing in the full version of Adobe Acrobat is worth the money. PDF files ensure that your documents will always have the same look and feel, regardless of what browser or platform users may have. Offering PDF files for download will also make your users happy because they only need to download the free Adobe Acrobat Reader to read your PDF documents.

✦ **Microsoft Excel:** As a spreadsheet, Excel can serve two very useful purposes. It can help you manage your content by providing you with a nice tool to manage your categorized data. With Excel, you can also save data in CSV format, which is the most common data format for importing into a database. So, for example, if you are providing your users with a list of the names and addresses of people in your association, then you might consider providing the information in CSV format, so that users can import the contact information directly into their own address book.

✦ **Microsoft Access (or equivalent):** Access is a database. If you create an e-commerce site, you'll find that your product data is best kept in a database, rather than in plain text. Access is the most commonly available database (though not necessarily the most robust), and is easily compatible with ColdFusion.

Prepping Content for the Web

When preparing your content for delivery to the Web, here are a few handy tips to keep in mind:

✦ **Have a plan:** If you haven't gone through the process of content development outlined previously in this chapter, your content is likely to be disorganized. Be sure you have an overview of your content, as well as an outline that shows all the various formats that your content will take and how you're choosing to categorize it.

✦ **Choose the right format:** Take a long, hard look at your content. Are you using the right format for certain types of content? Are your graphics in acceptable formats, such as GIF and JPEG? Are your downloadable items in PDF format? Be sure you're using the commonly accepted Web file formats, and if you're not, be sure to create some text to explain why you're not using standard formats.

✦ **Be consistent:** The Web relies on developers being at least somewhat consistent. So if you have a product data sheet available in PDF format, make sure that your other documents are in PDF format. Similarly, try to stick to the same audio and video formats. That way, when people get to your site, they'll know what to expect, and they're not likely to get frustrated.

✦ **Make your content more easily digestible:** One last thing to keep in mind: Just because you've written the Great American Novel and you want to put it on the Web doesn't mean that you should just put the whole thing up in one huge piece. The Web is made to deliver content in small chunks, and the best sites give viewers the facts first, and then let people delve deeper at their leisure. Remember, people are busy, and they may just need to get the facts quickly. For you as the developer, this means creating highlights, summaries, thumbnails, or charts that provide an introduction or an overview to your core content.

Chapter 3: Choosing the Right Tools for the Job

In This Chapter

✔ Developing a Web site with Dreamweaver

✔ Using Fireworks for design

✔ Creating illustrations with FreeHand

✔ Animating with Macromedia Flash

✔ Using ColdFusion to add dynamic content

✔ Maintaining your site with Contribute

You've probably heard that old saying, "A craftsman never blames his tools." Nowhere is that saying more appropriate than with Macromedia Studio MX 2004. With six incredibly powerful tools at your fingertips, you can create compelling and dynamic sites in no time flat.

Of course, even though a craftsman never blames his (or her) tools, a craftsman does need to know which tools to use for a given job, and sometimes, in the world of Web development, that's not always so clear. This chapter is designed to clarify this issue by highlighting the do's and don'ts of each of the Macromedia Studio products.

If you're already familiar with the products in Macromedia Studio, then just take a gander at the following section and then head right to Book I, Chapter 4.

Before You Begin: When Not to Use Macromedia Studio MX 2004

Although you certainly can use Macromedia Studio for every bit of your site development, some things are better done outside the tool suite:

✦ **Content development and management:** This is the process of developing the written content for the site, as well as managing the collection and status of each piece of content on the site. Products like Microsoft Word, WordPerfect, Microsoft Excel, and Microsoft Access are more appropriate tools for this job.

✦ **Project management:** This is the process of managing the steps of the project from start to finish, as well as where and how to allocate resources to the project. You may want to use Microsoft Project or Microsoft Excel to manage your project.

Using Dreamweaver MX 2004 for Web Development

No matter how graphic intensive or dynamic you want your site to be, you'll always come back to the fact that you have to build your Web site with something. In Macromedia Studio, Dreamweaver is the Web development workhorse. You can use Dreamweaver, shown in Figure 3-1, for a host of practical Web development tasks:

✦ Create and edit HTML or ColdFusion Markup Language code (or code using ASP, JSP, and the like).

✦ Create "Sites" — a confusing Dreamweaver term that means a place either locally on your computer or on a remote server where you keep all the content for your Web site. When your content is in a Dreamweaver Site, you can set up page templates and run various reports on your site content.

✦ Upload all your Web pages from your local computer to a Web server on the Internet that houses your site.

✦ Set up connections between your Web site and a database to make the site dynamic.

✦ Preview your work using Macromedia's Preview in Browser tools before you publish it on the Web.

✦ Review code for errors and badly formed code.

The best way to think of Dreamweaver is as the glue that binds your site together. Other Macromedia products like Macromedia Flash and Fireworks help to add flair and pizzazz to your site, but to actually include the files that these applications produce in your site requires the HTML and publishing tools that only Dreamweaver offers.

 Ultimately, most of your content ends up in an HTML or CFML (ColdFusion) page (or, depending on your server technology, an ASP, JSP, or other kind of page), so if you don't have Microsoft Word or WordPerfect, Dreamweaver can also be used to create content as you would in a word processing program.

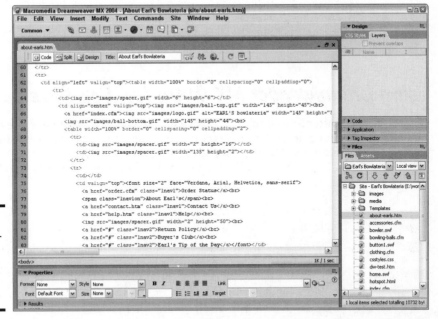

Figure 3-1:
Use Dreamweaver for many Web development tasks.

Designing with Fireworks MX 2004

Fireworks is easily the most versatile of all the tools in Macromedia Studio. As shown in Figure 3-2, Fireworks is primarily geared towards creating the graphical design of your site. With Fireworks, you can accomplish the following tasks:

✦ Create graphical elements that make up the look and feel of your site by using the Fireworks text and editing tools.

✦ Apply filters that create photo-quality effects for the imagery in your site.

✦ Manipulate text to be used in graphical elements.

✦ Use layers to manage the depth and positioning of elements on the screen during your graphics development.

✦ Slice up your page design into multiple images in preparation for integration into HTML using Dreamweaver.

✦ Use tools to optimize the size and color of images on your site.

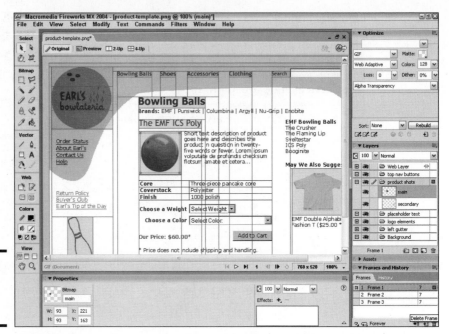

Figure 3-2:
The very
versatile
Fireworks.

These are just the core elements of Fireworks. In addition to being a powerful graphics development tool, Fireworks also incorporates elements of FreeHand, Dreamweaver, and even Macromedia Flash, providing you with additional functionality, such as the following:

✦ Creating vector images that can be used in Macromedia Flash animations.

✦ Creating basic animations and publishing your images as a Flash movie.

✦ Creating image rollovers that are common to most sites nowadays using the scripting language JavaScript.

✦ Generating the HTML to accompany your sliced images. Within the Web layer in Fireworks, you can divide an image into multiple pieces, each of which is called a *slice*. (See Book III, Chapter 6 for more information about slices.)

All told, you can use Fireworks for a variety of development tasks.

Illustrating with FreeHand MX

At first glance, with the flexibility of Fireworks, you may think that FreeHand MX is the odd man out in Macromedia Studio. Not true! Although many of the tools are identical to those you find in Fireworks, FreeHand offers illustrators and Flash animation developers a greater degree of control and integration in their work.

Some of the things that distinguish FreeHand (shown in Figure 3-3) from Fireworks include the following:

✦ A wider array of line art creation and manipulation tools

✦ Greater control of styles

✦ Better color management tools

✦ Increased integration with Macromedia Flash

✦ More import and export options

These distinctions may seem a bit subtle, and to some degree, they are. However, when you get down to the nuts and bolts of building Macromedia Flash animations, for example, you'll see that FreeHand provides nearly seamless integration with the product, offering you a more diverse palette for developing compelling animations.

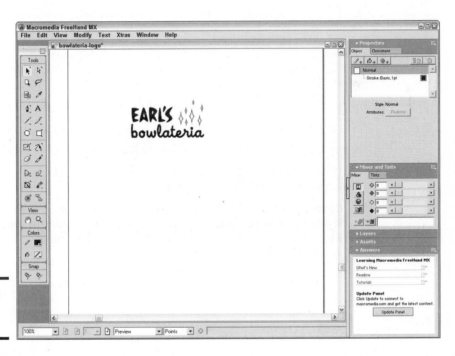

Figure 3-3:
FreeHand
in action.

Creating Animation with Macromedia Flash MX 2004

After you've got a few Web sites under your belt, you may find that HTML and graphics alone seem lifeless. Sure, they're necessary, but soon you'll begin to wonder what else you can do to add some pizzazz to your sites. That's where Macromedia Flash comes in. Macromedia Flash enables you to add animation, sound, and interactivity to your site.

Macromedia Flash, shown in Figure 3-4, can radically change the way your site works. Macromedia Flash allows you to create a more compelling user experience. Gone are the boundaries created by HTML and limited graphics. Although you still need help from the other Macromedia Studio products, you can think of Macromedia Flash as an entirely new development platform for building your site.

In order to view the Flash movies you create, visitors to your site will need to have the Flash plug-in installed in their browser. Luckily, almost everyone with a standard graphical Web browser like Internet Explorer, Netscape Navigator, or Safari has some version of the Flash plug-in installed.

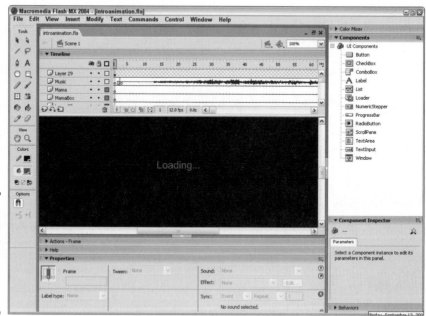

Figure 3-4:
Macromedia
Flash
changes
the way
you think
about a site.

Creating a Dynamic Site with ColdFusion MX 6.1 Developer Edition

Static HTML only gets you so far with Web development. After you've built that first-generation site, you may soon find that your Web site development needs have grown and you require more out of your development tools. What do we mean by more? Well, imagine you want to do any of the following:

✦ Customize the content of a site based on how a visitor got there.

✦ Personalize the site by letting users choose their own content.

✦ Open a store on the Internet with a host of product information contained in databases.

✦ Create interactivity in your site through the use of forms.

All these items go beyond what Dreamweaver or Macromedia Flash can provide as development tools. After you hit this proverbial Web development wall, it's time to turn to ColdFusion, which provides the following tools:

✦ A custom scripting language that enables you to query databases, create and test variables, and extend the functionality of your site through the use of specific ColdFusion tags and functions. For more information about ColdFusion's scripting language, be sure to check out Book VI.

✦ An application server (a program on a computer that serves a specific function) that reads the custom scripting language and turns it into HTML that people can see in their browser.

✦ An administrative component that enables you to configure all the different elements of your site, such as databases, virtual directories, log files that capture site tracking information, and e-mail features.

Managing Your Site with Contribute 2

By adding Contribute 2 to the Macromedia Studio family, Macromedia provides developers with a new tool to help them manage the content on their sites. Designed for the lay person, Contribute allows you to manage a handful of Web development tasks quickly and easily, including:

✦ Creating and editing Web pages on a site

✦ Adding images and links to a page

✦ Creating tables and text

✦ Publishing pages to a Web site

Now, you may be thinking that sounds an awful lot like what you do with Dreamweaver. In fact, Contribute, in a nutshell, is a tool that allows users to accomplish Dreamweaver-like tasks without jeopardizing any of the underlying code structure of a Web site. That goes for both site development and site maintenance.

During the development phase, if your site has many pages that share an identical design but need different content, the HTML developer can create a Dreamweaver template of the design, and non-technical colleagues can create multiple pages based on the template using Contribute, each page with its own content but all with a protected common layout.

When the site is up and running, Contribute allows people with no knowledge of HTML to make changes to content on the site. And built-in safeguards prevent two (or more) people from making changes to the same page at the same time.

Chapter 4: Best Practices for Web Development

In This Chapter

✔ **Understanding the basic steps of development**

✔ **Setting your site requirements**

✔ **Ensuring a smooth Web site build**

✔ **Testing your site**

✔ **Involving the right people at the right time**

*T*he late-night, caffeine-fueled, build-it-as-you-go model of Web development was fine when the industry was just getting started. However, Web development today is a more standardized practice and is subject to repeatable processes, just like other areas of software development. The result of the growing maturity in the industry is a set of "best practices" for Web development. Think of a *best practice* as an industry-accepted, commonly-agreed-upon way of performing a task or set of tasks.

Certainly, you can still build a Web site in more than one way. Best practices are designed just to give you some guidance in the following areas:

+ Ensuring that the site is easy to build and easier to maintain

+ Helping you avoid doing unnecessary work on a site

+ Confirming that your Web site is built according to industry standards

+ Making certain that you have the right people involved in the site development at the right time

Each of the sections of this chapter deals with a common aspect of Web development and provides you with the key points for making that part of the development run smoothly.

You should be aware that these tips and suggestions are not absolutes. Every site is a bit different, but you can use this chapter as a checklist guide for the kinds of things you *can* do. Your site may require more or less attention depending on your requirements.

Additionally, this chapter is limited to the general best practices for developing sites. Each of the chapters within Book II through Book VII covers the best way to perform operations with each of the individual Macromedia Studio MX 2004 products.

Following the Best Path of Development

The early days of Web sites saw a wide variety of methods and approaches to development, but today most common types of Web sites follow an accepted path from start to finish. Building a Web site takes six basic steps. The details within each step can be specific to the type of site you're building — product site, e-commerce site, and so on — but the basic steps remain the same.

Step one: Develop a site concept

Before you can build a site, you must have a mission and purpose for it. This process involves asking yourself and your colleagues a number of questions about whom you're trying to reach and why. Book I, Chapter 1 includes more information on this process.

Step two: Define your requirements

After you've decided what your site is all about, you need to come up with some basic requirements for the site. *Requirements* are the minimum standards that the site must conform to. These requirements break out along the following categories:

✦ **Feature requirements:** The basic set of site features and what those features need to accomplish.

✦ **Technical requirements:** The minimum technical specifications for the site. Table 4-1 includes the common technical requirements for Web sites.

✦ **Design requirements:** The aesthetic and accessibility requirements for the site. Design requirements may include things such as using the proper corporate colors, and accessibility requirements generally include things like adding a text-only version of a site so that it can be read by text readers (browsers designed for the visually impaired).

Table 4-1	Common Technical Requirements for Web Sites
Requirement	*Best Practice Option*
Screen resolution	800 x 600 pixels
Minimum browser support	Internet Explorer 5.0 and Netscape Navigator 6
Use of Web safe colors only	No longer required, as almost all monitors can display 16-bit color

Requirement	Best Practice Option
Minimum connection speed	56 kilobits per second (Kbps)
File extensions	Should still conform to the standard "dot and three characters" (`.htm`, `.cfm`, `.asp`, `.jsp`) where possible
Style sheets (Yes or No)	Yes
Dynamic HTML (Yes or No)	Yes
Web phone and PDA accessibility	No
Database of choice	Microsoft SQL Server

Step three: Generate content

During this step, you work to generate the various types of text, images, and so on that will make up the content of your site. Book I, Chapter 2 covers the details of generating content for Web sites.

Step four: Design the site

This step covers four different aspects of design, and in general, they follow this sequence:

1. **Complete the feature design.**

   In the second step of Web site development, you set out the requirements for features on the site. Here, you get down to the nitty-gritty and design exactly how those features will work. For example, if you want to collect mailing list information, you need to articulate precisely how the information is captured, what kind of response is sent to a user, and where the captured information goes.

2. **Work through the user interface design.**

   The user interface design is the way the site works, minus the aesthetics. It includes the composition of pages, the structure and look of the content, and it applies the logic of the feature design above.

3. **Consider the graphics design.**

   After the feature and user interface design are complete, your site is ready for the aesthetics. You may want to create graphics for logos, icons, navigation, sidebars, backgrounds, and other site elements.

4. **Complete the technical design of the site.**

   Truth be told, you can do the technical design after you complete the user interface design, but usually it ends up being the last design step. You must design the technical components that enable all the features of the site to be realized.

Step five: Build the site

After you've completed the design step, you're ready to start building the site. This includes generating all the code, supporting databases, generating HTML, and posting content. Building the site can take weeks, and you should keep a number of basic rules of development in mind when building your site. Here are the most critical ones:

✦ **Work internally.** Don't do all your development work on the site for everyone to see. Be sure to work on the site either internally (on your corporate network or your personal machine) or on a different URL than the final address. This way you can make all the mistakes you like and the real world isn't likely to see them.

✦ **Go wide, then deep.** A good strategy is to always build the structure of the site first, including the navigation, and then fill it in with the content within individual sections. Figure 4-1 shows the navigational structure of a typical site, with primary navigation running across the top and secondary navigation running down the left. Primary navigation allows visitors to get to the main sections of the site, while secondary navigation allows visitors to "drill down" to specific pages in the section.

✦ **Centralize your images.** Centralizing your images makes finding images and generating the proper code that much easier. The norm is to include all images in a folder called `images` at the root level of your site.

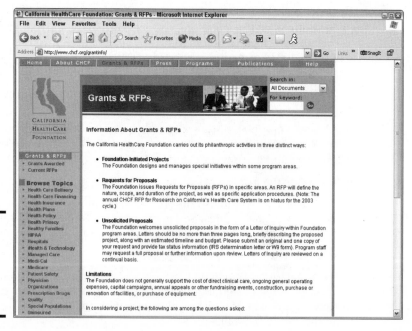

Figure 4-1:
The typical inverted L shape of a site's navigation.

✦ **Whenever possible, use relative paths.** Using a *relative path* simply means that your links from one file to another within your site — HTML files, images, PDFs, and so on — are relative to the location of the file you're currently working on. This makes changing links and moving things around in folders that much easier. Dreamweaver defaults to using relative paths. An absolute path (for example, `http://www.mysite.com/section/page.htm`) includes the site's URL, which is not only cumbersome but also difficult to use during development.

✦ **Keep filenames simple.** Always keep your filenames in lowercase letters, and don't include spaces in filenames, folder names, or URLs. This ensures that no matter what type of Web server your site is hosted on — Windows, Macintosh, or Unix — the files can be read by any Web browser.

✦ **Use folders to segment your content.** This provides your site with a structure that makes finding and managing your content and code easier.

✦ **Always comment your code.** Commenting code is a common software development practice. As you're writing your code, you add comments next to major features and functions so that someone else can understand your work if you're not there to explain it to them. Browsers ignore comments when displaying the page (but you can see comments, if they're in the code, by using your browser's View Source command). If the code is logically laid out with comments, managing it is much easier. Figure 4-2 shows what commented code looks like in Dreamweaver MX 2004. HTML comments always appear in this format: `<!-- comment here -->`. JavaScript, ColdFusion, and other types of Web code each have their own comment conventions.

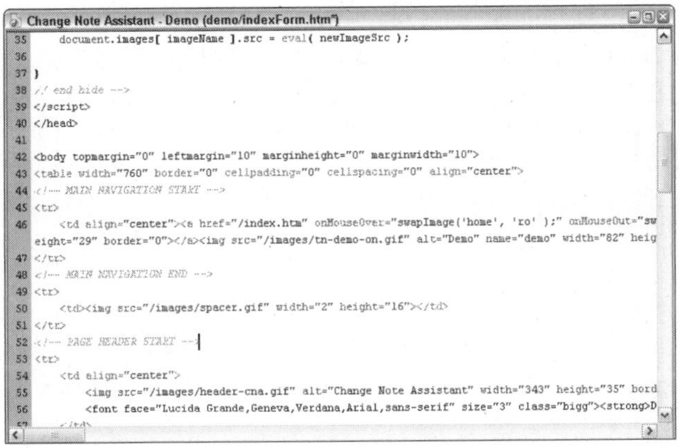

Figure 4-2:
Always
comment
your code!

✦ **Do everything you can to protect your applications.** Hacking is serious business, and the last thing you want to have happen is for your site to be compromised. Here are just some of the things you can do to ensure that your site is designed with security in mind:

- Always use digital certificates when sending users private information over the Internet. A *digital certificate* is a secure, encrypted digital key that ensures that only the user's Web browser and the server that issued the key can see the data being transmitted back and forth. You can find out more about digital certificates at `www.verisign.com`.

- If you're doing e-commerce, don't use Microsoft Access. Access isn't nearly as secure as Microsoft's SQL Server.

- Never query a database directly for a user's private information, such as username, password, or credit card numbers. With SQL, you can use stored procedures to query a database and mask the code from potential hackers. While stored procedures are outside the scope of this book, you can read more about them in Anthony T. Mann's *Microsoft SQL Server 2000 For Dummies*, published by Wiley Publishing, Inc.

- Always try to build your applications in three tiers. A three-tiered application, the concept of which is shown in Figure 4-3, ensures that the business logic for your site is separate from your display code and your database logic. This is more secure, *and* it makes changing components of your Web application easier because of the modular nature of a three-tiered application.

  In the three-tiered model, the Web browser can only talk to an intermediary application or object (sometimes called a COM object) and can only pass a finite set of variables to this intermediary. In turn, the intermediary negotiates with the data layer to retrieve only the specified information, which it passes back to the display layer. This ensures that the end user can't directly connect to the data layer.

✦ **Set up a mechanism for sharing files.** When you're working on the same files with more than one person, set up a convention for sharing the files, so as to avoid overwriting each other's work. Dreamweaver comes with some source control tools that help in this process, as does Contribute, but you may not want to rely just on their built-in protections. You should have an agreed-upon procedure for working on the same files.

Step six: Test and deploy your site

Before you can launch your site, you need to test it. Although test plans vary depending upon the sophistication of the site, here are four good things you should do when testing your site:

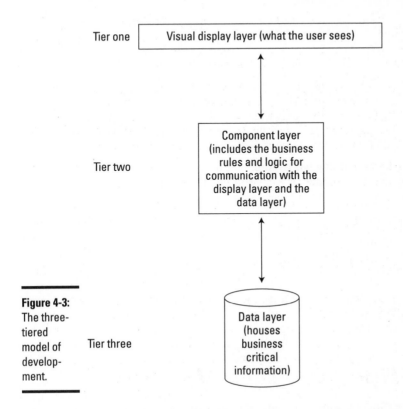

Tier one   Visual display layer (what the user sees)

Tier two   Component layer
(includes the business
rules and logic for
communication with the
display layer and the
data layer)

Tier three   Data layer
(houses
business
critical
information)

Figure 4-3:
The three-
tiered
model of
develop-
ment.

✦ **Check your site on multiple browsers.** Testing your site on various current and previous versions of browsers ensures that it works for the largest possible number of users. You should also check on different platforms as well (PC and Mac at the least).

You can get old versions of the Netscape browser at `http://wp.netscape.com/download/archive.html?cp=dowarc` and old versions of Internet Explorer at `www.oldversion.com/program.php?n=msie`. You can find a wide variety of old versions of many browsers at `http://browsers.evolt.org`.

✦ **Try your site with different Web connections of varying download speeds.** If you're building your site at work, you may have a very fast Internet connection. Try viewing and navigating your site using a dial-up 56 Kbps connection to see how well your site loads at that speed. If pages load within a few seconds, then your site is in good shape.

✦ **Test all of your forms and features.** Walk through each form, again preferably on multiple browsers and operating systems, to ensure that all your tools and forms work properly.

✦ **Enlist your friends and colleagues as site testers.** The more people that look at your site, the better. You're probably too close to the site by the time you've finished it anyway, and fresh eyes can see things you can't. Also, other people are likely to give you good feedback on structure and ease of use.

After you've finished testing your site, which generally takes at least a week, you should give yourself at least another week to fix any problems you've found during the testing phase.

When you're ready to roll out your site, a good idea is to do a soft launch first. A *soft launch* is when you launch a site but don't really tell anyone about it. People who already know something about you or may be looking for your site will start to check it out and may provide you with some additional feedback. But you won't be faced with a big barrage of people, and you'll have a chance to troubleshoot anything you may have overlooked in making the jump from working on a site internally to having a site out there live for the real world.

Getting the Right People at the Right Time

If you're building a site on your own, then you are always the right person at the right time. In most cases, however, you're building a site with a group of people. Some of these people are site builders, and others are around to approve content and give general direction. Keeping all the parts moving smoothly can be tricky. The following sections help you get the right people on board at the right time.

Building a team

Just how big is this project you're working on? How much money do you have to spend? When do you need it done? The answers to these three questions let you know just how big of a team you may need to build to complete your site. If you plan to assemble an internal team to build your site, these are the roles that you absolutely need:

✦ **Producer:** Perhaps this is you. The producer (sometimes also referred to as a Project Manager) manages all the resources of the project, internal and external. This means keeping the master budget and schedule, and providing all the resources with their tasks and deadlines. Largely overlooked, the producer is the conduit that keeps the project moving from start to finish.

+ **Programmer:** Programmers come in all shapes and sizes. Some can only do HTML, while others are adept at building all sorts of software applications. If you've got a smaller project, you should only need one programmer (who might also go by the title Engineer or Integrator), but if your project is larger, you should consider having an integrator for lower-level HTML coding and a senior programmer for more complex coding tasks.

+ **Designers:** Again, if you're building a smaller site, you can probably get away with having a designer who does both user interface design and graphical design. Alternatively, as the producer, you're probably qualified to handle the user interface duties as well as fill the feature design role. The larger the site, the more you'd want to look at separate specialists for user interface and graphical design.

+ **Content Specialists:** Generating content is always overlooked in building a team. Whether you have a contract writer or someone internal to your organization who is good at collecting and synthesizing data, it's always a good idea to have someone around dedicated to developing content for the site.

+ **Quality Assurance:** Someone's gotta test the site, and as we mention previously, you're probably not the ideal person to do it. The best testers are meticulous, accountant-types who like to poke and prod at things and find holes. A lot of times, this function can be contracted out.

+ **Approvers:** Unless you're building the site for yourself, then you're probably accountable to someone. Those would be your approvers, and yes, they're an essential part of the team, because ultimately, they are the ones who give you the yea or nay on whether your site gets up on the Internet!

If you were to contract out these resources through a single firm or through a variety of independent contractors, you'd still be looking for each of these skill sets. The method of employment doesn't really matter, though it's worth noting that it's generally cheaper to contract the resources yourself. Firms, on the other hand, offer complete teams, tried-and-true processes, and an existing code base (prewritten and tested code) that you don't generally get when you build an internal team from scratch.

Involving the right people at the right time

Knowing when to get people involved can be tricky. Ideally, you'd want everyone there all the time, but that can get expensive, so you want to get people on board at the right time for the right tasks. Table 4-2 includes many of the key milestones in a Web development project and who you really need to have involved during those parts of the process.

Table 4-2	When to Involve People in the Web Development Process
Key Milestone	*Who's Involved*
Site Conceptualization	Everyone
Requirements Gathering	Producer, Designers, Programmers, and Approvers
Generating Content	Producer, Content Specialists, User Interface Designers, and occasionally Graphic Designers and Programmers
Feature Design	Producer, User Interface Designer, and Programmers
User Interface Design	Producer and User Interface Designer
Graphic Design	Producer, Graphic Designer, Programmers, and Approvers
Build Phase	Everyone
Test and Deploy	Producer, Quality Assurance, Programmers, Approvers, and occasionally Designers

Book II

Dreamweaver MX 2004

The 5th Wave   By Rich Tennant

"What I'm looking for are dynamic Web applications and content, not Web innuendoes and intent."

Contents at a Glance

Chapter 1: Introduction to Dreamweaver MX 2004

In This Chapter

✓ **Exploring the new Dreamweaver MX 2004 interface**

✓ **Choosing between Design view and Code view**

✓ **Choosing among Standard, Expanded Table, and Layout modes**

✓ **Examining your site with the Files panel**

✓ **Exploring toolbar buttons**

✓ **Using panels and inspectors**

✓ **Getting help**

*I*f you're looking for a Web design tool that's both easy enough for beginners and sophisticated enough for Web design gurus, you've come to the right place. Dreamweaver MX 2004 from Macromedia is a powerful program that enables you to create almost any type of Web page. This chapter covers the Dreamweaver basics and introduces you to some of the program's essential tools.

Dreamweaver is the industry standard for Web site design and production. Whether you're interested in creating a site for fun, such as an online photo album or a site devoted to one of your hobbies, or for business, such as an online store, Dreamweaver's flexible interface provides simultaneous graphical and HTML editing. In other words, using Dreamweaver, you can not only lay out pages like an artist, you can also fine-tune the associated code like a programmer. Additionally, Dreamweaver's built-in FTP features enable you to upload your site to the Web in a snap, so that you can share your masterpieces with the world.

Exploring the New Dreamweaver MX 2004 Interface

With Dreamweaver MX, Macromedia integrated ColdFusion and HomeSite into one single, powerful interface, though you had the choice of working with that new interface or with the old Dreamweaver 4 interface (or, in Macromedia parlance, workspace). With Dreamweaver MX 2004,

Macromedia dropped the Dreamweaver 4 workspace and allows you to choose from only two versions of the Dreamweaver workspace: Designer style and HomeSite/Coder-Style.

Selecting a workspace on start-up

When you start Dreamweaver for the first time, you're asked to choose the way you want your workspace set up, as shown in Figure 1-1. You have two options:

Figure 1-1:
The Workspace Setup dialog box appears when you start Dreamweaver for the first time.

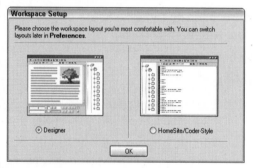

+ **Designer:** The WYSIWYG (What You See Is What You Get) interface, which shows the page you are working on much like it would be in a Web browser. This style is more appropriate for Web design novices working on basic HTML pages.

+ **HomeSite/Coder-Style:** The style that shows the page you are working on as an editable text document, which is appropriate for experienced coders and for pages on which you're editing ColdFusion Markup Language (CFML) or other dynamic code.

You can switch between the two styles, or even combine them, at the click of a button. See the "Introducing the Document Window" section, later in this chapter, for details.

Introducing the new Start page

After you've selected a workspace, when you launch Dreamweaver by double-clicking its icon on the desktop or by selecting it from the Windows Start menu, you'll see something new to Dreamweaver: a Start page, as shown in Figure 1-2. The Start page allows you to perform the following tasks with a single click of your mouse:

✦ **Open pages you've recently edited:** Simply click the file name of the page you want to open.

✦ **Create a new page in one of seven formats:** Simply click the type of page you want to create, from basic HTML to ColdFusion (CFML) to CSS (Cascading Style Sheet).

✦ **Create a new Dreamweaver Site:** Click the Dreamweaver Site icon (in the Create New column) to open the Site Definition wizard, which guides you through the process of setting up the directory location, FTP information, server technology (if applicable), and more for your Web site. See Book II, Chapter 3 for details on Dreamweaver Sites.

✦ **Create a new page based on Dreamweaver's built-in samples:** Click an option in the Create from Samples column to open the New Document dialog box and choose from the preset formatting options for that type of page.

The Start page also gives you fast access to a quick tour and set of tutorials for Dreamweaver, and to Macromedia's Dreamweaver Exchange page, where you can find lots of nifty widgets that extend Dreamweaver's capabilities.

If you find the Start page incompatible with your working methods, you can prevent it from appearing in the future by selecting the Don't Show Again check box at the lower-left corner of the page.

Book II
Chapter 1

Introduction to
Dreamweaver
MX 2004

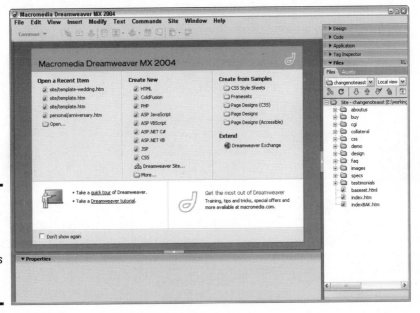

Figure 1-2:
The Start Page gives you one-click access to a variety of options.

Introducing the Document Window

Your primary workspace in Dreamweaver is the Document window, which appears automatically when you open a page in Dreamweaver. In the Document window, you construct your individual Web pages using panels and dialog boxes to format your work. The three primary views in Dreamweaver are as follows:

✦ **Design view:** The graphical view of your document, as shown in Figure 1-3. You can select this view by choosing View➪Design.

✦ **Code view:** This view shows the underlying code of your document. You can select this view by choosing View➪Code.

✦ **Split view:** As you may expect, this is a split screen view that includes both the Code and Design windows. You can select this view by choosing View➪Code and Design.

You can toggle between these views easily at any time by clicking their corresponding buttons at the top left of the Document window.

Code View button

Code and Design View button   Design View button

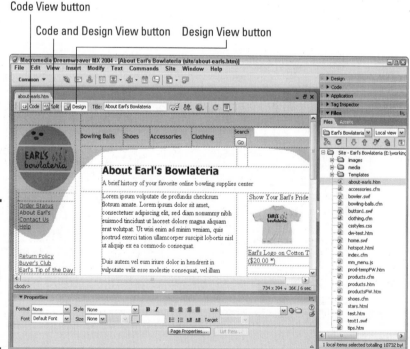

Figure 1-3: The Design view approximates what your page looks like in a Web browser.

When you have several documents open in a site, you can select which document you want to work on by clicking the document's name at the top of the Dreamweaver Document window. You can also click the Site tab in the Files panel to work on an entire site.

The Insert bar sits directly underneath Dreamweaver's main menu. It gives you quick access to eight sets of buttons you can use to insert everything from tables to Flash movies to form elements in your page. To select one of the eight categories, click the Insert bar's name (Common, Layout, and so on) and choose a new category from the drop-down list.

Choosing among Standard, Expanded Table, and Layout Modes

You can view content in your Document window using the Standard mode, the Expanded Table mode, or the Layout mode. The Standard mode is the default (Figure 1-3 shows a page in Standard mode, with the Insert bar set to Common). The Expanded Table mode makes it easier for you to select tables and cells (though if you want to resize the table or row or column, you need to do so in Standard mode). The Expanded Table mode is most useful for editing existing tables. The Layout mode provides a simpler interface for drawing and editing tables and table cells.

Two special tools are available only when working in Layout mode: the Draw Layout Cell button and the Draw Layout Table button. A table created with the Draw Layout Table tool is shown in Figure 1-4. Both of these tools can help you generate tables or table cells quickly and easily in Dreamweaver, and are described in more detail in Book II, Chapter 2.

To change to the Layout mode, select the Layout Insert bar at the top left of the Document window and click the Layout Mode button, or choose View⇨Table Mode⇨Layout Mode, or use the keyboard shortcut Ctrl+F6. When you're in Layout mode, press Ctrl+F6 or click the Layout Mode button to return to Standard mode.

To change to Expanded Table mode, select the Layout Insert bar at the top left of the Document window and click the Expanded Table Mode button at the top of the Document window, or choose View⇨Table Mode⇨Expanded Table Mode, or use the keyboard shortcut F6. When you're in Expanded Table mode, press F6 or click the Expanded Table Mode button to return to Standard mode. *Note:* The Expanded Table mode is not available in the Code View.

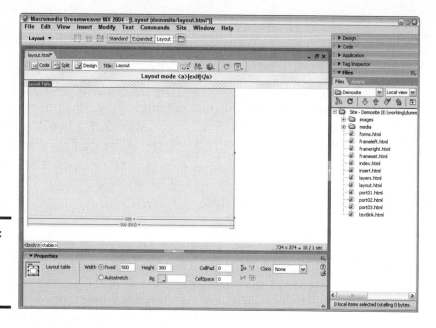

Figure 1-4:
A table drawn in Layout mode.

Examining Your Site with the Files Panel

Dreamweaver offers Web developers the opportunity to work on individual files that make up a Web site, as well as to manage their entire Web site, all through the Dreamweaver interface. This concept is called, not surprisingly, a *Site*; to avoid confusion, we call them *Dreamweaver Sites*. Dreamweaver Sites can include the following elements:

✦ HTML, CFM, ASP, and other files that make up the code of the site

✦ Graphics, such as GIF and JPEG files

✦ Documents, such as PDF files and DOC files

✦ Directories (folders that might contain any of the above)

Dreamweaver Sites are initially viewable within the Files panel (which is open by default; if the Files panel is not open, you can open it by pressing F8). To expand the Files panel so it fills your screen, or to collapse the panel back to panel size, click the Expand/Collapse button (the icon of the two-row, two-column box with an arrow in the middle, at the right of the panel).

The Web site management tools for Dreamweaver Sites are designed to give you total control over the way in which your Web site is built and maintained from your local computer. The key features of the Dreamweaver Site tools include:

✦ Asset management tools that help you manage all the files that make up your site. For example, these tools keep track of all your files and the links between files. Anytime you move a file, the tools will change the related links in other files.

✦ Basic source control to ensure that files don't get overwritten. These tools lock files so that when you're working on a particular file, others on your team can't edit that same file.

✦ Publishing tools that allow you to use FTP to upload the content from your site locally to the remote server where the site is housed.

✦ Utilities that create site maps, check links, check the HTML code, and run reports on who's been working on what.

Dreamweaver Sites are covered in more detail in Book II, Chapter 3.

Exploring Toolbar Buttons

Dreamweaver provides you with a number of useful view buttons (shown in Figure 1-5 and Figure 1-6) that you can use to see different views of your site or to perform various functions. You can easily switch among views to examine your site in different ways. Each Dreamweaver view offers specialized menus and tools to help you perform your work in that view. Certain views are available for an individual document or page, whereas other views are available for the entire site. At any time while you work, you can choose to preview your site in target Web browsers, which enables you to see your site from the user's perspective.

Refresh button

Get File(s) button

Put File(s) button

Figure 1-5:
The Files tab
of the Files
panel
includes
useful
buttons.

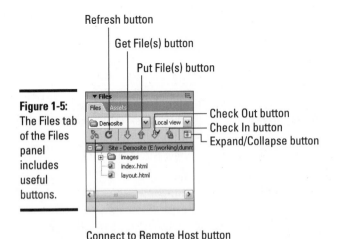

Check Out button
Check In button
Expand/Collapse button

Connect to Remote Host button

Figure 1-5 shows the following site-related buttons from the Files panel:

✦ **Connect to Remote Host button:** Connects your local computer and your Web host, allowing you to transfer files between the two computers.

✦ **Refresh button:** Refreshes the panel's view of files in the site if you've made a change to file names or file structures outside of Dreamweaver while the program was open.

✦ **Get File(s) button:** Downloads (retrieves) documents and files from the host.

✦ **Put File(s) button:** Uploads (sends) documents and files to the host.

✦ **Check Out File(s) button:** Locks files for editing by a single individual.

✦ **Check In button:** Replaces files on the server and makes them available for editing by unlocking them.

✦ **Expand/Collapse button:** Makes the Site tab full-screen with remote and local files side-by-side.

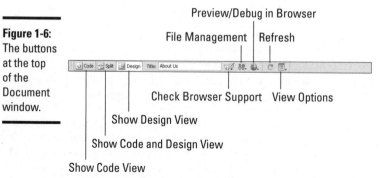

Figure 1-6: The buttons at the top of the Document window.

Figure 1-6 shows the following document-related buttons from the top of the Document window:

✦ **Show Code View button:** Enables you to view the HTML page code full-screen.

✦ **Show Split View button:** Allows you to view the HTML page code and the Document window at the same time.

✦ **Show Design View button:** Enables you to view the Document window full-screen.

✦ **Check Browser Support button:** Allows you to run a check on your code for browser compatibility.

✦ **File Management button:** Click and then select Get to retrieve files from the Web site host or select Put to send files to the host.

✦ **Preview/Debug in Browser button:** Click and select to preview or debug in your browser(s).

✦ **Refresh button:** Reloads your page so changes to the code are reflected in the Design view.

✦ **View Options button:** Click to select options (such as Word Wrap in Code View and the Ruler in Design view) to assist you in viewing your page.

Some of these items may be unavailable, depending on what view you're in and what you have selected in a document or panel.

Using Panels and Inspectors

You can use Dreamweaver panels and inspectors to enter details about all aspects of your Web site. These interfaces offer areas where you can add and format page features, set up navigation and behaviors, and manage the workflow of building your site.

Understanding the role of panels

A *panel* typically provides information about all instances of a particular page feature. For example, the Layers panel lists information about all the layers on the current page.

The Tag Inspector panel gives you easy access to various properties and behaviors specific to what object you have selected on your page. The Tag Inspector panel updates continually, depending on what you have selected on your page (if you have nothing selected on the page, the panel displays properties and behaviors of the whole page itself, as shown in Figure 1-7). Note that the Tag Inspector panel's name reflects the tag being inspected.

To switch among tabs in a panel, just click the tab names.

Figure 1-7: The Tag Inspector panel with general page properties displayed.

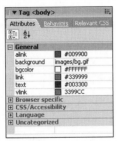

You can dock, expand, and collapse panels. See the section on customizing your work environment in Book III, Chapter 1 for information on working with panels.

Working with the Properties panel

The Properties panel, like the Tag Inspector panel, changes based on the individual document object you have selected on your page and contains details on attributes of the object. For example, selecting text on a page opens the Text Property inspector in the Properties panel, where you can format the size, font, color, link, and other attributes of the text. (Figure 1-4 shows the Properties panel with a Layout Table selected.) To make certain that the Properties panel is shown below the Document window, choose Window⇨Properties.

The Properties panel has a small down arrow in the lower-right corner, called an Expander button. Click the button to enlarge the Properties panel to view additional formatting options. In an expanded Properties panel, click the small up arrow in the lower-right corner to collapse the panel.

Getting Help

Dreamweaver offers a variety of tools to help you find the answer to virtually any question you have about the program. The Help tools provide basic information for beginners, as well as advanced references detailing HTML and JavaScript code.

You can get help by clicking the Help button — the small question mark — in the top-right corner of some panels. Similarly, you can open the Options menu in the top-right corner of any panel and select Help from the list.

You can also access help by using the Help menu located on the main menu. Just choose Help and then select one of the following options:

✦ **Getting Started and Tutorials:** Gives you quick access to basic information to get you up and running quickly, as well as to step-by-step tutorials where you can learn by doing.

✦ **Using Dreamweaver:** Provides definitions and itemized steps in performing routine Dreamweaver tasks. It contains Help Contents, Index, and Search categories.

✦ **Using ColdFusion:** Provides information about coding dynamic sites using ColdFusion technology.

✦ **Reference:** Opens the Reference tab of the Code panel offering a dictionary-style reference on CSS, HTML, Accessibility requirements, Sitespring tags, and JavaScript. You can also access the Reference tab of the Code panel by clicking the Reference button in the Document window.

✦ **Extensions:** Provides assistance in performing more advanced Dreamweaver tasks, especially tasks involving the integration of adjunct programs, such as Macromedia Flash, with Dreamweaver. This help option contains nitty-gritty information about application programming interfaces (APIs) — specific software interfaces that allow you to integrate Dreamweaver with databases, the C and Java programming languages, and much more.

✦ **Dreamweaver Support Center, and Macromedia Online Forums:** Connects you to the Web, where you can find constantly updated information on working with Dreamweaver, answers to Frequently Asked Questions, and program extensions. You can also join a developer's forum, where you can chat with other Dreamweaver users to get (and give) help.

Book II
Chapter 1

Introduction to
Dreamweaver
MX 2004

Chapter 2: Creating Basic Web Pages

In This Chapter

✔ **Setting ruler and grid options in the Document window**

✔ **Creating and opening pages**

✔ **Establishing page properties**

✔ **Working with text**

✔ **Working with images**

✔ **Adding links**

✔ **Working with tables**

✔ **Previewing your work**

The most significant (and, fortunately, the easiest) process in building a Web site is creating the individual pages that convey the site's content. Even if you plan on creating an ultra-hip site chock full of animation and interactive forms, you spend the vast majority of your site-building effort constructing basic Web pages comprised of words and images. This chapter shows you how to set up, color, and name individual Web pages. You also discover how to add basic elements, such as text, graphics, and tables, to your pages.

Setting Ruler and Grid Options in the Document Window

Dreamweaver offers you complete control over how you work in the Document window by providing two guide tools — rulers and a grid — to help you lay out your work accurately. You can customize a variety of guide tool attributes, such as ruler increments and grid snapping, to suit your personal preferences and speed Web page development.

Here's a brief look at all your options with rulers and grids:

✦ **Turning rulers on and off:** Using rulers — both horizontal and vertical — in the Document window can help you measure and position page elements. Toggle the rulers on and off by choosing View⇨Rulers⇨Show or by pressing Ctrl+Alt+R.

✦ **Moving and resetting the origin:** By default, the origin, or (0,0) coordinate, of a Dreamweaver ruler is set to the upper-left corner of the Document window. You can reposition it to any coordinate in the Document window by clicking the origin cross hairs and dragging them to new coordinates, which can be useful if you want to use the rulers to position elements of a table whose upper-left corner doesn't sit at (0,0) in the Document window. Reset the origin to its default position by choosing View➪Rulers➪Reset Origin.

✦ **Changing ruler measurement units:** You can change the ruler's measuring increment by choosing View➪Rulers and then choosing Pixels, Inches, or Centimeters.

✦ **Viewing the grid:** Dreamweaver provides a Document Window grid that can assist you in visually positioning and aligning page elements. You can toggle the grid on and off by choosing View➪Grid➪Show Grid or by using the keyboard shortcut Ctrl+Alt+G. The grid is shown in Figure 2-1.

✦ **Activating and deactivating grid snapping:** The Document window grid offers a snapping feature that causes a layer or Layout table/cell to automatically align precisely with the snap-to points you define, which can be useful when you draw, resize, or move a layer (see Book II, Chapter 5 for the skinny on layers). You can toggle grid snapping on and off by choosing View➪Grid➪Snap to Grid.

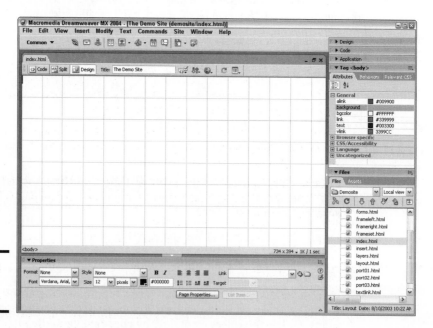

Figure 2-1:
The grid
is on.

Adjusting page size

When you design Web pages, you must consider how your target audiences will view them. People looking at your page may view it at any number of screen resolutions from 640 x 480 to 1024 x 768 or beyond. Your audience may even view your pages using WebTV, with a resolution of 544 x 376. Because pages appear differently at different resolutions, Dreamweaver offers you the ability to build your pages for a variety of monitor resolutions. The higher the resolution, the larger the workspace in your Document window.

If you want to size your pages, you must be in the Design workspace, and your Document window can't be maximized in the integrated workspace. To size your pages, click the Window Size Indicator (the height by width numbers and downward-pointing arrow at the bottom right of the Document window) and select a standard size — for example, 640 x 480 — from the drop-down list. (The Selecting Edit Sizes option on the drop-down list allows you to specify any height and width dimensions you want.)

 You can adjust how the grid appears in the Document window in the Grid Settings dialog box. To do so, open the Grid Settings dialog box by choosing View⇨Grid⇨Grid Settings and change any (or all) of the attributes that appear. When you finish, click the Apply button to view the effect of your changes. Click OK to accept the changes and close the dialog box.

Creating and Opening Pages

You have several ways to create a new page in Dreamweaver:

✦ On the Start page, scan through the Create New column and click the type of page you want to create from scratch.

✦ On the Start page, click one of the options in the Create from Samples column to open the New Document dialog box and make a new page with many common settings precoded.

✦ Choose File⇨New or use the keyboard shortcut Ctrl+N, which opens the New Document dialog box, from which you can create pages from scratch or from templates.

To open an existing page, do any of the following:

✦ On the Start page, click the name of the page in the Open Recent column.

✦ Double-click the page's filename in the Files tab of the Files panel.

✦ Choose File⇨Open or use the keyboard shortcut Ctrl+O, which opens the Open dialog box, which you can use to browse to the page you want to open.

Book II
Chapter 2

Creating Basic Web Pages

Establishing Page Properties

The Page Properties dialog box provides you with control over how several key page properties appear, including the title of the page, page background color, link colors, and page margins. Selections apply only to the current page, not to the entire site. Open a Page Properties dialog box similar to the one shown in Figure 2-2 by choosing Modify⇨Page Properties or by pressing Ctrl+J. Then make changes to any of the following in each of the five categories (Appearance, Links, Headings, Title/Encoding, and Tracing Image):

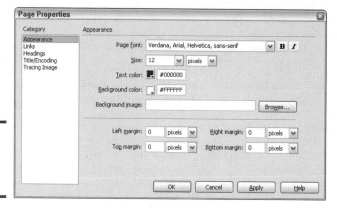

Figure 2-2:
The Page
Properties
dialog box.

✦ **Page Font, Font Size, Text Color, Background Color, Background Image:** Choose a font or set of fonts from the Page Font drop-down list; add a style (bold or italic) if desired. Click the Color box next to each property and pick a color from the Web safe color palette that appears, or enter a hexadecimal color code directly in any Color Code text field. You can also customize your own colors by selecting the color wheel and entering either RGB values or Hue, Saturation, and Luminosity values, as shown in Figure 2-3. For more information about using colors for the Web, see Book III, Chapter 2. Book III, Chapter 3 includes information on how to use the color picker to select colors in both Dreamweaver and Fireworks. For Background image, click the Browse button to locate the image file that you want to appear as the Document window background. If the image is smaller than the available background area, the image is *tiled* (repeated in a checkerboard fashion, like floor tiles) to fill the background.

Even if you choose to use a background image, select a complementary background color — the color shows while the background image is downloading.

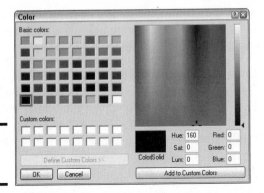

Figure 2-3:
The color picker.

- ✦ **Left Margin, Right Margin, Top Margin, and Bottom Margin:** Enter a number (in pixels) in these text fields to set up margins that affect how your page appears in modern browsers. Enter a whole number for the number of pixels of buffer space you want between the left, right, top, and bottom edges of your document and the content of the document.

- ✦ **Link Font and Size, Color for Links, Rollover Links, Visited Links, and Active Links:** Choose a font or set of fonts from the drop-down list; add a style (bold or italic) if desired. Click the Color box next to each property and pick a color from the Web safe color palette that appears, or enter a hexadecimal color code directly in any Color Code text field. You can also customize your own colors (see the preceding point on Text Color).

- ✦ **Underline Style:** Select an option from the drop-down list.

- ✦ **Heading Font, Sizes, and Colors:** Choose a font or set of fonts from the drop-down list; add a style (bold or italic) if desired. For as many of the six standard HTML heading levels as necessary, select a font size. If you choose a numeric value, the unit-of-measurement drop-down list to the right becomes active so you can select an option. Click the Color box next to each heading and pick a color from the Web safe color palette that appears, or enter a hexadecimal color code directly in any Color Code text field. You can also customize your own colors (see the preceding point on Text Color).

- ✦ **Title/Encoding:** Enter a page title in the text field. This title appears in the title bar area of the window both during construction in Dreamweaver and when the page is viewed in a Web browser. Select an Encoding format if your site requires the use of non-Western fonts (Japanese or Cyrillic, for example). If your site is in English, you can leave the setting at the default, Western European.

✦ **Tracing Image:** Click the Browse button to locate the image file you want to use as a guide for laying out your Web page in the Document window. This feature is handy for developers who prefer to mock up a portion of their Web page design in a graphics program and then re-create that design in their Web pages. Tracing images appear in Dreamweaver only as a pattern to help guide you in creating an actual Web page; the tracing image never appears on the finished Web page.

✦ **Image Transparency:** Drag the slider to adjust the visibility level of the tracing image. At 0 percent, the tracing image is invisible; at 100 percent, the image is completely opaque.

Click the Apply button to view the effect of any property you change. Click OK to accept your changes and close the Page Properties dialog box.

Working with Text

As we mention in Book II, Chapter 1, Dreamweaver has three different design views: Design, Code, and Split (Code and Design). The following sections apply when you're working in the Design view or Split view of Dreamweaver. In these views, you can enter and manipulate text on a Web page in Dreamweaver by using similar procedures to those you use when working with a word-processing document.

Adding, editing, and deleting text

To enter text on a page, click in the Document window and begin typing. Your mouse pointer appears as a blinking cursor that moves along with the text you enter. When you reach the end of a line, the text automatically wraps to the next line. Dreamweaver automatically adds the associated code for your new text in the HTML for the page.

To delete text from a page, in the Document window, select the chunk that you want to delete and press Backspace or Delete on your keyboard.

You can also modify how text appears on a page by editing its font, size, color, alignment, and other attributes. To modify text in the Document window, click and drag to select the text you want to modify. The Properties panel loads the Text Property inspector, as shown in Figure 2-4 (the Tag Inspector panel also reflects the selection). If the Text Property inspector is not open, choose Window➪Properties to open it. In the Text Property inspector, modify any of the following properties:

Figure 2-4:
The
Properties
panel with
the Text
Inspector
loaded.

✦ **Format:** From the Format drop-down list, select a default text style. Heading 1 is the largest style and Heading 6 is the smallest, but none of the headings correlates with a specific pixel size unless you set it to do so. Select Paragraph for the basic body text of your pages. Select Preformatted if you want spaces, tabs, and new lines in a paragraph to show up in a browser (ordinarily, when you add multiple spaces in a row or tabs to your HTML — this is particularly obvious in the Dreamweaver document's Code view — they appear as single spaces in a browser).

✦ **Font:** Select a font face from the Font drop-down list. Browsers show your text formatted as the first font in your selection that resides on the user's computer. Choosing Edit Font List allows you to add additional fonts you may have installed on your computer to the Font drop-down list. Most computers will have standard fonts like Arial and Helvetica and won't have less common fonts like, say, Univers or Futura.

✦ **Style:** Dreamweaver has been updated to work better with CSS styles. Styles defined within the document or in a linked stylesheet will be available from the Style drop-down list. You can also use the drop-down list to attach a stylesheet and create and edit styles.

✦ **Size:** Select a font size from the Size drop-down list. The options include none (choosing this option displays text in the default size), specific numbers, generic sizes XX-small to XX-large, and relative sizes Smaller and Larger. If you select a number, the unit-of-measurement drop-down list becomes available so that you can specify what the font size number refers to (pixels, ems, and so on).

✦ **Color:** Click the color box and select a text color from the Web safe color palette that appears. Alternatively, you may enter a hexa-decima color code directly in any color code text field. (To set the default text color for a page, check out the "Establishing Page Properties" section, earlier in this chapter.)

✦ **Bold or Italic:** Click the Bold button to make your selected text appear in bold. Click the Italic button to italicize your selected text. You can click either button or both.

✦ **Alignment:** Click an alignment button to align your text. Choices are Left, Center, Right, and Justify.

✦ **Link:** Type a URL in this field to transform selected text into a hypertext link. You can also use the Point to File tool to link to a file. To link to a file using this tool, just follow these steps:

1. **Open the Files panel by choosing Window⇨Files or by pressing F8.**

2. **Open the Explorer to the folder location that includes the file you want to link to by selecting the collapsing menu squares.**

   Alternatively, skip to Step 3 and hover your cursor over the folder that contains the file; the folder will expand so you can select the file within.

3. **Click and hold the Point to File button in the Text Property inspector and drag the pointer to the file you want to link to. Release the mouse button when the pointer is over the file.**

   The Point to File button looks like a compass without the needle or a clock face without hands or numbers. It's located to the right of the Links field.

   When you're dragging the button, a line appears from the origin point to your cursor, as shown in Figure 2-5.

   After you let go of the mouse button, the link to the file appears in the Link text field. If you select the Link drop-down list, it shows you your recent links as well.

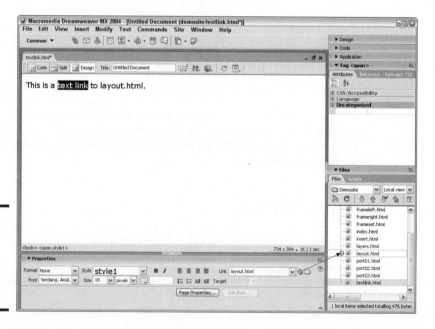

Figure 2-5:
The line helps you see which file you're choosing.

✦ **Target:** If you are linking the selected text, you can specify how the linked page will open when the user clicks the link by selecting one of the following options from the drop-down list:

- `_blank`: Opens the link in a new window.

- `_parent`: Opens the link in the parent of the currently opened window. If the window with the link in it is not in a frame, the linked page opens in the same window as the link. If the link is in a frame, the linked window will open in the parent frame or in the parent window of the frame with the link. See Book II, Chapter 4 for more information about frames.

- `_self`: Opens the link in the currently opened window; this is the default target.

- `_top`: Opens the link in the top-level window, replacing frames, if any.

✦ **List:** Click the Unordered List button next to the Target field to transform text into an unordered (bulleted) list; click the Ordered List button to transform text into an ordered (numbered) list.

✦ **Placement:** Click the Text Outdent button you find next to the Ordered List button to outdent (decrease the indent) the selected text; click the Text Indent button to indent the selected text. If you outdent an item in a bulleted or numbered list, the item will no longer be a list item.

Inserting a line break

When you want to start a new line in a word-processing program, you press the Enter key. If you press Enter in Dreamweaver, you create a paragraph break, which starts a new paragraph, creating a blank space between paragraphs. If you want to start a new line directly under another line of text and without the big space between lines, you need to insert a line break. In Dreamweaver, you create a line break by choosing Insert➪HTML➪Special Characters➪Line Break or by pressing Shift+Enter. Alternatively, you may click the Insert Line Break button from the HTML category of the Insert bar. Dreamweaver places the cursor at the start of the next line and inserts the line break HTML code.

Working with Images

Aside from entering text, manipulating images on a Web page is probably the most common Dreamweaver function you perform. You can add or delete an image and modify its properties to create an aesthetically pleasing layout that effectively conveys the information you want to deliver to the user.

To see how to place an image on the background of your page, check out the "Establishing Page Properties" section, earlier in this chapter.

Inserting an image

To insert an image on a page, follow these steps:

1. Choose Insert➪Image.

Alternatively, you can click the Insert Image button in the Common category of the Insert bar.

2. In the Select Image Source dialog box that appears (shown in Figure 2-6), click the image you want to insert.

If the image is outside the folder that holds your HTML document, use the Look In drop-down list to browse to the file you want.

3. Click OK to insert the image.

Note: Every image you want to include on a Web page should reside within the root folder of the current site (typically, you should have your HTML files in the site root folder — the master folder that holds everything on your site — and all your images in an images folder that's also in the site's root folder). If you attempt to insert an image from another location, Dreamweaver asks whether you want to copy the image to the current site root folder. Click Yes. In the Copy File As dialog box, you can enter a new name for the image in the File Name text field, or you can accept the current name and click the Save button.

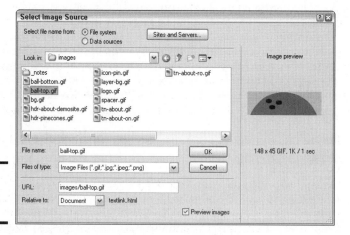

Figure 2-6:
Select an
image.

Always be sure you have saved your HTML file at least once before you insert an image into it. If your file isn't saved, Dreamweaver won't know where to place the image in relation to the file. After you've saved the file in a particular folder, the location is known and Dreamweaver can include the correct relative location of the image.

Put a check in the Preview Images check box at the bottom of the Select Image Source dialog box to view a thumbnail of the image before you select it for insertion. The preview area also tells you the size of the image and the expected download time.

Deleting or moving an image

To delete an image from a page, click the image in the Document window and press the Delete key on your keyboard.

If you want to move the image from one place on the page to another, you can click the image in the Document window, press Ctrl+X to cut the image, click the spot on the page where you want to move the image, and press Ctrl+V to paste the image. You can also move an image by clicking and dragging it to a new location.

Modifying an image

You can modify how an image appears on a page by editing its size and alignment, adding a border, and changing other attributes.

To modify an image, click the image in the Document window to select it. If the Image Property inspector does not appear, choose Window⇨Properties to open it.

To see all the options the Image Property inspector offers, click the down arrow in the bottom right-hand corner of the Image Property inspector. (Clicking the up arrow displays fewer options.)

You can do any of the following things to modify the way an image appears:

✦ **Resize the image:** Click and drag a sizing handle to change the dimensions of the image. To resize the image maintaining the same proportions, hold down the Shift key as you drag a sizing handle. You can also resize the image by typing new pixel dimensions in the W and H text fields in the Image Property inspector. Click the Resample button to conform the resized image to the new dimensions (otherwise resizing in Dreamweaver changes the dimensions in which the browser draws the image, but leaves the image file itself untouched — and image quality will suffer when the browser resizes the image). If you want the resized image to look its best, you may be better off resizing the image in Fireworks, because Fireworks gives you more control over the resizing process. To edit the image in Fireworks, select the image and click the Fireworks button in the Edit section of the Properties panel.

✦ **Align the image:** In the Image Property inspector, click an alignment button to position the image on the page (or within a cell if the image is located in a table cell). Alignment button choices are Left, Center, and Right. To align an image with special word wrapping, select one of the alignment options, which are detailed in Table 2-1, from the Align drop-down list that appears when you position your image near a bunch of text.

✦ **Add a border to the image:** In the Image Property inspector, enter a number in the Border text field to add a border of that thickness to the image. Border thickness is measured in pixels.

✦ **Pad an image with spaces:** In the Image Property inspector, enter a number in pixels in the V Space (V for vertical) text field for the space you want to appear between the top and bottom of the image and other page elements; then enter a number in pixels in the H Space (H for horizontal) text field for the space you want to appear between the image and page elements on either side of the image.

✦ **Make the image a link:** In the Image Property inspector, enter a URL in the Link text field.

✦ **Specify alternative text for the image:** In the Image Property inspector, enter alternative text in the Alt text field. (Specifying alternative text ensures that when viewers' browsers don't — or can't — display the image, some meaningful text appears instead, and also serves as an alternative for sight-impaired visitors to your page.)

✦ **Name the image:** In the Image Property inspector, enter a name in the text field next to the thumbnail image. (Naming an image is important if you want to refer to that image using a behavior or scripting language, such as JavaScript, but is otherwise unnecessary.)

✦ **Edit the image:** In the Image Property inspector, click the Edit button.

Dreamweaver allows you to optimize, crop, resample an image, adjust its brightness and contrast, and sharpen it by using the buttons in the Edit section of the Image Property inspector. If you want the most control over the process of editing the image, click the Fireworks button to open the image in Fireworks. You'll have the choice of working directly with the image or opening the source file the image came from. In most cases, you maintain the highest image quality by manipulating the pre-optimized source version of the image and then exporting it as a new GIF or JPEG. If you don't see the Fireworks icon in the Edit section of the

Properties panel when you select an image, you may have to set it (or another program) as your primary image editor. See Book II, Chapter 8 for instructions on making Fireworks your primary image editor.

✦ **Change the image file:** In the Image Property inspector, enter a different filename in the Src text field (or click the File Folder button to browse for image files).

✦ **Add an image map:** In Dreamweaver, you can add multiple hyperlinked hotspots to images to create an image map. In the bottom left of the Image Property inspector, you see an arrow pointer and some image tools (a rectangle, circle, and free form hotspot creator). With these tools, you can create hotspots on your images, and you can specify the following for each hotspot:

- The link location for the hotspot

- The target window for the link

- The alternate text for the hotspot

Table 2-1	Aligning an Image in Relation to Text
Alignment Option	*Effect on Image and Text Wrapping*
Default	Same as Bottom alignment
Baseline	Same as Bottom alignment
Top	Aligns the image top with the highest other inline element
Middle	Aligns the image middle with the text baseline
Bottom	Aligns the image bottom with the text baseline
Text Top	Aligns the image top with the text top
Absolute Middle	Aligns the image middle with the text middle
Absolute Bottom	Aligns the image bottom with the bottom of the text descenders
Left	Aligns the image flush left
Right	Aligns the image flush right

Working with Links

Linking your page to other Web pages enables you to direct visitors to related content on the Web. To insert a link, you must specify an image or some text to serve as the link; you must also specify the link location to which you want to send your visitors. The link can go to a page within your site or to a page elsewhere on the Web.

Inserting a link

To insert a link on a page, follow these steps:

1. Select the text or image you want to make into a link.

Doing so opens the Property inspector for your text or image. If the Property inspector does not appear, choose Window⇨Properties to open it.

2. In the Link area of the Property inspector, enter the destination URL of the link (text or image) that you created in Step 1.

The URL you specify can be any valid URL, for example, a Web page within your own site (`somePage.html`), a page on the Web (`http://www.someSite.com/somePage.html`), or even an e-mail address (`mailto:somebody@somewhere.com`).

Alternatively, you may click the File Folder button you see in the Property inspector to display the Select File dialog box. After you browse your computer using the Select File dialog box and select a file, click OK to make that file the target of a link.

To create an e-mail link quickly, click anywhere in your document and choose Insert⇨Email Link. Specifying the same value for the Text and E-mail fields that appear allows folks who haven't configured their Web browsers to handle e-mail automatically to see the e-mail address on the page. Then, they can copy and paste the e-mail address information into their e-mail program of choice.

Deleting a link

To delete a link from text or an image, without deleting the text or image itself, follow these steps:

1. Select the text or image you want to remove the link from.

The Property inspector for your text or image opens. If the Property inspector doesn't appear, choose Window⇨Properties to open it.

2. In the Property inspector, delete the URL from the Link text field.

Note that if you delete a linked image or linked text from a page, the link gets deleted along with the text or image.

Using named anchors

When you want to create a navigational link that connects users not only to a page, but also to a specific location on the page, you need to create a *named anchor*. Named anchors are frequently used for jumping to exact positions within a large block of text so that users don't have to scroll through paragraph after paragraph to find the information they need.

Setting up named anchors is especially useful when creating links from a directory or a table of contents to the content it presents.

Inserting a named anchor

Place an anchor anywhere on your Web page as follows:

1. **In the Document window, click at the position you want to insert the named anchor.**

2. **Click the Named Anchor button on the Common category of the Insert bar or choose Insert⇨Named Anchor.**

   The Named Anchor dialog box appears, as shown in Figure 2-7. If the Insert bar is set to a different category, click and hold the category name and select Common from the drop-down list.

3. **Type a name in the Anchor Name text field.**

4. **Click OK.**

**Book II
Chapter 2**

Creating Basic
Web Pages

Figure 2-7:
The Named
Anchor
dialog box.

 It's a good idea to insert the named anchor tag slightly above the actual position where you want the link to target. Doing so gives your targeted content a little padding on top. Otherwise, the top of your image or your first line of text appears flush with the top of the browser window.

Linking to a named anchor

To link to a named anchor, follow the procedure outlined in the "Inserting a link" section, earlier in this chapter, with the following modifications:

✦ **Linking to a named anchor on the current page:** In the Link text field of the Property inspector, type a pound sign (#) followed by the anchor name.

✦ **Linking to a named anchor on a different page:** In the Link text field of the Property inspector, type the page's URL followed by a pound sign and then the anchor name.

 Be sure not to include any spaces in the names of anchors. These may not be read by the various Web browsers.

Working with Tables

You can position objects (such as text blocks, images, or animations) relative to each other on a page in two basic ways:

+ **Using tables:** A time-honored Web tradition for page layout, tables are grids of cells defined by columns and rows. Cells can have set sizes and alignments and may contain anything you can put on a Web page, including other tables.

+ **Using layers:** Layers can be positioned precisely, and in Dreamweaver, layers are in some ways easier to use than tables. For instructions on how to lay out your Web page with layers, see Book II, Chapter 5.

Adding a table to a Web page can help you lay out page elements more easily in the Document window. Tables consist of as many holding areas, or cells, as you want, and you can place virtually any Web element, such as text or an image, into a cell. Cells are organized horizontally into *rows* and vertically into *columns*. Dreamweaver provides you with complete control over the size, position, color, and other attributes of your table. And you can edit these attributes at any time via the Table Property inspector.

Inserting a table

To insert a table into a Web page, just follow these steps:

1. **Click in the document where you want the table to go.**

2. **Choose Insert⇨Table or use the keyboard shortcut Ctrl+Alt+T, or click the Table button in the Common category of the Insert bar.**

The Insert Table dialog box appears, as shown in Figure 2-8. If the Insert bar is set to a different category, click and hold the category name and select Common from the drop-down list.

3. **Enter the number of rows and columns you want the table to have in the corresponding Rows and Columns fields.**

You can always add or remove rows or columns later.

4. **Use the Table Width field to set a width for the table.**

The width can be either a set number of pixels or a percentage of the area that bounds the table (the page itself, or, if the table is nested in a cell, that cell).

5. **In the Border Thickness field, enter a number for how many pixels thick you want the border of your table to be.**

If you don't want the table border to show (which you probably don't if you're using the table for page layout purposes), enter 0 (zero).

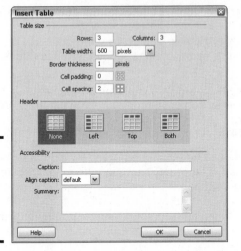

Figure 2-8:
Fill out the
Insert Table
dialog box
to create a
table.

6. **In the Cell Padding field, enter a whole number for the amount of pixels you want between the border of the cell and the text or object inside the cell.**

   The cell padding applies to the top, bottom, left, and right of the inside of each and every cell.

7. **In the Cell Spacing field, enter a number for the amount of pixels you want between the cells.**

   The cell spacing applies to the whole table; you can't have different cell spacing for individual rows or columns.

8. **If your table has a header row or header column (or both), click the button (None, Left, Top, or Both) that represents the header structure of your table.**

   The text in a header row has special formatting, which you can define in a stylesheet. If you're creating a table for layout purposes, you won't want a header row or column, so make sure None is selected.

9. **In the Accessibility section of the Insert Table dialog box, enter a caption and summary for the table if you need to describe the table for a sight-impaired audience.**

   If you're making the table for page layout purposes, leave these blank.

10. **Click OK.**

    The Insert Table dialog box disappears, and the empty table appears in your document.

An empty table is shown in Figure 2-9. To enter data into the table, just click on an individual cell and enter the content you want in that cell. You can modify any of the table's attributes by selecting the table and changing the attributes in the Properties inspector or the Tag Inspector panel.

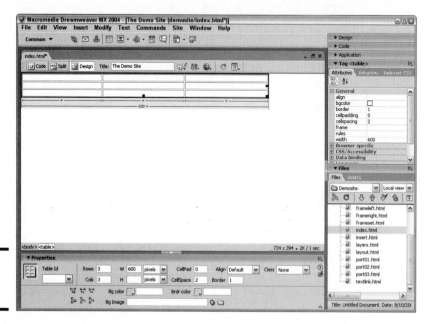

Figure 2-9:
A simple
table.

Deleting a table

To delete a table from a page, click the border of the table to select it and then press the Backspace or Delete key. Dreamweaver removes the table from your page and deletes the associated code in the HTML for the page. Naturally, everything that was in the table is also deleted from the page.

Using layout tables

The use of tables is central to the traditional way of building great Web pages (for information on laying out pages with layers, see Book II, Chapter 5). What happens, though, when you want to put an image right smack in the middle of a page, or when you want to have one column of information along the right side of the page, and a square text block at the bottom of the page? You can nest tables, which involves building new tables inside of cells of other tables. This is the tried and true method for a lot of developers, but creating nested tables is complicated and not at all fun, especially with complex pages.

Thankfully, Dreamweaver offers an easy way to work with complex tables called layout tables. With a layout table, you tell Dreamweaver where you want to put something on the screen, and the program generates all the required table work to make it happen.

To create a layout table, just follow these steps:

1. Click the Layout view button in the Layout category on the Insert bar.

If the Insert bar is set to a different category, click and hold the category name and select Layout from the drop-down list.

2. Click the Layout Table button (just to the right of the Layout view button).

3. Click and drag the cross hair to create the layout table of your choice.

A light green table appears, as shown in Figure 2-10, with the dimensions you gave it.

4. To create individual cells within that table, click the Draw Layout Cell button to the right of the Layout Table button and draw a cell anywhere within the table.

If you create a layout cell outside a layout table, Dreamweaver will create both the cell and the table to support it. Note that you cannot draw a new cell that overlaps an existing cell in the table.

Book II
Chapter 2

Creating Basic
Web Pages

Layout Table

Layout view Draw Layout Cell

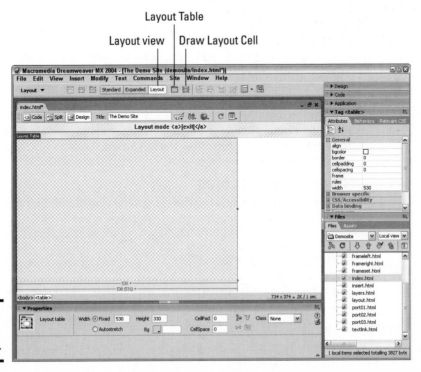

Figure 2-10:
Drawing a
layout table.

If you create a layout cell, you can immediately edit the cell you created. However, if you create a layout table, you either have to switch back to Standard view to edit the single cell of that table or create a layout cell within the table before you can edit the table.

Storing information in table cells

After you insert a table on a page, you can add or delete elements, such as text and images, in the table cells:

✦ **Adding an image to a cell:** To add an image to a table cell, click in a table cell and choose Insert⇨Image. Browse and select an image you want to add to the cell, and then click OK. (For more information on inserting images, flip to the "Inserting an image" section, earlier in this chapter.)

✦ **Adding text to a cell:** To add text to a table cell, click to position the cursor in a table cell and type the text you want placed inside the cell.

✦ **Deleting an image from a cell:** To delete an image from a table cell, select the image and press Backspace or Delete.

✦ **Deleting text from a cell:** To delete text from a table cell, select the text and press Backspace or Delete.

Previewing Your Work

Whether you're working in Code view or Design view, at some point you'll want to see the page as visitors to your site will see it: in a browser such as Internet Explorer or Netscape Navigator. If you have two or more browsers on your computer, you can preview your page in any of the browsers — without leaving Dreamweaver — by using the Preview in Browser feature.

To preview your page in your primary browser, choose File⇨Preview in Browser⇨*Browser Name* or use the keyboard shortcut F12. The keyboard shortcut for previewing in your secondary browser is Shift+F12.

Chapter 3: Creating and Using Dreamweaver Sites

In This Chapter

✔ **Defining a site in Dreamweaver MX 2004**

✔ **Whipping up your first site**

✔ **Establishing a remote connection**

✔ **Using advanced site options**

✔ **Publishing and maintaining your site**

✔ **Using source control**

reamweaver MX 2004 can be used to create many different kinds of Web pages. During the course of building a Web site, you'll add pages, graphics, links, and all sorts of related information into a single location to be posted eventually to a Web server on the Internet. After your site is complete, you'll probably want to make updates and fixes. Heck, you may even be making more than one site at the same time!

To help facilitate management of your Web site (or sites), Dreamweaver offers a suite of site management tools. These tools are collectively called a *Dreamweaver Site*. This chapter explores how you can use these tools to manage your Web site more easily.

Defining a Site in Dreamweaver MX 2004

Figure 3-1 shows a typical relationship between where you build your Web site (your desktop) and where the site actually lives on the Internet (a Web server). Dreamweaver Sites facilitate getting all the correct information from your desktop to the Web server and generally make the Web page creation process easier. Specifically, a Dreamweaver Site enables you to do the following:

✦ Move files seamlessly back and forth between your local machine and your Web server

✦ Keep all your site files in a single location

✦ Generate pages for your site based on templates that you create

✦ Run reports on the pages in your site to check links, page load, and other key functions

✦ Use source- and version-control to manage who works on what files and when they do it, which can prevent team members from accidentally overwriting each other's work when building or maintaining a site collaboratively

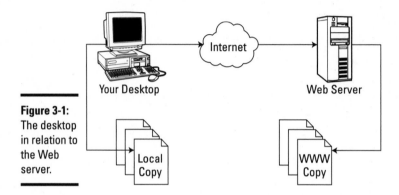

Figure 3-1:
The desktop in relation to the Web server.

Creating Your First Site

Earlier versions of Dreamweaver required every Web page you created or edited to be part of a Dreamweaver Site. With Dreamweaver MX 2004, Macromedia has removed that often-cumbersome requirement. Nevertheless, if you're working with a set of files regularly in Dreamweaver, or if you're managing several sites, you're likely to find using Dreamweaver Sites an efficient way of working.

You can create a site in Dreamweaver manually or by using a wizard, as the following sections describe.

Creating a site manually

This section shows you how to create a Dreamweaver Site manually. The following steps walk you through inputting the minimum amount of information that you need to enter to create your site. However, you can choose from a number of other options, and they are covered in the "Using Advanced Site Options" section, later in this chapter.

To create a basic site manually, follow these steps:

1. **Choose Site⇨Manage Sites.**

   The Manage Sites dialog box appears. You can also open the Manage Sites dialog box by choosing Manage Sites from the drop-down list in the Files panel that shows the current site.

2. **Click the New button.**

   A pop-up menu appears with the choices Site and FTP & RDS Server.

3. **Select Site.**

   The Site Definition dialog box appears, open to the Advanced tab by default. The Local Info options, shown in Figure 3-2, appear by default.

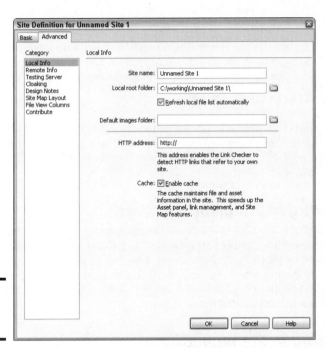

Figure 3-2:
Defining
your site.

4. **Set the options for your site by filling out each of the following pieces of information:**

   - **Site Name:** Choose a name that you can remember easily and that applies to the function of the site.

   - **Local Root Folder:** This is the location on your hard drive where you want to store the files that make up your site. Again, you should title the folder something intuitive and easy to remember. If you want to browse for a folder, just click the folder icon to the right of the text field.

- **Refresh Local File List Automatically:** When this option is selected, Dreamweaver refreshes the list of files in your site every time you copy a file into the site. The option is selected by default.

- **Default Images Folder:** This is the standard directory for images used on your site. Dreamweaver adds images here when you copy image files into your site. A good practice is to name this folder `images` (if your site is going to be hosted on a UNIX-based server, you need to be consistent about using upper- and lowercase letters in file-names and links to those files from your site). If you want to browse for the directory, just click the folder icon next to the text field.

- **HTTP Address:** This is the URL of your Web site. Dreamweaver uses this to verify that links in your site are working properly.

- **Enable Cache:** Selecting this option speeds up Dreamweaver's site management tools and is required for the Assets panel to work. See your documentation for information about using the Assets panel.

5. **Click OK to create the site.**

Dreamweaver creates a folder for your site if it doesn't exist on your hard drive, but it doesn't create the `images` directory within that folder. Thus, it's always a good idea to create your folders on the hard drive first, and then create your site.

Creating a site using a wizard

You may think that using a wizard to create a site is easier, which is true if you're creating a complex site. However, if you're creating a simple site (one that you'll be working on by yourself and that doesn't employ a server tech-nology or testing server, for example) the manual route is the way to go.

To use the wizard, follow these steps:

1. **Choose Site⇨Manage Sites.**

    The Manage Sites dialog box appears.

2. **Click the New button.**

    A pop-up menu appears with the choices Site and FTP & RDS Server.

3. **Select Site.**

    The Site Definition dialog box appears, open to the Advanced tab by default. (It just so happens that the Advanced tab has all the stuff for defining your site manually, whereas the Basic tab holds the Site Definition wizard.)

4. **Click the Basic tab to access the wizard, as shown in Figure 3-3.**

5. **Enter a name for your site in the appropriate text field, and then click Next.**

   The Editing Files, Part 2 page of the wizard appears.

6. **If your site is going to be dynamic, choose a server technology to process Web pages before they're sent to the user, and then click Next.**

   Select a technology by selecting the Yes radio button and selecting your Web serving technology from the drop-down list. Dreamweaver provides you with several server options, including several flavors of ASP, plus JSP, PHP, and (of course) ColdFusion. If you're not using a server technology, select the No radio button.

7. **In the new page that appears, choose how you want to edit your files, and then click Next.**

   If you have selected to use a server technology on the Editing Files, Part 2 page, then on the Editing Files, Part 3 page you get the Dynamic options shown in Table 3-1; if you're not using a server technology, you get the Static options. Click the radio button next to the option you want to choose.

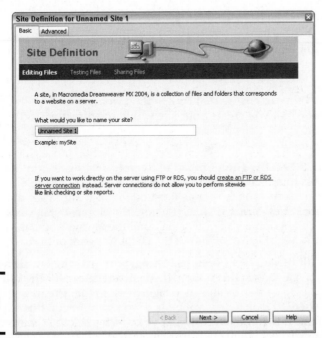

Figure 3-3:
Step one of
the wizard.

Table 3-1	Site Editing Options		
Option	*Description*	*Dynamic Option*	*Static Option*
Edit and Test Locally	Allows you to edit your files and test them locally using ColdFusion (or other technology) as your Web server.	Yes	No
Edit Locally, Then Upload to Remote Testing Server (Edit Local Copies on Your Machine, Then Upload to Server When Ready)	In this mode, you edit the files on your computer, and then manually upload them using Dreamweaver's FTP tools to move the files to a remote server.	Yes	Yes
Edit Directly on (Remote Testing) Server Using Local Network	This option allows you to edit files directly on a volume on your internal network.	Yes	Yes

8. **In the new page that appears, configure your testing environment, and then click Next.**

Based on the editing and testing methodology you chose in Step 7, you are asked to configure your testing environment. Here are the various options:

- **Edit and Test Locally:** For this method, you are asked to provide the local URL for testing. Usually, this is `http://localhost/folder`, where `folder` is the name of the root folder of your site.

  In order to ensure that this method works properly, always make sure that you create your site within the directory for `http://localhost` on your hard drive. For most Windows 2000 or XP computers, this location is `C:\inetpub\wwwroot\` by default.

- **Edit Locally, Then Upload to Remote Testing Server:** If you select this route, click Next to see a page where you can select a method of connecting to the remote location for your site. Your options are Local/Network, FTP, RDS (Remote Development Services, used in conjunction with ColdFusion), and the always popular, "I'll set this up later." Figure 3-4 shows the Local/Network option.

- **Edit Directly on (Remote Testing) Server Using Local Network:** If you've chosen this option, then you are asked for the URL of the remote server, as shown in Figure 3-5, so that Dreamweaver knows where to look to test your site. If you want to edit directly on the remote testing server using FTP or RDS, click the Create an FTP or RDS server connection text link on the first page of the wizard.

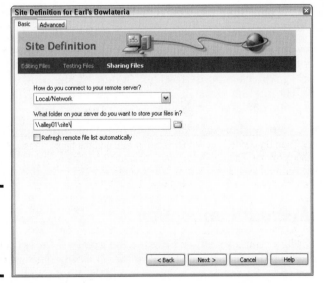

Figure 3-4:
Connecting
using your
local
network.

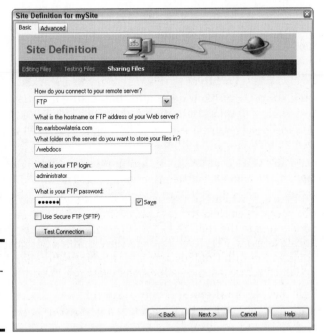

Figure 3-5:
FTP require-
ments for
editing
remotely.

9. **In the new page that appears, configure your file sharing options and click Next.**

Dreamweaver includes options for source control, which you can use to prevent team members from overwriting each others' work when collaborating. You can choose to enable it here by selecting the Yes radio button. File sharing is discussed in more detail in the section, "Using Source Control," later in this chapter.

10. **Review your settings and click Done to set up your site.**

The Site Definition dialog box closes. Click Done to close the Manage Sites dialog box.

Setting Up a Remote Connection

After you create your site, either by using the wizard or by setting it up manually, it's a good idea to get connected to the place where the remote version of your site (the one users will access via the World Wide Web) will live. Dreamweaver can connect to a remote server in a variety of ways. The route you choose depends largely on how you plan to build and maintain your site. You have essentially three different scenarios:

✦ **Creating and testing your site solely on your own computer:** For example, this may be the case if you're building your site for someone else, say a client. Here the remote server is your computer — not all that remote!

✦ **Creating your site on your computer, but testing it somewhere else:** This is the most common situation. Dreamweaver has three different delivery options for this scenario: FTP, Remote Development Services (RDS), and local network connection.

✦ **Creating and testing your site on a remote machine:** In this case, the options are the same as in the previous bullet. The only difference is that when you're editing, you're editing files directly on the remote location, leaving nothing on your local machine.

In many cases, your remote location is at an externally hosted Internet Service Provider (ISP). If you've got an account set up with an ISP, make sure to get the following information, which is required for Dreamweaver to set up a connection to your remote Web server:

✦ An IP address or a URL to be used when posting your files

✦ A folder on the remote server where you are supposed to keep your site files

✦ A username for your account

✦ A password for your account

To set up a remote connection, follow these steps:

1. **Choose Site⇨Manage Sites to bring up the Manage Sites dialog box, shown in Figure 3-6.**

Figure 3-6:
The
Manage
Sites
dialog box.

**Book II
Chapter 3**

Creating and Using
Dreamweaver Sites

2. **Select your site from the list on the left, and then click the Edit button.**

The Site Definition dialog box appears, open to the Advanced tab.

3. **From the Category list on the left, select Remote Info.**

Along the right side of the dialog box, the Local Info options are replaced with the Remote Info options. If you haven't set up a connection previously, all you see is the Access drop-down list.

4. **Select an option from the Access drop-down list.**

You can choose from several Access options in this list, including:

- **FTP:** The industry standard File Transfer Protocol.

- **Local/Network:** A location on your local (meaning office, home office, and so on) network.

- **RDS:** ColdFusion's Remote Development Services allows secure remote access to files within a ColdFusion application server.

- **SourceSafe Database:** SourceSafe is Microsoft's version control application, which helps prevent the accidental overwriting of files when you're collaborating with others to build the site. With Dreamweaver, you can integrate SourceSafe and use it for your version control.

- **WebDAV:** This stands for Web-based Distributed Authoring and Versioning. Like SourceSafe, it's a standard for version control and is used with Web servers like Apache Web Server and Microsoft's IIS.

5. Fill out the appropriate information for the connection type you selected.

Leave the source control settings alone for the moment, which are described in the "Using Source Control" section, later in this chapter. The following list describes the information needed for each connection type:

- **FTP:** In addition to the four items we note at the beginning of this section (host, folder, username, and password), you also need to select the Passive FTP check box if you plan to use Passive FTP (required for some servers). If there's a firewall you need to work through, you can click the Firewall Settings button to set the Firewall preferences in the dialog box that appears, as shown in Figure 3-7. Select the Use Secure FTP (SFTP) check box if you want to use encrypted secure logins (again, not likely). After you've added the necessary settings, you're able to connect to your ISP.

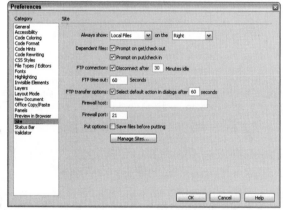

Figure 3-7:
Setting your
Firewall
preferences.

If you select Automatically Upload Files to Server on Save, Dreamweaver will automatically make a connection to the remote server and upload your file each time you save it.

Select the Enable File Check In and Check Out option if you're working in a collaborative environment and you want to ensure that other team members can't work on a file at the same time you're working on it. If you select this option, you need to add information that will identify you to your collaborators.

- **Local/Network:** Here, you only need to specify the location of the remote folder on the network or a local drive, which you can enter manually or by clicking the folder icon to browse the network for the folder location. You can also select the Refresh check box if you'd like the list of files on your site to be automatically refreshed when a new file is added.

- **RDS:** If you select RDS from the drop-down list, you need to click the Settings button next to the list to configure the RDS connection, as shown in Figure 3-8. To configure RDS, you need a host name (IP address or URL), port number (the default is 80), the directory of the site on the host, a username, and a password. If you don't want the password saved, then deselect the Save check box.

Figure 3-8:
The
Configure
RDS Server
dialog box.

- **SourceSafe:** As with RDS, with SourceSafe you have to click the Settings button next to the drop-down list. Then you specify the location of the SourceSafe Database Path (a path to an .ini file, usually on a network volume), the name of the project, a username, and a password. If you don't want the password saved, then deselect the Save check box.

- **WebDAV:** With WebDAV, you must also click the Settings button next to the drop-down list to configure the connection. You need the URL of the connection, a username, a password, and an e-mail address. If you don't want the password saved, then deselect the Save check box.

6. **Click OK to put the changes into effect.**

Using Advanced Site Options

If you used the wizard to create your site, you may have been struck by the array of questions asked. That's because you can configure a number of advanced settings with Dreamweaver. Most of them you're not likely to need, but just in case, we describe them in the following sections. You can access all these options by selecting the name of the item in the Category list of the Site Definition dialog box (refer to Figure 3-2).

Testing your server

Select Testing Server from the Category list on the Advanced tab of the Site Definition dialog box to access the options for setting up your testing server. If you're building a dynamic site, you need to have a Web server running that can process the pages and render them as HTML. (For more on how this is accomplished, see Book VI, Chapter 3.) To specify a Web serving technology, do the following:

1. Select a Web server from the Server Model drop-down list, as shown in Figure 3-9.

You have several options here, but if you're working within the Macromedia model, your selection is probably going to be ColdFusion.

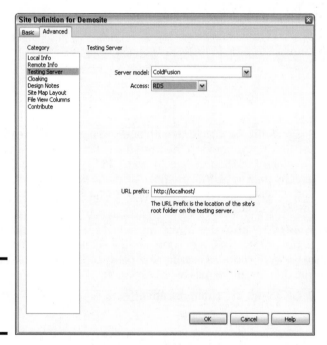

Figure 3-9: Choosing a testing server.

2. Select an Access type.

You can choose FTP or Local/Network. If you chose RDS on the Remote Info screen, you see an RDS option here as well. Choosing any of them provides additional fields for you to fill out, as specified for each Access type in the "Setting Up a Remote Connection" section, earlier in this chapter. Choose None if you don't want to use a testing server.

3. Click OK to save your settings.

Cloaking

Cloaking is a handy and appropriately named feature in Dreamweaver Sites. When enabled, *cloaking* allows you to hide different file types or folders from Dreamweaver's site tools. This can be especially helpful if you keep your raw asset files (your source Fireworks PNGs, Flash FLAs, and so on) in the same directory as the site itself, but you don't want the files uploaded or downloaded, included in reports, or otherwise touched by various Dreamweaver operations. To engage this feature, click the Advanced tab of the Site Definition dialog box and select Cloaking from the Category list on the left. Then select the Enable Cloaking check box, as well as the Cloak Files Ending With check box, and add the file extensions for the file types you want to mask. See the online Help files for more details.

Using Design Notes

Design Notes aren't really necessary unless you're working on your site collaboratively in Dreamweaver with other people. Then, Design Notes can be especially helpful. For example, you can use Design Notes to let others know the status of a given file. To engage Design Notes, click the Advanced tab of the Site Definition dialog box, select Design Notes from the Category list on the left, and then simply select the Maintain Design Notes check box. If you want to move the notes to the server when the site is published, so that other team members can access them, select the Upload Design Notes for Sharing check box.

Setting up a site map

If you select Site Map Layout in the Category list in the Site Definition dialog box, you can set up the specifics of how you'd like your site's Site Map to look. You can specify the following:

+ The home page for the site map, which can be different from the home page (`index.htm`) of the site

+ The number and width of the columns of the map

+ The labels for the site map icons

+ Whether or not to display items marked hidden

+ Whether or not to display dependent files

Selecting columns for the File view

For the File view, shown in Figure 3-10, you have six built-in columns to choose from: Name, Notes, Size, Type, Modified, and Checked Out By.

However, you can also add and remove your own columns by clicking the (+) and (–) buttons, respectively. For a column you create, you can also specify the following:

✦ The column name

✦ The column's Design Note association, if its contents relate to a specific Design Note

✦ The text alignment for the column

✦ The option to show or not show the column in the File view (***Note:*** The Name column cannot be hidden or moved.)

✦ Whether or not to share the column so other workers on the site can see it (***Note:*** You must have Maintain Design Notes checked to share a column.)

Enabling Contribute compatibility

To enable compatibility with Contribute 2, click the Advanced tab of the Site Definition dialog box and select Contribute from the Category list on the left. Select the Enable Contribute Compatibility check box if you plan to have people maintain your site using Contribute. Selecting this option allows you to perform many administrative functions related to Contribute. (For example, you can send Connection Keys based on your Dreamweaver Site setups.)

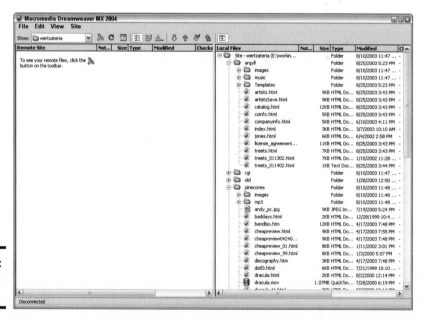

Figure 3-10:
The File
view.

Publishing Your Site

After you've set up a remote site in a Dreamweaver Site, publishing your site is a snap. To publish your site to a remote server, just follow these steps:

1. **If the Files panel isn't already open, open it by choosing Window⇨ Files or by pressing F8.**

2. **On the File tab, click the Expand/Collapse button (the button on the far right of the toolbar) to switch to File view mode.**

This brings up the File view shown in Figure 3-11.

3. **If you haven't connected to the remote server since you launched Dreamweaver most recently, click the Connection button at the left of the Files panel toolbar to establish a connection with the remote server.**

4. **Select a file and click the Put button on the toolbar (upward pointing blue arrow) to copy a file from the local server to the remote server or the Get button (downward pointing green arrow) to copy a file from the remote server to the local server.**

If you're copying files for the first time, simply select the site's root folder and click the Put button. To copy files from the Local to Remote servers, or vice versa, you can also simply click and drag the elements from local to remote, or vice versa. If you use this method, be careful to place files in the correct folders.

**Book II
Chapter 3**

Creating and Using
Dreamweaver Sites

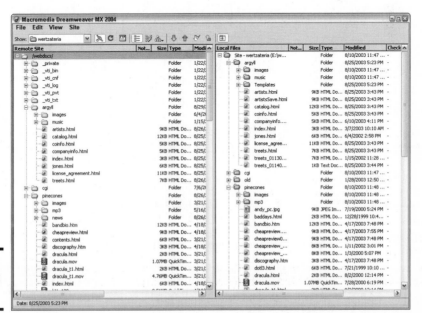

Figure 3-11:
Remote and
local sites.

If you ever want to see what's going on behind the scenes when you're copy-ing those files, just click the FTP button in the toolbar in File view. The Results panel appears/expands and shows you the remote connections being set and all the commands for the files being sent (the File view col-lapses back to the Files panel as well).

Maintaining Your Site

After your site is built, you want to make sure that it's running at peak effi-ciency. To help in this effort, Dreamweaver offers some valuable tools that can help you keep on top of the wide array of items that go into keeping your site running smoothly. We describe the two basic types of tools, reports and link checkers, in detail in the following sections.

Running reports

Reports encapsulate information about various aspects of your site at the time the reports are run, giving you a snapshot of things, such as which files on your site are currently being worked on by different team members, whether all the images on a selected page have Alt tags, and more. To run a report in Dreamweaver, just follow these steps:

1. **Choose Site⇨Reports.**

   The Reports dialog box, shown in Figure 3-12, appears.

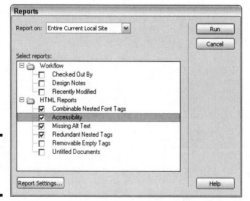

Figure 3-12:
The Reports
dialog box.

2. **Choose what you want to run the report against.**

   You can choose to run a report on the currently selected document, the entire site, selected files in the site, or a folder within the site. Select one of these options from the Report On drop-down list.

3. **Select the reports you want to run by selecting the check box next to their names.**

   You can run nine possible reports, across two categories:

   • **Checked Out By:** This report tells you what files in source control are currently being used by different members of the team. If you want the report to show only which files are currently checked out by a particular team member, click the Report Settings button at the bottom of the dialog box while the report is selected and add an individual's name to the text field in the Checked Out By dialog box that pops up.

   • **Design Notes:** This report prints out all the Design Notes associated with files on the site. To filter your results via the Design Notes dialog box, shown in Figure 3-13, click the Report Settings button while the Design Notes report is selected.

   • **Recently Modified:** This report shows which files have been modified within parameters you set by clicking the Report Settings button and specifying in the Recently Modified dialog box.

Book II
Chapter 3

Creating and Using
Dreamweaver Sites

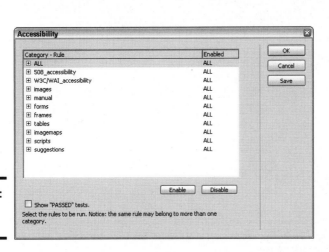

Figure 3-13: Filtering results.

   • **Combinable Nested Font Tags:** This report details locations in the code where overlapping Font tags could be merged. For example, if you change the size of a block of text, your code might contain something like this:

```
<FONT face="Arial"><FONT size="2">Some
    text.</FONT></FONT>
```

   When it could and should be

```
<FONT face="Arial" size="2">Some text.</FONT>
```

- **Accessibility:** If you run this report, the site files are scanned to find places where the code is not ADA (Americans with Disabilities Act) compliant. For more information about accessibility, browse to the W3C Web Accessibility Initiative pages at `www.w3.org/WAI/Resources/`.

- **Missing Alt Text:** This report looks for images to make sure they have Alt text (see the section on modifying an image in Book II, Chapter 2 for a little info on Alt text).

- **Redundant Nested Tags:** This report searches the code for locations where extra tags can be eliminated.

- **Removable Empty Tags:** If you're working in Design mode and moving lots of things around, sometimes the underlying code can be left with lingering, empty tags. This tool finds those empty tags.

- **Untitled Documents:** This report searches for pages that may have a filename but don't have a title.

4. **Click OK to run the reports.**

   The results appear in the Site Reports tab of the Results panel, as shown in Figure 3-14.

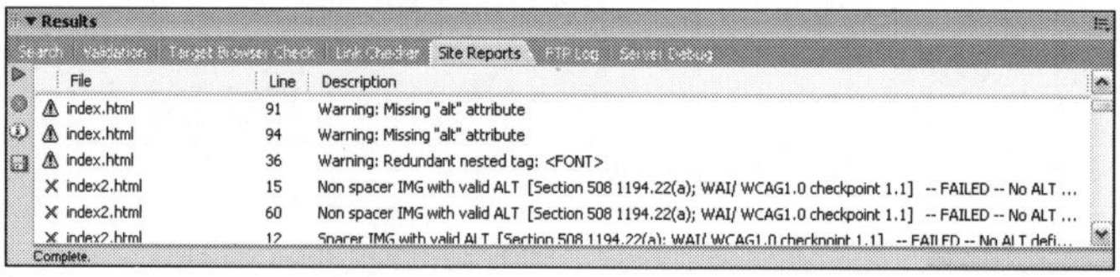

Figure 3-14:
The Results
panel.

Checking links

In addition to the reports that help clean up your code, Dreamweaver can also check the links on your site. To run the Link Check report, choose Site➪Check Links Sitewide or press Shift+F8. You see the results in the Link Checker tab in the Results panel. The report shows broken links, external links, and orphaned files.

Using Source Control

Source control allows team members to check out a document in your site, thereby locking it and making it uneditable by others until the team member who checked it out checks it back in again. This process is intended to ensure that files don't get overwritten accidentally and that data doesn't get lost during the development process.

In most large-scale software development projects, where you've got multi-tudes of people working on a single code-base, source control is critical. If your site requires that more than three people work on the same pages and code, you should consider taking advantage of this feature in Dreamweaver.

To set up source control, do the following:

1. **Choose Site⇨Manage Sites, select your site, and then click the Edit button to open the Site Definition dialog box.**

2. **Click the Advanced tab if it's not already open and select Remote Info from the Category list on the left.**

3. **Set your source control options at the bottom of the screen.**

When you enable file check in and check out, the following options become available:

- Check out files automatically when you open a document within the site

- Provide your name and e-mail address for site reporting and infor-mational purposes

You must have selected an Access option on the Remote Info screen before you can get the Check In/Check Out options to show up at the bottom of the page. See the "Setting Up a Remote Connection" section, earlier in this chapter, for more information about Access options.

4. **Click OK to save your settings.**

To work with a file after you've enabled source control, right-click the file from the Files panel and select one of the following options:

✦ **Get:** Retrieves the most recent version of the file and copies it locally.

✦ **Check Out:** Makes your local version the only editable version of a docu-ment and ensures that others can't open and save the file.

✦ **Put:** Copies the local version of your file to the remote location.

✦ **Check In:** Puts your local version of the file on the server and unlocks it so that others can check it out and work on it if need be.

Chapter 4: Punching Up Your Pages with Forms and Frames

In This Chapter

✔ Incorporating forms into your Web page

✔ Structuring your pages with frames

Two of the more popular Web page features, forms and frames, are also two of the most advanced features. You use them in your Web pages to serve the following functions:

✦ **Forms:** Enable you to gather information and feedback from the users who visit your Web pages. *Forms* can consist of text fields, buttons, check boxes, radio buttons, and drop-down lists, which enable the user to enter information or to choose among options you present.

✦ **Frames:** Enable you to construct sophisticated navigational schemes for your Web site. *Frames* are actually separate Web pages that are partitioned off so that two or more can be displayed in the same browser window at the same time. For example, one frame may be a navigational page consisting of a list of links to other pages; that frame remains in place in its portion of the browser window even when the user clicks a link to display a different Web page in the other frame.

In this chapter, you see how to work with these powerful features in Dreamweaver MX 2004.

Incorporating Forms into Web Pages

Forms on the Web serve the same purpose as the paper-based forms you fill out — they provide a structured format for gathering specific information. The difference is that Web-based forms usually require less time for keyboard-savvy users to fill out (and using Web-based forms also saves a few trees otherwise destined for a paper mill).

Dreamweaver offers you a number of handy tools for creating Web-based forms that you can easily include on your Web pages. You can incorporate everything from text fields to radio buttons, and you can create surveys, gather user data, and conduct e-commerce.

Creating Web-based forms requires two steps:

1. **Creating the form that users see and interact with, which we demon-strate how to do using Dreamweaver in this chapter.**

2. **Creating the processing program that accepts and processes form input, which we cover in more detail in Book VI, Chapter 4.**

Adding a form

Before you can insert specific form objects, such as check boxes, on your Web page, you must first add a form to the page so that the appropriate code is added to the HTML.

To add a form to a page, click in the Document window where you want to add the form and choose Insert⇨Form⇨Form or click the Form button from the Forms category on the Insert bar. (If the Insert bar is set to a different category, click and hold the category name and select Common from the drop-down list.)

Dreamweaver adds the form to the page as indicated by the red dashed lines and also adds the associated form tag to your HTML page code, as shown in Figure 4-1. You can now insert form objects inside the red dashed lines of the form.

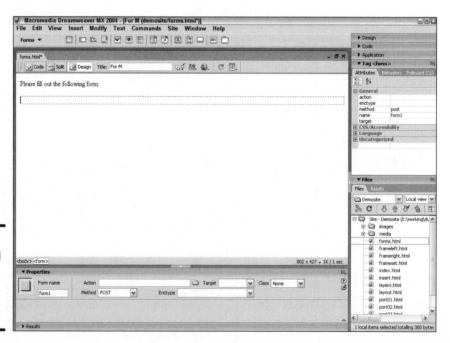

Figure 4-1:
The dashed lines mean you've created a form!

If you attempt to add a form object without first adding a form, a dialog box appears, asking whether you want to add a form tag. Click Yes to add both the form tag and the object to your page.

Specifying form properties

A form has six properties that you can set using the Form Property inspector: Form Name, Action, Method, Enctype, Target, and Class. Click the form to open the Form Property inspector. (If the Property inspector does not appear, open it by choosing Window⇨Properties.) Then specify the following properties:

✦ **Form Name:** Enter an alphanumeric name in the empty text field (the name should start with a letter, but it can be made up of both letters and numbers). The advantage of naming your form is that you can use the name to reference the form in a scripting language that you use to retrieve, store, and manipulate the form data.

✦ **Action:** Enter the URL of the application document/file that processes the form data. Alternatively, you can browse to the location by clicking the folder and making a selection in the Select File dialog box.

You can select the following three common actions:

- Enter the URL of a ColdFusion page that evaluates the form after it's been submitted.

- Enter the JavaScript program that runs after the user submits the form. The action appears as follows:

  `javascript:function()`

  Here, *function* refers to the name of your form-handling function.

- Enter a `mailto:` address where the form data goes after the user clicks the Submit button. A `mailto:` address appears similar to the following:

  `mailto:gruntworker@formhandling.com`

✦ **Method:** Select a method from the drop-down list for how the form data passes to the processing entity that you specified in the Action field. Choices are Default, GET, and POST. (Default and GET are the same.) GET sends the form data by appending it to the URL that the Action specifies. POST sends the form data as a separate entity. GET limits the amount of data that can pass along, but POST does not.

In other words, if you were to choose GET, the URL sent to the server might look something like `http://www.server.com/coldfusionpage.cfm&bowlingballcolor=blue`, with the form data stuck onto the end. If you were to choose POST instead, the URL would just look something like `http://www.server.com/coldfusionpage.cfm`.

Most of the time, whether you choose GET or POST doesn't really make a difference. However, there are times when you may want to choose one over the other. For example, for security purposes, you may not want information, such as a credit card number, ever being shown in a browser's history. And if the user might choose to bookmark the URL, whether or not to have all of the form data appear could affect your decision. If the form data included secure user information (such as the credit card example), then you probably wouldn't want to have the form data appear. However, if the form data includes search criteria, the user might want to bookmark the URL complete with the search parameters.

Data received at the specified `mailto:` address is not formatted for easy reading: It appears as strings of code with the form data embedded within it. This may depend on the encoding option, which we are about to discuss.

✦ **Enctype:** This is an optional attribute. For enctype, your choices are `application/x-www-form-urlencoded` (the default), and multipart/form-data. `application/x-www-form-urlencoded` replaces all blank characters in the text with a plus sign (+), and other non-printing characters with symbols and numbers. This is often necessary for the server to interpret the information it is receiving — for example, when you've used the GET method, the browser would not be able to process a URL with blank spaces in it. Multipart/form-data does not do this conversion, but instead transfers the information as a compound MIME document. Multipart/form-data is the method that must be used if you are using an `<INPUT TYPE="file">` element in the form. Instead of either of these two options, you can type in text/plain, which will also send the data unencoded; however, this is not a W3C standard.

✦ **Target:** This is also an optional attribute. If you do not specify a target, the server will assume that you want any information that is sent back to the browser (the URL of the response page, for example) sent to the same window or frame that your original form is in. If you wish the form submission's results to appear in a different frame or window, you must specify the name of the target window in this attribute.

✦ **Class:** You can apply a CSS (Cascading Style Sheet) class to the form as a whole and to some form elements in order to control how those form elements appear in a browser. For example, you can specify the color of a text field by assigning it a style. This attribute is also optional. For details on using CSS style sheets, take a look at *Cascading Style Sheets For Dummies*, by Damon Dean (published by Wiley Publishing, Inc.).

Labeling form objects

Dreamweaver enables you to provide descriptors for form objects and provide the user with directions about how to complete the information requested for each option. To add descriptors to form objects, simply position your cursor in the form and begin typing. Then insert the form object you want.

Using text fields

Text fields are blank text boxes that you can insert in your form to hold alphanumeric information that the user types. You can set up a text field to hold a single line of text, multiple lines of text, or a password, as follows:

✦ **Single line:** Provides space for the user to enter a single word or short phrase of text.

✦ **Multi line:** Provides space for the user to enter a longer string of text. Appropriate for a comment box.

✦ **Password:** Provides space for the user to enter a password. An asterisk or other placeholder appears in the text field for each character that the user types.

Book II
Chapter 4

**Punching Up
Your Pages with
Forms and Frames**

To add a text field, follow these steps:

1. **In the Document window, click where you want to add the text field and choose Insert⇨Form⇨Text Field, or click the Insert Text Field button on the Form category of the Insert bar.**

If the Insert bar is set to a different category, click and hold the category name and select Form from the drop-down list.

Dreamweaver adds a text field to your form, and a Text Field Property inspector appears. If the Text Field Property inspector does not appear, choose Window⇨Properties to open the inspector.

2. **Fill in the following fields of the Text Field Property inspector to define the parameters of the text field:**

- **TextField name:** Enter a name in the empty field. The field is referenced by this name in the HTML page code.

- **Char Width:** Enter a whole number for the approximate visible width of the field. (The width is approximate because text characters in your form are displayed differently according to users' browser settings.)

- **Max Chars:** (Applies to Single line and Password fields only.) Enter a whole number to indicate the maximum number of characters that the user can enter in the field. Max Chars can be different from Char Width.

- **Num Lines:** (Applies to Multi line fields only.) This specifies the height, in lines, of the form element, and may be affected by the setting for Wrap (see below).

- **Type:** Select a radio button for Single line, Multi line, or Password.

- **Init Val:** (Optional) Enter an alphanumeric word or phrase that occupies the text field when the user first encounters the field. Users can enter their own information over the Init Val. If you leave this attribute blank, the user will see a standard empty text field.

- **Wrap:** (Applies to Multi line fields only.) Select an option for text wrapping from the drop-down list. Options consist of Default, Off, Virtual, or Physical. Default and Off are the same and do not wrap text until the user presses the Enter key. The Virtual option wraps text on the user's screen but not when the form is submitted. The Physical option wraps text both on the user's screen and when the form is submitted.

- **Class:** (Optional) You may assign a CSS class to a text field to affect the appearance of the field or the text within it. For details on using CSS style sheets, look up *Cascading Style Sheets For Dummies*, by Damon Dean (published by Wiley Publishing, Inc.).

Setting up buttons

After a user enters data into a form, the user must then perform some sort of task to transmit the data from his or her computer to another computer that can process the information. Dreamweaver offers you three buttons you can use to activate your form: Submit Form, Reset Form, and None:

- ✦ **Submit Form:** After the user clicks this button, the form data scoots off to another computer based on the specified action. (You see how to set the action of a form in the "Specifying form properties" section, earlier in this chapter.)

- ✦ **Reset Form:** After the user clicks this button, it erases all data entered into the form, resetting each form field to its initial value.

- ✦ **None:** After the user clicks this button, it executes the programming function that the Web designer assigned to it (for example, performs a mathematical calculation or sends the user to a different URL).

Follow these steps to insert a button into your form:

1. **Click where you want to add the button in the Document window and choose Insert⇨Form⇨Button, or click Insert Button on the Form category of the Insert bar.**

If the Insert bar is set to a different category, click and hold the category name and select Form from the drop-down list.

Dreamweaver adds a button to your form and the Button Property inspector becomes visible. If the Button Property inspector does not appear, choose Window⇨Properties to open the inspector.

2. **Fill in the following fields of the Button Property inspector to define the parameters of the button:**

   - **Button name:** Enter a name in the empty text field. This name identifies the button in the HTML code.

   - **Label:** Enter the text that you want to appear on the button.

   - **Action:** Select a radio button to indicate the function of the button. Choices consist of Submit form, Reset form, and None.

   - **Class:** (Optional) You can assign a CSS style to affect the button's appearance (color, width, and the like).

You can create a graphical Submit button — a button created from a small image — by choosing Insert⇨Form⇨Image Field or by clicking the Image Field button in the Form category of the Insert bar. Then browse to the image file in your site or type the path to and name of the image file directly into the File Name field.

Adding other form elements

In addition to the text fields and buttons, you can add a variety of form elements that help your users give you information. Figure 4-2 shows some of the useful form elements you can add to your forms. To insert any of the elements you see in Figure 4-2, follow these steps:

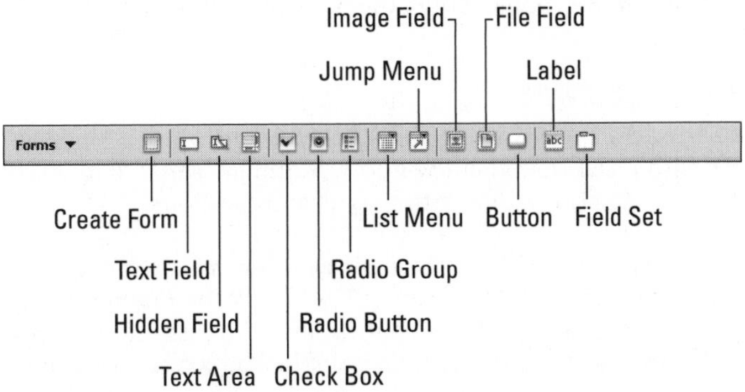

Figure 4-2:
Form
elements.

Image Field — *File Field*
Jump Menu — *Label*

Forms ▼

Create Form — *List Menu* — *Button* — *Field Set*
Text Field — *Radio Group*
Hidden Field — *Radio Button*
Text Area — *Check Box*

1. **Position your cursor in the area of the Document window where you want to add the element.**

2. **Click the appropriate button in the Form category of the Insert bar (see Figure 4-2), or choose Insert⇨Form Objects⇨*Desired Form Element.***

   If the Insert bar is set to a different category, click and hold the category name and select Form from the drop-down list.

Dreamweaver adds the element to your form, and the appropriate inspector appears. (If the appropriate inspector does not appear, open it by choosing Windows⇨Properties.)

3. **Fill in the fields of the inspector.**

   If you're adding a radio group, jump menu, or image, a dialog box will pop up and ask you for additional information. Fill in your choices for each of these.

4. **Click OK to apply your selections and close the dialog box.**

Structuring Pages with Frames

Frames are divisions of a Web page that enable you to load information independently into distinct regions of the browser window. Frames are useful if you want to display certain information on-screen while changing other information. You frequently see three-frame pages on the Web — the top frame shows the site's title graphic, the left frame shows the navigation bar, and the large body frame changes to show the content that you select.

A special HTML page called a *frameset* defines the structure and formatting of frames on your Web page. As you work with frames, be aware that you must always save the frameset page to lay out the size, position, and borders of your frames, along with the content that you want to display in each frame. And keep in mind that different browsers may draw the frames slightly differently, even if you specify exact pixel dimensions.

Adding frames

You can add a frame to a frameless Document window or to an existing frame within the Document window. Adding a frame to an existing frame divides the existing frame into two or more regions.

To add a frame, click the Document window or existing frame in the area where you want to add the frame. Then click the Frames button in the Form category of the Insert bar and choose from the list of options that pops up. You can also get to an equivalent list (the same options, some with slightly different names, and no icons) by choosing Insert⇨HTML⇨Frames⇨*Frame Option*, where *Frame Option* is one of the choices detailed in Table 4-1.

Table 4-1	Options for Creating Frames
Frame Option	*What It Does*
Left	Creates a vertical frame down the left side
Right	Creates a vertical frame down the right side
Top	Creates a horizontal frame across the top

Frame Option	What It Does
Bottom	Creates a horizontal frame across the bottom
Bottom and Nested Left	Splits the page in two — top and bottom — and creates a left frame in the top frame
Bottom and Nested Right	Splits the page in two — top and bottom — and creates a right frame in the top frame
Left and Nested Bottom	Splits the page in two — right and left — and creates a bottom frame in the right frame
Right and Nested Bottom	Splits the page in two — right and left — and creates a bottom frame in the left frame
Top and Bottom	Creates three frames
Left and Nested Top	Splits the page in two — right and left — and creates a top frame in the right frame
Right and Nested Top	Splits the page in two — right and left — and creates a top frame in the left frame
Top and Nested Left	Splits the page in two — top and bottom — and creates a left frame in the bottom frame
Top and Nested Right	Splits the page in two — top and bottom — and creates a right frame in the bottom frame

Book II
Chapter 4

Punching Up Your Pages with Forms and Frames

A third method of adding a frame is to drag the outer border of the current frame, or Alt+click in the inner border. You can then follow the steps in the next section to modify this new frame.

Modifying frames

You use the Frame Property inspector to select the source page that appears in a frame. You also use the Frame Property inspector to format the appearance of an individual frame. To modify a frame, follow these steps:

1. **If the Properties panel is not already open, open it by choosing Window⇨Properties or by using the keyboard shortcut Ctrl+F3.**

2. **In the Frames panel, Alt+click the frame that you want to modify the attributes of.**

    Note: You can't simply click a frame to open its associated Frame Property inspector. If you click a frame, you're actually clicking the source page that resides in the frame — a process identical to clicking in the Document window for that page. To select a specific frame, press the Alt key and click in the frame. You see the Frame Property inspector for an individual frame, and the selected frame is marked with a dashed line, as shown in Figure 4-3.

    A Frame Property inspector appears for the selected frame. If the inspector doesn't appear, open it by choosing Window⇨Properties.

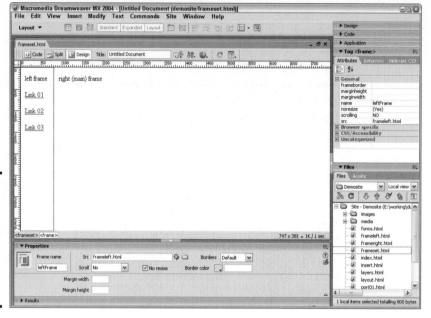

Figure 4-3:
Alt+click a frame to select it and see the Frame Property inspector.

3. **In the Frame Property inspector or the Attributes tab of the Tag Inspector panel, enter a name for your frame in the Frame Name text field.**

   This name is the name by which the frame is referenced in the Frames panel, target drop-down lists, and the HTML page code. The frame name must start with a letter, and you should not use hyphens, spaces, or periods. You should also avoid using JavaScript-reserved names, such as `top`. Although these words and symbols may be accepted, if you are using any scripting (JavaScript, VBScript) to manipulate your frames, the results may be inconsistent or wrong. It's a good idea to get into the habit of avoiding these words and characters. Word separation can be indicated by capitalization, and underscore characters can also be used.

4. **In the Src text field, enter the name of the source page whose content you intend to display in the frame.**

   Alternatively, you can click the Src folder and browse to select the source page.

5. **Select a scrolling option for your selected frame from the Scroll drop-down list. The options are as follows:**

   • **Yes:** Adds scroll bars to the frame, whether they're needed or not.

   • **No:** Doesn't add scroll bars to the frame, even if a scroll bar is needed to display the entire frame.

- **Auto:** Places one or more scroll bars in the frame if the frame contents exceed the frame boundaries.

- **Default:** Places one or more scroll bars in the frame, depending on the user's browser settings.

6. **Select the No Resize check box if you don't want the user to be able to resize the frame.**

    If you do want the user to be able to resize the frame, leave the check box deselected.

7. **Format the frame border appearance by selecting a choice from the Borders drop-down list:**

    - **Yes:** Creates a three-dimensional look for the borders. (This doesn't work in all browsers.)

    - **No:** Creates a single-color flat look for the borders, or if No is selected for each of the frames in a frameset, no border appears.

    - **Default:** Enables the user's browser to set how borders appear.

8. **Select a border color for the frame by clicking the Border Color swatch and selecting a color from the Color palette that appears.**

    Alternatively, you can enter a hexadecimal color code in the Border Color text field. This doesn't work in all browsers and is optional. If your frames don't have borders, then the border color will not apply.

9. **Enter a number in pixels in the Margin Width and the Margin Height text fields.**

    Margin Width specifies the horizontal standoff space between the frame content and the frame border. Margin Height specifies the vertical standoff space between the frame content and the frame border. This is in addition to any values that the page called into the frame already has assigned.

Deleting frames

To delete a frame, select the frame border and drag it to the edge of the parent frame or to the edge of the Document window — whichever is closer. If you only have two frames on the page, this action will result in a frameset with only one page in it.

Saving frames

Saving a frame means that you're saving the HTML page from which the source content of the frame originates. To save a frame, follow these steps:

1. **Select the frame by clicking in it.**

2. **Choose File⇨Save Frame.**

3. **The first time you save the frame, enter a name in the File Name text field of the Save As dialog box that appears, and then click the Save button.**

   Future saves require that you complete only Steps 1 and 2.

Saving framesets

Saving a frameset means saving the layout of frame positions, frame names, and border formatting on a page. Keep in mind that you must save individual frames to save the content contained in those frames. To save a frameset, follow these steps:

1. **Select the frameset by clicking one of its borders.**

2. **Choose File➪Save Frameset.**

   Note: This will not work if the frameset is nested.

3. **The first time you save the frameset, enter a name in the File Name text field of the Save As dialog box that appears, and then click Save.**

   Future saves require that you complete only Steps 1 and 2.

If you have made changes to individual frames — not just the frameset — since your last save, Dreamweaver asks if you want to save individual frames. Make sure that you do so.

Setting no-frames content

Text-based browsers and many older browsers frequently don't support frames and can't correctly display pages that you create by using frames.

To help ensure that the maximum number of users can view your page correctly, Dreamweaver offers you a method for building no-frames pages as companions to your frame-enabled pages. To create a no-frames page for your current frameset, follow these steps:

1. **Choose Modify➪Frameset➪Edit NoFrames Content.**

   A blank, NoFrames Content page appears in the Document window and replaces your frame-enabled page, as shown in Figure 4-4.

2. **On the NoFrames Content page, insert the content that you want to appear in NoFrames browsers.**

   This content can include text, images, and other page elements.

3. **Return to your frame-enabled page by choosing Modify➪Frameset➪ Edit NoFrames Content.**

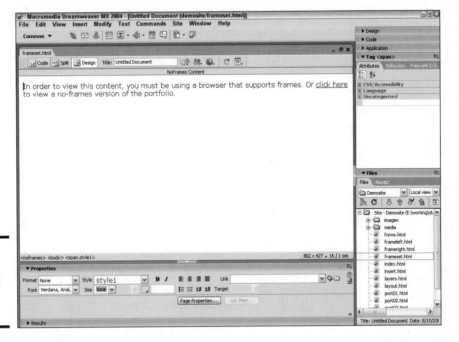

Book II
Chapter 4

Punching Up
Your Pages with
Forms and Frames

Figure 4-4:
An
alternative
NoFrames
page.

Targeting content

You can set up a two-frame frameset in which you use the left frame for navigation and the main frame to display any link that the user clicks in the navigation frame. Simply set up the link to target the main frame as the location where you want the selected HTML page to open.

Set up a target by following these steps:

1. **Select the text or image that you want to act as a link.**

Doing so opens the associated Property inspector. If the inspector doesn't appear, open it by choosing Window⇨Properties.

2. **In the Link field, enter the name of the HTML source page that will appear in the frame.**

Alternatively, you can click the Link folder and browse to select the source page.

3. **From the Target drop-down list, select the target frame where the link is to appear.**

All available targets are listed in the drop-down list, as shown in Figure 4-5. These targets include the names of all frames that you set up and also the following system-wide targets:

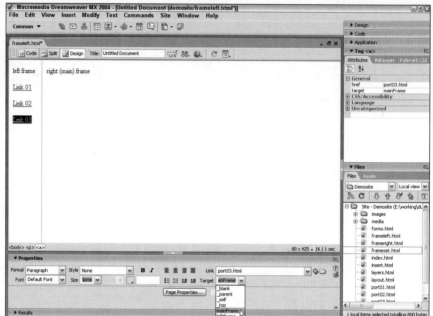

Figure 4-5:
Select a
target frame
for the link.

- **_blank**: Opens a new browser window and shows the link in that window. The current window remains open.

- **_parent**: Opens the link in a window that replaces the frameset containing the current page.

- **_self**: Opens the link in the current frame. The linked page replaces the page in the current frame. If you want the link to open in the current frame, you can select **_self**, or you can leave the Target area in the Property inspector empty.

- **_top**: Opens the link in a window that replaces the outermost frameset of the current page. (Same as **_parent**, unless you're using nested framesets.)

Targeting can work in more complicated framesets using the same basic process. Whichever frame you target is the one that will update when the user clicks a link targeting that frame.

Chapter 5: Laying Out Pages with Layers

In This Chapter

✔ Adding, selecting, and deleting a layer

✔ Placing objects in a layer

✔ Changing layer properties

✔ Nesting layers

To lay out the content of your Web page precisely, you can use tables (see Book II, Chapter 2), or you can use the latest and greatest layout aid: layers. You can think of layers in Dreamweaver MX 2004 as separate pieces of transparent paper that you fill with content (images, text, and so on) and shuffle, stack, position, and overlap until your Web page looks exactly the way you want.

Dreamweaver layers use a now common companion to HTML called Cascading Style Sheets (CSS) in order to place your content anywhere on the screen. However, you should be aware that Cascading Style Sheets are only supported in Internet Explorer and Netscape Navigator versions above 4.0. For more information about Cascading Style Sheets, check out *Cascading Style Sheets For Dummies,* by Damon Dean (published by Wiley Publishing, Inc.).

Before you begin working with layers, you may find it useful to have the Design panel open to the Layers tab. To do this, choose Window➪Layers, or if you're in hurry, simply press F2.

Adding a Layer

Adding a layer to the workspace of your Document window, shown in Figure 5-1, can be done using one of the following two methods:

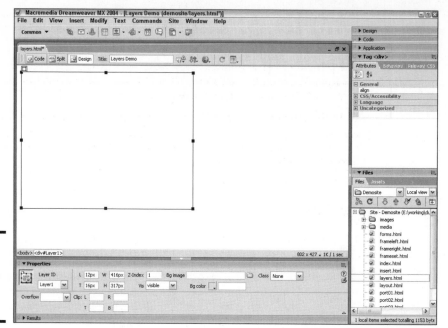

Figure 5-1:
Adding a
layer to the
Document
window.

✦ **Choose Insert⇨Layout Objects⇨Layer.** If there is nothing on the page already, as in this case, a new layer appears in the upper-left corner of your Document window.

✦ **Click the Draw Layer button (just to the left of the Standard button) on the Layout category of the Insert bar.** (If the Insert bar is not set to the Layout category, click the category name and choose Layout from the drop-down list.) Position the cross hair cursor anywhere in your Document window and click and drag until the layer obtains the dimensions you want. Release the mouse button.

If you set a layer's visibility to Hidden, it may be invisible in the Document window. To see it, simply click the name of the layer in the Layers tab of the Design panel. Now you can see the layer, even though its visibility remains set to Hidden. See the "Changing the visibility of a layer" section, later in this chapter, for details on Visibility settings.

Selecting a Layer

Selecting a layer enables you to identify which layer you want to affect when executing a layer operation, such as moving or naming the layer. Use any of the following methods to select a layer:

✦ In the Document window, click on the boundary of the layer. (Your cursor will turn into a four-pointed arrow when you place it over a layer boundary.)

✦ In the Document window, click anywhere inside the layer while holding down the Shift key. (***Note:*** This won't work if the insertion point is already inside the layer you want to select.)

✦ In the Layers tab of the Design panel, click the name of the layer.

Selection handles appear on the boundary of the layer to indicate that you have selected it.

Deleting a Layer

Deleting a layer removes the layer, the layer's contents, and the layer marker from the Document window. To delete a layer, select the layer and press the Delete or Backspace key.

Don't delete a layer if you want to remove it from one page and add it to another. Instead, cut the layer by choosing Edit⇨Cut. Open the page where you want to add the layer and choose Edit⇨Paste.

Placing Objects in a Layer

To add an object to a layer, click inside the layer and follow the normal procedure for adding the object. For instance, add text to a layer by clicking inside the layer and typing text; add other objects to a layer by clicking inside the layer and choosing Insert⇨*Object,* where *Object* is the name of the item you want to add to the layer.

Changing Layer Properties

You can change lots of properties of layers, including:

✦ **Background:** You can add a background image or color to a layer.

✦ **Name:** Naming a layer can help you keep track of objects on a complex page, and is necessary if you want to apply Behaviors to the layer.

✦ **Alignment:** You can align layers with each other.

✦ **Visibility:** Layers (and the objects on them) can be visible or invisible.

✦ **Position:** Layers can be nested inside other layers; they can also be stacked in different orders.

✦ **Size:** You can change the layer's height and width.

✦ **Location:** You can move a layer to any location on a page.

We show you how to edit each of these layer properties in the following sections.

Including a background image or color in a layer

By default, an unnested layer does not have a color or background image, and will just display what lies beneath it, as if it were transparent. (A nested child layer, if it's empty, will show the color or background image of its parent. For more about nested layers, see the section, "Nesting Layers," later in this chapter.)

You can change the background of any layer by adding a background image or color as follows:

1. Select the layer that you want to change the background of.

If the Layer Property inspector does not appear, open it by choosing Window⇨Properties.

2. In the Layer Property inspector, change one of the following:

• **Bg Image:** Click the folder to the right of the text field and browse to select a background image from the Select Image Source dialog box that appears. Click the Select button to accept your image choice and close the dialog box. The path to and name of the background image appear in the Bg Image field, and the image is added to the background of the layer. Figure 5-2 shows a layer with a background image.

• **Bg Color:** Click the color box (the little gray box with an arrow on it) and select a color from the color palette that appears. Alternatively, you can enter a hexadecimal number for a color in the Bg Color field. The new color appears in the background of the selected layer.

Naming a layer

The first layer you add to a page is automatically named Layer1; the second layer you add is named Layer2; and so on. You can change these default number names to other names that help you more easily distinguish layers when working with HTML and examining layers with the Layer Property inspector or Layers tab of the Design panel.

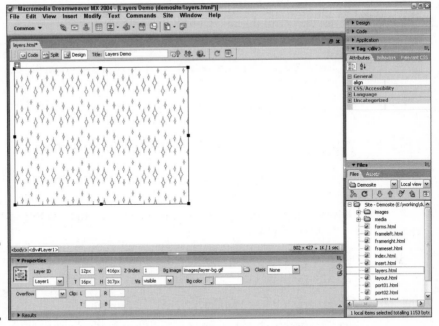

Figure 5-2:
An image
added to a
background.

To name a layer using the Layers tab of the Design panel, follow these steps:

1. **If the Layers tab of the Design panel is not already visible, choose
    Window⇨Layers or use the keyboard shortcut F2.**

2. **Double-click the Name column for the layer whose name you want to
    change.**

    The current name is selected.

3. **Enter a new name for the layer.**

Get in the habit of appropriately naming your layers as soon as you create
them. The name *BlueprintImageMap* helps you remember a layer's content
much better than *Layer15*. Remember that layer names cannot contain
spaces.

Aligning layers

Aligning layers with each other can help you precisely lay out visual content
in the Document window. You can align the top, left side, right side, or
bottom of layers.

To align layers, select the layers you want to align by pressing and holding the Shift key, and then clicking each layer in the Document window. Choose Modify➪Align and choose one of the following options from the submenu:

✦ **Left:** Assigns the x-coordinate of the last selected layer to all selected layers.

✦ **Right:** Aligns the right side of all selected layers with the right side of the last selected layer.

✦ **Top:** Assigns the y-coordinate of the last selected layer to all selected layers.

✦ **Bottom:** Aligns the bottom of all selected layers with the bottom of the last selected layer.

✦ **Make Same Width:** Gives all the layers the same width as the last selected layer.

✦ **Make Same Height:** Gives all the layers the same height as the last selected layer.

Changing the visibility of a layer

You can specify whether a layer is visible or hidden when a Web page *loads* — first appears in the user's browser window — and as a result of specific actions by the user. Visibility can change as many times as you want. Visibility options consist of the following:

✦ **Default:** The layer's initial visibility is the default setting, which is visible. To edit layer default settings, choose Edit➪Preferences and the Preferences dialog box (see Figure 5-3) appears, displaying the layer default settings that you can change.

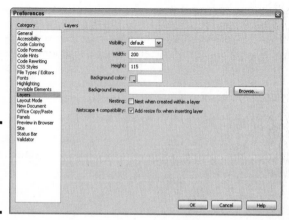

Figure 5-3:
Setting your default preferences for layers.

✦ **Inherit:** For a nested layer, the layer's initial visibility is the same as the visibility of its parent. For an unnested layer, selecting the inherit option causes the layer to appear as visible.

✦ **Visible:** The layer's initial visibility setting is visible.

✦ **Hidden:** The layer's initial visibility is hidden.

You can use either the Layer Property inspector or the Layers tab of the Design panel to set layer visibility. By setting layer visibility, you can create scripts that cause images to appear (or disappear) in response to user interaction. For example, you can create an image of a widget that appears on a Web page after a user clicks a link marked, <u>Click here to see our top-of-the-line widget!</u>

To set the initial visibility of a layer via the Layer Property inspector, select the layer in the Document window to open the Layer Property inspector. If the inspector does not appear, open it by choosing Window⇨Properties. Choose a visibility option from the Vis drop-down list.

Layering layers: Setting the z-index

The *z-index* of a layer indicates the layer's position in a stack of multiple layers. Z-indices are useful when you have a handful of layers — some containing transparent portions, some of different sizes — stacked one on top of the other. Changing the z-index of your layers lets you "shuffle" the layers — much as you shuffle a deck of cards — to create interesting visual effects.

Z-indices are measured in whole numbers and do not have to be consecutive — for instance, you can have three layers with z-indices of 1, 3, and 7, respectively. The layer with the largest z-index sits on top of the layer stack, and the layer with the smallest z-index sits on the bottom of the layer stack. Layers with larger z-indices obscure those with smaller z-indices. You can change the z-index of a layer in either the Layer Property inspector or the Layers tab of the Design panel.

To assign the z-index of a layer by using the Layer Property inspector, follow these steps:

1. **Select the layer to open the Layer Property inspector.**

   If the Layer Property inspector does not appear, open it by choosing Window⇨Properties.

2. **Enter a new number in the Z-Index field of the Layer Property inspector.**

To assign the z-index of a layer using the Layers tab of the Design panel, follow these steps:

1. **If the Layers tab of the Design panel is not already visible, choose Window⇨Layers or use the keyboard shortcut F2.**

2. **Click the Z column for the layer whose z-index you want to change.**

The current z-index is selected.

3. **Enter a new z-index for the layer.**

The new number appears in the Z column for the selected layer, as shown in Figure 5-4.

4. **Click anywhere outside the Z column or press the Enter key.**

Note that you can have multiple layers at the same z-index.

Figure 5-4:
Changing
the z-index
of the layer
named
"SuppText."

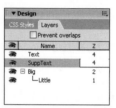

To assign relative z-indices to layers by reordering layers in the Layers tab of the Design panel, follow these steps:

1. **Open the Layers tab of the Design panel by choosing Window⇨Layers or by using the keyboard shortcut F2.**

The Layers tab lists layers in order of descending z-index. Nested layers are listed in descending order within their parent layer.

2. **Click the name of a layer for which you want to change the z-index.**

3. **Drag the layer name into a new list position and release the mouse button.**

As you drag, the selected layer is indicated by a thick line.

Figure 5-5 shows the effect of changing a z-index. In the top image, the z-index of the bowling pins is higher than the starry background image. As a result, the bowling pins are on top. Conversely, in the bottom image, the starry background image has the higher z-index value, and as a result, it's on top of the bowling pins. Dreamweaver reorders the list in the Layers tab and renumbers layer z-indices to reflect your change. Also, Dreamweaver updates the associated code for the layers' z-indices in the HTML source code for your page.

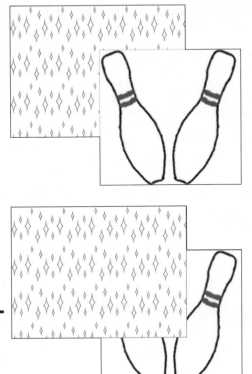

Figure 5-5:
The effect
of changing
z-indices.

Because you don't have to number the z-index of layers consecutively, consider leaving gaps between indices, in case you later want to add new layers into the middle of the stack. For instance, use only even numbers for your indices so that you can easily sandwich a layer with an odd-numbered z-index in between.

Moving a layer

You may want to move a layer to another location in the Document window or to a position relative to the grid or to other objects.

To move a layer, select the layer in the Document window and then reposition your selection by using one of the following three methods:

✦ Click and drag the layer to a new location and release the mouse button.

✦ Press the arrow keys you find on the numeric keypad on your keyboard to nudge the layer up, down, left, or right one pixel at a time. If you hold down the Shift key, every press of an arrow key moves the layer by 10 pixels.

◆ In the Layer Property inspector, enter a new value in the T (top) and L (left) fields to indicate the pixel coordinates of the layer's top-left corner.

When moving layers, you can choose to enable or prevent layer overlap, depending on how you want the final image montage to appear. You enable or prevent layer overlap by selecting or deselecting the Prevent Overlaps check box in the Layers tab of the Design panel.

Resizing a layer

Resizing a layer means changing its height and width dimensions. To resize a layer, select the layer and perform one of the following tasks:

◆ Click and drag a selection handle — one of the large dots on the layer boundary — until the layer obtains the dimensions you desire.

◆ In the Layer Property inspector, enter a new width in pixels at the W field and a new height in pixels at the H field. If the Layer Property inspector does not appear, open it by choosing Window⇨Properties.

You can change the height and width dimensions of multiple layers at the same time as follows:

1. **Press and hold the Shift key while selecting each layer you want to resize.**

If the Multiple Layers Property inspector does not appear, open it by choosing Window⇨Properties.

2. **In the Multiple Layers Property inspector, enter a new width in pixels in the W field and a new height in pixels in the H field.**

Nesting Layers

A *nested* layer is a layer that has all of its HTML code lying within another layer. The nested layer is often referred to as a *child* layer, whereas the layer on which it depends is called the *parent* layer. A child layer can be drawn completely inside its parent (as shown in Figure 5-6), in an intersecting arrangement with its parent, or completely unattached to its parent, depending on the effect you want to achieve. A nested layer inherits the same visibility of its parent and moves with the parent when the parent layer is repositioned in the Document window. Some versions of Netscape have issues with nested layers, so try to avoid using them if there is a simpler way to accomplish the same thing.

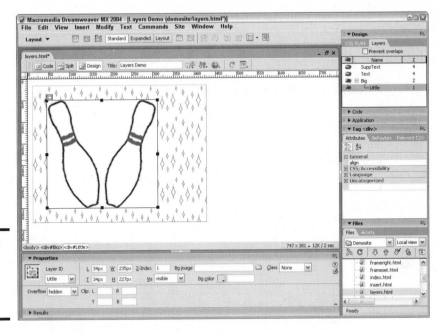

**Book II
Chapter 5**

Laying Out Pages
with Layers

Figure 5-6:
A layer
nested in
another
layer.

Enabling nesting

To create nested layers in the Document window, you must first enable nesting. To do so, follow these steps:

1. **Choose Edit⇨Preferences to open the Preferences dialog box or use the keyboard shortcut Ctrl+U.**

2. **In the Preferences dialog box, select Layers in the Category area.**

3. **Select the Nesting check box.**

4. **Click OK to close the Preferences dialog box.**

5. **In the Document window, choose Window⇨Layers to open the Layers tab of the Design panel.**

6. **In the Layers tab, make sure that the Prevent Overlaps option is deselected.**

Creating a new nested layer

Use either of these methods to draw a nested layer after enabling nesting:

✦ Click inside an existing layer and choose Insert⇨Layout Objects⇨Layer. A child layer of default size appears inside the parent layer.

✦ Select Layout Tools⇨Draw Layer in the Layout category of the Insert bar. Then click and drag your mouse in the parent layer, releasing the mouse button when the layer has reached the dimensions you desire.

If the dimensions of the parent layer are smaller than the dimensions of the child layer, the child layer will exceed the boundaries of the parent.

Nesting an existing layer

To change the nesting of an existing layer, follow these steps:

1. **Open the Layers tab of the Design panel by choosing Window⇨Layers or using the keyboard shortcut F2.**

2. **In the Layers tab of the Design panel, press and hold the Ctrl key while using the mouse to click and drag the intended child layer on top of its new parent.**

   The child is in the correct position when you see a box appear around the name of its intended parent layer.

3. **Release the mouse button.**

   The new child-parent relationship is shown in the Layers tab of the Design panel.

Dreamweaver draws the new child layer and updates the associated code for changed layer-nesting in the HTML source code for your page.

Collapsing or expanding your view in the Layers tab

You can change how you view the names of nested layers in the Layers tab of the Design panel by collapsing or expanding your view:

✦ **To collapse your view:** Click the minus sign (–) in front of a parent layer. Names of nested child layers for that parent are hidden.

✦ **To expand your view:** Click the plus sign (+) in front of a parent layer. Names of nested child layers appear underneath that parent layer.

Chapter 6: Using ColdFusion MX 6.1 Developer Edition in Dreamweaver MX 2004

In This Chapter

✔ **Exploring how ColdFusion is integrated into Dreamweaver**

✔ **Using the Tag Editor and the Insert panel**

✔ **Viewing database connections**

✔ **Using the Bindings tabs to get dynamic data**

✔ **Taking a brief look at Server behaviors and components**

*O*ne of the biggest changes that came with the previous version of Macromedia Studio was the integration of ColdFusion MX into Dreamweaver MX. For years, the two products had a symbiotic relationship, and as a result, their integration was an exceptionally smooth one. Dreamweaver was always better than ColdFusion as a graphical HTML editor. ColdFusion and its sister product, Macromedia HomeSite, were the better choices for the HTML editor who preferred a coder-friendly interface. This chapter provides the lowdown on the features in Dreamweaver that bring ColdFusion to life.

This chapter only covers the ColdFusion features that are available in Dreamweaver. For a complete run-down of ColdFusion and how it works, check out Book VI.

Understanding the Integration of ColdFusion and Dreamweaver

Before the MX version, Dreamweaver was largely geared toward the basics of HTML editing, such as creating and editing tables, graphics placement, text editing, and some basic site management tools. With the integration of ColdFusion, Dreamweaver became more robust, with a host of features that could make your site more dynamic.

Before Dreamweaver MX arrived, ColdFusion was made up of three components:

✦ A Web-based application server that read HTML and ColdFusion code and generated HTML for a browser to view.

✦ A scripting language that enabled users to perform a number of dynamic functions, such as querying databases and personalizing Web pages based on user input.

✦ A stand-alone development tool (ColdFusion Studio) that was used to create ColdFusion code and manage some parts of the application server.

In the previous version of Dreamweaver, ColdFusion Studio was simply integrated into the Dreamweaver interface. This resulted in a single product that incorporates both the WYSIWYG (What You See Is What You Get) interface that Dreamweaver users are accustomed to and the more developer-friendly ColdFusion Studio code environment. The other elements of ColdFusion remained largely the same.

In Dreamweaver, you can find ColdFusion features in the following areas:

✦ **Code view:** Select Code view by choosing View⇨Code. This is the development view that was traditionally associated with ColdFusion Studio. Figure 6-1 shows both the view from ColdFusion Studio 5 and the Code view in Dreamweaver MX 2004. You can see that a lot of the physical features look the same.

✦ **Insert bar:** If you've used the previous version of Dreamweaver, you'll notice a major interface change in the Insert function in Dreamweaver MX 2004. In the previous version, there was an Insert panel that utilized tabs to jump from section to section. In Dreamweaver MX 2004, when you click the name at the far left on the Insert bar, a listing of all the available sections (what Macromedia calls "categories") pops up. Scroll up or down and select a name to see the buttons in that category of the Insert bar. You find ColdFusion-specific functions in the Common, CFML, and Application categories.

✦ **Application panel:** To bring up the Application panel, choose Window, and then any of the following: Database, Bindings, Server Behaviors, or Components. This brings up the Application panel with the appropriate tab selected. Within the Application panel, you can configure databases, set up links to your remote site, and create ColdFusion components.

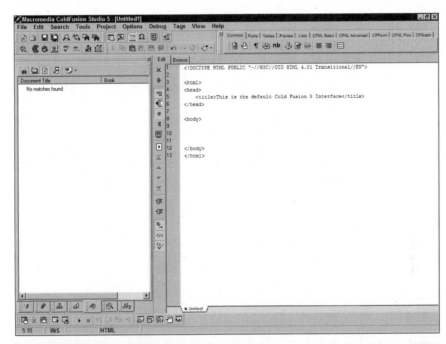

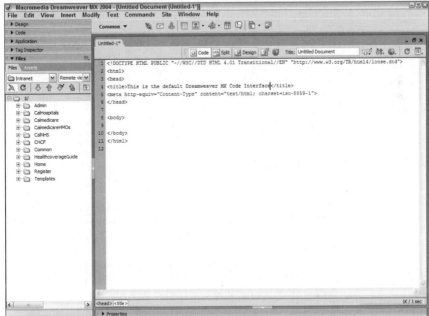

Figure 6-1:
Separated
at birth?

✦ **Code panel:** The Code panel, not to be confused with Code view, provides some valuable reference information about your code. (The Code panel is shown in Figure 6-2.) You can bring up the panel by choosing either Snippets or Reference from the Window menu:

- **Snippets tab:** With the Snippets tab, you can create reusable chunks (snippets) of code.

- **Reference tab:** The Reference tab gives you access to O'Reilly's reference guides to HTML, Javascript, and more, as well as guides to ColdFusion, ASP, and JSP.

Figure 6-2:
The Code
panel.

In previous versions of Dreamweaver, Code view also included a Tag Inspector, which reviewed the quality of your HTML code. That function is still there, though in Dreamweaver MX 2004, this feature has been given its own floating panel. You can still get to it by selecting Window⇨Code Inspector.

Using Features on the Insert Bar

When you have a ColdFusion page open, the Insert bar gives you access to a number of ColdFusion features, and using those ColdFusion features is pretty straightforward. Almost all the features include a Help button to explain to you precisely what the feature does.

To insert a ColdFusion feature, you follow these steps:

1. **Select the category in the Insert bar for the element you want to insert.**

You can choose from three ColdFusion categories: Common, CFML (ColdFusion Markup Language), and Application. The other categories are for regular Dreamweaver features.

2. **Click the icon of the feature you want to insert.**

   If the feature has parameters that need to be set, a dialog box will appear that allows you to set all the parameters for the selected feature. Figure 6-3 shows a dialog box for a Cfquery tag (with Cfquery, you can retrieve information from a database). For more information on how to use all these features, check out Book VI.

Book II
Chapter 6

Figure 6-3:
The Cfquery
dialog box.

Using ColdFusion MX 6.1 Developer Edition

If you move your mouse over an icon and keep it there, the name of the feature appears over the icon, allowing you to see what function that icon serves.

3. **Enter all the pertinent information in the dialog box for the element that you selected in Step 2.**

   Again, the information you must enter varies, depending on which tags or elements you selected.

4. **Click OK to insert the element.**

In Dreamweaver MX 2004, the ColdFusion commands have been consolidated from five tabs in the Insert panel to just three categories on the Insert bar. The Common category includes a Tag Chooser button, from which you can select ColdFusion CFML tags. Beyond that, all the ColdFusion features are either in the CFML or the Application categories on the Insert bar.

The CFML category includes access to the largest number of CFML tags and functions. Note that the last two icons on this category are entitled Flow and Advanced. This is where buttons from the old CFML Flow and CFML Advanced tabs landed. If you click these icons, you get pop-up menus, shown in Figure 6-4, which reveal a number of other functions that you can include in your documents. Here's a complete listing of the buttons in the CFML category:

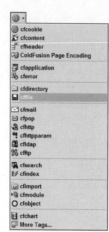

Figure 6-4:
The Flow
and
Advanced
pop-up
menus.

✦ **Server variables:** Creates server variables

✦ **cfquery:** Creates a <CFQUERY> tag

✦ **cfoutput:** Creates a <CFOUTPUT> tag

✦ **cfinsert:** Creates a <CFINSERT> tag

✦ **cfupdate:** Creates a <CFUPDATE> tag

✦ **cfinclude:** Creates a <CFINCLUDE> tag

✦ **cflocation:** Creates a <CFLOCATION> tag

✦ **cfset:** Sets the value of a variable

✦ **cfparam:** Creates a parameter

✦ **Comment:** Creates the comment arrows

✦ **Surround with #:** Surrounds the selected text with # signs

✦ **cfscript:** Creates a <CFSCRIPT> tag into which you can put ColdFusion
Script

Click the Flow icon to access to the following features:

✦ **cftry:** Creates a <CFTRY> tag

✦ **cfcatch:** Creates a <CFCATCH> tag

✦ **cfthrow:** Creates a <CFTHROW> tag

✦ **cflock:** Creates a <CFLOCK> tag

✦ **cfswitch:** Creates a <CFSWITCH> tag

✦ **cfcase:** Creates a <CFCASE> tag

✦ **cfdefaultcase:** Creates a <CFDEFAULTCASE> tag

✦ **cfif:** Creates a <CFIF> tag

✦ **cfelse:** Creates a <CFELSE> tag

✦ **cfelseif:** Creates a <CFELSEIF> tag

✦ **cfloop:** Creates a <CFLOOP> tag

✦ **cfbreak:** Creates a <CFBREAK> tag

Click the Advanced icon to access the following features:

✦ **cfcookie:** Enables you to specify the parameters of creating a cookie

✦ **cfcontent:** Enables you to specify how to create a content tag

✦ **cfheader:** Enables you to specify the parameters of creating a header

✦ **ColdFusion Page Encoding:** Sets your page encoding information

✦ **cfapplication:** Enables you to specify your application parameters

✦ **cferror:** Specifies error information

✦ **cfdirectory:** Allows you to work with directories (create, delete, list, and so on)

✦ **cffile:** Enables you to work with files (create, append, write, and so on)

✦ **cfmail:** Specifies how to send mail through ColdFusion

✦ **cfpop:** Specifies how to send messages through a POP server

✦ **cfhttp:** Specifies how to make an HTTP request

✦ **cfhttpparam:** Specifies how to set parameters for an HTTP request

✦ **cfldap:** Specifies how you can access an LDAP store

✦ **cfftp:** Specifies how to make an FTP request

✦ **cfsearch:** Builds you an interface to Verity to make searches

✦ **cfindex:** Builds you an interface to index a Verity search collection

✦ **cfimport:** Allows you to import a custom CF tag library or a JSP tag library

✦ **cfmodule:** Allows you to specify a module

✦ **cfobject:** Enables you to call a component

✦ **cfchart:** Specifies how to use ColdFusion's charting features

✦ **More Tags:** Brings up the Tag Chooser dialog box

**Book II
Chapter 6**

Using
ColdFusion MX 6.1
Developer Edition

Figure 6-5 shows the Application category of the Insert bar in Dreamweaver, which allows you to access the following ColdFusion features:

Figure 6-5:
Getting
at the
Application
features.

✦ **Recordset:** Allows you to connect to a database and retrieve data from that database and creates the `<CFQUERY>` tag for you

✦ **Stored Procedure:** Allows you to execute a stored procedure against an SQL database and specify parameters to be passed as part of that call

✦ **Dynamic Data:** Creates either dynamic text or a table, or populates various form elements with data from a database

✦ **Repeated Region:** Enables you to create a repeated region

✦ **Show Region:** Enables you to show or not show a specific area of content based on a set of criteria

✦ **Recordset Paging:** Creates dynamic page-scrolling arrows for a recordset

✦ **Display Record Count:** Shows how many records you have from a given query — first, last, and total number

✦ **Master Detail Page Set:** Creates a master detail page

✦ **Insert Record:** Creates a form to insert a database record

✦ **Update Record:** Creates a form to update a database record

✦ **Delete Record:** Creates a form to delete a database record

✦ **User Authentication:** Provides a series of tools to log a user in or out, or to restrict access to a page

Editing a Tag

After you've inserted a tag into your ColdFusion code, you may need to edit that tag. You can edit the code directly, or you can use the Tag Editor, which provides a cleaner way to see all the parameters for your tag. (***Note:*** Not all tags have this option. If you don't see Edit Tag in Step 3, then you know the tag you're working with doesn't support this feature.) To use the Tag Editor, follow these steps:

1. **If necessary, switch to the Code view in the Document window by choosing View⇨Code.**

2. **Place your cursor anywhere in the opening tag you want to edit.**

3. **Right-click and choose Edit Tag from the contextual menu.**

   The Edit Tag dialog box appears.

4. **Change the value in the dialog box, and then click OK to update the tag.**

   The value changes, depending on which tag you're editing.

Getting Data from a Database

You can set up a database connection using the ColdFusion Administrator, as described in Book VI, Chapter 6. Using the Dreamweaver interface, however, you can look directly into a database to see the tables and columns that make up a database when you're in Code view. More importantly, you can then easily add those tables and columns to your ColdFusion code simply by dragging them onto the screen. Here's how:

1. **Open the Application panel to the Databases tab by choosing Window⇨Database.**

   You see a list of the databases on your testing server. For this example, we use the CompanyInfo database, one of the sample databases that comes with ColdFusion.

2. **Click the plus (+) button next to the CompanyInfo database.**

   This shows you the views, tables, and stored procedures for the database.

3. **Expand the Employee table by clicking the plus (+) buttons next to the first Tables and then the Employee table.**

   All the columns in the table should now be visible, as shown in Figure 6-6.

4. **Click and drag the LastName column from the panel onto the work area.**

   You see that this adds the column name to the work area.

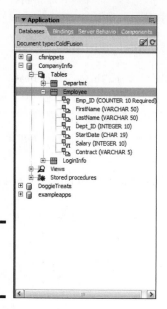

Figure 6-6:
The
Employee
table.

For the feature described in the previous steps to work, you need to have an active testing server configured, and you need to know the Remote Data Services password for your testing server. Check out Book VI, Chapter 2 for more information.

Now, by itself, this doesn't really accomplish a whole lot. All you've really done is drag a column name onto your work area. To really see it in action, try adding the following code text to your page, in between the <BODY> tags:

```
<CFQUERY name="DatabaseTest" datasource="CompanyInfo">
select LastName from Employee
</CFQUERY>

<CFOUTPUT query="DatabaseTest">
#lastname#<BR>
</CFOUTPUT>
```

Now, press the F12 key to preview the page in a Web browser, and you see a whole list of last names, as shown in Figure 6-7. If you'd like, try adding some other fields in the code between select and from, making sure that the fields are all separated by commas. If you then add the field name to CFOUTPUT, surrounded by pound signs (#), you see those fields displayed as well. For more information on accessing data from a database using ColdFusion, check out Book VI, Chapter 3.

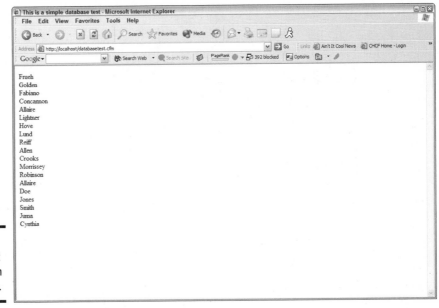

Figure 6-7:
Getting last
names from
a database.

Using the Bindings Tab

The Bindings tab of the Application panel provides another interface to data sources, and for someone unaccustomed to working with ColdFusion, it is an easy way to begin to understand CFML. *Binding,* in the Dreamweaver vernacular, is just a link between the page and some other datasource that provides data to the page. With this interface, you can build the same query we used in the example in the previous section, "Getting Data from a Database," as follows:

1. **Press Ctrl+N; in the New Page dialog box that appears, select Dynamic Page and ColdFusion, and then click the Create button.**

   This creates a new ColdFusion document.

2. **Save the document into a site that has a remote server configured to see the sample ColdFusion databases.**

3. **Switch to the Bindings tab by choosing Window⇨Bindings.**

4. **Click the plus (+) button and select Recordset (Query) from the drop-down list.**

   The Recordset dialog box, shown in Figure 6-8, appears.

5. **Type a name, such as** DatabaseTest**, into the Name field.**

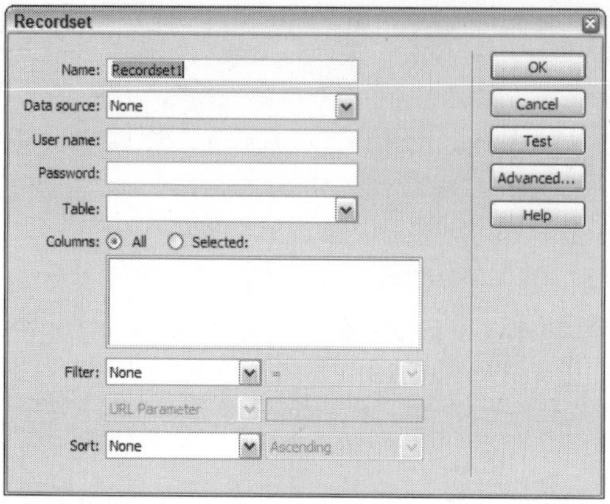

Figure 6-8:
The
Recordset
dialog box.

6. **Select CompanyInfo from the Data Source drop-down list.**

You may also need to input the username and password for the testing server. If you configured the remote testing server, then you should know the username and password. If not, then you may need to check with your organization's database administrator.

7. **Select the Employee table from the Table drop-down list.**

8. **Select the radio button labeled Selected from the Columns option, and choose LastName from the scroll list (it will show up when you select the radio button).**

9. **Leave the Filter and Sort fields set to None.**

These two tools, which you should try as you get more comfortable with using the Bindings tab, allow you to further refine and sort the data from the Employee table.

10. **Click OK to add the Binding.**

Dreamweaver adds a new record in the Bindings tab and the following code to the Code view:

```
<CFQUERY name="DatabaseTest" datasource="CompanyInfo">
SELECT LastName FROM Employee
</CFQUERY>
```

This code tells the server to get all the last names from the Employee table in the CompanyInfo database. When the page is read, this query retrieves the data and makes it available to be output.

11. **To make the last names output when the page is loaded, click and drag the LastName lightning bolt icon from the Bindings tab on the Application panel to the Document window.**

Dreamweaver creates the following code and adds it to your workspace:

```
<CFOUTPUT query="DatabaseTest">
#DatabaseTest.LastName#
</CFOUTPUT>
```

This tells ColdFusion to display the LastNames (all of them) when the page is loaded.

12. **Press F12 to preview the page.**

When the page loads, you'll notice that the names are output one right after another without anything in between them. You can add a line break (`<BR>`) or a comma after `#DatabaseTest.LastName#`, and ColdFusion will add the comma or line break after every record.

Queries are only one kind of Binding that Dreamweaver supports. You can see all the others when you click the plus (+) button on the Bindings tab. As you become more familiar with ColdFusion, you'll no doubt want to use some of these other kinds of Bindings, notably the Stored Procedure and the Form, Session, Client, and Application variables.

Introducing Server Behaviors and Components

The Server Behavior and Components tabs in the Application panel are similar in both design and concept to the Bindings panel. The following sections cover them only cursorily, because to use these tools to their fullest extent, you need an advanced working knowledge of ColdFusion and code development.

Understanding server behaviors

Server behaviors are code elements that make a request to the ColdFusion Server and receive some sort of data in return. If that sounds similar to the preceding Bindings example, it is! You can do that Recordset example from the earlier section, "Using the Bindings Tab," in the Server Behaviors tab. However, a number of more advanced server behaviors are beyond simple queries that you can do from this tab. Table 6-1 describes each of the server behaviors that Dreamweaver offers.

Table 6-1	Server Behaviors
Name	*Function*
Recordset	Makes a query to a data source
Stored Procedure	Passes information to a Stored Procedure
CFParam	Builds a `<CFPARAM>` tag

(continued)

Table 6-1 *(continued)*

Name	Function
Repeat Region	Allows you to create a repeated region
Recordset Paging	Creates forward, backward, first, and last links for a recordset
Show Region	Shows a region of content based on preset conditions
Display Record Count	Displays the record count for a recordset
Dynamic Text	Displays dynamic text based on a query
Insert Record	Inserts a record through a form
Update Record	Updates a record through a form
Delete Record	Deletes a record through a form
Dynamic Form Elements	Creates form elements based on a corresponding query and recordset
User Authentication	Creates all the code necessary to add user authentication to a site

Considering components

Components are reusable bits of ColdFusion code that can be used throughout your Dreamweaver Site. Dreamweaver comes with a number of sample components to show you how they work. In practical terms, though, you create your own components based on the needs of your site.

Suppose that you're building a site that sells boxes online, and you have a tool that calculates the volume of the various types of boxes that you sell. Because it's used globally by the site, this tool shouldn't be repeated in every single ColdFusion page. Instead, it should be in an area where all pages can access it and just pass along the value obtained by performing a calculation. If you built it as a component, this calculator could be accessed anywhere, and if there are ever any changes to the tool (say you changed from cubic feet to cubic meters), you'd only need to make the change once, instead of many times.

The Components tab provides developers with a framework for building these kinds of tools. From this tab, you can specify the following for a new component:

✦ General information about the component (such as its name and where it's located)

✦ Properties of the component (queries, arrays, strings, and so on)

✦ The functions associated with the component

✦ The arguments (data) the component will accept from another page or form

Chapter 7: Advanced Web Page Design Techniques

In This Chapter

✔ Creating hotspots

✔ Adding Flash text and button rollovers

✔ Adding a rollover behavior to an image

✔ Creating a navigation bar

✔ Inserting audio and video into your pages

✔ Using templates

✔ Validating your code

*I*n previous chapters of Book II, we focus on providing a good working knowledge of Dreamweaver MX 2004. Now we need to spend some time looking at the more advanced uses of Dreamweaver in Web development. In this chapter, we show you how to make images a bit more striking and how you can bring some other multimedia elements to life.

Creating Clickable Image Maps with Hotspots

You can designate certain areas of an image as *hotspots* — active areas that a user can click to open a link to another Web page or activate some other behavior. Hotspots can be shaped like rectangles, circles, or polygons (irregular objects). The coordinates of the hotspots are grouped into chunks of HTML code called *image maps*.

Creating a hotspot

Check out Figure 7-1. It shows a typical navigation bar for a site as a single JPEG image. The following procedure shows you how to create an image map for part of that image by adding hotspots:

1. **Select the image to which you want to add a hotspot.**

   The Image Property inspector appears. If the bottom half of the Image Property inspector is not visible, click the Expander button, which is the down arrow in the bottom-right corner.

Figure 7-1:
A typical
JPEG
navigation
image.

2. **In the Map area of the Image Property inspector, click the Hotspot button for the shape you want to draw.**

   You can choose a rectangle, a circle, or a polygon. Your mouse pointer becomes a cross hair cursor when you move it over the image.

3. **Draw the hotspot according to the shape you select:**

   • **Circle or rectangle:** Click your cross hair cursor on the image and drag diagonally to create a hotspot. Release the mouse button when the hotspot reaches your desired dimensions. The area you draw is highlighted light blue, and the Hotspot Property inspector appears.

   • **Polygon:** Click your cross hair cursor on the image once for each point. The area you draw is highlighted light blue, and the Hotspot Property inspector appears.

4. **In the Hotspot Property inspector, supply the following information:**

   • **Map:** Enter a unique name for the image map.

   • **Link:** Enter a URL or the name of an HTML file you want to open when the user clicks the hotspot. Alternatively, you can click the folder icon and browse to select the link from your files. *Note:* Completing this field is optional. Instead, you may choose to attach a behavior to the hotspot.

   • **Behaviors:** To attach a behavior other than a link to the hotspot, open the Behaviors tab of the Tag panel by choosing Window⇨ Behaviors or by using the keyboard shortcut Shift+F3. Then click the Add (+) button in the Behaviors panel, which opens a pop-up menu of available behaviors, including Check Plugin, Play Sound, Popup Message, Preload Images, and many others. Choose a behavior from the pop-up menu, complete the information in the dialog box that appears for your selected behavior, and click OK.

   • **Target:** Complete this field if you entered a link in the Link field, and you want the link to open in a window or frame other than the one you're linking from. Click the arrow and select from the drop-down list a target window where you want your selected link to appear. You can select from the following choices: _blank (opens the link in a new window), _parent (opens the link in the parent of the currently opened window; if the currently opened window was opened from another frame, the link will open in that frame), _self (the default; opens the link in the currently opened window; not selecting a Target produces the same effect), and _top (opens the link in the top-level window, replacing frames, if any). If you have created frames, you can also select a frame name from this list. (See Book II, Chapter 4 for more information about frames.)

- **Alt:** Enter the text you want to show when the user moves the mouse pointer over the hotspot. Alt text also makes information about the hotspot accessible to vision-impaired users.

Modifying a hotspot

If you need to change the size or shape of a hotspot after you've created it, or you need to change the link, target, or Alt information for the hotspot, use the following procedure to edit the hotspot:

1. **On an image in the Document window, click the hotspot you want to modify.**

   The Hotspot Property inspector appears. If the inspector does not appear, open it by choosing Window➪Properties.

2. **Edit the Link, Target, or Alt information you want to change in the Hotspot Property inspector.**

3. **If you want to reshape or resize the hotspot, select the Arrow tool in the Hotspot Property inspector, and then click any handle of the selected hotspot and drag the handle to a new location.**

4. **If you want to reposition the hotspot, select the Arrow tool in the Hotspot Property inspector, and then click anywhere within the hotspot and drag it to a new location.**

5. **You can delete a hotspot by selecting it and pressing the Delete key on your keyboard.**

Book II
Chapter 7

Advanced
Web Page
Design Techniques

Adding Flash Text Rollovers

A *text rollover* is text that changes color when users move their mouse pointer over it. (One color appears to "roll over" to the next color.) One way to create text rollovers in Dreamweaver is by adding *Flash text* to your pages, as described in the following section.

Flash text and Flash buttons are so called because Dreamweaver implements these features using the same code that Macromedia Flash MX 2004 (the animation program included in the Macromedia Studio MX 2004 suite) uses.

Adding Flash text

To add hyperlinked Flash text that changes color when users roll their mouse over it, follow these steps:

1. **Click in the Document window where you want to add Flash text.**

2. **Choose Insert⇨Media⇨Flash Text.**

   Your page must be saved before you can insert Flash text. If the page hasn't been saved at least once, an alert pops up to remind you to save the page so you can insert the Flash text.

3. **In the Insert Flash Text dialog box, shown in Figure 7-2, select a font from the Font drop-down list.**

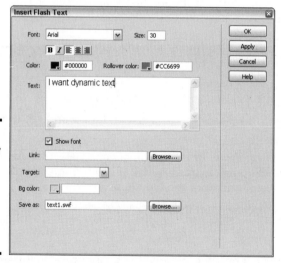

Figure 7-2:
Choose how you want the text to appear in the Insert Flash Text dialog box.

4. **Enter a point size for your text in the Size text field.**

5. **If you want, you can also format the text.**

   You can click the Bold button and/or Italics button. You can also click an alignment button. Alignment choices are Left, Center, and Right.

6. **Select a Color (initial color) and a Rollover Color (color the text changes to when users move their mouse pointer over it) by clicking the color swatch in each area and selecting a color from the color palette that appears.**

7. **Enter your text in the Text field. Select the Show Font option if you want to view the characters in the Text field in your selected font.**

8. **In the Link field, enter a URL or the name of the page you want to appear when the user clicks the Flash text.**

   Alternatively, you can click the Browse button to select a page from your files.

9. **In the Target area, click the arrow and select from the drop-down list a target window where the linked page will appear.**

   If you have created frames, you can select a frame name from this list, or you can select from the following choices:

   - `_blank`: Opens the link in a new window.
   - `_parent`: Opens the link in the parent of the currently opened window.
   - `_self`: Opens the link in the currently opened window; this is the default. Leaving the Target area empty produces the same result.
   - `_top`: Opens the link in the top-level window, replacing frames, if any.

10. **Select a Background color by clicking the Bg Color swatch and selecting a color from the color palette that appears, or type in a hexadecimal number.**

    Your Flash text appears over the background color you choose.

11. **Enter a name for your Flash text component in the Save As field or click the Browse button to select a name from your files.**

    You must save Flash text with an `.swf` extension.

12. **Click OK to create your Flash text and close the dialog box.**

To preview the rollover effect of your Flash text, select the Flash object in the Document window to open the Flash Text Property inspector. In the Property inspector, click the Play button to view your Flash text as it will appear in the browser window. Click the Stop button when you're done.

Changing Flash text

You can change an existing Flash text object by simply double-clicking the object in the Document window, or by clicking the object, and then clicking the Edit button in the Property inspector. Doing so opens the Insert Flash Text dialog box, where you can change various attributes of the object as we describe in the previous section.

Adding Flash Button Rollovers

Buttons that change appearance when users move their mouse pointer over them — called *button rollovers* — are so popular that Dreamweaver gives you a way to create them quickly and easily as Flash movies. To find out how to create button rollovers using images and behaviors instead of Flash button rollovers, see the "Inserting Image Rollovers" section, later in this chapter. (Book III, Chapter 5 describes how to make rollovers in Fireworks MX 2004 using images and behaviors.)

Adding a Flash button

To add a Flash button, follow these steps:

1. Click in the Document window where you want to add a Flash button.

2. Choose Insert⇨Media⇨Flash Button to open the Insert Flash Button dialog box, as shown in Figure 7-3.

Your page must be saved before you can insert a Flash button. If the page hasn't been saved at least once, an alert pops up to remind you to save the page so you can insert the Flash button.

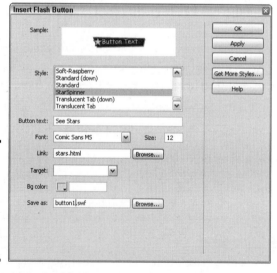

Figure 7-3: Add an interactive button with the Insert Flash Button dialog box.

3. In the Insert Flash Button dialog box, scroll through the button selections in the Style list and click to select a style.

You can preview the style in the Sample area of the dialog box — just point to the sample with your mouse to see the Flash button in action.

You can get new Flash buttons on the Macromedia Dreamweaver MX 2004 Web site by clicking the Get More Styles button in the Insert Flash Button dialog box. A Web page on Macromedia's site opens in your browser. Select the Flash Media option from the Categories drop-down list and scroll through the results as needed.

4. **If your selected button has a placeholder for text, enter the text that you want to appear on the button in the Button Text field.**

   Text centers within the button automatically. Button size is fixed, though, so you must make sure your text is brief enough to fit on the button.

5. **Select a font for your Flash button text from the Font drop-down list.**

6. **Enter a point size for your text in the Size field.**

7. **In the Link field, enter a URL or the name for the page that you want to appear when the user clicks the Flash button.**

   Alternatively, you can click the Browse button to select a page from your files.

8. **From the Target drop-down list, select a target window where the linked page will appear.**

   If you have created frames, you can select a frame name from this list, or you can select from the following choices:

   - _blank: Opens the link in a new window.

   - _parent: Opens the link in the parent of the currently opened window.

   - _self: Opens the link in the currently opened window; this is the default. Leaving the Target area empty produces the same result.

   - _top: Opens the link in the top-level window, replacing frames, if any.

9. **Select a Background color by clicking the Bg Color swatch and selecting a color from the color palette that appears.**

   Alternatively, you can enter a hexadecimal color code in the Bg Color field.

   Your Flash button displays with the background color you select.

10. **Enter a name for your Flash button in the Save As field or click the Browse button to select a name from your files.**

    The Flash button filename requires an .swf extension. Dreamweaver will add the extension automatically if you don't enter it.

11. **Click OK to create your Flash button and close the dialog box.**

To see what a Flash button looks like in action, select the button in the Document window to open the Flash Button Property inspector. In the Property inspector, click the Play button to view your Flash button as it appears in the browser window. Click the Stop button when you finish.

Changing a Flash button

To change an existing Flash button object, simply double-click the object in the Document window, or click the object, and then click the Edit button in the Property inspector. Doing so opens the Insert Flash Button dialog box, where you can change your button as we describe in the previous section.

Inserting Image Rollovers

An *image rollover* (often just referred to as a *rollover*) is a behavior that changes an image whenever users move their mouse pointer over the image. Rollovers add interactivity to a Web page by helping users to see what parts of the page are links to other Web pages.

A rollover is actually two images — one for normal display on a page (the original image) and one that is slightly modified for display when the image is rolled over (the rollover image). You can modify an image by changing the color or position, adding a glow or a shadow, or you can add another graphic — such as a dog changing from sleeping to wide-awake. For a rollover to work best, the normal and rollover states of the image should share the same width and height.

As with all images, you can't create the original image or the rollover image directly in Dreamweaver; you must use an image-editing program, such as Fireworks, to generate the images.

Insert a rollover by following these steps:

1. **Click inside the Document window where you want to insert the image rollover.**

2. **On the Common category of the Insert bar, click and hold the Image button and select Rollover Image from the pop-up menu.**

   The Insert Rollover Image dialog box appears, as shown in Figure 7-4. Alternatively, you can select Insert⇨Image Objects⇨Rollover Image.

3. **In the Insert Rollover Image dialog box, enter a unique name for the rollover in the Image Name field, making sure there are no spaces in the name.**

   The rollover is referred to by this name in the HTML page code. Keep in mind that this rollover name refers to the combined original image/rollover image pair.

4. **Enter the name of the original image file in the Original Image field or click the Browse button to select an image from your files.**

   The original image appears on the page when the user's mouse pointer is *not* over the image.

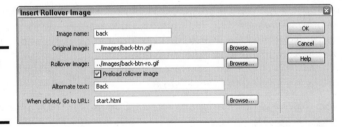

Figure 7-4:
Creating
an image
rollover.

5. **Enter the name of the rollover image file in the Rollover Image field or click the Browse button to select an image from your files.**

   The rollover image appears on the page when the user's mouse pointer is over the image.

6. **Select the Preload Rollover Image check box.**

   This feature makes the rollover action appear without delay to users as they move the mouse pointer over the original image. It is selected by default.

7. **Enter Alternate text for the image to make it accessible to vision-impaired visitors to your site.**

   This step is optional but recommended.

8. **If you want to make the rollover image a link, enter a URL of the page in the When Clicked, Go to URL text field.**

   Alternatively, you can click the Browse button to select a page from your files.

9. **Click OK to accept your choices and close the dialog box.**

To check the rollover, preview your page in a browser by choosing File⇨ Preview in Browser or by clicking the Preview in Browser button, and then use your mouse to point to the original image. You can also press F12 to preview in the default preview browser. If you haven't set a default preview browser, you will have to do so using the Preview in Browser category in Dreamweaver's Preferences dialog box. See Dreamweaver's help documentation for details.

Setting Up a Navigation Bar

A *navigation bar* is a group of buttons that users can access to move throughout your Web site. Buttons within a navigation bar may present users with options, such as moving backwards, moving forwards, returning to the home page, or jumping to specific pages within the site.

Each button in a navigation bar possesses properties similar to a rollover in that the button *changes state* — or appears differently — based on where the user is positioning the mouse pointer. However, a navigation bar button can possess as many as four different states:

✦ **Up:** The original state of the button

✦ **Over:** How the button appears when a user moves their mouse pointer over it

✦ **Down:** How the button appears as a user is clicking it

✦ **Over While Down:** How the button appears when the user moves their mouse pointer over it after clicking it and arriving on the page it represents

A navigation bar differs from individual rollovers in that clicking a navigation bar button in the Down state causes all other buttons in the bar to revert to the Up state.

To create a navigation bar, just follow these steps:

1. Select the Navigation Bar button from the Common category of the Insert bar or choose Insert➪Image Objects➪Navigation Bar.

Whichever method you choose, the Insert Navigation Bar dialog box appears, as shown in Figure 7-5.

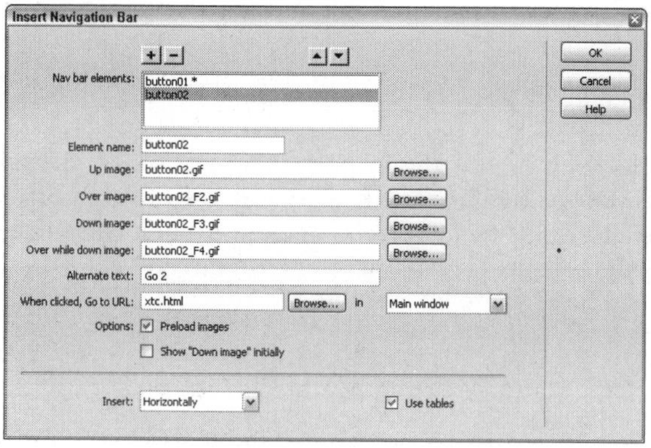

Figure 7-5:
From the Insert Navigation Bar dialog box, you can create an entire navigation bar.

2. In the Insert Navigation Bar dialog box, enter a name for the first button in the Element Name field.

The new button appears in the Nav Bar Elements field. Don't use spaces in the naming of any of these elements.

3. **For each state of the button — Up Image, Over Image, Down Image, and Over While Down Image — enter the name of the image file that you want to use in the associated field.**

   Alternatively, you can click the Browse button for each field and select an image from your files. You must supply the Up Image. All other states are optional and can be left blank.

   You don't need to use all four navigation bar button states — creating only Up and Down states works just fine.

4. **Enter Alternate text for the image to make it accessible to vision-impaired visitors to your site.**

   This step is optional but recommended.

5. **In the When Clicked, Go to URL text field, enter a URL or the name for the page you want to appear when the user clicks the navigation bar button.**

   Alternatively, you can click the Browse button to select a page from your files.

6. **From the In drop-down list, select a target window where you want the linked page to appear.**

   If you aren't using frames, the only option is to use the Main window.

7. **Click the Add Item (+) button to add another navigation bar button.**

   Repeat Steps 2 through 6 to format the new button.

   Note: You can remove any button already created by clicking its name in the Nav Bar Elements field and clicking the Remove Item (–) button. You can also reorder the sequence of the buttons as they will appear on the page by clicking a button name in the Nav Bar Elements field and clicking the up or down arrow button.

8. **In the Options area, select the Preload Images check box if you want the rollover effects to appear without delay when the user triggers them.**

9. **To set the current button to appear in the Down state when the user first sees the navigation bar (which you might do to indicate the current page is the one represented by the button), select the Show "Down Image" Initially check box in the Options area.**

   The Over While Down state works in combination with this option.

10. **Select Horizontally or Vertically from the Insert drop-down list to position the navigation bar horizontally or vertically.**

11. **To set up the button images in a table format, select the Use Tables check box.**

    This option is checked by default.

12. **Click OK to accept your choices and close the dialog box.**

To check the navigation bar, you must preview your page in a browser. Choose File⇨Preview in Browser or click the Preview in Browser button and use your mouse to point to the buttons.

To change elements of an existing navigation bar, choose Modify⇨Navigation Bar. The Modify Navigation Bar dialog box is nearly identical to the Insert Navigation Bar dialog box shown in Figure 7-5, except that you can no longer change the orientation of the bar or access the Use Tables check box.

Adding Audio and Video to Your Pages

You have two basic options, which are described in detail in the following sections, for adding downloadable audio and video to your Web pages:

✦ **Embedding:** You can embed an audio or video file to display a playback console on a Web page that users can use to play, rewind, and fast-forward the media file. (You can also embed an audio file and make it invisible to create a background audio effect.)

Users must have an appropriate plug-in installed on their machines to play the embedded audio or video file. To ensure maximum compatibility, you may wish to use SWFs to present audio and video.

✦ **Linking:** You can link to an audio or video file to give users the choice of whether or not to view that media file.

Keep in mind that most audio and video files are large — large enough that many folks impatiently click the Stop button on their browsers before a Web page chock-full of audio or video effects has a chance to finish loading. Keep the following basic rules in mind to help you use audio and video effectively in your Web pages:

✦ Use audio and video only when plain text just won't do.

✦ Keep your audio and video clips as short (and corresponding file sizes as small) as possible.

Embedding an audio or video clip

You can embed an audio or video file by following these steps:

1. **In the Document window, click the location in your page where you want to add an embedded audio or video file.**

2. **Click and hold the Media button in the Media category of the Insert bar and select Plugin from the pop-up menu, or choose Insert⇨Media⇨ Plugin.**

    The Select File dialog box, shown in Figure 7-6, appears.

Figure 7-6: Select a media file to import.

3. **In the File Name field in the Select File dialog box, enter the path or browse to the audio or video file that you want to embed and click OK.**

    If the file is outside your current root directory, Dreamweaver asks whether you want to copy the file to your site's root directory. Click Yes.

4. **In the Plugin Property inspector, size the Plugin placeholder to any dimensions you prefer.**

    You can either enter a width and height in the W and H text fields in the Plugin Property inspector, or you can drag a handle on the placeholder to manually resize.

    Test in all your target browsers (the browsers your users are likely to view your site with) to ensure that users can view all the audio playback controls or video area and controls.

You can click the Play button in the Plugin Property inspector to play your media file without previewing your page in a browser.

Embedding background music

Embedding *background music* (music that plays automatically after the user opens a page) in your page can be controversial because users may be unpleasantly surprised by audio when they are expecting silence, and because users have no way to turn off the music from within the browser. If you still want to embed background music in your page, follow these steps:

1. **In the Document window, click the location in your page where you want to add an embedded audio file.**

   This should be an out-of-the-way location, like the bottom of your page, so the embedded audio doesn't create an awkward space in your design.

2. **Click and hold the Media button in the Media category of the Insert bar and select Plugin from the pop-up menu, or choose Insert➪ Media➪Plugin.**

   The Select File dialog box appears.

3. **In the File Name field in the Select File dialog box, enter the path to the audio file that you want to embed and click OK.**

   If the file is outside your current root directory, Dreamweaver asks whether you want to copy the file to your site root. Click Yes.

4. **Enter a width and height of 2 in the W and H text fields in the Plugin Property inspector.**

5. **Click the Parameters button to open the Parameters dialog box.**

6. **In the Parameters dialog box, click the Add (+) button to add a new parameter.**

7. **Click in the Parameter column and type** hidden.

8. **Type** true **in the Value column.**

   Steps 7 and 8 hide the audio playback controls.

9. **Click OK to complete the process and close the dialog box.**

Linking to an audio or video clip

A simple and relatively trouble-free way to include audio and video clips on a Web page is to link the page to an audio or video file. Users can click the link if they want to hear or watch the clip. This selection opens a player outside the browser where the user can control playback.

You follow the same steps to create a link to an audio or video file that resides in your root folder as you do to create a link to a Web page (see Book II, Chapter 2); the only difference is that you specify a media file instead of a URL for the link.

Adding Other Media

Dreamweaver enables you to easily insert a number of other multimedia formats into your Web pages, including ActiveX, Java Applets, Macromedia Flash, and Shockwave. After inserting any of these media formats, you can set the control and playback features of the media in the Parameters dialog box. Additionally, you can fine-tune the media action on your page by using the Behaviors panel to create triggering actions that cause the media to play, stop, and execute other functions.

Follow these directions to insert other media:

1. **In the Document window, click the location in your page where you want to add a multimedia file.**

2. **Click and hold the Media button in the Common category of the Insert bar to view all the object types that you can insert, as shown in Figure 7-7, and select the icon of the type of media file you want to insert.**

Alternatively, you can choose Insert⇨Media⇨*Media Type,* where *Media Type* is the type of media file you want to insert.

**Book II
Chapter 7**

**Advanced
Web Page
Design Techniques**

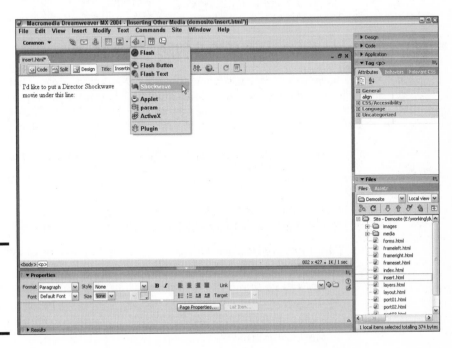

Figure 7-7:
Your
embedded
media
options.

The Select File dialog box appears.

- **For Applet, Macromedia Flash, and Shockwave files:** In the File Name field in the Select File dialog box, enter the path to the media and click OK. Your file is inserted, and the associated Property inspector appears. You can change the selected file in the Plugin Property inspector by typing a new name in the File text field or by browsing in the File folder to select a file (for Applets, use the Code text field). Select the Embed check box if you want Netscape Navigator users to have access to the Applet.

- **For ActiveX:** An ActiveX placeholder is inserted, and the ActiveX Property inspector appears. Enter the name of the ActiveX object you want to play in the Class ID text field. Select the Embed check box if you want Netscape Navigator users to have access to the ActiveX object.

3. **In the Property inspector for your selected media, enter dimensions in the W and H text fields to size the Media placeholder to any dimensions you choose.**

4. **In the Property inspector for your selected media, click the Parameters button to open the Parameters dialog box, where you can add parameters (like width, height, loop, and autoplay) appropriate to the selected media type.**

Using Dreamweaver MX 2004 Templates

Dreamweaver comes with many built-in layouts that you can use to create pages or Dreamweaver templates quickly. The layouts are predesigned pages with placeholder content. Make a new page from a layout, replace the placeholder content with real content, and voilà — a professionally designed page!

To create a new page based on a built-in layout, just follow these steps:

1. **Choose File⇨New.**

   The New Document dialog box appears.

2. **Select Table Based Layouts in the Category list on the left.**

   The Table Based Layouts appear in the middle column. Click any one to see a preview in the Preview area, as shown in Figure 7-8.

3. **When you've found the layout you want, select the Document option in the lower-right corner and click the Create button.**

   An untitled HTML page opens in the Document window, with placeholder content that you can replace with real content.

If you wanted to create your own template based on the built-in layout, you could select the Template option in the lower-right corner of the New Document dialog box.

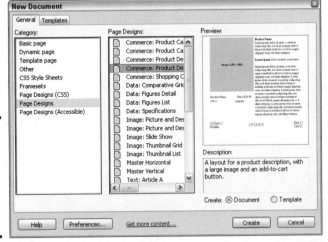

Figure 7-8:
The Commerce: Product Description layout is selected.

You don't have to use a built-in layout to create a Dreamweaver template: You can make a Dreamweaver template based on any Web page. One cool thing about Dreamweaver templates is that if you make a whole bunch of pages based on a template, you can change the template and all the pages based on it will be updated to match the template automatically. Another cool thing is that you can make a template that other people can use in combination with either Dreamweaver or Contribute 2 to create new pages that conform to the template's design.

To create a Dreamweaver template based on an existing HTML page, just follow these steps:

1. **Choose File⇨New.**

The New Document dialog box appears, with the General tab selected.

2. **Select Basic Page from the Category list on the left, and then select HTML Template from the list of Basic Pages that appear in the middle.**

You can also select Template Page from the Category list and choose HTML Template from the Template Page list that appears in the middle.

3. **Create your page layout.**

By default, nothing in the design of pages based on your template is editable. You must create editable regions in order to make a useful template.

4. **Click a table cell or other part of your layout that you want users to be able to fill with content and select Insert⇨Template Objects⇨ Editable Region, or use the keyboard shortcut Ctrl+Alt+V.**

   The New Editable Region dialog box appears. If you have a placeholder image already in the layout, you can right-click the image and choose Templates⇨New Editable Region from the contextual menu that pops up, or you can select the image and use the keyboard shortcut Ctrl+Alt+V.

5. **Name the region and click OK.**

   You can use the default name Dreamweaver gives to the region, but it's better if you name the region to reflect the content that will go into it (for example, name the region Product Description). Figure 7-9 shows a template with three editable regions. Editable regions are bound by a light blue box with region name at the top left.

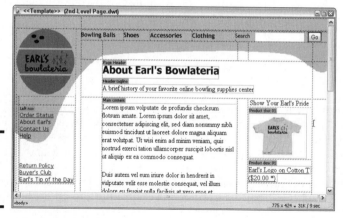

Figure 7-9: Editable regions in a template.

6. **Repeat Steps 4 and 5 until you have made editable regions out of all the areas of the page that you want to be editable in new pages based on the template.**

   Anything inside an editable region can be replaced in a page based on the template; anything outside the editable regions is locked and can't be changed in pages based on the template.

7. **Choose File⇨Save.**

   The Save As Template dialog box appears.

8. **Choose the site the template belongs to from the drop-down list, enter a name for the template in the Save As field, and click the Save button.**

   The template will now be available to anyone who has access to the Dreamweaver site, either through Dreamweaver or with Contribute.

You may turn any existing page into a template. Choose File⇨Save as Template when the page is open. If you try to close the template without having created editable regions (as described in the previous steps), Dreamweaver gives you a warning message saying that the template does not contain any editable regions. Click OK to close the warning dialog box, create the editable regions in your template, and choose File⇨Save to save your template.

To create an HTML page based on an existing user-created template, follow these steps:

1. **Click the Templates icon in the Assets tab of the File panel. All available templates for the selected site appear.**

   If the Files panel is closed, select Window⇨Assets or use the keyboard shortcut F11.

2. **Right-click the template you want to create the new page from and choose New from Template, as shown in Figure 7-10.**

   The page opens as an HTML page in the Document window.

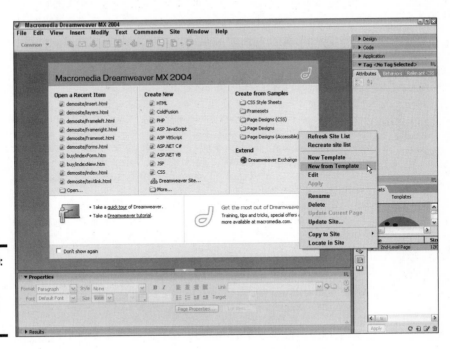

Figure 7-10: Creating a new page based on a template.

You can also create an HTML page based on a user-created template by choosing File➪New and choosing the template from the Templates tab of the New Document dialog box. (When you select the Templates tab, the dialog box's title bar changes to read New from Template and the Templates options appear, as shown in Figure 7-11.)

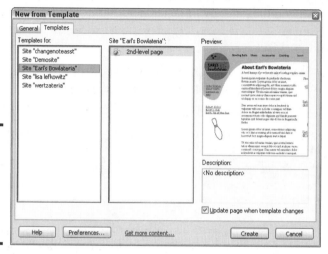

Figure 7-11: The Templates tab of the New Document dialog box.

Validating Your Code

Dreamweaver MX 2004 has a built-in code validator. The validator checks your HTML for errors (for example, unclosed <TD> tags, or tags with invalid attributes, such as <FONT width=113>). If you work exclusively in Design view, you may never need to use the validator. If you work in Code view, though, and you are creating long, complex pages, you may find it worthwhile to run the validator.

To validate your code (unless it's XML), select File➪Check Page➪Validate Markup. The Results panel opens and shows a list of warnings for any faults in the code.

To validate XML code, select File➪Check Page➪Validate as XML. Because XML has stricter requirements for well-formed code, you should take advantage of Dreamweaver's built-in validator if you're writing XML.

Chapter 8: Integrating Dreamweaver MX 2004 with Other Macromedia Products

In This Chapter

✔ Integrating Dreamweaver with Fireworks

✔ Integrating Dreamweaver with Macromedia Flash

✔ Integrating Dreamweaver with ColdFusion

✔ Integrating Dreamweaver with FreeHand

✔ Integrating Dreamweaver with Contribute

With the release of the Macromedia Studio MX 2004 suite, Macromedia brought Fireworks MX 2004, Macromedia Flash MX 2004, Dreamweaver MX 2004, ColdFusion MX 6.1 Developer Edition, and FreeHand MX closer together than ever before. Macromedia Studio MX 2004 also adds Contribute 2 to the mix. The applications in the suite have complementary — and in some cases overlapping — capabilities.

In order to take advantage of Dreamweaver's integration with Fireworks and Macromedia Flash, you need to make sure Design Notes are enabled. Design Notes are Macromedia Studio's way of tracking changes and establishing links between exported files (such as GIFs or JPEGs) and their source files (Fireworks PNG files, for example).

By default, Design Notes are enabled when you establish a new site. If you disabled them and wish to re-enable them, just follow these steps:

1. **In Dreamweaver, choose Site⇨Manage Sites.**

   The Manage Sites dialog box appears.

2. **Select the site by clicking it.**

   If you have a site open already, that site is already selected.

3. **Click the Edit button.**

   The Site Definition dialog box opens.

4. **If the Site Definition dialog box opens with the Basic tab selected, click the Advanced tab.**

The Advanced options appear.

5. **Select Design Notes in the Category list.**

The Design Notes options appear.

6. **Select the Maintain Design Notes check box, as shown in Figure 8-1.**

The Maintain Design Notes option is selected by default, but it can be toggled on and off in the Site Definition dialog box.

7. **If you're working on the site with others, make sure the Upload Design Notes for Sharing check box is selected.**

The Upload Design Notes for Sharing option uploads your Design Notes so that other people working on the site can have access to them. If you're the only person working on a site, you should deselect this option to speed file transfers.

8. **Click OK.**

Disabling Design Notes is simple: Just follow the preceding steps, but in Step 6, deselect the Maintain Design Notes check box.

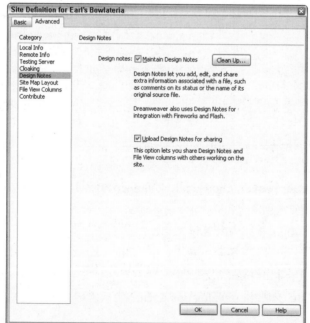

Figure 8-1:
Enabling the Maintain Design Notes option in the Site Definition dialog box.

With Design Notes enabled, you can move seamlessly back and forth between Dreamweaver and the other applications in the Macromedia Studio suite.

Integrating Dreamweaver with Fireworks

Fireworks is a Web design tool and Dreamweaver is an HTML editor, so you may expect that the two applications complement each other well. In fact, the two programs make a dynamite tag team.

The phrase *Roundtrip HTML* refers to the basic interaction between Fireworks and Dreamweaver. Essentially, if you generate your HTML in Fireworks and edit the code in Dreamweaver, Fireworks recognizes the changes you make in Dreamweaver. That goes for links, image maps, behaviors shared by both programs, and edited HTML text. If you make radical changes to the overall design of the page in Dreamweaver, however, Fireworks may not be able to reconcile the HTML with the Fireworks PNG source file. In those cases, Fireworks will write over your changed code with new code.

In order to take advantage of Roundtrip HMTL, you need to establish a few settings, both in Dreamweaver and in Fireworks. In Dreamweaver, you need to define a local site (see Book II, Chapter 3) and make Fireworks your primary image-editing application. To find out how, read the next section.

Making Fireworks your primary image editor

If you installed Dreamweaver along with the rest of Macromedia Studio, Fireworks is your primary image-editing application by default. However, if you changed that default setting, here's how to return to the setting of Fireworks as your primary image-editing application:

1. **In Dreamweaver, choose Edit⇨Preferences or use the keyboard shortcut Ctrl+U.**

The Preferences dialog box appears.

2. **Select File Types / Editors in the Category list.**

The File Types / Editors options appear in the Preferences dialog box, as shown in Figure 8-2.

3. **Select the** .png **extension in the Extensions list.**

The extension is highlighted.

4. **Click the plus (+) button over the Editors list.**

If Fireworks is already listed in the Editors list, you don't need to click the plus (+) button.

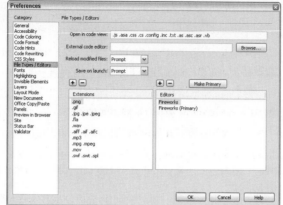

Figure 8-2:
The Dream-
weaver
Preferences
dialog box.

5. **If you need to add Fireworks to the Editors list, navigate to** `Fireworks.exe` **on your hard drive and double-click it.**

   If Fireworks is now the only application listed in the Editors area, it's the primary editor by default (Primary is in parentheses next to Fireworks).

6. **If you have more than one image editor in the Editors list, select Fireworks in the list and click the Make Primary button.**

7. **Repeat Steps 3 through 6 for the** `.gif`, `.jpg`, `.jpe`, **and** `.jpeg` **extensions.**

8. **Click OK.**

You may need to set a few preferences in Fireworks as well. See Book III, Chapter 8 for information on how to set Launch and Edit preferences in Fireworks.

Working with tables

Taking advantage of Roundtrip HTML means more than just setting preferences: You also need to know which application is best to use for particular types of changes. If you originally exported your HTML from Fireworks and wish to make major structural changes to the table that constitutes your HTML page, we recommend that you modify your original Fireworks PNG source file and re-export the HTML from there, rather than using Dreamweaver to modify the code. Using Fireworks to change the table structure ensures that the slices in your Fireworks PNG source file will correspond to the cells in your HTML table.

Here's how to edit a table in Fireworks (provided the table was created when you exported your page design as HTML from Fireworks) by launching it from within Dreamweaver:

1. **Select the table in Dreamweaver.**

   The Property inspector updates to display the parameters of the table.

2. **Click the Fireworks Edit button in the Property inspector.**

   If need be, you can navigate to the source Fireworks PNG file from within the Dreamweaver Property inspector. The source file opens in Fireworks.

3. **Make edits to the slices or guides as necessary.**

4. **Click the Done button when you're finished editing.**

   The Fireworks window closes, and Dreamweaver updates the table and images.

When you launch and edit a table in Fireworks, it may overwrite some changes you may have made to the table structure in your Dreamweaver code, if the changes you made in Dreamweaver are substantial. A warning notifies you when Fireworks will overwrite the existing Dreamweaver edits.

When you want to leave the table structure intact but need to rename or reoptimize an image, you can launch Fireworks from a selected image rather than a selected table. Editing a JPEG image from its Fireworks PNG source file rather than editing and resaving the already optimized image ensures the highest image quality.

To launch and edit a PNG source file from an optimized image placed in Dreamweaver (to change graphic text in a JPEG image, for example), follow these steps:

1. **Click the optimized image in the Dreamweaver Document window.**

   The Property inspector updates to display image parameters.

2. **Click the Fireworks Edit button in the Property inspector, as shown in Figure 8-3, or right-click the optimized image and choose Edit with Fireworks from the contextual menu that appears.**

   If Dreamweaver cannot locate the source Fireworks PNG file, you're prompted to navigate to the source file. When you do, the source PNG file opens in Fireworks. At the top of the Fireworks canvas, the words "Editing from Dreamweaver" show that Roundtrip HTML is in effect.

   Notice at the top left of the Property inspector that the Fireworks icon and the designation FW Image identify the selected image as one created in Fireworks. Note also the Fireworks Src text field at the bottom middle of the Property inspector, which shows the path and name of the source Fireworks PNG file.

3. **Edit the image within the context of your overall page design.**

   The new version of the image will be exported at the specified settings, which you may leave as is or change before clicking Done.

Figure 8-3:
The Dreamweaver Property inspector for an image.

Fireworks Edit button

Path and name of source PNG file

4. **Click the Done button at the top left of the canvas.**

The Fireworks window minimizes. When you look at the Document window in Dreamweaver, you see the new image.

You can also launch and edit a GIF or JPEG image directly in Fireworks, though it's always best to edit from the source PNG when possible, both to preserve image quality and to keep your source file in sync with your Web page. If you don't have a source PNG (or don't need to keep your source design file up to date) and you just want to tweak an image without changing its width and height, you can do so easily as follows:

1. **Double-click the image's filename or corresponding icon on the Files tab or Assets tab of the Files panel.**

Fireworks launches, and your image appears on the canvas.

2. **Make changes to the image.**

3. **Export the updated GIF or JPEG from Fireworks by choosing File⇨ Export or using the key command Ctrl+Shift+R.**

If necessary, navigate to the folder in which you keep the optimized images for your site. A prompt warns you that the file already exists. Click OK to replace the existing file.

4. **Close the file in Fireworks.**

When you close the file in Fireworks, an alert asks if you want to save changes to your file. If you want Fireworks to save the file as a PNG, click Yes. Otherwise, click No.

You can add a Fireworks-generated table to an open Dreamweaver document, whether the document is blank or has code already in it:

1. **Choose Insert⇨Image Objects⇨Fireworks HTML.**

The Insert Fireworks HTML dialog box appears.

2. **Type the pathname or click the Browse button and browse to the Fireworks HTML file.**

   If the HTML file you select was not generated by Fireworks, an alert informs you, and you won't be able to insert the HTML.

3. **Select the Delete File after Insertion check box if you don't need to save the Fireworks-generated HTML.**

   Unless you want a backup copy of the HTML, free from any edits you might make in Dreamweaver, you can safely delete it.

4. **Click OK.**

If you want to nest tables but still use Roundtrip HTML, one way to do it is to make a large table in Dreamweaver and insert Fireworks-generated tables in the cells. Then, if you need to change one of the inserted tables, you can select the table and edit it in Fireworks.

**Book II
Chapter 8**

Integrating
Dreamweaver
MX 2004

Integrating Dreamweaver with Macromedia Flash

You can create Flash buttons and Flash text without actually having Macromedia Flash installed on your computer, thanks to Dreamweaver's Flash commands. If you've installed Macromedia Studio, though, you'll probably prefer to create Flash movies in Macromedia Flash and let Dreamweaver write the code to embed Flash SWF files in your HTML pages.

Inserting a Flash movie into a Dreamweaver document

Inserting a Flash SWF movie into a Dreamweaver document is easy, and Dreamweaver offers easy access to many parameters of SWF movies directly from the Property inspector, though you can't edit a Flash SWF movie from within Dreamweaver.

To insert an SWF file into an existing Dreamweaver HTML document, follow these steps:

1. **Click the spot in the page where you want the Flash movie to go.**

2. **Choose Insert⇨Media⇨Flash (or use the keyboard shortcut Ctrl+Alt+F) or click and hold the Media button in the Common category of the Insert bar and choose the Flash icon.**

   The Select File dialog box appears.

3. **Navigate to the SWF file and double-click it, or click it once and click OK.**

You can type the name of the file in the File Name text field instead if you prefer. The Select File dialog box closes and your SWF movie is placed where the cursor was last active.

Working with the Property inspector

When an SWF file is selected in the Document window, the Dreamweaver Property inspector (shown in Figure 8-4) gives you access to many parameters for the display of the movie, including:

+ **Width and Height:** Unless specified otherwise here in the W and H fields, the SWF will display at the dimensions you set in Macromedia Flash's Document Properties dialog box.

+ **Loop:** You can toggle looping on or off by selecting or deselecting this check box.

+ **Autoplay:** You can toggle autoplay on or off by selecting or deselecting this check box. When Autoplay is selected, the SWF starts automatically when the HTML page loads in the user's browser window.

+ **V Space and H Space:** As with GIFs and JPEGs, you can set the vertical and horizontal spacing to provide margins between SWFs and other content that occupies the same table cell.

Figure 8-4:
The Dreamweaver Property inspector for SWF movies.

+ **Quality:** This drop-down list offers four options: High, Auto High, Auto Low, and Low. The Low option sacrifices image quality to increase smoothness in the flow of the animation.

+ **Scale:** This drop-down list gives you three choices: Show All, No Border, and Exact Fit.

+ **Align:** This drop-down list offers access to all the options for aligning the SWF within a table cell.

✦ **Background color (Bg):** A background color chosen here overrides the background color as set in Macromedia Flash's Document Properties dialog box.

The Property inspector also includes some other handy tools:

✦ **The Flash Edit button:** This button opens the source FLA file in the Macromedia Flash application.

✦ **The Reset Size button:** This button restores the SWF to its original dimensions.

✦ **The Play button:** This button allows you to see the SWF file in action without opening the page in a browser window.

✦ **The Parameters button:** This button allows you to customize parameters passed to the SWF.

The Flash Edit button in the Property inspector is grayed out if you do not have Macromedia Flash installed on your computer. When you want to edit an SWF, you need to go back to the FLA source file to make your changes, and then re-export the SWF. This is true except in the case of changing a link in an SWF file, in which case Dreamweaver adds a Design Note to pass the new link to the FLA source movie when you next launch and edit the FLA.

Editing a Flash movie in Dreamweaver

To edit a Flash movie from within Dreamweaver, just follow these steps:

1. **Select the SWF file by clicking it in the Dreamweaver Document window.**

The Property inspector updates to display the Macromedia Flash parameters. (Refer to Figure 8-4.)

2. **Click the Edit button in the Property inspector.**

If necessary, navigate to the FLA source file in the Locate Macromedia Flash Document File dialog box and double-click the FLA, or click it once and then click the Open button.

The source file opens in Macromedia Flash. The designation "Editing from Dreamweaver" confirms that Macromedia Flash was launched from within Dreamweaver.

3. **Edit the Flash movie source file.**

4. **Click the Done button at the top left of the Flash stage.**

Macromedia Flash exports an updated SWF to the proper directory, saves the FLA file to its current directory, and closes. The new SWF appears in the Dreamweaver Document window. If you changed the dimensions of the Flash movie, click the Reset size button to update the Dreamweaver code.

Editing a link in an SWF file in Dreamweaver

Editing a link in an SWF file is similar to editing a Flash movie, but you need to set up a few things beforehand:

✦ Establish a home page and dependent pages in the Site Map.

✦ Set the Site Map to display dependent files (as in Figure 8-5).

See the Dreamweaver Help files for details on setting up a Site Map.

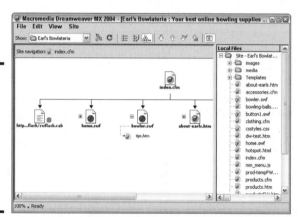

Figure 8-5:
The link from bowler.swf has been changed to tips.htm in the map view.

After you've done that, you can change a link in an SWF by following these steps:

1. **Right-click the link displayed under the SWF in the Site Map and choose Change Link from the contextual menu.**

   The Select HTML File dialog box appears.

2. **Navigate to the file to which you want to link and double-click it, or type a URL into the URL text field.**

3. **Click OK.**

You can also update a link in an SWF while updating the same link in other files by choosing Site⊃Change Link Sitewide and inputting the old and new links in the Change Link Sitewide dialog box that appears. Whether you change the link only in the SWF file or in an SWF file as part of a sitewide update, the FLA source file will not be updated until you launch and edit the SWF from Dreamweaver.

Integrating Dreamweaver with ColdFusion

Dreamweaver fully absorbed ColdFusion, in the sense that Dreamweaver became the working environment for ColdFusion. In Book VI, we describe how to set up your ColdFusion server, as well as concepts in programming; Book II, Chapter 6 offers the information you need to write CFML (ColdFusion Markup Language) using Dreamweaver.

Integrating Dreamweaver with FreeHand

Though you can publish FreeHand documents as HTML (complete with embedded SWF movies, URL links, and Flash actions), FreeHand MX is not as tightly integrated with Dreamweaver as Fireworks is.

FreeHand is primarily a print-oriented design application, so it's no surprise that it lacks the kinds of controls Fireworks offers for image slicing and optimization.

In other words, if you're designing for the Web, you'll find Fireworks a much better tool (not in the least for its solid integration with Dreamweaver). Nonetheless, if you ever find yourself with an HTML file published by FreeHand, rest assured that you can open and edit that file in Dreamweaver, as you can with an HTML file created in any application.

Book II
Chapter 8

Integrating
Dreamweaver
MX 2004

Integrating Dreamweaver with Contribute

From the beginning, Contribute was built with Dreamweaver in mind. Now with the release of version 2.0, Contribute has become more integrated with the Macromedia Studio suite, and Dreamweaver in particular, than ever.

See the section on enabling Contribute compatibility in Book II, Chapter 3 for a quick discussion of what to do if you haven't yet built your site and want others to maintain it using Contribute.

If you've built a site already and want to be able to administer it without leaving Dreamweaver, just follow these steps:

1. **Choose Site⇨Manage Sites.**

    The Manage Sites dialog box appears.

2. **Select the site you want to administer and click Edit.**

    The Site Definition dialog box appears.

3. **Click the Advanced tab.**

   The Advanced options become available.

4. **Click Contribute in the Category list.**

   The Contribute options load in the main part of the dialog box.

5. **Select the Enable Contribute Compatibility check box if it's not already selected.**

   If you haven't enabled Design Notes and Check In/Out, a dialog box appears to alert you to that fact. Click OK to enable them. The Contribute Site Settings dialog box appears.

6. **Enter your name and e-mail address in the Site Settings dialog box and click OK.**

   The dialog box closes, and new options appear in the Contribute page of the Site Definition window.

7. **Enter the remote site root URL (for example, `http://www.loungeboy.com`) in the Site Root URL text field, if it's not already there, and click the Test button.**

   Dreamweaver confirms the URL is accurate by connecting to the site.

8. **Click the Administer Site in Contribute button.**

   Either the Administrator Password dialog box appears, or, if there's no administrator for the site yet, a Contribute dialog box appears that asks if you want to be the administrator for the site.

9a. **If the Administrator Password dialog box appears, enter the password and click OK.**

9b. **If the Contribute dialog box appears, asking if you want to be the administrator (and you do want to be the administrator), click Yes.**

   The Administrator Password dialog box appears. Enter a password in the New Password text field, and re-enter it in the Confirm New Password text field below. Then click OK. Note that passwords are case-sensitive. (If the Contribute dialog box appears and you don't want to be the administrator, click No.)

   Contribute opens in the background, and the Administer Website dialog box appears, as shown in Figure 8-6.

10. **Make any changes to the Administer Website settings and click OK.**

    The Administer Website dialog box closes, and Contribute closes. For information on the Administer Website options, see Book VII, Chapter 3.

11. **Click OK in the Site Definition dialog box.**

12. **Click Done in the Manage Sites dialog box.**

**Book II
Chapter 8**

Integrating
Dreamweaver
MX 2004

Figure 8-6:
The
Administer
Website
dialog box.

For more information on creating new pages in Contribute based on
Dreamweaver templates, see the section on creating a new page in Book VII,
Chapter 2 and the section on using Dreamweaver templates in Book II,
Chapter 7.

Book III

Fireworks MX 2004

The 5th Wave   By Rich Tennant

"You know, I've asked you a dozen times not to animate the torches on our Web page!"

Contents at a Glance

Chapter 1: Introduction to Fireworks MX 2004

In This Chapter

✔ **Understanding the power of Fireworks MX 2004**

✔ **Touring the Fireworks MX 2004 interface**

✔ **Creating a customized work environment**

✔ **Setting your preferences**

Fireworks MX 2004 is the latest version of a graphics creation and editing program designed to streamline the process of making images for the Web. In the days before the original version of Fireworks, making graphics for the Web could be a frustrating and time-consuming process of trial and error. Not only that, but the results often looked pretty bad.

With products like Fireworks, all that has changed. This chapter gives you a brief introduction and tour of the product and shows you how to set up Fireworks to fit your working style.

Understanding the Power of Fireworks

The basic process of making graphics for a Web site can be divided into two major parts:

✦ **Creating the images:** This consists of drawing, importing, and manipulating pictures, as well as designing the overall page layout on the Fireworks canvas.

✦ **Optimizing the images:** This includes slicing the page layout into pieces, selecting the proper compression format and level for each piece, and exporting the individual pieces.

Fireworks has two different tools that make the process of creating graphics for a Web site easier: layers and slices. Layers are a mainstay of graphics development tools, such as Photoshop and FreeHand, and animation programs, such as Macromedia Flash. Layers make creating and editing graphics a simpler proposition. Slices, first introduced by Macromedia in the original version of Fireworks, offer an efficient way to divide a design into individually optimized Web graphics. Both layers and slices are described in more detail in the following sections.

Making designing easier with layers

We discuss layers in more detail in Book III, Chapter 5, but this section serves as an introduction to the benefits of layers.

Layers act like transparent sheets that can be stacked one on top of the other. You draw a separate element of the image on each transparency. Any area where you haven't put something remains transparent, so layers beneath show through. In a typical file you might have several text layers and many layers of backgrounds, icons, lines, shapes, and so on.

If you ever make mistakes or change your mind about things, layers can save you lots of time as you design your site. Suppose that you're doing calligraphy and illustration on fine paper. If you mess up one part of the image, the whole thing is often ruined because you only have one layer to work with: the paper. Short of cutting a piece out of the paper, you may not be able to delete your mistakes. Layers offer a practical approach to fixing your errors.

Using layers provides many benefits. Some of the most practical advantages include the following:

✦ You can change any element of your design — text, bitmap, or vector shape — without altering or destroying any other element.

✦ You can apply effects to layers that are grouped together, decreasing the amount of time it takes to edit an image. (Of course, you can also apply effects to individual layers.)

✦ You can easily move elements up and down in the stack of layers to change the visual effect on the screen.

✦ You can test new designs and effects in a snap because hiding and showing elements of an image is extremely easy.

Creating slices

We discuss slices in more detail in Book III, Chapter 6, but here's an introduction to the concept of slices. Imagine for a moment that you've created your masterpiece design for a new Web site. Your Fireworks file may include lots of different kinds of imagery, including the following:

✦ Logos

✦ Navigation buttons

✦ Header graphics, such as banners

✦ Photos

✦ Drawings

✦ Animations

Before you can create your Web page, you've got to get all of these graphics into a Web-friendly format, which is where slices come in. The idea is simple, yet elegant: include a special layer in the program that can never be removed, where you can create guides as to how you want the images to be "sliced" up into separate, individually optimized, and hyperlinked images. Figure 1-1 shows that special layer, called the Web layer, and some slices in action.

Slices provide some key advantages over traditional methods of creating images for the Web:

✦ You can slice a design into more than one image at a time.

✦ You can export multiple files in a single procedure.

✦ You can control exactly where images are sliced, which helps prevent you from making images with overlapping areas.

✦ You have an increased ability to optimize image size (and thereby reduce download time) by selecting the best optimization method for each slice.

Slices guarantee that the layout of your Web page appears nearly identical on every user's screen to the design you create in Fireworks. (If you have HTML text on your page, the appearance of that text may vary, depending on which browser and platform the user views your page with.)

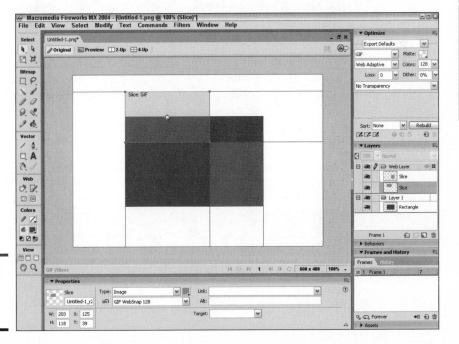

Figure 1-1:
The Web
layer and
slices.

Taking a Quick Tour of the Fireworks MX 2004 Interface

The Fireworks interface is set up to make accessing the tools quick and intuitive. When you start Fireworks, you'll notice that it doesn't create a new document automatically — instead, you see something new with Fireworks MX 2004: the Start Page, as shown in Figure 1-2. From the Start Page, you get one-click access to:

✦ **Open a Recent Item:** Just click the filename, or click the Open folder and browse to a file to open the image in Fireworks.

✦ **Create New:** Click the Fireworks File link to open a new, blank image.

✦ **Extend:** Click the Fireworks Exchange link to browse to a part of the Macromedia Web site that includes lots of free, downloadable cool tools and graphical elements created by users like you.

✦ **Tutorials:** Click the Take a Quick Tour of Fireworks link or the Take a Fireworks Tutorial link to go through a tutorial.

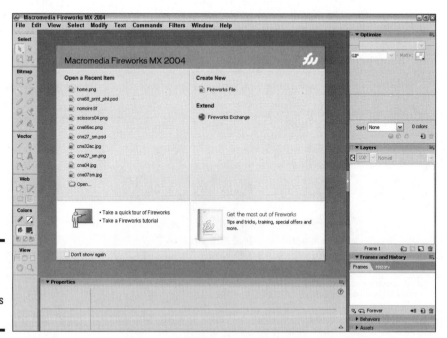

Figure 1-2:
The Start Page, new to Fireworks MX 2004.

If you don't want the Start Page to show up every time you launch Fireworks, click the Don't Show Again check box at the bottom-left corner of the page.

To create a new Fireworks file (called a PNG file), just follow these steps:

1. **Choose File⇨New, or click the Fireworks File link on the Start Page.**

The New Document dialog box appears.

2. **Choose the canvas size for your document.**

The default width and height are 500 pixels, and the default resolution is 72 pixels per inch. You can enter your own size in the fields provided and change the unit of measurement by selecting one from the drop-down list. You should leave the resolution at 72 pixels per inch unless you're designing for some medium other than the Web, like print.

3. **Select a color for the canvas.**

The default canvas color is white, but you can choose a custom color by selecting the Custom radio button and then using the eyedropper to choose a color from the color picker. You can also choose to have a transparent background by selecting the Transparent radio button.

4. **Click OK to create your new Fireworks document.**

When you click OK, you see something that looks a lot like Figure 1-3.

The Tools panel: A bird's-eye view

The panels lined along the left side of the screen are parts of the Tools panel, which provides access to all the tools you use to make and modify your graphics. The Tools panel divides tools into groups based on their function, as described in the following list:

✦ **Select:** Contains tools used to select an object, as well as tools used to crop or otherwise manipulate the canvas.

✦ **Bitmap:** Stores tools used to paint, draw, fill, and so on.

✦ **Vector:** Contains tools used to create and manipulate vector graphics. (See Book V, Chapter 1 for more on vector graphics.)

✦ **Web:** Holds tools, such as the Slice tool, that are designed specifically for getting images ready for the Web.

✦ **Colors:** Stows away tools that control the color(s) of objects.

✦ **View:** Holds tools that you can use to change your view of the canvas or the screen.

**Book III
Chapter 1**

**Introduction to
Fireworks MX 2004**

Quick Export button

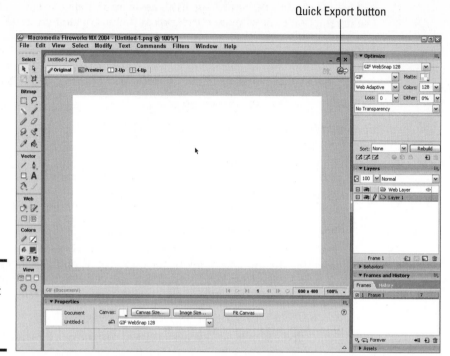

Figure 1-3:
The default
Fireworks
MX 2004
interface.

An arrow at the lower-right corner of a tool's icon indicates that the tool has one or more specialized variations. You can click the arrow to activate a pop-up menu that displays icons for the available variations.

The Tools panel: A bug's-eye view

This section gives you the lowdown on the tools you'll likely use the most in the Tools panel. An arrow at the bottom right of the tool icon indicates there are related tools available. Click the icon or the arrow to activate a pop-up menu so that you can choose from all the available tools. When a tool is selected, you can also cycle through the related tools by pressing certain keys on your keyboard (for example, select the Marquee tool and press M to toggle through the Marquee tools). The Tooltip for each tool includes the key you can press to cycle through the options on the tool.

You get to see the tools in action in subsequent chapters, but for now, here are the highlights for each of the three key categories of tools:

✦ **Select:** The following four tools (clockwise from top left) make up the Select section of the Tools panel:

- **Pointer/Select Behind tool:** Use the Pointer tool to select objects on the canvas by clicking on them or clicking and dragging an area that encompasses them. Use the new Select Behind tool when you want to click an object on the canvas that is covered by other objects.

- **Subselection tool:** Use the Subselection tool to select an individual object from a group.

- **Crop/Export Area tool:** Click the Crop tool and click-and-drag to select an area on the canvas to crop an image. When you *crop* an image, you discard everything outside the selected area from your image. After you have selected the area that you want to keep, double-click inside the area to crop. Use the Export Area tool to create a new image from the area you select. After you have selected the area you want to export, double-click inside the area to bring up the Export Preview window.

- **Scale/Skew/Distort tool:** This tool is inactive (as indicated by the dimmed icon) until you have selected an object on the canvas. Click this tool and click and drag the transform handles at the corners of the object to change its size and/or shape.

✦ **Bitmap:** The following ten tools (clockwise from top left) make up the Bitmap section of the Tools panel:

- **Marquee/Oval Marquee tool:** Click the Marquee tool and click and drag to select a rectangular area on the canvas. If you want to select a circle or oval area, use the Oval Marquee variation. When you select an area, you select all objects that fall completely within the area.

- **Lasso/Polygon Lasso tool:** Click the Lasso tool and click and drag on the canvas to select everything within an irregularly shaped area of the canvas. If the shape you want to select is made up of straight lines, use the Polygon Lasso.

- **Brush tool:** Click this tool to paint on the canvas. See Book III, Chapter 3 for more information about the very versatile Brush tool.

- **Eraser tool:** Click the Eraser tool to erase a swath through any bitmap object on the canvas.

- **Rubber Stamp/Replace Color/Red Eye Removal tool:** Click this tool to copy a selected area of a bitmap to another spot on the canvas. Alt+click the area that you want to copy, and then click and paint where you want the copy to go. Use the new Replace Color tool to swap one color for another wherever you click and drag the Replace Color brush on the canvas. Simply click with the new Red Eye Removal tool to replace red with black wherever you click the canvas.

- **Paint Bucket/Gradient tool:** Click this tool and then click a shape on the canvas to fill the shape with a solid color (Paint Bucket) or gradient. For details about gradients, see Book III, Chapter 4.

**Book III
Chapter 1**

**Introduction to
Fireworks MX 2004**

- **Eyedropper tool:** Click this handy tool to select a color from the swatches in the color picker or from any object on the canvas by clicking the desired color.

- **Blur/Sharpen/Dodge/Burn/Smudge tool:** Click this tool and click and drag on the canvas to soften the focus of (Blur) or bring into focus (Sharpen) an area of a bitmap image. Click the Dodge tool and click and drag on the canvas to lighten an area of a bitmap image. Click the Burn tool and click and drag to darken an area of a bitmap image. Click the Smudge tool and click and drag on the canvas to smear a part of an image into another part of the image, as if you were finger painting. You can set the parameters for these tools in the Property inspector.

- **Pencil tool:** Click the Pencil tool and click and drag to draw single-pixel-width lines. If you want control over the thickness and texture of the line you are creating, use the Brush tool.

- **Magic Wand tool:** Click the Magic Wand and click a bitmap to select contiguous areas of solid or similar colors in your image.

✦ **Vector:** The following six tools (clockwise from top left) make up the Vector section of the Tools panel:

- **Line tool:** Throw your ruler away! With the Line tool, you can draw a straight line every time. You can adjust the line's thickness, color, and other parameters in the Property inspector.

- **Pen/Vector Path/Redraw Path tool:** Click the Pen tool to create vector graphics by drawing vector paths. You can use the Pen tool to select points and let Fireworks connect the dots, or you can draw the shape yourself with the Vector Path tool. You can use the Redraw Path tool to change the shape of a vector graphic by clicking and dragging any of the points that define the shape.

- **Text tool:** Click this tool and click the canvas to place and edit text on the canvas. See Book III, Chapter 3 for information on how to make the most of the Text tool.

- **Knife tool:** Click this tool and click and drag a line to cut vector paths in two.

- **Freeform/Reshape Area/Path Scrubber (Additive)/Path Scrubber (Subtractive) tool:** Use the Freeform tool to reshape a vector path by pushing or pulling the stroke instead of moving the individual points that define it. Use the Reshape Area tool to pull a vector path as if you had grabbed it with your hand. Use the Path Scrubber tool to change the color, thickness, and various other properties of the vector path. If you have a graphics tablet, you can set the properties to vary based on variations in the pressure or speed you use in drawing.

- **Rectangle/Rounded Rectangle/Ellipse/Polygon tool:** Create vector shapes by clicking these tools and clicking and dragging on the canvas.

Across the aisle: The right-side panels

Four key panels appear on the right-hand side of the screen, opposite the Tools panel. These panels include the following:

✦ **The Optimize panel:** This panel enables you to set your export options (GIF or JPEG, quality level, and so on). See Book III, Chapter 6 for more information about the Optimize panel.

✦ **The Layers panel:** This panel contains all your layer options and information. The first layer is always the Web layer, which holds information about the coordinates of the slices. (See Book III, Chapter 6 for more about slices.)

✦ **The Assets panel:** This panel provides a way to centralize and organize links from Web objects to Web pages. Fireworks can actually generate your entire Web page — images, code, and all.

✦ **The Frames and History panel:** This panel gives you access to the Frames area, where you can navigate easily among the frames in your document. You use frames to make button rollovers and animations. (See Book III, Chapter 5 for more details.) This panel also allows you to view the History area, which is a list of your most recent actions.

The Property inspector

The Property inspector is docked to the bottom of the Document window. This panel changes automatically to reflect the settings for the currently selected tool or object.

The Property inspector allows you to see and adjust the parameters of whatever object or tool you select. If you're working on a text layer, for example, the Property inspector gives you immediate access to and complete control over the font, size, color, and other attributes of the text. When you select a shape, on the other hand, the Property inspector offers you easy access to controls over the shape's size, position on the canvas, color, texture, and more.

If you ever want to hide all the panels temporarily, press F4 or the Tab key. To make the panels visible, press F4 or the Tab key again.

Viewing and Previewing Your Work

While you work, you view the canvas with Original view selected. The other three view options at the top of the canvas allow you to preview what your optimized images will look like as follows:

+ **Original:** This is the default view in which you create and edit your design.

+ **Preview:** This view shows you what the page will look like when it is optimized for the Web, based on your current image optimization settings.

+ **2-Up:** This view offers previews of what optimized images will look like, but with a little something extra: a side-by-side comparison of the original image and an optimized version of the image, or two optimization settings.

+ **4-Up:** By selecting the 4-Up view, you can preview the original image and three different optimization settings at the same time. You can compare how they look and how big the resulting image file would be at each setting, as well as how long the image would take to download at a particular modem speed.

Because every image compresses a little differently, you can never predict exactly what an image might look like after it is optimized. The longer you work with Fireworks, the better you get at narrowing the optimization options before you preview; nevertheless, you may find it more efficient to preview before you export. For more information about the purpose and art of image optimization, see Book III, Chapter 6.

At the top right of the canvas is a feature introduced in the original Fireworks: a Quick Export button. The Quick Export button allows you to export files to, and even launch, other applications, such as Dreamweaver MX 2004, Macromedia Flash MX 2004, and FreeHand MX. Export options for Macromedia Director Shockwave Studio, Adobe Photoshop, and other programs are also available from the Quick Export button.

Customizing Your Work Environment

During different phases of the design process, you may find that you refer to some panels constantly but other panels not at all. Unless you have a gigantic monitor set to a high resolution, you'll need to collapse some less-frequently used panels to make room for more-frequently used ones.

Collapsing and expanding panels

Every panel's name is displayed at the left on the top title bar in the panel. To the left of the name sits a handy little arrow that points down to indicate the panel is expanded and points to the panel name if the panel is collapsed.

You can expand or collapse a panel in two ways:

+ Click the name of the panel.

+ Click the arrow to the left of the panel name.

When the panel expands, it makes room for itself by forcing the panels below it down — unless it's a panel on the bottom, in which case it forces the panels above it up. If there's not enough room on your monitor to show all the panels open at once, Fireworks collapses the panel directly beneath or above the one you expanded.

If you have a panel expanded but still can't see quite enough of it, you can drag the panel open wider or longer by clicking on the left or bottom edge of the panel and dragging it.

In addition to collapsing and expanding panels, you can also open and close panels. Check out Table 1-1, which includes the key commands for closing and opening panels.

Table 1-1	Keyboard Shortcuts for Opening and Closing Panels		
Panel	*Keyboard Shortcut*	*Panel*	*Keyboard Shortcut*
Tools	Ctrl+F2	Styles	Shift+F11
Properties	Ctrl+F3	Library	F11
Optimize	F6	Color Mixer	Shift+F9
Layers	F2	Swatches	Ctrl+F9
Frames	Shift+F2	Info	Alt+Shift+F12
History	Shift+F10	Behaviors	Shift+F3

To hide all panels at once, choose Window⇨Hide Panels, or use the keyboard shortcut F4.

Moving, docking, and grouping panels

When you open Fireworks for the first time, all the panels are docked and grouped in the default configuration. (Refer to Figure 1-3 to see this default configuration.) However, undocking and moving panels and putting them in custom groups is easy.

To move a panel, follow these steps:

1. Click the gripper at the top left of the panel.

The gripper is made up of two parallel lines of dots at the top left, on the panel's title bar.

2. Drag the panel to the spot on the screen where you would like it to go.

3. Release the mouse button.

You now see the panel in the position you selected, in its own window, as shown in Figure 1-4.

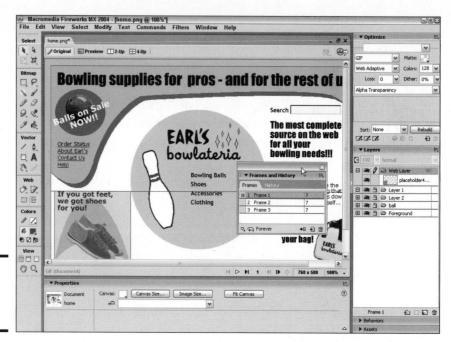

Figure 1-4:
An undocked panel.

When you move a panel, you automatically undock it, but you don't automatically dock it somewhere else when you release the mouse button. The panel remains floating in the Fireworks window until you dock it. To dock a panel, follow these steps:

1. **Place your cursor over the gripper at the top left of the panel.**

The gripper is made up of two parallel lines of dots at the top left, on the panel's title bar.

2. **Drag the panel to a docking area.**

A docking area is anywhere along the outer edge of the Document window or adjacent to a docked panel. When you have dragged the panel over a docking area, a rectangle appears on the screen to give you a preview of the space the panel would occupy if you docked it there.

3. **Release the mouse button.**

The panel is docked in its expanded state.

Fireworks allows you the option to consolidate or group panels, which provides a nice way to put the panels you like using together. To group a panel with another panel, follow these steps:

1. **Click the Panel Options icon (the three white lines and arrow) at the top right of the panel you want to add to a group.**

The Panel Options menu appears.

2. **Select the Group Layers With option.**

An additional pop-up menu appears.

3. **Choose the panel you want to group the currently selected panel with.**

The panel you added appears as a tab in the panel to which you added it.

Follow these steps to remove a panel from a group:

1. **Click the tab of the panel you want to separate from the group.**

2. **Click the Panel Options icon at the top right of the panel.**

The Panel Options menu appears.

3. **Select the Close Panel Group option.**

This closes not only the panel you want to close, but also any other panels in that group.

4. **Reopen any panels from the group that you didn't want to close by choosing them from the Window menu.**

If you have moved your panels around and docked them to accommodate a particular project or document, you can save your panel arrangement by choosing Commands⇨Panel Layout Sets⇨Save Panel Layout and giving your settings a name. You can then retrieve that layout set-up from the same location.

Setting Fireworks Preferences

Setting preferences allows you to customize the way Fireworks handles certain basic functions and displays certain items. To edit Fireworks preferences, choose Edit⇨Preferences or use the keyboard shortcut Ctrl+U.

As you can see in Figure 1-5, the Preferences dialog box has five tabs:

✦ General

✦ Editing

✦ Launch and Edit

✦ Folders

✦ Import

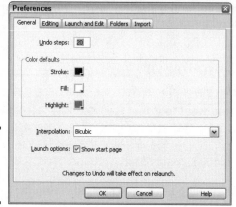

Figure 1-5:
The
Preferences
dialog box.

Setting General preferences

You can select the General tab on the Preferences dialog box and customize the following settings:

✦ **Undo Steps:** Set the value from 0 to 999. This setting affects Edit⟹Undo/ Redo and also increases the number of possible steps in the History panel. Be aware, however, that the more Undo steps you allow, the more memory Fireworks requires. You must close and relaunch Fireworks to use the new setting.

✦ **Color Defaults:** Set the default colors for Stroke (a line or border), Fill (the inside of a shape), and Highlight (the color that indicates what you currently have selected). To apply the changes to the default Stroke and Fill colors in the current document, you must click the Set Default Stroke/Fill Colors button in the Tools panel.

✦ **Interpolation:** Choose one of the four methods that Fireworks can use to render a change to the image size:

• **Bicubic Interpolation,** the default method, generally yields the highest-quality results.

• **Soft Interpolation** blurs the image slightly.

• **Bilinear Interpolation** gives a sharpness level somewhere in between Bicubic and Soft.

• **Nearest Neighbor Interpolation** sharpens edges.

For more details on changing image size, see Book III, Chapter 2.

✦ **Launch options:** Select this check box if you want to see the Start Page when you launch Fireworks; deselect the check box if you don't want to see the Start Page.

Setting Editing preferences

Select the Edit tab to access these editing preferences in Fireworks:

+ **Precise Cursors:** Select this check box if you prefer to use cross hairs as a cursor instead of the custom cursors for each tool.

+ **Delete Objects When Cropping:** Leave this check box selected if you want to delete objects and pixels that fall outside the area to which you crop your image.

+ **Brush-Size Painting Cursors:** Select this check box if you want the cursor size to represent the size of stroke you are about to make.

+ **Bitmap Option:** Select the Turn Off "Hide Edges" check box if you always want to see the path selection feedback of a selected object.

+ **Pen Tool Options:** You have two options here:

  • Select the Show Pen Preview check box if you want Fireworks to show what your path will look like (before you actually draw the line) based on the position of your cursor.

  • Select the Show Solid Points check box if you want selected points to appear hollow and deselected points to appear solid.

+ **Pointer Tool Options:** You have several options here:

  • Select the Mouse Highlight check box if you want an object's selection feedback (the box that indicates that an object has been selected) to activate when you roll the cursor over that object.

  • Select the Preview Drag check box if you want to see an object as you drag it.

  • Select the Show Fill Handles check box if you want to be able to drag handles to change the position, width, skew, and rotation of a gradient fill.

  • Set the value of the Pick Distance option from 1 to 10 to specify how close in pixels your cursor needs to be to an object for you to select it.

  • Set the value of the Snap Distance option from 1 to 10 to specify how close to a grid or guide in pixels an object must be before the object snaps to the grid or guide.

Setting Launch and Edit preferences

You set the Launch and Edit preferences to specify how you want Fireworks to act when it's launched from within other applications in the Macromedia Studio MX 2004 suite.

The options are the same whether you are choosing options under When Editing from External Application or When Optimizing from External Application:

✦ Select the Ask When Launching option if you want Fireworks to ask you whether or not to edit the PNG source file when you launch Fireworks from within another application.

✦ Select the Always Use Source PNG option if you want Fireworks always to find the source PNG for editing an image from within another application.

✦ Select the Never Use Source PNG option when you never want Fireworks to locate and make available for editing the source file for an image you are editing from within another application.

In most cases (with Macromedia Flash being an exception), if you edit an image by launching Fireworks from within another application, Fireworks attempts to locate the source PNG file for editing, regardless of the Launch and Edit preferences.

Setting Folders preferences

Fireworks comes with its own effects, textures, and patterns, but the application allows you to access additional materials for use in modifying bitmap images. Select the Folders tab to gain access to the following:

✦ **Photoshop Plug-Ins:** If you have Photoshop plug-ins you want to be able to use in Fireworks, select the Photoshop Plug-Ins check box. Use the dialog box to browse to the folder that holds those plug-ins.

✦ **Textures:** If you have additional textures you would like to access from within Fireworks, select the Textures check box. Use the dialog box to browse to the folder that has the texture files.

✦ **Patterns:** If you have additional patterns you would like to access from within Fireworks, select the Patterns check box. Use the dialog box to browse to the folder that has the pattern files.

If you change these preferences, you need to quit and relaunch Fireworks for the changes to take effect.

You can access the effects, textures, and patterns from the Property inspector when you select an object.

Setting Import preferences

Set the Import preferences to tell Fireworks how you want to convert Photoshop (.psd) files for editing in Fireworks:

+ **Layers:** Three options are grouped under this heading:

  - Select Convert to Fireworks Objects if you want Fireworks to make each Photoshop layer into an object on its own Fireworks layer.

  - Select the Share Layer Between Frames check box if you want each layer of the Photoshop file to be shared across all Fireworks frames.

  - Select Convert to Frames if you want Fireworks to import each Photoshop layer as a Fireworks frame. That can save you a few steps if the Photoshop file has layers that correspond to animation frames or button states.

+ **Text:** Three options are grouped under this heading:

  - Select Editable if you want to edit text layers from the Photoshop file using the Fireworks Text tool. The text may look slightly different in Fireworks, though it will be close.

  - Select Maintain Appearance if you need the text in Fireworks to look identical to the text in Photoshop but do not need to edit the text.

  - Select the Use Flat Composite Image check box if you want to import the Photoshop file as a flattened, one-layer image.

Getting Help

Fireworks offers several forms of assistance to users. If you can't find the answer to your question in this book, you have several good options available to you:

+ **The Help menu:** This menu offers links to appropriate parts of the Macromedia Web site and an indexed, searchable online manual.

  Press F1 to access the online manual at any time when you're using Fireworks. The online manual is always where we go first when we need to figure out how to do something in Fireworks.

+ **Fireworks tutorials:** There are two basic Fireworks tutorials, one on Graphic Design Basics and the other on Web Design Basics. You can download them from the Web by clicking the "Take a Fireworks Tutorial" link on the Fireworks Start page and then clicking the "Macromedia Fireworks MX Tutorials" link in the Macromedia Fireworks MX 2004 Documentation section at the top of the page. Then click to download the appropriate PDF and source files for your platform (PC or Mac). The tutorials are quick, easy, and very helpful to the novice.

+ **The installation CD-ROM:** The CD-ROM from which you installed Fireworks contains a couple of searchable, printable PDF files:

- The Using Fireworks PDF offers the basics.

- The Extending Fireworks PDF describes how you can use JavaScript to control every command and setting in Fireworks.

  You can copy the PDFs into the Fireworks folder on your hard drive so you don't have to rummage around for the installation CD when you have a question the Help menu can't answer.

✦ **Tooltips:** Tooltips are built into the Fireworks user interface. Hover the cursor over an interface element to see a brief description of the element's function or capabilities.

If none of these resources gives you an answer to your question, Macromedia offers both free Web-based support (including online forums) and fee-based support via e-mail and telephone.

Chapter 2: Fireworks MX 2004 Basics

In This Chapter

✔ **Creating a new Fireworks document**

✔ **Switching the view of your document**

✔ **Saving your documents**

✔ **Changing a document's size**

✔ **Understanding color management**

*I*n this chapter, we introduce some of the basic processes of working with Fireworks MX 2004. If you're a regular computer user, many of these processes will already be second nature to you. We show you how to create and save a Fireworks document, how to change the magnification of your document, and how to change the size of your document. We also offer an introduction to some issues regarding the way colors are displayed on the Web.

Creating a New Document

Before you can start creating or editing cool images with Fireworks, you need to start the program and either create a brand-new blank document or open an existing image that you want to change. You can open Fireworks in several ways:

✦ Select Fireworks MX 2004 from the Start menu.

✦ Click the Fireworks icon in your taskbar or double-click the icon on your desktop, if you have either of those options available.

✦ Double-click the icon of an existing Fireworks PNG file.

✦ Double-click the icon of any image associated with Fireworks. (During installation, you can choose which file types will be associated with Fireworks, including GIFs and JPEGs.)

No matter how you open Fireworks, you can create a new Fireworks document by following these steps:

1. **Choose File⇨New or press Ctrl+N.**

   The New Document dialog box opens, displaying options for the size and background color of your canvas, as well as the resolution of your document, as shown in Figure 2-1. The default for all these settings is determined by the settings of the most recently opened Fireworks document. If those settings are what you want, simply click OK. Otherwise, continue with the following steps.

Figure 2-1:
Set the canvas size and canvas color in the New Document dialog box.

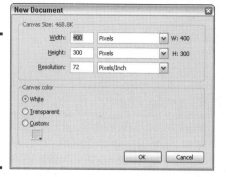

2. **Type numbers in the Width and Height text fields to set the width and height of your canvas; use the drop-down list to select whether you want the width and height of the canvas measured in pixels, inches, or centimeters.**

   If you're designing for the Web, pixels are most appropriate, because pixels are the basic display units on computer monitors. If you're designing for print, inches or centimeters may work better.

   You can use different units of measurement for the width and height, although it would probably be more confusing than helpful.

3. **Set the canvas color.**

   The default canvas color is white. You can also set the canvas to be transparent, which can be useful if you're making a graphic that you want to have a transparent background. If your Web page is going to use a particular color for the background, click the square to use the eyedropper to choose a color from the color picker, as shown in Figure 2-2.

4. **Click OK.**

   Your canvas opens to the specified size and with the specified background color.

Figure 2-2:
Use the color picker to select a custom background color for your canvas.

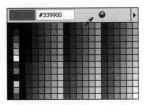

Changing Views of Your Document

After you start adding stuff to your canvas, you may find that you want to make adjustments too fine to eyeball with the canvas at 100 percent size. Fireworks offers several ways for you to increase and decrease the magnification of your canvas. Changing the magnification doesn't affect your document's size, it just changes your view of it, as if you're looking at your document through a magnifying glass.

To increase the magnification of the canvas so you can make fine adjustments, use one of the following methods:

✦ **Choose View➪Zoom In or press Ctrl+=.** Repeat as necessary to achieve the desired view.

✦ **Choose View➪Magnification, and then select a magnification percentage greater than 100 percent.** If you use this method, you can select your magnification percentage directly, rather than stepping through each level. Figure 2-3 shows this selection method.

✦ **Click the Magnification drop-down list at the bottom-right of the canvas and select from the list of preset magnification levels.**

✦ **Click the Zoom tool in the View section of the Tools panel, and then click on the canvas.** If you press Ctrl+Z, you can click and drag the Zoom tool to Zoom in on the selected area of the canvas.

If your canvas is larger than the window in which you are viewing it, you can decrease the magnification of the canvas so you can see the entire document by using one of the following methods:

✦ **Choose View➪Zoom Out or press Ctrl+-.** Repeat as necessary to achieve the view you want.

✦ **Choose View➪Magnification, and then select a magnification percentage less than 100 percent.** If you use this method, you can select your magnification percentage directly, rather than stepping through each level.

✦ **Click the Magnification drop-down list at the bottom of the canvas and select from the list of preset magnification levels.**

✦ **Click the Zoom tool in the View section of the Tools panel, and then hold down the Alt key and click on the canvas.** Notice that when you press the Alt key while the Zoom tool is over the canvas, the plus sign in the tool changes to a minus sign to indicate you can click to zoom out.

Several of the most common magnification levels can be accessed in one step with the key commands listed in Table 2-1.

Table 2-1	Magnification Shortcuts
Magnification Percentage	*Key Combination*
50%	Ctrl+5
100%	Ctrl+1
200%	Ctrl+2
300%	Ctrl+3
400%	Ctrl+4
800%	Ctrl+8
1600%	Ctrl+6

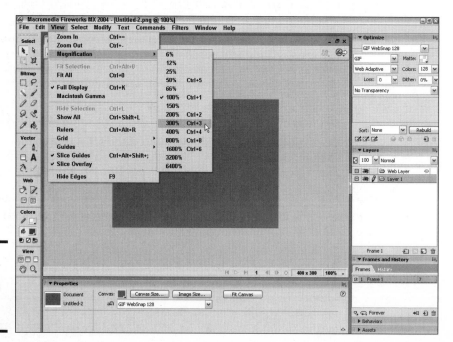

Figure 2-3:
Changing
the canvas
magnifi-
cation.

Saving Documents

You may have read this elsewhere, but it bears repeating: Save early and save often. We can't think of anything worse than working for hours on an image, getting it just perfect, and having a power outage or other mishap wipe out all that work in one cruel second.

Spare yourself the frustration of losing your work and save your documents often by choosing File⇨Save or by pressing Ctrl+S. When you save a file you created in Fireworks using this method, you save the file in the native Fireworks file format, PNG.

When you open and edit a TIFF, BMP, WBMP, GIF or JPEG, you can save as that file type, instead of saving the edited file as a PNG. To exercise the option, just save by choosing File⇨Save or by pressing Ctrl+S. If you've added Fireworks-specific things like slices or frames to your file, a dialog box appears, asking how you want to save the file. If you save the file as its original format, you'll lose any of those Fireworks-specific features.

You can still use the Undo command after you have saved, so it never really hurts to save your document. However, if you are concerned with preserving intermediate versions of a document, you can save versions, rather than saving over your previous work. If you want to try several different approaches to a design but don't want to clog one file with all of the approaches, use the Save As command and name the file with a slight variation. (For example, if your file is named homepage.png, you could name a second version homepage_v02.png.) When you Save As, any changes to the file since you last saved it will be saved in the new version of the file, not the old one.

To save a version of your document, follow these simple steps:

1. **Choose File⇨Save or press Ctrl+S to save the file in its current state, with its current name.**

2. **Choose File⇨Save As or press Ctrl+Shift+S.**

   The Save As dialog box appears, as shown in Figure 2-4.

3. **Type a new filename.**

   If you have already named the file, the current name is filled in for you, so you need to modify the filename in order to save the current version of the document.

4. **If you are editing a non-PNG file and want to save the file in its original format, use the Save As Type drop-down list to select the format.**

5. **Click OK.**

   The new version of the file is now open and ready for modification.

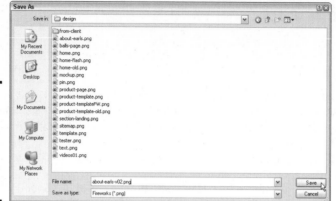

Figure 2-4:
Use the
Save As
command
to save
iterations of
your work.

Modifying Document Size

You can modify the size of your Fireworks document in two fundamentally different ways. With these methods, you're changing the actual dimensions of the document, not just the magnification of the canvas:

✦ **Changing the image size:** When you change the image size, Fireworks recreates the entire document, including everything on the canvas, at a different height and/or width.

✦ **Changing the canvas size:** When you change the canvas size, you do not change the size of the objects on the canvas, you only change the size of the space on which you put the material, as if you cut the top, bottom, or sides off a printed picture (or pasted extra strips on, if you're increasing the canvas size). You can use the crop tool to reduce the canvas size, or you can use a dialog box to increase or reduce the canvas size.

Changing the image size

To change the image size of your document, you use the Image Size dialog box, which is accessed by choosing Modify⇨Canvas⇨Image Size. When you change the image size of your document, you change the dimensions of the canvas and of everything on the canvas. If you shrink your image, Fireworks discards some of the data when it reorders the pixels to make the image smaller.

If you increase the size of your image, Fireworks *interpolates* data, which entails performing sophisticated calculations to decide what color of pixels to add and where to add them in order to make a larger version of the image. While Fireworks interpolates smartly, some amount of distortion is inevitable.

Using the Image Size dialog box, you can choose which method Fireworks uses to interpolate or resample pixels:

✦ **Bicubic interpolation:** Bicubic interpolation is the default method and generally yields the highest-quality results with the widest variety of images by taking an average of the nearest 16 pixels in the original image size to create a new pixel in the resized image.

✦ **Soft interpolation:** This method blurs the image slightly. Why would you want the resized image to be slightly blurred? Because resizing can result in visual inconsistencies in the image called *artifacts*. Blurring the image takes the edge off the artifacts, rather like a soft-focus lens makes a starlet's skin look smoother.

✦ **Bilinear interpolation:** The bilinear method gives a sharpness level somewhere in between Bicubic and Soft.

✦ **Nearest-neighbor interpolation:** This method sharpens edges, so it works best on images that don't have subtle gradients. If you use this method on a bitmap of a sunset, for example, you'll get *banding* — noticeable stripes of color instead of a smooth blending of colors.

When you shrink your image, Fireworks discards some pixels and replaces a few to smooth out the resized image. If you have a 400 x 300 image that you shrink to 240 x 180, and then you enlarge it back to its original size, the image you end up with will not be identical to the original image. However, as long as the size changes aren't extreme, you may not notice much of a difference.

If the Constrain Proportions check box is selected in the Image Size dialog box, as it is by default, and you change the width in the Pixel Dimensions part of the dialog box, the height in that part of the dialog box updates automatically, as does the width and height in the Print Size part of the dialog box. If you change the image resolution in the Print Size part of the dialog box, the width and height in both Pixel Dimensions and Print Size updates automatically.

The Pixel Dimensions and Print Size widths and heights are identical, they're just being measured with different units. (You can set Pixel Dimensions and Print Size to use the same units of measurement.)

To change the image size of your document, with the intention of displaying the image online, follow these steps:

1. **Choose Modify⇨Canvas⇨Image Size.**

The Image Size dialog box appears, with the current image size and resolution as the defaults, as shown in Figure 2-5.

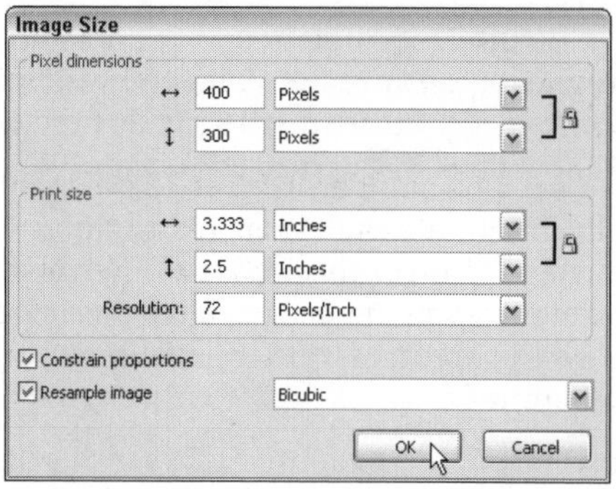

Figure 2-5:
Changing the image size.

2. **Type new numbers in the Width and Height text fields in the Pixel Dimensions part of the dialog box to set the new width and height for your image; use the drop-down list to select whether you want to change the width and height of the image based on pixels or percentages.**

If you're designing for the Web, pixels are most appropriate, because pixels are the standard units of computer monitor display. If you're designing for print, inches or centimeters may work better. If you want your new image to have the same *aspect ratio* (the ratio of width to height, for example, 4:3 for an image that is 400 x 300 pixels) as your current image, leave the Constrain Proportions check box selected. A padlock icon at the right indicates that proportions will be constrained.

If you want to stretch or squash everything in your image as if it were reflected in a funhouse mirror, deselect the Constrain Proportions check box and make sure the new width and height dimensions don't preserve the aspect ratio of the old width and height (the simplest way to do that is to change only height or only width).

You can use different units of measurement for the width and height, although doing so offers no advantages.

3. **Select a method for resampling your image, or leave at the default.**

Resampling settings (Bicubic interpolation or Soft interpolation, for example) are discussed earlier in this section.

4. **Click OK.**

The image resizes.

To change the image size of your document for the purpose of printing it, follow these steps:

1. **Choose Modify⇨Canvas⇨Image Size.**

   The Image Size dialog box appears, with the current image size and resolution as the defaults.

2. **Set the image resolution for print in the Print Size section of the Image Size dialog box.**

   Computer screen resolution is standardized at 72 dots per inch (dpi). Most printers nowadays print at resolutions of anywhere from 300 dpi to 2400 dpi. If you are designing for the Web and are working with a resolution of 72 dpi, changing the resolution here does not increase the resolution of any of your bitmaps (that's kind of like trying to focus a photograph after you've already taken it), but it ensures that the printout fills the page properly.

3. **Type new numbers in the Width and Height text fields in the Print Size part of the dialog box; use the drop-down list to change the measurement units, if desired.**

   If the Constrain Proportions check box is selected, as it is by default, and you want the printed image to have the same aspect ratio as the current image, skip to Step 4. You can deselect the Constrain Proportions check box and type new numbers in the Width and Height text fields if you want to stretch or smash your image.

   You can use different units of measurement for the width and height, although doing so offers no advantages.

4. **Leave the Resample Image check box selected unless you want to change the image size by changing the image resolution.**

   If you change the image resolution, you change the number of pixels per inch.

5. **Click OK.**

   The image resizes.

Changing the canvas size

Making the canvas size smaller is akin to removing strips from the outside of a drawing or painting. Whatever is on those strips gets discarded with the strips. In other words, when you reduce the canvas size, you are essentially cropping or cutting out a piece of the image.

Making the canvas size bigger is like sewing extra strips onto the outside edges of a canvas. You add space to the canvas without changing the size of anything already sitting on it.

To reduce the canvas size, follow these steps:

1. Choose Modify⇨Canvas⇨Canvas Size.

The Canvas Size dialog box opens, as shown in Figure 2-6. The default width and height dimensions when the dialog box opens are the current dimensions of the document.

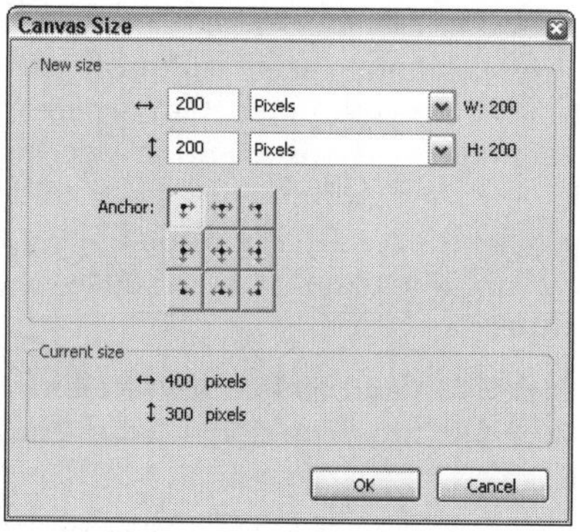

Figure 2-6:
Use the
Canvas Size
dialog box
to crop your
canvas.

2. Type new numbers for the width and height in the text fields, and select the measurement units for the width and height.

Your choice is, as elsewhere, pixels, inches, or centimeters.

3. Select the anchor area.

Because you are cutting off part of your canvas, you must set the anchor to tell Fireworks which edges of the canvas to discard:

- If you click one of the top three squares, Fireworks preserves the top and cuts off any pixels below the height you have set.

- If you click one of the middle three squares, Fireworks removes the top and bottom of the existing document.

- If you click one of the bottom squares, Fireworks cuts off any pixels above the height you have set.

- If you choose one of the left three squares, Fireworks discards any pixels to the right of the width you have set.

- If you choose one of the middle three squares, Fireworks chops off the pixels on either side of the width you have set.

- If you choose one of the right three squares, Fireworks lops off everything to the left of the width you have set.

4. Click OK.

The canvas resizes.

If you're not sure of the dimensions of the image you want, but you know which area of the current image you want to keep, you can reduce the canvas size by using the Crop tool. See Book III, Chapter 1 for information about how to use the Crop tool.

To increase the canvas size, just follow these steps:

1. Choose Modify⇨Canvas⇨Canvas Size.

A dialog box opens, showing the current document dimensions.

2. Type the new width and height in the Width and Height text fields and select the measurement units for the width and height.

You can choose pixels, inches, or centimeters.

3. Select the anchor area.

Because you are appending an area to your canvas, you must set the anchor to tell Fireworks where to put the new area:

- If you click one of the top three squares, Fireworks adds the space to the bottom of your current canvas.

- If you click one of the middle squares, Fireworks adds equal space to the top and bottom of your current canvas.

- If you click one of the bottom squares, Fireworks adds space to the top of your current canvas.

- If you click one of the left three squares, Fireworks adds space to the right of your current canvas.

- If you click one of the center three squares, Fireworks adds equal space to the left and right of your current canvas.

- If you click one of the right three squares, Fireworks adds space to the left of your current canvas.

4. Click OK.

The canvas resizes.

An Introduction to Color Management

The primary colors of light are Red, Green, and Blue (RGB). All the colors you see on a computer monitor are made up of varying amounts of those three colors. When you work in FreeHand MX, you have the option to design using CMYK colors (Cyan, Magenta, Yellow, and Black). CMYK is the process used in offset printing. If you are creating an image to be used for printing, be sure to set a resolution of at least 300 dpi in the Image Size dialog box before you put any bitmap objects in your Fireworks document. Better yet, use FreeHand to make the image; you can import the image into Fireworks if you want to deploy it on the Web. (See Book III, Chapter 8 for information about integrating Fireworks and FreeHand, and see Book IV for more about how to use FreeHand.)

Because Fireworks is made for Web design, it only uses the RGB color spectrum; all its color options are combinations of red, green, and blue. The following section explains how you use hexadecimal numbers to create different colors using the RGB color spectrum.

Hexadecimal numbers

When you are designing a Web page, you select a background color and HTML text colors. In HTML, colors are specified by using hexadecimal numbers — the # symbol, followed by six digits (from 0 through 9) or letters (A through F). Zero represents the bottom of the scale (zero luminosity) and F represents the top of the scale (full luminosity).

The hexadecimal number's six places operate as three pairs. The first pair represents red, the second pair represents green, and the third pair represents blue. For example, to make the background color for your page white, you would write the following code:

```
<BODY bgcolor="#FFFFFF">
```

In order to make white, you need to set each color to its highest luminosity, which is represented by the pair, "FF." If you wanted to put black text on your page, you could use the following code:

```
<FONT color="#000000">text</FONT>
```

In order to make black, you need to set each color to its lowest luminosity, which is represented by the pair, "00." If you don't understand what the code is all about in the examples above, see Book II on Dreamweaver MX 2004.

The hexadecimal expression of a pure RGB red is #FF0000; a pure green is #00FF00; and a pure blue is #0000FF. The number of possible colors is a bit mind-boggling: It's in the millions. Only a small subset of those possible colors is Web safe, though.

Web safe colors

In the early days of the Web, many computer monitors could display only 256 colors. Because 40 of those colors were reserved for the computer's operating system or were otherwise off-limits, that left 216 colors available for use on Web sites: the *Web safe colors*. When you set your monitor's resolution to the 8-bit display option, your monitor can show only that old set of 256 colors. What happens when you look at an image that has colors that don't fall into that set of 256? Your computer approximates the colors it can't display either by a process called dithering or by changing the colors to ones that it can display.

Dithering is the process of combining two or more colors in order to mimic another color. Offset printing uses an analogous process in order to make many colors out of the four CMYK ink colors. If you look at a color image in a newspaper or magazine through a magnifying glass, you see that it's made up of many little colored dots and holes. Viewed from a certain distance, those tiny dots blend together to form what appear to be solid colors. For example, you may see orange with your naked eyes, but if you look closely with a magnifying glass, you see alternating yellow and magenta dots on that newspaper or magazine page.

When a computer dithers a color, it patterns two colors to create the illusion of a third color. As with a color photo in a newspaper, this strategy works only to a limited extent. If you look closely, you can see the pattern. If the dithered color is used just for a line or some small page element, the dither may be rather innocuous. If, on the other hand, you select non-Web safe colors for your page background and/or text colors, people who view your site using a monitor set to 8-bit may have a difficult time trying to read the text on your Web site.

If users have their monitors set to 16-bit and they're looking at a 24-bit color, they get a dithered color also, but the higher resolution of 16-bit versus 8-bit means that the computer can choose closer colors, so the dither doesn't look as obvious. Note that the more colors you have in your image, the larger the file size.

So should you use only Web safe colors when you design your Web site? Isn't that terribly limiting? After all, the Web safe colors were not selected by designers, and there are some really ugly ones in the bunch!

Variability and Web design

One of the most frustrating aspects of Web design, especially for people trained in print design, is that many design elements cannot be accurately controlled. Monitor settings (both in terms of number of colors displayed and pixel resolution) vary from user to user, and colors on Macintosh monitors appear lighter than they do on PC monitors. Users can change the size of HTML text in their browsers, and they can drag their browser windows as wide or narrow as they see fit. Not only that, download rates may be anywhere from about 5K per second with a 56 Kbps modem, to twenty times that or more with cable or DSL modems.

As a result, Web design always starts with a consideration of the end user — the average person who's going to visit the site. If your Web site's audience is going to be made up mostly of college students who have high-speed Internet access in their dorms, or people working in large companies who have high-speed Internet access at their desks, you can get away with making image file sizes larger. You also can assume those people have their monitors set to 16-bit (thousands of colors) or 24-bit (millions of colors), since it looks better and all computers sold nowadays come with video cards that can display at least 16-bit color. What you know about your potential end users should affect your choices of colors for page background, HTML text, and GIFs.

If you have a mix of business users and home users, you have to make some compromises in page width, image quality, and other things. If your users are mostly older, you may want to make your default text size a little bigger than average, or you may be satisfied simply to design your page in such a way as to accommodate a larger text size. You should always try to choose a text color that contrasts fairly sharply with the background color.

Web designers have a phrase that describes what your design should be able to do so that all users can have a satisfactory experience on your site: Your design should *degrade gracefully*. That is, where you do not want to compromise quality or remove features to bring every user's experience down to the lowest common denominator, make sure that users with the least fancy equipment or with disabilities can still access your important content. For example, blind users will have access to any text on your site via screen reader software (which reads the text on your site aloud) or Braille software and hardware. For more information on accessibility issues and standards, visit the World Wide Web Consortium (W3C) Web site at www.w3.org.

Go ahead and use non-Web safe colors, but think about what you're using them for and how likely it may be that the people visiting your site may only be able to see them dithered.

In the early days of the Web, when most Web surfers had 8-bit monitors and used early browsers, designers would predither all their images. That way, images would look essentially the same to all users, whether the users had

8-bit displays or 16-bit displays. Nowadays, browsers have become more sophisticated, and monitors that display at 16-bit and higher are affordable to average computer owners. As a result, designers have decided that in certain cases, it's better to allow inconsistency in the realm of display in order to offer higher image quality to better-equipped users.

In keeping with tradition, though, Fireworks still uses the Web safe color palette as its default in the color picker.

In the next chapter, we get into the nitty-gritty of applying all this color stuff to the real-life situations of choosing colors for page backgrounds, HTML text, and the like.

Chapter 3: Working with Text, Shapes, and Images

In This Chapter

✔ **Entering and editing text**

✔ **Creating and changing shapes**

✔ **Working with bitmaps**

In this chapter, we explore the power that Fireworks MX 2004 gives you to write and edit text, make and manipulate vector shapes, and create and mutate bitmap images. The control that you have with Fireworks may sometimes seem overwhelming, but the number of its tools is limited and the concepts behind the tools are simple. And whether you have a clear idea about what you want, or you're interested in experimenting, Fireworks suits your needs.

Working with Text

Text is the most common element on most Web pages, much as text is the most common element in magazines and newspapers. Unlike with printed material, however, users can alter the size and appearance of HTML text to a certain extent. Some of the most important decisions you make in building your Web site involve how you present text on the screen. In general, a finished Web page has two kinds of text:

✦ **HTML text:** The text you see on the Web page that is created with HTML. This type of text is akin to the text in word-processing software such as Microsoft Word.

✦ **Graphic text:** The text that's embedded in an image, such as a JPEG or a GIF file. In other words, it's a *picture* of text.

Which method of presenting text is better for you and people viewing your Web site depends largely on the function of the text.

Some advantages of using HTML text include the following:

✦ HTML text is smaller (in kilobytes) and therefore loads faster in a user's Web browser.

✦ Visitors can vary the size of the text by changing settings in their browsers.

✦ Special software and hardware (in the case of Braille) can make HTML text available to blind users via audio or touch.

Remember, always use an ALT tag for graphic text. The ALT tag should say what the graphic text says, so blind users have access to it.

✦ Visitors to your site can select, copy, and paste HTML text into e-mails or word-processing documents, which can help spread the word you're trying to get out via your Web site.

On the downside, HTML text tends to be limited to very basic fonts — those available on all computers, notably Arial and Times — and can be presented in only a limited number of ways.

Graphic text, in contrast, is much more visually dynamic than HTML text, because it's part of an image. That's why graphic text is common for buttons and banners, which need to grab the user's attention. Some of the key advantages to using graphic text include the following:

✦ You can create text using any font that's installed on your computer.

✦ You can apply lots of different effects to text, like glows and drop-shadows.

✦ You have greater control of things like *leading* (the spacing between lines of text) and *kerning* (the spacing between letters).

Of course, using graphic text also has drawbacks. Users can't copy and paste text from a graphic, for example. Also, because the graphic text is part of an image, the size (in kilobytes) of the text is larger than that of plain HTML text.

Regardless of the kind of text you're creating, Fireworks can be of help. The following sections show how you can use the Fireworks text editing tools to create text as part of an image, as well as export text in HTML format.

If you want to include your main HTML text in your Fireworks document, or if you want to use placeholder text that will be replaced with final HTML text later in Dreamweaver, use the Fireworks text default, 12 point Arial or Verdana (with no anti-alias), in your page design. Using one of those settings gives you a good approximation of how the text will look on the HTML page you make from your design.

Creating text with the Text tool

Creating text with Fireworks is a snap, which is good because you do a lot of it when you're creating images and page mockups. To create some text, just follow these three easy steps:

1. **Select the Text tool by clicking the capital A in the Vector section of the Tools panel.**

   An I-shaped pointer appears, as shown in Figure 3-1.

2. **Move the pointer to the point on the canvas where you want to create the text.**

3. **Click on the canvas and type away.**

You can always move the text later, as well as change its font or color. We cover those details later in this chapter.

If the text you want to add already exists in a word-processing program, open the text document, select the applicable text, and copy it. Then select the Text tool in Fireworks, click on the canvas, and press Ctrl+V to paste the text. Your text appears in the default font.

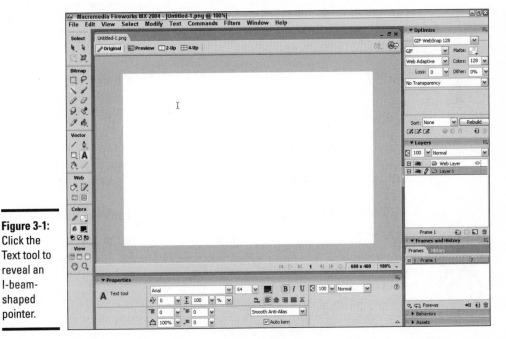

Figure 3-1:
Click the
Text tool to
reveal an
I-beam-
shaped
pointer.

If you're pasting text into your Fireworks document, set the width of the text box before you paste the text in. The default Fireworks text box expands outward to the right rather than downward. To set the width of the text box, select the Text tool from the Tools panel, and click and drag diagonally on the canvas to create a text box of the right size. If your text is too long to fit in the box you've created, the box expands downward automatically.

Selecting a font and changing its size

After you create a snippet of text, you can select it for editing in one of three ways:

✦ After selecting the Text tool, select the text you want to edit by clicking and dragging to highlight just the desired text.

✦ Using the Pointer tool, double-click the text you created. Doing so activates the Text tool and makes the text available for editing.

✦ Using the Pointer tool, click once on the text you've created. Doing so selects the entire text box. When you edit the text settings in the Property inspector, Fireworks applies the changes to all the text in the box.

After you select text, notice that the Property inspector switches automatically to show the available text properties that you can apply to your selected text, including bold, italic, various text alignments, and effects like drop shadow and glow.

You can change your text to a different font in one of two ways:

✦ Choose a font from the drop-down list (that's the list displaying the default font, Arial on the PC and Geneva on the Mac) in the Property inspector. The drop-down list displays all the fonts you have in your machine in alphabetical order. Note that as you scroll through the list, the list displays the name of the selected font using the font face itself so you can quickly see what each font looks like. Figure 3-2 shows the Property inspector when text is selected.

✦ Choose Text➪Font, and then select from the list of fonts displayed on the screen.

If you have tons of fonts and your favorite is way down the list, you can skip to it by clicking in the scrolling drop-down list in the Property inspector and typing the first letter of the font name on your keyboard. This jumps you to the first font available with that letter. You can then press the down-arrow key to find the font you're looking for. Press Enter to apply the font to the selected text. Unfortunately, this feature is not available on the Mac.

Figure 3-2:
The Property inspector puts all your text options within one click.

After you select a font, changing its size doesn't take any time at all. You can change a font size in Fireworks in one of two ways:

✦ **Use the Size field:** The Property inspector contains a field indicating the current size of the font you're working with. To change the text size, simply type the point size you'd like in the field and press Enter.

✦ **Use the Slider:** Click and hold the arrow at the right of the Size field and then slide it up. The text size increases. Similarly, slide it down and the text size decreases, as shown in Figure 3-3.

Figure 3-3:
Use the handy size slider to set your font size.

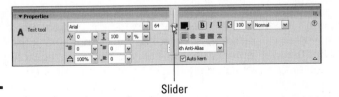

Slider

Adding a little color

By default, all text in Fireworks is black. Although black is handy and always in fashion, it's not the right color for every occasion. Changing font color in Fireworks is pretty easy. To change your color the basic way, just follow these steps:

1. **Select the Text tool and place the cursor next to the first word that you want to change the color of. Click and drag until you've selected all the text you want to make a different color.**

Alternatively, if you're using the Pointer tool, click the text once to select it.

2. Click the Color box to open the color picker.

The color picker appears on-screen, showing only Web safe colors by default (see Figure 3-4). Your mouse pointer changes to an eyedropper when you roll over the palette. The System Color Picker, which offers other color options, is discussed later in this section. You can move the eyedropper anywhere within the Fireworks window.

Figure 3-4:
Use the
eyedropper
to choose a
color in the
Color Picker.

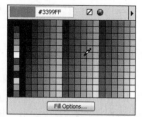

3. Using the eyedropper, click a color.

The square is now the color you have selected for your text. More importantly, your selected text is that color as well. If the text appears to be a different color than the square, that's because the text is high-lighted. Click anywhere on the canvas or click any tool to deselect the text and see the color applied to the text.

If you don't feel like moving your mouse all the way to the bottom of the screen, you can also change the color of your font by using the Colors area of the Tools panel. It works the same way as the color picker in the Property inspector, but you save moving that extra inch or so down the screen.

The color picker contains a number of different views. The default view is Web safe color cubes. You can switch views by clicking the right-facing triangle in the top-right corner of the color picker, and then selecting a new view from the list that appears. The other views include the following:

✦ **Swatches panel:** Displays your saved colors. If you have any saved colors, they show up here. If not, the panel displays the Web safe palette.

✦ **Continuous tone:** Shows the colors as they move from lighter to darker left to right across the color picker. These are the same colors as the Web safe color cubes, just arranged differently.

✦ **Windows OS:** Shows the 217 Web safe colors that are also the Windows operating system colors.

✦ **Mac OS:** Shows the system colors for the Mac operating system.

✦ **Grayscale:** Provides a range of grays from light to dark. Be warned though, only six grayscale colors are Web safe!

What if the color you want isn't in the Web safe palette? Well, thankfully, Fireworks provides you with a number of different coloring options. On the top of the palette is the System Color Picker (the color wheel near the middle of the top of the color picker). You can click the System Color Picker to see your other color options. The System Color Picker offers several other ways for you to choose a color, as shown in Figure 3-5:

✦ **RGB values:** Red, Green, and Blue are the colors that make up all the colors you can see on-screen.

✦ **Hue, Saturation, and Luminosity values:** A different way of telling the computer how to combine red, blue, and green.

✦ **The color matrix:** A visual representation of the Hue (the horizontal axis), Saturation (the vertical axis), and Luminosity (the extra strip on the right) values.

Figure 3-5:
The System Color Picker offers more options than the color picker.

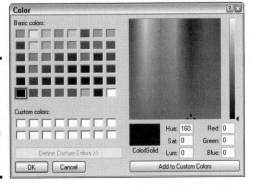

Using the color matrix gives you the most flexibility in choosing a color in that you can visually pick precisely the color you want. Here's how you use the color matrix:

1. **From the top middle of the color picker, select the System Color Picker.**

   The Color dialog box appears, as shown in Figure 3-5.

2. **Place your cursor over the color you want and click the mouse button.**

   You see a cross hair where you clicked. At the center of the cross hair is the color you chose. The higher you go in the matrix, the more saturated the color becomes. If you want to make the color darker or lighter, click the shade you want in the Luminosity bar next to the matrix, or click and move the slider to the right of the shade. Note that, at this point, you still haven't changed the color of the text on the canvas.

3. Click OK to apply the color to your text.

The color is applied to the selected text on the canvas.

If you want to use a color frequently, click the Add to Custom Colors button on the lower right after you select your custom color. That way, whenever you need to use that color, you can click its square in the color picker instead of having to remember its RGB values or trying to find it in the color matrix.

Manipulating text

After you have typed or pasted your text, you can change anything about it, from its color to its position on the page. The process of changing the color is identical to the process of applying color in the first place, and you'll find that editing, moving, and deleting text is just as easy.

Inserting text

To insert text, just follow these steps:

1. Choose the Text tool from the Tools panel.

An I-beam-shaped cursor appears.

2. Click the place in the text box where you want to add text.

A blinking vertical line indicates where your new text will be inserted.

3. Start typing, or paste text (Ctrl+V) that you have copied from elsewhere.

Deleting text

To delete text, do the following:

1. Choose the Text tool from the Tools panel.

2. Click the place in the text box where you want to delete text.

3. Click and drag over the text you want to delete.

The selected text is highlighted, as shown in Figure 3-6.

4. Press Delete or cut the text by pressing Ctrl+X.

The highlighted text disappears.

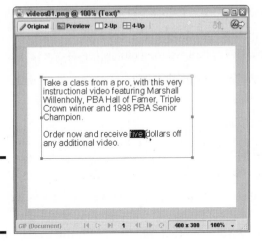

Figure 3-6:
Selecting
text in a
text box.

To delete an entire selection of text, select the Pointer tool, and then click once on the text box that you want to delete. After the text box is selected, press the Delete key to delete the text box and everything in it.

If you realize immediately that you deleted more than you intended, or deleted the wrong chunk of text, use the keyboard shortcut Ctrl+Z to undo the deletion.

Replacing text

To replace text, just follow these steps:

1. **Choose the Text tool from the Tools panel.**

2. **Click the place in the text box where you want to replace text.**

3. **Click and drag over the text you want to delete.**

   The selected text is highlighted, as shown in Figure 3-6.

4. **Start typing, or press Ctrl+V to paste in text you have copied from elsewhere.**

Moving text

To move text within a text box, do the following:

1. **Choose the Text tool from the Tools panel.**

2. **Click and drag over the text you want to move.**

   The selected text is highlighted, as shown in Figure 3-6.

3. **Choose Edit⇨Cut or press Ctrl+X to cut the text.**

4. **Click where you want to drop in the cut text.**

A blinking vertical line indicates where your text will be inserted.

5. **Choose Edit⇨Paste or press Ctrl+V to paste the text at the insertion point.**

To move a text box, follow these steps:

1. **Choose the Pointer tool.**

2. **Place the cursor anywhere over the text box.**

An outline appears in red to indicate that your cursor is over the text box.

3. **Click anywhere within the text box and, with the mouse button held down, drag to move the text box.**

Fireworks shows you where the text is moving to.

4. **Release the mouse button when the top left of your text is positioned where you want it.**

The text is relocated.

Changing text box dimensions

After you have moved your text box, you may find that the text is too wide, too narrow, too long, or too short to fit in its new position in your design. Do you have to change your text? Not necessarily. Fireworks allows you to adjust the dimensions of your text box, which may be all you need to do.

To change the width or length of a text box, just follow these steps:

1. **Choose the Pointer tool.**

2. **Place the cursor anywhere over the text box.**

An outline appears in red to indicate that you have rolled over the text box.

3. **Click anywhere within the text box to select it.**

The red outline changes to blue to indicate that you have selected the entire text box.

4. **Place the Pointer over one of the resize handles (the squares in the middle of the right-hand or left-hand side, which allow you to change the width of the box, and the squares in the corners, which allow you to change the width and height at the same time).**

The Pointer (the black arrow) automatically changes to the Subselection tool (the white arrow).

5. **Click a resize handle and drag the box to the desired width or length.**

6. **Release the mouse button to see the change.**

   If you widen your text box, Fireworks automatically shortens it. If you make your text box narrower, on the other hand, Fireworks makes the text box longer. If you drag the box longer than it needs to be to hold the text, the bottom of the box snaps to the lowest point your text reaches to at the width you dragged the box to.

Working with Vector Shapes

Fireworks gives you two ways to draw on your canvas:

✦ **Vector mode:** Uses points, lines, and shapes to define image elements

✦ **Bitmap mode:** Uses pixels to define image elements

Each method has advantages and disadvantages, and which mode you use depends on what you are attempting to do.

If you want to make a shape that you can easily tweak, resize, or export to Macromedia Flash or FreeHand later, you will want to work in vector mode. When you make a simple vector shape in Fireworks, what you are actually creating is a mathematical model of a series of points connected by lines. By adding, subtracting, or moving points, you can change the shape without changing any of its other qualities, such as the line (stroke), width, and texture.

Because a simple vector shape is more a mathematical description of an image than an actual image, its data size is small. Not only that, but a square of a particular color and stroke width and gradient fill is basically the same data size whether it's 10 x 10 pixels or 1000 x 1000 pixels on-screen. That becomes important in Macromedia Flash, in which smaller image data sizes mean faster downloads.

The basic building block of a shape is the path. The path by itself is just a set of coordinates; in order to make the path appear, you need to apply a *stroke*. A *stroke* in Fireworks is like a brushstroke in painting. Stroke properties include width, texture, and color. The thicker the brush, the thicker the stroke it makes. Of course, in Fireworks, you can make strokes with the Pencil and Pen tools, and with other tools as well.

Read on to discover how to create and edit vector shapes.

Making a good old-fashioned line

When you first create a line using the Line tool, it is a straight line (though it can be vertical, horizontal, or diagonal). To create a line in Fireworks, just follow these steps:

1. **Select the Line tool from the Vector part of the Tools panel.**

2. **Place your cursor over the spot where you would like your line to start.**

   When your cursor is over the canvas, it becomes a cross hair. The center of that cross hair is your point of contact with the canvas.

3. **Click where you want your line to start and, holding the mouse button down, move your cursor to where you want your line to end.**

4. **Release the mouse button.**

By default, the stroke of your line is 1 pixel in width.

By popular demand, Macromedia has introduced dotted and dashed lines to Fireworks MX 2004. You can access the dotted and dashed line stroke options in the Stroke Category pop-up menu in the Property inspector, as shown in Figure 3-7.

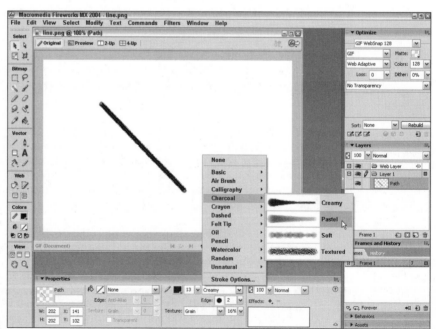

Figure 3-7: Select a stroke option from the Property inspector.

If you hold down the Shift key while you draw a line, you restrict the angle of the line to 45-degree increments.

Making simple shapes

Fireworks has easy-to-use tools for creating rectangles (including squares), ovals (including circles), and polygons. The tools for making all these shapes are grouped with the Rectangle tool in the vector section of the Tools panel. When you click the Rectangle tool and hold down the mouse button, a pop-up menu displays three basic tools at the top:

✦ **The Rectangle tool:** Use this tool to create squares and other rectangles.

✦ **The Ellipse tool:** Use this tool to create round shapes like circles and other ovals.

✦ **The Polygon tool:** Use this tool to create many-sided shapes (up to 360-sided). Use the Property inspector to set the number of sides before you draw on the canvas. The slider includes values from 3 through 25; for values greater than 25, you need to type a number in the field. By default, the Polygon tool creates pentagons. Add three points and you have an octagon, or delete two points to get a triangle.

See the section, "Making complex shapes," later in this chapter, for information on the tools below those three in the Rectangle tool pop-up menu.

To make a rectangle, follow these steps:

1. **Select the Rectangle tool from the Vector section of the Tools panel.**

2. **Place your cursor over the point on the canvas where you want the top-left corner of your rectangle.**

   Notice that the cursor has become a cross hair.

3. **Click and drag to the spot where you want the bottom-right corner of the rectangle, as shown in Figure 3-8.**

   To create a square, hold down the Shift key as you drag.

4. **Release the mouse button.**

   The shape appears on the canvas.

To make an oval, follow these steps:

1. **Select the Ellipse tool from the Vector section of the Tools panel by clicking on the Rectangle tool and holding the mouse button down until the pop-up menu with the Ellipse tool displays.**

Book III
Chapter 3

Working with Text, Shapes, and Images

2. **Place your cursor over the point on the canvas where you want the oval.**

   Your cursor becomes a cross hair.

3. **Click and drag to create the oval.**

   To create a circle, hold down the Shift key as you drag.

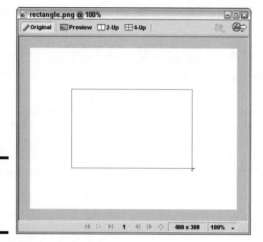

Figure 3-8:
Making a
rectangle
shape.

An oval doesn't have corners, so you may not be able to get precise placement when you make the shape. That's no big deal, though, because moving the shape is easy, as we describe later in this chapter in the "Editing, moving, and deleting shapes" section.

You can make an equilateral polygon (a shape in which all sides have equal lengths) by following these steps:

1. **Select the Polygon tool from the Vector section of the Tools panel by clicking on the Rectangle tool and holding the mouse button down until the pop-up menu with the Polygon tool displays.**

2. **At the right of the Property inspector, type the number of sides you want the polygon to have, or use the slider next to the Sides text field to set the number of sides.**

   By default, the polygon is five-sided. If you set the number of sides to 3 instead of 5, you draw a triangle. Set the number of sides to 6 and you draw a hexagon. You can make a shape with up to 360 sides — just don't expect us to know what a polygon with 360 sides is called!

3. **Place your cursor over the point on the canvas where you want the shape.**

   Your cursor becomes a cross hair.

4. **Click and drag to create the polygon.**

   The Property inspector changes to give you access to various properties of the polygon, including fill options, stroke options, and effects.

Making complex shapes

Fireworks MX 2004 introduces a new concept for creating shapes: AutoShapes. You can make these complex shapes simply by choosing them directly from the Rectangle tool's pop-up menu:

+ Arrow

+ Beveled Rectangle

+ Chamfer Rectangle

+ Connector Line

+ Doughnut

+ L-Shape

+ Pie

+ Rounded Rectangle

+ Smart Polygon

+ Spiral

+ Star

If you can't find the kind of shape you want to make in the Vector Shape tool pop-up menu, you can make a custom freeform shape. Believe it or not, making odd shapes is just as easy as making regular ones, and it may even be more fun!

The main tool you use to create complex shapes is the Pen tool, found in the Vectors section of the Tools panel. Like the Rectangle tool, the Pen tool comes with some variations, which you can access by clicking and holding the mouse button down on the Pen tool. The pop-up menu for the Pen tool displays the following variations:

+ **The Pen tool:** Use the Pen tool to place points on the page; Fireworks connects the dots for you.

+ **The Vector Path tool:** Use the Vector Path tool to draw as you would with a felt-tip marker. You can manipulate the path in ways unavailable if you'd used a bitmap tool (or a real felt-tip marker) — see "Editing, moving and deleting shapes," later in this chapter.

✦ **The Redraw Path tool:** Use the Redraw Path tool to change the length or shape of a path you have already created.

To make a freeform shape with straight lines, follow these steps:

1. **Select the Pen tool from the Vector section of the Tools panel.**

2. **Place the cursor over the canvas.**

Your cursor becomes a fountain pen.

3. **Click to make your starting point.**

4. **Move your cursor and click to create a second point.**

Fireworks connects the dots with a straight line.

5. **Move your cursor and click to create a third point, and, if you like, a fourth, fifth, tenth, or one hundred forty-second point.**

6. **If you want a closed shape, click again on your starting point to close the shape. Otherwise, double-click the end point to make an open shape.**

Making curved lines with the Pen tool can be a little difficult initially. If you know a few things about the Pen tool, using it to make curved lines will be a little easier. First of all, you can make two kinds of points with the Pen tool. Which kind you make determines whether the line connecting the dots is straight or curved:

✦ **Corner points:** These points anchor straight lines.

✦ **Curve points:** These points anchor curved lines.

If you simply click in various spots to make the shape, you automatically make corner points. To make a freeform shape with curved lines, as shown in Figure 3-9, do the following:

1. **Select the Pen tool from the Vector section of the Tools panel.**

2. **Place the cursor over the canvas.**

Your cursor becomes a fountain pen.

3. **Click to make your starting point.**

4. **Move your cursor and click a second point. Keeping the mouse button held down, move your cursor.**

Point handles (solid circles at both ends of a line that has the selected point in the middle) appear, which indicates that you have made a curve point. As you move the mouse, Fireworks previews the curve between the first and second point.

5. **Release the mouse button to make the curve.**

   Fireworks joins your first and second points.

6. **Move your cursor and click and drag to create as many curved lines as you wish.**

7. **If you want a closed shape, click again on your starting point to close the shape. Otherwise, double-click the end point to make an open shape.**

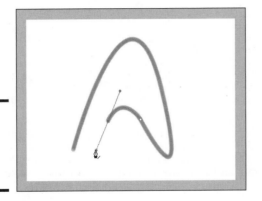

Figure 3-9:
Making a complex, curved shape.

Editing, moving, and deleting shapes

Altering a simple shape is nearly as easy as making a simple shape. If you make a shape using any of the tools grouped with the Rectangle, Ellipse, or Polygon tool, Fireworks thinks of the shape as a group of points. If you want to edit the shape, first you need to ungroup the points so you can move them.

To change the shape of a straight-sided simple shape (that is, a shape with nothing but corner points, like a rectangle), follow these steps:

1. **Select the Subselection tool (the white arrow) from the top of the Tools panel.**

2. **Click anywhere on the line defining the shape.**

   All the points, and the guide lines connecting them, highlight.

3. **Choose Modify⇨Ungroup or use the keyboard shortcut Ctrl+Shift+G to ungroup the points.**

The shape remains selected.

4. **Click and drag any point in the shape to the new location you want.**

You can also delete a point by clicking it and pressing the Backspace or Delete key.

If you want to edit a complex shape (like the one shown in Figure 3-9), you can use the Subselection tool to alter any of the curves:

1. **Select the Subselection tool (the white arrow) from the top of the Tools panel.**

2. **Click anywhere on the line defining the shape.**

All the points, and the guide lines connecting them, highlight.

3. **If the shape is grouped, choose Modify⇨Ungroup or press Ctrl+Shift+G to ungroup the points.**

4. **Click and drag a curve point to its new location, or click a curve point to make it active, and then click and drag one of the point handles to change the shape of the curve.**

Moving a shape is a piece of cake:

1. **Select the Pointer tool (the black arrow) from the top of the Tools panel.**

2. **Click anywhere on the line defining the shape and, keeping the mouse button held down, drag the shape to your desired location.**

You can also use the Subselection tool to move a shape, but you must be careful not to click a handle. If you click and drag a point handle, you move the point rather than the whole shape. If you change the shape by mistake, press Ctrl+Z to undo the change.

Deleting a shape is a very simple matter indeed. To delete a shape, do the following:

1. **Select the Pointer tool (the black arrow) or the Subselection tool (the white arrow) from the top of the Tools panel.**

2. **Click anywhere on the line defining the shape.**

3. **Press Delete key or Backspace.**

If you want to cut the shape and paste it somewhere else (in your current document, or in a different document), use the key command

Ctrl+X to remove the shape and Ctrl+V to paste it in your desired new location.

Splitting shapes

If you ever have occasion to split one shape into two shapes, you can call upon the services of the Knife tool. The Knife tool is only available when you have an ungrouped shape selected. When you don't have an ungrouped shape selected, the Knife tool is grayed out in the Tools panel.

To split a shape, follow these steps:

1. **Select the Pointer tool (the black arrow) or Subselection tool (the white arrow) from the top of the Tools panel.**

2. **Click anywhere on the line defining the shape you want to split.**

All the points, and the guide lines connecting them, highlight. Just as importantly, the Knife tool in the Vector section of the Tools panel becomes available. (If the Knife tool remains grayed out, press Ctrl+Shift+G to ungroup the shape and make the Knife tool available.)

3. **Select the Knife tool from the Vector section of the Tools panel.**

When you move your cursor over the canvas, it becomes a blade.

4. **Click and drag the cursor over the guide lines where you want the shape to split, as shown in Figure 3-10.**

New points show where the cut was made. You now have two shapes. If you want to move or edit either of the new shapes, select it with the Subselect tool.

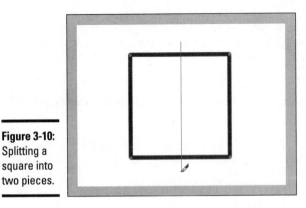

Figure 3-10:
Splitting a
square into
two pieces.

If you hold down the Shift key while dragging, you can constrain the split to 45-degree angles.

Adding a little color to your shapes

You can think of your shapes as having two parts: the path that defines the outside (which can have a stroke or not), and the inside (which can be empty or filled). The most basic stroke for a shape is a solid color; likewise the most basic inside for a filled shape is a solid color.

You can get pretty fancy with both strokes and fills (adding gradients, textures, and more, which we discuss in Book III, Chapter 4). However, we start with the basics: adding solid colors to strokes and fills.

Adding color to the stroke

The default color of strokes in Fireworks is black. So when you add color to the stroke, you're really changing the stroke's color from black to a color of your choosing.

To add or change the color of your stroke, just follow these steps:

1. **Select the Pointer tool (the black arrow) or Subselection tool (the white arrow) from the Tools panel.**

2. **Click anywhere in the stroke.**

   The stroke is highlighted to show that it is selected.

3. **Click the color box next to the Pencil icon in the Stroke part of the Property inspector.**

   The pointer assumes the shape of an eyedropper, and the Fireworks color picker appears. You can choose a color from the color picker, or place the eyedropper anywhere in the Fireworks window to select a color.

4. **Click to select the color the tip of the eyedropper is over.**

   The stroke changes color. For a refresher on the color picker, see the "Adding a little color" section, earlier in this chapter.

If your stroke is only 1-pixel wide, the highlight obscures the line and you can't see your change immediately. Don't worry, though. Just click anywhere on the canvas except the shape you just changed to deselect the shape so you can see it. (You can also deselect the shape by pressing Ctrl+D.)

To remove a stroke from a path, select the stroke and choose None from the Stroke Category pop-up menu in the Stroke part of the Property inspector.

Adding a fill color to the inside of the shape

Fills in Fireworks are empty by default. So when we say you add color to the fill, that's exactly what you're doing! Just as with adding color to a stroke, though, after you know how to add a color to the fill, you also know how to change the fill's color.

To add or change a fill color to your shape, just follow these steps:

1. **Select the Pointer tool (the black arrow) or Subselection tool (the white arrow) from the Tools panel.**

2. **Click anywhere in the shape.**

   The stroke highlights to show that the shape is selected.

3. **Click the square with the red line through it (next to the Paint Bucket icon) in the Fill part of the Property inspector.**

   The pointer assumes the shape of an eyedropper, and the Fireworks color picker pops up. You can choose a color from the color picker, or place the eyedropper anywhere in the Fireworks window to select a color.

4. **Select a color.**

   For a refresher on the color picker, see the "Adding a little color" section, earlier in this chapter.

 To remove an existing fill from your shape, follow the steps above, but at Step 4, click the Transparent button (the square with the red line through it at the top middle of the color picker).

Want to add a gradient or texture fill to your shape? See the section on adding gradients and textures to shape fills and bitmap selections in Book III, Chapter 4.

Working with Bitmap Images

Vector images are compact and versatile, but they don't accommodate the complexity of photographic images or illustrations. In a photographic image, any given pixel might be a completely different color than any of the pixels around it, so each pixel's color must be defined individually. That makes bitmaps big from a file-size perspective, but for photos on your Web site, bitmaps are the only way to go.

Fireworks offers an array of useful tools for making and manipulating bitmap images. You may use the bitmap tools to draw in Fireworks, but you're likely to be in bitmap mode mostly when you want to place and tweak imported images like photographs.

Exploring the bitmap drawing tools

The main bitmap drawing tools in Fireworks are the Brush and the Pencil tools. Those tools are somewhat interchangeable and using them is as intuitive as can be. On the other hand, each tool has an amazing amount of flexibility, so although you can start drawing with them quickly, it may take some time for you to become acquainted with their full capabilities.

Most of the flexibility of the tools is centered around the concept of *tips*. In the real world, the sharper a pencil, the thinner a line it draws. The thicker the end of a paint brush is, the thicker the line it makes, and the kind of bristles it has affects the texture of the line it makes. The same is true with the tools in Fireworks.

In Fireworks, however, each tip is associated with a tool (though all those tools are really just variations of the Pencil and Brush tools) to form a *stroke category,* as the following list describes:

✦ **Basic:** Hard Line, Hard Rounded, Soft Line, Soft Rounded

✦ **Air Brush:** Basic, Textured

✦ **Calligraphy:** Bamboo, Basic, Quill, Ribbon, Wet

✦ **Charcoal:** Creamy, Pastel, Soft, Textured

✦ **Crayon:** Basic, Rake, Thick

✦ **Dashed:** Basic Dash, Dash Double, Dash Triple, Dotted, Hard Dash, Heavy Dash

✦ **Felt Tip:** Dark Marker, Highlighter, Light Marker, Thin

✦ **Oil:** Bristle, Broad Splatter, Splatter, Strands, Textured Bristle

✦ **Pencil:** 1-Pixel Hard, 1-Pixel Soft, Colored Pencil, Graphite

✦ **Watercolor:** Heavy, Thick, Thin

✦ **Random:** Confetti, Dots, Fur, Squares, Yarn

✦ **Unnatural:** 3D, 3D Glow, Chameleon, Fluid Splatter, Outline, Paint Splatter, Toothpaste, Toxic Waste, Viscous Alien Paint

The tips run the gamut from basic to out-of-this-world. Figure 3-11 shows strokes made with three of the more complex tips. After you're familiar with the default stroke settings, you may want to customize the tips. The Edit Stroke dialog box offers you an amazing amount of control over stroke parameters like ink amount, flow rate, shape, and sensitivity. To open the Edit Stroke dialog box, select Stroke Options from the Stroke Category pop-up menu of the Property inspector, and click Advanced. See your documentation for further details.

 TIP

If you have a pressure-sensitive graphics tablet, you can set your drawing speed and pressure to modify how the stroke is placed on the canvas. Just enter your desired settings in the Sensitivity tab of the Edit Stroke dialog box.

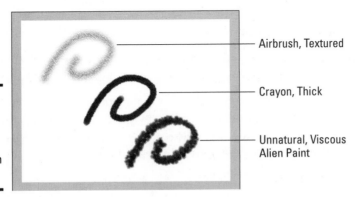

Figure 3-11: Lines made with some of the more exotic brush stroke tips.

Airbrush, Textured

Crayon, Thick

Unnatural, Viscous Alien Paint

To draw a line or shape using the Brush or Pencil tool, follow these steps:

1. **Select the Brush or Pencil tool from the Bitmap area of the Tools panel.**

   When you place your pointer over the canvas, the pointer takes the shape of a cross hair. The default tip for the Brush tool is also the default tip for the Pencil tool: 1-Pixel Hard.

2. **Select a color from the color picker in the tool's Property inspector.**

   For a refresher on the color picker, see the "Adding a little color" section, earlier in this chapter.

3. **Select a tip from the Stroke Category pop-up menu.**

   Each specialized tip has its own default edge size and texture.

4. **Click and drag on the canvas to make your line or shape.**

   The wider the brush, of course, the more pronounced the effect of a fancy tip. See Book III, Chapter 4 for more information on customizing the brush edge and texture.

Inserting a bitmap image

Inserting an existing bitmap image into a Fireworks document is something you're likely to do often if you're designing a Web page, whether the bitmaps are pictures of your products or pictures of your family.

To insert a bitmap image into your document, you can drag and drop the image onto the canvas from your desktop or a folder, or you can import the image. To import a bitmap image, follow these steps:

1. **Choose File⇨Import or press Ctrl+R.**

The Import dialog box appears.

2. **Navigate to the folder containing the image you want to insert.**

3. **Double-click the filename, or click the filename and click OK.**

The Import dialog box closes, revealing the canvas. The cursor changes into the Insertion Pointer — a right angle.

4. **Align the Insertion Pointer with the top-left point on your canvas where you want the inserted image to go.**

5. **Click to place the image.**

Selecting areas in a bitmap image

Fireworks allows you to select areas within an image in several different ways. The Marquee tool, Lasso tool, and Magic Wand tool will all be familiar to users of Photoshop. If you're new to these tools, read on for a brief rundown.

Using the Marquee tool

The Marquee tool has two guises, available by clicking and holding the Marquee tool until the pop-up menu appears:

✦ **The Marquee tool:** Use this tool to make rectangular selections.

✦ **The Oval Marquee tool:** Use this tool to make oval-shaped selections.

To select a rectangular or oval part of your bitmap, simply follow these steps:

1. **Select the Marquee tool or the Oval Marquee tool from the Bitmap part of the Tools panel.**

When you move your pointer over the canvas, it becomes a cross.

2. **Place the center of the pointer over one corner of the area you want to select.**

3. **Click and drag diagonally over the area you want to select.**

   The selected area is delimited by a flashing marquee — the marquee is rectangular if you selected the Marquee tool and oval if you selected the Oval Marquee tool.

Using the Lasso tool

The Lasso tool, like the Marquee tool, has two guises, available by clicking and holding the Lasso tool until the pop-up menu appears:

✦ **The Lasso tool:** Use this tool to make a freeform selection area by "drawing" the area.

✦ **The Polygon Lasso tool:** Use this tool to select a polygonal area by clicking points on the perimeter of the area.

To select an irregular area of your bitmap, follow these steps:

1. **Select the Lasso tool from the Bitmap part of the Tools panel.**

   When you place your pointer over the canvas, it becomes a lasso.

2. **Place the bottom tip of the pointer over the spot on the canvas where you want your selection to start.**

3. **Click and drag to create an outline of the area you want to select, as shown in Figure 3-12.**

   You must close the outline to make the selection. When your pointer is over the spot where you started your selection, a little filled square appears at the bottom right of the pointer. Click to close the selection shape.

Book III
Chapter 3

Working with Text, Shapes, and Images

Figure 3-12:
The Lasso tool allows you to select an irregularly shaped area.

To select a polygonal area of your bitmap, follow these steps:

1. **Select the Polygon Lasso tool from the Bitmap part of the Tools panel.**

   When you place your pointer over the canvas, it becomes a lasso.

2. **Place the bottom tip of the pointer over the spot on the canvas where you want your selection to start.**

3. **Click to establish the first point of the area you want to select.**

4. **Move your cursor to the second point of the area you want to select and click.**

   Fireworks connects the points with a straight line.

5. **Place your cursor and click on all points making up the polygonal selection.**

   You must close the outline to make the selection. Double-click to close the selection from the last-placed point to the first-placed point. Or, when your pointer is over the first-placed point (a little filled square appears at the bottom right of the pointer), click to close the selection shape.

Using the Magic Wand

The third bitmap selection tool is known as the Magic Wand tool. The Magic Wand tool selects an area of solid color or of similar colors. (You can set the wand's sensitivity level so it selects areas of more similar or less similar colors.)

To select a contiguous area of similar color in your bitmap, follow these steps:

1. **Select the Magic Wand tool from the Bitmap section of the Tools panel.**

   When you place your pointer over the canvas, it takes the form of a magician's wand.

2. **Place the pointer over the part of the image you want to select, and click.**

   A blinking marquee marks off the selected area. If too much area is selected, you need to make the wand more sensitive. Set the Tolerance level in the Property inspector to a lower number. If not enough area is selected, set the Tolerance level to a higher number (up to 255, at which setting you will probably select your entire bitmap).

Editing bitmaps: The basics

Fireworks allows you to manipulate bitmaps in all kinds of crazy and interesting ways, but naturally, it also allows you to do common everyday image-altering as well.

Perhaps the most basic bitmap editing tasks you can do are cropping, resizing, rotating, and distorting an image, which we cover in Book III, Chapter 4, along with basic filtering operations, like Blurring, Sharpening, and making color adjustments.

No introductory chapter on bitmap editing would be complete, though, without a quick look at the Eraser tool. As you may expect, the Eraser tool is the anti-brush. While the Brush tool adds a line or shape or pattern to a bitmap, the Eraser tool removes a line of pixels from a bitmap.

To erase pixels from your bitmap, follow these steps:

1. **Select the Eraser tool from the Bitmap part of the Tools panel.**

    The Eraser tool defaults to a circle, though you can set it to be square-shaped in the Property inspector.

2. **In the Property inspector, type a size, or use the handy slider to set the width of the Eraser.**

    The range goes from 1 to 100.

3. **Select the circle shape or square shape by clicking on one or the other.**

4. **Set the Edge by typing a number or using the slider.**

    The range goes from 0 to 100. Setting to zero gives a hard edge to your Eraser (a pixel is removed or not), while setting to 100 gives a fuzzy edge to the erased area.

5. **Set the Opacity of the Eraser by typing a number or using the slider.**

    The range goes from 1 to 100 percent. If you set the Opacity to 100 percent, the Eraser clears all the erased pixels entirely (except at the edges, if you have an edge of greater than 0 set). If you set the opacity to less than 100 percent, the Eraser creates a translucent effect, allowing whatever is under the bitmap to show through. The lower the opacity setting, the more the image underneath shows through.

6. **Click and drag on your image with the Eraser tool to rub out those unwanted pixels.**

    The pixels disappear as you drag the cursor over them.

Chapter 4: Transforming Text, Shapes, and Images

In This Chapter

✔ Scaling your images

✔ Distorting and skewing text and graphics

✔ Rotating and flipping graphics and text

✔ Adding gradients and textures

✔ Using filters

In the course of laying out the pages of your Web site, you may want to change the size or color of an image so that it fits more naturally into your design. In this chapter, we show you how to manipulate images, or parts of images, to create effects from subtle to extreme.

Scaling Graphics

When we talk about scaling graphics, we're talking about changing the size of a bitmap or vector shape on the canvas, not changing the size of your overall image (that is, everything on the whole of your canvas). To find out how to change the canvas size, see Book III, Chapter 2. You can change the size of an image element or selected part of an image element in two ways:

♦ **Use the Scale Transformation tool:** Click and drag the image object or selection. Employ this option if you want to figure out the proper size of the image by eyeballing it.

♦ **Change the numbers in the Property inspector:** Type numbers in the width and height boxes. Use this option if you have exact dimensions in mind for your image.

Both methods are fairly simple, and their results are identical (that is, whether you drag an object to a specific width or type that width into the Property inspector, the resized object will look the same).

Using the Scale Transformation tool

You can change the size of an object, either retaining its proportions or distorting it, by using the Scale tool. To change the size of an object by using
the click-and-drag method, follow these instructions:

1. **Click the Pointer tool or Subselection tool from the Select section of
   the Tools panel, and then click the object you want to resize.**

   For more information on selecting image objects or parts of image
   objects, see Book III, Chapter 3.

2. **Select the Scale tool — it looks a bit like a baseball diamond —
   from the Select section of the Tools panel or choose Modify⇨
   Transform⇨Scale.**

   A box with eight handles and a center point overlays the selected
   object.

3. **Click and drag one of the handles to scale the object as follows:**

   - **To scale the object while retaining its proportions:** Click one of
     the corner handles (make sure the cursor looks like a double-sided
     arrow) and drag the object to the desired size.

   - **To scale the object and distort its proportions:** Click and drag the
     middle handle on either the left or right side of the box around the
     object (make sure the cursor looks like a double-sided arrow) to
     change the object's width; or click and drag the center handle on
     either the top or bottom of the box around the object (make sure
     the cursor looks like a double-sided arrow) to change the object's
     height.

   By default, Fireworks continues to display the original box around
   the object, but it adds a version of the box with a dotted line to
   show the new dimensions as you drag, as shown in Figure 4-1.

   When the cursor looks like a three-quarter circle with an arrow, you
   can rotate the image instead of resizing it. See the "Rotating graphics" section, later in this chapter, for details on rotating images.

4. **Release the mouse button.**

   Fireworks redraws the image to your selected size.

5. **Click and drag to reposition the image, if necessary.**

   The cursor changes into a four-pointed arrow when you place it over
   the redrawn image, which indicates that you can move the image. (See
   Figure 4-2.) You can remove the transform handles by double-clicking
   the image, which will also change the tool to the Pointer tool.

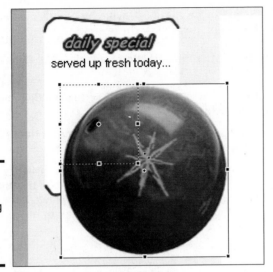

Figure 4-1:
Resizing an image using the click-and-drag method.

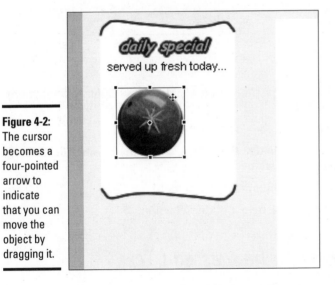

Figure 4-2:
The cursor becomes a four-pointed arrow to indicate that you can move the object by dragging it.

Resizing by entering numerical values

Sometimes you have a space with a defined width and height into which you want to place images of that exact width and height. If the images are not already sized to fit that space and you have calculated the exact proportions or you aren't worried about distorting the images, use the following method to resize the images.

To change the width and/or height of an image by typing in a new value for the width and/or the height, just follow these steps:

1. **Using the Pointer tool or Subselection tool, click the object you want to resize.**

   See Book III, Chapter 3 for more information on selecting image objects or parts of image objects.

2. **In the Property inspector, double-click or highlight the number in the Width field, as shown in Figure 4-3, and type in a new number.**

   If you cannot see the Width and Height fields, your Property inspector may be collapsed. To expand the panel, click once on the downward-pointing arrow at the bottom-right corner of the panel. If the Property inspector is not visible on-screen, press Ctrl+F3 to open it.

Figure 4-3:
Adjusting
the width of
a selected
object.

3. **If you are not going to change the height, press Enter to implement the width change.**

   Fireworks redraws the selection at the new width.

4. **If you are going to change the height, select the number in the Height field and type a new value.**

5. **Press Enter or click in another value field.**

   Fireworks updates the height of the selection.

Distorting and Skewing Images and Text

Changing the width but not the height of an image object, or changing the object's height but not the width, distorts the object along one axis. What if you want to stretch one corner of an object but leave the rest of the object more or less intact, or perform some other unusual stretching or shrinking? The Distort and Skew tools are at your disposal — they're just hiding behind the Scale tool. To access the Distort and Skew tools, click and hold the Scale tool in the Select section of the Tools panel and select one of the tools from the menu that pops up, or select the Scale tool and press Q on your keyboard until the tool you want appears.

What's the difference between skewing and distorting? Skewing is actually a particular kind of distortion:

✦ **Distorting:** Stretching or shrinking one or more sides of an image object.

✦ **Skewing:** Distorting an image object by stretching or shrinking two of its four sides while leaving the other two the same, or stretching or shrinking three of the four sides of the object's bounding box at once but not changing the dimensions of the fourth side. Skewing can create the illusion of perspective.

The Distort tool is far more versatile than the Skew tool:

✦ You can use the Distort tool to resize along one axis, in which case you are scaling the object.

✦ You can use the Distort tool to stretch or shrink three sides of an object at once, in which case you are skewing the object.

✦ You can use the Distort tool to create more complex forms of image manipulation by both scaling and skewing the object, for example.

Distorting an image

To distort an object by using the Distort tool, follow these steps:

1. **Click the Pointer tool or Subselection tool in the Tools panel, and then click the object you want to distort.**

2. **Select the Distort tool from the Tools panel or choose Modify⇨ Transform⇨Distort.**

   If you are selecting from the Tools panel, click and hold on the Scale tool in the Select section of the Tools panel and select the Distort tool from the pop-up menu. A box with eight handles and a center point overlays the selected object.

3. **Click and drag any handle.**

   By default, Fireworks continues to display the original box around the object, but it adds a version of the box with a dotted line to show the new dimensions as you drag, as shown in Figure 4-4. The cursor becomes a double-sided arrow as you place it over a center or middle handle.

   Note that when you try to drag handles too far (that is, if you try to drag a middle left handle above the top left handle, for example), the dotted line will stretch to wherever you drag the handle, but when you release the mouse button, the image snaps to the farthest allowable point in the direction you dragged. In short, a handle may not cross other handles.

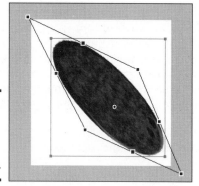

Figure 4-4:
Distorting
an image
to create a
weird effect.

4. **Click and drag any other handles.**

   You can stretch and squash the image by dragging as many handles as many times as you want.

5. **Press Enter or double-click anywhere on the canvas.**

   Fireworks updates the selection.

Skewing an image

To skew an image, follow these simple steps:

1. **With the Pointer tool or Subselection tool, click the object you want to skew.**

2. **Select the Skew tool from the Tools panel or choose Modify⇨ Transform⇨Skew.**

   If you are selecting from the Tools panel, click and hold on the Scale tool in the Select section of the Tools panel and select the Skew tool when the pop-up menu displays the Skew and Distort tools. A box with eight handles and a center point overlays the selected object.

3. **Click and drag any handle:**

   • The center handles on the top and bottom can skew a side of the image left or right.

   • The middle handles on the left and right can skew a side of the image up or down.

- The corner handles behave differently, depending on if you drag them along the left-right axis or along the up-down axis, but no matter which axis you drag along, they *spread* the selected side of the image along that axis. For example, if you select the top-left corner and drag up, the bottom-left corner stretches down proportionally.

By default, Fireworks continues to display the original box around the object, but it adds a version of the box with a dotted line to show the new dimensions as you drag, as shown in Figure 4-4. The cursor becomes a double-sided arrow as you place it over a center or middle handle. The arrow indicates in which directions you can drag the handle.

4. **Press Enter or double-click anywhere on the canvas.**

   Fireworks updates the selection, the transformation handles disappear, and the tool reverts to the Pointer tool.

Distorting and skewing text

In Fireworks, distorting text is as easy as distorting images. To distort the text in a text box, while leaving the text editable, just follow these steps:

1. **Click the Pointer tool or Subselection tool in the Tools panel, and then click the text box you want to distort.**

   You can also select the text box using the Text tool, but you cannot distort only part of the text in a text box. You can, however, Shift+click two text boxes and distort them together.

2. **Select the Distort tool from the Tools panel or choose Modify⇨ Transform⇨Distort.**

   If you are selecting from the Tools panel, click and hold on the Scale tool in the Tools panel and select the Distort tool from the pop-up menu. A box with eight handles and a center point overlays the selected text box.

3. **Click and drag any handle.**

   By default, Fireworks continues to display the original box around the object, but it adds a version of the box with a dotted line to show the new dimensions as you drag. The cursor becomes a double-sided arrow as you place it over a center or middle handle.

   Note that when you try to drag handles too far (that is, if you try to drag a middle right handle above the top right handle, for example), the dotted line will stretch to wherever you drag the handle, but when you release the mouse button, the image snaps to the farthest allowable point in the direction you dragged. In short, a handle may not cross other handles.

4. **Click and drag any other handles.**

   You can stretch and squash and drag as many handles as many times as you want.

5. **Press Enter or double-click anywhere on the canvas.**

   Fireworks updates the selection, as shown in Figure 4-5.

Figure 4-5:
Distorting
a text box
can give the
illusion of
perspective
to text.

To skew a text box, follow these simple steps:

1. **Using the Pointer tool or Subselection tool in the Tools panel, click the text box.**

   You can also select the text box using the Text tool, but you cannot distort only a part of the text in a text box.

2. **Select the Skew tool from the Tools panel or choose Modify⇨ Transform⇨Skew.**

   If you are selecting from the Tools panel, click and hold on the Scale tool in the Tools panel and select the Skew tool when the pop-up menu displays the Skew and Distort tools. A box with eight handles and a center point overlays the selected text box.

3. **Click and drag any handle.**

   By default, Fireworks continues to display the original box around the object, but it adds a version of the box with a dotted line to show the new dimensions as you drag. The cursor becomes a double-sided arrow as you place it over a center or middle handle. The arrow indicates in which directions you can drag the handle.

The center handles on the top and bottom can skew a side of the image left or right. The middle handles on the left and right can skew a side of the image up or down.

The corner handles behave differently, depending on if you drag them along the left-right axis or along the up-down axis, but no matter which axis you drag along, they *spread* the selected side of the image along that axis. For example, if you select the top-left corner and drag up, the bottom-left corner will stretch down proportionally.

4. **Press Enter or double-click anywhere on the canvas.**

   Fireworks updates the selection, the transformation handles disappear, and the tool reverts to the Pointer tool.

Rotating and Flipping Graphics and Text

As is the case with resizing, Fireworks allows you to rotate and flip everything on the canvas at once, but it also allows you to select individual graphic elements (image objects) and rotate or flip them independently.

Rotating graphics

You can rotate a graphic in two ways:

✦ **Rotate a preset amount:** Fireworks offers a quick way to rotate a graphic either 90 or 180 degrees around its center point.

✦ **Rotate any amount:** You can click and drag to rotate an image around its center point, or even move the point and rotate the image around a point not at the image's center.

To rotate a graphic by 90-degree increments, follow these steps:

1. **Select the object by using the Pointer tool or Subselection tool.**

   For more information on selecting image objects or parts of image objects, see Book III, Chapter 3.

2. **Choose how you want to rotate the object:**

   • **To rotate the object 180 degrees (turning it upside down):** Choose Modify➪Transform➪Rotate 180 Degrees.

   • **To rotate a graphic 90 degrees clockwise (to turn it sideways to the right):** Choose Modify➪Transform➪Rotate 90 Degrees CW, or use the key command Ctrl+Shift+9.

- **To rotate a graphic 90 degrees counter-clockwise (to turn it sideways to the left):** Choose Modify⇨Transform⇨Rotate 90 Degrees CCW, or use the key command Ctrl+Shift+7.

Rotating an object freehand requires a couple of extra steps, but it gives you much finer control over the degree of rotation. To rotate an object any amount about its center axis, just follow these steps:

1. **Select the object by using the Pointer tool or Subselection tool.**

2. **Choose Modify⇨Transform⇨Free Transform (or Scale, Skew, or Distort).**

   You can also use the keyboard shortcut Ctrl+T to access the Free Transform command.

3. **Place your cursor over the canvas.**

   The cursor changes into a rounded arrow, as shown in Figure 4-6.

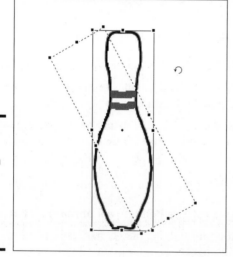

Figure 4-6:
Rotating a bowling pin image object so that it appears to be falling.

4. **Click and drag the cursor in any direction.**

   If you drag down or to the right, the image rotates clockwise; if you drag up or to the left, the image rotates counter-clockwise.

   If you hold down the Shift key while rotating your graphic, you restrict the angle of the rotation to 15-degree increments.

5. **Press Enter or double-click anywhere on the canvas.**

   Fireworks updates the selection, the transformation handles disappear, and the tool reverts to the Pointer tool.

Rotating text

In Fireworks, rotating text is pretty much like rotating a graphic. To rotate a text box in 90-degree increments, follow these steps:

1. **Click the Pointer tool or Subselection tool in the Tools panel, and then click the text box.**

You can also select the text box using the Text tool, but you cannot distort only a part of a text box.

2. **Choose how you want to rotate the text as follows:**

- **To rotate the text box by 180 degrees (turning it upside down):** Choose Modify➪Transform➪Rotate 180 Degrees.

- **To rotate a text box 90 degrees clockwise (to turn it sideways to the right):** Choose Modify➪Transform➪Rotate 90 Degrees CW, or use the key command Ctrl+Shift+9.

- **To rotate a text box 90 degrees counter-clockwise (to turn it sideways to the left):** Choose Modify➪Transform➪Rotate 90 Degrees CCW, or use the key command Ctrl+Shift+7.

To rotate text freehand, follow these simple steps:

1. **Use the Pointer tool or Subselection tool to select the text box you want to rotate.**

You can only distort the entire text box.

2. **Choose Modify➪Transform➪Free Transform (or Scale, Skew, or Distort).**

You can also use the keyboard shortcut Ctrl+T to access the Free Transform command.

3. **Place your cursor over the canvas.**

The cursor changes into a rounded arrow.

4. **Click and drag the cursor in any direction.**

If you drag down or to the right, the text box rotates clockwise; if you drag up or to the left, the image rotates counter-clockwise.

5. **Press Enter or double-click anywhere on the canvas.**

Fireworks updates the selection, the transformation handles disappear, and the tool reverts to the Pointer tool.

Flipping images

Fireworks allows you to flip images vertically and horizontally. Both manipulations are a snap.

To flip an image horizontally (making it a mirror image of what it was originally) or vertically (turning it upside down), follow these steps:

1. **Select the object you want to flip.**

2. **Choose Modify⇨Transform⇨Flip Horizontal to make a mirror image of the object; choose Modify⇨Transform⇨Flip Vertical to turn the object upside down.**

   Depending on which choice you make, your selection either flips horizontally, as shown in Figure 4-7, or vertically, as shown in Figure 4-8.

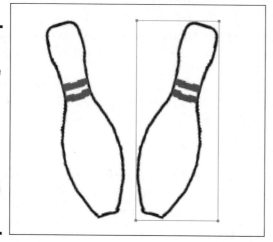

Figure 4-7:
The left image of the bowling pin has been duplicated, moved, and flipped horizontally to make the image of the bowling pin on the right.

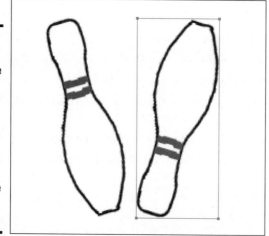

Figure 4-8:
The left image of the bowling pin has been duplicated, moved, and flipped vertically to make the image of the bowling pin on the right.

Flipping text

Fireworks allows you to flip text boxes vertically and horizontally. Both manipulations are a piece of cake.

Follow these steps to flip a text box horizontally (making it a mirror image of what it was originally) or vertically (turning it upside down):

1. **Select the text box you want to flip with the Pointer tool or Subselection tool.**

   You can also select the text box using the Text tool, but you cannot distort only a part of a text box.

2. **Choose Modify⇨Transform⇨Flip Horizontal to make a mirror image of the text box; choose Modify⇨Transform⇨Flip Vertical to turn the text upside down.**

   Your selection flips horizontally or vertically.

Adding Gradients and Textures to Shape Fills and Bitmap Selections

In Book III, Chapter 3, we show you how to fill a vector shape with a color. In this section, you find out how to treat your shape to a fancier filling: a gradient and/or a texture. Gradients and textures can add the illusion of depth to your images. They also increase the file size of your images because they are difficult to compress, so use them sparingly.

Introducing gradients

A *gradient* is a subtle blend of one color into another. A classic example of a gradient in nature is a sky at sunset (or sunrise, if you ever wake up that early). Near the horizon, the sky is a deep, bright orange; straight up, the sky is a dark blue. In between those two colors is a bunch of transitions: from bright orange to pale orange to pale blue to dark blue. The transitions are so subtle, it's difficult to say where one color leaves off and another begins. That's a gradient.

Fireworks ships with a wonderful array of useful gradient patterns, which you can access via a pop-up menu in the Property inspector:

- ✦ Linear
- ✦ Radial
- ✦ Rectangle
- ✦ Starburst
- ✦ Folds
- ✦ Ellipse

**Book III
Chapter 4**

**Transforming Text,
Shapes, and Images**

- ✦ Cone
- ✦ Contour
- ✦ Satin

- ✦ Bars
- ✦ Ripples
- ✦ Waves

While the black-and-white of this printed page may not quite do these gradients justice compared to what they look like in full color, you can still get a pretty good idea of the variety of the gradients, as shown in Figure 4-9.

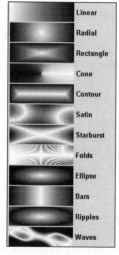

Figure 4-9: Fireworks ships with these gradient patterns.

You can choose any colors to make your gradients, but Fireworks also has the following handy preset gradient options:

- ✦ Black, White
- ✦ Blue, Red, Yellow
- ✦ Blue, Yellow, Blue
- ✦ Cobalt Blue
- ✦ Copper
- ✦ Emerald Green
- ✦ Pastels

- ✦ Red, Blue
- ✦ Red, Green, Blue
- ✦ Silver
- ✦ Spectrum
- ✦ Violet, Orange
- ✦ White, Black

To add a preset gradient fill to a vector shape, follow these steps:

1. **Select the Pointer tool or Subselection tool and click the shape.**

2. **Click and hold the Fill Categories box next to the Paint Bucket icon in the Property inspector.**

3. **Choose Gradient, and select a gradient type from the menu, as shown in Figure 4-10.**

   The default colors for gradients are black and white. If those are the colors you want for your gradient, congratulations! You're done! If not, continue with the next step.

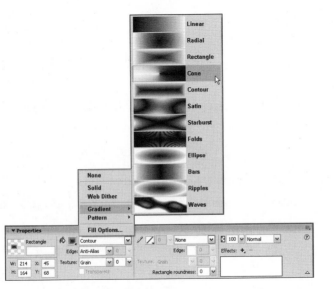

Figure 4-10: Selecting a gradient type.

Book III
Chapter 4

Transforming Text, Shapes, and Images

4. **Click the Fill Color box next to the Paint Bucket icon in the Property inspector.**

   A pop-up window, as shown in Figure 4-11, appears:

   • At the bottom is a preview pane, which shows what the gradient pattern will look like when applied to the shape. (The selected pattern in Figure 4-11 is Cone.)

   • In the middle of the window lies the Preset drop-down list, from which you can choose preset colors for your gradient.

   • At the top of the window is a simpler preview strip that shows color but not pattern information. Above and below that strip are sliders. The sliders above give you control over the opacity of each color in the gradient; the sliders below give you control over the amount of each color in the gradient.

Figure 4-11:
The gradient pop-up window has controls for color and opacity, a list of gradient presets, and a Preview pane.

5. **Select preset colors for your gradient from the Preset drop-down list.**

   The preview panes and the selected shape update.

   Notice that different presets have different numbers, or instances, of colors. The Cobalt Blue preset, for example, creates its opalescent glow with two instances each of three colors.

6. **Click anywhere outside the pop-up window to make it disappear.**

To add a user-defined gradient fill to a vector shape requires a number of steps, but it can be as simple or complex a process as you wish. Just follow these steps:

1. **Select the Pointer tool or Subselection tool and click the shape.**

2. **Click and hold the Fill Categories box next to the Paint Bucket icon in the Property inspector.**

3. **Select a gradient type from the pop-up menu (refer to Figure 4-10).**

   The default colors for gradients are black and white.

4. **Click the Fill Color box next to the Paint Bucket icon in the Property inspector.**

   A pop-up window appears (refer to Figure 4-11).

5. **Click the left color slider, as shown in Figure 4-12.**

   When you place the cursor over a slider, it becomes a solid black arrow with no stem. When you click and release the slider, the familiar color picker pops up. If you need a refresher on the color picker, see Book III, Chapter 3.

Figure 4-12:
Left: Picking the first color for the gradient.
Right: Adding a color.

6. **Select a color from the color picker.**

   Your cursor is an eyedropper in the color picker.

7. **If you want more than two colors in your gradient, click anywhere between the two default color sliders. If not, skip to Step 12.**

   Note that your cursor becomes an arrow with a small plus sign (+) when you move it between the existing color sliders. After you click, a new slider appears, and your cursor becomes a solid black arrow with no stem until you move it off the new slider.

   By default, the color of the new slider is the color in the strip directly above where you clicked.

8. **If you want to change the color of the new slider, click it and release.**

   When you click and release, the familiar color picker pops up.

9. **Select a color using the eyedropper.**

10. **If desired, move the new color slider left or right to change where the new color blends with the other colors.**

11. **If you want more than three colors in your gradient, repeat Steps 7 through 10.**

12. **Click the right color slider.**

13. **Select a color using the eyedropper.**

14. **If you want to, move any of the sliders horizontally to adjust where their respective colors fall in the gradient.**

15. **If desired, adjust the opacity of the entire gradient or vary the opacity of different parts of the gradient.**

    By default, the opacity of both ends is set to 100 percent (no background shows through). You can add and adjust opacity sliders just as you can color sliders, and they work in more or less the same way.

When you click an opacity slider, a pop-up window displays a slider that goes from 0 percent at the left (no gradient shows in front of the background) to 100 percent at the right.

16. **Click anywhere outside the pop-up window to make it disappear.**

After you've added a gradient fill to your shape, you can rotate, skew, move, and change the width of the gradient. See your documentation for details.

To remove a color slider or opacity slider (you must have at least two colors to make a gradient, of course), click and drag it up out of the gradient pop-up window. When you release the mouse button, the slider will be gone, and you'll have a less complex gradient fill.

Follow these steps to add a gradient fill to a bitmap selection:

1. **Select the part of the bitmap image you want to fill with a Tool from the Bitmap section of the Tools panel.**

In most cases, the Magic Wand tool is the best candidate for this job. For more information on selecting parts of image objects, see Book III, Chapter 3.

2. **Click the Color box next to the Paint Bucket icon in the Colors section of the Tools panel.**

The color picker appears.

3. **Click the Fill Options button at the bottom of the color picker.**

A new pop-up window appears in place of the color picker.

4. **Select a gradient pattern from the drop-down list.**

5. **Follow Steps 4 through 6 in the steps that describe adding a preset gradient fill to a vector shape or Steps 4 through 6 in the steps that describe adding a user-defined gradient fill to a vector shape.**

6. **Click the Paint Bucket tool, and then click anywhere in the selected area to apply the gradient fill.**

Adding textures

Adding textures to your fills and bitmap selections is even easier than adding gradients. You can even have fills with both a gradient and a texture, though we find that combining gradients and textures often diminishes the graphic power of both in a given image.

To add a texture to a vector shape, follow these steps:

1. **Select the Pointer tool or Subselection tool and click the shape.**

If the shape is transparent, you'll need to add a color or gradient fill. If the shape has a transparent fill (no fill), the Texture list box will be inactive.

2. **Click and hold the arrow in the Texture drop-down list — you'll find it under the Edge drop-down list in the Property inspector.**

3. **Select a texture from the drop-down list.**

   The drop-down list displays the built-in textures — if you have additional textures, select Other from the list and browse to the texture you want to use.

   When you release the mouse button, the texture is applied to the shape fill with the default opacity of 50%.

4. **Type a value or drag the slider in the Amount of Texture field (next to the Texture drop-down list) to set the opacity of the texture.**

   A setting of 0 does not show any of the texture, and a setting of 100 shows the texture at full (100 percent) opacity.

Adjusting Color Information and More with Filters

Fireworks has plenty of useful presets and defaults for the novice user, and enough tweakability to satisfy most any professional. Pros will especially appreciate the amount of control Fireworks gives users in the area of color adjustment.

You can accomplish many of the effects described in this section in two basic ways:

✦ **Using Live Effects:** This is a bit like making everything you look at appear yellow by putting on a pair of sunglasses. You're not changing the colors of whatever you're looking at, you're putting something between you and the object to change the appearance of the object. Live effects can be turned off and on without changing the pixels that make up the object to which the effects are applied. If the object in your Web page design is something that may change later or be repurposed elsewhere, perhaps with different effects applied, you can use Live Effects to apply *non-destructive* changes to the object in a particular PNG file. Live Effects can be applied only to whole objects.

✦ **Using Filters:** This method is considered *destructive,* because it alters the pixels in the bitmap. This is like making everything you see yellow by painting everything yellow. Though the process is destructive, it is not permanent — as long as you have the Undo command available.

We show you how to use the Filters method in the following three sections. For more about Live Effects, see Book III, Chapter 7.

Fine-tuning your colors

We touch briefly on the color adjustment tools at the end of Book III, Chapter 3, but here we go into a bit more detail. The color adjustment controls available from the Filters menu are as follows:

+ **Auto Levels:** In theory, an optimal image has an even distribution of dark tones, medium tones, and light tones. Auto Levels sets levels automatically so that shadows, midtones, and highlights are evenly distributed in your image.

+ **Brightness/Contrast:** Controls the overall luminosity of a selection and the contrast of color shades within a selection.

+ **Curves:** Offers a way to modify very specific colors without affecting others.

+ **Hue/Saturation:** Controls the tones and intensities of colors within a selection.

+ **Invert:** Allows you to reverse the colors in a selection to make something analogous to a photographic negative.

+ **Levels:** Like curves, levels allows you to modify colors, but it does so by letting you adjust shadows, midtones, and highlights of one of the three individual color channels (red, green, or blue) or all channels together.

To change the brightness or contrast of a graphic or selection, just follow these steps:

1. **Select a graphic or part of a graphic.**

   For more information on selecting image objects or parts of image objects, see Book III, Chapter 3.

2. **Choose Filters➪Adjust Color➪Brightness/Contrast.**

   A dialog box with separate sliders for brightness and contrast appears.

3. **If you wish to lighten or darken your selection, click and drag the Brightness slider.**

   The default position is at the center. You can drag left down to –100 units to darken the selection, or you can drag right up to 100 units to lighten the selection. If the Preview check box is selected, as it is by default, you can see the change to your selection when you release the mouse button.

4. **If you want to alter the relationship between the dark and light pixels in your selection, click and drag the Contrast slider.**

   The default position is at the center. You can drag left down to –100 units to reduce the contrast in the selection, or you can drag right up to 100 units to increase the contrast in the selection. If the Preview check box is selected, as it is by default, you can see the change to your selection when you release the mouse button.

5. **Click OK.**

All colors on a computer monitor are formed from the combination of the three color channels, red, green, and blue. You can change the curves for the individual color channels or for the combination of all channels. Curve adjustments can be made for bitmaps only, not shapes. If you want to adjust the color of a vector shape using curve values, convert it to a bitmap first (select the object and choose Flatten Selection from the Options menu in the Layers panel). To change the curve of the RGB channels, follow these steps:

1. **Select a graphic or part of a graphic.**

   For more information on selecting image objects or parts of image objects, see Book III, Chapter 3.

2. **Choose Filters➪Adjust Color➪Curves.**

   A dialog box with a grid appears, as shown in Figure 4-13. The grid's horizontal axis shows the original brightness of the pixels in your selection. The grid's vertical axis shows the new brightness of the pixels.

3. **Choose a channel from the Channel drop-down list.**

   Your choices are RGB (all channels), Red, Green, or Blue.

Book III
Chapter 4

Transforming Text,
Shapes, and Images

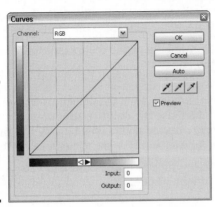

Figure 4-13: The default setting in the Curves dialog box is a diagonal line.

4. Click anywhere along the line in the grid and drag to adjust the curve.

When you click on the line, Fireworks generates a handle automatically. The end points always remain where they are, but you can add handles anywhere else on the line and drag them to new points. You can delete handles by dragging them up out of the dialog box. You can type a numerical value into the Input and Output text fields instead of dragging the line, if you prefer.

If the Preview check box is selected, as it is by default, you can see the changes when you release the mouse button after dragging a handle.

Clicking the Auto button restores the line to its original setting.

5. Click OK.

Follow these steps to change the hue, saturation, and/or lightness of a graphic or selection:

1. Select a graphic or part of a graphic.

For more information on selecting image objects or parts of image objects, see Book III, Chapter 3.

2. Choose Filters➪Adjust Color➪Hue/Saturation.

A dialog box with separate sliders for Hue, Saturation, and Lightness pops up.

3. If you want to change the basic color of your selection, click and drag the Hue slider.

The default position is at the center. You can drag left down to –180 degrees, or you can drag right up to 180 degrees. (You can think of the slider as a flattened circle, like a map of the Earth is a flattened globe.) If the Preview check box is selected, as it is by default, you can see the change to your selection when you release the mouse button.

4. If you want to alter the intensity of the colors in your selection, click and drag the Saturation slider.

The default position is at the center. You can drag left down to –100 units to reduce the color saturation in the selection, or you can drag right up to 100 units to increase the color saturation in the selection. If the Preview check box is selected, as it is by default, you can see the change to your selection when you release the mouse button.

5. If you want to alter the luminosity of the colors in your selection, click and drag the Lightness slider.

The default position is at the center. You can drag left down to –100 units to reduce the lightness of the selection, or you can drag right up to 100 units to increase the lightness of the selection. A setting of –100 gives you black, and a setting of 100 gives you white. If the Preview check box is selected, as it is by default, you can see the change to your selection when you release the mouse button.

6. **Click OK.**

If you want to change the hue and/or saturation of black or white pixels, select the Colorize check box, and then make your adjustments.

To invert the colors of a graphic or any selection, follow these steps:

1. **Select a graphic or part of a graphic.**

2. **Choose Filters⇨Adjust Color⇨Invert, or use the key command Ctrl+Alt+Shift+I.**

   The colors of your selection are inverted, as in a photographic negative.

The Levels command allows you to make color corrections to an image or selection by altering the balance of highlights, midtones, and shadows. The graphical representation of the distribution of shades is called a histogram.

To adjust the levels of an image or image selection, follow these steps:

1. **Select a graphic or part of a graphic.**

   For more information on selecting image objects or parts of image objects, see Book III, Chapter 3.

2. **Choose Filters⇨Adjust Color⇨Levels.**

   The Levels dialog box appears, as shown in Figure 4-14.

**Book III
Chapter 4**

Transforming Text,
Shapes, and Images

Figure 4-14:
The Levels
dialog box
includes a
histogram.

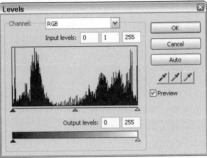

3. **Choose a channel from the Channel drop-down list.**

   Your choices are RGB (all channels), Red, Green, or Blue.

4. **Click and drag the Input shadows slider (the black triangle at the left under the histogram) as needed.**

   Note that the shadows slider cannot be dragged farther right than the midtones slider, because shadows must always be darker than midtones. The slider scale goes from 0 (no brightness, which is black) to 255 (full brightness, which is white). The midtones slider moves automatically when you move the shadows slider.

5. **Click and drag the Input midtones slider (the gray triangle in the middle under the histogram) as needed.**

   The midtones slider cannot be dragged farther left than the shadows slider nor farther right than the highlights slider. The midtones slider's scale goes from 0 to 10.

   Dragging the midtones slider to the right generally darkens the selection, and dragging it to the far left can create something resembling a posterization effect, in which transitions between colors are abrupt rather than smooth.

6. **Click and drag the Input highlights slider (the white triangle at the right under the histogram) as needed.**

   The highlights slider cannot be dragged farther left than the midtone slider, because highlights must be lighter than midtones.

7. **Click and drag the Output shadows and highlights sliders as needed.**

   These sliders can be moved past each other. Moving the darkness slider all the way to the right and the lightness slider all the way to the left inverts the colors in the selection.

8. **Click OK.**

   If you click Cancel, your adjustments will not be implemented. If you click the Auto button, Fireworks sets the optimal color balance automatically.

To let Fireworks set the optimal levels automatically, you can click the Auto button in the Curves and Levels dialog boxes, or you can select a graphic or part of a graphic, and then choose Filters⇨Adjust Color⇨Auto Levels.

Blurring and sharpening

Blurring a graphic or selection can add a sense of softness to an image; sharpening, on the other hand, can add a sense of solidity or hyper-reality to an image. *Note:* The Sharpen command cannot correct a blatantly out-of-focus photo; nothing can.

To blur an image or part of an image using Fireworks presets, simply follow these steps:

1. **Select a graphic or part of a graphic.**

   For more information on selecting image objects or parts of image objects, see Book III, Chapter 3.

2. **Choose Filters⇨Blur⇨Blur.**

   For a more pronounced effect, choose Filters⇨Blur⇨Blur More.

3. **Click OK.**

You can also use the Blur tool from the Bitmap section of the Tools panel to "paint" a blur across your image. If you want to blur multiple small parts of an image, you may find the Blur tool more effective.

If you want more control over the amount of blur of your image, you can employ the Gaussian Blur filter by following these steps:

1. **Select a graphic or part of a graphic.**

2. **Choose Filters⇨Blur⇨Gaussian Blur.**

   The Gaussian Blur dialog box appears.

3. **Click and drag the slider to set the radius of the blur.**

   The radius can be set from 0.1 (hardly noticeable blur) to 250.0 (near total blur).

4. **Click OK.**

To sharpen an image or selection using Fireworks presets, just follow these steps:

1. **Select a graphic or part of a graphic.**

2. **Choose Filters⇨Sharpen⇨Sharpen.**

   For a more pronounced effect, choose Filters⇨Sharpen⇨Sharpen More.

3. **Click OK.**

If you want more control over the amount and manner of the sharpening, you can use the Unsharp Mask filter. This filter works by strengthening the contrast between adjacent pixels, which makes for more sharply defined edges between areas of color. Actually, that's the way all the Sharpen filters

**Book III
Chapter 4**

**Transforming Text,
Shapes, and Images**

work, but with Unsharp Mask, you can create your own settings for three aspects of the sharpening process:

✦ **Sharpen Amount:** This is the amount of contrast introduced between adjacent pixels.

✦ **Pixel Radius:** This is the size of the area around each pixel that gets sharpened.

✦ **Threshold:** This setting determines which pixels get sharpened based on the existing contrast levels in the selection or image.

Follow these steps to sharpen an image or selection using the Unsharp Mask filter:

1. **Select a graphic or part of a graphic.**

   For more information on selecting image objects or parts of image objects, see Book III, Chapter 3.

2. **Choose Filters⇨Sharpen⇨Unsharp Mask.**

   The Unsharp Mask dialog box pops up.

3. **Click and drag the Sharpen Amount slider.**

   The slider goes from 1 percent (not very much) to 500 percent (very strong contrast).

4. **Click and drag the Pixel Radius slider.**

   The slider goes from 0.1 (hardly noticeable) to 250.0 (very strong effect).

5. **Click and drag the Threshold slider.**

   The slider goes from 0 (change all pixels) to 255 (change no pixels).

6. **Click OK.**

Using the other filters: Convert to Alpha and Find Edges

The Convert to Alpha filter makes your selection transparent. The lighter the pixel, the more transparent it becomes. White pixels, for example, seem to disappear, allowing the background to show through fully. Black pixels, on the other hand, remain black and completely opaque.

To convert a selection to Alpha, follow these simple steps:

1. **Select a graphic or part of a graphic.**

2. **Choose Filters⇨Other⇨Convert to Alpha.**

   The selection is converted.

3. **Click anywhere on the canvas or use the key command Ctrl+D to deselect your selection.**

The Find Edges filter makes a photograph look like a line drawing by greatly simplifying the color information in the image.

To use the Find Edges filter, just follow these steps:

1. **Select a graphic or part of a graphic.**

   For more information on selecting image objects or parts of image objects, see Book III, Chapter 3.

2. **Choose Filters⇨Other⇨Find Edges.**

   The selection takes on the appearance of a line drawing.

3. **Click anywhere on the canvas or use the key command Ctrl+D to deselect your selection.**

Using Extras: Lite Versions Bundled with Fireworks MX 2004

Fireworks allows you to use third-party filters as plug-ins, as demonstrated by the included "lite" versions of Alien Skin's Eye Candy 4000 (Bevel Boss, Marble, and Motion Trail) and Splat (Edges). These versions of the third-party software are not full-featured (hence the "lite" appellation), though grayed-out menu options give you a sense of what the full-featured version of the software can do.

Because these lite versions are not officially part of Fireworks, we do not cover them in this book. You can find information about the fully-functioning versions of these filters at www.alienskin.com.

Chapter 5: The Power of Layers and Frames

In This Chapter

✔ **Managing layers**

✔ **Using layers to mask images**

✔ **Using the Web layer**

✔ **Working with objects**

✔ **Managing frames**

✔ **Using frames to create animated GIFs and rollovers**

*E*verything you put on your canvas in Fireworks MX 2004 — everything you draw or type or paste or import — exists in a layer. In turn, every layer exists in a frame. Initially this seems simple enough, but it is more involved than it first appears. Layers can be shared by frames, and a single layer can contain a single object (a bitmap, shape, or text) or multiple objects. Things can actually get pretty complex in a large file, where you can have dozens of bitmaps, shapes, and text blocks.

Layers give you a way to organize your Fireworks PNG image so that you can easily turn groups of objects on or off (that is, make the groups of objects visible or hide them), put objects on top of or beneath other objects, lock groups of objects so they can't be modified, and find things easily.

Frames, on the other hand, offer a way to organize layers so you can export multiple states of buttons (different versions of the button, such as those that appear when the button is rolled over or clicked by the user) and animated GIFs quickly and easily.

The *canvas* is at the bottom of the stack of layers. It is not really a layer itself — it can't be expanded or collapsed, made visible or invisible, locked or unlocked, or deleted.

The *Web Layer,* the repository for slices and hotspots, is always the top layer, as you can see in Figure 5-1. You create slices in the Web Layer in order to cut your page design into individual images. After images have been sliced, they can be optimized, exported, and placed in HTML pages, where they may be hyperlinked. You create hotspots in the Web Layer to make images that can be exported for your Web page along with some HTML code that specifies areas in the image that are hyperlinked. The Web Layer can be made visible or invisible, and it can be locked and unlocked, but it cannot be deleted.

Figure 5-1:
The Layers panel displays a stack of layers in their collapsed state.

Managing Layers

Fireworks uses the concept of folders to describe how a layer functions. (Notice the little folder icons next to the layer names in Figure 5-1.) So you can think of a layer as a receptacle for "files" (image objects and text objects). The individual "files" can be copied or moved to other layers, deleted, named, renamed, and so on.

Take a closer look at the Layers panel. Looking left to right at an unexpanded layer, you can see the following across four columns:

✦ **The Expand/Collapse button:** A plus sign (+) in the box indicates that the layer can be expanded. A minus sign (–) in the box indicates that the layer can be collapsed. Click the control to toggle between expanded and collapsed views of the layer.

✦ **The Show/Hide layer button:** An eye appears in this column when the layer is visible on the canvas. When the layer is invisible on the canvas, the column is empty. Click in the column to toggle the layer's visibility on the canvas off and on. Note that when you export images from your PNG, only visible objects are exported.

✦ **The Lock/Unlock button:** If you click this column of a collapsed layer, a lock appears, indicating that none of the objects on that layer can be edited. If you click once on the layer name (in the fourth column) or turn on the Show/Hide layers button (in the second column), a pencil appears in the third column, indicating that the layer is unlocked and active. If the layer is unlocked and active, you can edit the objects in the layer. Only one layer can be active at a time, though any number of layers can be unlocked or locked.

✦ **The layer name:** By default, Fireworks names each layer for the order in which it was created. The first layer is called Layer 1, the second layer is called Layer 2, and so on. (To find out how to give the layer a more meaningful name, check out the "Renaming a layer" section, later in this chapter.) When the layer is active, the layer name is highlighted in the Layers panel.

Adding and deleting layers

When you add a new layer to your PNG, the new layer always gets added above the currently selected layer. You can add a layer in three easy ways:

✦ Click the Add/Duplicate Layer button (the folder with the plus sign on it) at the bottom middle of the Layers panel.

✦ Select Edit➪Insert➪Layer.

✦ Choose New Layer from the Layer panel's Options menu (the bulleted list icon at the right of the panel's title bar).

In either case, the New Layer dialog box appears, with the layer's default name highlighted. You need to type a new name for the layer and select the Share Across Frames option if you're making a multiple-frame document and you want the objects on the new layer you created to be visible on the other frames of your document. The newly created layer is active until you click another layer.

To delete a layer, click it in the Layers panel and drag it to the Delete button (the garbage can icon) at the bottom right of the Layers panel. You can also click the layer, and then click the Delete button in the Layers panel.

Making a layer active

As noted previously, only one layer at a time can be active. However, many objects on a layer can be editable simultaneously, which can come in handy when you want to move several objects the same amount and in the same direction. In order to change any object in a layer, you need to make the layer active:

✦ **Make a layer active:** Click an object on the canvas that's in that layer, or click the name of that layer in the Layers panel.

✦ **Make a layer inactive, but not locked:** Click an object on the canvas that's not in that layer, or click the name of another layer in the Layers panel.

Sometimes when you have an object from one layer selected and you click an object on another layer to make it active, the item you're trying to select won't highlight. Why not? Look closely: You have selected a new layer, just not the one you want. Often you find yourself in this position if you have a very large object on the bottom layer of your file — when you try to click something in front of it, Fireworks thinks you're trying to click the large object on the bottom layer and highlights it instead of the smaller object (the one you're trying to select) in front of it. Luckily, you can just click the object you want to select in the Layers panel to make it active.

Expanding and collapsing layers

Because files can contain many layers, and layers can contain many objects, and you have only so much room for the Layers panel, Fireworks allows you to expand and collapse a layer as needed:

✦ **Expand a layer:** Click the plus (+) button in the first column of that layer. Each object in that layer appears on its own line below the layer name. Each object has its own Show/Hide button, as well as a thumbnail of the object and a name.

✦ **Collapse a layer:** Click the minus (–) button. If the layer is active, it will remain so until you click another layer or an object on the canvas that resides on another layer.

Figure 5-2 shows the Layers panel with some layers collapsed and one layer expanded to show the objects it contains.

Figure 5-2:
Selecting an object on the canvas also selects it in the Layers panel.

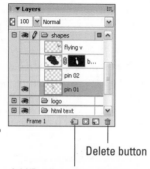

Delete button

Add/Duplicate Layers button

Making a layer visible or invisible on the canvas

The more complicated your designs get, the more you'll be *showing* and *hiding* layers, that is, making them visible or invisible. Luckily, showing and hiding layers is simple:

✦ **Make a layer visible (show a layer):** Click in the second column or the name column of the Layers panel.

✦ **Make a layer invisible (hide a layer):** Click the Hide Layer button (the eye icon) in the second column.

If you export your design as images (so you can use the images in a Web page), objects on hidden/invisible layers will not be exported. In other words, what you see on the canvas when you export is what you will get in your exported images folder.

Locking and unlocking a layer

Sometimes when you have a lot of overlapping objects, selecting some objects without selecting others can get difficult. One way to prevent objects from being accidentally moved or deleted is to lock the layer they're on. You can't lock individual objects, but you can move objects from one layer to another (say, from an unlocked layer to a layer you can then lock).

✦ **Lock a layer:** Click in the third column. If the column is blank when you click in it, the lock appears. If the column has a pencil in it, the pencil changes to a lock, and the pencil appears in an adjacent layer, if there is one.

✦ **Unlock a layer:** Click the lock in the third column of that layer. Unlocking a layer does not automatically make it active.

Renaming a layer

By default, each layer is named for the order in which it was created. The first layer is called Layer 1, the second is called Layer 2, and so on. If you have only a couple of layers in your document, that naming scheme may be sufficient. If you have dozens of layers, on the other hand, you'll want to place similar objects together on layers and then name the layers so you can tell with a quick glance at the Layers panel where the objects are.

To rename a layer from its default name, just follow these simple steps:

1. **Double-click the layer name.**

A simple dialog box appears. The current name is in the text field, in a highlighted state.

2. **Type a new name.**

You don't need to click in the text field, because the current layer name is already highlighted. If you want to keep part of the current name, use your mouse to select the part of the name you want to replace or remove and type over or delete it.

3. **If you have multiple frames in your document and you want this layer to be visible in the other frames, select the Share Across Frames check box.**

Otherwise, move on to Step 4.

4. **Press the Enter key.**

The dialog box closes, and your layer has a new name.

Moving a layer in front of or behind other layers

As you add layers to your PNG file, they stack up. The higher a layer appears in the Layers panel, the closer the objects in that layer are to the front of the canvas. Likewise, within a layer, the higher an object appears, the closer it is to the front of the canvas.

Figure 5-3 illustrates the relationship between objects, their position on the canvas, and their position in the Layers panel. The before part (on the top) of Figure 5-3 shows the bowling ball in front of both pins, and in the Layers panel, the object named "bowling ball" is above the "pin" objects. The after part (on the bottom) of Figure 5-3 shows the large pin in front of the bowling ball. The ball, in turn, is in front of a smaller bowling pin. In the Layers panel, the ball object is between the pin objects.

You can change the order of a layer or object as follows:

✦ **Move a layer or object in front of another:** Click the name column of the layer or object and drag it up. A black horizontal line appears when you roll over a spot where you can place the layer or object. Release the mouse button to drop the layer or object in its new location.

✦ **Move a layer or object behind another:** Click the name column of the layer or object and drag it down. A black horizontal line appears when you roll over a spot where you can place the layer or object. Release the mouse button to drop the layer or object in its new location:

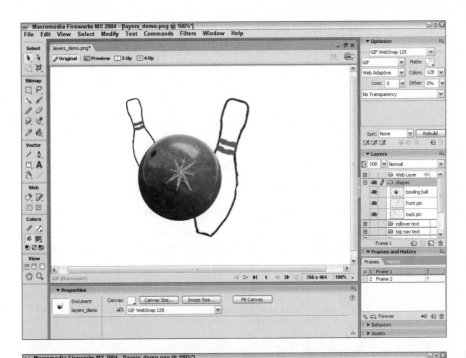

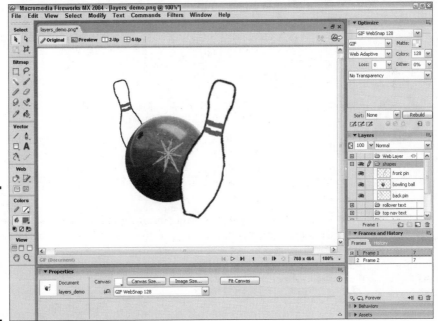

Figure 5-3:
Moving a
layer in the
Layers
panel,
before (top)
and after
(bottom).

Merging layers

Sometimes in the process of creating a PNG document, you'll find that you need all the objects you've made but you don't need them to be on so many layers. If you want to move one or two objects from one layer to another, you can do so using the method described in the previous section, "Moving a layer in front of or behind other layers." If, on the other hand, you want to move all the objects in one layer to another, and there are quite a few objects in each layer, you're better off merging the layers.

To merge all the objects on one layer into a single bitmap object in the layer immediately underneath, follow these steps:

1. **Click in the name column of the layer in the Layers panel.**

Make sure all the objects in the layer are highlighted. (If they're not, you may have clicked an object in the layer instead of the layer itself.)

2. **If necessary, drag the layer so it's on top of the layer you want to merge into.**

You use the Merge Down command later in this process, so you need to make sure the two layers are one on top of the other.

3. **Click the Options menu icon (it looks like a bulleted list) at the top right of the Layers panel and select Merge Down.**

The selected layer merges into the one below it. Note that the objects in the upper layer are combined into a single bitmap object in the new layer. Text in the new object is not editable, and vector shapes in the new object are now bitmaps.

You can also use the key command Ctrl+E to merge a layer into the one below it, or choose Modify⇨Merge Down.

To merge all the layers together into one, do the following:

1. **Click in the name column of any layer in the Layers panel.**

2. **Choose Modify⇨Flatten Layers.**

Your document now has a single layer. Each object remains separate from the others.

Using Layers for Masking

A *mask* is a layer that you create specifically to let some areas of an image show while other areas are hidden. Fireworks uses two kinds of masks — bitmap masks and vector masks (you can use text as a vector mask). What both kinds of masks have in common is what they do: When you lay a mask over an image, the mask blocks out parts of the image and lets other parts show through. Which parts show through and which are blocked out is determined by the shape of the mask, as Figure 5-4 demonstrates.

Figure 5-4:
This image was created by masking a beach with a photo of a dog.

When you use a *bitmap mask,* the grayscale values of the mask determine what, and how much, shows through. The lighter the pixel, the more the object or objects beneath show through. The darker the pixel, the less the stuff underneath shows through.

A *vector mask,* on the other hand, uses the shape outline of the vector object like a cookie cutter. However, Fireworks gives you a lot more flexibility than you have with a real cookie cutter! For example, you can *anti-alias* (smooth out jagged edges) and even feather (blur) the edges of your mask, or you can change the size of your mask at any time after you have created it.

Fireworks offers many ways to create masks. We cover the basics here, but you can always refer to the Fireworks Help files if you're interested in exploring masks more in-depth.

Creating a bitmap mask

To make a bitmap mask using an existing bitmap, follow these steps:

1. **If you want to mask multiple objects, group them by selecting them and using the key command Ctrl+G.**

2. **Select the object you want to use to make the mask.**

   You can select multiple objects to make a mask by Shift+clicking them, but if you do, Fireworks automatically makes a vector mask, not a bitmap mask. See the section "Creating a vector mask" if you want to make a vector mask using multiple bitmap objects.

3. **Choose Edit⇨Cut, or use the key command Ctrl+X.**

   Cut? That's right. You paste the shape in a couple of steps.

4. **Select the layer, object, or group you want to be visible through the mask by selecting it in the Layers panel or on the canvas.**

   The layer, object, or group is highlighted.

5. **Choose Edit⇨Paste as Mask.**

   All the parts of the masked image that fall outside the masking object disappear. In the Layers panel, the mask icon shows up in the third column, while a link icon and thumbnail of the mask shape show up next to the thumbnail of the masked image.

6. **If it's not already selected, select Alpha channel in the Property inspector.**

   When the mask is selected in the Layers panel, the Property inspector offers two options for a bitmap mask: Mask to Alpha Channel and Mask to Grayscale (the default), as shown in Figure 5-5. Mask to Alpha Channel uses the transparency of the mask bitmap, and Mask to Grayscale uses the brightness of the pixels in the mask bitmap.

Bitmaps can be represented as having four channels: Red, Green, Blue, and Alpha. The Red, Green, and Blue channels describe the amount of each of those colors in every pixel in the bitmap. The Alpha channel contains information about the level of transparency of each pixel in the bitmap.

Figure 5-5:
You can change the Mask setting in the Property inspector.

You can hide a mask temporarily by clicking it in the Layers panel and then choosing Disable Mask from the Layers panel's Options menu (the bulleted list icon at the top right of the panel). The mask icon disappears from the Show/Hide object column and a red X appears over the mask, indicating that the mask is disabled. To re-enable the mask, simply click it.

To make a bitmap mask by creating an empty mask and modifying it, follow these steps:

1. **Select the object you want to mask by clicking it on the canvas or in the Layers panel.**

2. **Click the Mask button at the bottom of the Layers panel or choose Modify⇨Mask⇨Reveal All.**

   The Mask icon is the rectangle with a dotted circle inside. Reveal All means the mask you have made will be completely transparent until you modify it.

3. **Select a paintbrush or other drawing tool and draw on top of the bitmap.**

   Wherever you draw, the mask blocks the image behind.

What if you want to do the opposite: Reveal what's underneath only where you draw? Easy! Just follow these steps:

1. **Select the object you want to mask by clicking it on the canvas or in the Layers panel.**

2. **Choose Modify⇨Mask⇨Hide All.**

   Hide All means the mask you have made will be completely opaque until you modify it, so when you first apply it, your masked object will seem to have disappeared.

3. **Select any color other than black.**

   Because the opaque areas of the mask are represented as black, the areas that you want to show through must be drawn using any other color.

4. **Select a paintbrush or other drawing tool and draw on top of the bitmap.**

   Wherever you draw, the mask reveals the image behind.

You can delete a mask by clicking it in the Layers panel, and then choosing Delete Mask from the Layers panel's Options menu (the bulleted list icon at the top right of the panel). When you delete a mask, a dialog box appears to give you the option to apply the mask before deleting it, which will change the masked image.

Creating a vector mask

To make a vector mask, such as the one shown in Figure 5-6, follow these steps:

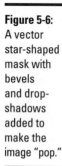

Figure 5-6:
A vector star-shaped mask with bevels and drop-shadows added to make the image "pop."

1. **Select a text block or vector shape by clicking on the shape on the canvas or in the Layers panel.**

The object is highlighted on the canvas and in the Layers panel.

2. **Drag the shape or text over the object or objects you want to mask.**

The layer with the shape doesn't have to be on top of the layers with the objects you want to mask, but it's easier to position the shape if you can see it!

3. **Choose Edit⇨Cut or use the key command Ctrl+X.**

You paste the shape in a couple of steps, so you need to cut it here.

4. **Select the layer or object you want to be visible through the mask by clicking it in the Layers panel or on the canvas.**

The layer or object is highlighted.

5. **Choose Edit⇨Paste as Mask.**

All the parts of the masked image that fall outside the mask shape or text disappear. In the Layers panel, the mask icon shows up in the third column, and a link icon and thumbnail of the mask shape appear next to the thumbnail of the masked image, as shown in Figure 5-7.

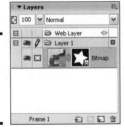

Figure 5-7:
An active
mask in
the Layers
panel.

Using the Web Layer

The Web Layer was the greatest innovation of the original version of Fireworks, and if it no longer seems revolutionary, it's still as handy a feature as you'll come across in making Web pages. The Web Layer allows you to cut your page layout into *slices,* which are pieces of your layout, held in place by HTML, that end up as individual images on your Web page. The Web Layer also allows you to name and optimize each slice individually, which means that you can find the best balance of file size and image quality for each piece of your layout. Just as importantly, because it's a repository for slice information, the Web Layer allows you to save slice coordinates, dimensions, and optimization settings along with everything else in your PNG file.

You never have to leave the Fireworks application to ready your images for the Web, and you don't have to write down or remember your image size, placement, and optimization settings if you ever need to remake an image. The Web Layer also allows you to see at a glance where your slices are, which helps you recreate your page design in HTML. For details about slices and image optimization (including when to use GIFs and when to use JPEGs), see Book III, Chapter 6.

Standard HTML pages are built on a grid system of cells organized into rows and columns. The rows and columns make up a *table.* You can have multiple tables on a Web page, and you can even have tables within tables within tables. You can set the height of each row and the width of each column individually, but you can't make a round cell or a triangular table.

If you use Fireworks to make your HTML, each slice you make in your PNG ends up as an image that fills a table cell in your Web page. It is possible to combine multiple images in a single cell, but Fireworks is not made to work that way.

Think of your Web page design as a rectangular sheet cake. The decorations on top of the cake can be all kinds of shapes, but when you cut the cake, you probably make rectangular slices, cutting right through text, slicing a single icing rose into four pieces, and so on. You ignore the design on the surface of the cake because you're more interested in slicing the cake quickly and controlling the size of each piece. You might make a few specially-cut pieces if somebody really wants the blue rose near the top or the exclamation points from the text that says, "Happy Birthday!!!"

When you are cutting up a Web page, you will want certain pieces to remain intact (a corporate logo or a navigation button, for example), but other objects will fit the HTML grid structure better if they are sliced into pieces or included with other objects on a single piece. If you have an object with round edges, you need to slice it into rectangles so it can be reconstructed on a Web page, like the bowling ball shown in Figure 5-8. The bowling ball will be recreated in HTML as three stacked rectangles. The middle slice in Figure 5-8 is selected, so its name and image compression type appear at the top left of the slice.

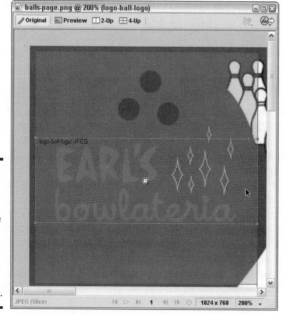

Figure 5-8:
A bowling ball divided into multiple slices so it can be reconstructed on a Web page.

Using the Slice tool

The Slice tool, which can be found in the Web section of the Tools panel, looks like a utility knife on a green square with red lines on each side. When you employ the Slice tool, the slices you create are added automatically to the Web Layer.

To make a slice in your PNG file, follow these steps:

1. **Select the Slice tool from the Web section of the Tools panel.**

2. **Click and drag diagonally on the canvas to make a rectangle.**

   The slice shows up as a green overlay on the canvas.

Using the Polygon Slice tool

The Slice tool has a partner "hidden" behind it in the toolbar: the Polygon Slice tool, which you can get to by clicking and holding the Slice tool until the pop-up menu containing the Polygon Slice tool appears, or by clicking the Slice tool and pressing K on your keyboard.

You can probably guess that the Polygon Slice tool allows you to make non-rectangular slices. But wait! Didn't we say that slices and images must be rectangular? The short answer is that the Polygon Slice tool doesn't create a non-rectangular slice — it creates a rectangular slice with a *polygonal hotspot* (a polygonal area that can be hyperlinked in combination with some HTML code) inside.

So what's the difference between a polygonal hotspot made by the Polygon Slice tool and one made by the Polygon Hotspot tool? The Polygon Hotspot tool doesn't make a slice, it just makes an irregularly-shaped linkable area in a slice. (A slice may contain many hotspots, each linked to a different page.) The Polygon Slice tool, on the other hand, makes both hotspots and slices. If you have a map of the United States, and you want each state to link to its own HTML page, use the Polygon Hotspot tool to make linked areas in the shape of each state. (For more information on the Polygon Hotspot tool, see Book III, Chapter 6.) If you just have a few irregularly shaped buttons, you can use the Polygon Slice tool to make a linkable image.

To make a polygonal slice, follow these steps:

1. **Select the Polygon Slice tool from the Slice tool menu in the Web area of the Tools panel.**

   If the regular Slice tool is showing, click and hold the Slice tool button to reveal the pop-up menu so you can select the Polygon Slice tool.

2. **Click a series of points to make a polygonal shape.**

   Fireworks automatically draws straight lines to connect each point to the last. You do not need to click the first spot to close the shape.

Working with Objects

In the world of Fireworks, an *object* is any self-contained bitmap, vector shape, or text block that can appear on the canvas. The object may include blank space, and you can make a single object out of many objects (as you do when you merge layers, which we discuss earlier in this chapter). In general, anything in your design that you want to be able to edit individually should be left as a single object.

Renaming an object in the Layers panel

By default, each object is named for its type (path, bitmap, and so on) but can be individually renamed. As with layers, being able to name objects in the Layers panel becomes crucial as you add more elements to your design. The Layers panel does contain thumbnails of each object, but if you have multiple similar objects in several places on the canvas, you may want a way to tell the objects apart in the Layers panel.

To rename an object, double-click the current name of the object in the Layers panel and type a new name in the text field that appears. Press Enter or click outside the text field to save the new name. Renaming an object makes it active. When the object is active, the line around the icon is highlighted and the column reverses to a black background with white text.

Moving an object between layers

You may want to move an object from the layer it was originally created on to a different layer. For example, you may want an object to be stacked on top of or under other items on the canvas and have other objects in the layer remain exactly where they are. Luckily, moving an object from one layer to another is a snap.

To move an object from one layer to another, click the name column of the object in the Layers panel and drag it to a new location. A black horizontal line appears when you roll over a spot where you can place the object. Release the mouse button to drop the object in its new location.

Setting an object's opacity/transparency

You can set each object's transparency independently by using the slider near the top left of the Layers panel. By default, objects are completely opaque, and the opaque object completely blocks out whatever objects are underneath it, as in Figure 5-3. You can make the objects on a layer semi-transparent, which allows the objects underneath to show through by an adjustable amount.

The extreme ends of the Opacity/Transparency scale are 100 percent opaque (which can also be thought of as 0 percent transparent) and 0 percent opaque (100 percent transparent). When you add an object to the canvas, its default opacity of 100 shows up at the top left of the Layers panel and in the object's Property inspector.

To adjust the transparency of a layer, follow these simple steps:

1. **Click the name column of the object you want to adjust or click the object on the canvas to select the object.**

   The object is highlighted on both the canvas and in the Layers panel.

2. **Click and drag the Opacity/Transparency slider to adjust how opaque the object will be.**

   The Opacity/Transparency slider is the button with the downward-pointing arrow located near the top left of the Layers panel, next to the Opacity text field. (You can find an identical slider in the Property inspector.)

3. **Release the mouse button when you get to the setting you want.**

You can also type a number from 0 to 100 into the text field next to the slider to set the object's transparency. Remember to press the Enter key to apply the new setting.

Fireworks can do a few fancier tricks with opacity. For example, you can set an opacity gradient, so some parts of your object are more transparent than others. See the next section on blending for more information on this topic.

Blending

Blending one object with another has to do with varying the transparency of the top object so some of the bottom object shows through. But blending in Fireworks involves more than just adjusting opacity. You can use a dozen blending modes in conjunction with the Opacity control and the colors of your objects to produce different blending effects:

✦ **Normal:** The default blending mode, normal, actually means there's no blending going on at all.

✦ **Multiply:** This mode multiplies the value of each pixel of the top object with each pixel of the objects underneath, which generally results in a darker color.

✦ **Screen:** This mode divides the value of each pixel of the bottom object by each pixel of the object on top and produces a lighter color.

✦ **Darken:** This mode replaces pixels of the top object that are lighter than the pixels in the object underneath with the darker pixels from below.

✦ **Lighten:** This mode replaces pixels of the top object that are darker than the object underneath with the lighter pixels from the object below.

✦ **Difference:** This mode subtracts the darker color from the color with more brightness, regardless of which is on top.

✦ **Hue:** This mode replaces the luminance and saturation of a pixel on top with those of the pixel underneath.

✦ **Saturation:** This mode replaces the hue and luminance of a pixel on top with those of the pixel underneath.

✦ **Color:** This mode replaces the luminance of a pixel on top with that of the pixel underneath, but keeps the hue and saturation of the top pixel the same.

✦ **Luminosity:** This mode replaces the hue and saturation of the pixel on top with those of the pixel underneath, leaving the luminance of the pixel on top.

✦ **Invert:** This mode changes the colors of the pixels in the object under-neath to their opposites, regardless of the colors of the object on top.

✦ **Tint:** This mode adds gray to the areas of overlap.

✦ **Erase:** This mode removes all pixels in the overlapping areas, leaving a hole in the canvas. Any objects underneath the object with a blend mode of erase will be invisible where the objects overlap.

Layers can have blending modes, but the blending mode settings of individual objects on the layer override the settings of the layer they're on. That means different objects on the same layer can have individualized blend settings. The blending mode of a *group* of objects, however, overrides the blending modes of individual objects within the group. Removing the blending mode of the group restores the blending modes of the individual objects.

To blend an existing object with whatever is under it, just follow these steps:

1. **Select the object you want to blend by clicking it on the canvas or in the Layers panel.**

2. **Select a blending mode from the drop-down list at the top-right of the Layers panel.**

When you release the mouse button, the blend mode takes effect.

3. **If you want, adjust the transparency of the object by typing a value between 1 and 100 in the Opacity text field next to the blending**

mode list or by using the Opacity/Transparency slider between the Opacity text field and the blending mode list.

Any objects that you put under the blended object will be affected by (or will affect) the blended object where both objects overlap.

You can also establish a blend's opacity and mode *before* you create an object by setting the properties of a drawing tool in the Property inspector, as shown in Figure 5-9. (***Note:*** Not all tools permit this.) Your settings will apply every time you use that tool. Remember, individual object blend settings override the blend settings of the layer the object is on.

To set the blend before you draw, follow these steps:

1. **Use the key command Ctrl+D or choose Edit⇨Deselect to make sure you don't have any objects selected.**

   If you have an object selected, you might accidentally change its blend mode when you're trying to set one for the object you're about to create.

2. **Select a drawing tool, such as the Brush tool.**

   Some tools cannot have their blends changed from the default, Normal.

3. **Select a color for the tool.**

   See the section on adding color in Book III, Chapter 2 if you don't know how to select a color for the tool. You can always change the color of the object later, but that can get complicated, especially if you have a special blend mode and opacity set.

4. **Select a blending mode from the drop-down list at the top-right of the Layers panel or from the identical list in the tool's Property inspector.**

5. **If desired, set an opacity for the tool by dragging the Layers panel's Opacity/Transparency slider (the button with the downward-pointing arrow between the Opacity text field and the blending mode list) or typing a value in the Layers panel's Opacity text field.**

   Alternatively, you can set the opacity in the rightmost section of the tool's Property inspector in the same way.

6. **Use the tool to make your vector shape or bitmap.**

   The tool's blend and opacity settings remain in effect until you change them. After you create an object, you can always adjust its blend and opacity settings. You may want to create a new layer (see the section "Adding and deleting layers") before making a new object. If you don't make a new layer, remember that the object's blend settings override the layer's blend settings.

**Book III
Chapter 5**

**The Power of
Layers and Frames**

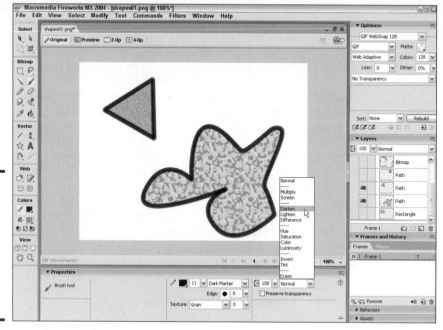

Figure 5-9:
You can set a tool's blending mode by using the tool's Property inspector.

Managing Frames

Given all that you can do with layers, you may be wondering why you would need these things called "frames." *Frames* are essentially sets of layers that enable you to do two things that layers alone can't accomplish:

✦ Export multiple button states (different versions of the button such as those that appear when the button is rolled over or clicked by the user) simultaneously

✦ Create and export animated GIFs (files that contain multiple GIF images displayed in sequence)

You can think of layers as stacked one on top of the other; frames, on the other hand, are better visualized as a series, each following the previous in the same location but at a later time, like a flip book. Each frame is distinct from the others. A given frame may share layers or objects with other frames, but the shared layers or objects are usually different from one frame to the next (the objects are a different color, have a different effect applied to them, or are at different coordinates). These differences make up multiple button states or animated GIFs.

The Frames panel (see Figure 5-12) displays frames in much the same way as the Layers panel displays layers, except that the Frames panel doesn't show the objects contained within each frame.

Like layers, frames can be duplicated, added, and deleted. You must have at least two frames in your Fireworks PNG file in order to export buttons with rollover states or animated GIFs.

Adding frames

By default, your Fireworks PNG has a single frame, which contains all the layers in the file. To add a frame to your file, just follow these steps:

1. **Click the Options menu (the bulleted list icon) at the top right of the Frames panel and choose Add Frames or Duplicate Frame from the menu.**

   Choose Duplicate Frame if you want the objects in the current frame to be copied to the new frames. Choose Add Frames if you want to add empty frames to your file. Either the Add Frames or Duplicate Frame dialog box (shown in Figure 5-10) appears, both of which have identical parameters.

Figure 5-10: The Duplicate Frame dialog box.

**Book III
Chapter 5**

**The Power of
Layers and Frames**

2. **Enter a number or click the arrow next to the text field to use a slider to set the number of frames you would like to add:**

   - For a simple rollover, you want one additional frame, for a total of two frames in your file.

   - If you want your button to have an on state as well as a highlight (rollover) and normal state, you want two additional frames, for a total of three frames.

   - If you want a highlight-while-on state, you want three additional frames, for a total of four frames.

   The slider goes from 0 through 10, but you can type in values higher than 10.

If your animated GIF has more than 20 frames, the file size may be prohibitively large. For complicated animations, you're better off using Macromedia Flash MX 2004.

3. **Select one of the options for where the new frames should be added in reference to the current one.**

You have the following options:

- **At the Beginning:** The first new frame becomes Frame 1 and the remaining frames are numbered sequentially, regardless of how many frames you currently have in your document, and regardless of which frame is currently active.

- **Before Current Frame:** The frames are added before the currently active frame.

- **After Current Frame:** The frames are added after the currently active frame.

- **At the End:** The new frames are the last frames, no matter how many frames you already have or which frame is currently active.

4. **Click OK.**

Deleting and editing frames

To delete a frame, click the frame in the Frames panel and drag it to the garbage can icon at the bottom right of the Frames panel. To delete multiple frames simultaneously, Shift+click all the frames in the Frames panel that you want to delete and, while the frames are highlighted, click the garbage can icon at the bottom right of the Frames panel.

You can select a frame for editing two ways:

+ **Click the frame in the Frames panel.**
+ **Click and hold the frame indicator at the bottom left of the Layers panel.** A drop-down list appears, giving you easy access to all the frames in your document. Simply select the frame you want to edit.

Renaming frames

Renaming frames is a simple matter: Double-click the frame's name in the Frames panel and type the new name in the text field that appears.

Using Frames to Create Rollovers and Animated GIFs

Now that you know how to make and manage frames, you're ready to use them! In this section we cover how to create rollovers and animated GIFs, both of which can add interest to your Web site.

Creating a rollover

Creating a button rollover is really just a matter of making two (or three or even four) versions of a button graphic, each on its own frame. Dreamweaver MX 2004 allows you to generate rollover code pretty easily, but you can also have Fireworks make the rollover code along with the HTML.

To make a simple button rollover, follow these steps:

1. **Make a button, or set of buttons, using the processes outlined in Book III, Chapters 3 and 4.**

The button can have text or an icon, it can have a shape or bitmap under the text or icon, and it can be any shape or size you like (but you probably want to keep it on the small side to limit file size and leave room on your page for content). For easy housekeeping, if you're creating a navigation bar, keep all the buttons for which you want to have additional states on the same layer.

2. **Make sure the layer on which you have your buttons is not shared across frames.**

By default, objects on layers are not shared across frames. If a layer is shared across frames, changes to any objects in that layer will be reflected in all frames. If a layer is shared across frames, the Shared icon (which resembles a ladder or strip of film with arrows on both sides) appears to the right of the layer name in the Layers panel.

To disable sharing across frames, double-click the layer and deselect the Share Across Frames check box.

3. **Add one frame after the current frame by clicking the New/Duplicate Frame button in the Frames panel or by choosing Add Frames from the Frames panel's Options menu (the bulleted list icon at the top right of the panel).**

4. **In Frame 2, edit the objects that make up your button to create a highlighted rollover state.**

The highlighted rollover state is the image that will swap in when the user rolls the cursor over the button.

You can make the text a different color or add a glow to it, or you can make the vector shape or bitmap a different color. There are too many options to mention here, really. Just make sure the difference is noticeable when the user moves a cursor over the button.

5. **Make a slice overlaying the button graphic.**

See Book III, Chapter 6 for details on making slices, or just check out the "Using the Slice tool" section, earlier in this chapter.

6. **Click and release the mouse button in the middle of the slice to access the Add Behavior pop-up menu, and choose the Add Simple Rollover behavior.**

   When a slice is active, you can see the Target icon in the middle of the slice. When you place your cursor over the target, it becomes a hand.

If you want to test the rollover, click the Preview tab at the top of the canvas to make the Preview pane active. Place your cursor over your button in the Preview pane to see the Rollover behavior in action. Next move the cursor off the button to see the button return to its normal state — that behavior is part of a Simple Rollover.

Adding an on state (for when the user is on the Web page the button represents) and a highlight-while-on state (for when the user rolls over the button on the Web page the button represents) are as simple as repeating Steps 3 and 4 above, and adding more behaviors via the Behaviors panel. See Book III, Chapter 7 for further details.

Creating an animated GIF

You may find that the easiest way to create an animated GIF is to build one frame, duplicate it, edit that frame, duplicate it, and so on. Fireworks has a display mode called onion skinning, which is especially handy for building animated GIFs. With onion skinning turned on, illustrated in Figure 5-11, you can see the frame you're working on, plus dimmed versions either of the next frame, the previous and next frames, or all frames. That can be very useful in helping you pace your animation to get the illusion of smooth motion.

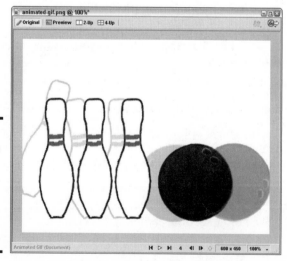

Figure 5-11: You can see the current frame plus other frames with onion skinning on.

To activate onion skinning, just follow these steps:

1. **Click the Onion Skinning button (the downward-pointing pentagon) at the lower left of the Frames panel.**

   The Onion Skinning menu pops up.

2. **Select one of the four options:**

   • **Show Next Frame:** Select the Show Next Frame option if you already have your frames set up and want to check frames two at a time.

   • **Before and After:** Select the Before and After option if you want to see the previous and next frames as well as the current frame.

   • **Show All Frames:** Select the Show All Frames option to see all the frames at once.

   • **Custom:** Select the Custom option if you want to set the number of frames visible at once and to customize their transparencies.

3. **Leave the Multi-Frame Editing option selected if you want to be able to edit the objects in the visible but not current frames.**

   Use the Select Behind tool to select objects in frames other than the current one.

When you duplicate a frame, you duplicate the objects in it. When you edit an object in a frame, though, you change only that instance of it. In our bowling ball animation, shown in Figure 5-11, we rotated the ball (as well as moved it left) in each frame to give the illusion that the ball is rolling. If we wanted to, we could have the ball be a different color in each frame as well.

Setting the frame rate

The frame rate is the speed at which each frame follows the previous frame. You can set the rate to be the same all the way through the animation, or you can set individually the amount of time each frame stays on-screen.

To set a constant frame rate, follow these steps:

1. **Click the first frame and Shift+click the last frame in the Frames panel to select all the Frames.**

   All the frames highlight.

2. **Double-click the frame delay column (the right-hand column) of any frame in the Frames panel.**

   The Frame Delay dialog box appears.

3. **Type a number in the Frame Delay text field to set the amount of time in hundredths of a second that each frame will remain on-screen.**

   If you want the frames to be on-screen for more than a second, the number you type should be over 100. For example, if you type 350, each frame will be on-screen for 3.5 seconds. You won't get much of an illusion of motion at that frame rate, however! The less time each frame is on-screen, the more frames of your animation will appear each second. The more frames per second, the smoother the animation looks. But the more frames you have in your animation, the bigger the file.

4. **Press Enter.**

To change the amount of time one frame stays on-screen, follow these steps:

1. **Double-click the frame delay column (the right-hand column) of any frame in the Frames panel.**

   The Frame Delay dialog box appears.

2. **Type a new number in the Frame Delay text field to set the amount of time in hundredths of a second that the frame will remain on-screen.**

3. **Press Enter.**

To loop or not to loop

Fireworks allows you to loop your animation, which causes it to automatically start over at the beginning after playing the last frame. You can have the GIF loop indefinitely, you can set it to play once (stopping at the last frame), or to play a designated number of times and then stop on the last frame.

The default for animated GIFs is to loop endlessly. To make a GIF that stops at the final frame, just follow these steps:

1. **Click the GIF Animation Looping button (the oval with an arrow) at the bottom of the Frames panel.**

   The Looping pop-up menu appears.

2. **Select a number of times you want the animation to repeat, or select No Looping if you want it to play only once.**

   Because you're setting the amount of times for it to repeat, if you select 1, that means the animation will play twice through and stop. Note that after you have made your choice, the choice appears next to the Loop button, as shown in Figure 5-12.

The Frames panel, shown in Figure 5-12, shows what mode of onion skinning is on, if any, and on which frames (first column); it also shows the frame name (second column), frame delay (third column), and looping information (bottom).

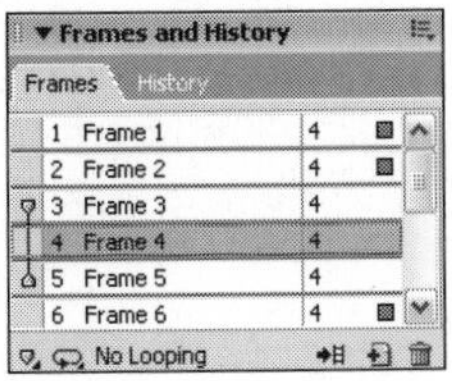

Figure 5-12:
The Frames panel shows the frames' settings.

Previewing animated GIFs

You can preview animated GIFs in the Preview pane (click Preview at the top of the canvas to view the Preview pane). The available controls are as follows:

✦ Go to first frame

✦ Play/Stop

✦ Go to last frame

✦ Go back one frame

✦ Go forward one frame

The animation plays at the frame rate you have set for it, and conveniently, you can adjust the frame rate in the Frames panel without leaving the Preview pane. Your animation will loop in the Preview pane, even if it's set not to loop for export. Onion skinning is not visible in the Preview pane.

Chapter 6: Slicing Up Content for the Web

In This Chapter

✔ **Investigating the advantages of using slices**

✔ **Creating and editing slices**

✔ **Optimizing images for the Web**

✔ **Previewing slices**

✔ **Relating hotspots and slices**

✔ **Exporting images**

*A*fter you have designed your page, you need to figure out how to translate your design to the Web. If you're planning to export HTML as well as images from Fireworks and plan not to mess with the code afterward, that's okay. When you want to make changes to the Web page, you can do so in Fireworks and then re-export the HTML and images.

Of course, you can also export all the images from Fireworks but generate the HTML code by hand. Regardless of your Web-coding skill level or your site maintenance needs, you'll want to slice and optimize your images, and luckily doing so is easy with Fireworks. The following section, "Exploring the Advantages of Using Slices," explains the whys and hows of slicing your design in Fireworks; for more information on image optimization, see the "Optimizing Your Images for the Web" section, later in this chapter.

Exploring the Advantages of Using Slices

When we introduce the Web Layer in the previous chapter, we offer the analogy that a design for a Web page is like a sheet cake. Of course, when you slice a cake, the point is to eat it. When you slice a page layout, like the one in Figure 6-1, the aim is to optimize (reduce the file size of) your images so that you can reconstruct your design with HTML in such a way as to balance image quality with download time.

Slicing your design offers two advantages:

✦ **Individually optimized images:** Each sliced image can be compressed by a different amount using the most appropriate method, giving you maximum control over the balance between image quality and download time.

✦ **Gradual download:** The browser displays each sliced image as it is downloaded to the user's computer, so the page appears to build gradually. Users are much more engaged by watching this process than by staring at a blank screen waiting for a complete page to load all at once!

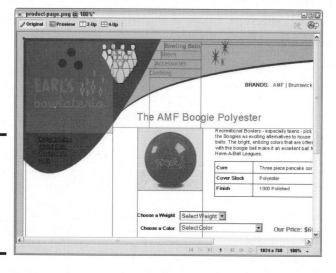

Figure 6-1:
This layout
is sliced
where
we have
images to
export.

When you use slices in combination with frames, you gain other advantages (for more on frames, see Book III, Chapter 5). The main advantage is that you can export multiple images simultaneously from a single slice, which is the easiest way to make buttons that change based on user actions. (See the "Exporting Images" section, later in this chapter, for the details.)

A Web page made up of a single image may be simple to make but may take too long to download on a dial-up modem because the image file is so large. That's where slices come in. Although there's no minimum or maximum number of slices that you can make on a page, you don't want to make too many slices. Having lots of teeny-weeny images can result in a page that loads *too* gradually. It's a question of balance.

Every image tag in a Web page's HTML code results in a call to the Web site's host server. The more images you have on your page, the more requests for images the browser has to make, and the more images the server has to send. That can feel like having a waiter bring you a salad one piece of lettuce at a time — with you having to request each piece!

Creating and Editing Slices

In Book III, Chapter 5, we cover the basics of how to make a slice, but here we give you some more details. So you don't have to flip back to the previous chapter, here's a reminder on how to make a slice in your Fireworks PNG file:

1. **Select the Slice tool from the Web section of the Tools panel.**

2. **Click and drag diagonally on the canvas to make a rectangle.**

The slice shows up as a green overlay on the canvas.

The default appearance of the slice is as a bright green semi-transparent overlay. You can change the default color of slices in the Preferences settings. You can also change the color of an individual slice in the Property inspector when you have the slice selected. Changing a slice color does not affect the underlying image in any way.

One handy feature of the Slice tool is its snap feature. If you have navigation buttons on the left side of your page, you may want the buttons all to be the same width to simplify your HTML. When you have a single slice made for your first button and you click and drag to make the slice for the second button, Fireworks will snap to the identical width when your cursor is within a few pixels of it. Of course, you can also make sure they're the same width by typing a value into the width text field, or by copying and pasting the slice.

Naming a slice

When you name a slice, you're doing more than making it easy to identify in the Layers panel — you're also naming the image for export. For that reason, when you name a slice, you want to avoid using spaces or any special characters that are illegal in filenames. You should also limit any name to no more than 27 characters (otherwise, Macintosh users will not get to see the image).

To name or rename a slice, just follow these steps:

1. **Double-click the current name of the slice in the Layers panel.**

A text field pops up, as shown in Figure 6-2. By default, slices are named "Slice." If you don't see the slices, you may have to expand the Web layer by clicking the plus (+) button at the left.

Figure 6-2:
Naming a
slice that
contains
a top
navigation
button.

2. **Type a new name for the slice.**

3. **Press Enter.**

You may notice that when a slice is selected, the Property inspector gives you access to the slice's name, dimensions, position on the page, and more. You can also change the name of the slice in the Property inspector rather than in the Layers panel.

Moving a slice

After you have created a slice, you may find yourself needing to move it. For example, if you moved some elements in your design a few pixels one way or the other, the image underlying the slice may have shifted enough that you need to adjust the slice's position. You can choose between three basic ways of moving a slice:

✦ Move a slice by clicking and dragging the slice. (In most cases, you'll probably want to use this method.)

✦ Use the arrow keys to move a slice.

✦ Change the X and Y coordinates of the slice in the Property inspector.

Be aware that if you overlap slices on the canvas, the overlapped area will only appear in the image created from one of the slices — the one that appears higher in the Layers panel.

To move a slice using the click-and-drag method, just follow these steps:

1. **Click the slice on the canvas.**

You can click anywhere on the slice except the corners and the center. Clicking a corner or the center of a slice gives you special options.

2. **Hold down the mouse button and drag the slice to its new location.**

If you want finer control when you move a slice, you can use the arrow keys to move a slice as follows:

1. **Select the slice by clicking it on the canvas or in the Layers panel.**

2. **Press the appropriate arrow key.**

> Each time you press an arrow key, the slice moves by one pixel. If you hold down the Shift key and then press an arrow key, the slice moves by ten pixels.

Sometimes when you want to line something up along one axis, the easiest way to do that is to select slices and type the new X or Y coordinate for each slice. The top-left corner of the canvas always has the coordinates (0, 0), and coordinates are expressed in the form (X, Y). If your design is 800 pixels wide and 600 pixels high, the bottom-right corner has the coordinates (800, 600).

To move a slice when you know the exact pixel coordinates to which you want to move it, follow these steps:

1. **Select the slice by clicking it on the canvas or in the Layers panel.**

> The Property inspector changes to give you access to slice parameters.

2. **If you want to change the slice's horizontal position, type a numerical value in the Property inspector text field labeled X: and press Enter.**

> Your slice shifts left if you type in a lower number or right if you type in a higher number.

3. **If you want to change the slice's vertical position, type a numerical value in the Property inspector text field labeled Y: and press Enter.**

> Your slice shifts up if you type in a lower number or down if you type in a higher number.

Resizing a slice

Sometimes after you make a slice, you decide you need to resize the underlying image. After you resize the image, you want to resize the slice. You may also need to resize a slice if you draw the slice quickly and don't make it big enough. As with moving a slice, resizing a slice can be done by clicking and dragging or by typing new values.

To resize two dimensions of a slice at once using the click-and-drag method, follow these steps:

1. **Click a corner of the slice.**

> You must click a handle at one of the corners in order to resize the slice. If you click anywhere inside the slice (except the exact center) and drag, you move the slice instead of resizing it.

**Book III
Chapter 6**

**Slicing Up Content
for the Web**

2. **Drag the handle on the corner of the slice to the desired new location.**

If you only want to change the height, click and drag the top or bottom border of the slice. If you only want to change the width, click and drag the left or right border of the slice. Note that when your cursor is over the border, it changes into the Resize cursor, two parallel lines with an arrow pointing outward from each line, as shown in Figure 6-3.

Figure 6-3:
Dragging the right edge of a slice to make it wider. Note the Resize cursor.

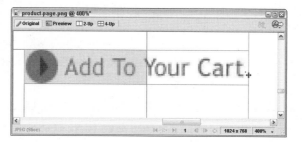

When you're creating slices, their edges snap to edges of already created slices, so you may find it difficult to get the edge of a slice where you want it. You can zoom in until you reach a magnification at which you can resize the slice so it doesn't snap to the edge of the other slice, or you can use the text fields in the Property inspector to change the selected slice's dimensions.

To resize a slice by typing new values, follow these steps:

1. **Select the slice by clicking it on the canvas or in the Layers panel.**

   The Property inspector changes to give you access to the slice's parameters.

2. **If you want to change the slice's width, type a new numerical value in the text field labeled W: and press Enter.**

   If you increase the width, you add pixels to the right side of the slice. If you decrease the width, you take pixels away from the right side of the slice.

3. **If you want to change the slice's height, type a new numerical value in the text field labeled H: and press Enter.**

   If you increase the height, you add pixels to the bottom of the slice. If you decrease the height, you take pixels away from the bottom of the slice.

Duplicating a slice

If you have a series of buttons, each of which is to be the same width and height, you can make one slice and duplicate it as many times as you need. Of course, you also need to move each duplicated slice to overlay a different button and name each slice according to the button it overlays. To duplicate a slice, just follow these steps:

1. **Select the slice by clicking it on the canvas or in the Layers panel.**

2. **Choose Edit⇨Duplicate or use the key command Ctrl+Alt+D.**

A duplicate slice appears on top of, but slightly offset from, the slice you duplicated.

If you clone the slice instead of duplicating it (Edit⇨Clone or Ctrl+Shift+D), the new slice appears directly on top of the old one.

You can also copy and paste a slice, though that's essentially the same as cloning, except that it takes an extra step!

3. **Move the slice to its proper location.**

See the "Moving a slice" section, earlier in this chapter, for instructions.

Optimizing Your Images for the Web

In order to understand the process of optimization, you need to know about image compression. When you compress an image, you reduce its file size by reducing the amount of data in the file. The two main types of image compression are

✦ **Lossy:** Some data is discarded from the image to make the file smaller.

✦ **Lossless:** The data in the image is described in a more efficient way, which makes the file smaller.

The two main compression methods used to format images for the Web are

✦ **JPEG:** A lossy method, best used for photographs, gradients, and other complex, variegated images.

✦ **GIF:** A generally lossless method, best used for images with large areas of flat color, like company logos. It also allows for images with transparent backgrounds.

Not sure which compression method to use for a particular slice? That's where the Preview panes come in. You can use a Preview pane any time you have slices. They show you what the image will look like at your chosen compression setting (or settings). See the section, "Previewing Slices," later in this chapter, for the details.

One way to deal with compression is to make a setting when you first make the slice and make the fine adjustments later. It doesn't really matter, though. You can just leave each slice at the default setting until you're ready to export.

Working with the options in the Optimize panel

By default, the Optimize panel resides at the top right of the Fireworks window. If it's not visible onscreen, choose Windows➪Optimize or press F6 to open it. Figure 6-4 shows the Optimize panel as it appears when it is expanded and a slice is selected.

Figure 6-4:
The Optimize panel with a default JPEG setting selected.

The top drop-down list displays a saved setting. A *saved setting* is a group of optimization options that includes the export file format and options appropriate to the selected export file format (read on to discover more about the main export file formats — JPEG and GIF — and the options specific to each).

Under the Saved Settings drop-down list is the Export File Format drop-down list. If you use a default setting from the Saved Settings drop-down list above, Fireworks automatically shows the file format in the lower list. Otherwise, you have to select the export file format. We only look at JPEGs and GIFs, because they are by far the most common Web formats, but the full list of file formats that Fireworks can export is noted in the sidebar, "Other export file types."

We discuss the options displayed in the Optimize panel in the following sections, "Making a JPEG" and "Making a GIF." The Options button (the bulleted list icon) at the top right of the Optimize panel provides access to the Options menu, which offers its own set of choices. The items in the Options menu vary, depending on the file type you have selected in the Export File Format drop-down list.

When you have JPEG selected, the Options menu offers the following:

✦ **Save Settings:** This option allows you to preserve your current compression setting as a preset, which you can then select from the Saved Settings drop-down list in the Optimize panel. Presets (custom or not) can be useful for *batch processing* images (automating the export of multiple images that use the same settings).

✦ **Delete Settings:** This option does what you would expect — it deletes your custom compression settings.

This option deletes *all* the settings.

✦ **Optimize to Size:** This handy option allows you to set a target file size for your slice. Fireworks then makes the appropriate compression settings to produce a file of your specified size.

✦ **Export Wizard:** The Export Wizard walks you through the steps of exporting an image with a series of dialog boxes.

✦ **Progressive JPEG:** If you have this option selected when you export a slice, your JPEG will contain two versions of your image. The first is a low-resolution version of the image that loads relatively quickly to a browser. The second, which fills in over the first, is a higher-resolution version. Although the time it takes for this type of image to become visible is shorter, the overall download time is longer.

If your JPEG needs to be large (in terms of width and height) *and* high-quality, you should consider exporting it as a progressive JPEG.

Macromedia Flash cannot dynamically import progressive JPEGs.

✦ **Sharpen JPEG Edges:** Select this option if image clarity is a priority (if, for example, you have small text in the image). Note that clarity makes for larger file sizes.

✦ **Show Swatch Feedback, Load Palette, Save Palette:** These options apply to 8-bit graphics (including GIFs; JPEGs are a 24-bit format). Custom palettes are sets of colors to which you can limit images. See your documentation for further details.

✦ **Help, Group Optimize With, Close Panel Group:** These options don't relate to JPEGs per se. See Book III, Chapter 1 for more information about general panel options.

When you have GIF selected from the Export File Format drop-down list, the Options menu makes some JPEG-specific options unavailable but offers the following GIF-specific (8-bit graphic specific) options:

✦ **Interlaced:** An interlaced GIF is similar to a progressive JPEG. A low-resolution version of the graphic loads first (and fast), and the image slowly transitions until it is at its maximum resolution. As with progressive JPEGs, the image loads faster initially, but the final version of the image doesn't load as quickly as it would if it weren't interlaced. (You can also export an interlaced PNG.)

✦ **Remove Unused Colors:** When this option is selected, as it is by default, Fireworks removes any color from the image's palette that isn't used by the image. Smaller palettes mean smaller file sizes.

Under the Optimize panel name is the Saved Settings drop-down list, which offers seven default settings (two for JPEGs and five for GIFs). You can choose between two default settings for JPEGs:

• **JPEG — Better Quality:** Makes a high-quality image, which results in a bigger file size and a longer download time.

• **JPEG — Smaller File:** Makes a small file, with a corresponding loss in image quality.

For information about the default GIF settings, see the section, "Making a GIF," later in this chapter.

The rest of the parameters in the Optimize panel vary based on what export file format you choose, so we discuss them in the following sections in the context of how to export JPEGs and GIFs.

Making a JPEG

Because JPEG is a lossy compression method, you will want a fair amount of control over just how much data gets discarded from your image. The higher the amount of compression, the lower the image quality — but also the smaller the file size and consequently the faster the download time. Fireworks gives you a few options so you can maximize image quality while minimizing file size.

Using the default JPEG settings

To use a default setting is easy. Just follow these steps:

1. **Select the slice by clicking it on the canvas or in the Layers panel.**

2. **Select either JPEG — Better Quality or JPEG — Smaller File from the Settings drop-down list in the Optimize panel.**

   The Image Type, Quality, and Smoothing drop-down lists update according to your chosen setting. You can further refine these settings if you like, as outlined in the following section.

Other export file types

Fireworks can export these other image types in addition to JPEGs and GIFs:

✔ **PNG:** The native file format for Fireworks is PNG. You should be aware that Fireworks stores extra information in PNGs that is not available to other applications opening the same file. PNGs can have transparent backgrounds and can be viewed in some browsers. PNG is a Macromedia Flash-friendly format.

✔ **WBMP:** A 2-bit format (black and white only) created especially for wireless devices, such as PDAs and cell phones.

✔ **TIFF:** This format is often used for print materials.

✔ **BMP:** Bitmap is the native image format for PCs.

Fireworks on the Macintosh can export an image in the Mac-native image format, PICT.

Using custom JPEG settings

To make or edit a custom JPEG setting, follow these steps:

1. **Select the slice by clicking it on the canvas or in the Layers panel.**

2. **Select JPEG from the Export File Format drop-down list in the Optimize panel.**

3. **Type a number in the Quality text field or use the slider (click the button next to the text field with the downward-pointing arrow to activate the slider) to set the image quality.**

   You can enter any whole number from 0 to 100, with 0 representing the lowest quality and 100 the highest.

   If part of your image needs to be a higher quality than the rest, follow the next set of instructions, which describe using the Selective Quality option.

4. **Set the smoothing, if necessary.**

   Smoothing blurs the image a little, reducing its quality but also reducing its file size. You can type or select any whole number from 1 through 8, with 1 representing the least blurring and 8 representing the most blurring. If you don't want smoothing, leave it at its default setting, 0.

The Selective Quality option in the Optimize panel allows you to compress different parts of your image by different amounts. In some cases, using Selective Quality can be a great alternative to cutting a photograph into different slices set at different compression levels.

Here's how to use the Selective Quality option:

1. **Click the Original button at the top left of the canvas if you are not already viewing the Original pane.**

2. **Use a Selection tool to select the area of the image that you want to compress differently than the rest of the image.**

   Make sure you're in the Original view, not in a Preview pane.

3. **Choose Modify➪Selective JPEG➪Save Selection as JPEG Mask.**

   Your JPEG mask shows up as a pink overlay.

4. **Select JPEG from the drop-down list in the Optimize panel, if it's not already selected.**

5. **Click the Selective Quality button (the pencil and paper) in the Optimize panel.**

   The Selective JPEG Settings dialog box, shown in Figure 6-5, appears.

Figure 6-5:
The Selective JPEG Settings dialog box offers a few simple options.

6. **Make sure the Enable Selective Quality check box is selected in the Selective JPEG Settings dialog box (it is checked by default).**

7. **Type a number from 0 to 100 in the text field.**

   Zero represents the lowest quality; 100 represents the highest quality. This number should, of course, be different from the number in the Quality field discussed previously.

8. **Change the overlay color if you don't like the default overlay color.**

   The overlay color does not affect the exported image.

9. **Select the Preserve Text Quality check box if you want to preserve the quality of any text within your selection, regardless of the overall compression settings.**

This is a handy shortcut that you can use with or without a JPEG mask.

10. **Select the Preserve Button Quality check box if you want to preserve the quality of any buttons within your selection, regardless of the overall compression settings.**

11. **Click OK or press Enter.**

Making a GIF

Okay, when we said the GIF compression method is generally lossless, we meant this: You can make lossless GIFs, but you can also make lossy GIFs if you need to. GIFs compress image data in a couple of ways:

✦ **By keeping track of the data more efficiently:** GIFs group adjacent pixels of the same color in each row of the image so the pixels can be described as a group instead of as individual pixels. The fewer colors you have in each row, and the more pixels of the same color are together in a line, the better GIF compression works.

✦ **By limiting the number of colors in an image:** You can create custom palettes (sets of colors) or use the specialized built-in palettes that Fireworks offers. If you compress your image with a palette that doesn't contain all the colors in the image, Fireworks substitutes colors from the palette, effectively reducing the number of colors in the GIF as compared to the source image.

Sometimes you can simulate the appearance of the lost color by dithering two colors from the palette. The section on Web safe colors in Book III, Chapter 2 has more about dithering.

Using the default GIF settings

Fireworks offers several default Saved Settings for GIFs (available from the Saved Settings drop-down list at the top of the Optimize panel):

✦ **GIF Web 216:** This setting limits the colors in your GIF to the basic Web safe palette.

✦ **GIF Web Snap 256:** This setting limits the number of colors in your GIF to 256, while snapping any colors close in appearance to Web safe colors to the Web safe palette.

✦ **GIF Web Snap 128:** This setting limits the colors in your GIF to 128, while snapping any colors close in appearance to Web safe colors to the Web safe palette.

✦ **GIF Adaptive 256:** This setting limits the colors in your GIF to the 256 most common in the GIF. Other colors are changed to the closest color in the palette. This setting will give you the highest fidelity GIF version of your image.

✦ **Animated GIF Web Snap 128:** This setting is the same as GIF Web Snap 128, but for animated GIFs.

Using custom GIF settings

To make a basic GIF that doesn't use a Fireworks default setting, just follow these steps:

1. **Select a slice by clicking it on the canvas or in the Layers panel.**

2. **Select GIF from the Export File Format drop-down list in the Optimize panel, which is shown in Figure 6-6.**

The Optimize panel, shown in Figure 6-6, displays the setting for a top navigation button. Note that transparency appears as a checkerboard pattern in the palette. Note also that because this is a custom setting, the Saved Settings field is blank.

Figure 6-6: A button's settings in the Optimize panel.

3. **Set the compression mode by selecting one from the Indexed Palette drop-down list (right below the Export File Format drop-down list).**

Palettes are sets of colors. For GIFs, the palettes may contain no more than 256 colors. For Web images, choose from the top four:

- Adaptive
- Web Adaptive
- Web 216
- Exact

For more information about these palettes, see the Fireworks Help files.

4. **Type a number in the Colors text field or use the drop-down list to set the number of colors in your palette, if you're not compressing using the Web 216 or Exact settings.**

   The fewer colors you have in your palette, the smaller the file size of your image. If you have fewer colors in the palette than in your image, however, Fireworks must substitute colors, deteriorating image quality. If your image has more than 256 colors, you may get better results using a JPEG setting.

5. **If there are more colors in your image than in your palette, and if you prefer dithering to straight one-for-one color substitutions, type a percent in the Dither text field or use the slider (click the button next to the text field with the downward-pointing arrow to activate the slider) to set a percentage from 1 to 96.**

   The more you dither, the fewer colors you need in your palette. Unfortunately, dithering can look bad up close and increases the file size.

Making a transparent GIF

To make a GIF with transparent areas, which allows the HTML page background color or background image to show through, follow these steps:

1. **Select a slice by clicking it on the canvas or in the Layers panel.**

2. **Select GIF from the Export File Format drop-down list in the Optimize panel, if GIF is not already selected.**

3. **Select Index Transparency from the Transparency drop-down list.**

   The default is No Transparency. Even when you don't have a background in your PNG file, you still need to select Index Transparency to make a GIF with transparent pixels.

4. **Click the eyedropper button with the equal sign (=) to select a color in the palette or on the canvas that you want to make transparent.**

   The three transparency eyedropper buttons are at the bottom left of the Optimize panel. The selected color becomes transparent in the palette in the Optimize panel. If you're viewing a Preview pane, the transparency will appear (or disappear, as it were) on the canvas.

5. **Use the eyedropper with the plus sign (+) to select additional colors to make transparent, if desired.**

   You can use the eyedropper with the minus sign (–) to restore opacity to a color that has been made transparent, if necessary.

Previewing Slices

You can optimize your slices as you make them, or you can make all your slices first and then optimize them all at once. Either way, if you're having trouble deciding on the best method or amount of compression to use on a slice, you can use one of the three Preview panes to help you make an informed decision. Just click one of the following buttons at the top of the canvas:

+ **Preview:** This view shows a single version of your canvas, where you can see what your slices will look like and how big their files sizes will be at your current compression settings. Click a slice to preview it.

+ **2-Up:** This view puts two versions of your canvas side-by-side, so you can compare the original image with a compressed version of the image, or you can compare two compressed versions to each other. Click a slice on either side to preview it on both sides.

+ **4-Up:** This view divides the work area into quadrants, so you can compare three compression settings at once to the original image. Click a slice in any quadrant to preview the settings in all quadrants.

In the Preview panes, slices that are not currently selected look slightly pale, as if viewed through a fogged-up window. Selected slices look as they will when exported, given their current settings (including transparencies, which appear as checkerboards), as shown in Figure 6-7.

Figure 6-7: The checker-board behind the Bowling Balls button indicates the slice's back-ground is transparent.

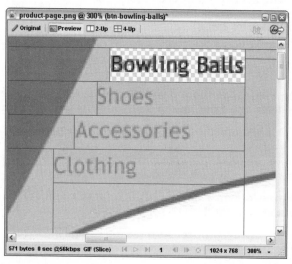

The Preview pane

You can select the Preview pane by clicking the Preview button at the top left of the image's window, right above the canvas.

The Preview pane previews more than just the appearance of your image; it also shows you the image's projected file size *and* the amount of time it would take for a file that size to download at a particular download speed. (The default is 56 Kbps, or the approximate speed of a dial-up modem.)

In Figure 6-7, you can see the file size, export file format and download time stats at the bottom left, below the canvas. Because a 56 Kbps modem can download at a rate of 5K per second, and this image is a little over 0.5K, the download time shows as 0 sec (less than 1 second).

When you change the settings in the Optimize panel, the size and download time information at the bottom of the Preview pane update automatically. The Optimize panel works the same way, whether you're looking at a Preview pane or the default Original pane.

The 2-Up view

You can select the 2-Up view simply by clicking the 2-Up button at the top left of the image's window, above the canvas.

The 2-Up view sets two versions of the canvas side by side. At the bottom of each pane is an indicator of which view is in the pane and some of its vital statistics. In Figure 6-8, the pane on the right shows what the image would look like as a JPEG with the settings as shown at the bottom of the pane, and the pane on the left shows what the image would look like if exported as a GIF with the settings as shown at the bottom of the pane.

You can click in either pane to select the slice, and then adjust its settings in the Optimize panel. You can set the magnification of both panes several ways:

✦ You can use the Magnifying tool in the View section of the Tools panel.

✦ You can choose Zoom In, Zoom Out, or a preset Magnification setting from the View menu.

✦ You can select a zoom setting from the drop-down list at the bottom-right of the window.

To toggle between an optimized setting and the original image, click the indented button at the left just below the canvas. A pop-up menu allows you to select Original (No Preview) or Export Preview.

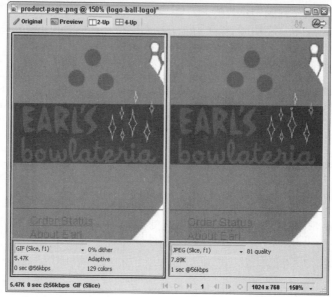

Figure 6-8:
Comparing two possible compression settings side by side in the 2-Up view.

You can use the Hand tool from the View section of the Tools panel to move the canvas (select the Hand tool and then click and drag on the canvas), or just hold down the Space bar while you click and drag (whatever tool you're using becomes the Hand tool automatically). When you move the canvas in one pane, the canvas also moves in the other pane.

To select a different slice than the one currently selected, click the Pointer tool from the Tools panel, and then click a slice in either pane or in the Layers panel. The slice becomes active in both panes simultaneously.

The 4-Up view

You can select the 4-Up view by clicking the 4-Up button at the top left above the canvas. When you first open the 4-Up view, the top-left quadrant displays the Original view, and the other three panes have identical compression settings. To change the settings in one pane, click in the pane to select it, and then change its settings in the Optimize panel. In fact, the concept, properties, and processes of using the 4-Up view are identical to those of the 2-Up view; you just get two extra panes.

Figure 6-9 shows the 4-Up view. Comparing the three compression settings, it seems the one that best balances visual quality with file size is the GIF pane at the bottom right.

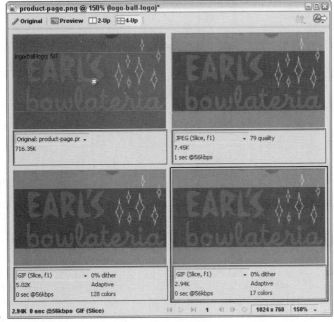

Figure 6-9:
Comparing three possible compression settings using the 4-Up view.

Relating Hotspots and Slices

Slices can only be rectangular, which is fine if your buttons are rectangular. But what if you want to create non-rectangular HTML links to other Web pages? You have two choices:

✦ **Use the Polygon Slice tool to make a polygonal slice.** This works best if the area that you want to use as a hyperlink is fairly isolated from other slices. See Book III, Chapter 5 for details.

✦ **Use a Hotspot tool to draw hotspots on an image.** Fireworks will create the underlying image plus what is known as an *image map*. An image map is some HTML code representing coordinates for hyperlinked polygonal hotspots. *Hotspots* are areas on an image that have been coded to respond to user actions.

Typically, the hotspots are hyperlinked to Web pages. In Figure 6-10, the bowling ball could be linked to a page about bowling balls, while the pin could be linked to a page with a list of bowling alleys. Hotspots are great, but use them sparingly so you don't add too much code to your HTML or tax the user's processor with too many instructions.

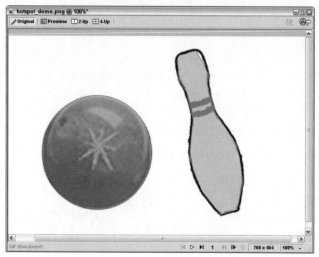

Figure 6-10: The Circle Hotspot tool works best for a bowling ball, and the Polygon Hotspot tool works best for the pin.

If that all sounds too technical, don't worry. You don't need to know all the ins and outs of HTML to make an image map — Fireworks takes care of that for you. All you have to do is create hotspots in the shapes you want, and export HTML with your images. See Book III, Chapter 7 for details.

Exporting Images

You can export images in two ways: one by one or all at once. You can have Fireworks generate HTML at the same time as you export your images, or you can export the images only and write the code yourself in Dreamweaver. (The code Fireworks generates is less efficient and more difficult to edit than code you would write in Dreamweaver.)

Exporting a single image

To export a single image, follow these steps:

1. **Right-click a slice and select Export Selected Slice from the contextual menu.**

   An Export dialog box appears, with default values set for exporting a single image.

2. **Navigate to the folder into which you want to put your image.**

3. **Leave the Save as Type setting at the default, Images Only.**

4. **If necessary, rename the image.**

5. **Leave the Slices setting at the default, Export Slices.**

6. **Leave the Selected Slices Only and Current Frame Only check boxes selected.**

7. **Click the Save button.**

Exporting multiple image slices

To export all the image slices in a PNG file at once, if you plan to write the HTML yourself, follow these steps:

1. **Choose File⇨Export or use the key command Ctrl+Shift+R.**

   The Export dialog box appears, with default values set for exporting multiple images and HTML, as shown in Figure 6-11.

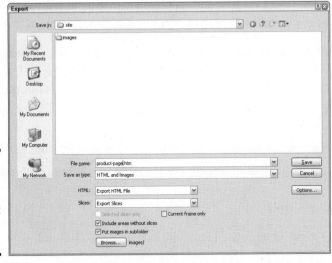

Figure 6-11: The Export dialog box set to export HTML and images.

Book III Chapter 6

Slicing Up Content for the Web

2. **Select Images Only from the Save as Type drop-down list.**

   The options below the Save as Type drop-down list update to reflect your selection.

3. **Leave the Slices setting at the default, Export Slices.**

4. **Deselect the Include Areas without Slices check box if you need only the sliced images to build your HMTL page.**

5. **If you have rollover images that you want to export, make sure that the Current Frame Only check box is deselected.**

   Remember, it takes multiple frames to make rollover images.

6. **Click the Save button.**

Exporting an animated GIF

When you export an animated GIF, you'll notice that beyond the default Images Only option in the Save as Type drop-down list, there's also a Macromedia Flash SWF option. Although that option does allow you to make some additional settings, chances are that if the ultimate format of the animation is to be an SWF file instead of a GIF file, you would be better off opening the PNG file in Macromedia Flash and exporting from there. Why? Because Macromedia Flash offers more powerful authoring and editing tools, many more export parameters than Fireworks, and ActionScript for adding complex interactivity to your animation.

To export an animation as an animated GIF (not a Flash SWF movie), follow these simple steps:

1. **Make sure you have selected Animated GIF in the Optimize panel's Export File Format drop-down list.**

2. **Choose File➪Export or use the key command Ctrl+Shift+R.**

   The Export dialog box appears, with default values set for exporting animated GIFs.

3. **Navigate to the folder into which you would like the GIF to go.**

4. **Leave the default Images Only setting in the Save as Type drop-down list.**

5. **Click Save.**

There's lots more to the Export function than we've outlined in this section. For information on exporting HTML and other export options, see the section about advanced export functions in Book III, Chapter 7.

Chapter 7: Advanced Fireworks MX 2004 Tools

In This Chapter

✔ **Using advanced export options**

✔ **Creating image maps and advanced button rollovers**

✔ **Making your pages interactive with behaviors**

F ireworks MX 2004, like all the applications in the Macromedia Studio MX 2004 suite, is deep and rich. In this chapter, we introduce some of the application's more advanced capabilities, such as the following:

✦ **Exporting HTML code with JavaScript.** (*JavaScript* is a coding language that you can use to make elements of your Web page change based on user feedback, among other things.) If you have added behaviors to your Fireworks PNG, you've added JavaScript to the HTML that Fireworks will generate.

✦ **Creating image maps with hotspots.**

✦ **Setting up button behaviors that go beyond simple rollovers.** (See Book III, Chapter 5 for instructions on how to create simple button rollovers.)

✦ **Using the Image Swap behavior to make an image on your Web page change when the user rolls over a separate image.**

Using Advanced Export Options

In Book III, Chapter 6, we describe how to export images, but not how to export HTML or other types of files. If you're designing a Web page and you have behaviors or hotspots in your Fireworks PNG file, you will want to export HTML along with your images, because the HTML and JavaScript code make hotspots and behaviors work in Web pages.

The first step in exporting any type of file from Fireworks is to choose File⇨Export or press Ctrl+Shift+R to bring up the Export dialog box, shown in Figure 7-1. The Save as Type drop-down list in the Export dialog box offers access to an array of extra options:

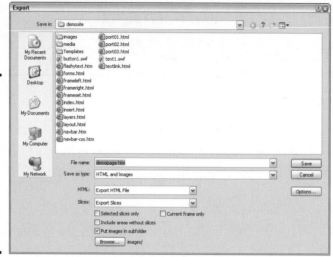

Figure 7-1:
The Export dialog box offers different options, depending on which Save as Type option you choose.

✦ **HTML and Images:** Exports HTML (or other Web language) code as well as images.

✦ **Images Only:** Exports images at your chosen optimization settings.

✦ **Dreamweaver Library (.lbi):** Exports Library items as well as images. (*Library items* are snippets of HTML code you can use in Dreamweaver to make site maintenance easier.)

✦ **CSS Layers (.htm):** Allows you to export layers, frames, or slices as Cascading Style Sheet layers, so Fireworks generates both images and CSS-based HTML code, placing each layer, frame, or slice in its own CSS layer (for information about working with CSS layers in Dreamweaver, see Book II, Chapter 5).

✦ **Director (.htm):** Exports either layers or frames as images that can be imported into Macromedia Director MX for use in Shockwave movies. (Director is not part of the Macromedia Studio suite.)

✦ **Layers to Files:** Exports each layer in the current frame as a separate image file, which can be useful if you're planning to use the layers to build an animation in another application.

✦ **Frames to Files:** Exports each frame as a separate image file, which can be useful if you're planning to use the frames to build an animation in another application.

✦ **Lotus Domino Designer:** Exports either the top four layers, the top four frames, or the first four frames of each slice as separate files. Domino is an IBM Web application server/collaboration tool.

+ **Macromedia Flash SWF:** Exports an SWF file, which can be viewed via the Flash browser plug-in and imported into Macromedia Flash. Macromedia Flash is a much more flexible authoring tool for SWFs.

+ **Illustrator 7:** Exports either the current frame, leaving layers intact, or exports a document in which frames have been converted to layers. Illustrator is a design program from Adobe (the company that also makes Photoshop).

+ **Photoshop PSD:** Exports the PNG as a layered Photoshop document (PSD). You can choose to maintain editability of text layers and effects, which may result in variations in appearance between the two files, or to maintain the appearance by giving up editability of text and effects. Remember, your PNG's Web layer won't be exported.

Although you may want to export any of these types of files, in this section we focus on the HTML and Images option, which is the one that you're likely to use most often.

Readying your PNG for HTML export

If you're using Fireworks to generate your HTML code, chances are you have buttons in your design that you want linked to other pages on your site. Or perhaps you have one or more hotspots in your PNG, and you want those hotspots to link to other pages on your Web site. Naturally, Fireworks makes it easy for you to add URLs to create the hyperlinks for buttons and hotspots. All you need to do is plan ahead: You should have HTML document names for all the pages to which you want to link from your current page.

To add a URL to an existing slice or hotspot in the document's Web layer (see Book III, Chapter 6 for information on creating slices), just follow these steps:

1. **Select the slice or hotspot by clicking it on the canvas or in the Layers panel (if necessary, open the Layers panel by pressing F2 and/or expand the panel by clicking the panel name).**

The Property inspector is updated to show information about the selected slice or hotspot.

2. **Click in the Link text field in the Property inspector.**

If you have added links to other slices or other hotspots, those links appear as drop-down list choices in the Link text field.

3. **Type a URL.**

If you are linking to a page on your own site and all your HTML pages are in the same folder, simply type the name of the HTML document (for example, `index.htm` or `help.htm`). You must type the name of the document exactly as it appears. (If you type `index.htm` but your home page is actually `index.html`, the link will not work.)

If you are linking to a page not on your site, include the complete URL (such as `http://catalog.dummies.com/booksanddownloads.asp`).

4. **Press Enter or click anywhere on the canvas.**

Exporting HTML with your images

If you want, you can tell Fireworks to generate the HTML along with the optimized images for your Web page and let that be the end of it. If you plan to make any changes to the HTML in Dreamweaver or another HTML editor, however, you can set some options to control the way Fireworks sets up tables in the HTML it generates, which can make your Web page maintenance a little easier down the line.

To export HTML and images that you plan not to update, or that you plan to update in Fireworks rather than Dreamweaver, follow these steps:

1. **Set up a folder structure for your Web site on your hard drive.**

   You should have a master folder that holds every file for your site. Inside the master folder, you may wish to put an `images` folder, which can hold all your images, keeping them separate from the HTML documents. You can have your HTML documents and image files all mixed together in the master folder, but if you have lots of images, you'll find the image files easier to locate and work with if you create a separate folder for them.

2. **Check to make sure all the right layers are visible (or not visible) in your PNG file.**

   Remember, only visible layers and objects are included in the exported image files.

3. **In Fireworks, choose File⇨Export or press Ctrl+Shift+R.**

   The Export dialog box appears.

4. **Navigate to the Web site's master folder.**

   If you haven't created a master folder for your Web site, you can create a folder by clicking the standard Windows Create New Folder icon to the right of the Save In drop-down list.

5. **Type a name for your page in the File Name text field if the default is not what you want your HTML page to be named.**

   The default HTML file extension in the Macromedia Studio suite is `.htm`, but `.html` is also acceptable.

6. **Select HTML and Images from the Save as Type drop-down list.**

The options below this drop-down list update to reflect your choice.

7. **Select Export HTML File from the HTML drop-down list.**

If you select Copy to Clipboard instead of Exporting HTML File, Fireworks exports the code to a temporary location (your computer's Clipboard), from which the code can be pasted into an existing document. If you select Copy to Clipboard, you can simply open any type of text document and press Ctrl+V to paste the HTML into the file.

Export HTML File has myriad options available. See the upcoming section, "Setting the export HTML file options," for more information.

8. **Select Export Slices from the Slices drop-down list.**

If you haven't made slices in your PNG file but you have placed guides in the file, you can select the Slice Along Guides option, and Fireworks cuts up your design based on the guides.

9. **Leave the Current Frame Only check box deselected unless you have multiple frames in your document, at least one of which you do not want to export.**

10. **Leave the Include Areas without Slices option selected unless you have a plan to deal with areas you didn't slice.**

If you're using a background image, for example, or you want to use transparent spacer GIFs, you may not need images from the nonsliced areas — if there are any.

11. **Select the Put Images in Subfolder check box if you want your images to be exported to a folder inside your site's master folder.**

It's important to decide when you export where your images are going to live, because your HTML document will include links to the images. The links will be expressed as pathnames to the images relative to the location of the HTML document.

12. **Click the Save button.**

The HTML file is saved to your site's master folder, and the images are saved either to that same folder or to a folder within that folder, as specified in Step 11.

Setting the export HTML file options

When you click the Options button in the Export dialog box, the HTML Setup dialog box opens, as shown in Figure 7-2. In the HTML Setup dialog box, you can view and modify the default settings that determine the structure of the exported HTML document.

Book III
Chapter 7

Advanced
Fireworks MX
2004 Tools

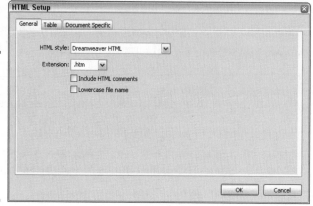

Figure 7-2:
The HTML
Setup dialog
box opens
when you
click
Options in
the Export
dialog box.

You can access settings on the three tabs in the HTML Setup dialog box:

✦ **General:** Allows you to change the default HTML style — different HTML editors have different styles of writing and displaying the code — and file extension. With Fireworks MX 2004, the different kinds of code include CFML, ASP, and more. You can also choose whether or not Fireworks should put comments in the HTML document. (*Comments* are notes in the HTML source code that typically contain information about the structure of the code, such as `<!- Left navigation starts here ->`. Comments are not displayed by the browser. If you want to be able to launch and edit entire tables from Dreamweaver, be sure you've selected the Include HTML Comments check box.) Select the Lowercase File Name check box if you want to make the names of the HTML file and all exported images all lowercase, even if you might have named images with uppercase and lowercase letters in your PNG.

✦ **Table:** Allows you to customize the way Fireworks sets up tables. The default is that Fireworks puts a one-pixel high spacer row at the top and a one-pixel wide spacer column on the right to hold the design in place. You can choose to have Fireworks nest tables (put one table inside another) instead. You can also tell Fireworks to recreate parts of your design that lack objects as cells with background-transparent spacer GIFs in the HTML, to leave the cell empty, or put in a non-breaking space. A spacer GIF is a one-pixel by one-pixel transparent image that you can set to any height and width in your HTML to hold open an otherwise empty table cell.

✦ **Document Specific:** Allows you to customize image naming based on table structure and/or image function. For example, for slices with multiple frames, Fireworks appends _f2, _f3, and so on, to the filename. If the images from Frame 2 of your PNG are buttons in their rollover state, you may prefer to have Fireworks append -o or -over to the filename. If you want all images to have identical Alt tags, enter the desired word or phrase in the Default ALT tag text field. If your PNG file contains a Nav Bar Image (see the "Creating advanced button rollovers" section, later in this chapter), you can select the Export Multiple Nav Bar HTML Files check box if you want Fireworks to generate separate HTML files for each button in the navigation bar. The Include Areas without Slice Objects check box is selected by default; leave it selected for most consistent results. Select the UTF-8 Encoding check box if you want to use multiple character sets (Hebrew and English, for example) in your HTML.

The Set Defaults button on the Document Specific tab allows you to save any new settings you make, which is particularly useful if you like to use a specific naming convention for button rollovers and on states. When you adjust the Document Specific settings to your liking and click the Set Defaults button, your adjusted settings become the new default Document Specific settings.

Setting Up Image Maps and Button Rollovers

Fireworks writes image maps and JavaScript into the HTML code you export, provided that you have hotspots (which Fireworks uses to make image maps) or behaviors (which Fireworks uses to make JavaScript) in your PNG. The following two sections outline how to set up image maps (which allow you to make several distinct hyperlinks from a single image) and complex button behaviors (which make the button image change based on a user action like rolling the mouse over the image or clicking the image).

Fireworks can show slices and hotspots overlapping, but you should be careful not to overlap either. Fireworks will not export any part of a slice that's under another slice. (The slice on top includes the overlapped area; the slice underneath is cut off.) Likewise, whichever hotspot is on top in the Layers panel overrides the hotspot underneath.

Creating image maps with hotspots

The three hotspot tools allow you to create hotspots shaped like rectangles, circles, or polygons. You can also use the Polygon Slice tool to create a hotspot, though as a rule you should use the hotspot tools unless you are making a single, isolated hotspot. (For more information on the Polygon Slice tool, see Book III, Chapter 6.)

To create a circular or rectangular hotspot using a hotspot tool, just follow these steps:

1. **Select a hotspot tool from the Web section of the Tools panel.**

Click and hold on the Rectangle Hotspot tool to access the pop-up menu containing the Circle Hotspot tool, if necessary.

2. **Click and drag over the area you want to become a hotspot.**

3. **Type a URL in the Link text field in the Property inspector and press Enter.**

   You can add URLs as you make the hotspots, or you can create all of your hotspots and then select each one and add a URL in the Property inspector.

4. **Make more hotspots as needed.**

When you create hotspots using the Polygon Slice tool, you're actually making rectangular images with linked areas inside. As a result, Fireworks makes a separate image map for each slice. That's fine if you're only making one polygonal slice, but if you're making several adjacent hotspots, you're better off using the Polygon Hotspot tool or making your image map in Dreamweaver. (See Book III, Chapter 6 for information about how to use the Polygon Slice tool.)

Making a polygonal hotspot is only a little bit more involved than making a rectangular or circular hotspot. To make a polygonal hotspot, just follow these steps:

1. **Select the Polygon Hotspot tool from the Web section of the Tools panel.**

   Click and hold on the Rectangle Hotspot tool to access the pop-up menu containing the Polygon Hotspot tool.

2. **Click on the canvas to establish the first point of your polygon.**

3. **Click on a second point.**

   Fireworks draws a line connecting the points.

4. **Continue to click until you have drawn the shape you want.**

   You don't need to click again on the first point to close the shape. Be aware that the more points you make, the more code is required to reproduce your hotspot as an image map, so you may want to avoid making hotspots that have more than six or seven points. Note how the polygonal hotspot for the bowling pin in Figure 7-3 sacrifices perfect coverage of the pin to make a simpler shape, which means less code.

5. **Type a URL in the Link text field in the Property inspector and press Enter.**

   You can add URLs as you make the hotspots, or you can create all of your hotspots and then select each one and add a URL in the Property inspector.

6. **Click the Polygon hotspot tool and then deselect the last hotspot you made by using the key command Ctrl+D or choosing Select↔Deselect.**

   Deselecting ensures that you won't inadvertently add an extra point to your Polygon hotspot.

When it comes time to export your images, you need to export HTML as well as images in order to get the image map that Fireworks makes from your hotspots. See the "Exporting HTML with your images" section, earlier in this chapter, for more details.

Dreamweaver has its own tool for creating hotspots and image maps. You can also use that tool to edit hotspots and image maps generated by Fireworks. See Book II, Chapter 7 for more details.

Creating advanced button rollovers

In Book III, Chapter 5, we discuss how to use frames in conjunction with text and drawing tools to make the images (one per frame for each button) for a simple button rollover, which provides all the information you need if you plan to use Dreamweaver to generate the rollover code.

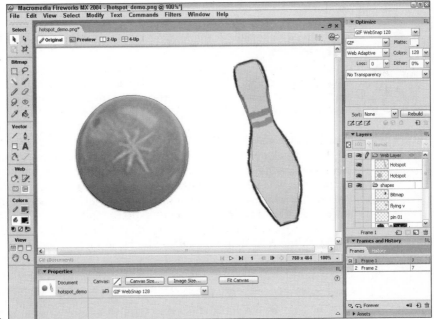

Figure 7-3: The Circle Hotspot tool is the obvious choice for the bowling ball; the Polygon Hotspot tool works best for the pin.

If you want to export the rollover code for a two-state button (normal and rollover/highlight) from Fireworks, you need to add a behavior to the slice by taking these steps:

1. **Right-click the slice for which you want to create rollover code, or select the slice and click the behavior handle (the round icon) in the center of the selected slice.**

A contextual menu appears.

2. **Choose Add Simple Rollover.**

A second way to add rollover behavior to a button is to use the Behavior panel:

1. **If the Behavior panel is not currently open, choose Window⇨ Behaviors or use the keyboard shortcut Shift+F3.**

2. **Click the Add Behavior (+) button at the top left of the Behaviors panel.**

A menu appears.

3. **Choose Simple Rollover from the menu.**

You have set up a behavior that swaps the image in Frame 1 with the image in Frame 2 when a user rolls a cursor over the button on your Web page. The behavior also swaps the image back when the user moves the cursor off the button.

 If you want to check out your rollover in action without building your Web page, click the Preview button at the top of the canvas and move your cursor over the slice.

Your button can have up to four states. Fireworks uses the image in Frame 1 for the normal, default state, Frame 2 for the Rollover state, Frame 3 for the Down state, and Frame 4 for the Over While Down state. If you want to include a down state for your button, and you have a third frame in your PNG with the image for an additional button state, follow the preceding steps to add a rollover state, and then do the following:

1. **Click the Add Behavior button at the top left of the Behaviors panel.**

A menu appears.

2. **Choose Set Nav Bar Image from the menu.**

The Set Nav Bar Image dialog box appears.

3. **Click OK.**

Now, when a user clicks the button in your exported HMTL, the button will change from the rollover state to the down state.

Figure 7-4 shows what the Behaviors panel looks like after you add the Simple Rollover and Set Nav Bar Image behaviors. You can use the add behavior (+) button to add a behavior and use the minus (–) button to remove a behavior from a slice.

Figure 7-4:
The
Behaviors
panel
shows
the actions
assigned
to a slice.

If the three-state button is linking to another page, adding a down state doesn't give you much bang for your buck because the linked page may appear in the browser window before the user even has a chance to notice that the button changed.

You may want to include an over-while-down state for your button (sort of an extra rollover) if you are using the down state of the button to indicate the current page. If so, make sure you have a fourth frame with the image for an extra button state, add the Rollover and Set Nav Bar Image behaviors as discussed previously, and then do the following:

1. **Double-click the Set Nav Bar Image line in the Behaviors panel.**

The Set Nav Bar Image dialog box appears.

2. **Select the Include Over While Down State (Frame 4) check box.**

If the button is for the current page, select the Show Down Image upon Load check box as well.

3. **Click OK.**

Remember to select the Export Multiple Nav Bar HTML Files check box on the Document Specific tab of the HTML Setup dialog box if you want Fireworks to generate separate HTML files for each button in the nav bar (see the "Setting the export HTML file options" section, earlier in this chapter, for more information).

Bringing Interactivity to Your Pages with Behaviors

Fireworks can generate JavaScript that does more than merely change the state of a button. For instance, you can set a behavior that swaps one image for another image elsewhere on the page when you roll over a button or hotspot. You can also use Fireworks to generate pop-up menus.

The Swap Images behavior

A button rollover is an image swap — you swap the image for one button state with the image for another state. But you can roll over a button and have a different image on the page swap. For example, you could set up a rollover behavior for two or more buttons to show different color choices for a product, so that when the user rolls over a button for color choices, the image of the product changes to show the appropriately colored version. If you want the image swap and page download to be pretty quick, you should limit the number of images to be swapped and limit the file size of each swapped image.

To add the Swap Image behavior to a trigger slice and target slice, create the frames, images, and slices, and then follow these steps:

1. **Click the slice that you want to use to trigger the image swap.**

You can click the slice either on the canvas or in the Layers panel.

2. **Click the Add Behavior (+) button at the top left of the Behaviors panel (if the Behaviors panel isn't visible, press Shift+F3 on your keyboard).**

A menu appears.

3. **Choose Swap Image.**

The Swap Image dialog box, shown in Figure 7-5, appears.

4. **Select the targeted slice by clicking its name (in the box on the left) or by clicking its representation (in the box on the right).**

When you click in either box, both boxes update to show your selection.

5. **Using the Frame No. drop-down list, select the frame number the rollover should trigger.**

The drop-down list shows all the frames in your PNG file.

You can also select the Image File radio button and navigate to an existing image file outside your PNG to swap in. Be aware, though, that for the rollover to work correctly in all browsers, the default target image and swapped target image must be the same height and width.

Figure 7-5:
The Swap
Image
dialog box
allows you
to choose
the
swapped
image by
name or
position on
the page.

6. **Leave the Preload Images and the Restore Image onMouseOut check boxes selected.**

Preloading the swapped image ensures there won't be a delay the first time the user rolls over the button that triggers the swap. The trade-off is that the Web page takes longer to load initially.

Restoring the image to default prevents the swapped image from "sticking." If you want the swapped image to remain in place until the user rolls over another button, deselect the Restore Image onMouseOut check box.

7. **Click OK.**

A line on the canvas from the center of the trigger slice to the target slice shows that one slice triggers a behavior in the other, as shown in Figure 7-6.

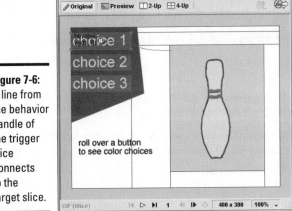

Figure 7-6:
A line from
the behavior
handle of
the trigger
slice
connects
to the
target slice.

**Book III
Chapter 7**

**Advanced
Fireworks MX
2004 Tools**

You can have multiple buttons trigger a rollover in the same slice, and you can have a single button trigger rollovers in multiple slices. Of course, the more big rollovers you have on the page, the longer the page takes to load. On the other hand, rollovers provide useful feedback (and instant gratification) to the user, and Fireworks makes producing them a snap.

Generating pop-up menus

Pop-up menus are a great way to cram a lot of navigation into a small space because they only appear when a user rolls over a button or hotspot. Fireworks allows you to specify many of the parameters of the menus' appearance. To start with, you can choose whether the links in your pop-up menus are made of text or images. In a nutshell, that choice boils down to this:

✦ **Linked text:** This option ensures faster download but less control over the appearance of the text, because the text is HMTL.

✦ **Linked images:** This option makes for a slower download but gives you more control over the appearance of the text, because the text is graphic.

You can also customize the position of the menu relative to the slice that triggers it, the color of the text and cell background for both normal and rollover states, and more. In fact, there are so many options, we can't cover them all here! After you've got the basics, though, you'll be poised to explore all the options, if you so desire.

To make a basic one-level pop-up menu with linked text, follow these steps:

1. **Select a slice by clicking it on the canvas or in the Layers panel (if necessary, open the Layers panel by pressing F2 and/or expand the panel by clicking the panel name).**

2. **Click the Add Behavior (+) button at the top left of the Behaviors panel (if the Behaviors panel is not visible, press Shift+F3).**

A pop-up menu appears.

3. **Choose Set Pop-up Menu from the Add Behaviors pop-up menu.**

The Pop-up Menu Editor, shown in Figure 7-7, appears, with the Content tab active by default.

4. **Click under the Text column of the Pop-up Menu Editor and type the text as you would like it to appear in your menu.**

5. **Press Tab or click under the Link column of the Pop-up Menu Editor and type or select the URL or filename for the page you want your text to link to.**

If you have any existing links already on your page, they appear in a drop-down list in the Link column.

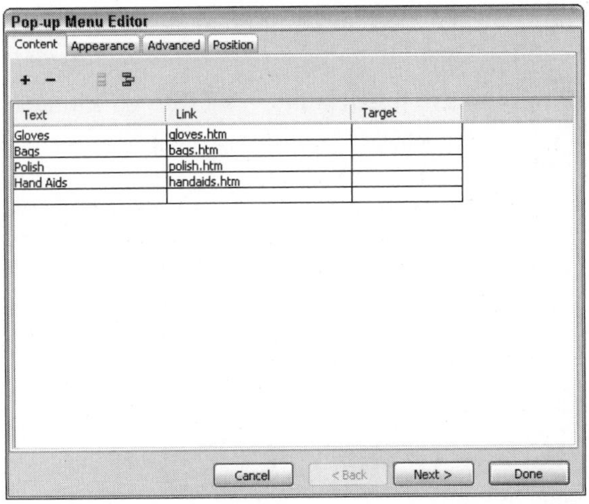

Figure 7-7:
The Content tab of the Pop-up Menu Editor, with a few items added.

6. **If you want the link to open in a new window or different frameset, tab over to or click in the Target column to set the target for the link.**

If you simply want the linked page to open in the user's current browser window, leave this column blank, as shown in Figure 7-7. For information on other Target options, see the discussion of links in Book II, Chapter 2, or the discussion of framesets in Book II, Chapter 6.

7. **Repeat Steps 4 through 6 for each item in your menu.**

You can add rows to the list of menu items by clicking the Add Menu button (the plus sign at the top left), or by pressing the Tab key until a text field appears in the Text column.

8. **Click the Next button at the bottom of the Pop-up Menu Editor.**

The Appearance tab becomes active.

9. **For the Cells option, make sure the HTML radio button (the default selection) is selected.**

If you want to use images instead of HTML text, you need to select the Image radio button. Each navigation item is in its own table cell.

10. **Select Vertical Menu or Horizontal Menu from the drop-down list.**

**Book III
Chapter 7**

**Advanced
Fireworks MX
2004 Tools**

11. **Select the Font face, size, style, and alignment.**

Of course, this isn't necessary if you're using graphics rather than HTML text.

12. **Using the appropriate Text and Cell color swatches, select the text color and cell background color for the Up (normal) state.**

If you don't want to use the defaults, click the color boxes to open the color picker. At the bottom of the dialog box, you can see a preview of your menu, as shown in Figure 7-8.

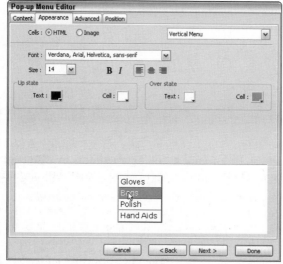

Figure 7-8: The preview shows what the menu will look like after you change each parameter.

13. **Using the appropriate Text and Cell color boxes, select the text color and cell background color for the Over (rollover) state.**

If you don't want to use the defaults, click the color boxes to open the color picker. At the bottom of the dialog box, you can see a preview of your menu.

14. **Click the Next button at the bottom of the Pop-up Menu Editor.**

The Advanced tab becomes active.

15. **Adjust any of the parameters in the Advanced tab as needed.**

All these settings can be previewed at the bottom of the dialog box, except Menu Delay:

- **Cell Width and Cell Height:** By default, Fireworks sets the cell width and cell height automatically, based on the content, but you can select Pixels from the drop-down list and type in a custom width and/or height.

- **Cell Padding and Cell Spacing:** Cell padding is the space between the edges of the cells and the text within the cells. The default Cell Padding setting is 3. Cell spacing is the space between the edge of one cell and the edge of an adjacent cell. The default Cell Spacing setting is 0.

- **Text Indent:** Text indent is the number of pixels from the left (in a vertical menu) or from the top (in a horizontal menu) to the text, not including the gaps introduced by cell padding and cell spacing. The default Text Indent setting is 0.

- **Menu Delay:** Menu delay is the amount of time your menu stays on-screen after the user's mouse rolls off the menu. It is adjusted in milliseconds (ms), or thousandths of a second. The default, 1000 ms, is one second.

- **Border:** The border of your pop-up menu can be turned on or off (and adjusted if on), and the colors that make up the border are customizable.

16. **Click the Next button at the bottom of the Pop-up Menu Editor.**

The Position tab becomes active.

17. **Click a Menu Position icon.**

The X and Y coordinates, which represent the top-left corner of the menu relative to the slice, update. You can type your own values for the X and Y coordinates if you want to customize them.

18. **Click Done.**

The Preview pane that you access at the top of your canvas does not allow you to see the pop-up menu in action. In order to preview your pop-up menu in action, you must choose File➪Preview in Browser or use the key command F12. Any Web browser installed on your computer can be used to preview your menu, as long as you have JavaScript enabled on that browser.

Pop-up menus are a tricky business, and their appearance can vary in different browsers. Be sure to test all your target browsers to make sure they display the menus acceptably.

When you make a slice active that has a pop-up menu behavior attached, an outline shows on the canvas in Fireworks where the pop-up menu will appear when the user rolls over the slice.

To edit the pop-up menu, click the behavior handle (the round icon in the middle of the slice, visible when the slice is selected) and choose Edit Pop-up Menu, or double-click the Behavior in the Behaviors panel.

Chapter 8: Integrating Fireworks MX 2004 with Other Macromedia Products

In This Chapter

✔ **Integrating Fireworks with Macromedia Flash**

✔ **Integrating Fireworks with Dreamweaver**

✔ **Integrating Fireworks with FreeHand**

✔ **Integrating Fireworks with Director**

With the release of the Macromedia Studio MX 2004 suite, Macromedia brought Fireworks MX 2004, Macromedia Flash MX 2004, Dreamweaver MX 2004, ColdFusion MX 6.1 Developer Edition, and FreeHand MX closer together. Fireworks MX 2004 adds CFML and other server-side languages to its Roundtrip HTML capabilities, so Fireworks recognizes changes made in Dreamweaver (and vice versa) in a wider variety of Web page formats than ever.

The applications in the suite have complementary, and in some cases, even overlapping, capabilities. We explore some of those capabilities in the next few pages but start by pointing out one of the key features you'll find in Fireworks: the Quick Export button, shown at the upper-right corner of the canvas in Figure 8-1.

Figure 8-1:
In Fireworks, the Quick Export button is a small Fireworks icon with an arrow at the right.

When you click the Quick Export button, a menu appears (see Figure 8-2) that offers one-click access to the following options:

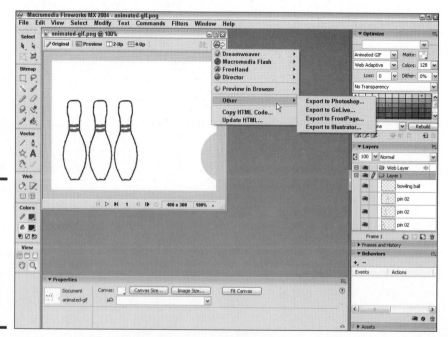

Figure 8-2:
The Quick Export button gives you one-click access to several options.

✦ **Dreamweaver:** Export HTML, Update HTML, Copy HTML to Clipboard, and Launch Dreamweaver

✦ **Macromedia Flash:** Export SWF, Copy, and Launch Flash

✦ **FreeHand:** Export to FreeHand, Copy Path Outlines, and Launch FreeHand

✦ **Director:** Source as Layers, Source as Slices, and Launch Director

✦ **Preview in Browser:** View in Primary Browser, View in Secondary Browser, and Set Primary and Secondary Browser

✦ **Other:** Export to Photoshop, Export to GoLive, Export to FrontPage, and Export to Illustrator

The Quick Export button may include additional options, depending on what exports you may have done previously from your Fireworks PNG file.

When you export using the Quick Export button, you may use defaults, but you also have access to all the regular options available from the Export dialog box. See Book III, Chapter 7 for information on advanced export options.

Integrating Fireworks with Macromedia Flash

You can open, edit, and export animated GIFs in both Macromedia Flash and Fireworks. If you're creating an animated GIF only as an alternative to an SWF (for users who come to your Web page who don't have the Flash plug-in), you'll want to use Macromedia Flash to generate the GIF and SWF (Shockwave Flash) animations. Macromedia Flash was built as a powerful animation program, which means that it offers more flexibility, more sophisticated animation tools, and more advanced export options for animations than Fireworks.

Exporting files from Fireworks to Macromedia Flash

Sometimes all the sophistication and flexibility that Macromedia Flash provides is more than you want or need. You may find Fireworks a more congenial environment for creating or editing simple, silent, non-interactive animations for the Web, whether as animated GIFs or SWFs.

Fireworks can export SWFs, but behaviors won't be exported from Fireworks with the SWF. Nor will masks, live effects, some text formatting, and numerous other features of your PNG. If you want to work with elements of your PNG in Macromedia Flash, you don't need to export it — you can simply import it into Macromedia Flash. (See Book V, Chapter 10 for details on the advantages of and restrictions on importing Fireworks PNGs.)

Nevertheless, if you want to export a simple SWF animation from Fireworks, it's a snap. Just follow these steps:

1. **Choose File⇨Export, or use the key command Ctrl+Shift+R.**

   The Export dialog box appears.

2. **Change the filename from the default, if necessary.**

3. **Select Macromedia Flash SWF from the Save as Type drop-down list.**

4. **Click the Options button if you plan to import the file into Macromedia Flash for editing; otherwise, click OK.**

   Clicking the Options button opens the Macromedia Flash SWF Options dialog box, which gives you control over objects, text, JPEG quality, frame rate, and which frames to export:

   - **Objects:** Select the Maintain Paths radio button if you want vector shapes to be editable, but you don't mind if their appearance shifts a little. Select the Maintain Appearance radio button if you want the shapes to look identical, but you don't need to edit them within Macromedia Flash.

   - **Text:** Select the Maintain Editability radio button if you want to be able to change the text after the SWF has been imported into Macromedia Flash. Select the Convert to Paths radio button if you want the text to appear the same in Macromedia Flash and don't plan to edit it.

   - **JPEG Quality:** Type a number between 1 and 100 or use the slider to select a number to set the optimization for JPEGs (to activate the slider, click the button with the downward-pointing arrow next to the JPEG Quality text field). For more information on JPEG quality settings, see Book III, Chapter 6.

   - **Frames:** Select the All radio button if you want all the frames in your PNG to be in the exported SWF. If you want only a select series of frames to be exported, select the From radio button, and in the text fields, type the number of the first and last frame in the PNG that you want in the SWF.

   - **Frame Rate:** Type the number of frames per second at which you want your exported SWF to run.

Of course, you can also click the Quick Export button and choose Macromedia Flash⇨Export SWF, as shown in Figure 8-3.

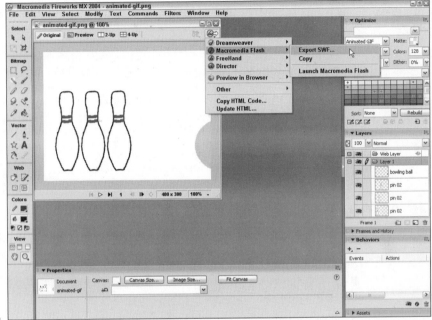

Figure 8-3:
Taking the Quick Export shortcut to export a multiple-frame PNG as an SWF is easy.

You can't import or open SWFs in Fireworks, but you can import or open Fireworks PNGs in Macromedia Flash. Read on to find out how.

Importing files into Macromedia Flash from Fireworks

If you want to design a Macromedia Flash-based Web page, you can do so in Fireworks, but you'll need to import the PNG into Macromedia Flash and create the interactivity in Macromedia Flash.

Macromedia Flash can import PNG files, either as flattened files (with or without *alpha transparencies,* which are transparent or semi-transparent areas) or as sets of editable Library items. Macromedia Flash can't import slice information, Live Effects, or JavaScript behaviors, but it can preserve different button states on their respective separate frames. For more information on what Macromedia Flash can and cannot import in a PNG, see Book V, Chapter 10.

And of course, Macromedia Flash can import JPEGs and regular GIFs, so you can export those formats from Fireworks for easy import into Macromedia Flash.

Macromedia Flash cannot dynamically load progressive JPEGs. See Book III, Chapter 6 for information on progressive JPEGs.

Macromedia Flash can import SWFs that were created in and exported from Fireworks, but keep in mind that many benefits of SWFs are not available in SWFs exported from Fireworks. (See the section, "Exporting files from Fireworks to Macromedia Flash.") If you want interactivity in your SWF, you're better off designing objects in Fireworks (or FreeHand) and then importing the Fireworks PNG (or FH11 file) into Macromedia Flash. Of course, you also have the option to author the movie using only Macromedia Flash.

Integrating Fireworks with Dreamweaver

Fireworks is a Web design tool, and Dreamweaver is an HTML editor (XML editor, ColdFusion editor, and so on). The two programs have overlapping capabilities, and they have complementary capabilities. Not only that, but they're designed to work together to make Web page creation and modification a breeze.

Basically, if you generate your HTML in Fireworks and edit the code in Dreamweaver, Fireworks recognizes the changes you make in the other application. That goes for links, image maps, behaviors shared by both programs, and HTML text. Macromedia coined the term *Roundtrip HTML* to describe the way the two programs work together.

Setting preferences

You need to establish a few settings, both in Dreamweaver and in Fireworks, to work with Roundtrip HTML. In Dreamweaver, you need to define a local site (see Book II, Chapter 3) and make Fireworks your primary image-editing application (see Book II, Chapter 7).

In Fireworks, you should set a few preferences. Just follow these steps:

1. **Choose Edit➪Preferences or use the key command Ctrl+U.**

   The Preferences dialog box appears.

2. **Click the Launch and Edit tab to make it active.**

   You use the two drop-down lists for specifying the treatment of Fireworks source files: When Editing from External Application and When Optimizing from External Application.

3. **Select one of the three options from the When Editing from External Application drop-down list:**

   - **Always Use Source PNG:** This option means that when you launch Fireworks from within another application, the original PNG source file for the Web page or table will open in Fireworks.

   - **Never Use Source PNG:** If you select this option, when you launch Fireworks from within another application, the exported GIF or JPEG you select will open in Fireworks.

     JPEG is a lossy format, so if possible, you'll want to edit the image from the original source file. For more information about lossy compression, see Book III, Chapter 6.

   - **Ask When Launching:** Choosing this option means that every time you launch Fireworks from within another application, you will be prompted to specify whether you want to edit the PNG source file or the exported optimized image.

4. **Select one of the three options from the When Optimizing from External Application drop-down list.**

   The options are identical to those in the When Editing from External Application drop-down list.

5. **Click OK.**

Editing PNGs

When you're editing your Web page in Dreamweaver, you may find that it's not working quite the way you wanted it to. You may add text to one cell and find that it creates a misalignment of an image in the adjacent cell in the table that makes up your page. Perhaps you need to slice an image differently. In cases like these, you'll want to edit your PNG source file, instead of making massive changes in Dreamweaver that can make your PNG source file out of sync with the Web page it represents. Luckily, you can launch and edit your Fireworks PNG source file from within Dreamweaver by following these steps:

1. **Click the optimized image in the Dreamweaver document window.**

   The Property inspector updates to display image parameters.

2. **Click the Fireworks Edit button in the Property inspector, as shown in Figure 8-4, or right-click the optimized image and choose Edit with Fireworks from the contextual menu that appears.**

   If Dreamweaver cannot locate the PNG automatically, the Find Source dialog box appears. Click Yes, because you want to locate the PNG source file for the image you selected for editing. Navigate to the source file in the Open dialog box and either double-click the PNG file's icon or click the file's icon and click Open. The source PNG file opens in Fireworks. At the top of the canvas, the words "Editing from Dreamweaver" show that Roundtrip HTML is in effect.

Figure 8-4:
The Fireworks Edit button in the Dreamweaver Image Property inspector.

Fireworks Edit button

3. **Edit the image and/or slice as needed.**

4. **Adjust any Optimization settings if necessary.**

   See Book III, Chapter 6 for information about optimizing images.

   The new version of the image will be exported at the new settings you specify or at the previous settings if you opt not to change them.

5. **Click the Done button at the top left of the canvas.**

   The Fireworks window closes, and the new image is visible in the Document window in Dreamweaver.

If you don't need to change anything about the image but its optimization settings, you can select the images and click the new Optimize in Fireworks Edit button in Dreamweaver's Property inspector. A special Optimize Images dialog box appears, where you can edit optimization settings. Just click the Update button when you've made the adjustments.

Working with tables

When you export HTML from Fireworks, you export code that tells a browser where each slice goes by establishing a table with cells arranged in rows and columns to correspond with your slices. If you want to take advantage of Roundtrip HTML for editing tables, make sure your Export settings include Dreamweaver HTML as the HTML Style and that you've set the option to include HTML comments (see Book III, Chapter 7 for details). If you want to make major changes to the table structure after you start editing the HTML in Dreamweaver, whether or not that requires reslicing images, you should launch from Dreamweaver and edit the table in your Fireworks PNG source file:

1. **Select the table in Dreamweaver.**

   The Property inspector updates to display the parameters of the table.

2. **Click the Fireworks Edit button in the Property inspector.**

   If need be, you can navigate to the source PNG file from within the Dreamweaver Property inspector by clicking the File icon next to the Edit button. The source file opens in Fireworks.

3. **Make edits to the slices, guides, and images as necessary.**

   You can even edit the HTML in text slices if you wish.

4. **Click the Done button (to the left of the Editing from Dreamweaver icon at the top of the canvas) when you are finished editing.**

   The Fireworks window closes, and Dreamweaver updates the table and images.

If you have made substantial changes to table structures in Dreamweaver, though, Fireworks may not recognize the code. In that case, when you launch and edit the table in Fireworks, Fireworks will overwrite the changes you made in Dreamweaver. A prompt notifies you when Fireworks will overwrite the existing Dreamweaver edits.

What if you accidentally delete the PNG source file, or you don't have a copy of it in the first place? The Fireworks Reconstitute Table feature can save the day. Fireworks can make an existing HTML table with image slices into an editable PNG — as long as no tables are nested in the table you want to reconstitute — and can even import behaviors and pop-up menus created in Fireworks or Dreamweaver. If you have multiple, non-nested tables on the page (tables stacked one on top of the other, for example), Fireworks opens a PNG for each table.

To create new PNGs from an HTML file with multiple, non-nested tables, follow these steps:

1. **Choose File⇨Reconstitute Table.**

   The Open dialog box appears.

2. **Navigate to the HTML file and double-click to open it or select the file and then click Open.**

   Each non-nested table in the HTML opens in its own window, with slices named and in place, and rollover behaviors attached.

To create a new PNG from the first table in an HTML file that has multiple tables, follow these steps:

1. **Choose File⇨Open.**

The Open dialog box appears.

2. **Navigate to the HTML file and double-click to open it or select the file and then click Open.**

The first table in the file opens in Fireworks, with slices named and in place, and rollover behaviors attached.

To add the first table in an HTML file with multiple tables to an existing PNG, follow these steps:

1. **Choose File⇨Import.**

The Open dialog box appears.

2. **Navigate to the HTML file and double-click it or select the file and click Open.**

The insert pointer appears when you place the cursor over the canvas.

3. **Place the pointer at the top-left corner of where you want the imported table to go and click.**

The table — slices, images, JavaScript, and all — appears. Objects are spread in layers based on table structure.

You can also import XHTML, CFML, UTF-8 encoded files, and more. (See the Using Fireworks PDF on your Macromedia Studio installation CD for details.) After you export the reconstituted table from Fireworks, you can take advantage of Roundtrip HTML from that point on.

Integrating Fireworks with FreeHand

FreeHand is a vector graphics application, so it shares many capabilities with Fireworks. The main difference between the programs is that FreeHand is best used to create images primarily for print design (because it has more extensive drawing capabilities), and Fireworks is made to be used primarily for Web page design.

Print and Web design jobs use different color modes:

✦ **CMYK:** Offset printing, the four-color process used to create most mass-produced printed materials, utilizes the color mode CMYK (*C*yan, *M*agenta, *Y*ellow, and blac*K*).

✦ **RGB:** Though some Web graphics may be made using the Grayscale or other modes, by and large, graphic production for the Web uses the RGB (*R*ed, *G*reen, *B*lue) mode, because RGB is the mode used for computer monitors.

Changing an image from one mode to another requires a *conversion* process. If you have designed a page in Fireworks but you want to repurpose the design for a print piece, you should import it into FreeHand to perform the conversion from RGB to CMYK. Some colors may shift slightly, because the two modes do not share all colors. For more information, see Book IV, Chapter 6.

Despite the differences in color mode for print and Web design jobs, document portability between FreeHand and Fireworks is pretty seamless. You can open FreeHand files (.fh11) in Fireworks and Fireworks PNGs in FreeHand. Some features of Fireworks PNGs may not be available or translate to FreeHand, and some FreeHand options and settings may not be available when you open an FH11 document in Fireworks, including Live Effects and slices. (See the Fireworks Help files for a complete list.)

Importing FreeHand files into Fireworks

To import a FreeHand MX file (or any FreeHand file from version 7 or later) into Fireworks, follow these steps:

1. **Choose File➪Import or use the key command Ctrl+R.**

   The Import dialog box appears.

2. **Navigate to the FreeHand file and double-click it, or select it and then click the Import button.**

   The Vector File Options dialog box, shown in Figure 8-5, appears.

3. **Adjust any settings that you wish to change from the file-specific defaults:**

   • **Scale:** Scale sets the scale of the imported file using a percentage. If you change the scale, the width and height change automatically to reflect the scaling percentage. Bitmap objects are not affected by this setting.

   • **Width and Height:** You can set the width and height of the imported file by typing numbers in the text fields and selecting pixels, inches, or centimeters from the drop-down lists.

   • **Resolution:** Standard screen resolution is 72 dpi (pixels/inch). If the file you're importing is at another resolution, you may want to import it at the standard screen resolution, because files at print resolution tend to be bigger and slower, and the final resolution of your Web images will be 72 dpi.

Figure 8-5:
The Vector
File Options
dialog box
allows you
to set
various
options
when you
import a
FreeHand
file into
Fireworks.

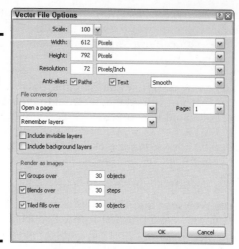

- **Paths and Text:** Select the check boxes for Paths and Text if you want them to be anti-aliased (for smoothed edges) on import, and select Crisp, Strong, or Smooth from the drop-down list to control the anti-aliasing. You can change these settings later from the Property inspector.

  You can use the File Conversion settings to control how Fireworks imports multi-page documents.

- **Include Invisible Layers:** By default, layers that are turned off in FreeHand do not get imported to Fireworks. Select the Include Invisible Layers check box if you want to import objects on layers that are turned off.

- **Include Background Layers:** Select the Include Background Layers check box if you want the objects on the background layer(s) of the FreeHand file to be imported into Fireworks.

  The Render as Images settings allow you to convert complicated shapes and fills to bitmaps.

4. **Click OK.**

   The Vector File Options dialog box closes and the pointer changes to the right-angled Insert cursor when you place it over the canvas.

5. **Put the cursor where you want the top-left corner of the imported file to go and click.**

   The imported files objects are placed in the current frame of the Fireworks document.

If you don't want to import the whole FreeHand file, you have a couple options. If you have enough room on your monitor to have Fireworks and FreeHand open side-by-side, you can drag and drop shapes and bitmaps from one application to the other.

Alternatively, you can copy and paste vectors and bitmaps from one application to the other. To copy and paste a vector object from Fireworks to FreeHand, just follow these steps:

1. **Select a vector shape in Fireworks by clicking it on the canvas or in the Layers panel.**

2. **Choose Edit⇨Copy or use the keyboard shortcut Ctrl+C.**

   If you want to copy only the outline of the shape, you can use the Fireworks command Copy Path Outlines from the Edit menu or from the Quick Export button.

3. **Paste the shape into an open FreeHand document by choosing Edit⇨ Paste from the FreeHand menu or using the key command Ctrl+V.**

   Your vector shape, including outline and fill information, appears in the FreeHand document.

When you copy and paste or drag a vector shape with a FreeHand pattern fill into Fireworks, if the pattern fill is not available in Fireworks, it will be lost.

Editing Fireworks objects in FreeHand

You can copy bitmaps, text, and vector art from Fireworks into FreeHand easily. Just follow these steps:

1. **In Fireworks, select the bitmap, text, or vector object and copy it by pressing Ctrl+C or by choosing Edit⇨Copy.**

2. **Open FreeHand, if it's not already open, and open a new document by pressing Ctrl+N or selecting File⇨New, if you don't already have a document open.**

3. **Select Edit⇨Paste or use the key command Ctrl+V.**

   The Fireworks PNG Import Settings dialog box appears.

4. **Select a file conversion method from the File Conversion drop-down list, unless you want to import the Fireworks document as a single flattened bitmap, in which case you may skip to Step 7.**

**Book III
Chapter 8**

Integrating Fireworks
MX 2004 with Other
Macromedia Products

Your options for file conversion are

- **Open frames as pages:** Converts frames in the Fireworks document into pages in the FreeHand document. If you select this option, select the Remember Layers check box if you want the layers from the Fireworks document to be preserved for each page in the FreeHand document.

- **Open frames as layers:** Converts frames in the Fireworks document into layers in the FreeHand document.

5. **From the Frame drop-down list, select which individual frame from the Fireworks document that you want to copy to FreeHand, or select All to import all frames.**

6. **For objects and for text, select the radio button for one of the following two options:**

   - **Rasterize If Necessary to Maintain Appearance:** When you select this option, certain properties (gradients, drop-shadows, and the like) lose their editability, but the object maintains its appearance.

   - **Keep All (Paths or Text) Editable:** When you select this option, certain properties of the vector shape or text may shift in appearance, but text or vector properties of the object remain editable within FreeHand.

7. **Select the Import as a Single Flattened Bitmap check box if you want to import the object as you see it on your canvas in Fireworks.**

   If you're pasting in text or a vector object, the object will no longer be editable as text or a vector object, because it becomes a bitmap. If you select this check box, the rest of the options in the Fireworks PNG Import Settings dialog box become irrelevant, so they are grayed out.

8. **Click OK.**

   The dialog box closes and the bitmap or vector object you copied from Fireworks is added to the FreeHand document.

Integrating Fireworks with Director

The MX version of Director (Macromedia's flagship multimedia authoring application) wasn't released at the time the original Macromedia Studio suite came out, but has become available since. Fireworks and Director can work together nicely if, for example, you want to edit a Director bitmap cast member using the capabilities of Fireworks (in Director, objects like bitmaps, shapes, and text are referred to as *cast members*). Macromedia's Web site gives you access to a Fireworks Import Xtra, which you need to download and install if you are working with Director Shockwave Studio version 8.0 or earlier.

You can use Fireworks to create GIFs, JPEGs, 32-bit PNGs (with or without transparencies), and HTML (with interactive and/or animated content), all of which can be imported into Director.

The Quick Export button gives you easy access to two Director export modes:

✦ **Source as Layers:** This mode exports each layer. You should use this mode for layered PNG files or animations.

✦ **Source as Slices:** This mode exports slices and behaviors in the form of optimized images and HTML with JavaScript. You should use this mode for rollover buttons or other interactive content.

Whichever option you select, the Export dialog box opens. The Trim Images check box in the Export dialog box is selected by default when you export to Director. The Trim Images option crops each layer or frame to remove space outside the objects in each layer or frame. In other words, if your canvas is 800 x 600 pixels, and you have an animation that uses only 25 percent of the canvas, selecting the Trim Images check box will cause Fireworks to crop the extra 75 percent out of each layer it exports.

You can also launch Fireworks from within Director to edit and optimize cast members. To do so, you first want to set Fireworks as your external image-editor by choosing File⇨Preferences⇨Editors from within Director and selecting Fireworks for bitmap graphics.

Book IV

FreeHand MX

The 5th Wave   By Rich Tennant

Rothman
Paint Drying Equip.
TV Test Pattern Design
Sap Buckets

"Maybe it would help our Web site if we showed our products in action."

Contents at a Glance

Chapter 1: Introduction to FreeHand MX

In This Chapter

✔ **Introducing FreeHand**

✔ **Appreciating vector graphics**

✔ **Navigating the interface**

✔ **Introducing the drawing tools**

*I*n this chapter, you get to know FreeHand MX up close and personal. We show you what you can do with FreeHand and give you a tour of the interface. In this chapter, we introduce you to the drawing tools that you use to create vector objects. We also show you how to come to grips with those pesky inspectors and panels that are lurking about the interface, just waiting for you to try your hand at FreeHand.

Introducing FreeHand MX

First and foremost, FreeHand is an illustration program. You use it to create illustrations for use in a variety of applications. FreeHand has sophisticated drawing tools that you use to create shapes for your illustration. The shapes range from ho-hum circles and rectangles to freeform shapes limited only by your imagination. You can specify the color of the shape (known as a *fill*) and whether the shape has an outline (known in FreeHand-speak as a *stroke*).

The shapes you create with the drawing tools are vector-based. What? You say you don't know what a vector is, Victor? Well, if you have to know right now, you can fast-forward to the section, "Understanding the Role of Vector Graphics."

You combine the shapes you create with text objects, and if your design requires, you can add a photograph to the illustration. Photo-realistic images are also known as bitmaps, which you should not confuse with the Windows-only BMP image format, which also goes by the name of bitmap.

When you have many objects in a document, it can be hard to select individual shapes. And sometimes you've got so many objects, it's hard to see the vectors for the bitmaps or text objects. The designers of FreeHand give you an easy way to organize a busy document: layers. When you select a layer, you can add objects to the layer and then arrange them just the way you want. When you've got it just right, you can lock the layer and begin working on another layer. No matter what you do on the new layer, you can't inadvertently mess up your locked layer — until you unlock it, that is.

Prior versions of FreeHand allowed you to create documents with vector objects and bitmaps for print purposes. The current version of FreeHand gives you increased support for creating objects for the Web. You can export your document, or just selected objects from your document, in a wide variety of formats. And if it has been a long day and you've had all the FreeHand you can handle, you can save the document in FreeHand's native FH11 format for another day's work. When you save a document in FreeHand's native format, you can edit all objects in the document and, if needed, add more or delete existing objects.

Using Illustration Tools for the Web

When you have a program with as much power as FreeHand, you can easily create documents for Web pages. The sophisticated drawing tools in FreeHand make it possible for you to create the basis for Web page buttons that you can add to a document you're creating in Dreamweaver, or for that matter, buttons for a Flash movie. You can assign links to the buttons. When you're finished with the document, you can export selected objects, or an entire document, in Web-friendly image formats.

The illustration tools in FreeHand also make it possible for you to create artsy-fartsy interfaces for your Flash movies and banners for your Web pages. If you create a FreeHand document with multiple pages, you can also export the whole thing as a Macromedia Flash SWF movie.

Understanding the Role of Vector Graphics

Vector objects are comprised of lines and curves that are redrawn mathematically, which results in a small file size. Vector-based graphics are resolution-independent, which means that you can increase their size without losing image fidelity. By contrast, bitmaps cannot be enlarged without losing fidelity. Figure 1-1 shows an enlarged vector object alongside an enlarged bitmap. (Which one would you rather use in that snazzy Web site you're planning?)

When you create a vector object, you have point-by-point control over the shape of the object. Vector objects have straight points and curve points. You can specify which type of point is created when you create freeform shapes with the Pencil tool. When you use the shape tools, the point type is predetermined, but you can change them in a heartbeat. A curve point has handles that you can click and drag to modify the shape. Figure 1-2 shows a vector object with straight and curve points.

Vector object   Bitmap

Figure 1-1:
Bitmaps
become
grainy when
enlarged
(right), but
vector
objects
remain razor
sharp when
enlarged
(left).

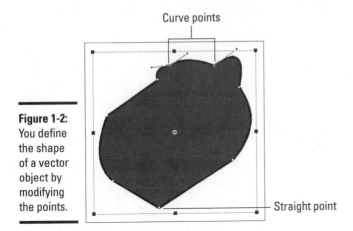

Curve points

Figure 1-2:
You define
the shape
of a vector
object by
modifying
the points.

Straight point

Investigating the FreeHand MX Interface

The FreeHand interface has many components. When you launch FreeHand and create a new document, you get an interface with a document window, a toolbar docked on the side of the interface, a status bar (Windows only) at the bottom of the interface, and some panels and inspectors aligned along the right side of the interface, as in other Macromedia Studio products like Fireworks and Macromedia Flash. The FreeHand workspace is shown in Figure 1-3.

When you launch the Windows version of FreeHand, you'll see a blank gray screen, and the interface is lightly shaded and inactive. To create a new document and start working, just press Ctrl+N or choose File➪New from the main menu.

Exploring the document window

In the center of the interface, you find what looks like a blank piece of paper. (The Macromedia designers put a border and a drop shadow around it so you can find it.) This is the document you are creating, and unless you're creating illustrations of polar bears in a blizzard, the document won't stay white and blank for long.

The area outside of the document is known as the *pasteboard*. No, you can't paste sticky notes on it to remind yourself to pick up milk on your way home, but you can use it as a staging area for items you intend to use in the document, but don't quite know where yet. Objects outside of the document area will not normally be printed or exported, but they are saved with the FreeHand document.

Around the border of the document, you find a vertical and horizontal scroll bar that you can use to pan to different parts of the document. Scroll bars come in handy when you magnify the document or if the document has multiple pages.

TIP

FreeHand has lots of contextual menus. Contextual menus contain commands and options relevant to a selected item or workspace. You access the commands in a contextual menu by right-clicking on the specific item or workspace.

Figure 1-3:
The
FreeHand
workspace
is your key
to creating
vector
objects.

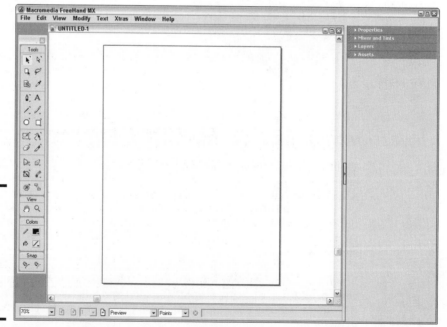

Using the drawing tools

On the left side of the interface, you find the toolbar, which shows various tools neatly grouped and stacked. On the toolbar, you find your drawing tools and other tools that you use to modify vector objects, move them, reshape them, and more. We know you're probably chomping at the bit to find out what these tools do. Don't worry. We show you how to use most of the drawing tools in Book IV, Chapter 2. The other tools are discussed in detail throughout Book IV as they pertain to different tasks you perform with FreeHand.

In FreeHand, your tools are displayed on a floating toolbar by default. The toolbar itself is neatly labeled *Tools* and your tools are divided into two columns. Because it is a *floating* toolbar, you can click and drag it anywhere in your workspace, dropping your tools at any convenient location. If you don't like the spot you've dropped the tools, you can click the title bar and then drag and drop to reposition the toolbar. Figure 1-3 shows how the tools look as a floating toolbar.

You can, however, lock the Tools toolbar to the top or bottom of the screen if you're more comfortable having the tools stay in the same location at all times. Just click the toolbar's title bar and drag the toolbar to the top or bottom of the application window. A thick black outline previews where the toolbar will go; release the mouse button when the outline sits where you want the toolbar.

To select a tool, click its icon. If you're not sure what a particular tool does, hold your cursor over the tool for a second or two, and a ToolTip will appear.

ToolTips are enabled by default. If you prefer to work without ToolTips, you can turn them off by choosing Edit⇨Preferences. In the Preferences dialog box, click the Panels tab and then deselect the Show ToolTips option.

Many of the tools have keyboard shortcuts, which is a convenient way to quickly change from one tool to another. Some of the tools have two keyboard shortcuts, a letter and a number. Table 1-1 shows the keyboard shortcuts for frequently used tools listed in the order in which they appear on the toolbar.

Table 1-1		Keyboard Shortcuts for Tools	
Tool	*Shortcut*	*Tool*	*Shortcut*
Pointer	V or 0 (zero)	Subselect	A or 1
Page	D	Lasso	L
Text	T	Pen	P or 6
Bezigon	B or 8	Pencil	Y or 5

(continued)

Table 1-1 *(continued)*

Tool	Shortcut	Tool	Shortcut
Line	N or 4	Rectangle	R
Polygon	G or 2	Ellipse	O or 3
Freeform	F or 9	Knife	K or 7
Hand	H	Zoom	Z

Working with toolbars

In addition to the drawing tools, you have other tools to simplify your life as a FreeHand illustrator. They're tucked away as menu commands, but you can get them anytime you need them by choosing Window⇨Toolbars and then selecting one of the following:

✦ **Main:** Use this toolbar, which is open by default, to duplicate many menu commands. On this toolbar, you find icons to open a document, save a document, print a document, import graphics, open frequently used panels, and more.

✦ **Text:** Use this toolbar to format text objects in your documents. You can choose font style, font size, font color, and specify paragraph alignment, along with other options that are discussed in Book IV, Chapter 3.

✦ **Controller:** Use the Controller toolbar to test a document you plan to export as a Flash movie. You use the VCR-like controls to play the movie and use the other icons to export the movie.

✦ **Info:** Choose this toolbar to see information about objects you select. The Info toolbar displays the type of object selected, the current position of the cursor, as well as the object's coordinates when you drag it to a different position in the document.

✦ **Xtra Operations:** Use this toolbar to transform and distort the path of one or more selected objects in your document. We show you how to use the available options from this toolbar in Book IV, Chapter 5.

✦ **Xtras:** Use this toolbar to access FreeHand plug-in tools, such as the Arc tool and Fisheye Lens tool. We show you how to use these tools in Book IV, Chapter 5.

✦ **Envelope:** Use this toolbar to transform shapes or object groups by applying an envelope to them. When you distort or warp the envelope, every shape or object within it is distorted or warped in the same way.

When you choose one of these toolbars, it appears as part of the main toolbar at the top of the interface. However, you can drag the toolbar into the workspace if this suits your working preference. If you exit FreeHand and leave several toolbars in the workspace, the program doesn't clean up after you; it assumes you're perfectly capable of keeping your workspace tidy and figures you want the toolbars in these positions. Every time you launch FreeHand, the workspace is laid out as you last left it.

Perusing the panels

When you launch FreeHand, you find several panel groups aligned along the right-hand side of the screen. Panel groups are combinations of panels that you use to create or modify items for your FreeHand document. For example, the Color Mixer tab of the Mixer and Tints panel gives you all the tools you need to mix up a sky-blue-pink, or any other color your artistic muse or client requires.

Each panel within a group has its own tab. If you don't like a panel group's position, you can click on the bulleted list in the top right of the panel, select Group Mixer With from the menu that appears, and then select the panel you want to add the tab to. You can collapse panel groups when you're finished with them, or close them entirely to clear the workspace. You can also create custom panel groups to suit your working preferences. By default, the following panels are shown when you launch FreeHand:

✦ **Properties:** The Properties panel includes two tabs: Object and Document. The Object tab enables you to modify properties of the currently selected object on the screen, while the Document tab enables you to modify the default properties of the entire document. When you select an object, at the top of the Object tab you find a list of properties of the object. The list may contain branches, that is, sets of properties that are dependent on a property (branches are indented under the property on which they're dependent). When you select a property from the list (simply click to select), editable options for the property appear at the bottom of the panel. The properties that may appear, depending on the type of object, are

- **Object:** If you click on the name of a vector object, the bottom of the panel displays the height, width, and position on the page of the object. For text objects, the basic text parameters — font, size, and styling — are shown. You can change any of these parameters by entering new values; a task we show you in Book IV, Chapter 4. If you click the name of a bitmap, the position, dimensions, scale, and other parameters appear at the bottom of the panel.

- **Stroke:** A stroke is a theoretical line that defines the perimeter of an object; to make the stroke "real," you give it attributes like width, color, and texture. If you select a stroke in the list, the bottom of the panel updates to show you the editable attributes of the stroke. If you don't like what you see, you can change the stroke by choosing different options. We show you how to modify strokes in Book IV, Chapter 6.

- **Fill:** If you select the fill of a text or vector object, the bottom of the panel displays editable properties of the current fill (color, as well as pattern, gradient, or the like, as applicable). We show you how to define an object's fill in Book IV, Chapter 2.

- **Effects:** If you have an effect on the object (bevel, drop-shadow, and so on), you can click it in the list to display various editable properties of the effect at the bottom of the panel.

✦ Depending on the object or property selected in the list, the following buttons may be active:

- **Add Stroke:** Click the Add Stroke button (the one with the pencil on it) to add a stroke to the selected object.

- **Add Fill:** Click the Add Fill button (the one with the paint can on it) to add a fill to the selected object.

- **Add Effects:** New to FreeHand MX, you can also add effects through the Object tab. Select your object, and then select the Add Effects button to add many cool effects, including blends, sketch, and transformation effects.

- **Remove Branch:** Click the Remove Branch button (the one with the trash can and three parallel lines) to remove a selected property and any properties dependent on it.

- **Remove Item:** Click the Remove Item button to delete the selected property or object from the list.

✦ **Mixer and Tints:** The Mixer and Tints panel contains two tabs: the Color Mixer tab and the Tints tab. You use the Color Mixer to mix a color. You can mix the color using the CMYK (Cyan, Magenta, Yellow, Black) color model, RGB (Red, Green, Blue) color model, HLS (Hue, Lightness, Saturation) color model, or the System Color Picker. After you mix a color, you can add it to the Swatches panel, a task we show you how to perform in Book IV, Chapter 6. You use the Tints tab to specify the percentage or hue of the original color. We show you how to tint reds, greens, blues, and other popular rainbow colors in Book IV, Chapter 6.

✦ **Layers:** You use the Layers panel to add layers to a document and manage layers within a document. We show you how to work with layers in Book IV, Chapter 2.

✦ **Assets:** The Assets panel includes three different tabs: Styles, Swatches, and Library. You use the Styles tab to duplicate, edit, or delete styles being used in your document. The Swatches tab is for creating a color palette for objects in your document. The Library tab, as you might expect, includes a set of ready-made objects that you can use in your document.

✦ **Answers:** The Answers panel gives you quick access to all the help features in FreeHand, including tutorials.

In addition to the default panels that are active when you launch FreeHand, you can access several others by selecting Window⇨*Panel Name* (substitute *Panel Name* for the name of the appropriate panel). These panels include

✦ **Navigation:** Use the Navigation panel to assign URL links to objects and text in your FreeHand documents.

✦ **Halftones:** Use the Halftones panel when you add screened objects to a document. The only time you'd need to use halftones is when you're preparing a document for a postscript-printing device at a service center. Halftones are beyond the scope of this book.

✦ **Align:** Use the Align panel to align objects in your document. We show you how to get your objects in alignment (without visiting a chiropractor) in Book IV, Chapter 4.

✦ **Transform:** Use the Transform panel to move, rotate, scale, skew, or reflect a selected object. We show you how to fold, spindle, and otherwise mutilate objects with the Transform panel in Book IV, Chapter 5.

You can move a panel group to any desired position in the workspace by clicking the panel title bar and then dragging and dropping it to the desired position. Figure 1-4 shows two panels side by side. The panel on the left is the shy, reclusive type as it is currently collapsed, while the panel on the right is strutting its stuff in the expanded position.

Figure 1-4:
A tale of
two panel
groups.

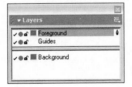

Here are a few final tips on how to navigate and manage panels:

✦ If you use a panel group frequently, collapse the panel group and move it to a convenient position in the workspace.

✦ When you have a panel group open with the Windows version of FreeHand, you can switch between panels by pressing Ctrl+Tab.

✦ To clear the workspace of all panel groups, choose View⇨Panels (or press F4).

✦ To display hidden panels, choose View⇨Panels (or press F4).

Modifying groups

Macromedia's FreeHand design team worked long and hard to come up with an optimum layout for panels and inspectors. They grouped panels and inspectors in a logical manner. However, like everything else, the way panels are grouped is not cast in stone, and if you're one of those folks who like different strokes, you can change the way panels and inspectors are grouped as follows:

**Book IV
Chapter 1**

**Introduction to
FreeHand MX**

1. **Choose View⇨Panels to bring up the default FreeHand panel grouping.**

2. **Select the name of the panel or inspector you want to group differently.**

The panel or inspector appears. Alternatively, you can click the panel's or inspector's tab to select it.

3. **Make sure the tab you want to move is the active tab.**

To make a tab active, simply click it. If the panel doesn't have tabs, you can skip this step.

4. **Click the bulleted list near the upper-right corner of the panel.**

5. **Choose Group *Name* With, where *Name* is the name of the panel or inspector.**

6. **Choose the name of the panel group you want to group the panel or inspector with, as shown in Figure 1-5.**

The panel or inspector is added to the group you specified and banished from its former home.

FreeHand has contextual menus, lots of them. Contextual menus contain commands and options relevant to a selected item or workspace. You access the commands in a contextual menu by right-clicking the selected item or workspace.

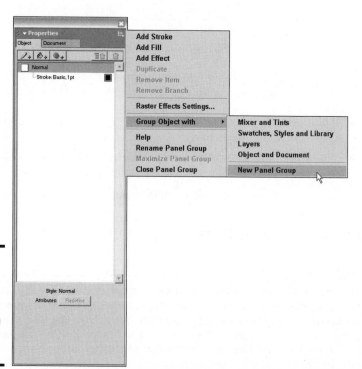

Figure 1-5:
You can group a panel or inspector in a different group.

Chapter 2: Understanding FreeHand MX Basics

In This Chapter

✓ Creating a new document

✓ Working with text

✓ Adding shapes to the document

✓ Using the Pen tool

✓ Adding color to a shape

✓ Introducing layers

✓ Saving documents

*W*hen you create an illustration with FreeHand MX, you start by launching the program and creating a new document. After that, you can begin creating your masterpiece. This process can involve getting the word out by adding text, creating artwork by making standard shapes with the shape tools or freeform shapes with the Pen tool, and setting a dividing line between elements in your illustration with the Line tool. When you create objects for your illustrations, you can outline the object by defining a stroke and add color to the object by defining the object's fill. After you've created the document, you can save it for future editing and refinement. When your document is complete, you export the document to its intended destination.

In this chapter, you get an overview of the typical FreeHand workflow. We also show you which tools you can use to create objects for your illustrations and point you in the right direction for additional information and tips.

Creating FreeHand Documents

The default size for a FreeHand document is 612 x 792 points (8½ x 11 inches), which is letter size. You can modify the document size and add pages to the document by using the Document tab of the Properties panel. You also use the Document tab to set the bleed value — the amount of "spillover" of content that will be physically trimmed from the printed document — and final output resolution of the document. You can also modify parameters, such as the page orientation and the way thumbnails are displayed in the Document tab. If you want, you can also create a Master Page to maintain the continuity of all pages in the document. A Master Page has elements that will be used on every page of the document, such as a text header with the client's logo. We show you how to create Master Pages in the "Creating a Master Page" section, later in this chapter.

Creating a new document

You begin a FreeHand project by creating a new document. Creating a new document gives you a blank page that you use to assemble the artwork for your illustration. You can create a new document one of two ways:

✦ Choose File⇨New Document.

✦ Click the New Document icon that looks like a blank letter in the Main toolbar. To open the Main toolbar, choose Window⇨Toolbars⇨Main.

After you create a new document, it appears in the center of the Document window, as shown in Figure 2-1.

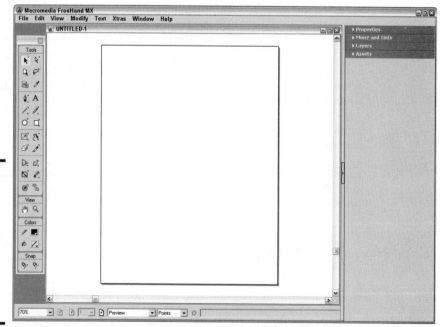

Figure 2-1: Every FreeHand project begins with a blank document. It's a FreeHand law.

Modifying documents with the Properties panel

You use the Document tab within the Properties panel to change the orientation of the document, change the size of the document, and so on. If the Properties panel is open but the Object tab is active, you can click on the Document tab, shown in Figure 2-2, to make it active. If the Properties panel is not open, choose Window⇨Document.

Figure 2-2:
Use the Document panel to change the size of the document.

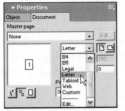

Changing the document size and orientation

If you need to change the size of a document, you use the Document tab of the Properties panel. You can choose from a standard document size, or create a custom size. You also use the Document tab to change the document orientation from portrait (vertical) to landscape (horizontal). To modify the document size and orientation, follow these steps:

1. **If necessary, click the Document tab in the Properties panel to make it active.**

   If the Properties panel is not open, choose Window⇨Document. The Document tab of the Properties panel opens (refer to Figure 2-2).

2. **Select the Page Size drop-down list.**

   The Page Size drop-down list appears and provides you with a series of page size options.

3. **Choose one of the preset options.**

   The first five presets are European sizes. The available presets are as follows:

   • **A3:** Creates a document sized 841.89 x 1190.55 points.

   • **A4:** Creates a document sized 595.27 x 841.29 points.

- **A5:** Creates a document sized 419.52 x 595.27 points.
- **B4:** Creates a document sized 708.66 x 1000.60 points.
- **B5:** Creates a document sized 498.89 x 708.66 points.
- **Legal:** Creates a document sized 612 x 1008 points.
- **Letter:** Creates a document sized 612 x 792 points.
- **Tabloid:** Creates a document sized 792 x 1224 points.
- **Web:** Creates a document sized 550 x 400 points, which incidentally is the default size for a Flash movie. The default orientation for this preset is Landscape.
- **Custom:** Choose this preset, and the x and y fields become available. You can then enter values in these fields to create a document of the desired size.

The measurements in the preceding list are shown in points, the default FreeHand unit of measurement. You will see different values if you change to a different unit of measurement. (To change to a different unit of measurement, choose one from the Units drop-down list at the bottom of the Document window.) For example, if you change the unit of measurement to inches, Letter size is 8.5 x 11 inches.

4. **Click the desired orientation button.**

   You can choose from Portrait to create a document that is taller than it is wide, or Landscape to create a document that is wider than it is tall.

Adding pages to a document

If you use FreeHand to create storyboards or Flash movies, you can add as many pages as you need to get the job done. When you add pages, you can format them using a previously created Master Page. To add one or more pages to your document, follow these steps:

1. **If necessary, click the Document tab in the Properties panel to make it active.**

   If the Properties panel is not open, choose Window➪Document. The Properties panel appears with the Document tab selected.

2. **Click the arrow near the upper-right corner of the panel.**

   The Options menu appears, as shown in Figure 2-3.

3. **Choose Add Pages.**

   The Add Pages dialog box, shown in Figure 2-4, appears.

4. **Enter a value for the number of pages you want to add.**

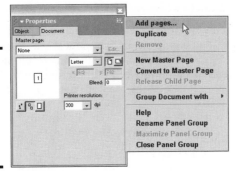

Figure 2-3:
Use the
Properties
panel to get
to the
Options
menu.

Figure 2-4:
Adding
pages
to your
document.

5. **If you have created a Master Page (see "Creating a Master Page," later in this chapter), select a Master Page from the Make Child of Master Page drop-down list. If you don't want to use a Master Page to format the document, skip to Step 6.**

   When you choose an option from this drop-down list, the new page inherits the characteristics of the selected Master Page. *Note:* This option is unavailable if you've changed the page size.

6. **Accept the default document page size, or select the Page Size radio button and select a different page size from the drop-down list.**

   You can choose a default page size, or you can select Custom to enter your own values for document size.

7. **Click OK.**

   FreeHand adds the pages to your document. Alternatively, you can click Cancel to void the operation.

You can also add a page by clicking the Add Page button (the page with a plus sign in it) at the bottom of the Document window.

You can also duplicate a page, remove a page, or convert the current page to a Master Page by choosing Window➪Document, clicking the arrow near the upper-right corner of the Document tab, and then choosing the appropriate command from the Options menu.

Creating a Master Page

If you need to create a multipage document that you want to use as a Flash movie or as a storyboard, you can use the Document tab in the Properties panel to create a Master Page that you can apply to any or all pages in the document. A *Master Page* is like a template; it has common items and attributes that are applied to all children of the Master Page. To create a master document, follow these steps:

1. **If necessary, click the Document tab in the Properties panel to make it active.**

   If the Properties panel is not open, choose Window⇨Document. The Document tab in the Properties panel appears.

2. **Click the arrow near the upper-right corner of the Document tab.**

   The Options menu appears (refer to Figure 2-3).

3. **Choose New Master Page from the menu.**

   FreeHand creates a blank page entitled New Master Page-01. If you don't like the name, there's not much you can do about it; the designers of FreeHand make sure the name is cast in stone.

4. **Create the elements that you want to appear on all pages that use this Master Page.**

   For example, you can create a text header with your client's logo.

You can create as many Master Pages as needed for a document by following the preceding steps. New Master Pages will be appended by the next available Master Page number.

To format an existing page using a Master Page, follow these steps:

1. **If necessary, click the Document tab in the Properties panel to make it active.**

   If the Properties panel is not open, choose Window⇨Document. The Document tab within the Properties panel opens.

2. **Navigate to the page you want to format using a Master Page.**

   You navigate to the page by clicking its thumbnail in the Document tab, or by using the Hand tool to scroll from one page to another in the Document window. You can also choose the page number from the Go To Page drop-down list at the bottom of the Document window.

3. **Select the desired page from the Master Page drop-down list.**

   The page inherits the characteristics of the selected Master Page.

TIP

To covert a regular page to a Master page, select Convert to Master Page from the Options menu in the top right of the Properties panel.

Editing a Master Page

You're on the home stretch of a project when all of a sudden your boss or client rears his or her head and wants you to change the document. You mumble some choice words under your breath until you remember you've formatted most of the pages in the document using a Master Page. When you edit a Master Page, all instances of pages to which the master is applied are updated as well. To edit a Master Page, follow these steps:

1. **Select a page that you formatted using a Master Page.**

2. **If necessary, click the Document tab in the Properties panel to make it active.**

   If the Properties panel is not open, choose Window⇨Document. The Document tab of the Properties panel opens.

3. **Click the Edit button.**

   FreeHand refreshes the Document window to display the Master Page.

4. **Edit the Master Page as needed.**

5. **To apply your changes, select another document from the Window menu on the Main toolbar, or click the Close (X) button for the window.**

   All pages formatted with the Master Page are updated to reflect your edits. If you closed the window with the Master Page, the most recently edited page remains open.

Changing the Document Tab Thumbnail Display

When you create a document with multiple pages, you can display thumbnails of the pages in the Document tab of the Properties panel. When you view pages in this manner, you can use the Page tool (a mahvelous device we show you how to use in the next section, "Using the Page Tool") to rearrange the order of the pages. Follow these steps to modify the way thumbnails are displayed in the Document tab:

1. **If necessary, click the Document tab in the Properties panel to make it active.**

   If the Properties panel is not open, choose Window⇨Document. The Document tab of the Properties panel opens.

2. **Click one of the buttons at the lower-left corner of the Document tab:**

   • The first button displays each page as tiny thumbnails.

   • The second button displays each page as medium-size thumbnails.

   • The third button displays a thumbnail of the selected page only.

   The page thumbnails are displayed according to the button you selected. FreeHand will remember your change the next time you open the Document tab.

You can also use the Document tab of the Properties panel to set Bleed and Resolution. When you print a document, FreeHand places registration marks and crop marks according to the document size you specify. Registration marks are the little cross hairs placed on the sides of a document that are aligned to get perfect registration of all the colors in the printing process. Crop marks are the long tick marks at the corners of the page that tell the printer where to trim the printed sheet. The Bleed value is a margin for error for the printer's page-trimming process. When you enter a bleed value, the registration marks are moved in from the edge of the page without changing the document size. If you're using a desktop printer and you add a bleed value to the document, you may need to increase the page size by that amount in your printer's setup dialog box, otherwise you'll get this error message: "This document will not fit in the selected page size." Refer to your printer manual to determine the maximum resolution the printer is capable of producing as well as how to modify the page size.

Using the Page Tool

When you create a multipage document, you use the Page tool to rearrange the order of pages and select and delete pages. You find the Page tool — it looks like a document with an arrow in it — with all the other FreeHand tools, as you can see in Figure 2-5. To use the Page tool on a multipage document, do the following:

1. **Deselect all objects, place your cursor inside the Document window, and then right-click.**

   The contextual menu appears.

2. **Choose View⇨Fit All.**

   FreeHand refreshes the Document window to display all pages in the document.

3. **Select the Page tool from the Tools panel.**

Page tool   Bounding box of page being moved

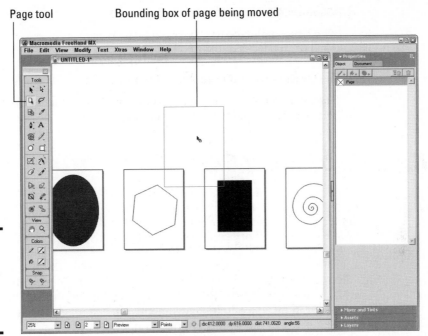

Figure 2-5:
You use the
Page tool to
select and
rearrange
pages.

4. Click a page to select it.

After selecting a page, you can move it to a different position. This is
like rearranging the papers on your desk, but you can't get messy and
overlap document pages. Figure 2-5 shows a multipage document being
rearranged with the Page tool.

You can also use the Document tab of the Properties panel to rearrange
pages. Open the Document tab and then switch to a view that shows thumbnails of all the pages in your document. Click a page thumbnail to select it
and drag it to a new location.

Opening Existing Documents

We know. We haven't shown you how to save a document yet, and here's
a section about opening them. Well, when you first begin working with
FreeHand, you may need to open existing FreeHand documents created by
someone else, and you usually open existing documents before you can edit
and save them, so here goes. To open an existing document, follow these
steps:

1. **Choose File⇨Open.**

The Open dialog box appears.

2. **Navigate to the folder where the file is located.**

3. **Select the file, and then click Open.**

FreeHand displays the document and associated pages in the Document window. You can now edit the document.

Using the Document Grid

When you create documents, you may need to enlist visual aids to help you place objects with precision. Visual aids are a definite benefit if you're dealing with a small monitor, or if you're working with a large monitor, but you have managed to work your way into wearing trifocal glasses.

Your first line of optic defense is the document grid, which is a series of equally spaced vertical and horizontal dotted lines. To view the document grid, choose View⇨Grid⇨Show. You can use the grid intersections as anchor points for items you add to a document. You can toggle the grid on and off at will, as well as modify other grid parameters. Note that the grid only shows up onscreen, not in the printed document.

After you enable the grid, you can give it a magnetic personality by choosing View⇨Grid⇨Snap to Grid, which causes objects you create to snap to grid intersections. If you're creating an illustration for duck hunters, enabling the Snap to Grid feature is an easy way to get your ducks in a row.

After you display the grid, you can modify the grid spacing to suit the document you are creating:

1. **Choose View⇨Grid⇨Edit.**

The Edit Grid dialog box appears.

2. **Enter a value in the Grid Size field.**

This is the new grid spacing using the default document unit of measure.

3. **Select the Relative Grid check box.**

This option is disabled by default. Selecting this option causes objects when moved to snap to the same relative position within different grid spaces. Do not select this option if you want objects to snap to grid intersections.

4. Click OK to apply the changes.

FreeHand resizes the grid to the value you specified.

Using Rulers

FreeHand has yet another visual aid you can use: rulers. To view rulers, choose View⇨Page Rulers⇨Show.

You can modify the rulers' unit of measure by choosing View⇨Page Rulers⇨ Edit.

Creating guides

After you display rulers, you can create guides to further aid in aligning objects in your document. You can create as many vertical and horizontal guides as you need, essentially making a custom grid, where the guide lines don't need to be equally spaced or fill the screen. You do not need to delete guides when you print the documents, because the guides don't get printed. You can create guidelines by dragging them from the rulers, and if needed, position them precisely using menu commands.

To create a guide, follow these steps:

1. Click one of the rulers and drag into the Document window.

Click the horizontal ruler to create a horizontal guide; click the vertical ruler to create a vertical guide. As you drag, a blue line designates the guide's current position. You can use the opposite ruler to view the current location of the guide.

2. Release the mouse button when the guide is in the desired position.

A FreeHand guide is added to your document. If the guide isn't positioned perfectly, you can click it and drag it to a new position. If you need to precisely position a guide, please refer to the next section, "Editing guides."

If you have both the grid and guides showing, the workspace can become a bit cluttered. We recommend that you only use one or the other.

You can customize the way that guides behave as follows:

✦ **Snap to guides:** Objects snap to guides by default. To disable snapping to guides, choose View⇨Guides⇨Snap to Guides. To enable snapping, choose the command again.

✦ **Hide and show guides:** When you add guides to a document, they are visible by default. You can hide guides by choosing View⇨Guides⇨Show or clicking the check mark icon at the left of the Guides row in the Layers panel. To view hidden guides, choose View⇨Guides⇨Show again or click the empty space at the left of the Guides row in the Layers panel.

✦ **Lock and unlock guides:** When the guides are positioned the way you want them, you can lock them by choosing View⇨Guides⇨Lock. To unlock all guides, choose the command again. You can also lock and unlock the guides by clicking the Lock icon in the Guides row of the Layers panel.

Editing guides

If in spite of your best efforts, a guide is in the wrong place, you can precisely position it where you want. To reposition an improperly placed guide, follow these steps:

1. Choose View⇨Guides⇨Edit or double-click the guide that you want to edit.

The Guides dialog box, shown in Figure 2-6, opens. If you have multiple guides in your document, they are listed by type and position.

Figure 2-6: You can move a guide precisely using the Guides dialog box.

2. Select the guide you want to edit.

The guide is highlighted. If you double-clicked a guide to open the dialog box, the guide is already selected. If you have a multipage document, you also need to enter the number of the page whose guides you want to edit or use the buttons at the top of the dialog box to navigate from one page to another.

3. Click the Edit button.

The Guide Position dialog box opens, showing the coordinate of each guide.

4. **In the Location field, enter the position (coordinate) where you want the guide to appear, and then click OK.**

   The Guide Position dialog box closes and the new location is recorded in the Guides dialog box.

5. **Click OK to reposition the guide.**

   The Guides dialog box closes and the guides get a move on.

When you choose View⇨Guides⇨Edit Guides, you can use the Guides dialog box to add a guide, remove a guide, or release a guide (turn it into an object).

Adding Text to Your Illustration

When you use FreeHand to create an illustration, you can use the Text tool to add text to vector and bitmap objects. You can do so much with text in FreeHand that it truly boggles the mind. This section gets you up and running with the Text tool, but we show you the whole enchilada on text in Book IV, Chapter 3. To add text to your document, follow these steps:

1. **Select the Text tool — it looks like a capital letter A — from the Tools panel.**

2. **Click the location where you want the text to appear in your document.**

3. **Type.**

   It's really that simple.

4. **When you're finished typing, click anywhere outside of the text box.**

   The Text tool reverts to the Pointer tool, which you can now use to move the text box to another location.

After you create text, you can change text characteristics to create wonderfully artistic text for your illustration. We show you how to do everything with text — short of writing the next Great American Novel — in Book IV, Chapter 3.

Creating Predefined Shapes

The easiest way to add vector shapes to your illustrations is by using the shape tools. In this section, we show you the tools you can use to add shapes to your illustrations, as well as how to add the shape to a document. Some of the tools have parameters that you can define, such as the number of sides in a polygon. We show you how to set these parameters and more in Book IV, Chapter 4.

You can use the following tools (available from the Tools panel) to add shapes to your illustrations:

✦ **Rectangle tool:** You use this tool to add rectangles (and squares) to your illustrations. The rectangles can have rounded corners or not.

✦ **Polygon tool:** You use this tool to add star-like shapes to your illustrations. In fact, you can specify whether you use the tool to draw a polygon or a star. You can also specify the number of sides for the polygon. To access the Polygon tool, click and hold the Rectangle tool, and then select the Polygon tool from the pop-up menu.

✦ **Ellipse tool:** You use this tool to draw ovals (or circles), or as high-brow designers refer to them, ellipses.

To add a shape to your document, follow these steps:

1. **Select a drawing tool from the Tools panel.**

If you click the tool once, you draw a shape using the last settings specified for the tool. If the tool has definable parameters, you can choose new parameters by double-clicking the tool. Tools that have modifiable parameters have an inverted L to the upper right of their icons. Tools with other tools hidden underneath them have a gray arrow to the bottom right of their icons. The drawing tools are shown in Figure 2-7, along with the boxes you use to color shapes and outlines.

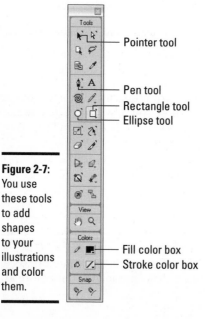

Figure 2-7:
You use these tools to add shapes to your illustrations and color them.

— Pointer tool

— Pen tool
— Rectangle tool
— Ellipse tool

— Fill color box
— Stroke color box

2. **Click the place inside the document where you want the shape to appear, and then drag diagonally to create the shape.**

   As you drag, FreeHand creates a preview of the shape. If you hold down the Shift key while creating a shape, the shape width and height remain equal. In other words, if you hold down the Shift key while using the Rectangle tool, you create a square; hold down the Shift key while using the Ellipse tool, and you create a circle.

3. **Release the mouse button when the shape is the desired size.**

   FreeHand adds the shape to your document. After creating a shape, you can move it to a different location with the Pointer tool, or you can modify the shape by selecting it and setting available properties in the Object tab of the Properties panel. We show you how to modify a shape using the Object tab in Book IV, Chapter 4.

Creating Custom Shapes with the Pen Tool

You use the Pen tool to create freeform vector objects. The Pen tool gives you point-to-point control over the shape you create. You can use the Pen tool to create an open path or a closed path (the beginning and ending points meet to create an outline). You can even use the Pen tool to trace an image on another layer. (We show you how to add layers to a document in the upcoming section, "Working with Layers.")

To create a shape with the Pen tool, follow these steps:

1. **Select the Pen tool from the Tools panel.**

2. **Click the place in the document where you want to add the first point.**

   When you click, you create a straight point; if you click and drag, you create a curve point. You create a straight point when you want to create a straight line segment, a curve point when you want a curved line segment.

3. **Click the spot where you want the second point to appear.**

   Remember to click and drag if you want a curve point. A curve point has handles that you use to modify a curved line segment. You modify handles with the Pointer tool or with the Subselection tool. The Subselection tool — the white-headed arrow at the top-right of the Tools palette — is covered in detail in Book IV, Chapter 4.

4. **Continue adding points to define your shape.**

   You can double-click the Pen tool icon to select the Show Pen Preview option, which will provide a preview of the path that will be created when you make the next point.

5. **To complete an open path, double-click to define the last point; to complete a closed path, click the first point.**

   Your shape is finished. Now you can use the Pen tool to create another shape or to modify the shape that you just created.

 If you are looking to create straight lines in combination with curved shapes, then the Bezigon tool offers you greater control and flexibility than the Pen tool. To use it, click and hold the Pen tool in the Tools panel. A pop-up menu appears, and you can select the Bezigon tool to active it. The Bezigon tool works similarly to the Pen tool, but with a major difference: When you hold down the Alt key when creating points, the subsequent point will automatically be constructed as a uniform curve!

Using the Line Tool

You use the Line tool to create straight lines. You can modify the line style and width in the Object tab of the Properties panel, a task we describe in the upcoming section, "Creating Outlines."

To use the Line tool, follow these steps:

1. **Select the Line tool from the Tools panel.**

2. **Click the point where you want the line to begin and drag to create the line.**

   As you drag the tool across the document, FreeHand creates a preview of the line. If you hold down the Shift key while using the tool, you constrain the line to a predefined angle. (To predefine the angle, choose File⇨Document Settings⇨Constrain and enter the value in the dialog box.) As you drag, a filled square will appear at the pointer-end of the line whenever it gets to a 45 or 90 degree angle.

3. **Release the mouse button when the line is the desired length.**

   FreeHand creates a straight line using the old tried and true method of following the shortest distance between the beginning and ending points.

Coloring Shapes

If you use a shape tool that creates a closed path or use the Pen tool to create a closed path, you can add color to the resulting shape by defining a fill. You can also add a fill to an open path. (Choose Preferences⇨Object and select the option to Show Fill for New Open Paths to add a fill automatically when you draw an open shape. To add color to a shape, you use the Fill color box.)

Using the Fill color box

The Fill color box is near the bottom of the Tools panel, yet it's one of the most important tools in the whole lot. After all, a shape without color is kind of drab. Of course, you can opt for the minimalist look and create a shape with no fill and a stroke, in which case, you get an outline.

To define a fill for an object, follow these steps:

1. **Click the Fill color box (the box to the right of the paint bucket) in the Colors section of the Tools panel.**

   The color picker appears.

2. **Move your cursor over the color cubes.**

   Your cursor becomes an eyedropper. As you move your cursor over the color cubes, the window in the upper-left corner of the palette refreshes and displays the color your cursor is currently over. A Tooltip displays the color's hexadecimal value and RGB value, as shown in Figure 2-8. If you're working for print instead of the Web, you may wish to use Swatches instead of the default color cubes. Click on the triangle at the top right of the color picker and select Swatches from the pop-up window to use swatches. See your documentation for details on using Swatches.

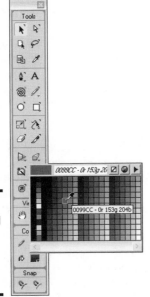

Figure 2-8:
You can add color to an object by defining a fill.

3. **Click a color to select it or click the No Color button (the box with the diagonal red slash through it next to the color wheel at the top of the window) if you want a shape with just an outline (stroke).**

The swatch in the Fill color box refreshes to show the color you selected. This color is used to fill any new shapes you create until you select a different fill color. If you select no color, a diagonal red slash (/) appears in the Fill color box.

Changing a shape's fill color

If a shape's fill color doesn't suit your (or your client's) fancy, you can easily change it. You can also create a custom fill using the Fill button in the Object tab of the Properties panel, a colorful operation we show you how to do in Book IV, Chapter 4.

Follow these steps to change a shape's fill color:

1. **Select the shape.**

2. **Click the Fill color box. (Refer to Figure 2-8.)**

The color picker appears and your cursor becomes an eyedropper as you move it over the palette.

3. **Click a color to select it.**

You can click in the color picker. The swatch in the Fill color box changes to the color you selected, as does the color of the shape you selected. *Remember:* You can revert from a filled shape to an unfilled shape by clicking the No Color button. If you select No Color, the diagonal red slash appears in the Fill color box.

Creating Outlines

You can create an object with no fill, select a stroke color, and you've got an outline. If you create an object with no fill and no stroke, well . . . you've got nothing. But seriously, you use the Stroke color box to select an outline color for an object. If you need to change the stroke width, or style, you can access the stroke's properties using the Object tab in the Properties panel, which is covered in detail in Book IV, Chapter 4.

Using the Stroke color box

You use the Stroke color box to choose a color for the outlines of the shapes you add to your illustration. You can select any color from the color picker or the System Color Picker (covered in Book IV, Chapter 6), or you can choose to go sans stroke.

Follow these steps to select a stroke color:

1. **Click the Stroke color box next to the icon that looks like a pencil.**

The color picker appears.

2. **Move your cursor over the palette.**

Your cursor becomes an eyedropper. As you move your cursor over the color swatches, a Tooltip displays the color's hexadecimal and RGB values. The window in the upper-left corner of the color picker refreshes to show the color your cursor is currently over.

3. **Click a color to select it.**

If the shape you are creating won't have a stroke, click the No Color button. After you select a color, the palette closes, and the selected color is displayed in the Stroke color box. If you click the No Color button, a diagonal red slash appears in the Stroke color box. The color you choose is applied to all shapes you create until you follow the preceding steps to select another stroke color.

Changing an object's stroke color

If you create an object and the object's outline (stroke) is not to your liking, you can change it at any time. You can also add a stroke to a shape that doesn't have one.

To change the stroke color of an object:

1. **Select the object by clicking on it with your mouse.**

2. **Click the Stroke color box.**

The color picker appears.

3. **Move your cursor over the palette.**

Your cursor becomes an eyedropper. As you move your cursor over the color swatches, a Tooltip displays the color's hexadecimal and RGB values. The window in the upper-left corner of the color picker refreshes to show the color your cursor is currently over.

4. **Click a color to select it.**

To remove a stroke from an object, click the No Color button. You can also choose a color from the System Color Picker by clicking the System Color Picker button to the right of the No Color button. After you select a color, the color picker closes and the color is applied to the object's outline.

Working with Layers

Layers are like thin sheets of clear plastic on top of your illustration. You can see what's underneath the plastic. In FreeHand, you use layers to organize your objects. You can also use layers to trace an object on a lower layer, such as a complex bitmap image. Layers simplify your life as a FreeHand illustrator, especially when you create a document with a lot of stuff.

When you create a new document, FreeHand gives you three layers to work with: Foreground, Background, and Guides. Only objects on the Foreground layer, or layers above the separation line, are printable. The separation line is a horizontal black line in the Layers panel.

You use the Layers panel to create and otherwise manage layers. To open the Layers panel, choose Window⇨Layers. The Layers panel is shown in Figure 2-9.

Figure 2-9:
Use the
Layers
panel to
manage the
layers in
your
document.

Creating layers

You can create a new layer whenever you need it. When you create a new layer, it becomes the drawing layer until you select another layer to work with. You create a new layer by following these steps:

1. **Choose Windows⇨Layers.**

   The Layers panel becomes activated.

2. **Click the Options button (the bulleted list icon in the upper-right corner of the panel).**

   The Options menu appears.

3. **Choose New.**

   FreeHand creates a new layer with the default name of Layer followed by the next available layer number, such as Layer-1. You'll know it's the active layer because there will be a little pen next to the name of the layer.

4. **Enter a new name for the layer by clicking and dragging to highlight the default name, typing a new name, and pressing Enter.**

   This step is optional. You can rename the layer at any time. We strongly advise you to get in the habit of giving your layers descriptive names, especially if you're creating documents with multiple layers.

You can duplicate the currently selected layer and all objects on it by opening the Layers panel, clicking the Options button (the bulleted list icon in the upper-right corner of the panel), and then choosing Duplicate from the Options menu.

After you select a layer, it becomes the active layer. You can use the Layers panel to perform any of the following tasks:

✦ **Hide and unhide objects:** Click the check mark in the left column to hide all objects on the selected layer. Click the column again to unhide the layer.

✦ **Display objects as keylines:** To display objects on a selected layer as keylines (they look like outlines with an X through them), click the filled dot in the center column of the Layers panel. The filled dot becomes hollow and a keyline of each shape is displayed.

✦ **Lock and unlock layers:** Click the open padlock icon in the third column to lock the layer. After you lock a layer, the icon changes to a closed padlock and you cannot edit or select objects on the layer. Click the padlock again to unlock the layer.

✦ **Hide and display layers:** Click the Options button (the bulleted list icon in the upper-right corner of the Layers panel) and choose All Off from the Options menu to hide all layers or choose All On to display all hidden layers.

Editing layers

When you use layers to organize a complex illustration, objects on top layers eclipse underlying objects on lower layers. You use the Layers panel to rearrange the order of layers and to perform other tasks, such as merging layers. You can also merge objects into a single layer when you've got everything just the way you want it.

To edit layers, choose Window⇨Layers to activate the Layers panel (if it's not already open and expanded), and then perform any of the following tasks:

✦ **Move layers:** Select a layer in the Layers panel and drag it up or down to a different position to change the way objects are displayed.

**Book IV
Chapter 2**

**Understanding
FreeHand MX
Basics**

✦ **Make layers non-printable:** Select a layer in the Layers panel and drag it below the separation line to make the layer non-printable.

✦ **Move objects between layers:** You can move an object to a different layer by selecting it in the Document window, and then in the Layers panel, click the name of the layer to which you want to move the object.

✦ **Merge layers:** To merge several layers into a single layer, select the layers in the Layers panel, click the Options button (the bulleted list icon in the upper-right corner of the Layers panel), and choose Merge Selected Layers from the Options menu. Hold down the Shift key to select multiple contiguous layers; hold down the Ctrl key to select non-contiguous layers.

✦ **Merge foreground layers:** To merge all foreground layers into a single layer, click the Options button (the bulleted list icon in the upper-right corner of the Layers panel), and then choose Merge Foreground Layers from the Options menu.

✦ **Remove layers:** You can remove a selected layer by clicking the Options button (the bulleted list icon in the upper-right corner of the Layers panel) and choosing Remove from the Options menu. If the layer you are removing contains objects, FreeHand displays a warning dialog box to that effect. Click Yes to delete the layer and all objects on it.

Saving Documents in FreeHand

When you finish creating a document, or you've had all the fun with FreeHand that you can handle for the day, or at any point while you're working, you can save your document. You can save the document as a FreeHand file, a FreeHand template, or an Editable EPS file. Save the document as a FreeHand file and you can edit the elements in the document when you reopen it. When you open a document saved as a template, you can use the elements in it as the basis for a new document. Saving a document as a template is useful if you do repetitive work for a client that uses the same elements in all the documents, such as the client's logo and address. You add additional elements to the template as needed and use the Save As command to save the revised template as a document. When you save the file as an Editable EPS file, you can work with the file in another illustration program that supports the EPS format, such as Adobe Illustrator or CorelDraw. When you save a document in any of these formats, you can later reopen and edit the document. *Note:* You are limited to saving a single page document when you choose the Editable EPS format.

In addition to saving documents, you can also export FreeHand documents into a number of different graphics formats, including JPEG, GIF, PNG, TIF, and BMP.

Saving FreeHand files

You can save a FreeHand document whenever you need to. When you save a document that has been edited since it was last saved, an asterisk (*) appears after the document's name in the document title bar. To save a document, follow these steps:

1. Choose File⇨Save or press Ctrl+S.

The Save Document dialog box opens.

2. Enter a name for the document and navigate to the folder where you want to save the file.

3. Choose the file format you want the document saved as.

You can choose from the following: FreeHand Document (`.fh11`), FreeHand Template (`.ft11`), or Editable EPS (`.eps`).

4. Click the Save button.

FreeHand saves the document to the specified folder.

When you save a previously saved file, the Save Document dialog box does not appear, and the file is saved using the same filename in the same location as the previous iteration of the file.

You can save your work using a different filename. This option is handy when you're making lots of edits and saving a file frequently. You can save a master version of the file, and then save a working version of the file using a different filename. If you run into a computer glitch and the working version of the file becomes corrupt, you can always revert to the master copy (or another previous version) of the file. You also use the Save As command to save a FreeHand template that you have added elements to in order to create a new document. To save a file using a different filename:

1. Choose File⇨Save As or press Ctrl+Shift+S.

The Save Document dialog box opens.

2. Enter a name for the document and navigate to the folder where you want to save the file.

3. Choose the file format you want the document saved as.

You can choose to save the document in one of the following formats: FreeHand Document (`.fh11`), FreeHand Template (`.ft11`), or Editable EPS (`.eps`).

4. Click the Save button.

FreeHand saves the renamed document to the specified folder.

Book IV Chapter 2

Understanding FreeHand MX Basics

Computers can be cranky creatures and are subject to system overloads, which may cause your machine to crash when you least expect it. In order to avoid losing hours of work, save your work early and save your work often.

Exporting files in other formats

You can create FreeHand illustrations for a wide variety of uses. You can create images for the Web, illustrations for print, and Flash movies, to name a few. When you need to use the finished illustration for a specific application, you export the file in the necessary format. You can also save the original as a previous-version FreeHand document. To export a file, follow these steps:

1. **Choose File⇨Export.**

   The Export dialog box appears.

2. **Enter a name for the file and specify the folder to which you want the file saved.**

3. **Choose the export file format. You can choose to export the file as one of the following:**

   - A bitmap file using the BMP, GIF, JPEG, PNG, or TIFF file formats.
   - A vector file using the EPS or EMF file format.
   - A Flash movie using the SWF format. You can import the end result into Macromedia Flash, or embed the movie in an HTML document for viewing on the Internet.
   - A FreeHand 8, 9, or 10 file.
   - An Adobe Illustrator file, versions 1.1, 3.0/4.0, 5.x, 7.x, or 8.8.
   - A PICT file (Macintosh only).
   - A DXF file for use in 3D applications.
   - A PDF file for viewing with the Adobe Acrobat Reader. The file may also be printed from the Acrobat Reader.
   - An RTF file for use in a word processing application.

4. **Click the Save button.**

   FreeHand exports the file in the format you specify.

Chapter 3: Using the FreeHand MX Text Tools

In This Chapter

✓ Creating text

✓ Editing text

✓ Creating text styles

✓ Creating text columns

✓ Converting text to paths

✓ Aligning text to a path

*I*f you need to add text to an illustration, you use the Text tool. If you want the text to jump up and get someone's attention, FreeHand MX gives you the tools to create really cool looking text. You can convert text to vector objects, align text to paths, and much more. In fact, you can do so many cool things with text in FreeHand, it would take forty or fifty pages to show you all of them. Unfortunately, we don't have that much space, but this chapter shows you the important features of working with text in FreeHand, so you'll have plenty to work with.

In this chapter, we show you how to stylize your text by modifying fonts, point size, and more. We explain how to use the Object tab of the Properties panel to modify your text, as well as how to format your text. And if you want to make your text jump through hoops, we show you how to do that by aligning text to a path.

Creating Text Using the Text Tool

When you need to add text to an illustration, the first step is to call on the Text tool. After you select the Text tool, you can create an auto-expanding text box that grows wider as you enter more text, or you can create a text box that is sized to fit a specific area of the illustration, in which case FreeHand automatically wraps text to a new line as needed. You can specify the font size, color, and other text attributes before or after you enter text.

Creating auto-expanding text boxes

When you select the Text tool and create text in the document, the default text block (box) is auto-expanding, which means the box gets wider as you enter more text. To create an auto-expanding box of text, follow these steps:

1. **Select the Text tool from the Tools panel.**

   The Text tool is the handsome-looking tool that's identified by a capital A. As you move the tool into the Document window, your cursor becomes an I-beam.

2. **Click the spot in your illustration where you want the text block to begin.**

   A flashing vertical line signifies that FreeHand is ready for you to enter text.

3. **Begin typing.**

   Your text appears in the document.

4. **Press Enter to create a new line.**

   Any text you type now appears on a new line. If you want a text box that automatically wraps text from line to line, you need to create a fixed-size text box, which we show you how to create in the next section.

5. **Click anywhere outside of the text box when you are finished entering text.**

   The Pointer tool is selected.

Creating fixed-size text boxes

When you create a fixed-size text box, you constrain the text to the size of the box. When text reaches the side of the box, FreeHand automatically wraps new text to the next line. To create a fixed-size text box, follow these steps:

1. **Select the Text tool from the Tools panel.**

2. **Click the point in the illustration where you want the text to appear, and then drag diagonally to define the size of the text box.**

   As you drag, FreeHand displays a dashed rectangle that gives you a preview of the box's current size.

3. **Release the mouse button when the text box is the desired size.**

   FreeHand creates a rectangular bounding box.

4. **Begin typing.**

   When you enter enough text to reach the side of the text box, FreeHand wraps the text to the next line.

5. **Click anywhere outside of the text box when you finish entering text.**

   FreeHand reverts to the Pointer tool that you can now use to resize or move the text box. Figure 3-1 shows an auto-expanding text box and a fixed-size text box.

You can add additional text to a text box by selecting the Text tool or Pointer tool and clicking the text box at the point where you want to add text. If you double-click a text box with the Pointer tool, it reverts to the Text tool. If you're using the Text tool, you need only click once.

You can remove any empty text blocks from your document by choosing Xtras⇨Delete⇨Empty Text Blocks.

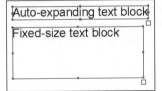

Figure 3-1:
A tale of two text boxes.

Using Text Rulers

When you create text, FreeHand displays a text ruler above the text. The text ruler is similar to the ruler you find at the top of the workspace of popular word processing programs. You use the text ruler in a similar manner. You can change the indent of paragraph text and change the position of tabs by dragging the icons at the top of the text ruler. After you finish entering text and select another tool, the text ruler is no longer visible. To view the text ruler, double-click the text box with the Pointer tool. Figure 3-2 shows a block of text with its attached text ruler.

Text rulers are enabled by default. Choose View⇨Text Rulers to hide text rulers from view. Choose the command again to show text rulers.

First line indent marker

Tab markers

Left indent marker

Figure 3-2:
Use the text ruler to change the indent of paragraph text and the position of tabs.

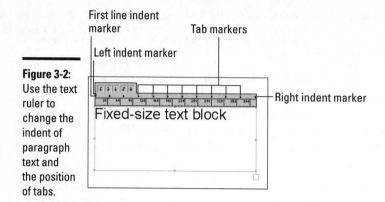

Right indent marker

Checking the Spelling of a Text Selection

If you're like many designers, when you enter text, your fingers are flying across the keyboard, especially when you have copious amounts of text to stuff into a document. Sometimes your fingers are moving so fast that you transpose letters and end up with some spelling errors. To safeguard against exporting a document with spelling errors, you can spell check your text selections:

1. **Choose Text⇨Spelling.**

The Spelling dialog box appears.

2. **Click the Start button.**

FreeHand begins checking your document for spelling errors. If it finds a spelling error, the suspect word is highlighted in the field at the top of the dialog box. Possible substitutes are listed in a field underneath the suspect word, as shown in Figure 3-3.

Figure 3-3:
Checking for misspelled words.

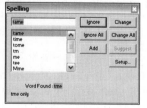

3. **If the spell checker finds a word not listed in its dictionary, you can choose one of the following options by clicking the appropriate button:**

- **Ignore:** If you choose this option, the spell checker ignores the word and checks the rest of the document for errors.

- **Change:** Choose this option after you select a word from the suggestions list so that the spell checker can replace the suspect word with the correctly spelled one that you selected.

- **Ignore All:** If you choose this option, the spell checker ignores this and all future instances of the suspect word. This option is handy when your document has several instances of a person's name or something else that would not be found in the dictionary but is spelled correctly.

- **Change All:** Choose this option when you select a word from the suggestions list so that the spell checker can replace this and all future occurrences of the suspect word.

- **Add:** If you choose this option, the spell checker adds the suspect word to its dictionary.

After you click a button, the spell checker continues searching the rest of the document for misspelled words.

You can select some basic preferences for the spell checker. You can access these options by clicking the Setup button from the main Spelling dialog box. Those options include:

✦ **Find Duplicate Words:** When selected, this feature ensures that the spell checker will show you when the same word appears sequentially (such as "the the" appearing in a sentence). By default, this option is selected.

✦ **Find Capitalization Errors:** If selected, this option causes the spell checker to look for anomalies in capitalization, including capital letters in the wrong place and two sequential capital letters. By default this option is selected.

✦ **Ignore Words with Numbers:** As you might expect, when selected, this option ensures that the spell checker ignores words that include numbers in them. By default, this option is selected.

✦ **Ignore Internet and File Addresses:** If selected, this option ensures that the spell checker ignores Web addresses, such as `www.dummies.com`, and file addresses, such as `C:\Program Files`. By default, this option is selected.

✦ **Ignore Words in UPPERCASE:** This option ignores words or acronyms that are all in uppercase letters. By default, this option is selected.

✦ **Add Words to Dictionary:** This is the only option that is not a check box. The two options available for this tool are selectable as radio buttons. The first option, Exactly as Typed, adds words to the dictionary just as they are typed. The All Lowercase radio button adds words to the dictionary in lowercase, no matter how they look when they are added. By default, the Exactly as Typed option is selected.

You can find and replace text and other objects in your FreeHand documents by choosing Edit⇨Find and Replace⇨Text. Follow the prompts in the dialog box to quickly locate text in your document.

Editing Blocks of Text

After you create a block of text, you can use the Pointer tool to move it or to resize a fixed-size text box. You can also convert an auto-expanding text box to a fixed-size box, and vice-versa.

Moving and deleting text

After you create a block of text, you can move or delete it as needed by following these steps:

1. **Select the Pointer tool from the Tools panel, and then click the text block to select it.**

   A bounding box appears around the perimeter of the text box.

2. **To move the selected text box, click it and drag it to a new location.**

   The cursor changes to a four-headed arrow when you place it over the bounding box to click and drag. The text box is moved.

3. **To delete the text box, press the Delete or Backspace key.**

   The text box is gone. Alternatively, you can delete a selected text box by choosing Edit⇨Clear.

Resizing text boxes

If you create fixed-size text boxes, you can modify the width and height as needed. To resize a fixed-size text box, select the text box with the Pointer tool and do one of the following:

+ **Resize a text box:** To resize the text box, click and drag the corner handle. The text reflows to the new dimensions of the text box.

+ **Proportionately resize a text box:** To proportionately resize the text box, click the handle on any corner, and then while holding down the Shift key, drag away from the center of the text box to make it larger, or towards the center to make it smaller. Text inside the box reflows to the new dimensions.

When you resize a text box using one of these methods, the text size remains unchanged. You can resize the text as you resize the text box by doing the following:

1. **Select the Pointer tool from the Tools panel, and then click the text block to select it.**

   FreeHand draws a bounding box around the text box.

2. **Click the handle at any corner of the text box, and while holding down the Shift and Alt keys, drag the handle until the text box is the desired size.**

   The text box is proportionately resized and the text is resized as well.

If you drag the middle handle on either side, or the center top or bottom handle, you don't resize the text, you change the text spacing. If you move either of these handles towards the center of the text box, individual characters overlap, leaving you with a jumbled, illegible mess. If you drag the top center or bottom center handle, you adjust the leading (line spacing) of the text. Moving the handles toward the center of the box can create overlapping lines, but dragging outward from the center can give your text a light, airy feel by increasing the distance between lines.

Changing text box characteristics

You can change the characteristics of a text box at any time. For example, if you have a fixed-size text box, you can convert it to an auto-expanding text box, and vice versa.

To convert an auto-expanding text box to a fixed-size text box, follow these steps:

1. **Select the Pointer tool from the Tools panel, and then click the text box to select it.**

2. **Double-click one of the middle handles on the sides of the text box and one of the middle handles on the top or bottom of the text box.**

   You can now resize the text box by clicking any corner handle and dragging. *Remember:* You can proportionately resize the text box by holding down the Shift key while dragging.

Any text that is added that doesn't fit within a fixed-size text block will not be visible, and the Text Overflow icon appears at the bottom-right corner of the text block. Stretch the text block from a corner point to see the added text.

To convert a fixed-size text box to an auto-expanding text box, follow these steps:

1. **Select the text box with the Pointer tool.**

**Book IV
Chapter 3**

Using the
FreeHand MX
Text Tools

2. **Double-click one of the middle handles on the sides of the text box and one of the middle handles on the top or bottom of the text box.**

FreeHand shrink-wraps the box around the text inside. When you add additional text to the box, it will expand to accommodate the additional text. *Remember:* You can create a new line by pressing Enter.

Formatting Text

When you create text for a FreeHand document, you can format the text before you type it in, or you can select all the text in the text box after the fact and do your formatting then. You can specify the font style, font size, font color, paragraph alignment, and much more.

You have three tools at your disposal for choosing text attributes: menu commands, the Object tab of the Properties panel, and the Text toolbar. We give you a brief overview of the menu commands and the Text toolbar, but we focus on the Properties panel, FreeHand's formatting powerhouse:

✦ **Menu commands:** You can use the menu to specify font type, font size, style, paragraph alignment, leading, baseline shift, and case (capitalization). To format selected text using a menu command, choose Text, choose a category from the menu, and then choose the desired command from the submenu. For example, choose Text➪Size➪12 to change the font size to 12.

✦ **The Text toolbar:** You use the Text toolbar to select a font, specify the font size and paragraph alignment, and so on. You can even use the Text toolbar to attach text to a path, as described in the upcoming section, "Working with Text and Paths." The Text toolbar is shown in Figure 3-4, and like other FreeHand toolbars, you can leave it floating in the workspace or dock it below the menu bar. To use the Text toolbar, choose Window➪Toolbars➪Text.

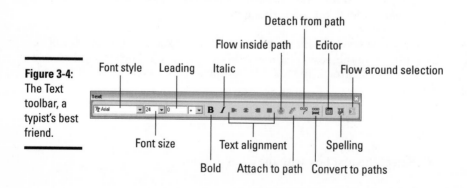

Figure 3-4: The Text toolbar, a typist's best friend.

Detach from path

Flow inside path   Editor

Font style   Leading   Italic   Flow around selection

Font size   Text alignment   Spelling

Bold   Attach to path   Convert to paths

✦ **The Object tab in the Properties panel:** You can choose your font type, style, size, and alignment using the Object tab in the Properties panel. You can choose these parameters before or after creating a text box. To open the Properties panel, choose Window⇨Object. Make sure that your text box is selected, and you'll see a text block appear in the Object tab, as shown in Figure 3-5. Choose from one of the five buttons to specify parameters when working with text:

- **Character:** You use this section of the Object tab to choose a font type, font size, style, paragraph alignment, leading, kerning, and baseline shift. You can also apply effects to text in this section, as well as choose a text style. The character button is the top one (with "abc" on it).

- **Paragraph:** You use this section of the Object tab to specify paragraph spacing and indentation, and answer the age-old question: "To hyphenate or not to hyphenate?"

- **Spacing:** You use this section of the Object tab to scale characters and specify spacing between letters and words.

- **Columns and Rows:** You use this section of the Object tab to display a block of text as columns and rows.

- **Adjust Columns:** You use this section of the Object tab to specify how text flows between columns and rows.

Paragraph

Character

Figure 3-5:
You use the
Object tab
in the
Properties
panel to
format text
and much
more.

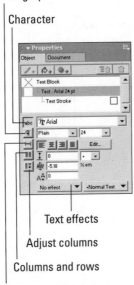

Text effects

Adjust columns

Columns and rows

Spacing

Choosing a font type, size, and style

You can choose a font style and size before you begin typing or after you create a block of text. If you choose the font style after creating your text, you have the added benefit of seeing a preview of the font, as it will be applied to your text. To choose a font style, follow these steps:

1. Create a block of text.

You know the drill. Select the Text tool, click inside the document, and type.

2. Click anywhere outside of the text box to deselect the Text tool.

The block of text is still selected, and the Pointer tool is now the active tool.

3. Click the Character button in the Object tab of the Properties panel.

The character properties are displayed. If the Properties panel is not open to the Object tab, choose Window⇨Object or press Ctrl+F3.

4. Click the triangle to the right of the Font Name field and scroll through the drop-down list.

The fonts you have installed on your system show up in the Font Name drop-down list. As you scroll through the list, the first few words of the selected text are displayed with the font style applied, as shown in Figure 3-6.

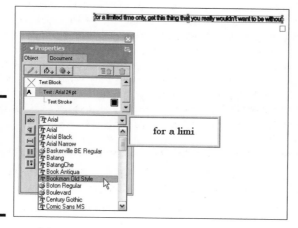

Figure 3-6:
Choosing a font type in the Object tab in the Properties panel.

5. **Click a font name to select it.**

6. **Select a size from the Text Size drop-down list.**

   You can also enter your own value in this field if you want the text to be sized differently than the preset values. If you type a value into this field, you must press Enter to apply the size.

7. **Select one of the following options from the Style drop-down list:**

   - **Plain:** Choose this default style if you like plain text.

   - **Bold:** Choose this style to boldface the text.

   - **Italic:** Choose this style to italicize the text.

   - **BoldItalic:** Choose this style to boldface and italicize the text.

8. **Close the panel to apply the characteristics to the text.**

   If needed, you can also use this section of the Object tab to apply effects to text, apply a style to the text, and more.

If you like to mix and match font types, styles, and so on, within a block of text, double-click the text to activate the Text tool and select the letters or words in the block of text that you want to style differently. After selecting the letters or words, open the Object tab of the Properties panel to set the parameters for the text selection.

Creating text styles

When you add text to a document, FreeHand uses the default Normal Text style to format the text. You can modify the text using menu commands or the Object tab in the Properties panel, however, the changes only apply to the block of text you are creating. If you're creating a document with lots of text that spans different pages, formatting each new block of text can become a nuisance, especially when they're all the same. After you decide on text formatting options for a document, you can save the formatting as a style, which you can then apply to any block of text with a click of the mouse. To create a text style, follow these steps:

1. **Select the Text tool from the Tools panel and create a block of text.**

2. **Format the text using the font style, size, and other attributes that will remain constant throughout the document.**

3. **Choose Window⇨Styles or press Shift+F11.**

   The Styles tab of the Assets panel, shown in Figure 3-7, opens.

Figure 3-7:
You can create a custom text style using the Styles panel.

4. **Click the Options button (the bulleted list icon in the upper-right corner of the panel) and choose New from the Options menu.**

   A new entry, in the form of a box with Aa in the middle of it, appears in the Styles tab. In the Object tab of the Properties panel, you'll see that the style will be given the default name of Style, appended by the next available style number (Style-1, for example). If you're creating more than one style for the document, you can rename the style to better reflect what the style applies to.

After you create a text style, you can apply the style to any text box on any page in your document. To apply a text style, follow these steps:

1. **Select the block of text to which you want to apply a style.**

2. **Choose Window⇨Styles or press Shift+F11.**

   The Styles tab of the Assets panel opens and all styles currently in use for the document are displayed.

3. **Click the name of the style you want applied to the text.**

   The text is formatted to the style's parameters.

In FreeHand MX, renaming a style is a bit more complicated than it was in previous versions. By default, items in the Styles tab are shown in "Previews only" format, which is to say they show a small preview of the style itself. To rename a style, you must first change the layout of the styles to either "Compact list views" or "Large list views" by clicking the Options button (the bulleted text icon in the top right of the Assets panel) and selecting a layout option. After this is complete, you can double-click on your style, enter a name for it, and press Enter to save it.

Choosing a text color

If language can be colorful, so should text. When you add color to text, you accentuate the text and make it stand apart from other elements in an illustration. You can apply the same color to an entire block of text, or select individual letters from a block of text and choose a different color for each. To specify the color for a block of text, follow these steps:

1. **Select the Pointer tool from the Tools panel, and then click the text box to select it.**

If you only want to apply a color to an individual letter or word in a text box, double-click the text box to activate the Text tool, and then highlight the letter or word you want to select a color for.

2. **Click the Fill color box (next to the paint bucket) in the Tools panel.**

The color picker appears.

3. **Click a color to select it.**

You've got colorful text!

Some illustrators like to choose a different color for the first letter in a paragraph to draw the viewer's eye to the paragraph. You can also draw attention to the first letter in a paragraph by specifying a larger font size.

Aligning your text

When you create a block of text, the text is aligned by default to the left side of the text box. You can modify the text alignment to suit the illustration that you are creating. You can change the text alignment at any time by following these steps:

1. **Using the Pointer tool from the Tools panel, select the block of text whose alignment you want to modify.**

2. **Click the Character button in the Object tab of the Properties panel.**

The character properties are displayed. If the Properties panel is not open to the Object tab, choose Window⇨Object or press Ctrl+F3. The Character button is the one with the "abc" on it.

3. **Click the appropriate button to apply one of the following alignments to the selected text:**

- **Left:** Aligns the text to the left side of the text box; this is the default alignment. The right side of the text will be ragged.

- **Center:** Aligns each line of text to the center of the text box.

- **Right:** Aligns text to the right side of the text box. The left side of the text will be ragged.

- **Justify:** Spaces the text so that it flows to fill the text box, leaving no ragged edges.

Changing paragraph settings

When you create several paragraphs of text in a block, you can change the formatting of the paragraphs to suit your illustration. You can modify the paragraph indentation and how the tabs are spaced using the Object tab of the Properties panel:

1. **Select the block of text whose paragraph settings you want to modify by clicking it with the Pointer tool.**

2. **Choose Window⇨Object or press Ctrl+F3.**

The Properties panel opens to the Object tab.

3. **Click the Paragraph button.**

The Paragraph section of the Object tab opens, as shown in Figure 3-8.

Below

Above

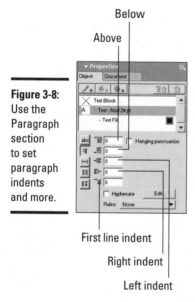

Figure 3-8:
Use the
Paragraph
section
to set
paragraph
indents
and more.

First line indent

Right indent

Left indent

4. **Enter a value in the Above field or in the Below field, or both.**

The values you enter in these fields determine how much space appears above or below the paragraph. If you enter values in both fields, FreeHand creates a space above and below each paragraph in the text box.

5. **Select the Hanging Punctuation check box to place punctuation, such as quotation marks, outside of paragraph margins.**

6. **Enter a value in the Left and Right Indent fields.**

   These values determine how far a paragraph indents from the left and right borders of the text box. A positive value indents the text inside the text box, and a negative value places the text outside the text box or column.

7. **Enter a value in the First Line Indent field.**

   This value determines how far the first line of a paragraph indents from the left indent of the paragraph.

8. **Select the Hyphenate check box to enable automatic hyphenation for the block of text.**

9. **Press Enter.**

   Your changes are applied to the selected block of text.

Formatting text in columns and rows

If you like your text neatly arranged, you can do that in FreeHand. You can format a block of text to be displayed in rows and columns, which is the equivalent of creating a table. After you format text into columns and rows, you can control how the text flows between columns and rows. Follow these steps to format a block of text into columns and rows:

1. **Select the block of text you want to format into columns and rows.**

2. **Choose Window⇨Object or press Ctrl+F3.**

   The Properties panel opens to the Object tab.

3. **Click the Columns button (fourth from the top).**

   The Columns section of the Object tab opens, as shown in Figure 3-9.

4. **Enter a value in the Columns field.**

   This determines the number of columns in the text box.

5. **Enter a value in the Column Spacing field.**

   This value determines the distance between columns.

6. **Enter a value in the H field.**

   This value determines the height of each table cell.

7. **Enter a value in the Rows field.**

   This value determines the number of rows in the text box.

Column height

Columns

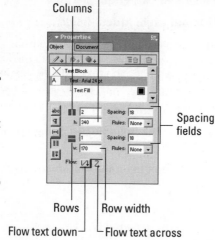

Figure 3-9:
You can
format a text
block into
rows and
columns.

Spacing
fields

Rows │ │ Row width

Flow text down ┘ └ Flow text across

8. Enter a value in the Row Spacing field.

This value determines the amount of space between the rows in the
text box.

9. Enter a value in the W field.

This value determines the width of each cell.

10. Click the desired Flow button.

The option you choose determines how the text flows within the table.
The left button flows text down all rows in a column and then into the
next column. The right button flows text across all rows and then down
to the next column.

If the text isn't flowing between rows and columns to your liking, you can
modify text flow by opening the Object tab of the Properties panel, and then
clicking the Adjust Columns button — the bottom button in the list on the
left. When the Adjust Columns section of the Object tab appears, select the
Balance Columns check box to balance the flow between columns.

Scaling text horizontally

You can adjust the width of characters in a text block to suit your design.
You can make characters wider or narrower. This option gives you a bit of

artistic latitude when a font is almost, but not quite, perfect for your needs. To scale text horizontally, follow these steps:

1. **Using the Pointer tool from the Tools panel, select the block of text you want to scale.**

   If you select a block of text with the Pointer tool, the changes will be applied to all text and subsequent text you enter in the text box. To scale individual words in a text block, double-click the text box with the Pointer tool, and then select the word(s) or character(s) you want to scale.

2. **Choose Window⇨Object or press Ctrl+F3.**

   The Properties panel opens to the Object tab.

3. **Click the Spacing button.**

   The Spacing section of the Object tab opens.

4. **In the % field, enter the value by which you want the text scaled.**

   This value is a percentage of the text's original size. Enter a value larger than 100 to increase the text width, or lower than 100 to shrink the text.

5. **In the Spacing % fields, enter values in the Min, Opt, and Max fields for Words and Letters:**

   • **Word:** The values you enter for Word affect the space between words in a selected block of text. A value of 100 is the standard spacing for words. Values less than 100 move words closer together, and values higher than 100 move words apart.

   • **Letter:** The values you enter for Letter change the percentage deviation from the standard spacing between letters. The standard letter spacing is 0. Enter a higher value for more space between letters and a lower value to move letters closer together.

   To precisely space letters and words, enter the same value in the Min, Opt, and Max fields.

6. **In the Keep Together field, enter a value for the number of lines to be kept together when scaling text columns.**

   Enter a value of 2 to prevent the first or last line of a paragraph being isolated at the top or bottom of a column.

7. **Select the Selected Words check box to prevent a line break when scaling selected text.**

8. **Close the Properties panel or select another text option to modify.**

   The selected text is scaled by the values specified.

Copying attributes between text boxes

If you're like many illustrators, you'll be working on a document, get a blinding flash of insight, and come up with a better design for something. If this happens when you're creating a new block of text, you can quickly copy the attributes from the new block of text to other text boxes in your document. You can copy settings from the Text Character, Spacing, and Paragraph sections of the Object tab of the Properties panel. To copy attributes from one text box to another, follow these steps:

1. **Select the text box whose attributes you want to copy.**

2. **Choose Edit➪Copy Attributes.**

   The attributes are copied to the Clipboard.

3. **Select the text box to which you want to paste the attributes.**

4. **Choose Edit➪Paste Attributes.**

   FreeHand pastes the copied attributes to the selected block of text.

Adding visual effects to text

You can create some pretty snazzy text using FreeHand by selecting an exciting font and modifying it with the Object tab of the Properties panel. If you need more pizzazz than that, you can apply visual effects to text. You can choose from effects like the ever-present drop shadow, or other unique effects, such as highlighting text. Figure 3-10 shows the effects that you can choose from.

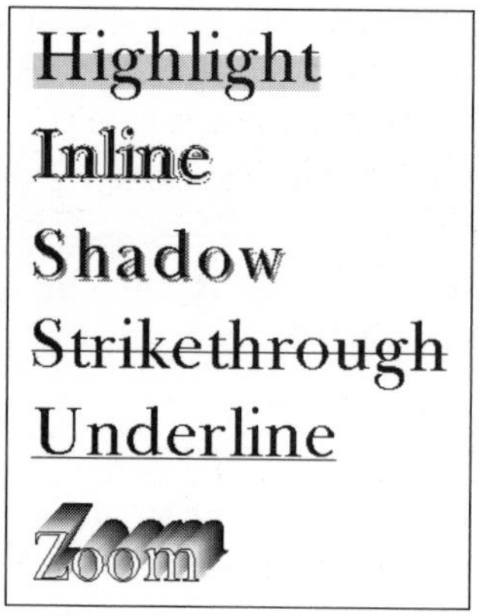

Figure 3-10:
You can achieve interesting results by applying an effect to text.

Highlight
Inline
Shadow
Strikethrough
Underline

Follow these steps to add a visual effect to text in a document:

1. **Select the Pointer tool from the Tools panel and double-click a text box.**

The text is selected and the Text tool is active.

2. **Select the text to which you want to apply a visual effect.**

You can select an individual letter, a word, or the entire text box.

3. **Choose Window⇨Object or press Ctrl+F3.**

The text properties will show up on the Object tab.

4. **Click the Effects button at the bottom-left of the Object tab and choose one of the following:**

- No Effect (the default)
- Highlight
- Inline
- Shadow

- Strikethrough
- Underline
- Zoom

5. **Press Enter or click outside the text box.**

FreeHand applies the effect to the selected text. Be aware that these effects will not be retained if the text is converted to paths.

Adjusting the Spacing and Position of Characters and Lines

When you create paragraph text, you have more options than just font type, size, and alignment. You can also specify the space between paragraph lines, which is known as *leading*. Another parameter you can modify is *kerning*, which is the space between two characters. You can also modify the *baseline shift* of a word or letter in a block of text, which causes the selected word or letter to be raised above or below the baseline of the other characters in the text block.

Adjusting leading

To adjust leading for a block of text, follow these steps:

1. **Select the Pointer tool from the Tools panel and click a text box to select it.**

2. **Choose Window⇨Object or press Ctrl+F3.**

The Properties panel opens to the Object tab.

3. **Click the Character button.**

4. **Enter a value in the Leading field.**

   Enter a number to specify the leading value. The value is applied according to the option you select in Step 5.

5. **Choose one of the following options from the Leading Type drop-down list:**

   - **Plus (+):** Specifies a point value to be added to the current font size.

   - **Equal (=):** Specifies leading equal to a value.

   - **Percent (%):** Specifies leading as a percentage of the current font size.

6. **Close the Properties panel to apply your changes or select another text parameter to modify.**

   The change is applied to the selected text box.

Adjusting kerning

To adjust kerning for a block of text, follow these steps:

1. **Select the Pointer tool from the Tools panel and click a text box to select it.**

   Selecting a text box determines the kerning for the entire block of text, also known as *range kerning*. To modify kerning between individual words or characters, double-click the block of text and place your cursor between the characters or words for which you want to modify kerning.

2. **Choose Window⇨Object or press Ctrl+F3.**

   The Properties panel opens to the Object tab.

3. **Click the Character button.**

4. **Enter a value in the Kerning field and press Enter.**

   The value you enter is a percentage of the space of the letter M for the text font. To decrease the kerning between words or characters, enter a negative value, such as −10, which will decrease the kerning by 10 percent.

5. **Press Enter, or choose another text parameter to modify.**

   Your specified kerning is applied to the text.

Adjusting baseline shift

You can modify baseline shift by following these steps:

1. **Select the Pointer tool from the Tools panel and double-click the text box that contains the word or character whose baseline shift you want to modify.**

   Your cursor becomes an I-beam.

2. **Select the word or character whose baseline shift you want to modify.**

   The word or character is highlighted.

3. **Choose Window⇨Object or press Ctrl+F3.**

   The Properties panel opens to the Object tab.

4. **Click the Character button.**

5. **In the Baseline Shift field, enter the value by which you want the baseline shifted.**

   By default, this value is in points. (If you've changed to a different unit of measurement, for example, pixels, the value will be in pixels.) To shift the selected text above the baseline, enter a positive value. To shift the selected text below the baseline, enter a negative value. For example, entering a value of –15 shifts the selected text 15 points below the baseline.

6. **Press Enter, or choose another text parameter to modify.**

   The text is shifted by the amount specified.

Working with Text and Paths

When you create a line of text, it flows in a line from point A to point B. This is the time-honored standard for creating text. But wait, you're an illustrator, and FreeHand is an illustration program. You say you want text that swoops and swirls like a roller coaster? Or perhaps you want your text characters to look a little different. If that's your artistic vision, we show you how to achieve it in the upcoming sections.

Converting text to a path

You can convert a block of text, or a single letter, into a path. When you do this, the letter or text block is no longer editable as text, but you can have a field day distorting the text by manipulating points with the Subselection tool or by using the Freeform tool. (We show you how to use the Subselection tool in Book IV, Chapter 4.)

If you're trying to convert text that has special effects being applied to it, be warned. When you convert the text to a path, you'll find that your special effects will disappear.

Here's how you convert text to a path:

1. Select the block of text that you want to convert to a path.

This technique works best with single letters or initials, for example, the letters used to make a client's logo. This technique also works best if the text is large.

2. Choose Text⇨Convert to Paths or press Ctrl+Shift+P.

FreeHand converts the text to a vector object. Characters with counters (holes: e, g, b, d, o, a, and so on) become Compound Paths. Figure 3-11 shows a letter after being converted to paths. The converted letter has been further modified with the Freeform tool.

Figure 3-11:
You can create editable vector objects when you convert text to paths.

Aligning text to a path

If you (or your client) have the hankering for an illustration with unique text, you can easily achieve this goal by attaching text to a path. You create text that swoops and swirls by attaching text to an open path, or you can create stylized text by attaching it to a closed path, such as an ellipse. To align text to a path:

1. Select the text and the path.

You can select both objects by dragging the Pointer tool around the text and the path, or by selecting either the text or the path, and then selecting the other while holding down the Shift key.

2. Choose Text⇨Attach to Path or press Ctrl+Shift+Y.

The text develops a magnetic attraction for the path.

After you've attached your text to a path, you can move the text along the path if it isn't exactly where you want it. See the "Modifying the alignment of text along a path" section, later in this chapter, for details.

Aligning text to both sides of an ellipse

Another effect that you can achieve with FreeHand is attaching text to the top and bottom of an ellipse. If you have a client that wants you to display text above and below a logo, this is the path — pun intended — to take. To attach text to the top and bottom of an ellipse, follow these steps:

1. **Create an ellipse.**

   For more information on creating an ellipse, see Book IV, Chapter 4.

2. **Use the Text tool to create a block of text.**

   Create the text that appears above and below the ellipse in the same text block. Press Enter after you create the text that appears above the ellipse, and then type the second line of text.

3. **Select the ellipse, and then while pressing the Shift key, select the text.**

4. **Choose Text⇨Attach to Path.**

   The text on the first line attaches to the top of the ellipse, and the text on the second line attaches to the bottom of the ellipse, as shown in Figure 3-12.

Figure 3-12: You can attach text to both the top and bottom of an ellipse.

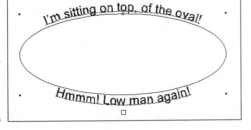

If you have an object in your illustration and you want a block of text to flow around it, select the object and move it so it overlaps the text. Then choose Modify⇨Arrange⇨Bring to Front to bring the object in front of the text. Then choose Text⇨Flow Around Selection. In the Flow Around Selection dialog box that appears, click the Text Wrap button (the button on the right), and then in the text fields, enter the size of the margins you want between the text and the object.

You can flow text inside an object. Create an object, such as an ellipse or polygon, and then create a block of text. Select the text and object, and then choose Text⟿Flow Inside Path. Whoosh! The text appears inside the shape.

Modifying the alignment of text along a path

After you attach text to a path, you can modify where the text aligns to the path. You can modify which side of the path text appears on, as well as move the text to a different point along the path. To modify the alignment of text along a path, follow these steps:

1. **Using the Pointer tool from the Tools panel, select the text whose alignment along a path you need to change.**

2. **Choose Window⟿Object or press Ctrl+F3.**

   The Object tab in the Properties panel opens.

3. **Select the Show Path check box if you want the path displayed as well as the text.**

4. **From the Top and Bottom Alignment drop-down list, select one of the following:**

   • **None:** Select this option if the text is attached to a path that is not visible.

   • **Baseline:** Aligns the baseline of the text to the path.

   • **Ascent:** Aligns the text to the bottom of the path.

   • **Descent:** Aligns the text to the top of the path.

5. **From the Orientation drop-down list, select one of the following options:**

   • **Rotate around path:** Orients the text with the rotation of the path.

   • **Vertical:** Orients the text vertically to the path.

   • **Skew Horizontal:** Skews the text horizontally along the path.

   • **Skew Vertical:** Skews the text vertically along the path.

6. **In the Inset section, enter a value in the Left field, and then press Enter to move the text to a different position along the path.**

   This is the distance you want the text offset to the right along the path. If the text is attached to an ellipse, enter a negative value to move the text to the left.

   When you enter a value in the Left field, the value in the Right field is automatically updated. For example, if you enter a value of 10 in the Left field, this value is added to the Right field. The value in the Right field is where the text ends. If you're a math whiz, you can enter a value in the Right field, however, it's easier to enter a value in the Left field.

If you prefer, you can change the text alignment along a path by manually moving it. To manually align text along a path, follow these steps:

1. **Use the Pointer tool from the Tools panel to select the block of text whose alignment to a path you want to modify.**

The text is selected and a small triangle appears to the left of the text, as shown in Figure 3-13.

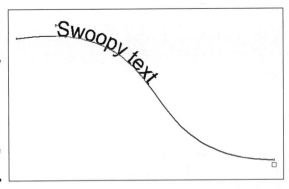

Figure 3-13:
Move the
text along
the path by
clicking and
dragging the
triangle.

2. **Click the triangle and drag the text to a new location along the path.**

As you drag the triangle, FreeHand creates a gray shape the size of the text that gives you a preview of the current location of the text along the path.

3. **Release the mouse button when the text is in the desired location.**

Chapter 4: Creating Illustrations with FreeHand MX

In This Chapter

✔ **Creating shapes**

✔ **Selecting objects**

✔ **Modifying shapes**

✔ **Creating groups**

✔ **Arranging and aligning objects**

✔ **Slicing objects**

*W*hen you create an illustration in FreeHand MX, you have a multitude of options to work with. With a bit of practice, you can create some interesting shapes for your illustrations and modify them to suit your artistic muse or your client's vision. The results you can achieve are only limited by your imagination and sense of experimentation. The FreeHand tools, although many, are relatively simple to use, which gives you the freedom to concentrate on your creation without having to worry about an overly complicated tool.

In this chapter, we show you how to create an illustration using the marvelous array of tools in FreeHand. We explain how to use the available tools to create shapes, and then use panels or other tools to modify those shapes. In Book IV, Chapter 5, we show you how to transform the shapes you create to put your own unique touch on an illustration.

Using Predefined Shapes

In Book IV, Chapter 2, we introduce the shape tools. The shape tools look kind of ho-hum when you see them in the Tools panel; but when you click one of them and use it to add a shape to your illustration, things start looking up. And if you double-click an innocuous little tool button, you may get a dialog box with tool options that allow you to modify the base shape into something truly cool, or modify the way the tool draws. In this section, we show you how to use the shape tools to create shapely shapes. We also point out which tools have additional options. Figure 4-1 shows the shape tools and the shapes you can create with them.

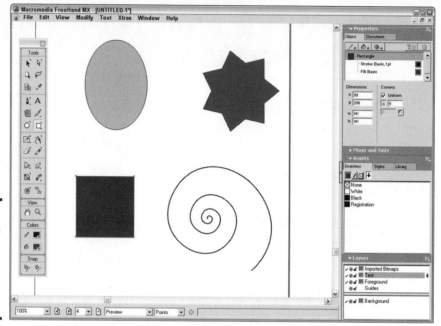

Figure 4-1:
Cool shapes
are just a
click and
drag away
with these
tools.

Creating rectangles and squares

If you need a rectangle in your illustration, or its equally dimensioned
cousin, the square, you use the Rectangle tool. Rectangles make wonderful
borders for Web site headers or frames for text. If your illustration calls for
rectangles with rounded corners, the Rectangle tool can give you this as
well. To add a rectangle to your illustration, follow these steps:

1. **Select the Rectangle tool from the Tools panel. (Refer to Figure 4-1).**

   If you're creating a garden-variety rectangle, skip to Step 5. If you want a
   rectangle with pizzazz, read on.

2. **Double-click the Rectangle tool.**

   The Rectangle Tool dialog box appears.

3. **To make the corners rounded, enter a value for the corner radius.**

   Enter a low value for gently rounded corners, or a high value for corners
   with curves that rival those of an Italian sports car.

4. **Click OK.**

   The dialog box goes on hiatus until you double-click the tool again.

5. **Click and drag inside the document to draw the rectangle.**

   As you drag, FreeHand draws a bounding box to give you a preview of the shape's current size. If you hold down the Shift key while dragging, you constrain the shape to a square. If you hold down the Alt key, the shape is created from the center outward.

6. **Release the mouse button when the shape is the desired size.**

   FreeHand creates the rectangle.

Creating polygons

If you like many-sided shapes, the Polygon tool's got your name written all over it. Actually, it has a polygonal shape emblazoned on it, but you can satisfy your need for many-sided shapes with this tool. You can create polygons and star-shaped objects with the Polygon tool. You'll also be happy to know that you can specify how many sides the shape has. To create a polygon, follow these steps:

1. **Select the Polygon tool (refer to Figure 4-1) by clicking and holding on the Rectangle tool and selecting Polygon when the pop-up menu appears.**

   You can create a polygon using the tool's current settings by clicking and dragging inside the document. For other options, you need to open the Polygon Tool dialog box.

2. **Double-click the Polygon tool.**

   The Polygon Tool dialog box opens, as shown in Figure 4-2.

Figure 4-2:
You can create a polygon or star with the Polygon tool.

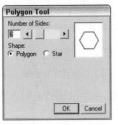

3. **Drag the slider to specify the number of sides.**

   Alternatively, you can enter a value higher than 3 in the field. The slider stops at 20, but you can manually enter any number in the field. (If you create a polygon with lots of sides, it ends up looking like a circle.)

4. **Select the Polygon or Star radio button.**

This determines whether you draw a polygon or a star. If you select Star, you can specify the angle of the sides by following the next step. If you select Polygon, you're done; go to Step 7.

5. **In the Star Points section, select Automatic or Manual.**

If you select Automatic, FreeHand determines the angle based on the number of sides you specify.

6. **If you specify Manual, drag the slider to specify the angle of the star sides.**

As you drag the slider, the preview window refreshes to show you the star's shape with the current settings.

7. **Click OK.**

The dialog box closes.

8. **Click and drag inside the document to create the shape.**

As you drag, FreeHand creates a preview that shows the current size of the shape. Hold down the Shift key while dragging to create a shape that is as wide as it is tall. Hold down the Alt key to draw the shape from the center out.

9. **Release the mouse button when the shape is the desired size.**

A star is born. That is, unless you choose the Polygon option.

Creating ellipses

The ellipse is a wonderful shape, a curved wonder that makes ends meet. If your illustration calls for a circular or oval shape, the Ellipse tool is right up your alley. And if you're creating an illustration of a bowling alley, you can use the Ellipse tool to create a bowling ball and use the Rectangle tool to create an alley. To create a shape with the Ellipse tool:

1. **Select the Ellipse tool by clicking on it in the Tools panel.**

It's the tool with a circle for an icon. (Refer to Figure 4-1.) The Ellipse tool has no parameters to modify.

2. **Click the spot in the document where you want to create an ellipse and then drag diagonally.**

As you drag the tool, FreeHand creates a preview of the shape's size. If you hold down the Shift key while dragging, you constrain the shape to a circle. If you hold down the Alt key, you create the shape from the center out.

3. **Release the mouse button when the ellipse is the desired size.**

FreeHand creates the ellipse.

Creating spirals

If you're familiar with previous versions of FreeHand, you might initially think that the Spiral tool was phased out in FreeHand MX. Not true! The Spiral tool just has been buried a bit more in the interface. Spirals are fun shapes that you can use to good effect when creating whimsical illustrations. You can use a spiral to create a reasonable facsimile of a corkscrew, just the thing if your client sells fine — or not so fine — wines. To add a spiral to an illustration, follow these steps:

1. **Select the Spiral tool by clicking and holding down on the Line tool in the Tools panel, and then selecting Spiral from the pop-up menu. (It looks like a wound-too-tight spring.)**

You can create a spiral using the tool's current settings by dragging in the document. If you want a custom spiral, take the following steps.

2. **Double-click the tool.**

The Spiral dialog box opens, as shown in Figure 4-3.

Figure 4-3: Use this dialog box to specify how your soaring spiral swirls.

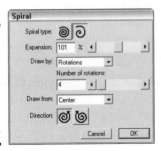

3. **In the Spiral Type section, select one of the following options:**

- Click the left button to create a spiral with an evenly spaced, concentric radius.

- Click the right button to create a spiral with an expanding radius that becomes wider with each spiral. When you click the right button, an extra option appears. Drag the slider to set the expansion rate. Alternatively, you can enter a value in the text field.

4. **From the Draw By drop-down list, select one of the following options to specify the manner in which FreeHand draws the spiral:**

- **Rotations:** Choose this option to specify the number of rotations the spiral has, regardless of its size. When you choose this option, set the number of rotations by dragging the slider. Alternatively, you can enter a value in the text field.

- **Increments:** Choose this option to create more rotations as the spiral grows larger. When you choose this option, specify the spacing between each interval by dragging the slider or by entering a value in the Increment Width text field. To create a shape with expanding spirals, enter a value in the Start Radius text field.

5. **From the Draw From drop-down list, select one of the following options:**

   - **Center:** Choose this option, and you draw the spiral by clicking the center point and then dragging to place the spiral's ending point.

   - **Corner:** Choose this option, and you draw the spiral by clicking to place one ending point of the spiral and then dragging to set the other.

   - **Edge:** Choose this option, and you draw the spiral by clicking to create the end point and then clicking to set to center point.

6. **Click a Direction button to determine which way your spiral swirls.**

   Click the left button for a counterclockwise spiral, the right button for a clockwise spiral.

7. **Click OK.**

   The Spiral dialog box closes.

8. **Click anywhere in the document and then drag to define the size of the spiral.**

   As you drag, FreeHand creates a preview of the spiral's current size. Hold down the Alt key to draw the spiral from the center, regardless of the option you choose in the Spiral dialog box.

9. **Release the mouse button when the spiral is the desired size.**

   FreeHand draws the spiral.

Creating Freeform Shapes

The Pencil tools represent another major interface change in FreeHand MX. In the previous version of FreeHand, a single Pencil tool had three formats: Freehand, Variable Stroke, and Calligraphic Pen.

Now, in FreeHand MX, these functions are separated into their own tools:

- ✦ **Pencil tool (formerly Freehand tool):** Draws a simple line the width of the currently selected stroke.

- ✦ **Variable Stroke Pen tool:** Creates an artistic brush-like stroke.

- ✦ **Calligraphic Pen tool:** Creates a stroke that looks like it was created with a calligrapher's pen.

You can use these tools to create anything from a simple squiggly line to an expressive calligraphic stroke. The following sections show how best to utilize these three tools.

When you use the tools, keep in mind that if you set attributes for the stroke and fill while you have the Pointer tool selected, those attributes become the default attributes for all the drawing tools. You may find it advantageous to set the Stroke and Fill attributes with the Pointer tool selected, before you begin using the three tools we introduce in this section. You can change the default attributes at any time by selecting a non-drawing tool (like the Pointer or Subselection tool) and editing them. And, of course, you can set attributes different from the defaults as you use each of the tools.

Using the Pencil tool

To use the Pencil tool, follow these steps:

1. **Select the Pencil tool from the Tools panel.**

   To create a line using the tool's current settings, click inside the document and drag to create the line.

2. **For more options, double-click the Pencil tool.**

   The Pencil Tool dialog box, shown in Figure 4-4, opens.

Figure 4-4:
Adjust the
stroke width
and more.

3. **Drag the slider next to the Precision field.**

   This setting determines how much FreeHand smoothes the line as you draw. Choose a low value to smooth minor variations as you draw, or choose a high value to allow minor variations as you draw. Alternatively, you can enter a value in the text field.

4. **Select the Draw Dotted Line check box.**

   This setting is optional. If you select it, FreeHand creates a dotted line preview as you draw (note that the actual line you draw will be solid; only the preview will be dotted). This option speeds redraw and is recommended if you use FreeHand on a computer with a slower processor.

Book IV
Chapter 4

Creating
Illustrations with
FreeHand MX

5. Click OK.

The Pencil Tool dialog box closes.

6. Click and drag inside the document to create a line.

As you drag the tool across the document, FreeHand creates a preview of the line. If you hold down the Alt and Shift keys while using the tool, you constrain the line to a predefined angle. (To predefine the angle, choose File⇨Document Settings⇨Constrain and enter a value in the dialog box; the default angle is 45 degrees).

7. If you choose the Variable Stroke tool or Calligraphic Pen tool by clicking and holding the Pencil tool and selecting either tool from the pop-up menu, you can vary the stroke by 1/8 of the tool's Width setting by doing one of the following as you draw:

- To decrease the stroke width, press the left-arrow key.

- To increase the stroke width, press the right-arrow key.

- If you draw with a pressure-sensitive tablet, vary the pressure you apply to the tablet to vary the stroke width.

8. Release the mouse button when the line is the desired length.

FreeHand draws the line. At this point, you can add to the line by placing the tool over the last or first point. Your cursor becomes a plus sign (+), indicating that the path can be extended.

Using the Variable Stroke Pen tool

The Variable Stroke Pen tool is a handy tool when you're looking to make swoopy lines that go from being small to large, or vice versa. To use the tool, just follow these steps:

1. Select the Variable Stroke Pen tool from the Tools panel by clicking and holding the Pencil tool and selecting the Variable Stroke Pen tool from the pop-up menu that appears.

If you start drawing with it, it will make a line that looks just like the Pencil tool. However, for more magic, continue through the following steps.

2. Double-click the Variable Stroke Pen tool.

The Variable Stroke Pen dialog box opens.

3. Set your precision and dotted line options.

You can change the precision of the line by dragging the slider or by entering a number in the Precision field. 1 is the smallest value, and 10 is the highest. The higher the number, the more points FreeHand will add to the lines you create, giving you more precise control over the line. If you want the preview of the line as you draw (but not the line itself) to be dotted instead of solid, select the Draw Dotted Line check box.

4. **Select the Auto Remove Overlap check box if you want FreeHand to create composite paths when line segments overlap, rather than keeping the lines discreet.**

5. **Set the minimum and maximum width of the stroke.**

   You can either use the sliders to change the values in each of the fields or manually input the min and max values.

6. **Click OK to save your settings.**

   When you have your settings saved, you can really experience the magic of this tool. As you're drawing, hold down the right- or left-arrow keys to dynamically increase or decrease the width of the line.

Using the Calligraphic Pen tool

The Calligraphic Pen tool is not likely to be your first tool of choice, but it is equally as cool as the Pencil tool and the Variable Stroke Pen tool. Practically speaking, the Calligraphic Pen tool is a tool that you should really only use if you're drawing using a pressure-sensitive tablet — but if you can write calligraphy using a mouse or a trackball, more power to you! As you would expect, this tool creates angled lines, similar to a calligraphy pen.

You use the tool like you use the others, by selecting it from the menu that pops up when you click and hold the Pencil tool in the Tools panel. Similarly, you can double-click the tool to bring up the Calligraphic Pen dialog box. There, you can specify the following items:

✦ **Precision:** The number of points associated with the calligraphic line you're drawing. The higher the number, the more points on the line.

✦ **Draw Dotted Line:** Select this check box if you want the preview of the line you're drawing to be dotted as you draw instead of solid. Only the preview of the line is dotted; the drawn line's stroke and fill (as set in the Object tab of the Properties panel) appear when you release the mouse button.

✦ **Auto Remove Overlap:** Select this check box if you want FreeHand to create composite paths when line segments overlap, rather than keeping the lines discreet.

✦ **Width:** Select the Fixed or the Variable radio button to choose a width. If you choose Variable, you can enter values for the minimum and maximum width for the line.

✦ **Angle:** Click and hold on the wheel to change the angle of the line. This angle will make your line more or less angular, depending upon the value you choose.

Selecting Objects

When you create a document and add stuff (a technical term for objects) to the illustration, you place the stuff where you think it belongs. Thankfully, your initial placement isn't cast in stone. If you need to move, or otherwise modify, an object, you have to first select it. If the object you're modifying is a path, you can select individual points along the path. In the upcoming sections, we show you how to use the Selection tools to select stuff.

Using the Pointer tool

You use the Pointer tool to select an object or several objects in your document. To use the Pointer tool, select it from the Tools panel (it's at the top left of the panel, with the solid black left-pointing arrow for an icon) and do one of the following:

✦ Click an object to select it. If the object has no fill, click the object's stroke (the border line that makes up the object).

✦ Click and drag a marquee around several objects to select them.

✦ Click an object, and then while holding down the Shift key, click other objects to add them to the selection.

After selecting an object or group of objects, dots appear to signify the border of each object or group. You can now drag the objects to a different location or use the Object panel of the Properties panel to change the parameters of the object(s). If you select a path, the dots that comprise the path appear.

If you are using a tool other than the Pointer tool, you can momentarily select the Pointer tool by pressing and holding the Ctrl key. Use the tool to select objects; release the Ctrl key to revert to the previous tool.

The Pointer, Subselection, and Lasso tools share common settings. The Subselection tool is the white-headed arrow to the right of the Pointer tool; the Lasso tool is directly beneath the Subselection tool. By default, objects or points must be completely encompassed by a marquee in order to be selected. You can vary the sensitivity of these tools by doing the following:

1. **Double-click the Pointer tool, Subselection tool, or Lasso tool.**

The tool's dialog box appears.

2. **Select the Contact Sensitivity option.**

Select this option if you want the ability to select objects that are only partially encompassed by a marquee. This option is deselected by default.

3. **Click OK.**

The new settings are applied to the tool and remain in effect until you open the dialog box and choose a different option.

Using the Subselection tool

You use the Subselection tool to select individual objects, select individual points along a path, or select an object that is nestled within a group. To make a selection with the Subselection tool, follow these steps:

1. **Select the Subselection tool from the Tools panel.**

   It's the tool with the icon that looks like a hollow arrow pointing left. You find it right next to the Pointer tool at the top of the Tools panel.

   To momentarily select the Subselection tool while using the Pointer tool, hold down the Alt key. After using the Subselection tool, release the Alt key to revert to the Pointer tool.

2. **To make a selection, do one of the following:**

   - Click an object. This selects an object, even when it's in a group.

   - Click a path to select it.

   - Click an individual point along a path. Note that you must first select the path, and then select the point.

   - Select a group of points by dragging a marquee around them.

3. **After creating a selection, you can move it with the Pointer tool.**

To momentarily select the Subselection tool while using a tool other than the Pointer tool, hold down the Ctrl+Alt keys. Release the keys to return to the previously used tool.

To modify a path between two points, select the path with the Subselection tool, and then click and drag anywhere between two points. As you drag, FreeHand modifies the path between the two points.

The Subselection tool has a few other nifty tricks up its sleeve: You can use it to modify the radius of corners on rectangles and polygons (simply click any corner and drag toward the center of the shape), or to create arcs in ellipses (simply click the handle and drag toward the center of the ellipse; when you release the mouse button, your ellipse becomes a PacMan!).

Using the Lasso tool

You use the Lasso tool to select objects by drawing a shape around them instead of by clicking them. To make a selection with the Lasso tool (the tool that looks like a cowboy's lariat), follow these steps:

1. **Select the Lasso tool by clicking it on the Tools panel.**

2. **Click and drag to define a marquee around the object(s) you want to select.**

   FreeHand creates a dashed bounding box, giving you a preview of the selection area.

3. **Release the mouse button when the bounding box surrounds the object(s) you want to select.**

   The objects are selected. You can now move the objects with the Pointer tool or modify them in the Object tab of the Properties panel.

Editing Objects with the Object Tab

The completely overhauled FreeHand Object tab in the Properties panel is a multifaceted workhorse you use to change a variety of parameters, depending on the object you select. In FreeHand MX, you can control the stroke, fill, and effects of an object, all from this single interface. When you select an object with the Pointer tool, the Object tab of the Properties panel automatically displays the current stroke, fill, and effect parameters for that object, as shown in Figure 4-5. If the object is a rectangle, ellipse, or polygon, the panel also shows its size and position information, all of which can be edited on the Object tab. For rectangles and polygons, you also have access to corner properties.

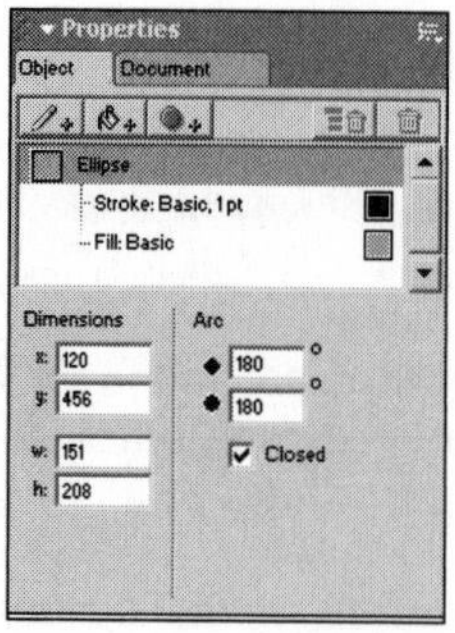

Figure 4-5: Inside the newly revised Object tab.

To change an object's position and size, follow these steps:

1. **Using the Pointer tool, select the object whose characteristics you want to modify.**

2. **Choose Window⇨Object or press Ctrl+F3.**

   The Object tab of the Properties panel opens. If the selected object is a rectangle, polygon, or ellipse, the tab displays the object's dimensions and location. If the selected object is an open or closed path, the tab displays the object's stroke, fill, number of points in the path, odd or even fill, whether the path is open or closed, and the flatness of the curve. In order to see the position, group the object.

3. **To change the position of the object, enter new values in the X and/or Y fields.**

4. **To change the object's dimensions, enter new values in the Width and/or Height fields.**

   Note that this does not resize the object proportionately unless the ratio of the new values you entered in the width and height fields matches the ratio of the original values.

5. **Press Enter to apply the changes.**

   The object is resized and/or repositioned. You can close the Properties panel, or leave it floating in the workspace.

A number of other powerful options reside within the Object tab of the Properties panel, specifically those that add and edit strokes, fills, and effects. These options are all covered in detail in Book IV, Chapter 5.

Grouping and Ungrouping Objects

At times, it's advantageous to create a group of objects. When you select several objects and create a group, the group behaves as a single object. You can move the group with the Pointer tool, resize the group with the Object tab of the Properties panel, and modify the stroke and fill of every object in the group at once by changing the stroke and fill settings in the oft-mentioned Object tab. If you need to edit an individual object in a group, select it with the Subselection tool, and then perform the needed task.

You can create a group at any time, for example, when you've arranged several elements to create an illustration of a face. You can create a group by selecting objects from different layers. When you do this, the objects are moved to the current drawing layer, yet they retain their stacking order. To create a group, follow these steps:

1. **Select the objects you want to group.**

   You can select objects with the Pointer tool, Subselection tool, or Lasso tool.

2. **Choose Modify⇨Group.**

   Four dots appear to signify the border of the group.

**Book IV
Chapter 4**

**Creating
Illustrations with
FreeHand MX**

After you have created a group, you can select an individual object in the group by doing one of the following:

✦ Select the Subselection tool and click the object you want to select.

✦ Select the Pointer tool, hold down the Alt key, and click the object you want to select.

 If you have objects underneath other objects in a group, you can select them by holding down the Ctrl and Alt keys while right-clicking to cycle through the objects in the group.

To ungroup objects, follow these steps:

1. **Select the object group with the Pointer tool.**

2. **Choose Modify➪Ungroup.**

The group is disbanded, and you can now edit each object individually. Yoko goes into hiding.

 After you create a group, you can nest another object or group by selecting the object or group, selecting the object or group you want to nest the item in, and then choosing Modify➪Group.

Arranging Objects

When you add objects to an illustration, they are stacked on top of each other, and the objects on top of the stack in a layer eclipse the objects below. You can change the stacking order of objects at any time by following these steps:

1. **Use the Pointer or Subselection tool to select the object whose order in the stack you want to rearrange.**

2. **Choose Modify➪Arrange and choose one of the following commands from the submenu:**

• **Bring to Front:** Moves the selected object to the front of the stack.

• **Move Forward:** Moves the selected object ahead of the next object in the stack.

• **Move Backward:** Moves the selected object behind the next lower object in the stack.

• **Send to Back:** Moves the selected object to the back of the stack.

After applying one of the Arrange commands, the object's order in the stacking layer is changed.

When you use the Arrange command, you modify the stacking order on the drawing layer. If there are layers above or below the drawing layer (the currently selected layer), objects on those layers will affect the overall appearance of your illustration. In order to achieve the desired result, you may have to move the object to another layer. For more information on layers, see Book IV, Chapter 2.

 You can also modify the stacking order by cutting or copying an object, selecting an object in the document, and then choosing Edit⇨Special⇨Paste in Front or choosing Edit⇨Special⇨Paste Behind. Note that this changes the stacking order, but not the position of the pasted object.

Aligning Objects with the Align Panel

When you have several objects in a document, you may need to align them. This is a fairly easy process using FreeHand's object chiropractor: the Align panel. You use the Align panel to align objects to each other or to the document. You can also use the Align panel to distribute objects relative to the other objects in the selection or relative to the document. When you choose one of the distribution options, the objects are spaced equally. You can also use the panel to align points along a path.

To align objects, follow these steps:

1. **Use the Pointer or Subselection tool to select the objects or points you want to align.**

2. **Choose Window⇨Align.**

The Align and Transform panel, shown in Figure 4-6, appears, open to the Align tab. The tab consists of two drop-down lists on the right and a preview window on the left. The preview window gives you an abstract visual representation of the currently selected options.

The preview window has nine squares in the center and four mitered edges. You can align the objects by double-clicking one of these squares or mitered edges. For example, if you double-click the mitered edge at the top of the window, objects are aligned to the top; double-click the mitered edge on the left side and objects are aligned to the left. If you double-click the square in the top-right corner, objects are aligned to the top and right; double-click the square in the center and objects are aligned to the center. The drop-down lists update to match the preview window. Likewise, when you select options from the drop-down lists, the preview window updates to display an idealized representation of the chosen list option. The following steps walk you through selecting the options.

Book IV Chapter 4

Creating Illustrations with FreeHand MX

Figure 4-6:
You use this
panel to
bring your
objects into
alignment.

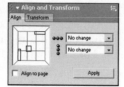

3. **Select the Align to Page check box to align or distribute objects relative to the page.**

   This aligns selected objects relative to the page. For example, objects can be aligned to the top-right corner of the page. If this option is not selected, objects are aligned or distributed relative to their current positions in the document. For example, if you have selected several objects in the document, and you double-click the left edge with the Align to Page option selected, the objects are aligned to the left border of the document. Without this option selected, all the objects are aligned to the leftmost of the selected objects.

4. **To align the selected objects, do one of the following:**

   - Click one of the squares or edges in the Alignment window.

   - Select one of the following options from the Horizontal drop-down list: No Change, Align Top, Align Center, or Align Bottom.

   - Select one of the following options from the Vertical drop-down list: No Change, Align Left, Align Center, or Align Right.

5. **To distribute the selected objects, do the following:**

   - Select one of the following options from the Horizontal drop-down list: No Change, Distribute Tops, Distribute Centers, Distribute Bottoms, or Distribute Heights. For example, if you select the Distribute Tops option, the objects are equally spaced according to the top of each object.

   - Select one of the following options from the Vertical drop-down list: No Change, Distribute Lefts, Distribute Centers, Distribute Rights, or Distributes Widths. For example, if you select the Distribute Lefts option, selected objects are distributed (spaced) according to the left side of each object.

6. **Click the Apply button.**

   The objects are aligned or distributed according to the options you select. If the alignment or distribution isn't as you'd expect — this may happen the first few times you use the panel — choose Edit⇨Undo (or press Ctrl+Z), and then perform the alignment or distribution again.

Slicing Objects with the Knife Tool

You can use the Knife tool to create two paths from a closed path, such as a circle or rectangle, or you can use the tool to slice an open path in two. For example, you can use the Knife tool on a circle or oval to create a curved path that otherwise would be difficult to create.

After you slice an object or path one time, you are left with two editable paths. If you use the Knife tool to take several swipes at the shape, you're left with a lot of editable paths. You can vary the Knife tool settings to vary the width of the slice, and whether the tool makes a straight slice or freehand slice.

To use the Knife tool, follow these steps:

1. **Use the Pointer tool to select the object or path you want to slice.**

2. **Select the Knife tool from the Tools panel.**

   You can use the tool using the previous settings or change the settings.

3. **Double-click the Knife tool to change the settings.**

   The Knife Tool dialog box, shown in Figure 4-7, appears.

Figure 4-7:
The slice and dice settings for the Knife tool.

4. **Select one of the following Tool Operation options:**

   - **Freehand:** Select this default option to make a freehand cut. If you hold down the Alt and Shift keys while using the tool, you constrain the line to a predefined angle (to predefine the angle, choose File⇨Document Settings⇨Constrain and enter a value in the dialog box; the default angle is 45 degrees).

   - **Straight:** Select this option to make a straight cut. Hold down the Shift key to constrain the tool to horizontal when dragging left to right, vertical when dragging up or down, or 45 degrees from the horizontal when dragging diagonally.

5. **Drag the Width slider to determine the tool's effective cutting area.**

   A value of 0 creates a thin cut, while higher values create two cuts separated by the width you choose. Alternatively, you can enter a value in the Width text field.

6. **Select one of the following check boxes:**

   - **Close Cut Paths:** Select this check box, and FreeHand closes the paths you create with the tool and displays the stroke and fill of the original path.

   - **Tight Fit:** Select this check box, and the tool closely follows the path you draw with your mouse or tablet.

7. **Click OK.**

   The Knife Tool dialog box closes.

8. **Click and drag across the object.**

   As you drag, FreeHand displays the tool's path.

9. **Release the mouse button to complete the operation.**

   FreeHand slices and dices the shape into paths.

After you use the Knife tool, you have two (or more) paths. To select an individual path, select the Pointer tool and click anywhere outside of the document to deselect any selected paths. You can then click a path to select it, and then move it to a different location or modify it using the Object tab of the Properties panel.

Chapter 5: Transforming Text, Shapes, and Images

In This Chapter

✔ Importing bitmaps

✔ Scaling objects

✔ Modifying an object's shape and position

✔ Tracing images

✔ Combining shapes

✔ Using Xtras tools

Thanks to the diversity of the software toolset and menu commands, FreeHand MX allows you to put your own stamp of creativity on your designs by creating preset shapes and modifying the shapes to suit your creative muse (and your client). In addition to modifying shapes, you can combine two or more shapes to create something truly unique.

In this chapter, we show you how to modify shapes with tools and menu commands. We also show you how to create new shapes by blending one shape into another, by using the Combine menu commands to combine shapes, by cutting one shape from another, and more.

Working with Bitmap Images

Vector objects are FreeHand's claim to fame; however, sometimes you have to add a photo or other bitmap image to an illustration. If you use FreeHand to create brochures, flyers, or package designs, you'll probably need to incorporate bitmaps into your work.

You can import images that have been saved in the following formats: TIFF, EPS, GIF, JPEG, PICT (Mac only), PNG, Targa, and BMP (PC only). After you have a bitmap image in an illustration, you can modify the bitmap using certain menu commands and the Xtra tools. For example, you can scale, skew, flip, or rotate the bitmap. You can also use the drawing tools to augment a bitmap image. For example, you can use the Rectangle tool to create a snazzy border for a bitmap. You can also use the Text tool to plop some text on top of the bitmap. To import a bitmap, follow these steps:

1. **Choose File⇨Import.**

   The Import Document dialog box appears.

2. **Navigate to the folder that contains the bitmap you want to import.**

3. **Select the bitmap file and click the Open button.**

   Your cursor becomes a right angle. This signifies the upper-left corner of the bitmap image you are importing.

4. **Click the spot in the document where you want the bitmap to appear.**

   The bitmap is placed in the document and the Pointer tool becomes active. You can now move, scale, skew, flip, or rotate the bitmap.

To create a snazzy border or frame for the bitmap, select the Rectangle tool from the Tools panel and create a rectangle slightly bigger than the bitmap. Choose Modify⇨Arrange⇨Send Backward to move the rectangle behind the bitmap. You may wish to center the rectangle and bitmap by choosing Modify⇨Align⇨Center Horizontal and Modify⇨Align⇨Center Vertical. You can then use one of the Xtras tools or operations to modify the rectangle (Emboss works well), and then group the bitmap and rectangle. We show you how to use the Xtras tools in the upcoming section, "Using the Xtra Tools to Change a Shape."

Modifying Objects

You have a great deal of latitude in how you can modify an object after you create it. You can scale, skew, flip, or rotate an object using menu commands or tools. In the upcoming sections, we show you how to accomplish these object makeovers without breaking a sweat. The tools you can use to modify objects all live in the FreeHand Tools panel, though some less-used tools are hidden behind the more popular ones. Figure 5-1 shows the tools you commonly use to modify objects.

If you're a perfectionist, you probably prefer to move and resize objects with mathematical precision. Don't be alarmed. There are others like you in the world. In fact, many of them are graphic designers, which is why Macromedia created menu commands to scale, resize, and move objects. The cool thing about these commands is that when you invoke one, the others all pop up in the Transform tab of the Align and Transform panel. Talk about convenience. In the upcoming sections, we show you how to use each command.

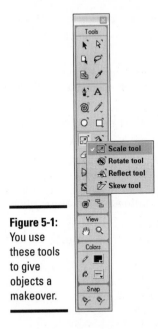

Figure 5-1:
You use
these tools
to give
objects a
makeover.

Scaling graphics

Sometimes you make things just a bit too large and you've got to cut them
down to size, or vice versa. For an object in your illustration, you cut it
down to size (or make it bigger) by scaling it. You can scale an object manually, or you can use a menu command.

Scaling graphics manually

You can scale an object manually either from one of its corners or from its
center. To scale the object from one of its corners, follow these simple steps:

1. **Select the Pointer or Subselection tool from the Tools panel.**

2. **Click any corner and drag left, right, up, or down.**

Dragging away from the object will increase the size of the object.
Dragging into the object will make it smaller. Hold down the Shift key
while you drag to change the size proportionately. As you drag,
FreeHand displays the outline of the shape's current size.

3. **Release the mouse button when the shape is the desired size.**

FreeHand resizes the object.

**Book IV
Chapter 5**

Transforming Text,
Shapes, and Images

To scale an object from its center, just follow these steps:

1. **Select the Scale tool from the Tools panel.**

   The Scale tool is the one that has a black arrow inside a blue square. When you place the cursor over the page, it becomes a small circle with four long and four short lines radiating out.

2. **Click inside the object and drag left, right, up, or down.**

   Dragging left makes the object narrower; dragging right makes it wider. Dragging up makes the object taller; dragging down makes it shorter. To scale the object proportionately, hold down the Shift key as you drag left or down to make the object smaller or right or up to make it larger. As you drag the tool, FreeHand displays the outline of the shape's current size.

3. **Release the mouse button when the shape is the desired size.**

   FreeHand resizes the object.

Using the Scale command

To resize an object with mathematical precision, you can use the Scale command. If that's the route you want to take, follow these steps:

1. **Use the Pointer or Subselection tool to select the object you want to scale.**

2. **Choose Modify⇨Transform⇨Scale or double-click the Scale tool in the Tools panel.**

   The Transform tab of the Align and Transform panel opens to the Scale section, as shown in Figure 5-2.

Figure 5-2:
Scale and
make
copies in
one fell
swoop.

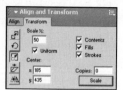

3. **Enter a value in the Scale field.**

   This value is the percentage of the object's original size. Enter a value larger than 100 to increase the object's size; enter a value lower than 100 to decrease the size.

4. **Select one or more of the following check boxes:**

   - **Contents:** Scales the contents of a clipping path with the rest of the path.
   - **Fills:** Scales the object fill as you scale the object.
   - **Strokes:** Scales the object's stroke as you scale the object.

5. **Select the Uniform check box to scale the object proportionately.**

   This is the default scaling option. If you deselect this check box, the H and V fields appear. To scale the object vertically, enter a value in the V field; to scale the object horizontally, enter a value in the H field, or enter the desired values in both fields to scale both dimensions.

6. **In the Center section, enter values in the X and/or Y fields.**

   Changing the value in either field moves the object's center of rotation.

7. **Enter a value in the Copies field to create copies of the object as you scale it.**

   When you enter a value in this field, FreeHand leaves the original object unaltered and creates the number of copies you specify. Each copy will be incrementally larger or smaller, creating copies that are sized incrementally along a path between the original object and the last copy.

8. **Click the Scale button.**

   FreeHand scales the object, and if you enter a value in the Copies field, it blends the copies with the original.

If you like really radical transformations, select an object, and then select the Freeform tool (it's next to the Scale tool in the Tools panel, and its icon looks like a backward "S" with a black arrow pointing to a red dot on the line). Move your cursor toward the object, and then click and drag to modify the shape. FreeHand morphs the shape like it was made of virtual Silly Putty. You can get more pronounced results by clicking and dragging a point to warp the shape.

Skewing and distorting objects

In this section, we show you how to skew. Skewing is great fun. And if you skew up, you can undo the change. If you wanted to make an image of a car look like it was accelerating or rapidly coming to a halt, you could skew the image to the left or right.

Skewing an object manually

To skew an object manually, follow these steps:

1. **Use the Pointer or Subselection tool to select the object you want to skew.**

**Book IV
Chapter 5**

**Transforming Text,
Shapes, and Images**

2. **Click and hold the Scale tool in the Tools panel and select the Skew tool from the pop-up menu (refer to Figure 5-1).**

You can skew an object vertically or horizontally, relative to a side of the object, or relative to the center of the object.

3. **To skew the object, do one of the following:**

- Click above or below the object and drag left or right to skew the object horizontally, or drag left or right and up or down to skew the object vertically and horizontally relative to the side from which you are skewing.

- Click to the right or left of the object and drag up or down to skew the object vertically, or drag up or down and left or right to skew the object vertically and horizontally relative to the side from which you are skewing.

- Click inside the object and drag left or right to skew horizontally, or drag up or down to skew vertically, or drag up or down and drag left or right to skew horizontally and vertically relative to the center of the object.

As you skew the object, FreeHand creates an outline of the shape's current configuration. For best results, hold down the Shift key while you drag to constrain the skewing to a predefined angle (to predefine the angle, choose File⇨Document Settings⇨Constrain and enter a value in the dialog box; the default angle is 45 degrees).

4. **Release the mouse button when the shape has been skewed to perfection.**

FreeHand skews the shape.

Using the Skew command

If you or your client has a skewed outlook on an illustration, you can easily get this point across to your viewing audience by skewing one or more objects with the Skew command. You use the command to precisely skew — as opposed to skewer, something the Knife tool is good at — an object horizontally or vertically. To use the Skew command, follow these steps:

1. **Use the Pointer or Subselection tool to select the object you want to skew.**

2. **Choose Modify⇨Transform⇨Skew or double-click the Skew tool (if the Skew tool isn't visible, click and hold the Scale tool in the Tools panel and select the Skew tool from the pop-up menu).**

The Align and Transform panel opens, conveniently bookmarked at the Skew section of the Transform tab, as shown in Figure 5-3.

Figure 5-3:
You can
really skew
up when
you use this
command.

3. **Enter a value in the H and/or V fields.**

   These values are in degrees. Enter a positive value in the H field to skew the object to the right; enter a negative value to skew the object to the left. Enter a positive value in the V field to skew the object up; enter a negative value to skew the object down.

4. **Select one or both of the following check boxes:**

   - **Contents:** Select this check box to skew the contents of a clipping path along with the rest of the path.

   - **Fills:** Select this check box to skew a tiled fill along with the rest of the object.

5. **In the Center section, enter values in the X and/or Y fields.**

   If you enter a different value in either of these fields, the object's center of rotation changes. FreeHand uses this center when skewing the object.

6. **Enter a value in the Copies field.**

   If you enter a value, FreeHand does not skew the original object and creates the number of copies specified. The original object is unchanged and each copy is skewed by the specified amount; the last copy is skewed to a value that is the product of the number of copies and the skew value you specify.

7. **Click the Skew button.**

   The object gets skewed.

Rotating objects

No self-respecting graphics program would leave a graphic designer without a means of rotating an object. FreeHand doesn't surprise you here. You can rotate an object or group with the Rotate tool. And if you like to rotate your objects with a degree of precision (pun intended, a circle after all is 360 degrees), you can use a menu command to do that.

Rotating objects manually

If you prefer menu commands, fast-forward to the "Using the Rotate command" section. If you prefer freeform rotation, follow these steps:

**Book IV
Chapter 5**

Transforming Text,
Shapes, and Images

1. **Use the Pointer or Subselection tool to select the object you want to rotate.**

2. **Click and hold the Scale tool in the Tools panel and select the Rotation tool from the pop-up menu (refer to Figure 5-1).**

   You can use the tool to rotate an object using a corner or the center as the point of reference.

3. **To rotate the object, do one of the following:**

   - Click any corner and drag to rotate the object relative to the corner point clicked. If you click beyond the corner boundary of the object, FreeHand uses the spot you click as the center of rotation.

   - Click the center of the object and drag to rotate the object relative to its center.

   As you drag the tool, FreeHand creates an outline of the object's current position and a diagonal line to show you the angle of rotation. The center point of all rotation with the Rotation tool is where the mouse is clicked on the page. The further you drag the mouse out after clicking its point of rotation, the higher the degree of accuracy you have.

4. **Release the mouse button when you have rotated the object to the desired position.**

   FreeHand redraws the object in its new position.

Using the Rotate command

When you need to put a different spin on an object, you can use the Rotate command. You specify the number of degrees the object rotates, and you can even spin some copies of the original object. Follow these steps to use the Rotate command:

1. **Use the Pointer or Subselection tool to select the object you want to rotate.**

2. **Choose Modify⇨Transform⇨Rotate or double-click the Rotate tool.**

   The Align and Transform panel appears with the Rotate section of the Transform tab selected, as shown in Figure 5-4.

Figure 5-4:
It spins! It copies! It's the rotate command.

3. **Enter a value in the Rotation Angle field.**

This is the number of degrees you want the object to rotate. Enter a negative value to rotate the object in a clockwise direction.

4. **Select one of the following check boxes:**

- **Contents:** Select this check box to rotate the contents of a clipping path with the rest of the path.

- **Fills:** Select this check box to rotate a tiled fill with the rest of the object.

5. **In the Center section, enter values in the X and/or Y fields.**

If you enter a different value in either of these fields, the object's center of rotation changes. FreeHand spins an object around the center of rotation.

6. **Enter a value in the Copies field.**

If you enter a value, the original object is not rotated and FreeHand creates the number of copies you specify, rotating each copy by the amount specified. The last copy is rotated to an angle that is determined by the number of copies and the degree of rotation. For example, if you create three copies with a rotation of 15 degrees, the last object is rotated 45 degrees.

7. **Click the Rotate button.**

FreeHand spins the object.

Flipping objects

We're sure you've seen those cute pictures of identical twins standing next to each other. They look like bookends. If you want the bookend effect in a FreeHand illustration, you can flip a copy of an object. Or you can flip an object to point it in the opposite direction. In this section we give you instructions to flip for.

Reflecting objects manually

You can flip an object with the Reflect tool. When you flip an object, you create a mirror reflection of the object. If you need to flip an object to keep your illustration from being a flop, follow these steps:

1. **Use the Pointer or Subselection tool to select the object you want to flip.**

2. **Click and hold the Scale tool in the Tools panel and select the Reflect tool from the pop-up menu (refer to Figure 5-1).**

3. **Click the document to specify the centerline FreeHand uses to flip the object.**

If you hold the mouse button, FreeHand creates a vertical line to show you the centerline and an outline of the shape's position, which also allows you to rotate the reflected object (see the next step).

4. **If desired, drag up or down to rotate the reflected object from the centerline.**

As you drag, FreeHand moves the outline to give you a preview of the reflected object's current position.

5. **Release the mouse button.**

FreeHand flips the object and places it on the other side of the spot you clicked, at a distance equal to the object's former position from the centerline.

Using the Reflect command

You can flip an object vertically or horizontally with the Reflect command. And if your design calls for it, you can use the command to create a mirror image alongside of or below the original. To use the Reflect command, do the following:

1. **Use the Pointer or Subselection tool to select the object you want to reflect.**

2. **Choose Modify⇨Transform⇨Reflect or double-click the Reflect tool.**

The Align and Transform panel appears, and it's in a reflective state of mind, as shown in Figure 5-5.

Figure 5-5:
Objects flip
over the
reflect
command.

3. **In the Reflect Axis field, enter a value between 0 and 90 to reflect the object horizontally; enter a value between 90 and 180 to reflect the object vertically.**

4. **Select one or both of the following check boxes:**

   • **Contents:** Select this check box to reflect the contents of a clipping path along with the path.

   • **Fills:** Select this check box to reflect a tiled fill with the rest of the object.

5. **Enter a value of 1 in the Copies field.**

By default, this field has a value of 0. Entering a value of 1 will create a mirror image of the original along with the original for a bookend effect.

6. **Enter values in the X and Y fields to determine the center axis along which the object is reflected.**

    Unless you're a math whiz, it's easier to double-click the object and then drag the center handle (it looks like a gear) to the desired position.

7. **Click the Reflect button.**

    The Align and Transform panel says, "Om," and the object is reflected.

If you like transforming objects with menu commands, you can save yourself some time by keeping the Align and Transform panel in your workspace. To open the Align and Transform panel, choose Window⇨Panels⇨Transform or press Ctrl+M. After the panel is open, click the appropriate button to move, rotate, scale, skew, or reflect a selected object. After you complete the transformation, grab the panel's handle (the five dots to the left of the panel name) and drag to the right. A thick black line appears to show where you can "dock" the panel. Release the mouse button when the black line shows up where you'd like the panel to sit.

If the Align and Transform panel isn't docked, you can also open it by double-clicking any of the transformation tools (the ones grouped with the Scale tool in the Tools panel).

Using the Move command

You can move objects anywhere in your document with the Pointer tool. However, when precision is needed, only a good menu command will do; in this case the Move command. If you need any object in your document to get a move on with precision, follow these steps:

1. **Use the Pointer or Subselection tool to select the object you want to move.**

2. **Choose Modify⇨Transform⇨Move.**

    The Align and Transform panel appears with the Move section selected, as shown in Figure 5-6.

Figure 5-6:
Click the
Move
button, and
the object's
gonna
move.

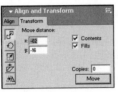

Book IV
Chapter 5

Transforming Text,
Shapes, and Images

3. **Enter a value in the X field and/or Y field.**

This is the distance in pixels (or the unit of measure you specify for the document) you want the object to move along each axis.

4. **Select one or both of the following check boxes:**

- **Contents:** Select this check box to move the contents of a clipping path with the rest of the path.

- **Fills:** Select this check box to move a tiled fill with the rest of the object.

5. **Enter a value in the Copies field.**

If you enter a value in this field, FreeHand does not move the original object and creates copies equally spaced along a path between the original object's position and the position that results by applying the values entered in each field.

6. **Click the Move button.**

FreeHand moves the object and makes the number of copies you specify.

You can also nudge a selected object by pressing one of the arrow keys on your keyboard. Hold down the Shift key while moving the object to increase the nudge distance by a factor of ten. To customize the nudge distance, choose File⇨Document⇨Settings⇨Cursor Distance. The Cursor Distance dialog box appears. Enter a value in the Shift+Arrow Key text field and click OK.

Giving an object some perspective

The Perspective tool allows you to take an object — such as a circle, rectangle, polygon, or text — and align it to a perspective grid to make the object look like it has dimension. Now, you may be wondering how that's any different than the Skew tool. The Skew tool creates a rhombus outline, making a parallelogram out of the object: the top and bottom edges will be parallel to each other, and the sides will be parallel to each other. In contrast, the Perspective tool makes all sides vanish to a set of vanishing points. The top and bottom converge (or diverge if you're looking at it that way), and the sides are either constrained vertically, or converge upwards (or downwards, depending on what you're doing).

To give an object perspective, just follow these steps:

1. **Create an object on the canvas, or select an already created object.**

As noted previously, the object can be a polygon, circle, rectangle, text, or an open or closed path.

2. **Show the Perspective grid by choosing View⇨Perspective Grid⇨Show.**

This brings up the default Perspective grid for the page, as shown in Figure 5-7. You can modify the Perspective grid by selecting View⇨Perspective Grid⇨Define and changing the number of vanishing points (that's what creates the distance depth), the size of the grid squares, and the colors used for the grid.

3. **Select the Perspective tool from the Tools panel (the Perspective tool looks like a blue parallelogram with a light green fill and some light blue parallel lines in front) and click the object you want to give perspective.**

4. **Move the object to where you'd like it on the grid, and while keeping the mouse button held down, use the arrow keys to place the object in the proper perspective grid.**

   When you use the arrow keys, a wireframe of your object appears and moves from grid cell to grid cell as you press the arrow keys. This takes a little getting used to, and depending upon which arrow key you press, the object may move around a lot on the grid. But after you play with it for a bit, you'll get the hang of it.

5. **Release the mouse button to create the perspective for your object.**

   FreeHand puts the object in perspective.

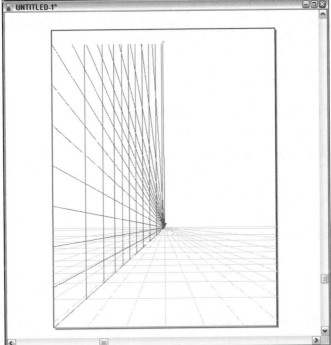

Figure 5-7:
Now that's
some
perspective!

Extruding an object

If you have designs on becoming a 3D graphical artist, then there's no better place to get started than FreeHand. In addition to being able to create 2D objects and giving them depth perception, now you can actually take a 2D object and turn it into a 3D object by using the Extrude tool.

To use the Extrude tool to transform a 2D object into a 3D object, just follow these steps:

1. **Select the Extrude tool from the Tools panel — the tool that looks like a 3D elongated cube, found to the right of the Perspective tool.**

2. **Click and drag the tool on the object to apply the extrusion effect.**

3. **Release the mouse button to apply the effect.**

While the Perspective and Extrude tools are cool to watch in action, they generally require more processing power than the other, basic tools. If you're using FreeHand on an older machine, you could find yourself waiting around, staring at your screen as you turn that 2D polygon into a 3D polygon.

Scaling, skewing, and rotating with the Pointer tool

When you first glance at the Pointer tool, you might think all it can do is select objects. But this tool has the strength of three tools — the Rotate tool, the Scale tool, and the Skew tool — when you use it in combination with Transformation Handles (the boxes that appear along the perimeter of an object when you select it). You can use the tool to scale, skew, and rotate in a constrained or freeform manner. To transform an object with the Pointer tool, follow these steps:

1. **Select the Pointer tool from the Tools panel.**

2. **Double-click the object you want to transform.**

   When you double-click the object, a bounding box with eight Transformation Handles along the perimeter appears. A circular handle in the center that looks like a gear also appears, as shown in Figure 5-8.

3. **After double-clicking the object, you can do any of the following to transform the object's shape:**

   • **To change the object's height:** Move your cursor toward the handle on the center top or bottom of the object. When your cursor becomes a two-headed vertical arrow, click and drag up or down.

- **To change the object's width:** Move your cursor toward the handle on the middle right or left of the object. When your cursor becomes a two-headed horizontal arrow, click and then drag right or left.

- **To scale the object:** Move your cursor toward any corner point. When your cursor becomes a dual-headed diagonal arrow, click and drag toward the object or away from it. Hold down the Shift key while dragging to scale the object proportionately.

  When scaling an object proportionately with the Pointer tool, be sure to release the mouse button before releasing the Shift key; otherwise the object may not scale proportionately.

- **To move the object's center of rotation:** Click the handle that looks like a gear and drag it to a different location. You can drag the handle anywhere in the document.

- **To rotate an object:** Move your cursor beyond the object's bounding box. When your cursor becomes a curved two-headed arrow, click and drag to rotate the object. FreeHand rotates the object relative to its center of rotation, the little gear-like handle that you can move anywhere to change the center of rotation.

- **To skew the object horizontally:** Move your cursor between the center and one of the corner points on the object's top or bottom. When your cursor becomes two horizontal lines with arrows going in opposite directions, click and drag left or right. If you move your cursor diagonally, the object will rotate and skew at the same time.

- **To skew the object vertically:** Move your cursor between the center and one of the corner points on the left or right side of the object. When your cursor becomes two vertical lines with arrows going in opposite directions, move your cursor up or down. If you move your cursor diagonally, the object rotates around its center point and skews at the same time. You can hold down the Shift key while you drag to prevent the object from rotating while it skews.

Transformation handles

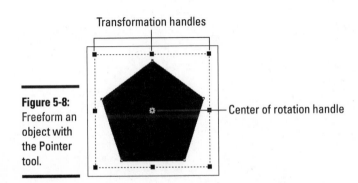

Figure 5-8: Freeform an object with the Pointer tool.

Center of rotation handle

4. Release the mouse button when the object is transformed to the desired shape.

The object is transformed.

5. You can now drag other handles to further change the object, or double-click anywhere beyond the object's bounding box.

If you press the Tab key or double-click beyond the bounding box, the super Pointer tool swoops into a phone booth and resumes its former guise as the mild-mannered Pointer tool. The object is still selected.

Using the Trace Tool

You use the Trace tool to trace all or part of a bitmap image or any other FreeHand object. When you use the Trace tool, you transform the pixels in the bitmap into vector paths and shapes. The default settings for the Trace tool are optimized to produce good results without taxing your system. However, you can modify the settings if your computer has a powerful processor and lots of memory. Follow these steps to use the Trace tool:

1. Double-click the Trace tool. (It's just below the Perspective tool in the Tools panel and resembles the Magic Wand tool you find in Fireworks MX.)

The Trace Tool dialog box opens, as shown in Figure 5-9.

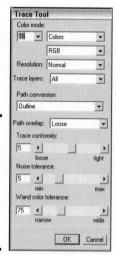

Figure 5-9:
You can
specify the
degree of
accuracy
with which
the Trace
tool traces.

2. **From the first Color Mode drop-down list, select an option.**

   You can use as few as 2 colors to trace a bitmap, or as many as 256. Choosing a higher value creates more vector objects, and your computer takes longer to perform the operation.

3. **Select Colors or Grays from the next Color Mode drop-down list.**

   If you select Grays, the traced image will be grayscale.

4. **If you're tracing a color image, select the RGB color model or CMYK color model from the third Color Mode drop-down list.**

   Select the RGB color model if your illustration will be displayed on a monitor; select CMYK if your illustration will be printed.

5. **From the Resolution drop-down list, select High, Normal, or Low.**

   Selecting Medium or High results in a more faithful rendition of the original bitmap; however, this produces more vector objects and takes longer for your computer and printer to process.

6. **Select one of the following options from the Trace Layers drop-down list:**

   - **All:** FreeHand traces all layers.

   - **Foreground:** FreeHand traces only the foreground layer.

   - **Background:** FreeHand traces only the background layer.

7. **From the Path Conversion drop-down list, select one of the following options:**

   - **Outline:** Select this option, and FreeHand traces the outline of blocks of color in the bitmap and creates closed, filled paths. If you select this option, the Path Overlap field opens. Select None for tracing text objects and line art, select the Loose option to trace an image made up of large areas of single colors, or select the Tight option for best results when tracing images like JPEGs with millions of colors.

   - **Centerline:** Select this option, and FreeHand traces the center of strokes. Use this option when you are tracing a vector illustration with lots of line work and few fills. If you select this option, the Uniform Lines option is selected by default. Deselect the Uniform Lines option to create paths with varying stroke widths.

   - **Centerline/Outline:** Select this option to trace an object with the end result being vector objects with both strokes and fills. Contiguous areas of color will be outlined with a stroke. If you select this option, enter an Open Path Below value between 2 and 10 pixels. When tracing, FreeHand leaves any paths below this value open.

**Book IV
Chapter 5**

Transforming Text,
Shapes, and Images

8. **Drag the slider to specify a value for Trace Conformity.**

You can specify a value between 0 and 10. Select a low value for a loose rendering of the original bitmap; a higher value for a more precise rendering of the image with more points.

9. **Drag the slider to specify a value for Noise Tolerance.**

This setting determines how FreeHand deals with muddy areas of color, scan lines, or other noise in a low-quality image. You can specify a value between 0 and 10. Choose a higher value to remove more noise from the original.

10. **Drag the slider to set a value for Wand Color Tolerance.**

This value determines how FreeHand treats neighboring areas of color. If you choose a low value, FreeHand blends colors of similar hues; if you choose a high value, FreeHand creates more colors when tracing.

11. **Click OK.**

The Trace Tool dialog box closes.

12. **Click one corner of the area you want to trace and drag the tool to define the area you want traced.**

As you drag the tool, FreeHand creates a dotted marquee showing you the current selection area. Hold down the Shift key to constrain the selection to a square area.

13. **Release the mouse button when you have selected the desired area.**

FreeHand traces the object.

Creating New Shapes by Combining Shapes

Did you ever wish you could combine a rectangle with a triangle and an oval to create a freeform sculpture? With FreeHand, you can combine shapes to create something new by choosing a menu command. To combine two or more shapes into a new shape, follow these steps:

1. **Use the Pointer tool to select the shapes you want to combine.**

Hold down the Shift key and click to select multiple shapes. You can select as many shapes as you need. The shapes must overlap, unless you're using the Blend command.

2. **Choose Modify⇨Combine and choose one of the following commands from the submenu:**

- **Blend:** Creates a blend between the selected shapes. When you choose this command, FreeHand creates new shapes between the original shapes. By default, FreeHand places 25 steps in the blend, but you can change the number of steps in the Object tab of the Properties panel.

- **Union:** Joins the selected objects into a single object. If you choose this command with filled objects, the new object inherits the fill of the object that was highest in the stack.

- **Divide:** Creates new shapes where the shapes intersect.

- **Intersect:** Creates a new shape that encompasses the area where the original shapes overlap.

- **Punch:** Cuts the object highest in the stack out of the objects underneath.

- **Crop:** Creates new paths by cropping to the area where the paths overlap.

After you choose one of the Combine commands, FreeHand creates new shapes. Figure 5-10 shows the different shapes you can create with the commands.

Figure 5-10:
If you want neat shapes, choose a command from the Combine submenu.

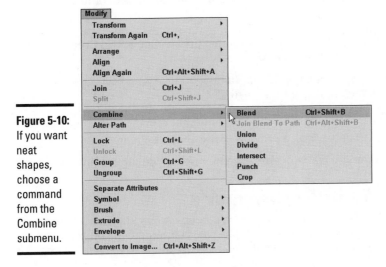

Using the Xtra Tools to Change a Shape

You use the Xtra tools to create interesting shapes and modify existing ones. Instead of using a whole lot of pages to write about each tool, in the next sections, we show you how to use some of the more popular Xtra tools. We leave it to you to explore the others at your own leisure. To use an Xtra tool, choose Window➪Toolbars➪Xtra Tools, and the toolbar shown in Figure 5-11 appears.

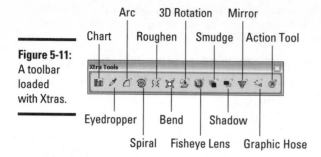

Figure 5-11:
A toolbar
loaded
with Xtras.

Using the Arc tool

You use the Arc Xtra tool to create . . . you guessed it: Arcs. To use the Arc
tool, follow these steps:

1. **Double-click the Arc tool on the Xtra toolbar, as shown in Figure 5-11.**

The Arc Tool dialog box opens.

2. **Select one of the following options: Create Open Arc, Create Flipped
Arc, or Create Concave Arc.**

When you select an option, a window in the dialog box gives you a preview of the arc the option creates.

3. **Click and drag on the canvas.**

As you drag the tool, a preview of the shape is created.

4. **When the arc is the desired shape, release the mouse button.**

Using the 3D Rotation tool

You use the 3D Rotation tool to give a garden-variety shape, such as a rectangle, the illusion of perspective. The tool is interactive; you click and drag
until you get the result you want. Follow these steps to use the 3D Rotation
tool:

1. **Use the Pointer tool to select the shape to which you want to add
perspective.**

2. **Select the 3D Rotation tool from the Xtra Tools toolbar (see Figure 5-11).**

3. **Click and drag.**

As you drag, FreeHand draws a preview of the shape.

4. **Release the mouse button when the shape is as desired.**

   FreeHand completes the 3D rotation.

You can modify the settings for the 3D Rotation tool by double-clicking it and modifying the settings in the 3D Rotation dialog box.

Using the Smudge tool

You use the Smudge tool to create ghost images of an object. It almost looks like someone repeatedly mashed a rubber stamp while moving along a straight line; each image is more faded than the last until the effect fades away. To use the Smudge tool, follow these steps:

1. **Use the Pointer tool to select the object you want to smudge.**

2. **Select the Smudge tool from the Xtra Tools toolbar, as shown in Figure 5-11.**

   Your cursor becomes a pointing finger.

   Double-click the Smudge tool to open the Smudge Tool dialog box. Within this dialog box, you can specify the final stroke and fill colors by dragging a color swatch from the Swatches, Tint, or Color Mixer panels into the appropriate field in the Smudge Tool dialog box.

3. **Click and drag in the direction you want the smudges to appear.**

   As you drag, an outline of the shape signifies the current position of your cursor and a straight line is drawn from the object's original position to the current position of the cursor. The straight line indicates the path of the smudges.

4. **Release the mouse button when the smudge path is acceptable.**

   FreeHand creates some smudges.

Using the Shadow tool

You use the Shadow tool to create a drop shadow for a vector object in your document. You use the tool interactively by simply clicking where you want the shadow to appear. To create a shadow, follow these steps:

1. **Use the Pointer tool to select the object you want to give a shadow.**

2. **Select the Shadow tool from the Xtra Tools toolbar (see Figure 5-11).**

3. **Click and drag.**

   As you drag, FreeHand creates an outline of the shadow's current position and a straight line from the corner of the original object to the shadow.

4. **Release the mouse button when the shadow is in the desired position.**

FreeHand creates a shadow using a tint of the original fill.

You can vary the opacity of the shadow and change several other parameters by double-clicking the Shadow tool and specifying different parameters in the Shadow dialog box.

You'll find two other useful tools are on the Xtra Tools toolbar: the Bend tool and the Graphics Hose tool. The Bend tool bends vector objects. If you need to add many identical graphic elements, such as flowers or leaves, to an illustration, the Graphics Hose tool is the tool you need. Double-click the Graphics Hose tool to fill the graphic hose with preset objects from the Contents list, set your parameters, and then click away.

Using Xtra Operations to Modify Shapes

You use the Xtra Operations toolbar to modify shapes and more without a lot of extra work. Many of the tools on this toolbar are duplicated as menu commands. To open the Xtra Operations toolbar, shown in Figure 5-12, choose Window⇨Toolbars⇨Xtra Operations.

Most of the tools shown in Figure 5-12 have been covered previously. We urge you to experiment with the others, but unfortunately, we have no more space left to cover them. We're going to squeeze in an introduction to one more tool, though: the Emboss tool.

Figure 5-12:
The Xtra Operations tools.

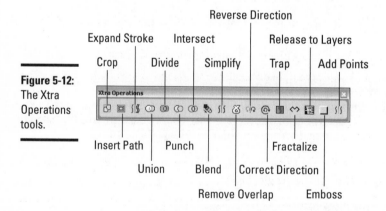

The Emboss Xtra Operations tool is cool for things like buttons and just plain old fancy objects. The Emboss tool has so many options, it would take a half-hour long infomercial — The Amazing Emboss-O-Matic — to explain them all. We give you the condensed version of how to use the Emboss tool:

1. **Use the Pointer tool to select the object you want to emboss.**

2. **Double-click the Emboss tool from the Xtra Operations toolbar, as shown in Figure 5-12.**

   The Emboss dialog box opens, as shown in Figure 5-13.

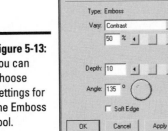

Figure 5-13: You can choose settings for the Emboss tool.

3. **Click a button to select an emboss style. The available styles are: Emboss, Deboss, Chisel, Ridge, or Quilt.**

   The buttons look just like the effect you get when you apply the effect to an object.

4. **From the Vary drop-down list, select Color or Contrast.**

   If you select Contrast, use the slider to set the contrast level (drag the slider to the left to decrease contrast and to the right to increase contrast). If you select the Color option, the Highlight and Shadow fields become available. Click each color swatch to choose a color from the color picker.

5. **Drag the slider to choose a Depth setting.**

6. **Enter a value in the Angle field.**

   This determines the angle from which the light source comes. Alternatively, you can click and drag the dial slider.

7. **Click the Apply button to preview the object with the current settings.**

   If the object is embossed to your liking, proceed to Step 8; otherwise, choose different settings and click the Apply button to preview the object with the new settings.

8. **Click OK.**

   The object gets embossed.

Chapter 6: Exploring the Color Management Tools

In This Chapter

✔ **Working with color**

✔ **Creating a color palette**

✔ **Mixing a color**

✔ **Using the Eyedropper tool**

✔ **Modifying strokes and fills**

*W*hen you create a FreeHand MX illustration, you can work with as much or as little color as you want. You can use color sparingly if you're creating an illustration for the Web, or you can use lots of color if you're creating illustrations for print. FreeHand gives you a wide variety of color tools to work with. You can mix colors, create color palettes, load color palettes, and more. If you like bright, vibrant objects that look three dimensional in your illustrations, you can use the Fill options in the Objects tab of the Properties panel to create a gradient fill (a gradual transition between two or more colors).

In this chapter, we show you how to use the FreeHand color tools to add vibrancy to every illustration you create. We explain how to work with the different color models to mix up colors, as well as how to use the Swatches tab of the Assets panel to create a color palette for your document. If you prefer to stick with a given color, but want lighter variations of it, we detail how to do this with the Tints tab of the Mixer and Tints panel.

Before you begin creating an illustration, consider its final destination. Are you creating an illustration for print or for the Web? If you're creating an illustration for print, choose colors from the CMYK palette. If you are having a service center print the illustration, find out what system they use for color matching and choose all your colors from that color system. We show you how to choose from a color system in the section, "Using the Swatches Tab of the Assets Panel."

If you're creating an illustration for viewing on a computer, use colors from the RGB color model. If you're creating a document for Web viewing, remember the old Zen maxim: Less is more. If your viewing audience accesses the Internet using dial-up modems, the fewer colors you use, the smaller the file size, and thus the quicker the download time.

Using the Mixer Tab

You use the Mixer tab of the Mixer and Tints panel to mix up any color of the rainbow for your objects. You can mix a color using one of three color models, or you can use the System Color Picker to add a splash of color to your illustration (Mac users can select colors from Crayons, a Spectrum, and more). The neat thing about the Mixer tab is that you're dealing with values. If you have a set of values for a color (say that lovely chartreuse your client uses for a logo), you can match that color exactly by entering the values in the appropriate section of the Mixer tab. In the next few sections, we explain how to use each color model to mix up a shade of chartreuse, or whatever other color you fancy for your illustration. To open the Mixer tab, shown in Figure 6-1, choose Window⇨Color Mixer or press Shift+F9.

RGB

CMYK

Figure 6-1:
You can mix
a color
using one of
the three
color
models.

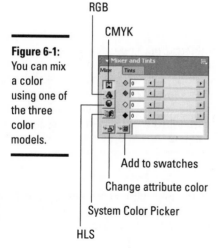

Add to swatches

Change attribute color

System Color Picker

HLS

After mixing a color, you can apply it to an object or add it to the Swatches tab of the Assets panel. We cover these colorful tasks in the upcoming section, "Working with the Mixer Tab."

Mixing a CMYK color

When you mix a color using the CMYK color model, you mix percentages of Cyan, Magenta, Yellow, and blacK. If your document is destined for print, this is the color model you should choose. Follow these steps to mix a color using the CMYK color model:

1. **Choose Window⇨Color Mixer or press Shift+F9.**

The Mixer and Tints panel, previously shown in Figure 6-1, opens.

2. **Click the CMYK button, which is the top button.**

   The Mixer tab goes into CMYK mode.

3. **Drag the sliders to mix the color.**

   As you drag the sliders, the color swatch on the right side at the bottom of the panel changes to reflect the current values, as shown in Figure 6-2. The values in each field update as well. Alternatively, you can enter known values in each field to match a known color, or click the arrows to increment the values.

Color value sliders

Color component values

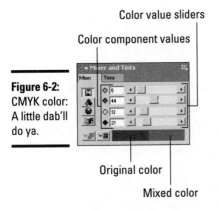

Figure 6-2:
CMYK color:
A little dab'll
do ya.

Original color

Mixed color

Mixing an RGB color

When you create illustrations that will be displayed on a Web site or as part of a CD-ROM presentation, you use the RGB (*R*ed, *G*reen, *B*lue) color model. You have 256 values (values from 0 to 255) of each color to work with. For example, if you create an RGB color with the following values (R=255, G=0, B=0), you get bright red; the following values yield bright blue (R=0, G=0, B=255), the values for black are (R=0, G=0, B=0), and so on. When you combine the possible permutations, you end up with millions of colors. To mix an RGB color, follow these steps:

1. **Choose Window⇨Color Mixer or press Shift+F9.**

   The Mixer and Tints panel opens to show the Mixer tab (refer to Figure 6-1).

2. **Click the RGB button, which is the second one from the top in the panel.**

   The Mixer tab is reconfigured, as shown in Figure 6-3.

Color value sliders

Color component values

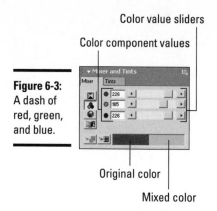

Figure 6-3:
A dash of
red, green,
and blue.

Original color

Mixed color

3. **Drag the sliders to mix the color.**

As you drag the sliders, the color swatch on the right side at the bottom of the panel changes to reflect the current values. The values in each field also update. Alternatively, you can enter values in the text fields, which by the by, is the proper way to match a known color value.

Mixing an HLS color

FreeHand uses HLS (*H*ue, *L*ightness, *S*aturation) color; you may see this color model referred to as HSB (*H*ue, *S*aturation, *B*rightness) in other programs. When you mix a color using the HLS color model, you choose a hue, specify the lightness of the color, and how saturated the color is. The HLS model is actually a color wheel. The hue is a value between 0 and 360 degrees. Values for light and saturation vary between 0 and 100. To mix an HLS color, follow these steps:

1. **Choose Window⇨Color Mixer or press Shift+F9.**

The Mixer and Tints panel opens with the Mixer tab selected (refer to Figure 6-1).

2. **Click the HLS button, which is the third one from the top in the panel.**

The Mixer tab is reconfigured, as shown in Figure 6-4.

3. **Click inside the color wheel and drag to select a hue.**

As you drag, the color swatch at the bottom of the panel changes to reflect the color your cursor is currently over. The values in the Hue and Saturation fields update as well.

Color component values

HLS color wheel

Figure 6-4:
You can mix
colors form
the HLS
color wheel.

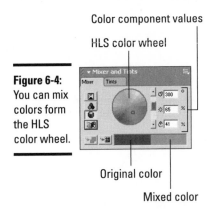

Original color

Mixed color

4. **Drag the slider to select a value for Lightness.**

   The values vary from 0 (black) to 100 (white). Alternatively, you can
   enter a value in the Lightness field.

5. **To specify saturation, enter a value in the Saturation field.**

   You can enter a value between 0 and 100. Low values create a grayer
   variation of the color; higher values increase saturation, creating a more
   vibrant color. Alternatively, you can drag the point in the color wheel,
   towards the center to decrease saturation, or away from the center to
   increase saturation.

After you mix up a color, click the button for another color mode to see the
component values for the new color in that color mode.

Mixing a color from the System Color Picker

Your operating system uses specific colors to display the icons, buttons,
and text of the software you use. You can use a color from the System Color
Picker in your FreeHand illustrations (Mac users can choose a color from
Crayons, a Spectrum, Grayscale, CMYK, RGB, HSB, Web-safe colors, and
more). To mix a color from the System Color Picker, follow these steps:

1. **Choose Window⊏➪Color Mixer or press Shift+F9.**

   The Mixer and Tints panel opens to show the Mixer tab (refer to
   Figure 6-1).

2. **Click the System Color Picker button, which is the fourth one from
   the top in the panel.**

   The Color dialog box opens, as shown in Figure 6-5.

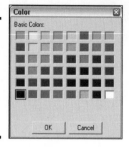

Figure 6-5:
You can
choose a
color from
the System
Color
Picker.

3. **Click a color to select it.**

   Half of the bar at the bottom of the Mixer tab of the Mixer and Tints panel refreshes to show the color you select. The component values for the color are displayed in the text fields for the color mode you choose. If you want to see the values for the color in CMYK, RGB, or HLS, click the appropriate button on the Mixer tab.

Working with the Mixer Tab

After you use the Mixer tab to mix the perfect hue, you can apply it directly to an object, use it for the current fill color, or add it to the Swatches tab of the Assets panel. We show you how to use the Swatches tab of the Assets panel to create a color palette in the upcoming section, "Using the Swatches Tab of the Assets Panel."

Using the Mixer tab to apply color to an object

When you mix a color with the Mixer tab, you can apply it directly to the stroke or fill of an object in your document. To apply a color from the Mixer tab to an object, follow these steps:

1. **Click the swatch shown in the right half of the rectangular bar at the bottom of the Mixer tab.**

   A square appears at the end of your cursor.

2. **While holding down the mouse button, drag toward the object you want to apply the color to.**

3. **Release the mouse button when your cursor is over the stroke or fill of the object, whichever you want to change.**

   The color is applied to stroke or fill of the object.

Using the Mixer tab to change the current fill or stroke color

If you're getting ready to create several objects and you want to use the same stroke or fill color on these objects, you can replace the current stroke or fill color with one you mix in the Mixer tab and create away. To use a color mixed in the Mixer tab as the current fill or stroke color, follow these steps:

1. **Click the swatch shown in the right half of the rectangular bar at the bottom of the Mixer tab.**

   A square appears at the end of your cursor.

2. **While holding down the mouse button, drag towards the Fill or Stroke color box.**

   You can find these boxes in the Colors section of the Tools panel.

3. **Release the mouse button when your cursor is over the Fill or Stroke color box.**

   The swatch in the Fill color box or Stroke color box changes to the color you mixed in the Mixer tab. If you have an object in the document selected, its fill or stroke color changes as well.

Adding a color to the Swatches tab of the Assets panel

If you mix a color you're going to use repeatedly in the document, you can add it to the Swatches tab. To add a color from the Mixer tab to the Swatches tab of the Assets panel, follow these steps:

1. **Choose Window⇨Color Mixer or press Shift+F9.**

   The Mixer and Tints panel opens.

2. **Mix a color.**

   If you don't know how to mix a color, read the preceding section, "Using the Mixer Tab."

3. **Click the Add to Swatches button at the lower-left corner of the Mixer tab — it's the one to the right of the Change Attribute Color button.**

   The Add to Swatches dialog box opens.

4. **Accept the default name for the color or enter one of your own.**

   FreeHand uses the component values to name the color. When the color is added to the Swatches tab of the Assets panel, a small rectangular swatch of the new color is added as well. If you give the color a unique name, it will be easier to find if you're creating an illustration with lots of colors. To give the color a unique name, type the name and press Enter.

5. **Choose Process or Spot.**

   This option refers to how the color is separated for the output device. Process colors are printed on four separate pages using the four process (CMYK) inks. Spot colors are not separated and are printed on a separate plate.

6. **Click Add.**

   The color is added to the Swatches tab of the Assets panel.

Creating Color Tints

When you create a color tint, you create a lighter variation of the original color. You create a color tint by varying the percentage of the original color with the Tints tab of the Mixers and Tints panel. After you create a color tint, you can apply it directly to an object, add the tint to the Swatches tab of the Assets panel, or use it as the current fill or stroke color. To create a color tint, follow these steps:

1. **Create a color using the Mixer tab of the Mixer and Tints panel.**

2. **Click the Tints tab on the panel.**

   The Tints tab opens, as shown in Figure 6-6.

Tint value windows

Slider

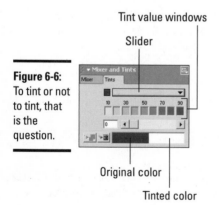

Figure 6-6:
To tint or not
to tint, that
is the
question.

Original color

Tinted color

3. **Drag the slider to specify the percentage of the original color that will be used to create the tint.**

   As you drag the slider, the swatch at the bottom-right of the panel updates to display the new tint. Compare this to the swatch at the bottom-left of the panel, which is the original color. Alternatively, you can tint the color by clicking one of the squares (tints of the original color in ten percent increments) or by entering a value in the field.

4. **After creating the tint, do one of the following:**

   - Click the color swatch shown in the right half of the rectangle at the bottom of the panel, and then drag and drop the color on an object in the document.

   - Click the color swatch shown in the right half of the rectangle at the bottom of the panel, and then drag and drop the color on the Fill color box to replace the current fill color with the tint, or drag and drop the color on the Stroke color box to replace the current stroke color with the tint. If you have an object selected while doing this, the object's stroke or fill color is changed as well. ***Note:*** The Fill color box and the Stroke color box are both found on the Tools panel.

   - Click the Add to Swatches button to add the tint to the Swatches tab of the Assets panel. After you click the button, the Add to Swatches dialog box appears. For more information, read the "Adding a color to the Swatches tab of the Assets panel" section, earlier in this chapter.

 If the Mixer and Tint panel is open at the same time as the Swatches tab of the Assets panels, you can click the color swatch at the bottom of either the Mixer tab or the Tint tab in the Mixer and Tint panel, and drag and drop it into the Swatches tab, and the color is added to the palette.

Using the Swatches Tab of the Assets Panel

When you create an illustration that uses the same colors on each page or for several objects, mixing the color each time you need it is time-consuming and counterproductive. You can save a considerable amount of time if you add the colors you use frequently to the Swatches tab of the Assets panel. You also use the Swatches tab to organize and apply colors from standard preset color-matching systems. This option is handy if you're creating a document that will be printed by a service center. If you're creating a document for a Web page, you can also choose a color from the Web safe color library. Another option you have with the Swatches tab is saving the current color palette for future use. To open the Swatches tab, shown in Figure 6-7, choose Window⇨Swatches or press Ctrl+F9.

The Swatches tab shown in Figure 6-7 already has colors added to it. The default colors when you create a new document are None, Black, White, and Registration. You cannot rename or delete these colors. Black is a spot color that is used for the black separation plate when printing a process color. The registration color, a combination of CMY and K, all at 100%, is used for crop or trim marks and prints solid on separations.

Figure 6-7:
You use the Swatches tab to create a color palette and more.

You can differentiate color types in the Swatches tab of the Assets panel as follows:

✦ **Process colors:** The names of process colors are italicized.

✦ **Spot colors:** The names of spot colors are displayed with plain type.

✦ **RGB colors:** RGB colors display a triangular icon with red, green, and blue spheres after the color's name. Colors derived from the HLS color wheel or the System Color Picker are displayed as RGB colors as well.

✦ **CMYK colors:** CMYK colors are displayed with no icon.

After you open the Swatches tab of the Assets panel, you can do any of the following:

✦ **Apply a color to an object:** You can apply a color to the stroke or fill of an object by selecting the color and dragging and dropping it on an object. Alternatively, you can apply a color by selecting an object, clicking the Fill, Stroke, or Stroke and Fill button at the top of the Swatches tab, and clicking the desired color's name in the Swatches tab.

✦ **Modify a color:** You can modify a color in one of two ways:

   • **Mixer tab:** You can modify a color in the Swatches tab by opening the Mixer tab and dragging and dropping a color from the Swatches tab to the left side of the rectangular color swatch at the bottom of the Mixer tab.

   • **Tints tab:** You can modify a color in the Swatches tab by opening the Tints tab and dragging and dropping a color from the Swatches tab to the left side of the rectangular color swatch at the bottom of the Tints tab.

✦ **Change the stroke color:** You can change the current stroke color by selecting a color from the Swatches tab and then dragging and dropping it on the Stroke color box on the Tools panel.

✦ **Change the fill color:** You can change the current fill color by selecting a color from the Swatches tab and then dragging and dropping it on the Fill color box on the Tools panel.

Adding preset colors to the Swatches tab

You can add a color to the Swatches tab of the Assets panel from either the Mixer tab or the Tints tab, as outlined earlier in the chapter. If you fast-forwarded to this section and need to know how to add a color to the Swatches tab from the Mixer tab, read the section, "Adding a color to the Swatches tab"; to add a tint to the Swatches tab, read the section, "Creating Color Tints." In this section, we show you how to add colors to the Swatches tab from preset color matching systems. To add a color from a preset color matching system to the Swatches tab, follow these steps:

1. **Choose Window⇨Swatches.**

   The Swatches tab of the Assets panel opens.

2. **Click the Options menu (the bulleted list icon at the upper-right corner of the Assets panel) and choose one of the preset color matching sets.**

   If the document you're creating will be printed commercially, find out the system they use for color matching. For example, they may use one of the PANTONE or Munsell matching systems. If the document you're creating will be displayed on a Web page, choose Web Safe Color Library. When you choose a color matching system, a dialog box appears.

3. **Select a color (or colors) from the Library dialog box.**

   You can select additional contiguous colors by clicking them while holding down the Shift key and non-contiguous colors by holding down the Ctrl key.

4. **Click OK.**

   The Library dialog box closes and FreeHand adds the selected color(s) to the Swatches tab using the color's default library name.

You can also double-click a color to add it the Swatches tab, which will close the dialog box.

Renaming a color

You can rename any color in the Swatches tab, except the default colors: None, Black, White, and Registration. If you give a color a unique name, you'll have an easier time selecting it from the Swatches tab. To rename a color, follow these steps:

1. **Choose Window⇨Swatches.**

   The Swatches tab of the Assets panel opens.

2. **Double-click the color you want to rename.**

   The color's name is highlighted.

**Book IV
Chapter 6**

**Exploring the Color
Management Tools**

3. **Type a new name for the color and then press Enter.**

The color is renamed.

Exporting a color palette

When you create an ideal color palette, you can export the palette for use in documents you create in the future. This option is handy if you do work for a client that uses specific color combinations for their text and logo. You create the palette by adding colors to the Swatches tab as outlined previously in this chapter in the "Adding a color to the Swatches tab," "Creating Color Tints," and "Adding preset colors to the Swatches tab" sections. After you create the palette (also known as a Color Library), you can export it by following these steps:

1. **Choose Window⇨Swatches or press Ctrl+F9.**

The Swatches tab of the Assets panel opens.

2. **Click the Options menu (the bulleted list icon at the upper-right corner of the Assets panel) and choose Export.**

The Export Colors dialog box, shown in Figure 6-8, opens.

Figure 6-8:
You can create a custom Color Library from the Swatches tab.

3. **Select the colors you want to export.**

To select a color, click it. Hold down the Shift key to add a selection of contiguous colors to the selection, or hold down the Ctrl key to add individual noncontiguous colors to the selection.

4. **Click OK.**

The Create Color Library dialog box appears.

5. **Enter a name in the Library Name field.**

Choose a meaningful name that describes the type of colors in the library, or enter the name of the client you use the colors for.

6. **In the Filename field, accept the default name of CUSTOM, or enter another name for the library.**

If you intend to store more than one library, change the name to one that reflects the contents of the library. When you import the Color Library into a future document, this is the name you look for.

7. **Click Save.**

FreeHand saves the library in the Colors folder (in FreeHand's Settings folder) and the colors in it appear on the Swatches tab.

Adding custom colors to the Swatches tab

After you save a color palette as a library, you can use any or all colors from the palette in new illustrations by adding them to the Swatches tab of the Assets panel. To add colors from a custom library to the current Swatches tab, follow these steps:

1. **Choose Windows⇨Swatches or press Ctrl+F9.**

The Swatches panel opens.

2. **Click the Options menu (the bulleted list icon at the upper-right corner of the Assets panel) and select the custom color library by clicking its name.**

The Library dialog box opens.

3. **Select the colors you want to add to the Swatches tab.**

Select an individual color by clicking its swatch. To add contiguous colors to the selection, hold down the Shift key and click the top and bottom colors you want to add. To add noncontiguous colors to the selection, hold down the Ctrl key and click the individual colors you want to add.

4. **Click OK.**

The colors are added to the Swatches tab.

You can also copy and paste or drag and drop named colors from one open FreeHand document to another. The colors will be added to the Swatches tab automatically.

Using the Eyedropper Tool

You use the Eyedropper tool to sample a color. You can sample the color from an object in your document, the Stroke color box, the Fill color box, or from the following panel tabs: Mixer, Tints, and Swatches. To sample a color with the Eyedropper tool, follow these steps:

1. **Select the Eyedropper tool from the Tools panel.**

It's the tool with an eyedropper for an icon.

2. **Sample a color by doing one of the following:**

- Click an object in the document window.

- Click a color swatch in any of the following panel tabs: Mixer, Swatches, or Tints.

After you sample a color, hold down the mouse button and drag and drop the color to any of the following:

- **A different object in the document:** Do this when you sample a color from one object that you want to apply to another.

- **An object in the document:** Do this when you want to sample a color from a panel tab.

- **The color swatch in the Mixer tab:** Do this when you want to modify a color using the Mixer tab.

- **The color swatch in the Tints tab:** Do this when you want to tint an existing color.

- **The Swatches tab:** Do this when you want to add a sampled color to the Swatches tab.

3. **Release the mouse button.**

The sampled color is applied to the object or added to the tab you dropped it on.

Modifying Strokes

You use the Object tab of the Properties panel to change the color of a stroke, its width, and other parameters. If the stroke is a single line, you can add arrowheads to the head and/or tail of the stroke. The Object tab of the Properties panel has enough options to fill up a whole lot of pages. You'll never use many of the options, so we spare you a lot of excess verbiage by showing you how to modify a basic stroke in this section. To modify a stroke using the Object tab of the Properties panel, follow these steps:

1. **Use the Pointer tool to select the stroke you want to modify.**

You select a path, or modify an object's stroke (outline) by selecting the object.

2. **Choose Windows⇨Object or press Ctrl+F3.**

The Object tab of the Properties panel opens, displaying the Stroke tools, as shown in Figure 6-9.

Stroke color

Stroke type

Figure 6-9:
You can
modify a
stroke's
appearance
with the
Object tab
of the
Properties
panel.

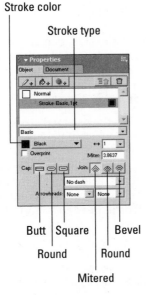

Butt | Square | Bevel

Round | Round

Mitered

3. **Click the stroke in the list of Object properties to show the options for the stroke you want to edit.**

4. **To change the stroke's color, click and drag a color from the Swatches tab of the Assets panel onto the box to the right of the stroke indicator.**

Similarly, you can also click the Stroke color box on the Tools panel and select a color from there.

5. **Select an option from the Width drop-down list.**

Alternatively, you can enter the desired value in the Width field.

6. **Click a button in the Cap section to determine the path end.**

The available options are Butt, Round, or Square.

7. **Click a button in the Join section to determine how path ends join.**

   The available options are Mitered, Round, and Bevel.

8. **Enter a value in the Miter field.**

   This value is applicable if you choose a miter join. Enter a value between 1 and 57. If the line length exceeds this value, it will be squared off instead of mitered.

9. **To have a dashed stroke, select an option from the Dash drop-down list.**

10. **To apply an arrowhead to an open path, select an option from each of the Arrowheads drop-down lists.**

    Use the left Arrowheads drop-down list to select an arrowhead for the start of the path; use the right Arrowheads drop-down list to select an arrowhead for the end of the path. You can select different arrowheads for each end of the path. You can also have an arrowhead at one end of the path and no arrowhead at the other.

    The settings you specify are applied to the selected stroke. When you create a new stroke, the stroke is created using the previous settings.

You can use the Object tab to set stroke settings for all future strokes you create. Deselect all objects in the document, select a non-drawing tool, such as the Pointer tool, and then set stroke characteristics as outlined in the previous steps. The characteristics will be applied to all future strokes until you modify the settings in the Object tab.

If you like artistic brush strokes, select a path, open the Object tab, and then select Brush from the Stroke Type drop-down list. (Refer to Figure 6-9.) You can make the stroke look like it was painted with an artist's brush or an airbrush.

Modifying Fills

When you add color to a shape, you give it a fill. You can modify the fill at any time using the Object tab of the Properties panel. The Object tab is filled with all manner of different fill options. In fact, it has so many options; it would fill a chapter of its own. In the upcoming sections, we show you the most commonly used fill options.

Creating a basic fill

You can create or modify a basic fill through the Object tab in the Properties panel. A basic fill is pretty simple; it only has one color. When your design calls for a basic fill, here's how you create one with the Object tab:

1. **Use the Pointer tool to select the object whose fill you want to modify.**

   Alternatively, deselect all objects in the document, select a non-drawing tool, and the fill you create is applied to all future shapes you create.

2. **Choose Window➪Object or press Ctrl+F3.**

   The Object tab of the Properties panel opens.

3. **Click Fill: Basic beneath the object box in the list area of the panel.**

   By default, fills are defined as Basic and are colored black, as shown in Figure 6-10.

Figure 6-10: Basic fills are . . . basic.

4. **Choose a color from the Fill drop-down list.**

   These are the colors currently in the Swatches tab of the Assets panel. Alternatively, you can select a color by clicking the swatch in the Mixer or Tint tabs of the Mixer and Tints panel and dragging and dropping the color on the current color swatch in the Object tab.

   After you select a color, it is applied to the selected object, or if you have no objects selected, the fill will be applied to all closed paths you create until you modify the fill.

   If there is no default fill created for an object you're working on, you can create one by clicking the Paint Bucket button on the Object tab. This will add a fill of the default color (which is usually black) to the object.

Creating a gradient fill

When you create a gradient fill, you create a gradual transition of two or more colors. In FreeHand, you can create the following types of gradient fills: linear, radial, contoured, logarithmic, rectangle, or cone. Figure 6-11 shows a comparison of the six gradient fill types.

Linear   Radial   Contour

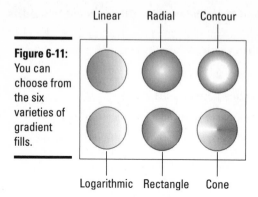

Figure 6-11:
You can
choose from
the six
varieties of
gradient
fills.

Logarithmic   Rectangle   Cone

When you create a gradient fill, you specify each color in the fill and where
the color is blended. To create a gradient fill, follow these steps:

1. **Use the Pointer tool to select the object to which you want to apply
   the gradient fill. The object must have a closed path.**

   Alternatively, you can deselect all objects in the document, and the fill
   you create will be applied to closed paths you create from this point
   forward.

2. **Choose Window⇨Object and, from the Object tab, select Fill: Basic
   from the area underneath the object name in the middle list area.**

3. **From the Fill Type drop-down list, select Gradient.**

   The Object tab is reconfigured, as shown in Figure 6-12.

Fill type

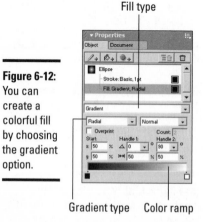

Figure 6-12:
You can
create a
colorful fill
by choosing
the gradient
option.

Gradient type   Color ramp

4. **Select the appropriate gradient type from the drop-down list beneath the Fill Type drop-down list.**

You can choose Linear, Radial, Contour, Logarithmic, Rectangle, or Cone. The default gradient fill blends black and white, but you can choose any color.

5. **Click the color swatch at either end of the color ramp (the rectangle at the bottom of the tab) and choose a color from the color picker.**

The color swatch refreshes to show the color you selected. Alternatively, you can click the color swatch in the Mixer or Tint tabs and drag and drop the color onto the color swatch on the color ramp.

6. **To add additional color points to the gradient, click a color swatch from the Mixer tab of the Mixer and Tints panel or from the Swatches tab of the Assets panel and drag and drop it to the desired position on the color ramp.**

You can add as many color points as needed to define your fill. After adding another color point, you can select a different color by using any of the methods outlined in Step 5. If you need to move a color pointer, click the color pointer and drag it to a different position on the color ramp. To remove a color point, click it and drag it off the color ramp.

7. **Set the options for the type of gradient you've selected.**

Each of the gradients has slightly different options for tweaking the fill pattern. In general, though, they include starting points for the gradient, the angle of the gradient, and the width of the gradient.

Creating a tiled fill

When you create a tiled fill, you copy a shape from within the document and use it to create a fill that displays the copied object tiled within another object. You can specify how large the tiled object is and change the fill's position within the filled object. To create a tiled fill, follow these steps:

1. **Use the Pointer tool to select the object (or objects) that you want as the basis for your tiled fill.**

2. **Choose Edit⇨Copy or press Ctrl+C.**

The object is copied to the Clipboard.

3. **Use the Pointer tool to select the object you want to fill.**

**Book IV
Chapter 6**

**Exploring the Color
Management Tools**

4. **Choose Window⇨Object and select Tiled from the Fill Type drop-down list in the Object tab of the Properties panel.**

The Object tab is reconfigured to create tiled fills.

5. **Click the Paste In button.**

The copied shape is pasted into the window and is tiled within the object you are filling.

6. **To resize the object, enter values in the X and Y fields.**

Enter values lower than 100 to make the object smaller and values larger than 100 to increase the size of the tiled object. As you enter values, the object's fill changes to reflect the new parameters. Enter the same value in each field to resize the object proportionately.

7. **Enter values in the X and Y Offset fields.**

The values you enter move the fill within the object to which it is applied. Enter positive X values to move the tiled fill to the right, and negative X values to move the tiled fill to the left. Enter positive Y values to move the fill up, and negative Y values to move the fill down.

8. **Drag the circular dial to set the fill's angle.**

Hold down the Shift key to constrain the changes to 45-degree increments. Alternatively, you can enter a value in the Angle field. Figure 6-13 shows the Object tab being used to create a tiled fill as well as the object the tiled fill is being applied to.

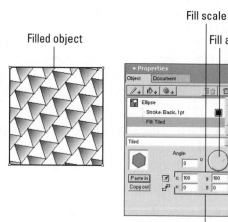

Figure 6-13: It's not ceramic, but it is tile.

Fun with color, FreeHand style

You can also modify colors in your documents by choosing Xtras⇨Colors and choosing a command from the submenu. You can use these commands to lighten, darken, or desaturate process colors, as well as randomize colors, sort named colors, and more. We urge you to experiment with these powerful commands to further your use of color in FreeHand.

Using FreeHand's other fill types

Getting into the nitty-gritty details of how to use FreeHand's other fill types goes a little beyond the scope of this book, but we did want to at least mention what they're used for, lest you see them in the Fill Type drop-down list and think, "Hey, I got robbed! Nobody told me about these." Briefly, here's what the other Fill types are designed to do:

✦ **Custom Fill:** Nine custom fills are available, and they include things like bricks, circles, and grass. Each of the fills is editable.

✦ **Lens:** The Lens fill allows you to set up your fill using common photo-realistic effects, such as transparency, lighten, darken, invert, and monochrome. Again, each of these effects is editable to your liking.

✦ **Pattern:** The Pattern fill is fun, because you can watch your object change as you click on little boxes in a grid in the Object tab.

✦ **Postscript:** Postscript fills are standardized repeating patterns. You won't be able to see them onscreen — they only appear when you print your document on a PostScript printer. Onscreen (and when output from non-Postscript printers) they show up as rows of the letter C. Postscript fills don't scale when you scale an object; they have set sizes. If you're looking for a place to get started on understanding postscript, including links to other sources on the Net, check out www.postscript.org.

✦ **Textured:** Textured fills work almost exactly like the pattern fills, except that the fills are more interesting. For this type, they include burlap, denim, sand, and coarse gravel.

Chapter 7: Integrating FreeHand MX with Other Macromedia Products

In This Chapter

✓ Integrating FreeHand with Fireworks

✓ Integrating FreeHand with Macromedia Flash

✓ Integrating FreeHand with Dreamweaver

Macromedia Studio MX 2004 is a complete package that offers graphic designers and Web designers a wonderful set of tools to work with. The applications share some common components, and the interfaces are similar, making it easy to branch out from one Macromedia Studio application to another. In addition to sharing common interface elements, Macromedia applications can use items created in other Macromedia applications. For example, you can create a multipage FreeHand document and export it as a Flash movie. You can also take advantage of FreeHand's superior illustration tools to create objects that would be difficult or impossible to create with Flash or Fireworks. You can then export the objects for use in a Fireworks document that will be used in a Dreamweaver MX 2004 Web design, or incorporate the objects in a Flash movie or application. You can also publish a FreeHand document as HTML that you can modify in Dreamweaver.

In this chapter, we show you some of the ways FreeHand integrates with other Macromedia applications. We explain how to export illustrations as images for the Web and how to export a multipage document for use as a Flash movie.

Integrating FreeHand with Fireworks

When you create artwork in FreeHand, you can export it for use in a Fireworks MX 2004 document. You can do this if you prefer the drawing toolset in FreeHand, but you also need to use the enhanced Web graphics features in Fireworks to create documents for Web pages. Fireworks also features enhanced optimization tools that enable you to optimize an image for an intended destination, producing a document with the smallest possible file size with acceptable image quality. You can export documents as image files, or as AI (Adobe Illustrator) or EPS (Encapsulated PostScript) files, that can be opened in Fireworks. For information on file types you can open in Fireworks, refer to Book III, Chapter 8.

In addition to exporting your documents to Fireworks, you can simply save them as FH11 files and open them directly in Fireworks. Should you choose to go this route, your layers will be maintained. However, once you edit the file in Fireworks, you'll need to save it in the native Fireworks format (PNG).

Even though you can export a FreeHand document as a PNG file, when you open the file in Fireworks, all objects and layers are flattened and cannot be edited.

You can also get FreeHand objects into Fireworks by dragging and dropping. To do this, create your artwork in FreeHand, and then launch Fireworks. You then need to resize both application windows so that they are tiled side by side. At this point, you can drag an object from a FreeHand document into a Fireworks document.

Integrating FreeHand with Macromedia Flash

If you've used Macromedia Flash, you know the software has a wonderful toolset for creating animations; however, traditional graphic illustrators may find the drawing tools somewhat quirky. Even though Macromedia Flash has a powerful Pen tool that enables you to create open and closed paths, if your background is in graphic illustration, you'll find the more powerful FreeHand toolset preferable. In this regard, you can create a multipage document using the FreeHand drawing tools to create characters that change from page to page. In the upcoming sections, we show you how to animate the artwork you create in FreeHand and export the document as a Flash SWF movie file.

Creating animations

When you want to animate objects that you intend to use in Flash movies, you place the objects on separate layers. You can animate objects, groups, or blends. If you want to animate a single object and make it appear to move from one point of the page to another, follow these steps:

1. **Use the Pointer tool to select the object you want to animate, press the Alt key, and drag to duplicate the object.**

   As you drag, FreeHand creates a preview of the duplicate's current position.

2. **Release the mouse button when the duplicate object is in the desired position.**

   After you create the duplicate, you can use any tool to modify the shape. Do this when you want the shape to morph during the animation. For that matter, you can create a different object instead of creating a duplicate, and then follow the remaining steps to morph from one shape to another.

3. **Select the Blend tool from the Tools panel.**

   The Blend tool, represented by the icon with three shapes (a blue star in front and a red circle in the back), is to the right of the Trace tool.

4. **Click the original object and drag to the duplicate object.**

   FreeHand creates a blend between the original and the duplicate objects.

5. **If desired, leave the blended object selected and adjust its properties in the Object tab of the Properties panel.**

   By default, the blend consists of 25 steps. You can change the number of steps as well as other properties.

6. **Choose Xtras⇨Animate⇨Release to Layers.**

   The Release to Layers dialog box appears.

7. **Accept the default Sequence option and click OK.**

   FreeHand releases the objects to layers.

After you release the blend to layers, you can preview the animation as it will appear in the Macromedia Flash Player. *Note:* The animation sequence is determined by the stacking of layers, and goes from the bottom layer up. Objects on the Background layer are shown on all frames of the animation.

To preview the animation as a Flash movie, follow these steps:

1. **Choose Window⇨Movie⇨Test.**

   FreeHand creates an SWF file and opens the movie in another window. When the window opens, the animation does not automatically play.

2. **You control the movie by choosing Window⇨Movie and choosing one of these commands:**

   - **Play:** Restarts the movie after you stop it.
   - **Stop:** Stops the movie.
   - **Rewind:** Rewinds the movie to the first frame.
   - **Step Forward:** Advances the movie to the next frame.

**Book IV
Chapter 7**

**Integrating
FreeHand MX**

- **Step Backward:** Rewinds the movie to the previous frame.
- **Export:** Opens the Export Movie dialog box.
- **Movie Settings:** Opens the Movie Settings dialog box.

After you preview the movie, close the SWF preview window. The file you made the movie from is open in the FreeHand window.

Using ActionScript

When you create a document in FreeHand with the intention of exporting it as a Flash movie, you can integrate ActionScript in the Flash movie. ActionScript adds a degree of interaction to a Flash movie. You can assign ActionScript to objects in your FreeHand movie that cause the movie to advance to another frame, stop, enable users to drag an object from one place to another, and so on. You choose which event causes the ActionScript to execute; for example, the downstroke or upstroke of a mouse click. The ActionScript is embedded in the Flash movie you export. You can assign one of the following actions to an object in a FreeHand document:

✦ **Go To:** Advances the movie to another frame or scene.

✦ **Play:** Plays the movie frame by frame.

✦ **Stop:** Stops the movie.

✦ **Print:** Prints the frame.

✦ **Full Screen:** Displays the movie in Full Screen mode, regardless of the document size.

✦ **Start/Stop Drag:** Causes the object to be draggable, based on the event you choose; for example, when a user presses the mouse button.

You can assign ActionScript to a bitmap image or object in your FreeHand document by following these steps:

1. **Use the Pointer tool to select the object to which you want to assign ActionScript.**

2. **Select Window⇨Navigation.**

   The Navigation panel appears, as shown in Figure 7-1.

3. **Select an action from the Action drop-down list.**

   You can select any of the actions listed in the previous bullet list.

4. **Select the event that triggers the action from the Event drop-down list.**

   For more information on ActionScript events, refer to Book V, Chapter 8.

Figure 7-1:
Some
options
in the
Navigation
panel
may be
unavailable,
depending
on other
options
selected.

5. **If the action you select requires parameters, the Parameters drop-down list becomes active. Select the parameter that suits the way you want the action to execute.**

   For more information on ActionScript parameters, refer to Book V, Chapter 8.

6. **Close the Navigation panel.**

   The action is added to the object. Test the movie to make sure the action executes properly.

Exporting Flash movies

After you create an animation and add ActionScript to objects in the document, you can export the document as a Flash movie. You can export the movie for the Macromedia Flash Player 7. To export your document as a Flash movie, follow these steps:

1. **Choose File⇨Export.**

   The Export Document dialog box appears.

2. **From the Save as Type drop-down list, select Macromedia Flash SWF.**

3. **Click the Setup button.**

   The Movie Settings dialog box, shown in Figure 7-2, appears.

4. **In the Optimization section, select compression options from the Path Compression and the Image Compression drop-down lists.**

   The default compression setting is Medium. Select a higher setting to create a smaller file size with lower image quality. Select a lower setting for higher image quality at the expense of a larger file size.

**Book IV
Chapter 7**

**Integrating
FreeHand MX**

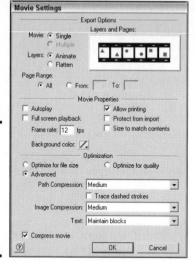

Figure 7-2:
Control
movie
parameters
with the
Movie
Settings
dialog box.

5. **If your document has dashed lines, you can convert them to individual objects by selecting the Trace Dashed Strokes check box.**

   If you select this option, FreeHand creates an individual object for each dash. This results in a larger file size, but you can edit each dash as an object if you import the movie into Macromedia Flash. If you don't convert the dashed lines to individual objects, they will be converted to solid lines.

6. **Select one of the following options from the Text drop-down list:**

   - **Maintain Blocks:** Select this option if you want to be able to edit the text when you import the file into Macromedia Flash.

   - **Convert to Paths:** Select this option, and FreeHand converts text objects to paths that cannot be edited as text in Macromedia Flash. This results in a smaller file size.

   - **None:** Select this option, and FreeHand does not export text objects with the Flash movie.

7. **In the Export Options section, select a Page option.**

   This determines how many pages of the document are exported as frames. Select the All option to export all pages, or enter specific page numbers in the From and To fields.

8. **If your document has more than a single page, select the single or multiple option from the Movie radio button.**

   If you select the Single option, all the pages in your document will be exported as a single movie. If you select the Multiple option, each page will be exported as a separate movie.

9. **Select one of the following options from the Layers radio button:**

- **Animate:** Select this option to export each page as a separate SWF file. Layers on each page are converted to frames.

- **Flatten:** Select this option to export each page of the document in a single SWF file. Layers on each page are flattened to a single image.

10. **Accept the default frame rate of 12 fps (frames per second) or enter a different value.**

This value is the number of frames that result in one second of playback in the Flash movie. Enter a lower value for a smaller file size that may cause jerky motion when the movie is played; enter a higher value for smoother motion at the expense of a larger file.

11. **Select the Autoplay option (enabled by default), and the movie begins playing as soon as it loads into the Macromedia Flash Player.**

Deselect this option if you have added ActionScript that causes the movie to begin playing when a user clicks an object in the Flash movie.

12. **Select the Full Screen Playback option, and the exported Flash movie expands to fill the user's screen.**

The user can exit full-screen mode by pressing the Esc key.

13. **Select the Protect from Import option, and the movie cannot be imported into Macromedia Flash MX 2004, or any previous version.**

This option prevents other animators from dissecting your handiwork in any version of Macromedia Flash. Do not select this option if you intend to use the exported Flash movie as part of another production you are editing in Macromedia Flash.

14. **Click OK.**

The Movie Settings dialog box closes.

15. **Enter a name for the file and specify the folder to which you want the file saved.**

16. **Click the Save button.**

FreeHand exports the file as an SWF movie.

A new feature in FreeHand MX allows you to edit the Flash source file of an imported SWF file by selecting the SWF and clicking the FreeHand to Flash button in the Object tab of the Properties panel. Edit the movie in Macromedia Flash and click the Save button. Macromedia Flash exports the updated movie and closes. The updated SWF shows up automatically in FreeHand.

Integrating FreeHand with Dreamweaver

The artwork that you create in FreeHand can be exported in formats you can use in a Dreamweaver HTML document. You can export documents as JPEG or GIF files. You can also export documents as SWF files that you can then embed in Web pages you create within Dreamweaver.

In addition, you can add navigation links to objects in your FreeHand documents and publish the document as an HTML file. If this piques your curiosity, please read the following sections.

Adding navigation links

You can add a navigation link to any object in a FreeHand document. This option is handy when you intend to publish the document as an HMTL file. To add a navigation link to an object in a FreeHand document, follow these steps:

1. Use the Pointer tool to select the object to which you want to add the link.

You can add a link to a text object, a path, or a bitmap image. However, if you assign a link to an open path, you don't give the user much of a target area to click.

2. Choose Window⇨Navigation.

The Navigation panel opens, as shown in Figure 7-3.

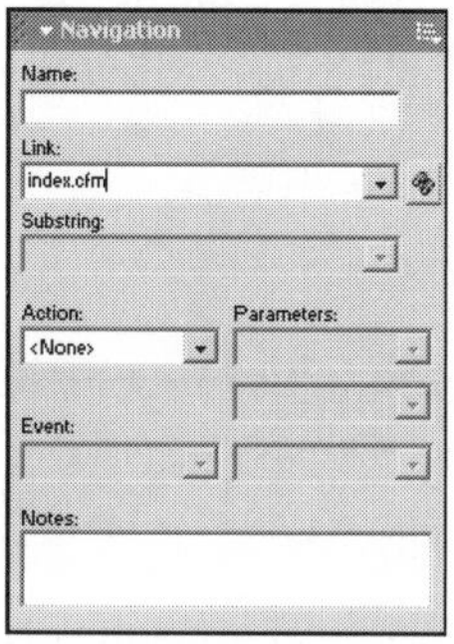

Figure 7-3:
We've typed a URL in the Link field of the Navigation panel.

3. In the Link field, enter the URL you want linked to the object.

This is the Web page that appears in the user's browser when the link is clicked. If the Web page is at the same Web site, you only need to enter the filename of the page you want opened when the link is clicked; for example: `myPage.htm`. If the file is in a different directory, you need to enter the relative path to the file; for example, `htmldocs/myHtmldoc.htm`. If the Web page resides at another Web site, you need to enter the absolute path to the Web page, such as `http://www.dasdesigns.net/about.htm`.

4. Close the Navigation panel.

The link is assigned to the object and will be written as HTML code when the document is published as an HTML file.

Publishing a document as HTML

When you create a FreeHand document that you intend to use as a Web page, you can publish the document as an HTML file that you can edit in Dreamweaver. When you publish a FreeHand document as an HTML file, FreeHand writes the HTML code needed to display the objects and bitmaps in the document in a Web browser, as well as to create any links you assigned to objects in the document. To export a FreeHand document as an HTML file, follow these steps:

1. Choose File⇨Publish as HTML.

The HTML Output dialog box opens, as shown in Figure 7-4.

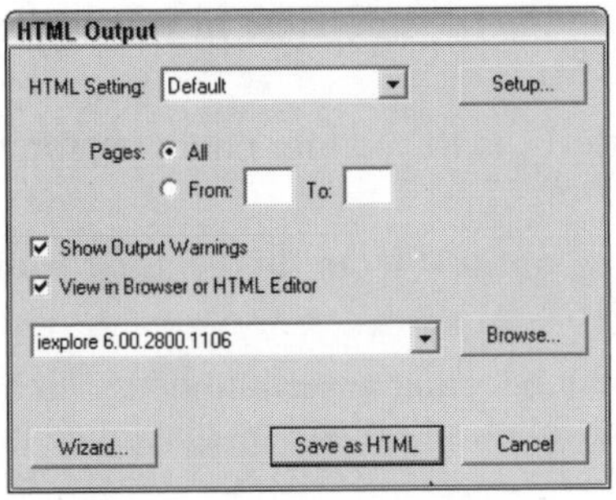

Figure 7-4: Exporting a FreeHand file as HTML.

2. Click the Setup button.

The HTML Setup dialog box appears, as shown in Figure 7-5.

3. In the Document Root field, enter the folder where the files for your Web site are stored.

If you're using the file in a Web site you've already created in Dreamweaver, store the file in the same directory as your Dreamweaver HTML documents.

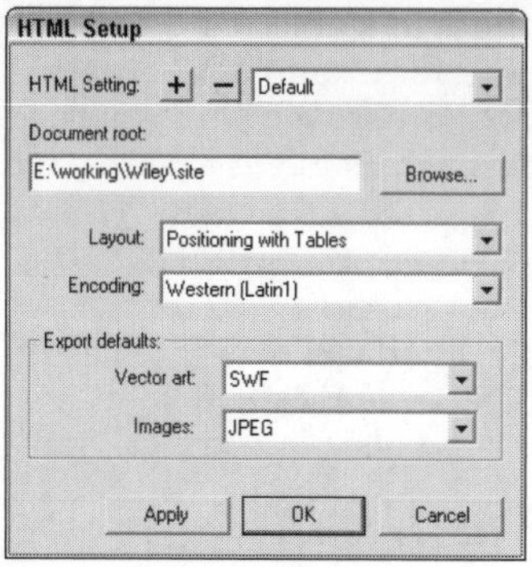

Figure 7-5:
Customizing
the HTML
setup.

4. **Select one of the following options from the Layout drop-down list:**

   • **Positioning with Layers:** Select this option, and FreeHand creates HTML code that positions the objects using HTML layers. This option precisely places each object in the document. Browsers capable of decoding HTML 3.0 or greater support layers.

   • **Positioning with Tables:** Select this option, and FreeHand creates an HTML document with a table. Each object in the document is placed in a table cell. Overlapping objects are sliced or combined to fit table cells. Most popular Web browsers support tables.

5. **Select the option applicable to the language in your document from the Encoding drop-down list.**

   The default, Western (Latin 1), is the proper encoding format for the English language.

6. **Select one of the following options from the Vector Art drop-down list: GIF, JPEG, PNG, or SWF.**

   This option determines which format FreeHand uses when converting paths in your document to images that will be displayed in a Web browser.

7. **Select one of the following options from the Images drop-down list: GIF, JPEG, PNG, or SWF.**

   The option determines the file format FreeHand uses to convert bitmap images in your document into images that are displayed when the HTML document is loaded into a Web browser. If the image has millions of colors, choose JPEG. If the image has large areas of solid color, choose GIF.

8. **Click OK.**

   The HTML Setup dialog box closes, and you're back at the HTML Output dialog box.

9. **Select an option for Pages.**

You can publish all pages as HTML documents, or specify a range of pages to publish.

10. **Select the Show Output Warnings option (selected by default), and FreeHand displays the HTML Output Warnings dialog box when converting the document to HTML.**

The HTML Output Warnings dialog box warns you of any potential anomalies that would prevent the page from displaying properly in a Web browser.

11. **Select the View in Browser or HTML Editor option.**

This option is selected by default. When the document is converted, FreeHand opens the exported HTML document in your default Web browser. You can specify another Web browser or HTML editor by clicking the Browse button and using the Open dialog box to navigate to the folder where the browser or HTML editor is located.

12. **Select the Save as HTML option.**

FreeHand converts the file to HTML format and the HTML Output Warnings window appears (it may be hidden behind the browser window). The file is displayed in your default browser if you choose this option. If the file is displayed in a browser, you can check to make sure the links are working properly. When the file is saved, if you didn't specify otherwise in Step 3, FreeHand creates a folder named FreeHand HTML Output and saves the HTML file to it. Within the FreeHand HTML Output folder is a subfolder named Images that stores the vector and bitmaps artwork from the document.

After you publish a document as HTML, you can edit the file by opening it in Dreamweaver, modifying the document to suit the Web site it will be displayed at, and then uploading the file to a Web site. When you upload the HTML file, you will have to upload any associated images from the Images folder as well.

**Book IV
Chapter 7**

**Integrating
FreeHand MX**

Book V

Macromedia Flash MX 2004

The 5th Wave   By Rich Tennant

"Well, shoot — I know the animation's moving a mite too fast, but <u>dang</u> if I can find a 'mosey' function anywhere in the toolbox!"

Contents at a Glance

Chapter 1: Introduction to Macromedia Flash MX 2004

In This Chapter

✔ **Familiarizing yourself with Macromedia Flash**

✔ **Introducing vector graphics**

✔ **Investigating basic moviemaking principles**

✔ **Creating a Flash document file**

✔ **Exploring the Macromedia Flash interface**

✔ **Viewing movies**

✔ **Setting preferences in Macromedia Flash**

✔ **Getting help**

If you're creating a Web site, Macromedia Flash isn't a necessity. If this is the case, the question becomes: When and why do you use Macromedia Flash? The answer is simple: You use Macromedia Flash when you want your Web site to make greater use of animation, sound, and interactive graphics. And now, two different flavors of Macromedia Flash MX 2004 are available. Standard Macromedia Flash MX 2004 is available for people like you and us, and the hard-core developer can buy Macromedia Flash MX Professional 2004. For this book, we're just looking at good old-fashioned Macromedia Flash by providing an introduction to Macromedia Flash and its capabilities.

Understanding What Macromedia Flash Is and How It Works

If someone asks you what Macromedia Flash is, you can quickly say, "It's a Web animation program." However, that statement, while true, doesn't do justice to Macromedia Flash's wide-ranging capabilities.

Recognizing what Macromedia Flash can do

Macromedia Flash is a rich program. It is fully programmable and uses its own language, called ActionScript. Only your creativity limits what you can do with Macromedia Flash. The following list points out Macromedia Flash's major features and may help you decide if you want to use Macromedia Flash on your Web site:

✦ Animate text and graphics, including changing their color and visibility.

✦ Create your own graphics or import graphics from another program, such as FreeHand MX or Fireworks MX 2004.

✦ Design Web buttons, still or animated, that link users to other pages or sites or perform other programmed actions.

✦ Add sound and video to your Web site.

✦ Add interactivity to your site by enabling viewers to choose where they go and what they see or hear. You can also create forms for viewers to fill out, poll viewers' interests, and customize a site for each viewer.

✦ Create a user interface, including scroll bars, check boxes, list boxes, forms, and more.

You can design an entire Web site using Macromedia Flash. For example, you can use Flash buttons to create your menu and place the content of your Web site on the Timeline. (The *Timeline* is the collection of frames and layers that make up a Flash movie.) Macromedia Flash gives you complete artistic freedom when designing your site, while designing in HTML can be limiting. For example, HTML significantly limits your placement of objects. On the other hand, when using Macromedia Flash, you need to be careful that the site displays quickly and is easy to navigate. Also, updates and server-side connectivity may be more complex and time-consuming with Macromedia Flash.

Creating content for a Web site in Macromedia Flash

Using Macromedia Flash has two components. First you create the Flash document and publish it to a format that a browser can read. Then you (or others) view the Flash content in a browser. To create Flash content, follow these basic steps:

1. **Create your Flash animation in Macromedia Flash and save it as a Flash document.**

This document has an .fla extension and is often called an FLA file. (Chapters 2 through 6 and Chapters 8 and 9 in Book V explain the features that Macromedia Flash offers for creating Flash documents.)

2. **Use the Publish command in Macromedia Flash to save your FLA file as a Flash movie.**

The Flash movie has an .swf extension and is often called an SWF file. When you publish the movie, Macromedia Flash also generates the HTML code that you need to insert the SWF file into your Web page. See Book V, Chapter 7 for detailed instructions.

You sometimes see an FLA file referred to as a movie file. However, current Macromedia usage is to call the SWF file a movie. You sometimes see the SWF file called a Shockwave file, which explains the letters SWF. However, Macromedia no longer uses this terminology for the SWF file.

3. **Insert the HTML code into your Web page (or create a new Web page and add the HTML code).**

The HTML code refers to the SWF file.

After taking these three steps, you follow the procedures that you use for any Web site — uploading the HTML and SWF files.

Using Macromedia Flash on a Web site

To view a Flash movie, you need the Macromedia Flash Player. Macromedia Flash Player 6 is the latest player as of this writing. After you have the Macromedia Flash Player installed, your browser automatically uses the player to display the Flash animation. The Macromedia Flash Player is a free download from the following Web site:

www.macromedia.com/shockwave/download/index.cgi?P1_Prod_Version=ShockwaveFlash

Although the vast majority of people who access your Web site will have the Macromedia Flash Player on their computers already, it is a good idea to include a button or link on your Web site that connects to this URL so that people can easily find and download the player if they need it.

Appreciating the Unique Nature of Vector Graphics

Most graphics that you see on a Web site are bitmap files. A *bitmap* is a graphic image that's made up of many tiny dots (bits), which are very close together. The various colored dots create the pattern that your eyes see as a picture. When the dots are displayed on a computer screen, they're called *pixels*. To get a bitmap graphic into Macromedia Flash, you import it. See Book V, Chapter 3 for more details about importing graphics.

Bitmap graphics can create very large file sizes (although compression can make the files smaller). Large file sizes mean that your Web page takes longer to display in a Web browser. Also, bitmaps don't scale very well, and they're difficult to transform. If you need to enlarge a bitmap, you start to see the individual dots, which results in a grainy graphic image.

Macromedia Flash creates vector graphics. Unlike bitmaps, *vector graphics* are defined by equations that specify location, direction, and color. White space is not recorded. The equations result in small file sizes, and that provides a faster display on your Web site. Moreover, vector graphics are easily scalable. No matter how large or small you make your graphic, it always looks clear. And finally, with vector graphics, it's easy to transform an image like a circle into another image, like a triangle.

Not all graphics can be created using vectors. Photographs and other complex designs usually need bitmaps to be displayed in all their glory. Often you will use a combination of bitmap and vector graphics.

Exploring Basic Moviemaking Principles

Macromedia Flash uses a classic moviemaking structure, which contains the following components:

✦ **The Stage:** The Stage contains all your content, which includes graphics and text.

✦ **Frames:** A frame represents a small unit of time, such as $\frac{1}{12}$ of a second. Each frame contains a tiny section of the animation.

✦ **The Timeline:** The Timeline contains all the frames. You use the Timeline to manipulate your content over time and thus create the animation.

The Stage

The Stage, shown in Figure 1-1, is a simple rectangle on which you place all your content. You change the content on the Stage from frame to frame to create animation. You generally use the drawing and editing tools in the Tools panel to draw and edit the content on the Stage. In this respect, Macromedia Flash is a graphic program like many others. You can create text, circles, lines, and so on, and you can specify the color of the objects that you create. You can save the graphics in standard Web site bitmap formats — JPEG, GIF, and PNG.

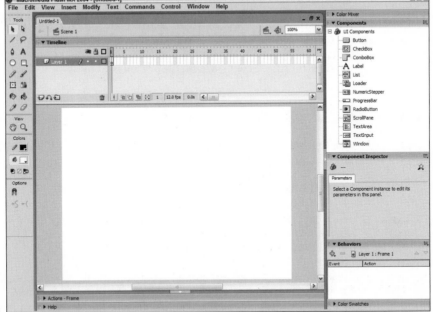

Figure 1-1:
The main
screen
contains
everything
that you
need to
create great
animations.

In the section, "Setting document properties," later in this chapter, we
explain how to specify the size and color of the Stage.

The Timeline and frames

You can think of the Timeline (refer to Figure 1-1) as the frames in a film reel.
The difference is that Macromedia Flash's Timeline is electronic, rather than
on film. Each frame covers a specific period of time. The default frame rate
is 12 frames per second (fps), which means that each frame covers $\frac{1}{12}$ of a
second. You use the frames in the Timeline to control the flow of the animation. You click a frame to make it current. By specifying which frames contain animation, you determine when animation starts and stops. Book V,
Chapter 5 explains more about working with the frames in the Timeline.

Layers

In Figure 1-1, you can see the Layer list, which includes the default Layer 1,
to the left of the Timeline. Layers are covered in Book V, Chapter 4, but for
now you should understand that you can separate the content on the Stage
into layers. Layers help organize your content so that your graphics and animations don't "bump" into each other. You should also use separate layers
for ActionScript and sounds.

Scenes

A scene is simply a way to organize the Timeline. You can use the default Scene 1 (refer to Figure 1-1) and ignore scenes altogether. However, when your animations become more complex, scenes help you keep track of your movie structure. Scenes are further discussed in Book V, Chapter 5.

Creating a Flash Document File

The first step in creating a Flash document is to start Macromedia Flash MX 2004. In most cases, you have a shortcut on your desktop. Double-click it to start Macromedia Flash. If you don't have a shortcut, choose Start⇨ Programs⇨Macromedia⇨Macromedia Flash MX 2004.

When you start Macromedia Flash, you're immediately in a new movie. To open an existing movie, choose File⇨Open, locate the FLA file, and double-click it. You often start by creating or importing graphics.

To save a Flash document as an FLA file for the first time, choose File⇨Save. Choose a location on your hard drive or network, type a name, and click the Save button. After the first save, just choose File⇨Save to save your latest changes.

Taking a Quick Tour of the Macromedia Flash Interface

The Macromedia Flash interface exists to help you create animation. While the interface has several components and is very customizable, you will soon find it easy to use. Refer to Figure 1-1 to see one way of viewing the interface.

Menus

Most of the commands that you use in Macromedia Flash are on the menus. Macromedia Flash doesn't make extensive use of the toolbars that are so familiar from other programs. The following is a summary of the menu items and their main features:

✦ **File:** Open, close, and save files; import and export files; print a Flash document; publish documents (to create SWF movie files); and close Macromedia Flash.

✦ **Edit:** Undo and redo actions; cut, copy, and paste; delete, duplicate, and select objects on the Stage; copy and paste frames from the Timelines; edit symbols (which is covered in Book V, Chapter 3); set preferences; and create keyboard shortcuts.

✦ **View:** Zoom in and out, change how Macromedia Flash displays objects and text, choose which parts of the screen you want to display, and snap objects to pixels on the Stage or other objects.

✦ **Insert:** Insert symbols, insert and delete frames on the Timeline, insert layers, and create animation (see Book V, Chapter 5).

✦ **Modify:** Edit layers, scenes, the Stage, symbols, frames, and graphic objects on the Stage.

✦ **Text:** Format text.

✦ **Command:** Create automated tasks that can be used repeatedly on a variety of objects.

✦ **Control:** Play and rewind animation, test movies and scenes, activate some interactive features, and mute sounds.

✦ **Window:** Display panels and toolbars.

✦ **Help:** Get help on Macromedia Flash and ActionScript.

Most of the menu commands are discussed in detail in the rest of this book.

Table 1-1 lists some of the commonly used keyboard shortcuts for the menu commands. After you get used to them, you'll find that they're faster than using the menu. Later in this chapter, we explain how you can create your own keyboard shortcuts.

It may be helpful to photocopy this table and post it near where you work.

Table 1-1	Handy Keyboard Shortcuts
Menu Command	*Keyboard Shortcut*
File➪New	Ctrl+N
File➪Open	Ctrl+O
File➪Save	Ctrl+S
File➪Import	Ctrl+R
Edit➪Undo	Ctrl+Z
Edit➪Redo	Ctrl+Y
Edit➪Cut	Ctrl+X

(continued)

Table 1-1 *(continued)*

Menu Command	Keyboard Shortcut
Edit⇨Copy	Ctrl+C
Edit⇨Paste	Ctrl+V
Edit⇨Paste in Place	Ctrl+Shift+V
Edit⇨Copy Frames	Ctrl+Alt+C
Edit⇨Paste Frames	Ctrl+Alt+V
View⇨Hide Panels	F4
Insert⇨Convert to Symbol	F8
Insert⇨New Symbol	Ctrl+F8
Insert⇨Frame	F5
Insert⇨Keyframe	F6
Modify⇨Group	Ctrl+G
Modify⇨Break Apart	Ctrl+B
Control⇨Play	Enter
Control⇨Rewind	Ctrl+Alt+R
Control⇨Test Movie	Ctrl+Enter
Window⇨Align	Ctrl+K
Window⇨Color Swatches	Ctrl+F9
Window⇨Actions	F9
Window⇨Library	Ctrl+L or F11

Timeline

The Timeline doesn't tell you *what* is happening; it tells you *when* something is happening. However, the Timeline does give you clues about the content of your animation. Figure 1-2 shows a Timeline with plenty of action. (Book V, Chapter 5 is all about using the Timeline to create animation.)

If the Timeline isn't displayed, choose View⇨Timeline. Note that each layer has its own Timeline so that you can see the sequence of events separately for each layer. (See Book V, Chapter 4 for more information about the Timeline, layers, and the Layer list.) The Timeline has the following features (see Figure 1-2):

✦ **Layer list:** The Layer list helps you organize your content. For example, Figure 1-2 shows separate layers for different objects, sounds, and actions (ActionScript programming).

✦ **Insert a layer:** Use the New Layer button to add a new layer.

Layer list   Keyframe with no content

Playhead   Sound

Figure 1-2:
A busy
Timeline.

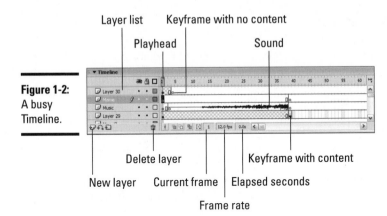

Delete layer   Keyframe with content

New layer   Current frame   Elapsed seconds

Frame rate

+ **Delete a layer:** Use the Delete Layer button to delete a layer.

+ **Playhead:** The playhead indicates the current frame.

+ **Current frame:** The Current Frame box also displays the current frame.

+ **Frame rate:** The Frame Rate box displays the current frame rate, which is the number of frames that play per second in an animation.

+ **Elapsed seconds:** The Elapsed Seconds box displays the number of seconds that have passed from the beginning of the movie to the current frame, at the current frame rate.

+ **Action:** A small *a* in a frame indicates that the frame contains ActionScript to control the animation.

+ **Keyframe with no content:** A *keyframe* is a frame that contains a change in the animation. If you insert a keyframe but don't put anything in that keyframe, the Timeline displays an unfilled circle.

+ **Keyframe with content:** When a keyframe contains any object, the Timeline displays a filled circle.

+ **Sound:** When you insert sound into an animation, its wave appears on the Timeline.

+ **Motion tween:** A *motion tween* is motion animation that Macromedia Flash calculates automatically from the first and last keyframes. The Timeline shows motion tweens in light blue.

+ **Shape tween:** A *shape tween* is shape (morphing) animation that Macromedia Flash calculates automatically. The Timeline shows shape tweens in light green.

The Tools panel

The Tools panel includes all the tools that you need to create and edit graphics. The Tools panel contains the following sections:

✦ **Tools:** Select, draw, and edit graphic objects and text

✦ **View:** Pan and zoom

✦ **Colors:** Specify the color of lines and fills

✦ **Options:** Specify options for the buttons in the Tools section

Figure 1-3 shows the Tools panel in detail, and you can also see the options for the Brush tool. See Book V, Chapter 2 for further explanation about the Tools panel.

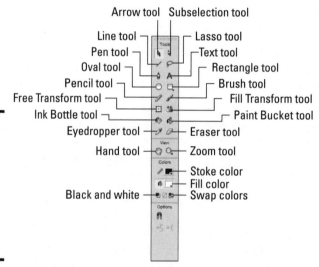

Figure 1-3: Use the Tools panel to create graphics, view your drawing, and specify colors.

All the tools in the Tools panel have keyboard shortcuts. It's very convenient to pick a tool using your left hand on the keyboard while your right hand is on the mouse (or perhaps vice versa if you're left-handed). Table 1-2 lists keyboard shortcuts for many of the tools in the Tools panel.

Table 1-2		Keyboard Shortcuts for Tools panel Tools	
Tool	*Shortcut*	*Tool*	*Shortcut*
Arrow	V	Brush	B
Subselection	A	Free Transform	Q
Line	N	Fill Transform	F

Tool	Shortcut	Tool	Shortcut
Lasso	L	Ink Bottle	S
Pen	P	Paint Bucket	K
Text	T	Eyedropper	I
Oval	O	Eraser	E
Rectangle	R	Hand (Pan)	H
Pencil	Y	Zoom	M, Z

Panels

You use panels to specify settings (such as colors) or to view information about objects. You can access the panels from the Window menu, and panels also have their own Options menus. Click the menu icon in the upper-right corner of a panel to display its Options menu.

You can organize the Macromedia Flash screen for your convenience. For certain tasks, you may want one group of panels open; for other tasks, you may want a different group available, or none at all. Follow these guidelines when working with panels:

✦ **Save panel layouts:** If you like to work with certain panels open most of the time, you can save panel configurations. Just display the panels that you want and choose Window⇨Save Panel Layout. Type a name for the layout, and click OK. The next time that you want to see that layout, choose Window⇨Panel Sets. You'll see your layout listed on the submenu. Choose it to restore your panel layout.

✦ **Dock:** The panels can be docked at the edge of the screen so that they don't cover up the Stage. To dock a panel, drag it by its *grabber* (the five dots next to the name of the panel) to the right or bottom of the screen until it displays a rectangular border. (See Figure 1-4.) To undock a panel, drag the grabber away from the edge of the screen.

✦ **Hide/Display panels:** Press F4 or Tab to toggle hiding and displaying all the panels.

✦ **Stack:** You can stack panels one on top of the other to save space. Drag the panel by its grabber beneath another panel. (See Figure 1-4.)

✦ **Expand and Collapse:** You can collapse a panel to just a title bar when you need more space on your screen — this option makes it easy to reopen the panel when you need it again. You can either click the panel's title bar or click the Expand/Collapse arrow at the left side of the title bar. (See Figure 1-4.)

Title bar

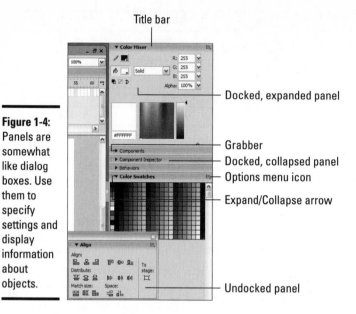

Docked, expanded panel

Grabber
Docked, collapsed panel
Options menu icon
Expand/Collapse arrow

Undocked panel

Figure 1-4:
Panels are
somewhat
like dialog
boxes. Use
them to
specify
settings and
display
information
about
objects.

Specific panels are covered throughout the book as appropriate. For example, Chapter 2 includes a discussion of colors as well as the panels that you
need to use to create and work with colors.

The Properties panel

The Properties panel is a special panel that you use almost all the time. The
Properties panel is context-sensitive, which means that it changes depending on what you are doing. For example, if you are working with text, you see
all the possible text properties, as shown in Figure 1-5. If you select a rectangle, you see the properties of that shape. Usually, you keep the Properties
panel open at the bottom of the screen, either expanded or collapsed. The
Properties panel has its own special Expand/Collapse arrow at its lower-
right corner that you use to display additional properties.

To set the properties of an object, select the object and enter the properties
in the appropriate boxes of the Properties panel. Specific details about the
Properties panel are explained throughout the rest of the book in the context of the topics of each chapter.

Library

Every Flash document file has its own Library. Whenever you import a
graphic, video, or sound, Macromedia Flash saves it in the Library. If you save

a graphic object as a symbol (see Book V, Chapter 3 for details), the object goes in the Library as well. The Library stores every object that you may use again. These objects all have names so that you can easily find them.

Figure 1-5:
The Properties panel lets you inspect and change the properties of your objects.

To use an object from the Library, click the keyframe on the Timeline where you want the object to appear and drag the object from the Library onto the Stage. (Keyframes are explained in Book V, Chapter 5.) You can drag an object from the Preview window or from the item's listing. Figure 1-6 shows a Library with several types of objects.

Figure 1-6:
The Library contains named objects that are saved with a Flash document file.

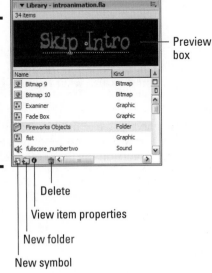

— Preview box

Delete

View item properties

New folder

New symbol

To keep your Library from becoming overwhelming, use the following Library tools:

✦ **Use folders:** Organize your Library items into folders. To create a new folder, click the New Folder icon. Then drag items onto the folder's name. Double-click a folder to expand or collapse it.

✦ **Sort:** You can alphabetize Library items by any column. Click the heading of the column. To reverse the sort order, click the Sort Order icon.

✦ **Rename:** Double-click any item, and type a new name.

✦ **Delete:** Select an item, and click the Delete (Trashcan) icon. Macromedia Flash warns you that this action cannot be undone.

✦ **Update:** If a sound, video, or bitmap file that you have imported has changed, you can update the Library to use the latest version of that file. Click the menu icon in the upper-right corner of a panel to display its Options menu, and then choose Update.

You're not limited to using items in your current document's Library. You can open a Library from any Flash document and drag any of its items into your movie. Choose File➪Import➪Import to Library, and choose the file. The new Library opens as a stacked panel on your current Library panel.

To see some sample Library items, choose Window➪Common Libraries. You find a good assortment of sounds and symbols that come with Macromedia Flash.

Viewing the Stage

As you work, you often need to zoom in to see part of the Stage more closely or zoom out to see the entire Stage. You may also want to *pan* — to move the display in any direction.

At the upper-right corner of the Timeline, you can find the Zoom drop-down list, as shown in Figure 1-7. Click the arrow to set the zoom percentage; choose a higher zoom setting to see objects on the Stage more clearly.

Figure 1-7:
Zooming in.

Another way to zoom in and out is to use the Zoom tool in the View section of the Tools panel, which is shown in Figure 1-8. Follow these steps to use the Zoom tool:

1. **Choose the Zoom tool.**

The Options section displays the plus and minus icons.

2. **Choose the plus icon to zoom in or the minus icon to zoom out.**

3. **Click anywhere on the Stage to zoom in or out.**

To pan, choose the Pan tool, in the View section of the Tools panel, and drag on the Stage in any direction. You can also use the scroll bars to pan.

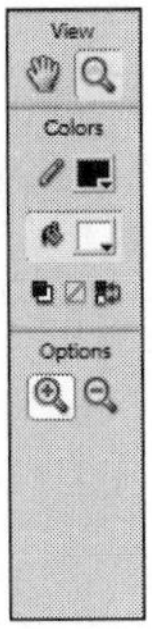

Figure 1-8:
The View
section of
the Tools
panel.

Setting Movie and Macromedia Flash Preferences

Macromedia Flash offers lots of opportunities to customize the way it looks and functions. It's worthwhile to take a look at these features to make your work flow as smoothly as possible.

Setting document properties

One of the first things you do when you start a movie is to set the size and color of the Stage, along with other properties that apply to the entire Flash document. You can adjust these settings using the Properties panel or the Document Properties dialog box. To use the Properties panel, follow these steps:

1. **Choose Window⇨Properties to display the Properties panel, if it isn't already open.**

If the Properties panel isn't expanded, click its title bar to expand it.

2. **Click the Stage to make sure that no other object is selected.**

The Properties panel looks like the one shown in Figure 1-9.

Figure 1-9:
The
Properties
panel when
no objects
are
selected.

3. **To change the Stage size, click the Size button.**

   The Document Properties dialog box, shown in Figure 1-10, opens.

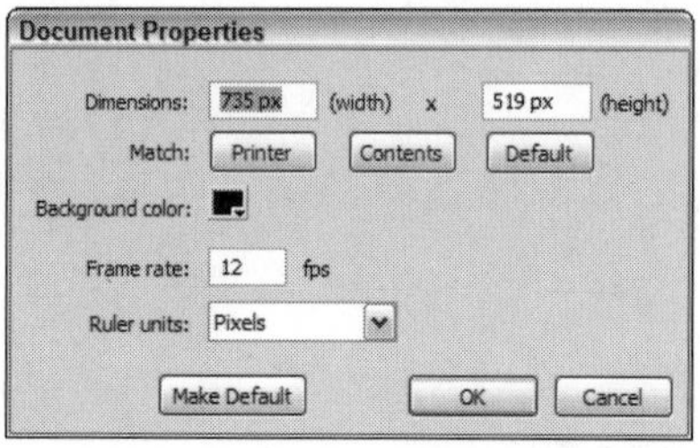

Figure 1-10:
The
Document
Properties
dialog box.

4. **Type the new width and height of the Stage in the Dimensions text fields, and click OK.**

5. **To change the frame rate (the speed at which Macromedia Flash plays the frames), type a new number in the Frame Rate text field.**

   The default is 12 frames per second (fps).

6. **To change the Stage color, click the Background Color box. Choose a new color from the color picker.**

   For more about colors, see Book V, Chapter 2.

If you use the Document Properties dialog box, you have more options. Follow these steps to modify the properties of your Flash movie:

1. **Choose Modify➪Document.**

   The Document Properties dialog box appears. (Refer to Figure 1-10.)

2. **To change the Stage size, type the new width and height of the Stage in the Dimensions text fields.**

As a shortcut, click the Match Printer button to set the Stage size to match the current paper size, or click the Match Contents button to set the Stage size to the minimum size needed to encompass all the objects.

To get the smallest possible Stage size, put all your objects at the upper-left corner of the Stage.

3. **To change the units that are used on the ruler, use the Ruler Units drop-down list and select an option.**

   You can choose from pixels (the default), inches, centimeters, millimeters, and points.

Setting preferences

You can customize a number of settings to suit your personal needs. The main switchboard is the Preferences dialog box, which is shown in Figure 1-11 with the General tab selected.

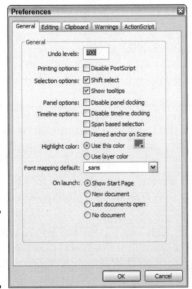

Figure 1-11:
The
Preferences
dialog box.

The General tab contains the following options:

✦ **Undo Levels:** This is the number of commands that Macromedia Flash remembers so that you can undo them. You can enter a value from 0 to 300. The default is 100.

✦ **Printing Options — Disable PostScript:** This option disables PostScript output when you print to a PostScript printer in Windows. Select this check box only if you have trouble printing to a PostScript printer.

✦ **Selection Options — Shift Select:** By default, you have to press Shift to select more than one object. If you don't press Shift, the first object is deselected. Uncheck this item to enable you to select additional objects without pressing Shift.

✦ **Selection Options — Show Tooltips:** This option shows Tooltips over toolbars and buttons when you pass your cursor over them. Deselect this check box to make the Tooltips disappear.

✦ **Panel Options — Disable Panel Docking:** This option prevents panels from docking. Docked panels lock to the side of the Macromedia Flash window without covering up the Stage where you work.

✦ **Timeline Options — Disable Timeline Docking:** This option prevents the Timeline from docking.

✦ **Timeline Options — Span Based Selection:** This option allows you to click between two keyframes to select the entire section between them.

✦ **Timeline Options — Named Anchor on Scene:** Selecting this option automatically creates a named anchor at the beginning of each scene. A named anchor enables Web site users to use their browser's Back and Forward buttons to navigate within a Flash movie, from anchor to anchor.

✦ **Highlight Color:** This option sets the color of the box around selected symbols and groups. Select the Use This Color option to specify another color, or select the Use Layer Color option to use the layer's outline color.

✦ **Font Mapping Default:** This option specifies which font to use when you open a Flash document that contains a font that you don't have installed.

✦ **On Launch:** With this option, you can specify what happens when you start Macromedia Flash. You can choose to have it start with a new document, show a start page, open the last open document, or have no document open.

The Editing tab contains options that are related to the Pen tool and text, as follows:

✦ **Pen tool — Show Pen Preview:** When this option is selected, Macromedia Flash displays a preview of the line or curve segment before you click the next point. This is a helpful option for visualizing the final result of the graphic.

✦ **Pen tool — Show Solid Points:** Deselect this option to show unfilled points at vertices.

✦ **Pen tool — Show Precise Cursors:** This option means that you will see a small cross hair rather than the default pen-shaped cursor; the cross hair can be handy for more precise placement of points.

✦ **Vertical text — Default Text Orientation:** This option sets vertical text as the default and is useful for some Asian fonts.

✦ **Right to Left Text Flow:** This option sets the default for vertical text so that vertical lines flow from right to left (used for some Asian fonts).

✦ **No Kerning:** This option removes kerning from vertical text.

✦ **Project Settings:** With this option, you can choose to close project files when you close Macromedia Flash as well as save project files when running the test project or publish project features.

The Pen tool and text are covered in Book V, Chapter 2.

The Clipboard tab enables you to set preferences for bitmaps, gradients, and text that are pasted in from FreeHand. (See Book IV for more about FreeHand.) The following items are available on the Clipboard tab:

✦ **Bitmaps — Color Depth:** This option sets the color depth for bitmaps that are copied to the Clipboard — for Windows only.

✦ **Bitmaps — Resolution:** This option sets the resolution of bitmaps that are copied to the Clipboard — for Windows only.

✦ **Bitmaps — Size Limit:** This option specifies a size limit in kilobytes for RAM (memory) that is used for a bitmap on the Windows Clipboard. If you have large images, you can increase this number. The default is 250K.

✦ **Bitmaps — Smooth:** This option applies anti-aliasing to bitmaps in Windows to smooth their edges.

✦ **Gradients:** This option specifies the quality of gradients that you copy to the Windows Clipboard for use in other applications.

✦ **FreeHand Text:** This option enables text that is pasted from FreeHand to be edited in Macromedia Flash.

The Warnings tab lists situations in which Macromedia Flash displays a warning message. The check boxes are all selected by default. If you find a warning unnecessary, deselect the appropriate check box.

The ActionScript Editor tab customizes how ActionScript looks and functions in the Action panel. ActionScript is Macromedia Flash's proprietary programming language that adds advanced interactivity to Flash movies; see Book V, Chapter 8 for more about ActionScript. The ActionScript editor includes the following functions:

✦ **Automatic Indentation and Tab Size:** By default, ActionScript that you type in Expert mode is indented. The default tab size (indentation) is four spaces. You can remove or change the tab size.

✦ **Code Hints and Delay:** Code hints provide a pop-up menu to help you complete your code based on what you're typing. You can remove code hints or delay their display.

✦ **UTF Settings:** You can choose to set your files to UTF-8 on Open/Import and Save/Export, or you can accept the default settings for encoding of Unicode characters. UTF-8 is an ASCII-preserving encoding method for Unicode, the Universal Character Set.

✦ **Text:** This option specifies text font and size in the ActionScript editor.

✦ **Syntax Coloring:** This option sets the colors for each syntax type of code.

✦ **Language:** To customize your settings for ActionScript 2.0, click this button.

When you finish specifying preferences, click OK.

Creating your own keyboard shortcuts

You can change any shortcut and create your own. To create shortcuts, choose Edit➪Keyboard Shortcuts to open the Keyboard Shortcuts dialog box, as shown in Figure 1-12.

You can't change the set of shortcuts that come with Macromedia Flash. However, you can create a duplicate set of shortcuts and modify the duplicate. Give the duplicate a new name, such as MyShortcuts.

The following buttons, located at the top of the Keyboard Shortcuts dialog box, can help you manage your shortcuts:

✦ **Duplicate Set:** Duplicates a shortcut set

✦ **Rename Set:** Renames a set of shortcuts

✦ **Delete Set:** Deletes a set of shortcuts

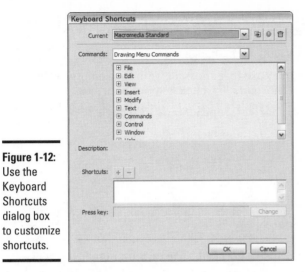

Figure 1-12:
Use the
Keyboard
Shortcuts
dialog box
to customize
shortcuts.

After you have a new set of shortcuts from the Commands drop-down list of
the Keyboard Shortcuts dialog box, choose the types of commands that you
want to change. You can change any of the following types of commands by
selecting their name from the Commands drop-down list:

✦ **Drawing Menu Commands:** Commands from the Drawing menu

✦ **Drawing Tools Commands:** Tools in the Drawing toolbox

✦ **Test Movie Menu Commands:** The menu that appears when you choose
Control➪Test Movie

✦ **Actions Panel Commands:** Commands that control the look and functioning of the Actions panel

Click the plus sign (+) on the list of commands (not all will have the plus (+)
sign) to display all the commands and their current shortcuts. To create a
new shortcut, follow these steps:

1. **Choose the command that you want.**

2. **Click the Add Shortcut button.**

Macromedia Flash adds a new shortcut.

3. **Press the key (for example, A) for the shortcut that you want to use.**

You must press Ctrl in conjunction with the shortcut key. If you are
attempting to create a shortcut that is already assigned, that command

is displayed. You can decide to override the shortcut, or you can choose another key for your shortcut.

- To use that shortcut, click Change.

- If you don't want to use that shortcut, with the <empty> value selected on the Shortcuts list, click Remove Shortcut.

4. To change another shortcut, repeat Steps 1 through 3.

5. Click OK.

Getting Help

If you need more help than you can find in this book, use Macromedia Flash's Help system and tutorials.

To open Help, choose Help➪Using Flash. The opening screen looks like Figure 1-13.

Tutorial

Macromedia Flash includes both a set of lessons and a tutorial. Choose Help➪Lessons➪Introduction to start with the lessons, which are more basic than the tutorial.

Figure 1-13:
Use the
Help feature
when you
have a
question.

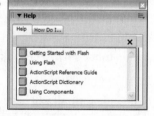

To try the tutorial, choose Tutorials from the main Help screen. (See Figure 1-13.) If you have the printed manual, you can find the tutorial in Chapter 1. (The printed tutorial is easier to use than the electronic version.)

Chapter 2: Using the Graphics Tools

In This Chapter

✓ Understanding when to use the Flash tools

✓ Creating shapes and text

✓ Modifying shapes and text

✓ Working with colors

This chapter shows you how to use the drawing and editing tools in Macromedia Flash MX 2004 to create graphics and text. To produce great animation, you need great graphics, so read on.

Choosing When to Use the Macromedia Flash Tools

Book V, Chapter 1 explains the difference between vector and bitmap graphics. You should use the Macromedia Flash drawing tools when you want to create vector graphics for fast download times.

To create more detailed graphics, you may want to use Fireworks MX 2004 or FreeHand MX, because they have more advanced creation and editing tools. You may also want to use these programs to edit existing bitmaps. On the other hand, you may have bitmaps, such as a photograph or complex logo, that's only available as a bitmap. To use any bitmap, import it. (See Book V, Chapter 3 for the scoop on importing graphics.)

Creating Shapes and Text

You use the Tools panel to create shapes and text in Macromedia Flash. See Figure 2-1 for the details of the Tools panel. The Tools section of the Tools panel offers many tools for creating and editing images. Most tools have options that specify how the tool works.

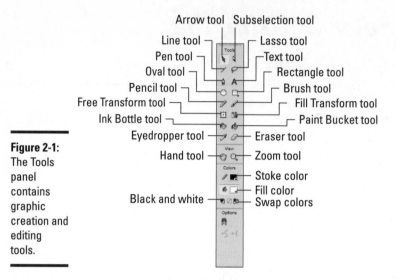

Arrow tool   Subselection tool

Line tool ———   ┌— Lasso tool
Pen tool ———   ┌—Text tool
Oval tool ———   ┌— Rectangle tool
Pencil tool ———   ┌— Brush tool
Free Transform tool ———   ┌— Fill Transform tool
Ink Bottle tool ———   ┌— Paint Bucket tool
Eyedropper tool ———   ┌— Eraser tool
Hand tool ———   ┌— Zoom tool
  ┌— Stoke color
  ┌— Fill color
Black and white ———   ┌— Swap colors

Figure 2-1:
The Tools
panel
contains
graphic
creation and
editing
tools.

When creating shapes in Macromedia Flash, you need to keep in mind what happens when two or more shapes touch, as follows:

✦ If the shapes are the same color, they combine. You can use this technique to create complex shapes.

✦ If the shapes are different colors, the top shape replaces and cuts out the bottom shape.

✦ If you use the Pencil or Line tool to intersect any other shape, the line and other shape are cut at their intersection.

If you don't see the Tools panel, choose Window⇨Tools to make it visible.

Line tool

The Line tool draws straight lines. You can continue to draw connected lines to create any shape you want.

To draw a line, follow these steps:

1. **Choose the Line tool from the Tools section of the Tools panel.**

2. **From the Properties panel, choose a color by clicking the Stroke Color box.**

If the Properties panel is not visible, choose Window⇨Properties to make it appear.

You can also find the Stroke Color box in the Colors section of the Tools panel. A *stroke* is another word for a line or the outline of any shape in Macromedia Flash.

3. **Type a stroke weight (width) in the Stroke Height box of the Properties panel, or click the arrow next to the point size box and use the vertical slider to choose a stroke weight.**

4. **Choose a stroke style from the Stroke Style box of the Properties panel.**

   To create a custom stroke style, click the Custom button in the Properties panel.

5. **Click the Stage where you want to start the line and drag (while holding the mouse button down) to the ending point.**

6. **Release the mouse button.**

To constrain the line to multiples of 45 degrees, press Shift while dragging.

Oval tool

An oval has both a stroke (outline) and a fill color. Use the Oval tool to draw ovals and circles, as follows:

1. **Choose the Oval tool from the Tools section of the Tools panel.**

2. **From the Properties panel, choose a stroke color by clicking the Stroke Color box and choosing a color.**

   If the Properties panel is not visible, choose Window⇨Properties to make it appear.

   You can also find the Stroke Color box in the Colors section of the Tools panel. As with the Line tool, you can also set a stroke weight and style.

3. **From the Properties panel, choose a fill color by clicking the Fill Color box.**

4. **Click the Stage where you want the upper-left portion of the oval to be, and drag (while holding the mouse button down) diagonally to the lower right.**

5. **Release the mouse button.**

To create a circle, press Shift as you drag the mouse.

Rectangle tool

Like an oval, a rectangle has both a stroke and a fill. You can draw rectangles and squares with the Rectangle tool as follows:

1. **Choose the Rectangle tool from the Tools section of the Tools panel.**

2. **From the Properties panel, choose a stroke color by clicking the Stroke Color box and choosing a color.**

   If the Properties panel is not visible, choose Window⇨Properties to make it appear.

   You can also find the Stroke Color box in the Colors section of the Tools panel. As with the Line tool, you can also set a stroke weight and style.

3. **From the Properties panel, choose a fill color by clicking the Fill Color box.**

4. **To draw a rectangle with rounded corners, click the Rounded Rectangle Radius button (the button with the curved black line and the little blue semi-square underneath it) in the Options section of the Tools panel, type a radius, and press Enter.**

   The larger the number entered in the Corner Radius field, the softer the curve in the rectangle's edges.

5. **Click the Stage where you want the upper-left corner of the rectangle to be, and drag (while holding the mouse button down) diagonally to the lower right.**

6. **Release the mouse button.**

To create a square, press Shift as you drag the mouse.

Polystar tool

In addition to the Rectangle tool, Macromedia Flash MX 2004 includes a tool for creating other kinds of polygons. To use the Polystar tool, follow these steps:

1. **Click and hold down the Rectangle button in the Tools section of the Tools panel.**

2. **Select the Polystar icon from the menu that appears.**

3. **In the Properties panel, click the Options button.**

   This opens the Tool Settings dialog box, as shown in Figure 2-2.

4. **Select a style of polygon from the Style drop-down list.**

   The Polygon option creates a true polygon, while the Polystar option creates a multipointed star.

5. **Enter the number of sides for the polygon or polystar.**

   The larger the number of sides, the closer to a circle a polygon will be. For the polystar, more points creates a starburst-like effect.

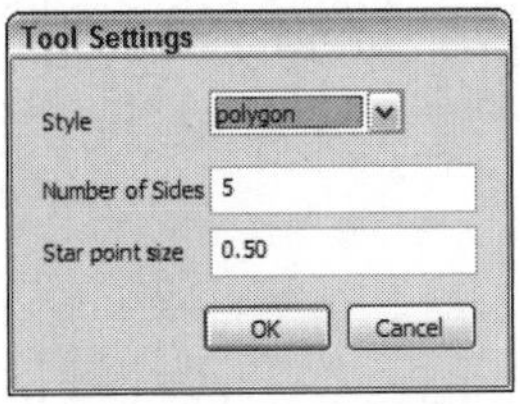

Figure 2-2:
The Tool
Settings
dialog box
allows you
to customize
the look of
your
polygon.

Tool Settings	
Style	polygon
Number of Sides	5
Star point size	0.50
	OK Cancel

6. **Enter a value for the star point size.**

   The larger the star point size, the more dull the polystar will be, making it look closer to a circle.

Pencil tool

The Pencil tool is somewhat like a real pencil. You can draw artistic shapes with it. To draw with the Pencil tool, follow these steps:

1. **Choose the Pencil tool from the Tools section of the Tools panel.**

2. **From the Properties panel, choose a stroke color by clicking the Stroke Color box and choosing a color.**

   If the Properties panel is not visible, choose Window➪Properties to make it appear.

   You can also find the Stroke Color box in the Colors section of the Tools panel. As with the Line tool, you can also set a stroke weight and style.

3. **Click the Pencil Mode button in the Options section of the Tools panel, and from the pop-up menu, choose one of the following:**

   - **Straighten:** Straightens wiggly lines and changes sloppy rectangles, ovals, and triangles to perfect ones.
   - **Smooth:** Smoothes out curved lines.
   - **Ink:** Slightly smoothes and straightens, but mostly leaves your drawings the same.

4. **Click the Stage where you want the drawing to start and drag on the Stage.**

   You can draw angles and curves.

5. **Release the mouse button.**

To constrain each line segment to 90-degree angles, press Shift as you drag the mouse. To refine how the options work, choose Edit⇨Preferences and click the Editing tab. Use the Smooth Curves and Recognize Shapes drop-down lists. When you're done, click OK.

Pen tool

You can use the Pen tool to draw straight lines and curves. The Pen tool offers the greatest editing control and the most control over curves. Using the Pen tool takes some practice, but soon you'll find it to be very flexible.

To better see how a Pen tool drawing will look, choose Edit⇨Preferences and click the Editing tab. Select the Show Pen Preview check box. Click OK.

Follow these steps to work with the Pen tool:

1. **Choose the Pen tool from the Tools section of the Tools panel.**

2. **From the Properties panel, choose a stroke color by clicking the Stroke Color box and choosing a color.**

   If the Properties panel is not visible, choose Window⇨Properties to make it appear.

   You can also find the Stroke Color box in the Colors section of the Tools panel. As with the Line tool, you can set a stroke weight and style.

3. **You can draw either straight segments or curves, as follows:**

   • **To draw a straight segment:** Click the start point, and click the end point. Do not drag. Click additional points to add segments. Double-click to finish.

   • **To draw a curve:** Click the start point and move the mouse in the desired direction; then click and drag in the direction of the curve. Continue clicking and dragging to create additional curves. Double-click to finish.

To close a figure, place the cursor near the start point until you see a small circle, and then click. Press Shift as you draw to constrain the lines or curves to 45-degree angles.

Brush tool

The Brush tool fills areas with a brush-like effect. You can vary the shape and width of the stroke. The Brush tool creates fills, so you use the Fill Color button to set the color. To draw with the Brush tool, follow these steps:

1. **Choose the Brush tool from the Tools section of the Tools panel.**

2. **From the Properties panel, choose a fill color by clicking the Fill Color box and choosing a color.**

   If the Properties panel is not visible, choose Window➪Properties to make it appear.

   You can also find the Fill Color box in the Colors section of the Tools panel.

3. **Choose a brush mode by clicking the Brush Mode button in the Options section of the Tools panel and choosing one of the following options:**

   - **Paint Normal:** Paints wherever you brush, including over other objects on the same layer. (See Book V, Chapter 4 for more details on layers.)

   - **Paint Fills:** Fills enclosed and blank areas, but doesn't cover strokes.

   - **Paint Behind:** Paints blank areas of the Stage, but doesn't cover fills or strokes.

   - **Paint Selection:** Fills in a selected area.

   - **Paint Inside:** Paints inside any enclosed area where you start your brush or on the Stage if you don't start in an enclosed area. Doesn't cover strokes.

4. **Choose a brush size by clicking the Brush Size drop-down list in the Options section of the Tools panel.**

5. **Choose a brush shape by clicking the Brush Shape drop-down list.**

   If you have a pressure-sensitive pen and tablet, you see a pressure button in the Options section. You can then dynamically vary the width of the brush according to how much pressure you put on the pen as you draw.

6. **Click the start point, and then drag to draw with the brush.**

Press Shift as you draw to constrain your shapes to 90-degree angles.

TIP

If you want your gradient fill to be independent of the background, make sure that the Lock Fill option button is not selected. If, however, you're creating more than one stroke and you want it to appear as if the gradient is in the background and being applied to both strokes, select the Lock Fill option button.

Paint Bucket tool

The Paint Bucket tool fills enclosed shapes. You can create the enclosed shape with many of the other tools in the Tools panel. You can also use the Paint Bucket tool to change the color of existing fills. To fill an enclosed area, follow these steps:

1. **Choose the Paint Bucket tool from the Tools section of the Tools panel.**

2. **From the Properties panel, choose a fill color by clicking the Fill Color box and choosing a color.**

   If the Properties panel is not visible, choose Window➪Properties to make it appear.

   You can also find the Fill Color box in the Colors section of the Tools panel.

3. **Click the Gap Size button in the Options section of the Tools panel, and from the pop-up menu, select an option if you need to fill in a shape that is not completely enclosed.**

   You can choose from Don't Close Gaps to Close Large Gaps.

4. **Click inside the enclosed area to fill the shape.**

Ink Bottle tool

The Ink Bottle tool outlines an existing shape or changes the color of an existing stroke (outline). Follow these steps to use the Ink Bottle tool:

1. **Select the Ink Bottle tool from the Tools section of the Tools panel.**

2. **From the Properties panel, choose a stroke color by clicking the Stroke Color box and choosing a color.**

   If the Properties panel is not visible, choose Window➪Properties to make it appear.

   You can also find the Stroke Color box in the Colors section of the Tools panel. You can set a stroke weight and style as well.

3. **Click anywhere on the shape.**

If the shape has no stroke outline, Macromedia Flash adds a stroke. Otherwise, Macromedia Flash changes the shape's color, width, and style to the settings that you choose.

Text tool

Sooner or later, you may need to explain what all those animations you have created mean, so you'll probably need some text. Macromedia Flash offers many text options, both simple and advanced. To create text, follow these steps:

1. **Choose the Text tool from the Tools section of the Tools panel.**

2. **In the Properties panel, shown in Figure 2-3, specify the font, size, color, and other properties.**

If the Properties panel is not visible, choose Window⇨Properties to make it appear.

Figure 2-3:
Use the
Properties
panel to
set the
properties
of your text.

3. **Click the Stage and start typing, as follows:**

- To specify the width of the text (when creating a paragraph), click at the upper-left corner where you want the text to start and drag to the right margin.

- To create text that expands as you type (for a single line of text), just click.

You can specify the following text properties in the Properties panel:

✦ **Text type:** Use the Text Type drop-down list to specify one of the following types of text:

- **Static:** Regular text.

- **Input:** Text that users type in their browser. Input text is one way of making your Web site interactive. Use input text for forms or to enable users to set values that affect the animation.

- **Dynamic:** Text that is displayed from another source, such as another Web site, another movie (SWF) file, or an external file. This is great for weather, sports scores, and so on.

✦ **Font:** The font or typeface. Select from the drop-down list.

✦ **Font size:** Type a number or use the vertical slider to choose a size.

✦ **Color:** Click the Text (fill) Color box to choose a color.

✦ **Bold/Italic:** Click the Bold button or the Italic button to make the text bold or italic.

✦ **Justify:** Click one of the Justify buttons to make the text justified to the left, center, or right, or full justified (justified to reach both the left and right margins).

✦ **Character spacing:** Adjust the *tracking,* which is the spacing between a series of letters.

✦ **Character position:** Select Superscript to create text above the normal position or Subscript to create text that is below the normal position. For normal text, just keep it at Normal.

✦ **Auto Kern:** *Kerning* is the spacing between two specific letters. You may adjust the kerning of certain letters, such as A and V, that appear to be too far apart. Select the Auto Kern check box to turn kerning on; deselect it to turn kerning off.

✦ **Aliasing:** By default, all text is *aliased,* or smoothed. If you want the text to appear anti-aliased, or jagged, click this button.

✦ **Format:** Click the Format button to open the Format Options dialog box, where you can set paragraph formatting, as follows:

- **Indent:** The indentation of the first line of a paragraph.

- **Line Spacing:** The spacing between lines, measured in points. If your text is 18 points, for example, set a line spacing of 18 points to double-space the text.

Click the Expand/Collapse arrow at the lower-right corner of the Properties panel for more advanced text options.

Modifying Shapes and Text

If you create something on a computer, you'll inevitably have to change it. Sometimes you change your mind, and other times you just need to make adjustments to get the effect that you want.

Selection tool

The first step in changing an object is to select it. To select an object or group of objects, choose the Selection tool (the dark arrow at the top left of the Tools panel) and use one of the following techniques:

+ To select one object, click the object.

+ To select several graphic objects that touch each other, double-click one of the objects. (This doesn't work with symbols. See Book V, Chapter 3 for more about symbols.) To select a rectangle's stroke and fill, double-click the fill.

+ To select several objects that do not touch, click away from the objects and drag diagonally to create a bounding box around the objects that you want to select. Macromedia Flash selects all objects that are completely inside the box.

See the section, "Reshaping with the Selection tool," later in this chapter, for information on reshaping objects using the Selection tool.

The Selection tool has a Snap button in the Options section of the Tools panel. When you click this button, objects that you move snap to other objects so that you can attach two objects precisely. The Snap option also snaps new objects that you create to existing objects.

Lasso tool

Another way to select your objects is to lasso 'em. Use the Lasso tool when you want to select a number of objects but can't get them in a rectangular bounding box. You can drag the mouse and create a free-form shape or use straight-line segments, as follows:

1. **Choose the Lasso tool from the Tools panel.**

2. **Choose the type of lassoing you want, as follows:**

   • **To lasso free-form:** Click anywhere on the Stage, drag around the objects that you want to select, and then release the mouse button.

   • **To lasso with straight-line segments:** Choose the Polygon button from the Options section of the Tools panel. Click anywhere on the Stage, and continue to click at each segment's end point. Double-click to finish.

Moving and copying objects

You can move and copy objects on the Stage in many ways. The best method varies with the circumstances and your personal preferences. Move and copy objects using the following methods:

✦ **Select and drag:** Use the Selection tool to select an object. Then move the cursor over the object until you see the four-arrow cursor. Click and drag to move the object. Press and hold Ctrl while you drag to copy the object.

✦ **Arrow keys:** Select an object and use the arrow keys to move the object one pixel at a time in the direction of the arrow.

✦ **Properties panel:** Select an object and open the Properties panel. Click the Expand/Collapse arrow at the lower-right corner to display the expanded panel. Use the X and Y text fields to set a new location for the object.

✦ **Cut, copy, and paste:** Select an object; then press Ctrl+X to move (cut) it or Ctrl+C to copy it. If you want, click another layer or frame. Then press Ctrl+V to paste the object.

Eraser tool

To delete any object, select it and press Delete. However, to erase part of an object, use the Eraser tool, as follows:

1. **Choose the Eraser tool from the Tools panel.**

2. **Select the eraser size and shape from the Eraser Shape pop-up menu in the Options section of the Tools panel.**

3. **To specify how the Eraser tool works, choose an option from the Eraser Mode pop-up menu:**

 • **Erase Normal:** Erases anything that you drag across.

 • **Erase Fills:** Erases only fills.

 • **Erase Lines:** Erases only strokes.

 • **Erase Selected Fills:** Erases only selected fills.

 • **Erase Inside:** Erases only fills where you first click. Use this option to erase only fills inside an enclosed area, but leave other fills alone.

4. **With the Faucet option (in the Options section of the Tools panel) deselected, click and drag to erase.**

To erase an entire fill, select the Faucet option (in the Options section of the Tools panel) and click the fill. This method is equivalent to selecting a fill and pressing Delete, as if the faucet washed away all the color.

Reshaping with the Selection tool

You can reshape and modify objects using the Selection tool when the objects are not selected. You can reshape both end points (including corners) and middles (whether straight or curved), as shown in Figure 2-4, as follows:

✦ **End points:** Place the cursor over the end point of a line or curve segment. You see a small corner shape near the cursor. Click and drag to change the location of the end point.

✦ **Middles:** Place the cursor over the middle of any line or curve segment. You see a small curved shape near the cursor. Click and drag to reshape the segment.

Figure 2-4:
Reshape
end points
and middles
of fills
and lines
with the
Selection
tool.

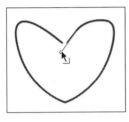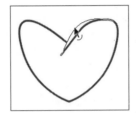

Subselect tool

The Subselect tool looks like the Selection tool, but the Subselect tool is a white (instead of black) arrow. Both the Selection tool and the Subselect tool reshape objects, but the Subselect tool uses a more sophisticated technique. When you are using the Subselect tool, the shape displays anchor points that you can move or delete. When you click an anchor point, *tangent lines* — lines that are parallel to the curve at the anchor point — appear and enable you to change the direction of the curve. You can reshape strokes or fills that were created with the following tools:

✦ Pen   ✦ Oval

✦ Pencil   ✦ Rectangle

✦ Line   ✦ Brush

To reshape objects with the Subselect tool, follow these steps:

1. **Choose the Subselect tool from the Tools panel.**

2. **Click a stroke or the edge of a fill to display the anchor points.**

3. **Drag any anchor point to modify the shape.**

4. **To change the direction of a curve, select its anchor curve and then drag the tangent line's handles (the dots at either end of the tangent line).**

To delete an anchor, select the object and then click the desired anchor point. The anchor point then turns dark. Then press Delete.

Free Transform tool

The Free Transform tool is the heavyweight of editing tools — it can do almost anything. To use this tool, choose the Free Transform tool from the Tools panel and select an object. The object displays a special bounding box that includes handles and a central *transformation point,* as shown in Figure 2-5.

Figure 2-5:
The
bounding
box of
the Free
Transform
tool.

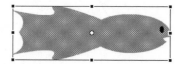

You can use the Free Transform tool in the following ways:

✦ **Move:** Place the cursor over the object. When you see the four-arrow cursor, click and drag.

✦ **Rotate:** Place the cursor just outside (but not on) any corner handle. When you see a circular arrow cursor, click and drag.

✦ **Scale while maintaining proportion:** Place the cursor on any corner handle. When you see a broken two-arrow cursor, click and drag inward or outward.

✦ **Scale either the height or width:** Place the cursor on any side handle. When you see a two-arrow cursor, click and drag inward or outward.

✦ **Skew (slant either horizontally or vertically):** Place the cursor anywhere on the bounding box, but not on a handle. When you see the parallel line cursor, click and drag in any direction.

✦ **Move the transformation point:** Place the cursor on the transformation point at the center of the bounding box. When you see a small circle cursor, click and drag in any direction. The transformation point is used as a base for rotation and scaling.

✦ **Taper:** Choose the Distort option of the Free Transform tool from the Options section of the Tools panel. Place the cursor on any corner handle, and press Shift as you click and drag inward or outward. (See Figure 2-6 for an example of tapering.)

Figure 2-6:
Tapering the fish makes its back end wider.

✦ **Distort:** Choose the Distort option of the Free Transform tool from the Options section of the Tools panel. Click and drag any handle to distort the bounding box. (See Figure 2-7 for an example of distortion.) ***Note:*** The Distort option works on shapes, but not on symbols (see Book V, Chapter 3 for more on symbols), text, or groups. (Groups are explained in the "Grouping" section, later in this chapter.)

Figure 2-7:
Distort the upper-right corner of the goldfish, and it looks more like a shark.

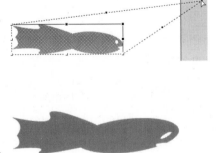

✦ **Warp:** Choose the Envelope option of the Free Transform tool from the Options section of the Tools panel. Drag any anchor point or tangent line handle to warp the bounding box.

The Envelope option, shown in Figure 2-8, works on shapes, but not on symbols, text, or groups.

Figure 2-8:
Fine-tune
shapes
using the
Envelope
option of
the Free
Transform
tool.

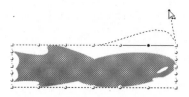

When you select an object — for example, a circle — with the Free Transform tool, you'll notice that the tool selects the object, but not the stroke around the object. To select both the object and its stroke, click the Free Transform tool and drag it around the entire object. This creates one bounding box for both the fill and the stroke.

Straightening and smoothing with the Selection tool

You can straighten lines and smooth curves with the Selection tool. Both processes reduce the number of changes in direction. You can repeat the process until Macromedia Flash can't straighten or smooth anymore. Follow these steps to straighten lines and smooth curves:

1. **Choose the Selection tool from the Tools panel.**

2. **Select the shape that you want to modify.**

3. **To straighten, click the Straighten button from the Options section of the Tools panel. To smooth, click the Smooth button.**

4. **Continue to click the Straighten or Smooth button until you like the result.**

Optimizing curves

A process called *optimizing curves* is similar to smoothing curves. Optimizing a curve reduces the number of individual elements that the curve contains and can help reduce the size of your Flash document file. Follow these steps to optimize curves:

1. **Choose the Selection tool from the Tools panel.**

2. **Using the Selection tool, select the object that you want to optimize.**

3. **Choose Modify⇨Shape⇨Optimize.**

The Optimize Curves dialog box appears, as shown in Figure 2-9. You can select Use Multiple Passes for a slower, more thorough approach. If you select the Show Totals Message check box, the amount of optimization displays after you close the dialog box.

Figure 2-9:
The
Optimize
Curves
dialog box.

4. **Choose the amount of smoothing by using the slider in the dialog box.**

5. **Click OK.**

Carefully check the results after optimizing. Sometimes small objects disappear! If you don't like the results, choose Edit⇨Undo and try again with a different Smoothing setting.

Softening edges

To create a soft look around the edges of a shape, follow these steps:

1. **Choose the Selection tool from the Tools panel.**

2. **Using the Selection tool, select a shape.**

3. **Choose Modify⇨Shape⇨Soften Fill Edges.**

The Soften Fill Edges dialog box opens, as shown in Figure 2-10.

Figure 2-10:
The Soften
Fill Edges
dialog box.

4. **In the Soften Fill Edges dialog box, set the distance.**

   The distance is the width of the softened part of the edge, in pixels (by default).

   Macromedia Flash uses the units that you set in the Document Properties dialog box to measure the distance. Choose Modify⇨Document to change the measurement units.

5. **Enter the number of steps, that is, the number of concentric rows in the softened edge.**

6. **Select Expand or Inset.**

   The Expand option creates the softened edges outside the shape. The Inset option creates the softened edges within the shape.

7. **Click OK.**

Flipping

A great way to make symmetric shapes is to draw half the shape, copy it, and flip the copy either vertically or horizontally. You can then move the two shapes together, as shown in Figure 2-11. To flip an object, follow these steps:

Figure 2-11: Create this shape by copying the crescent, flipping it horizontally, and then moving the two shapes together.

1. **Choose the Selection tool from the Tools panel.**

2. **Using the Selection tool, select the object.**

3. **Choose Modify⇨Transform⇨Flip Vertical or Flip Horizontal.**

Transferring properties with the Eyedropper tool

The Eyedropper tool transfers stroke and fill properties from one object to another. To transfer properties, follow these steps:

1. **Choose the Eyedropper tool from the Tools panel.**

2. **Select a stroke or fill.**

If you select a stroke, the Ink Bottle tool is activated. If you select a fill, the Paint Bucket tool is activated.

3. **Click another stroke or fill.**

Macromedia Flash transfers the properties of the stroke or fill to the second object.

Grouping

You often want to work with several objects at one time. Instead of having to select all the objects each time you want to move or copy them, you can group them and work with them as one object. To group objects, select them and choose Modify⇨Group.

You can edit one element of the group by following these steps:

1. **Choose the Selection tool from the Tools panel.**

2. **Double-click the group.**

Macromedia Flash dims other objects on the Stage.

3. **Edit any element of the group.**

4. **To return to regular editing, double-click any blank area on the Stage with the Selection tool.**

Alternatively, you can choose Edit⇨Edit All.

To ungroup objects, select the group and choose Modify⇨Ungroup.

Breaking objects apart

You can break apart text into letters, and then break apart the letters into shapes. After letters are broken apart into shapes, you can edit them like any other shape. You can also break apart symbols (see Book V, Chapter 3), groups, and bitmaps. (See the section, "Working with bitmap fills," later in this chapter, for more information.)

Aligning objects

To get a professional look, you may want to make sure that objects are properly aligned and equally distributed. To align and distribute objects, follow these steps:

1. **Choose the Selection tool from the Tools panel.**

2. **Using the Selection tool, select the objects.**

3. **Choose Window⇨Align.**

The Align panel, shown in Figure 2-12, appears.

Figure 2-12:
Use the Align panel to align and equally space objects, such as buttons for your Web site.

4. **Choose the options that you want in the Align panel, as follows:**

- Use the top row to align the selected objects horizontally or vertically.

- Use the middle row to evenly distribute objects horizontally or vertically by their edges.

- Use the Match Size buttons to match the size of selected objects by width, height, or both.

- Use the Space buttons to distribute objects by the spaces between them.

- Use the To Stage button to align or distribute objects relative to the Stage.

To center an object on the Stage, click the To Stage button on the Align panel. Then click the middle Align Vertical and Align Horizontal buttons. However, if you haven't panned or scrolled your display, you can use a quicker method — cut and paste the object. Macromedia Flash pastes the object at the center of the display.

Working with Colors

By default, Macromedia Flash works with a Web safe palette of 216 colors. These colors are likely to appear the same in all browsers. However, you can create your own colors. You can also design gradients that vary from one color to another. Another technique is to fill objects with bitmap images. This is explained in the "Working with bitmap fills" section, later in this chapter.

Creating solid colors

You can create a solid color when you need to take more artistic license than the standard Web safe palette allows. Follow these steps to create a solid color:

1. Choose Window⇨Design Panels⇨Color Mixer.

The Color Mixer panel, shown in Figure 2-13 with the Solid option active, opens.

Figure 2-13: The Color Mixer panel is the place to create new colors.

You can specify colors using the RGB (Red, Green, Blue) or HSB (Hue, Saturation, Brightness) systems. You can see the current system by the letters that are next to the text fields in the panel. In Figure 2-13, you can tell that the RGB system is active because the text fields are labeled R, G, and B. To choose a different system, click the menu icon in the upper-right corner of the panel to open the panel's Options menu and choose the color system that you want. You can also use the color space in the panel to specify a color.

2. Select Solid from the Fill Style drop-down list.

3. Click the Stroke Color or Fill Color icon (to the left of the Stroke or Fill box), depending on whether you want to change a stroke or a fill.

You can use this color later for either a stroke or a fill if you save the color as a swatch, as outlined in Step 6.

4. Type the color specifications in the text fields, or click a color in the color space and use the slider to make the color lighter or darker.

5. Use the vertical slider next to the Alpha field or text field to set the transparency of the color.

A higher alpha percent is more opaque.

6. To save the color, create a color swatch by clicking the Options menu icon in the upper-right corner of the panel and choosing Add Swatch.

Your new color is now displayed in the Stroke Color or Fill Color box in the Properties panel and in the Colors section of the Tools panel. You can use any of the tools to work with that color. If you add a color swatch, you can continue to use that color later by choosing it from the color palette that opens when you click the Stroke Color or Fill Color box.

Creating gradients

Gradients blend one color (lighter with darker) or many colors in either a linear or radial (circular) pattern. Gradients give the appearance of shading and three dimensions. To create a gradient, follow these steps:

1. Choose Window⇨Design Panels⇨Color Mixer.

The Color Mixer panel opens.

2. From the Fill Style drop-down list, select Linear or Radial to specify the type of gradient that you want to create, as shown in Figure 2-14.

Figure 2-14:
Use the
Color Mixer
panel to
create
gradients.

3. Choose a pointer underneath the horizontal gradient bar.

The pointer becomes black when you select it so that you know it is active.

4. Use one of the following methods to select a color for that pointer:

- Click the Fill Color box and choose a color.

- Specify a color using one of the methods of creating a new color that were described in the previous section.

- Use the color space to specify a color.

5. **Repeat Steps 3 and 4 for all the pointers.**

   You add a pointer when you want to add a new color to the gradient. Three pointers result in a three-color gradient. To add a pointer, click just beneath the gradient bar where you want the pointer to appear. To delete a pointer, drag it off the gradient bar.

6. **To save the gradient, click the menu icon in the upper-right corner of the Color Mixer panel and choose Add Swatch from the Options menu that appears.**

Editing fills

After you create your gradient or bitmap fills, you may decide that you want to change them. (Bitmap fills are explained in the next section.) To edit a fill, follow these steps:

1. **Choose the Fill Transform tool from the Tools panel.**

2. **Click a gradient or bitmap fill.**

   Macromedia Flash places a boundary and editing handles around the fill, which varies with the type of fill, as shown in Figure 2-15.

Figure 2-15:
When you edit a fill, you see an editing boundary around the fill.

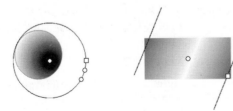

3. **Make one or more of the following changes:**

   - **Move the fill's center:** Drag the small circle at the center of the fill.

   - **Change the fill's width or height:** Drag the square handle inward or outward.

   - **Rotate a fill:** Drag the circle on the editing boundary (the endmost circle for a radial gradient).

   - **Scale a bitmap fill:** Drag the corner square boundary inward or outward.

- **Scale a radial gradient:** Drag the middle circular handle on the editing boundary inward or outward.
- **Skew a bitmap fill:** Drag a circular handle on the top or side.

Working with bitmap fills

You can create a fill with a bitmap that you have imported. (See Book V, Chapter 3 for more on importing bitmaps.) To create a fill with a bitmap image, follow these steps:

1. **Choose File➪Import.**

   The Import dialog box appears.

2. **Choose the bitmap file that you want, and click Open.**

   The bitmap appears on the Stage.

3. **Choose Modify➪Break Apart.**

   This action selects the entire image as a fill rather than as a single color when the eyedropper is used (in the next step).

4. **Choose the Eyedropper tool from the Tools section of the Tools panel.**

5. **Click the bitmap image.**

   The Paint Bucket tool is activated, and the Fill Color button (in the Colors section of the Tools panel and in the Properties panel) displays the bitmap image.

6. **Click the object that you want to fill.**

   You may have to move the bitmap image that you imported if it covered your object. Notice that the bitmap is tiled — that is, repeated throughout the filled area.

Chapter 3: Working with Symbols

In This Chapter

✔ **Understanding the importance of symbols**

✔ **Working with graphic symbols**

✔ **Working with movie clip symbols**

✔ **Working with button symbols**

A *symbol* is any object or group of objects, an animation, or a Web button. You give the symbol a name and save it in the Library. (See Book V, Chapter 1 for a discussion of the Library.) In this chapter, you find out about symbols and how to use them.

Appreciating the Importance of Symbols

You need to know about symbols if you want to work in Macromedia Flash MX 2004. The following are the three types of symbols:

✦ **Graphic:** The simplest type of symbol, and a useful way to save groups of objects that you want to reuse. You can also animate graphic symbols.

✦ **Movie clip:** A little movie that you put inside your big movie. You can apply ActionScript, Macromedia Flash's programming language, to a movie clip or within a movie clip to specify how it functions. The movie clip has its own Timeline, and you generally insert the movie clip on the Timeline of the main Flash movie to let it play. Movie clips can be placed inside each other, or *nested*. Movie clips are useful for building complex animation and an interactive Web site.

✦ **Button:** You use buttons when you want your site viewers to click to go to another page or create some other effect. You use ActionScript to specify what happens when a viewer clicks a button.

The rest of this chapter explains how to create and work with graphic, movie clip, and button symbols.

Symbols are the building blocks of complex graphics and animation in your Flash documents. Symbols have the following qualities:

✦ You can easily use symbols repeatedly by dragging them from the Library onto the Stage. Each time you drag something from the Library onto the Stage, that's called an *instance* of the symbol. Individual instances can be resized.

✦ Symbols reduce your file size (for faster browser display) because Macromedia Flash only stores the symbol definition once and remembers one object instead of many.

✦ Symbols (or text or grouped objects) are required for most animation.

✦ Symbols keep their integrity, so you can put other objects in front of them or behind them without the objects being joined or cut out.

Working with Graphic Symbols

You usually create a graphic symbol from objects that you have already created. For example, you may have a background that consists of a sky, grass, flowers, and the sun. Saving these objects as a symbol reduces file size and ensures that if you copy or move the background, all its components come along for the ride.

Working with instances of symbols

When you drag a symbol from the Library, the copy on the Stage is called an *instance.* You can have many instances of one symbol in a Flash document. You can change an instance so that it differs from its original symbol, and the original symbol in the Library remains intact. To change an instance, follow these steps:

1. **Select the instance by clicking it on the Stage with the Selection tool.**

Remember that changing an individual instance does not change the symbol itself.

2. **Use the Properties panel to do one or more of the following:**

• Change the brightness, color, or transparency by selecting an option from the Color drop-down list. Select Advanced from the Color drop-down list to change both color and alpha (transparency) at the same time.

• Change an instance's type (graphic, movie clip, or button) by selecting an option from the Symbol Behavior drop-down list.

You can also change the properties of an instance using ActionScript. For more information on ActionScript, see Book V, Chapter 8. If you need to refer to a symbol instance in your ActionScript, you can give that instance a name so that it has a unique name. Select the instance and enter the name in the Instance Name text field of the Properties panel.

3. **Use the Free Transform tool (or other editing tools) in the Tools panel to rotate, scale, or skew the instance.**

Creating graphic symbols

To create a graphic symbol from existing objects, follow these steps:

1. **Using the Selection tool from the Tools section of the Tools panel, select the objects that you want to convert to a symbol.**

2. **Choose Insert⇨Convert to Symbol, or press F8.**

    The Convert to Symbol dialog box appears, as shown in Figure 3-1.

Figure 3-1:
Convert an object to a symbol.

3. **In the Name text field, enter a name for the symbol.**

    Some people start the names of their symbols with a code that indicates the type of symbol. For example, you could start your graphic symbols with gr_ and then add the name of the symbol. This type of nomenclature automatically alphabetizes your symbols by their type and helps to make clear which type of symbol you are using.

4. **Select Graphic from the Behavior list of symbol types.**

5. **Click OK.**

    The objects that you selected are now one object, surrounded by a selection border. The symbol has also been stored, automatically, in the Library.

You can achieve the same result by creating an empty symbol and then adding your objects. Follow these steps to do so:

1. **Choose Insert⇨New Symbol to open the Create New Symbol dialog box.**

   Make sure that no objects are selected when you perform this step. The Create New Symbol dialog box is the same as the Convert to Symbol dialog box (refer to Figure 3-1).

2. **In the Name text field, enter a name for the symbol.**

3. **Select Graphic from the Behavior list of symbol types.**

4. **Click OK.**

   You now find yourself in symbol-editing mode and are no longer on the main Timeline.

5. **Draw the objects for your graphic symbol.**

   All these objects become part of your symbol.

6. **Choose Edit⇨Edit Document to exit symbol-editing mode and return to the main Timeline.**

   The symbol is now in the Library and disappears from the screen.

Using graphic symbols

To insert an instance of a symbol, drag it from the Library onto the Stage. You can drag from the symbol's icon in the Library list or from its preview at the top of the Library window.

You can also use a graphic symbol (and any other type of symbol) from another Flash document file, as follows:

1. **Choose Import⇨Import to Library.**

   This opens the Import to Library dialog box, where you can browse for Flash files.

2. **Choose the file that contains the symbol that you want.**

3. **Click the Open button.**

   Macromedia Flash opens another Library window.

4. **Drag symbols from the new Library window onto the Stage.**

Editing graphic symbols

If you change the original symbol, every instance of the symbol that you have inserted is also changed. This feature can save you lots of time if you need to change the shape of all your buttons, for example. To edit a symbol, follow these steps:

1. **Select any instance of the symbol on the Stage.**

Although you start by selecting an instance of the symbol, when you edit it, as described in Step 2, you are editing the symbol, not the instance.

2. **Right-click the symbol instance and choose one of the following:**

- **Edit in place:** This option allows you to edit a symbol while still viewing other objects on the Stage. The other objects are dimmed so that you can distinguish them from the symbol.

- **Edit:** If you select this option, you perform your edits in symbol-editing mode, which allows you to edit a symbol separately from the main Stage and Timeline. You see only the symbol.

- **Edit in New Window:** This option opens a new window, where you edit the symbol. You see only the symbol.

3. **Edit the symbol by changing its color, shape, or effects.**

4. **Choose Edit⇨Edit Document to return to the main Timeline, or if you chose Edit in a New Window, click the window's Close button.**

You see all the instances of the symbol change to reflect the edits.

To return to individual objects, you can break apart any instance of a symbol. Select the instance, and choose Modify⇨Break Apart.

Creating and Working with Movie Clip Symbols

Movie clips can be used for a number of reasons and in a number of different ways. These ways are described as follows:

- ✦ Use a movie clip to create animation that you want to insert or load onto the main Timeline.

- ✦ Use a movie clip whenever you need to control its functioning with ActionScript. (For more information on ActionScript, see Book V, Chapter 8.) For example, you can use ActionScript to control the size or color of a movie clip. You can also put ActionScript inside a movie clip to tell the movie to stop at a certain frame. You cannot control a graphic symbol with ActionScript.

- ✦ You can use movie clips to create interface elements, such as check boxes, radio buttons, and scroll bars. This type of movie clip is called a *component* and is covered in Book V, Chapter 8.

✦ You can also use movie clip symbols whenever you want to insert animation into the main Timeline but keep the original movie in the Library for reuse. Figure 3-2 shows a movie clip in symbol-editing mode that will be an animation of a bouncing ball. If you want several bouncing balls on your Web site, you can drag the movie clip onto the Stage as many times as you want.

You can create a movie clip symbol from scratch or convert animation that you have created on the main Timeline to a movie clip. To create a movie clip symbol from scratch, follow these steps:

1. **Choose Insert⇨New Symbol to open the Create New Symbol dialog box.**

   Make sure that no objects are selected when you perform this step.

2. **In the Name text field, enter a name for the symbol.**

3. **Select Movie Clip from the Behavior list of symbol types.**

4. **Click OK.**

   You now find yourself in symbol-editing mode and are no longer on the main Timeline, as shown in Figure 3-2. In Figure 3-2, you can see the movie clip icon and the name of the movie clip, Bouncing Ball, just below the layer list.

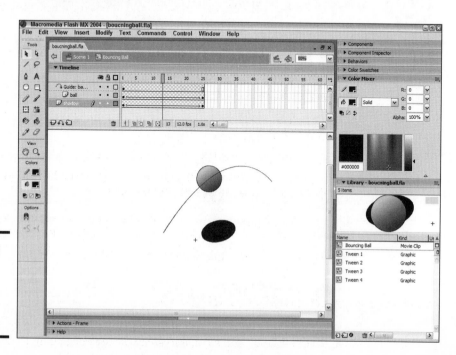

Figure 3-2:
Creating a symbol in symbol-editing mode.

5. **Create the objects or animation for your movie clip symbol.**

6. **Choose Edit⇨Edit Document to exit symbol-editing mode and return to the main Timeline.**

   The symbol is now in the Library and disappears from the screen.

Sometimes you create some animation on the main Timeline and later realize that you need to turn that animation into a movie clip. Follow these steps to create a movie clip from an animation:

1. **On the layer listing, click the first layer on the list, press Shift, and then click the last layer.**

   All the layers are now selected. See Book V, Chapter 4 for coverage of layers.

2. **Choose Edit⇨Copy Frames.**

3. **Make sure that no single objects on an individual frame are selected, and choose Insert⇨New Symbol.**

   The New Symbol dialog box appears.

4. **In the Name text field, enter a name for the symbol.**

5. **Select Movie Clip from the Behavior list of symbol types.**

6. **Click OK to close the dialog box and enter symbol-editing mode.**

7. **Click the first frame of the Timeline.**

   This is the Timeline for the movie clip, not the whole movie.

8. **Choose Edit⇨Paste Frames.**

   The frames are copied into the active layer.

9. **Choose Edit⇨Edit Document to return to the main Timeline of the movie and exit symbol-editing mode.**

   The movie clip symbol is now saved in the Library.

10. **Delete the original animation by selecting all the layers (as you did in Step 1) and choosing Insert⇨Remove Frames.**

You drag a movie clip onto the Stage just like a graphic symbol. Editing a movie clip is also the same as editing graphic symbols. See the section, "Working with Graphic Symbols," earlier in this chapter, for detailed steps.

Working with Button Symbols

Buttons are a major component of Web sites. You can use buttons as links to move to other pages and sites, and some buttons trigger more complex actions, such as stopping music or starting an animation.

A button has the following *states,* which you define when you create the button:

✦ **Up:** The appearance of the button when the mouse cursor is not over the button.

✦ **Over:** The appearance of the button when the mouse cursor is over the button, but not clicking it.

✦ **Down:** The appearance of the button when the button is being clicked.

✦ **Hit:** The area of the button that responds to the mouse. This area is invisible. The hit state is often the same as the down state, because it just defines the active area of the button.

A common technique is to design a button that changes color or size when the cursor passes over the button and then changes again when clicked. This technique provides feedback that the button has responded to the user. Figure 3-3 shows a button's four states.

Figure 3-3:
The four button states: up, over, down, and hit. Notice how each state has a slightly different fill.

Creating simple button symbols

Creating a button involves designing the look of the button for the first three states and the size of the button for the Hit state. Often, you add text to the graphic so that people know what the button is for. Follow these steps to create a button:

1. **Choose Insert⇨New Symbol.**

The Create New Symbol dialog box appears.

2. **In the Name text field, type a name for the button.**

3. **From the list of behaviors, select Button and click OK.**

You now see the Button Timeline. The dot in the Up frame indicates that the frame is a keyframe. (See Book V, Chapter 5 for more information on keyframes.) The Up frame is active.

4. **Draw the button for the Up state.**

   You can create the graphic with Macromedia Flash's drawing tools, an imported graphic, or an instance of a symbol.

   Place the graphic for all the button states at the center of the display. (Book V, Chapter 2 explains how to center objects.) If the button images aren't all in the same place, the button shifts when the viewer passes the cursor over or clicks the button.

5. **Click the Over frame, and choose Insert➪Keyframe.**

   The graphic that you created for the Up state is still on the Stage.

6. **Draw the button for the Over state.**

   Use the graphic for the Up state and change it (or leave it the same if you want), or delete the graphic and draw a new one in its place.

7. **Click the Down frame and choose Insert➪Keyframe.**

8. **Create the graphic for the Down frame (as in Step 6).**

9. **Click the Hit frame and choose Insert➪Keyframe.**

10. **Create the shape that defines the active area of the button.**

    This shape should completely cover all the graphics of the other states. Usually a rectangle or circle is enough. If you ignore the Hit frame, Macromedia Flash uses the boundary of the objects in the Up frame.

    If you use text for the button, viewers have to hit the letters precisely, unless you create a hit area around the text.

11. **Choose Edit➪Edit Document to return to the regular Timeline.**

To place a button on the Stage, use the Selection tool to drag the button from the Library to create an instance of the symbol. To edit a button, double-click it in the Library.

Adding pizzazz to buttons

Buttons don't have to be simple. You can make your buttons more interesting in the following ways:

✦ **Add a sound:** You add a sound to a button's Timeline in symbol-editing mode in the same way that you add a sound to a frame on the main Timeline. See Book V, Chapter 6 for information on adding sounds.

✦ **Add animation:** Create a movie clip symbol, as described in the section, "Creating and Working with Movie Clip Symbols," earlier in this chapter. Click the keyframe of the button's Timeline that you want to contain the movie clip; for example, click the Over keyframe. Delete any existing graphic, and drag a movie clip symbol that contains animation from the Library onto the screen.

✦ **Add interactivity:** In order for the button to do something, it needs some ActionScript. Drag an instance of the button onto the Stage, and select that instance by clicking it once with the Selection tool. Then use the Actions panel to add ActionScript to the button. See Book V, Chapter 8 for specific information about using ActionScript.

Testing buttons

After you have created a button, you should drag an instance of it onto the Stage and test it. To test simple buttons, follow these steps:

1. **Choose Control⇨Enable Simple Buttons.**

2. **Pass the cursor over the button, and click it to see if the effects work.**

3. **To select the button by clicking it, choose Control⇨Enable Simple Buttons again to disable the button.**

If your button contains movie clips, you need to test the entire movie to test the button. Choose Control⇨Test Movie, and test the button. To close the movie window, click its Close button.

Chapter 4: Making Your Life Easier with Layers

In This Chapter

✔ **Getting familiar with layers**

✔ **Working with layers**

✔ **Changing layer options**

✔ **Using folders to manage layers**

*L*ayers are a way to organize your Flash document. Layers are an important part of creating a movie for the following reasons:

✦ **Layers keep objects from bumping into each other.** If you draw two circles and overlap them, they either merge or one creates a cut out of the other. However, if you put the two circles on two separate layers, they each remain whole.

✦ **Each animated object must be on its own layer.** If you want more than one object on the Stage at a time, you need to create a new layer.

✦ **ActionScript and sounds should have their own layer.** This allows you to easily find and troubleshoot any problems as well as to avoid potential conflicts.

✦ **Special types of layers let you create special effects, as follows:**

  • **Mask layers:** Mask layers create a "keyhole" through which you can see layers beneath it.

  • **Guide layers:** Guide layers direct animation along a path.

In addition, you can use layers for your own organizational purposes. For example, you can put text on a separate layer. Then, to focus on just the text, you can hide all the other layers. In this chapter, we explain how to create and manage layers.

Layers add a third dimension to the organization of your Flash document. The Stage lays out your graphics in the horizontal (X-axis) and vertical (Y-axis) dimensions. Using layers is like adding a Z-axis, enabling you to place graphics on top of each other as if they were on successive transparent sheets.

The Timeline, of course, adds the fourth dimension — time. Layers are intimately connected to the Timeline. For each layer, Macromedia Flash adds a row of frames in the Timeline.

Working with the Layer List

You work with layers on the Layer list, which is to the left of the Timeline, as shown in Figure 4-1. The Layer list contains the following features:

✦ **Default layer:** You start a new movie with the default layer, Layer 1.

✦ **Active layer:** The active layer is highlighted. When you create objects, they go on the active layer.

✦ **Show/Hide Layers:** You can show or hide objects on any layer by clicking the Show/Hide icon for that layer.

✦ **Lock/Unlock Layers:** You can lock any layer so that objects cannot be selected or edited. Click the Lock icon for that layer. To unlock a layer, click the Lock icon again.

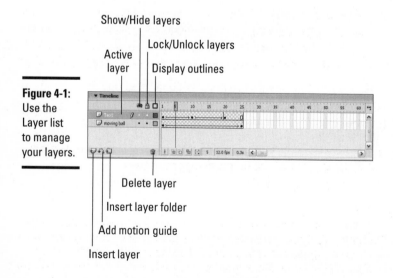

Show/Hide layers

Lock/Unlock layers

Active layer

Display outlines

Figure 4-1: Use the Layer list to manage your layers.

Delete layer

Insert layer folder

Add motion guide

Insert layer

+ **Display Outlines:** You can display objects on a layer as outlines. Each layer uses a different outline color. Outlines may help you see objects on all layers more clearly. Click the Outlines icon for any layer.

+ **Insert Layer:** To insert a layer, click the Insert Layer button below the Layer list.

+ **Insert Motion Guide:** To add a motion guide layer, click the Insert Motion Guide button below the Layer list. See the section, "An introduction to guide layers," later in this chapter, for more information on guide layers.

+ **Insert Layer Folder:** You can organize layers into folders. Click the Insert Layer Folder button below the Layer list.

+ **Delete Layer:** To delete a layer, select it and click the Delete Layer button, or drag the layer to the Delete Layer button.

Working with Layers

When you open a new movie, it has one layer, called Layer 1. As you work, you create, delete, move, and copy layers. You also name your layers. Choose a naming system that makes sense to you. *Note:* If the names are too long, you won't be able to see the whole name in the Layer list, so don't get too extravagant. You can drag the right border of the Layer list to the right to see more of the layer names.

Creating layers

When you need to create a new layer, click the Insert Layer button at the bottom of the Layer list (refer to Figure 4-1) or choose Insert⇨Timeline⇨ Layer. The new layer appears above the active layer and becomes the active layer.

You can also create a new layer by right-clicking a layer in the Layer list and selecting Insert Layer from the contextual menu that appears.

You should rename the new layer immediately after you create it. Double-click the layer name, type a new name, and press Enter.

Using layers

When you draw an object, it appears on the active layer, which is the layer that is highlighted and has a pencil icon next to its name in the Layer list. To draw on a different layer, click the name of the layer that you want to use. When you click a new layer, Macromedia Flash selects all the objects on that layer. To deselect the objects, click any empty area (on the Stage or in the gray space around the Stage).

Editing layers

You often need to make changes to layers or move objects from one layer to another. Keeping your layers organized is an important part of keeping your entire movie under control.

Selecting layers

When editing layers, you may want to select more than one layer at a time, such as when you need to move more than one layer at a time. To select a group of layers that are all together, click the first layer name on the Layer list, press and hold down Shift, and click the last layer of the group. To select layers that are not together, click the first layer, press and hold down Ctrl, and click any additional layers that you want to select.

Moving objects from one layer to another

You often draw objects before you realize that they need to be on a separate or different layer. For example, you can only have one object on a layer that you are animating. If you draw additional objects on that layer, you should move them to another layer. First create a new layer, if necessary. (See the section, "Creating layers," earlier in this chapter.) To move objects from one layer to another, follow these steps:

1. **Select the frames that represent the objects that you want to move by using the Selection tool.**

   The layer that contains the objects is also made current. To select more than one frame, select the first frame, press and hold down Shift, and then select the last frame.

2. **Choose Edit⇨Cut.**

3. **In the Layer list, click the layer to which you want to move the objects.**

4. **Choose Edit⇨Paste in Place.**

   The objects appear to be in the same location, but they are now on a new layer.

Distributing to layers

A great feature is the ability to distribute all objects on a layer to separate layers. For example, to animate each letter of a word, you should put each letter on a separate layer. For example, you may want to animate the letters of the word *now* so that each letter flies onto the Stage separately. Follow these steps to do so:

1. **Select the text or objects using the Selection tool.**

For the purposes of this example, select the Text tool from the Tools section of the Tools panel, type **now** in a single frame, and then select the text.

2. **If you are working with text, choose Modify⇨Break Apart.**

You see a separate box around each letter. Each letter is now a separate object.

3. **Choose Modify⇨Timeline⇨Distribute to Layers.**

Each object or letter is now on a separate layer. Macromedia Flash automatically creates the layers for you. In the "now" example, Macromedia Flash creates three layers, named n, o, and w for each of the three letters.

The objects also remain on their original layer. You can delete that layer if you want and keep only the copies on the individual layers.

Renaming layers

If the content of a layer changes, you should rename the layer to something that is appropriate to its content. To rename a layer, double-click the layer name in the Layer list, type the new name, and press Enter.

Deleting layers

To delete a layer, select the layer in the Layer list and click the Delete button (it looks like a trashcan) at the bottom of the list. (Refer to Figure 4-1.)

Deleting a layer deletes *everything* on that layer. Be aware that you may not be able to see everything on the layer, because you see only what is on the Stage in the current frame. To see what is on a layer throughout the Timeline, follow these steps:

1. **Right-click the layer name in the Layer list, and choose Hide Others from the contextual menu that appears.**

2. **Click the first frame on the Timeline.**

3. **Press Enter to run the animation.**

Copying layers

You can copy an entire layer, and if you do, all the objects on that layer are copied as well. Follow these steps to copy a layer:

1. **Select the layer by clicking the layer's name in the Layer list.**

   Selecting the layer selects all the objects on the layer.

2. **Choose Edit⇨Copy Frames.**

3. **Choose Insert⇨Layer to create a new layer.**

4. **Choose Edit⇨Paste Frames.**

Reordering layers

Macromedia Flash displays objects in the order of their layers, from the top down. In other words, objects on the top layer appear in front of objects on the next layer on the list. You can reorder the Layer list to change what objects appear in front on the Stage. See Figure 4-2 for an example.

Figure 4-2:
By changing the layer order, you change which objects appear in front on the Stage.

To move a layer to a different spot in the Layer list, click and drag the layer's name to the desired location, and then release the mouse button.

An introduction to guide layers

A *guide layer* is a special type of layer that is invisible when your Flash document is published and played as a movie. Guide layers have the following main purposes:

✦ **Drawing guide:** You can place gridlines on the Stage to help you lay out the objects on the Stage, or you can import a bitmap and use it as a guide to help you draw using the graphics tools. The content on the guide layer is invisible when the movie is published, but having the extra layer helps you draw.

✦ **Motion guide:** You can place a path on a guide layer that controls the animation of an object. This process is described in more detail in Book V, Chapter 5.

To create a drawing guide layer, follow these steps:

1. **Click the Insert Layer button on the Layer list.**

2. **Right-click the layer and choose Guide from the contextual menu that appears.**

The layer icon changes to the guide icon that looks like a hammer.

Using mask layers

A *mask layer* hides everything on its connected masked layers, except what's inside the objects that are on the top mask layer. It, in effect, masks the content on the lower layers. Masks are often used to create a spotlight effect, where you only see what is in the spotlight and everything else is hidden. You can see this effect in Figure 4-3, where the circular mask hides everything outside of the circle. The circle is on a *mask layer,* and what you see inside the circle is on a *masked layer.*

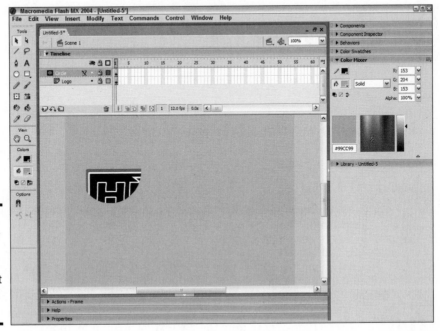

Figure 4-3:
The circular mask hides everything except what is inside the circle.

To create a mask layer, follow these steps:

1. **On the top layer of the Layer list, create the objects that you want to be visible through the mask.**

2. **With the top layer selected, click the Add Layer button at the bottom of the Layer list.**

3. **Draw a shape, such as a circle, on this new layer.**

4. **Right-click the new layer and choose Mask from the contextual menu that appears.**

   In the Layer list, the mask layer is locked and the masked layer is both locked and indented. (Refer to Figure 4-3.)

To edit a mask or masked layer, click the lock next to the layer name in the Layer list. Unlocking these layers removes the mask effect. After you have finished editing, click the lock column next to the layers' names again to redisplay the mask effect.

To link a layer to a mask layer, drag the layer directly underneath a mask layer. The layer is indented. To display the mask effect, make sure that the layer is locked by clicking it under the Lock column in the Layer list.

Changing Layer Options

You can control the visibility, editability, and display of objects on layers. These tools are very helpful when you are trying to isolate certain objects for editing or animation.

Altering the visibility of objects

You can hide all the objects on a layer. If you have a lot of objects on the Stage and want to edit objects on one layer, you can hide other layers that you don't need to see at the moment.

Don't forget about objects on hidden layers. These objects still appear in your published movie.

To hide a layer, click beneath the Eye icon on the layer's row. An X appears in the Eye column to show you that the layer is hidden. Click the X to unhide the layer.

To hide all layers except one, right-click the layer that you want to see and choose Hide Others from the contextual menu that appears.

Locking and unlocking layers

You can lock the objects on a layer so that you cannot edit them. You may find yourself inadvertently selecting objects that you want to leave alone. This can get annoying, but you can easily avoid the situation by locking that layer.

To lock a layer, click beneath the Lock icon on the layer's row. A lock appears in the Lock column. Click the lock to unlock the layer.

To lock all layers except one, right-click the layer and choose Lock Others from the contextual menu that appears.

Setting layer properties

Many of the layer controls that we discuss in this chapter are combined in the Layer Properties dialog box, as shown in Figure 4-4. Most of the time, you just use the controls on the Layer list or the contextual menu that you see when you right-click a layer. However, the Layer Properties dialog box does have some unique features.

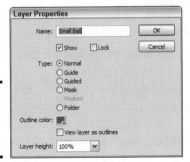

Figure 4-4:
The Layer
Properties
dialog box.

To open the Layer Properties dialog box, select the layer that you want to modify and choose Modify➪Timeline➪Layer Properties. You can use this dialog box to do the following things:

✦ **Rename the layer:** Type a new name in the Name text field.

✦ **Show/Hide the layer:** Select or deselect the Show check box.

✦ **Lock/Unlock the layer:** Select or deselect the Lock check box.

✦ **Change the type of layer:** You can turn a layer into a guide, guided, mask, masked, or folder layer.

✦ **Change the outline color:** Click the Outline Color swatch to choose a new color.

+ **Turn outlines on/off:** Select or deselect the View Layer as Outlines check box.

+ **Change layer height:** Select a percentage from the Layer Height drop-down list. This increases the physical size of the layer to make it more viewable.

When you finish making changes, click OK to close the Layer Properties dialog box.

Using Folders to Manage Layers

If you have many layers, you can organize them into folders. For example, you may want to put all your layers containing text in one folder.

To create a folder, click the Insert Layer Folder icon at the bottom of the Layer list. A new folder appears above the current layer. Double-click the folder name, and enter a name that describes the folder's contents.

Use the following tips to manage folders:

+ **Put layers in a folder:** Drag layers onto the folder's row.

+ **Collapse and expand individual folders:** Click the arrow at the left of the folder's icon.

+ **Expand and collapse all folders:** Right-click the Layer list, and choose Expand All Folders or Collapse All Folders from the contextual menu that appears.

+ **Remove a layer from a folder:** Expand the folder, if necessary, and drag the layer above the folder name or to another location where it doesn't darken a folder.

+ **Hide or lock an entire folder and its layers:** Click beneath the Eye or Lock icon on the folder's row.

+ **Reorder folders:** You can change the order of folders, which also changes the order of its layers. Just drag any folder up or down.

+ **Delete folders:** Select the folder and click the Delete (trashcan) icon.

Deleting a folder deletes all the layers in the folder and everything on those layers. Macromedia Flash warns you of this if you try to delete a folder.

Chapter 5: Creating Animation

In This Chapter

✔ Touring the Timeline

✔ Understanding frames and keyframes

✔ Creating animation frame-by-frame

✔ Creating tweened animation

✔ Creating interactive animation

✔ Working with scenes

Macromedia Flash MX 2004 is basically an animation program, so this chapter on animation is central to the whole purpose of Macromedia Flash. In this chapter, we provide the information you need to create motion and shape animation.

Getting Familiar with the Timeline

The Timeline lays out your animation in time. In order to animate, you need to be thoroughly familiar with the Timeline (shown in Figure 5-1) and its special coding.

As you can see in Figure 5-1, every fifth frame on the Timeline is numbered and each layer has its own row in the Timeline. (For more information on layers, see Book V, Chapter 4.)

Scene name   Playhead   Frame view

Figure 5-1:
The Timeline
provides a
great deal of
information
about your
animation.

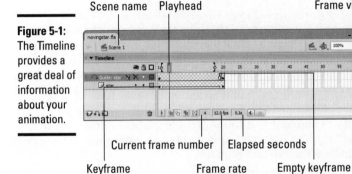

Current frame number   Elapsed seconds

Keyframe   Frame rate   Empty keyframe

If the Timeline isn't visible, choose Window⇨Timeline. You can collapse the Timeline by clicking its Collapse/Expand arrow at the left side of its title bar.

Understanding the frame rate

The frame rate is the speed at which Macromedia Flash plays the animation. The default frame rate is 12 frames per second (fps). You can have only one frame rate per document. To change the frame rate, follow these steps:

1. **Double-click the Frame Rate box at the bottom middle of the Timeline.**

   The Document Properties dialog box appears.

2. **In the Frame Rate text field, enter a new number in frames per second.**

3. **Click OK.**

When you use a frame rate that is too slow, the animation appears jerky. Increasing the frame rate may make animation appear smoother, but a frame rate that is too fast can appear blurred. The default frame rate of 12 fps is a good place to start.

The Internet connection rate and the size of the file also affect the rate of animation. A large file (often due to large graphics or sounds) and a slow Internet connection can make the animation stutter. Your viewers will get the best results if you reduce the size of the file as much as possible. In Book V, Chapter 7, we explain how to optimize files for the Web.

Working with the Timeline

You can work with the Timeline in the following ways:

✦ **Go to a frame:** Click the frame on the Timeline to go to a particular frame. If you want to work on a specific layer, click the frame in that layer's row.

✦ **Change size and appearance of the frames:** To modify the frames as they appear in the Timeline, click the Frame View button in the upper-right corner of the Timeline and choose one of the options from the menu. You can change the width and height of the frames, turn coloring of frames on and off, and choose to display a small thumbnail of the frame's content in each frame.

✦ **Add a label or comment to a frame:** To add a label or comment to a frame in the Timeline, select a frame and type a label name in the Frame Label text field in the Properties panel.

✦ **Select frames:** Click a frame and drag across the frames you want to select. (You can also click the first frame, press Shift, and click the last frame you want to select to select all the frames in between.)

✦ **Copy and paste frames:** Select the frames you want to copy, choose Edit⇨Timeline⇨Copy Frames, click where you want the frames to go, and choose Edit⇨Timeline⇨Paste Frames.

✦ **Move frames:** Select the frames you want to move and drag them to the desired location.

✦ **Add a frame:** To add a frame, right-click on the frame to the left of where you want to create a frame and choose Insert Frame from the contextual menu that appears.

✦ **Delete frames:** Select the frames you want to delete. Right-click and choose Remove Frames.

✦ **Add a keyframe:** Right-click on the desired frame and choose Insert Keyframe from the contextual menu.

✦ **Change the length of an animation:** Press Ctrl and click and drag the first or last keyframe of the animation to the right or left.

✦ **Scroll along the Timeline:** Use the horizontal scroll bar to scroll along the Timeline. Use the Vertical scroll bar (which appears when you have too many layers to display) to scroll through the layers.

Onion skinning

When you animate an object, you can display some or all of the animated frames at once, using an effect known as *onion skinning*. Onion skinning produces overlapping translucent images like the translucent layers of an onion. See Figure 5-2 for an example of onion skinning.

To work with onion skinning, use the buttons under the Timeline:

✦ **Onion skin:** Turns on onion skinning and adjusts the Onion markers to customize the number of frames that display the effect.

✦ **Onion skin outlines:** Displays single-color outlines of your animation.

✦ **Edit multiple frames:** Enables you to edit any of the frames on the Timeline, regardless of the current frame.

✦ **Modify onion markers:** Displays a menu that enables you to always show the markers (even when onion skinning is off), anchor the markers so they don't follow the playhead (current frame marker), and set the number of frames that the markers cover.

Onion markers

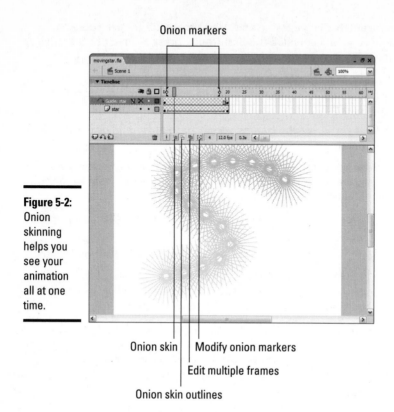

Figure 5-2:
Onion
skinning
helps you
see your
animation
all at one
time.

Onion skin | Modify onion markers

Edit multiple frames

Onion skin outlines

Using Frames and Keyframes

A frame is actually a unit of time, based on your frame rate. You can place
content on any frame, but you can only change content on a keyframe. Use a
keyframe whenever you want to start or stop an animation or make any
object appear or disappear.

To introduce any new object onto the Stage, you must have a keyframe.
Insert a keyframe by right-clicking to the left of where you'd like the
keyframe and selecting Insert Keyframe from the contextual menu. Click the
keyframe on the layer where you want the object to appear, and then do one
of the following:

✦ Draw something by using the Macromedia Flash drawing tools. (See
Book V, Chapter 2.)

✦ Import a bitmap. (See Book V, Chapter 3.)

✦ Drag an object onto the Stage from the Library. (See Book V, Chapter 1.)

You can create two types of animation in Macromedia Flash:

✦ **Frame-by-frame:** In frame-by-frame animation, each frame is a keyframe and contains a slight change in your objects so that when you play the Flash document, you see a smooth animation. This type of animation is time-consuming and creates bigger files, but it may be necessary to create complex effects. Cartooning is mostly done using frame-by-frame animation.

✦ **Tweening:** In tweening, the first and last frames of the animation are keyframes, and Macromedia Flash calculates everything in between. You can tween motion and shapes (*morphing*). Tweening is faster to create than frame-by-frame animation and creates small file sizes. The only down side to tweening is that it can't be done with any type of object except vector graphics.

Creating Animation Frame-By-Frame

When your animation does not have a simple pattern, such as movement of one object in a direction or the change of one shape to another shape, you need to use frame-by-frame animation. A common example of frame-by-frame animation is cartooning, where a figure needs to move in complex ways or a mouth moves in synchrony with speech.

To create frame-by-frame animation, follow these steps:

1. **Right-click a frame in the current layer where you want the animation to start and choose Insert Keyframe from the contextual menu.**

2. **Draw or import your image.**

Book V, Chapter 2 is all about creating graphics. To import an image, choose File⇨Import.

3. **Right-click the next frame and choose Insert Keyframe again.**

4. **Change the graphic slightly to create the second frame of the animation.**

5. **Repeat Steps 3 and 4 as necessary until you have completed your animation.**

See Figure 5-3 for an example of frame-by-frame animation.

During the process, press Enter to play back your animation and check your work.

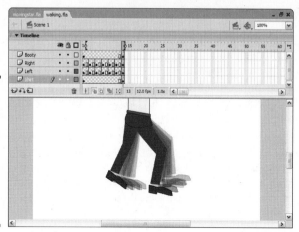

Figure 5-3:
This frame-
by-frame
animation of
the legs
moving is
shown
using onion
skinning.

Creating Tweened Motion Animation

Motion tweening moves a single symbol instance, text object, or grouped set of objects either in a straight line or along a path that you draw (often with the Pencil tool).

Although you can motion tween only one object at a time on any layer, you can tween other objects on other layers to create the overall look of many objects being animated.

You can also change the size, rotation, skew (slant), color, and transparency of symbol instances as you motion tween them. To make these changes to text or groups, convert them to symbols. See Book V, Chapter 3 for a discussion of symbols.

Preparing to tween

You can only put one object — symbol instance, text, or group — on the layer where you are animating. The first step is to create the object you want to animate and make sure that nothing else is on that layer. Often, you create a new layer just for your animation.

Decide how you want your object to move. Do you want its color, size, or rotation to change? After you have decided, you are ready to tween.

The Macromedia Flash Controller is like a control panel for a CD or video player. The Controller is helpful when you animate because it offers controls for rewinding and playing your animation. To open the Controller, choose Window➪Toolbars➪Controller.

Creating a simple tween

Before you tween, open the Properties panel by choosing Window⇨ Properties. To create a simple motion tween that moves the object along a straight line, follow these steps:

1. **On your animation layer, insert a keyframe where you want the animation to start.**

   To add a keyframe, right-click on the frame to the left of where you want to create a keyframe and choose Insert Frame from the contextual menu.

2. **Click the keyframe and create the object or objects you want to animate.**

   You cannot tween plain graphics. If necessary, turn your object or objects into a symbol (see Book V, Chapter 3) or a group (see Book V, Chapter 2). Text is fine as it is. You can also import a graphic or drag an instance of a symbol from the Library onto the Stage.

3. **Insert a keyframe where you want the animation to end.**

   The longer the span of frames is, the slower the animation. You can always adjust the length of a tween later, as explained in the "Working with the Timeline" section, earlier in this chapter.

4. **Click the last keyframe and then move the object to its new location using the Selection tool.**

   At this point, you can also change the object's color properties and transparency by using the Color box in the Properties panel. In addition, you can use the Free Transform tool or other Macromedia Flash commands to change the object's size, rotation, and skew, as shown in Figure 5-4.

5. **Select the range from keyframe to keyframe by clicking the first keyframe and dragging to the last keyframe.**

   If the span of frames is too long to show, click the first keyframe, scroll to the last keyframe, press Shift, and click the last keyframe.

   You can click anywhere between the keyframes and get almost the exact same result as the technique in Step 5. The last keyframe isn't tweened, but the result looks the same when you play the animation.

6. **From the Tween drop-down list in the Properties panel, select Motion.**

   If you changed the object's size, select the Scale check box in the Properties panel to tween the size.

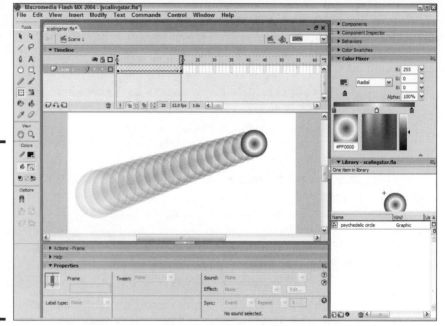

Figure 5-4:
A simple
motion
tween
including
scaling.
Onion
skinning
shows all
the frames
outlined.

7. **If you want to rotate the object during the tween (in addition to any rotation you created in Step 4), select CW (clockwise) or CCW (counter-clockwise) from the Rotate drop-down list in the Properties panel, and then enter the number of rotations in the Rotation Count text field.**

   To test your animation, click the first keyframe and press Enter or use the Controller to rewind and play your animation.

You can accelerate or decelerate the speed of the tween. To accelerate from beginning to end, enter a value between –1 and –100 in the Ease text field in the Properties panel. To decelerate, use a value between 1 and 100.

See Figure 5-4 for an example of a ball that moves along a diagonal line. The ball also becomes smaller, so that it appears to recede in the distance as it moves.

Motion tweening along a path

To tween along a path that is not a straight line, you need to draw the path on a guide layer. (See Book V, Chapter 4 for the steps to create a guide layer.) Your animation is on the guided layer that is associated with the guide layer. Figure 5-5 shows an example of a motion tween along a path.

To create an animation that moves along a path, follow these steps (which start just like the steps for simple motion tweening):

1. **On your animation layer, insert a keyframe where you want the animation to start.**

   To add a keyframe, right-click on the frame to the left of where you want to create a keyframe and choose Insert Frame from the contextual menu.

2. **Click the keyframe and create or import the object or objects (symbol instance, group, or text) you want to animate.**

3. **Insert a keyframe where you want the animation to end.**

4. **Select the range from keyframe to keyframe by clicking the first keyframe and dragging to the last keyframe, or click anywhere between the two keyframes.**

5. **From the Tween drop-down list in the Properties panel, select Motion.**

6. **In the Properties panel, select the Snap check box to snap the object to the path.**

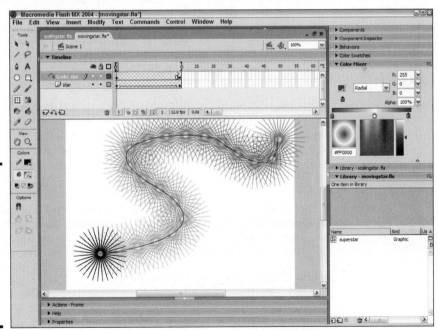

Figure 5-5:
The star moves along a path. Here you see the effect shown with onion skinning on.

7. **If you want the object to rotate in the direction and angle of the path, select the Orient to Path check box.**

8. **Right-click the object's layer and select Add Motion Guide.**

   The new layer is added. The layer is labeled Guide, and the object's layer is indented beneath it.

9. **On the guide layer, draw your path using the Pen tool.**

10. **Click the first keyframe of the object's layer and drag the object by its registration point (a small plus or circle) to the beginning of the path until the registration point snaps to the path.**

11. **Click the last keyframe of the object's layer and drag the object by its registration point to the end of the path until the registration point snaps to the path.**

12. **Press Enter to play the animation.**

If you need to change your path, use the Macromedia Flash editing tools to edit the path you created. You can use the Selection or Subselection tools to edit the path. (See Book V, Chapter 2 for details.)

The guide path is not visible in the published movie. However, you often don't want to see the path even in your document, so you can more easily visualize the animation. Just click the eye column of the guide layer to hide it.

Creating Tweened Shape Animation

If you want your objects to change shape, you need shape tweening, often called *morphing*. Unlike motion tweening, shape tweening works only with plain vector objects, usually ones that you create with the Macromedia Flash drawing tools. You cannot shape tween a symbol instance, text, or a group unless you break them apart by choosing Modify⇨Break Apart.

To turn text into shapes, choose Modify⇨Break Apart twice. The first time only breaks apart the text into individual letters. The second time you choose Modify⇨Break Apart, you create shapes from the individual letters. However, remember that you can have only one animated object on a layer. You can break apart text once, and then choose Modify⇨Distribute to Layers to put each letter on a separate layer. If you want to shape tween the letters, break apart each letter a second time.

Creating a simple shape tween

To shape tween a shape, follow these steps:

1. **On a new layer, right-click the frame where you want the animation to start and select Insert Keyframe.**

2. **Create the beginning shape.**

3. **Insert a keyframe where you want to end the animation.**

4. **With the second keyframe selected, create the ending shape.**

You can create the end shape by erasing the first shape and drawing a new one or by modifying the first shape.

5. **If you want to change color, you can simply choose another color for the ending shape from the Color box in the Properties panel.**

6. **If you want to change transparency, open the Color Mixer panel (Window⇨Design Panels ⇨ Color Mixer) and change the Alpha percentage in the Alpha text field.**

You can also change the color in the Color Mixer.

7. **Click between the keyframes or select the entire span of the tween.**

8. **Select Shape from the Tween drop-down list in the Properties panel.**

9. **From the lower section of the Properties panel, select Angular from the Blend drop-down list if your tween shape has straight lines and sharp corners. Select Distributive for more curvy shapes.**

You may need to click the Collapse/Expand arrow at the lower-right corner of the Properties panel to display the lower section of the Properties panel.

10. **To play the animation, click the first keyframe and press Enter.**

Using shape hints for more control

When you create your first shape tween, you may find that Macromedia Flash calculated the transformation differently than you imagined it. You can give Macromedia Flash cues, called *shape hints,* that tell it which part of the original shape moves where, as shown in Figure 5-6.

Figure 5-6:
Shape hints show where points on your beginning shape will end up.

To use shape hints, follow these steps:

1. **Create a shape animation as described in the section, "Creating a simple shape tween."**

2. **Click the first keyframe of the animation.**

3. **Choose Modify⇨Shape⇨Add Shape Hint or press Ctrl+Shift+H.**

   A small red circle with the letter "a" inside it appears on the Stage.

4. **Drag the shape hint to the desired area in your shape.**

5. **Click the ending keyframe of the animation.**

   You again see a small circle with the letter "a" inside it on the Stage.

6. **Drag the shape hint to the area in your shape where you want the beginning hint to move.**

7. **Repeat Steps 3 through 6 to place additional shape hints.**

8. **Press Enter to play the animation and check the results.**

If you want, you can remove or hide existing shape hints:

+ To remove a shape hint, drag it off the Stage.

+ To display and hide shape hints, select the layer and keyframe with the shape hints and choose View⇨Show Shape Hints.

You may get better results if you place the hints counterclockwise, starting from the upper-left corner of your shape.

Adding Basic Interactivity to Animation

You often need to control how your animation works. For example, you may want some animation to loop or to stop at a certain point. You may also want to enable viewers to control the animation. Buttons commonly allow users to stop the animation (perhaps some introductory animation for your Web site) or turn off the sound. You introduce interactivity and control by using ActionScript, the Macromedia Flash programming language.

The following sections offer a few ideas for using ActionScript in animation. We cover interactivity in detail in Book V, Chapter 9.

Go To

You don't need to play your animation from beginning to end. You can add ActionScript (often simply called *actions*) to control the playing of the frames. The goto action tells the movie to go to a different frame. At that point, you can tell the animation to stop or to play.

Say that you want your animation to play from Frames 1–24, but then you want the last half to loop over and over again. On Frame 24, you can add a goto action and tell Macromedia Flash to go to Frame 12 and play. The animation goes to Frame 24, and then loops back to Frame 12 again. In this situation, the first 11 frames play only once, but Frames 12 through 24 play over and over in a loop.

In another situation, you may want animation to play from Frames 1–24 and then go to Frame 50 and stop. You may be using Frame 50 to display a menu. In this case, you use the goto and stop actions.

Stop

Sometimes, you just want to stop the animation. For example, movie clips automatically loop. If you want them to play just once and then stop, you add a stop action in the last frame. For any animation, you can add a stop action at the end to make sure that everything stops at the same time.

Play

After you stop an animation, you may want to play it again. You can use the play action to play a movie when certain conditions are met. If the conditions are not met, the movie does not play (due to a stop action).

On (mouse event)

The on action is used for buttons, which are explained in Book V, Chapter 3. To add interactivity, you specify what happens when the button is clicked or released, when a mouse cursor passes over or off the button, or when a mouse cursor is dragged over or off the button. For example, a common use of the on action would be to specify that when the button is clicked, you go to a different frame or URL, such as another page on the Web site.

Working with Scenes

A *scene* is a section of an animation. You can divide up your animation into scenes, each with its own Timeline. The scenes play back in the order you set. The purpose of creating a scene is to help you organize your animation. By default, you work in Scene 1. The current scene name is displayed beneath the Layer list. To create a new scene, choose Insert⇨Scene.

To manage your scenes, choose Window➪Scene. The Scene panel opens, as shown in Figure 5-7.

Figure 5-7: The Scene panel helps you manage scenes.

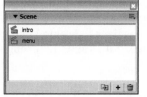

You can use the Scene panel to work with scenes in the following ways:

✦ **Change scene order:** Drag a scene's name in the Scene panel to a new location to change the order of the scenes.

✦ **Rename a scene:** Double-click a scene's name, type a new name, and press Enter to rename a scene.

✦ **Add a scene:** Click the Add Scene button at the bottom of the Scene panel to add a scene.

✦ **Delete a scene:** Select a scene and click the Delete Scene button at the bottom of the Scene panel to delete a scene.

✦ **Duplicate a scene:** Select a scene and click the Duplicate Scene button at the bottom of the Scene panel to create a copy of a scene.

✦ **View a scene:** Select the scene in the Scene panel to view the scene.

Chapter 6: Adding Sound and Video

In This Chapter

↙ **Introducing sound and video formats**

↙ **Working with sounds**

↙ **Working with video clips**

You can make the Web experience richer by adding sound and video to your Web pages. Sounds can range from a simple clicking noise when a user clicks a button to music and narration. You can also include video in your Web site.

Exploring Sound and Video Formats

Both sound and video files come in many formats. Before you can use sound or video, however, you need a file that Macromedia Flash MX 2004 can import.

Sound file formats

You can use the following sound file formats in Macromedia Flash:

+ **AIFF:** This is the standard sound format for Macintosh computers. These files usually have filenames with the .aif or .ief extensions.

+ **WAV:** This is the standard format for Windows machines. These files usually have filenames with a .wav extension.

+ **MP3:** This is a highly-compressed format that maintains high quality sound.

If you have QuickTime 4 or higher installed on your computer, you can import Sound Designer II, Sun AU, and System 7 or higher sounds.

A sound file has several properties that affect its quality and size. You can often adjust these properties to reduce file size without noticeably affecting quality. For sophisticated adjustments, you probably need a sound-editing program, such as SoundForge. Here are the basic properties of a sound file:

✦ **Sample rate:** The *sample rate* is the number of times in kilohertz (kHz) that an audio signal is sampled when it's recorded digitally. A higher sample rate results in higher quality sound but also yields a larger file size.

✦ **Bit rate:** The *bit rate* is the number of bits (pieces of data) used for each audio sample. Sixteen-bit sounds are clearer, but 8-bit sounds are smaller and may be good enough for simple sounds, such as a button click.

✦ **Channels:** *Channels* are the number of streams of sound in a file and are either mono or stereo. Mono may be just fine and uses half the amount of data as stereo.

You can find a sound's properties when you import the sound into Macromedia Flash, as explained in the upcoming section, "Importing sounds."

Video file formats

The type of video formats you can use depends on some other software that supports their playback:

✦ **If you have QuickTime 4 or later installed:** You can import AVI, MPEG (MPG), MOV, and DV formats.

✦ **If you have DirectX 7 or later installed:** You can import AVI, MPEG (MPG), and WMV/ASF (Windows Media File) formats.

Because video files are usually very large, they are always compressed by using a *codec.* The word *codec* stands for *co*mpression/*dec*ompression. The same codec decompresses the video file when it is used. You need to have the codec that was used for the video file on your computer in order to import the video file. The same applies to the audio track in a video file.

Working with Sounds

Working with sounds in Macromedia Flash involves at least two steps — importing the sound and placing it in a movie. You can also do basic sound edits in Macromedia Flash.

Importing sounds

To import a sound, follow these steps:

1. **Choose File⇨Import⇨Import to Library.**

The Import dialog box appears.

2. **Select the sound file you want to import and click Open.**

   The sound goes into the Library.

To see a sound's properties, open the Library, right-click the sound and choose Properties from the contextual menu that appears.

Placing a sound in a movie

After a sound is in the Library, you can place it in your movie. You need to decide when it starts, when it ends, or whether you want to loop the sound.

To place a sound, follow these steps:

1. **Create a new layer for the sound by choosing Insert⇨Timeline⇨ Layer.**

2. **Right-click the frame and choose Insert Keyframe from the contextual menu.**

   This inserts a keyframe on the sound's layer where you want the sound to start.

3. **Press Ctrl+L to open the Library or select Window⇨Library.**

   Scroll down to the sound file you're looking for in the Library.

4. **Drag the sound to the Stage.**

   The sound extends to the next keyframe, if one exists.

5. **To specify settings for the sound, open the Properties panel by choosing Window⇨Properties.**

6. **Expand the Properties panel, shown in Figure 6-1, using the Expand/ Collapse arrow in the lower-right corner.**

Figure 6-1:
Specifying
sound
settings.

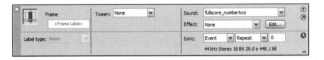

7. **From the Sound drop-down list, choose the sound for which you want to specify settings.**

   All the sounds you have imported are listed.

8. **To create a special effect, select an effect from the Effect drop-down list.**

   You have the following choices:

   - **None:** No special effect (the default).

   - **Left channel:** Plays the sound from only the left speaker.

   - **Right channel:** Plays the sound from only the right speaker.

   - **Fade left to right:** Starts playing from the left speaker and moves to the right speaker.

   - **Fade right to left:** Starts playing from the right speaker and moves to the left speaker.

   - **Fade in:** Starts playing softly and increases the volume.

   - **Fade out:** Starts playing loudly and decreases the volume.

   - **Custom:** If you edit the sound, as explained in the next section, your sound has a custom effect.

9. **Select a synchronization type from the Sync drop-down list.**

   You can choose from the following options:

   - **Event:** Plays the sound from its first keyframe until it ends (even if the movie stops), replays the sound whenever that keyframe plays, and the entire sound downloads before it plays. This choice is ideal for button sounds that you want to play whenever the button is clicked. Event is the default synchronization type.

   - **Start:** Plays the sound like the Event option, but if the keyframe is replayed before the sound is finished, the Start option doesn't replay the sound.

   - **Stop:** Stops playing the sound.

   - **Stream:** Synchronizes the sound with the animation, shortening or lengthening the animation to match the length of the sound. Macromedia Flash may skip frames if necessary.

10. **If you want to loop or repeat the sound, select either Loop or Repeat from the drop-down list beside it.**

    If you select Loop, the movie will simply repeat over and over again. If you select repeat, you'll be asked to enter the number of repeats in the field provided.

11. **Press Enter to play the animation and hear the sound.**

    Press Ctrl+Enter to test the movie if you're working on a complex animation.

Editing sounds

Macromedia Flash contains its own simple sound-editing tool. For example, you can delete some of the beginning or end of the sound if you don't need it. You can also change the volume. To edit a sound, follow these steps:

1. **Click a frame that contains a sound.**

2. **Open the Properties panel by choosing Window⇨Properties.**

   If necessary, click the Collapse/Expand arrow at the lower-right corner to expand the Properties panel fully.

3. **Click the Edit button within the Properties panel.**

   The Edit Envelope dialog box, shown in Figure 6-2, appears. In this context, *envelope* just means the entire snippet of music.

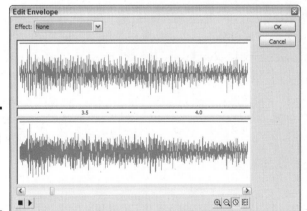

Figure 6-2:
You can edit sounds in the Edit Sounds dialog box.

You can edit the sound as follows:

- **Change the volume:** Drag an envelope handle (see Figure 6-2) up to increase volume or down to decrease volume. Click an envelope line to add a handle so that you can change the volume at that location.

- **Delete the beginning of the sound:** Drag the Time In control to the right.

- **Delete the end of the sound:** Scroll to the end of the sound and drag the Time Out control (the ending control) to the left.

You can use the Zoom In and Zoom Out buttons (refer to Figure 6-2) to change the magnification in the Edit Envelope dialog box. You can also use the Frames and Seconds buttons to change the display between frames and seconds.

Setting sound properties

You can control the properties of a sound to further compress it. If you need to specify different properties for different sounds, set the properties when you place the sound in your movie:

1. **Open the Library by choosing Window⇨Library or by pressing Ctrl+L.**

2. **Double-click the sound icon next to the sound for which you want to see the properties.**

The Sound Properties dialog box, shown in Figure 6-3, appears.

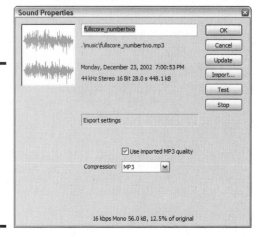

Figure 6-3:
You can set the properties for individual sounds in the Sound Properties dialog box.

The top part of the dialog box lists the sound's name, original location, and statistics. At the bottom of the dialog box, use the Compression drop-down list to select the file format you want:

- **Default:** Leaves the sound unchanged.

- **ADPCM:** Enables you to convert stereo to mono and to choose a sampling rate and bit rate. Used for short sounds.

- **MP3:** Enables you to convert stereo to mono and to choose a bit rate and quality. MP3 is an efficient compression method and is used for longer, more complex sounds, especially music.

- **Raw:** Enables you to convert stereo to mono and to choose the sampling rate. Raw uses no compression.

- **Speech:** Enables you to choose a sampling rate. This option uses compression specially designed for speech.

As you choose an option, you see the resulting statistics at the bottom of the dialog box.

3. **Click the Test button to hear the result of your choice.**

You can also set sound properties for all sounds at once when you publish your movie. (See Book V, Chapter 7.)

Working with Video Clips

A new feature of Macromedia Flash MX 2004 is the ability to embed video clips in your Flash movie. A video clip can be live action or animation created with an animation program that outputs a video file format. **Note:** Macromedia Flash may not be able to handle very long video files. You also have no direct control over the video frames.

To use a video, follow these steps:

1. **Select a key frame already on your Timeline (or create a new keyframe by right-clicking a frame and choosing Insert Keyframe from the contextual menu that appears).**

2. **Choose File⇨Import⇨Import to Library.**

   The Import dialog box appears.

3. **Choose the video file you want and click the Open button.**

   The Video Import Wizard appears, as shown in Figure 6-4.

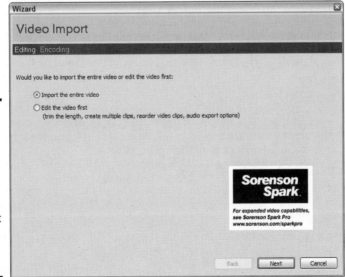

Figure 6-4:
The Video Import Wizard provides all the steps you need to follow to get video into your Flash movie.

4. Select either the Import the Entire Video or the Edit the Video First option.

Most Windows video formats, such as AVI or WMV, are not editable before import. QuickTime, however, is editable. If you select Edit the Video First option, you're presented with a number of options, such as combining clips and editing them to include only the parts you want to see. In either case, when you're ready to move on, click the Next button.

5. Select a compression profile.

You can select from one of the five compression algorithms that Macromedia Flash offers by selecting it from the drop-down list, or you can create your own by selecting the Create Your Own Profile option.

6. To choose the frequency of keyframes in the video clip, drag the Keyframe Interval slider.

A *video* keyframe is separate from a *Timeline* keyframe. A *video* keyframe stores the entire image data as compared to the changes from the previous frame that are stored in regular frames.

A keyframe interval of 0 adds a single keyframe at the beginning of the video stream and no other keyframes.

7. Select the Synchronize Video to Macromedia Flash Document Frame Rate option to match the video frame rate to the Flash movie frame rate.

If your video seems to display poorly, try deselecting this option.

8. From the Number of Video Frames to Encode per Number of Flash Frames drop-down list, select a ratio.

The default is 1:1, which plays one video frame for each Flash frame. A ratio of 1:2 would play one video frame for every two Flash frames. A 1:2 or higher ratio reduces file size, but reduces smoothness of playback as well.

9. Click OK.

If the video clip is longer than the span of keyframes into which you are placing the video, a message displays, asking if you want to add enough frames necessary to play the entire clip.

10. Click Yes to add the frames.

Chapter 7: Publishing Movies

In This Chapter

✔ **Publishing movies the easy way**

✔ **Optimizing movies for speedy download times**

✔ **Generating HTML and graphics**

After you finish creating your Flash document, you need to publish it in SWF movie format. You then use HTML code to insert the SWF movie in a Web page so that browsers can display the animation. In this chapter, we explain how to get your animation onto your Web site.

Publishing Movies the Simple Way

If you don't need to change any settings, you can immediately publish your file by choosing File⇨Publish. For more control, choose File⇨Publish Settings to open the Publish Settings dialog box, as shown in Figure 7-1.

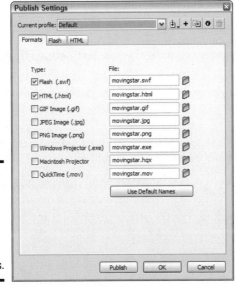

Figure 7-1:
Use the Publish Settings dialog box to publish your movies.

By default, Macromedia Flash MX 2004 creates two files: The SWF file and an HTML file that contains the HTML code needed for your Web page. You can also export your document to other formats by selecting the format you want on the Formats tab. We discuss the HTML code and other export formats in the "Generating HTML and Graphics" section, later in this chapter.

Macromedia Flash creates all these files by using the name of your Flash document and tacking on various filename extensions. If you want to specify the filenames, deselect the Use Default Names check box and enter your own filenames in the text fields.

To post your movie on your Web site, you use the HTML code either by itself or within another Web page. Then you upload both the Web page and the SWF file as you would any other Web page and image.

Macromedia Flash has a lot more options for you to tweak. To set these options, click the other tabs of the Publish Settings dialog box and select the options you want before clicking the Publish button.

Click the Flash tab, shown in Figure 7-2, to see the options for creating the SWF file. You can set the following options:

✦ **Version:** Saves in previous version formats for backward compatibility.

✦ **Load Order:** Controls the loading order of layers in your document for the first frame (which usually takes the longest to display).

Changing the load order can affect how your ActionScript code functions.

✦ **ActionScript Version:** Here you can select the version of ActionScript you'd like to run in your movie. You can click the Settings button to specify the classes to be exported if you select ActionScript 2.0 from the drop-down list.

✦ **Generate Size Report:** Creates a text file that details the size of the frames of your movie, so that you can make adjustments if a movie is loading slowly.

✦ **Protect from Import:** Helps prevent the SWF file from being imported into an FLA file that others could then modify.

Never trust that your SWF is completely safe. Tools to undo this option are available on the Web.

✦ **Omit Trace Actions:** Reduces file size by deleting trace actions if you used them in your ActionScript to help you debug your code.

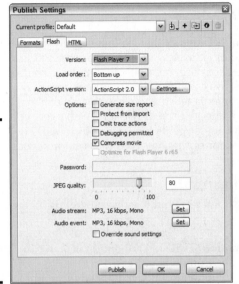

Figure 7-2:
Use the
Flash tab of
the Publish
Settings
dialog box
to set
options for
the SWF
movie file.

✦ **Debugging Permitted:** Enables you to use the Macromedia Flash Debugger feature to debug errors in ActionScript.

The debugger allows you to troubleshoot ActionScript problems from within your browser. You can protect this feature with a password.

✦ **Compress Movie:** Compresses your Flash document, especially text and ActionScript. *Note:* This feature is only compatible with the Flash Player 6 or later.

✦ **Optimize for Flash Player 6:** This feature optimizes your movie for playback on the Flash Player 6.

✦ **Password:** Enables you to enter a password for debugging so that those without the password cannot debug your movie.

✦ **JPEG Quality:** Sets the quality of bitmaps. Higher quality looks better, but means a larger file size.

✦ **Audio Stream:** Sets the audio compression for all stream sounds in the movie, if you haven't set individual settings in the Sound Properties dialog box. Click the Set button to set the compression. See Book V, Chapter 6 for more information on stream sounds.

✦ **Audio Event:** Sets audio compression for all event sounds in the movie. Click the Set button to set the compression.

✦ **Override Sound Settings:** Overrides settings in the Sound Properties dialog box and applies settings here to all sounds in your movie.

Optimizing Movies for Speed

As you work, you should always design for fast display on a Web site. You can't control the speed of your viewers' Internet connections or how fast their computers' processors are, but you can definitely control the size of your movie file. Before you publish your document, you may want to look it over from within Macromedia Flash and see how you can make it more efficient. After you publish and test the movie on a Web page, you may find that you need to make some adjustments for faster download. The following four sections offer some tips for optimizing your movies for speedy display.

Simplifying graphics

You can simplify the graphics in your movie and greatly increase its speed. Here are some pointers:

- **Use tweened animation:** Tweened animation is faster than frame-by-frame animation. (See Book V, Chapter 5.)

- **Don't animate bitmaps:** Macromedia Flash needs to store the location of each pixel in a bitmap, and that greatly increases file size. In fact, avoid bitmaps altogether as much as possible.

- **Turn everything into symbols:** Even backgrounds should be symbols. You can also put symbols inside of symbols. (See Book V, Chapter 3.)

- **Group objects:** Groups also reduce file size. (See Book V, Chapter 2.)

- **Optimize curves:** Optimizing curves reduces the number of lines in your graphics. (See Book V, Chapter 2.)

- **Use solid lines:** Avoid dashed and dotted lines. Especially avoid custom lines. (See Book V, Chapter 2.)

- **Use the Pencil tool rather than the Brush tool:** The Brush tool requires your document to store more information. (See Book V, Chapter 2.)

- **Use the Web safe color palette:** Avoid custom colors. (See Book V, Chapter 2.)

- **Use solid fills rather than gradients as much as possible:** Gradients are more complex to calculate.

- **Avoid transparency:** As much as possible, avoid using alpha values of less than 100 percent.

Optimizing text

Text takes up more bytes in your file than vector graphics. Here are some options for reducing the load:

✦ **Reduce the number of fonts:** Use simpler fonts, fewer font styles (bold, italic), and fewer fonts overall. Use device fonts (sans, serif, and typewriter) if possible.

The three device fonts display correctly in any browser and on any computer.

✦ **Put text into your HTML document:** Not all text needs to be in your Flash document. If you can put some of your text in HTML format, you'll get faster download times.

Minimizing the size of sound files

Sound and music can really hog up the download stream. (See Book V, Chapter 6 for details about working with sounds.) You can use the following techniques to minimize the size of sounds:

✦ **Compress sounds:** Use the Sound Properties dialog box (right-click the sound in the Library and choose Properties from the contextual menu) to fine-tune settings for individual sounds or compress sounds using the sound settings (Audio Stream and Audio Event) on the Flash tab of the Publish Settings dialog box, described earlier in this chapter. Use the MP3 format whenever possible.

✦ **Remove silent areas:** Edit sounds to remove unnecessary beginnings and endings by adjusting the Time In and Time Out controls.

✦ **Reuse sounds:** You can reuse a sound with different in and out points or loop different parts of the same sound.

✦ **Don't loop streaming sound:** It's not necessary, and the browser continually downloads it.

Testing download time

Macromedia Flash can simulate various Internet connection speeds and give you feedback on which frames may cause a delay in download time. Don't miss out on this excellent tool. If the results indicate delays, go back and adjust your movie until everything displays quickly. You don't want to lose your Web site visitors because they get impatient while waiting for your Flash movie to download! Follow these steps to test your movie's download time:

1. **Choose Control⇨Test Movie.**

2. **From the menu bar of the new window, choose View⇨Download Settings and choose a download speed.**

3. **From the menu bar of the new window, choose View⇨Bandwidth Profiler.**

The Bandwidth Profiler is shown in Figure 7-3.

Figure 7-3:
The
Bandwidth
Profiler
shows the
frames that
will display
slowly on a
Web site.

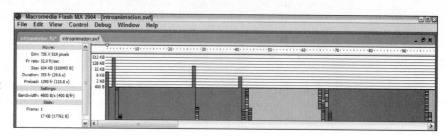

4. **Choose View⇨Simulate Download to simulate playing the animation over an Internet connection.**

Watch for any jerkiness and listen for any breaks in the sound.

5. **Choose View⇨Streaming Graph to see all the frames that may cause delays or View⇨Frame by Frame Graph to see the size of each frame.**

These are just two ways of viewing the information. You can use either view. Click on any bar (which represents a frame) to see the information for that frame. Frames that extend above the red horizontal line may cause a delay in the display of the movie.

6. **Choose File⇨Close to close the movie testing tools.**

A short delay in the first frame is often acceptable as Macromedia Flash downloads all the information. After the first frame, you should try to avoid any delays because they result in pauses or uneven animation.

Although the best solution is to minimize delays, another possible choice is a preloader, a short animation that plays over and over while the main animation is loading. If you want your viewers to get to your movie quickly, work to reduce file size rather than using a preloader. If the artistry and special effects are primary, then use a preloader.

Generating HTML and Graphics

When you publish your Flash document, you also generate the HTML code that you need to create a Web page that plays your animation. You can also export your movie in several other graphic and animation formats.

Creating HTML code

You can use the HTML code that Macromedia Flash generates to create a new Web page that contains nothing but your movie, or you can insert the

HTML code into an existing Web page that may contain many other components. On the HTML tab of the Publish Settings dialog box, you can specify the following settings:

✦ **Template:** Specifies the content of the HTML file. The Flash Only (the default) option includes only `<OBJECT>` and `<EMBED>` tags. Other templates add code to detect earlier Flash Players or offer other features. To see what each template does and which formats you need to choose, select the template and click the Info button.

✦ **Dimensions:** Controls the size of the movie in the browser. The default option, Match Movie, matches the width and height of your Stage. You can also specify the size in pixels or by percent.

✦ **Playback: Paused at Start:** Pauses the movie until your viewer clicks a button (that you have coded to start the movie) or right-clicks and chooses Play. By default, this option is off, so that the movie plays automatically.

✦ **Playback: Loop:** Repeats the movie over and over. By default, this option is on.

✦ **Playback: Display Menu:** On by default, this option displays a contextual menu if viewers right-click. The menu allows viewers to play, loop, and print the movie. However, not all viewers know that this contextual menu exists.

✦ **Playback: Device Font:** Substitutes anti-aliased fonts (that look smoother) for fonts not available on the user's computer. This option is not selected by default.

✦ **Quality:** Sets the quality of playback. Choose one of the following:

 • **Low:** Uses no anti-aliasing (smoothing).

 • **Auto low:** Starts at low quality and switches to the highest quality that the user's computer (detected by the Macromedia Flash Player) can handle.

 • **Auto high:** Starts at high quality and switches to a lower quality if the user's computer (detected by the Macromedia Flash Player) cannot handle high quality.

 • **Medium:** Uses some anti-aliasing, but doesn't smooth bitmaps.

 • **High:** Uses anti-aliasing for everything except tweened bitmaps (the default).

 • **Best:** Uses anti-aliasing for text, unanimated bitmaps, and tweened bitmaps.

✦ **Window Mode:** Specifies how the movie's window relates to the rest of the page in Internet Explorer 4.0 and higher on the PC. Choose Window (a separate window), Opaque (an opaque background), and Transparent (a transparent background).

✦ **HTML Alignment:** Aligns the movie in the browser window. You can choose Default (centered), Left, Right, Top, or Bottom.

✦ **Scale:** Specifies how the movie is placed in its boundaries when you use the Pixels or Percent option of the Dimensions setting and the width and height are therefore different from the movie's original size. The choices are Default (Show All), No Border, Exact Fit, and No Scale.

✦ **Flash Alignment:** Specifies how the movie fits in the movie window (not the browser window). The Horizontal setting can be Left, Center, or Right. The Vertical setting can be Top, Center, or Bottom.

✦ **Show Warning Message:** Displays warning messages if there are problems during publishing.

Creating graphic files

You can create GIF, JPEG, and PNG graphic files from a frame of your Flash movie. Each type of graphics file has its own options. By default, Macromedia Flash creates the image from your first frame.

To add a label to a frame, click the frame and open the Properties panel (Window⇨Properties). Expand the Properties panel by using the Collapse/Expand arrow at the bottom-right corner. Type the label name in the Frame text field. You can name a frame anything you want. Certain names, such as the #Static label, have specific meanings for how Macromedia Flash functions.

GIF files

GIF files have limited colors but allow transparency. Select the GIF check box on the Formats tab of the Publish Settings dialog box. when you do that, you'll see a GIF tab appear. Then click the GIF tab, where you have the following settings:

✦ **Dimensions:** Select the Match Movie option to match the size of the Stage. To use a different size, deselect the Match Movie option and type the new dimensions.

✦ **Playback:** Select either the Static (a single image) or Animated (an animated GIF of the entire movie) option. If you select Animated, you can choose to loop continuously or repeat a specified number of times.

✦ **Options:** You have several options to choose from:

- **Optimize Colors:** Select the Optimize Colors option to remove unused colors.

- **Interlace:** Select the Interlace option to load in increments of greater resolution (starting from fuzzy).

- **Smooth:** Select the Smooth option to anti-alias the artwork.

- **Dither Solids:** Select the Dither Solids option to approximate colors not available on the GIF color palette.

✦ **Transparent:** Allows you to set transparency (alpha) of the background.

✦ **Dither:** *Dithering* is the approximation of a color from a mixture of other colors when the desired color is not available. This option defines the type of dithering. You can choose Ordered dithering, which provides good-quality dithering without much increase in file size, or you can choose Diffusion dithering, which provides top-quality dithering for the 216 Web safe colors but makes for a larger file size.

✦ **Palette Type:** Defines the GIF color palette. If you choose an adaptive palette, a unique color palette is created for the GIF. You can then choose the maximum number of colors. If you choose a custom palette, click the ellipsis button and choose a palette file. To save a palette of colors that you use in Macromedia Flash, choose Window⇨Design Panels⇨Color Swatches, click the Options menu icon in the upper-right corner of the Color Swatches panel, and choose Save Colors.

JPEG files

JPEG files allow for many colors but do not allow transparency. They decompress when downloaded, taking up more memory. Select the JPEG check box on the Formats tab of the Publish Settings dialog box. Then click the JPEG tab (it appears after you select the JPEG check box), where you have the following settings:

✦ **Dimensions:** You can match the size of the Stage or specify another size.

✦ **Quality:** Choose the quality. Higher quality means a better picture but a larger file size.

✦ **Progressive:** Displays the JPEG file in increments of greater resolution (starting from fuzzy) as it downloads in a browser.

PNG files

PNG files offer many colors and transparency, too. Select the PNG check box on the Formats tab of the Publish Settings dialog box. Then click the PNG tab (it appears after you select the PNG check box), where you have the following settings:

✦ **Dimensions:** You can match the size of the Stage or specify another size.

✦ **Bit Depth:** Controls the number of colors the image can contain and the availability of transparency (alpha). More colors — and adding transparency — increase the file size.

✦ **Options:** You have several options to choose from:

- **Optimize Colors:** Select the Optimize Colors option to remove unused colors.

- **Interlace:** Select the Interlace option to load the PNG file in increments of greater resolution (starting from fuzzy).

- **Smooth:** Select the Smooth option to anti-alias the artwork.

- **Dither Solids:** Select the Dither Solids option to approximate colors not available on the GIF color palette. Same as for GIF images (explained previously).

✦ **Dither:** If you choose an 8-bit depth, use the same Dither settings as for GIF images. This option is not available for other bit depths.

✦ **Palette Type:** If you choose an 8-bit depth, use the same Dither settings as for GIF images.

✦ **Max Colors:** Same as for GIF images.

✦ **Palette:** Same as for GIF images.

✦ **Filter Options:** Determines the method of compression (the method of combining pixels in an image). Choose from the following options:

- **None:** No compression.

- **Sub:** Filters adjoining pixel bytes, going horizontally.

- **Up:** Filters vertically.

- **Average:** Uses both horizontal and vertical.

- **Path:** Creates an algorithm using the three nearest pixels to predict the next pixel.

- **Adaptive:** Provides the most accurate colors.

Creating QuickTime movies

QuickTime is a video format that plays on the QuickTime player. To use QuickTime movies, you need to have QuickTime 4, 5, or 6 installed.

The Macromedia Flash Player doesn't always keep up with QuickTime versions. A movie that you create in Macromedia Flash may not work with the latest version of QuickTime.

Select the QuickTime check box on the Formats tab of the Publish Settings dialog box. Click the QuickTime tab that appears, where you have the following settings:

✦ **Dimensions:** You can match the size of the Stage or specify another size.

✦ **Alpha:** If you have combined a QuickTime movie with a Flash movie, this option sets the transparency of the Flash track within the QuickTime movie. A QuickTime movie can contain a separate layer with the Flash movie. The Auto option makes the Flash track transparent only if it is on top of other tracks. The Alpha-transparent option always makes the Flash track transparent. The Copy option makes the Flash track opaque, hiding all content behind it.

✦ **Layer:** Specifies how the Flash track is layered with the QuickTime content. Choose from Auto (Flash track on top if Flash content appears in front, otherwise on the bottom), Top (Flash track on top), and Bottom (Flash track at the bottom).

✦ **Streaming Sound:** Select the Use QuickTime Compression check box to export sound to a QuickTime soundtrack. Click Setting to specify how the sound is compressed.

✦ **Controller:** Creates a control panel to play the movie. Choose None if you have created your own controller or don't want viewers to have any control. The Standard option displays the QuickTime controller. The QuickTime VR option offers special panoramic and 3D viewing features.

✦ **Playback:** Select the Loop check box to repeat the movie, the Paused At Start check box to let viewers use the Controller to start the movie, or the Play Every Frame check box to disable skipping frames and sound to maintain timing.

✦ **File:** The Flatten (Make Self-Contained) option combines the Flash movie with imported content into a QuickTime movie. If you don't select the Flatten check box, the QuickTime movie references the Macromedia Flash SWF file.

Creating self-playing movies

Self-playing movies are called *projectors*. A projector doesn't require a separate Macromedia Flash Player and is ideal when you are putting a Flash movie on a CD-ROM. To create a projector, select the Windows Projector or the Macintosh Projector check box on the Formats tab of the Publish Settings dialog box. Then click the Publish button. The result is a file with an `.exe` extension (for PCs) or an `.hqx` extension (for Macs). The projector file is larger than an SWF file, but users can download it from a Web site and play it without needing the Flash Player.

Exporting movies and images

Export a movie or image, instead of publishing it, when you need to use it in another application. For example, you can export a frame as a GIF file and insert it into a PowerPoint presentation. If you already have the HTML code and just want to update an SWF file, you can export instead of publish:

1. **Select the frame you want to export, if you are exporting an image.**

2. **Choose File⇨Export Image or File⇨Export Movie.**

3. **Type a name for the image or movie.**

4. **From the Save as Type drop-down list, select a file type.**

5. **Click Save.**

A dialog box may appear if the format you choose has settings that you can specify. These settings are the same as you have when you publish a file and are explained in the section, "Generating HTML and Graphics," earlier in this chapter. You can export the following file types:

✦ Adobe Illustrator (.ai)

✦ Encapsulated PostScript (.eps)

✦ Drawing Exchange Format (.dxf)

✦ Windows Bitmap (.bmp)

✦ Metafile (.emf/.wmf)

✦ FutureSplash Player (.spl)

✦ Graphics Interchange File (.gif)

✦ Joint Photographic Experts Group (.jpeg/.jpg)

✦ QuickTime (.mov)

✦ PICT Sequence (.pct)

✦ Portable Network Graphic (.png)

✦ Video for Windows (.avi)

✦ Windows Audio (only) (.wav)

Chapter 8: Getting Interactive with ActionScript

*F*lash documents are fully programmable using the built-in language, ActionScript. Before we go any further, let's be clear: You don't need to be a programmer to use ActionScript. Nonprogrammers can do a lot with ActionScript. However, if you are a programmer, you certainly have an advantage. In this chapter, we explain how a nonprogrammer uses ActionScript.

Exploring the Role of ActionScript

Although you can do many interactive tasks without ActionScript, including some of those in the following list, ActionScript gives you the ability to control your movies. Here are some things you can do with ActionScript:

+ Create a button to take your viewers to another Web page.

+ Loop a movie clip through a small range of frames.

+ Let your viewers drag objects on your Web site to new locations. (An example would be a site where viewers drag images of furniture onto a floor plan to see if it fits.)

+ Create a preloader, a short animation that plays while a longer movie loads.

+ Set the properties, such as location and size, of movie clip instances. (See Book V, Chapter 3 for an explanation of movie clips and instances.)

+ Create an animated *mask* (a shape that hides everything on the Stage except what is just behind the shape).

+ Play or stop animation.

In certain cases, you need to use ActionScript. For example, a button is useless without some ActionScript. You can create wonderful animation with no ActionScript at all, but adding ActionScript opens many possibilities for interactivity on your Web site, and it's easy to use after you get some practice.

Because ActionScript tells your movie what action to take, the code is often called *actions*. Adding ActionScript is the same as adding actions.

ActionScript is very similar to JavaScript, a programming language used on Web pages.

Using Actions in Your Movies

Macromedia Flash MX 2004 offers a wide variety of actions that you can use, the basics of which we cover here. You can get more information several ways:

✦ Choose Help➪ActionScript Dictionary.

✦ Take a tutorial by choosing Help➪Using Flash➪Tutorials➪Introduction to ActionScript Tutorial.

✦ Pick up a copy of *Macromedia Flash MX ActionScript For Dummies*, by Doug Sahlin, published by Wiley Publishing, Inc.

To add actions, you use the Actions panel (Window➪Development Panels➪ Actions), which is shown in Figure 8-1 as it appears when you select a frame.

Actions list   Script pane   View options

Title Bar Expand/Collapse arrow   Debugging options

Insert a target path   ActionScript Help

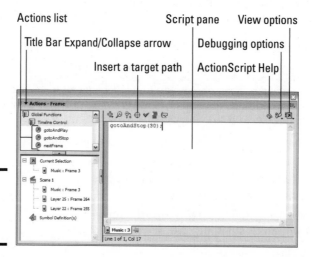

Figure 8-1:
Using the
Actions
panel.

As part of the split of Macromedia Flash into two products, Macromedia Flash MX 2004 and Macromedia Flash MX Professional 2004, the Actions panel has been completely reworked. Even in the entry-level version of Macromedia Flash, the Actions Panel has completely eliminated the visual interface for ActionScript of previous versions in favor of a code-only view. While this makes the products more similar, it actually makes the interface vastly more confusing for the budding ActionScript user.

The Actions panel has the following features:

+ **Title Bar Expand/Collapse arrow:** Use this arrow at the top-left of the panel to expand the Actions panel, as shown in Figure 8-1, and to collapse the Actions panel so that you see only the title bar.

+ **Actions list:** Choose actions and other ActionScript components from this list. Underneath the Actions list, you'll see a status pane that includes exactly where you are in your Flash document.

+ **Script pane:** Displays ActionScript.

+ **Insert a target path:** Click this button to open a dialog box where you can choose from named instances in the drawing if you need to refer to another object.

+ **Options area:** At the top right of the Actions panel are three buttons that allow you to set various options in the panel. When clicked, the book icon brings up the ActionScript Help in the Help panel. Click the stethoscope icon (interesting choice!) to bring up a pop-up menu with code debugging options. And finally, click the View Options button to add line numbers, see the key commands for ActionScript commands in the reference, and to invoke the word wrap feature.

Timeline Control actions

The first grouping of actions in the Actions panel, which you can open by choosing Window⇨Development Panels⇨Actions, contains the Timeline Control actions. In Macromedia Flash MX 2004, these actions are part of the Global Functions suite of ActionScript functions. These actions control the Timeline of a movie, and they are the most commonly used functions. You can choose from the following actions:

+ `gotoAndPlay`: This action tells your movie to go to a different frame and then continue to play at the new frame.

+ `gotoAndStop`: This action tells your movie to go to a different frame and then stops the movie at the new frame.

+ `nextFrame` and `prevFrame`: This action will take you to the next or previous frame.

- ✦ nextScene and prevScene: This action will take you to the next or previous scene in the scene order.

- ✦ play: This action tells a movie to start playing.

- ✦ stop: This action stops a movie from playing.

- ✦ stopAllSounds: This action stops any sounds from playing.

It's important to note that all of these actions are case-sensitive. So, be sure that you've got them input in the Script pane properly or your ActionScript won't work properly.

Browser/Network actions

The Browser/Network category contains actions that connect your movie to the world outside it. Here's a sample of some of the more common actions in this category:

- ✦ fscommand: This action is an advanced command that enables you to control other applications. You can use this command to execute JavaScript on the Web page.

- ✦ getURL: This action creates a hyperlink to another Web page or Web site.

- ✦ loadMovie: This action loads either a single SWF file or JPEG image.

- ✦ unloadMovie: This action unloads a loaded movie.

Movie Clip Control actions

Movie Clip Control actions control movie clips, of course. Some of the more commonly used actions are noted here:

- ✦ duplicateMovieClip: This action makes a copy of a movie clip.

- ✦ on: This action defines the mouse event that triggers the action. It is used for buttons and is added automatically when you are adding ActionScript to a button.

- ✦ onClipEvent: This action specifies the event that triggers a movie clip action. It is inserted automatically when you add an action to a movie clip.

- ✦ removeMovieClip: This action deletes a movie clip, usually one created with the duplicateMovieClip action.

- ✦ setProperty: This action sets various size, visibility, and position properties of a movie clip.

- ✦ startDrag: This action makes a movie clip draggable on the browser screen. You can add this action to a button inside a movie clip, so that the movie clip responds to the mouse.

+ stopDrag: This action stops a drag that was started with startDrag.

+ updateAfterEvent: This action updates the display of a movie clip after a specified event, such as dragging.

Advanced actions

If you're ready to do a little programming, you can use many more options. For example, ActionScript contains a large number of built-in *methods,* which modify symbol instances. ActionScript programmers create *variables* that store values and use them later on in the script. You can create code that executes only if and when certain conditions exist. For more information, see Macromedia Flash's ActionScript dictionary, which you can access by choosing Help⇨ActionScript Dictionary.

To help you understand what you've written, you can (and should) add comments that explain what is going on. *Comments* are lines within the ActionScript code that are ignored when the code is processed. To add a comment, place two forward slashes (//) before the comment text.

Here are some basics about how to write ActionScript:

+ You can use operators such as + and *or* to calculate values.

+ You can use built-in functions to obtain information about objects before you change them.

+ You can change certain properties of objects with setProperty, such as

  • Alpha (transparency)

  • Height

  • Rotation

  • Visibility (yes or no)

  • Height and width

  • X and Y location

  • X and Y scale

Creating Frame Actions

You can add actions to three places: frames, buttons, and movie clips. When you add actions to movie clips, you add it to the instance (copy) of the movie clip symbol that you insert on the Stage. You can also insert actions on the Timeline of movie clips.

Movie clips have their own Timeline and therefore their own set of frames.

If you add an action to a frame, the action is executed when the animation reaches that frame. For example, if Frame 20 has an action to go to Frame 1, when Frame 20 is loaded, the movie jumps to Frame 1. You can use frame actions to load a movie clip at a certain frame, to stop a movie from running, or to automatically send the user to another URL or another frame.

To add an action to a frame, follow these steps:

1. **Create a new layer by right-clicking a layer and selecting Insert Layer from the contextual menu.**

   A common name for this new layer would be Actions. (You can put actions on existing layers, but we recommend placing actions on a special layer so that you can easily find them.)

2. **Click a keyframe on the new layer.**

   Because the action means a change occurs in that frame, you need a keyframe. If necessary, insert a keyframe by right-clicking and choosing Insert Keyframe from the contextual menu that appears.

3. **If it is not open already, open the Actions panel by choosing Window⇨Development Panels⇨Actions.**

   If the panel is open but collapsed, click the Expand/Collapse arrow on the Actions panel's title bar. (Refer to Figure 8-1. Notice that the title bar of the Actions panel says Actions - Frame because you have clicked a keyframe.)

   See Book V, Chapter 1 for more on managing panels.

4. **To choose an action, click a category (such as Global Functions) and a subcategory (such as Timeline Control) from the upper-left pane of the Actions panel, and then double-click the action you want (or drag it to the Script pane).**

   If the action needs parameters to specify how it works, you can mouse over the ActionScript on the Script pane and see what values the ActionScript function can accept.

5. **Type the required parameters in the parameter text fields or choose them from the drop-down lists.**

   Each action requires different parameters. The appropriate parameters for an action appear when the ActionScript is inserted and when you highlight a line of ActionScript containing that action. For information about the parameters required for any action, choose Help➪ActionScript Dictionary and locate the action from the alphabetical list.

Some parameters display an Expression check box at the right. Select the check box if you want the parameter to be considered as an expression, which means that the ActionScript can calculate its value. Macromedia Flash defines an *expression* as any combination of ActionScript symbols that represent a value. Deselect the check box if you want the parameter to be considered literally. (For example, the word "Hello" should be considered literally as a string of text.) Also, in many cases, you need to refer to another object, such as a movie clip. Click the Insert a Target Path button to get a list of appropriate objects.

To get the Actions panel out of the way, click the Collapse/Expand arrow on its title bar. Press Ctrl+Enter to test your movie and see the result of your ActionScript.

For a detailed list of actions, see the section, "Using Actions in Your Movies," earlier in this chapter.

For example, to add a `gotoAndPlay` action that sends the movie from the last keyframe to Frame 20 and plays from there, follow these steps:

1. **If Frame 20 is not a keyframe, right-click Frame 20 and choose Insert Keyframe.**

2. **Click the last keyframe.**

3. **Open the Actions panel (choose Window➪Development Panels➪ Actions or click the Actions panel's Expand/Collapse arrow).**

4. **On the upper-left pane of the Actions panel, click Actions, and then click Timeline Control.**

5. **Double-click** `gotoAndPlay`.

6. **Input either the frame number or the name of the frame and scene inside the parentheses.**

   If you include the frame number, you would just input the number. If you include the scene, include the name of the scene followed by a comma, followed by a space and the frame. The frame can be either a number or, if the frame has a label, the label name. In this example, you would type **20** between the parentheses.

7. **Test the movie (press Ctrl+Enter) to check that it goes from the last keyframe to Frame 20.**

Creating Button Actions

Buttons are your key to interactivity on your Web site. Buttons are especially attuned to the actions of the mouse. You can add ActionScript to a button that executes an action when the user passes the mouse pointer over the button or clicks it. For information on creating buttons, see Book V, Chapter 3.

To add an action to a button, follow these steps:

1. **Create the button, or if you created the button earlier, drag an instance from the Library onto the Stage.**

2. **Select the button and open the Actions panel, if it is not already open, by choosing Window⇨Development Panels⇨Actions.**

   If the panel is open but collapsed, click the Expand/Collapse arrow on the Actions panel's title bar. (Notice that the title bar of the Actions panel says Actions - Button because you have selected a button.)

3. **From the upper-left pane of the Actions panel, choose a category (such as Global Functions) and subcategory (such as Browser/Network), and then double-click an action (such as getURL).**

   The getURL action sends the user to the URL that you specify. You can also drag the Action from the Action list to the Script pane using the Selection tool.

4. **If the action requires parameters, click the line of code that contains the action itself and enter the necessary information in the parameter text fields.**

   For more information about the parameters required by each action, consult the ActionScript dictionary. Choose Help⇨ActionScript Dictionary.

To add an action to a button, you need to specify what type of mouse action activates the ActionScript. Because the mouse option determines when the action takes place (such as when the mouse button is released), it is called an *event.* You can choose from the following button events:

✦ **Press:** The action is executed when the viewer clicks the mouse button.

✦ **Release:** The action is executed when the viewer releases the mouse button. This is the most commonly used button event, because the release of the mouse button means that the viewer has completed the click.

✦ **Release Outside:** The action is executed when the viewer releases the mouse button outside the hit area.

+ **Key Press:** The action is executed when the viewer presses the specified key. Use this in addition to a mouse event to enable viewers to use the keyboard instead of the mouse. A commonly used key is the Enter key.

+ **Roll Over:** The action is executed when the viewer passes the mouse cursor over the button's hit area, but doesn't click.

+ **Roll Out:** The action is executed when the viewer leaves the hit area.

+ **Drag Over:** The viewer passes the mouse cursor over the button's hit area while holding down the mouse button.

+ **Drag Out:** The viewer leaves the hit area while holding down the mouse button.

As an example, to add a `getURL` action to a button that functions when the button is clicked, follow these steps:

1. **Create the button.**

   For instructions, see Book V, Chapter 3.

2. **From the Library (Window⇨Library), drag an instance of the button onto the Stage.**

   The button should have a border around it, indicating that it is selected.

3. **Open the Actions panel (choose Window⇨Development Panels⇨Actions or click the Actions panel's Expand/Collapse arrow).**

   The Actions panel should say Button on its title bar. If it doesn't, click the button again.

4. **From the upper-left pane of the Actions panel, click Actions, and then click Browser/Network. Double-click `getURL`.**

   Your code in the Script pane should look like this:

   ```
   getURL();
   ```

5. **In the Script pane, enter the URL you've chosen inside quotes.**

   If the URL is within a Web site, it can be local, meaning that you don't need `http://`. If you want the button to send viewers to another site, you need the full URL, including the `http://`.

6. **To specify a target window for the URL, add it after the URL in the `getURL` function as displayed in the Script pane.**

   These are the same options used with the `<A>` tag in HTML:

   • `_self`: Opens the URL in the same window.

   • `_blank`: Opens the URL in a new window.

- _parent: When frames are used and one file is nested inside another, opens the URL where the inner file was.

- _top: When frames are used, loads the URL in the topmost frame, and the new page fills the entire window.

If you wanted to load a new window, and your URL is www.somesite.com, the resulting ActionScript would look as follows:

```
getURL("http://www.somesite.com", "blank");
```

Even though Flash doesn't add the quotes in for you when you add the getURL function to the Script pane, you will need quotes around both the URL and the target.

7. Add the appropriate button code around the getURL function.

As noted previously, you have several button event options. To call the URL when the button is pressed, you'd add the following code around the getURL function:

```
on (Press) {
  getURL("http://www.somesite.com", "_blank");
  }
```

8. Choose Control⇨Test Movie and click the button to check if the getURL action works.

If you used a local URL, the button won't work unless the movie is published and uploaded to the domain for that URL.

Chapter 9: Creating Interfaces with Components and Forms

In This Chapter

✔ **Inserting components**

✔ **Building forms**

Macromedia Flash MX 2004 is not limited to creating animation. You can use Macromedia Flash to develop an entire interface, including buttons, menus, forms, scroll bars, and more. Macromedia Flash includes a set of interface elements called components that you can use to efficiently add interfaces and interactivity to your Web site. In this chapter, we show how you can use components and create forms with Macromedia Flash.

Macromedia Flash can create very innovative interfaces. As long as you keep your Macromedia Flash interfaces user-friendly and easy to understand, your viewers will appreciate the new look and feel. Scroll bars created with Macromedia Flash are a lot cooler than the ones created in most professional programs because you can customize how they look and function. Creating scroll bars and other interface elements for your Web page with Macromedia Flash may actually be easier than with other, more complex programming environments, although some of these techniques require a bit of ActionScript programming to make them fully functional.

Components are actually movie clip symbols that contain a set of defined parameters and properties. (For an explanation of movie clip symbols, see Book V, Chapter 3.) You can specify the values of these parameters and properties when you create your Flash document. Using these components ensures that your interface items work together and in a similar manner. Because of the programming that has been done in advance to create the parameters and properties, you need to do less programming for each Flash document you create.

You can customize the appearance of components to match the rest of your Web site's style. If you know some ActionScript, you can even create your own components, and you can find components that Flash developers have created on Flash resource Web sites.

Adding Components

Components can be as simple as a check box or as complex as an entire graphical user interface. The following list represents a majority of the components included in Macromedia Flash MX 2004:

✦ **Radio buttons:** Radio buttons are small round buttons. Users can select one choice from several options.

✦ **Check boxes:** Users can select or deselect each check box.

✦ **Push buttons:** Clicking a button makes something happen, like a button symbol in Macromedia Flash. (See Book V, Chapter 3 for more information on working with buttons.)

✦ **Combo boxes:** Combo boxes provide drop-down lists.

✦ **List boxes:** List boxes enable you to offer users a scrolling list of choices.

✦ **Scroll panes:** Scroll panes enable you to create scrollable windows for movie clips.

✦ **Label:** A label is a simple one-line text descriptor that accompanies a field.

✦ **Loader:** A loader loads a movie or a graphic file into memory.

✦ **ProgressBar:** This handy component will show your viewers the progress of a file being loaded.

✦ **TextArea:** A multiline text area that can accept text inputs.

✦ **TextInput:** Unlike the multiline text area, the TextInput accepts only a single line of text.

✦ **Numeric Stepper:** This handy component is great for drop-down-like lists. Use it to make lists of numbers that can be incremented or decremented depending on the keystroke.

✦ **Window:** The Window component creates a window within your Flash movie. This window can have a specific size, as well as header text and even a Close button.

The procedure for working with a component is similar for all the components. However, individual items vary. The general procedure is as follows:

1. **Open the Components panel by choosing Window⇨Components.**

The Components panel is shown in Figure 9-1.

2. **Drag one of the components onto the Stage.**

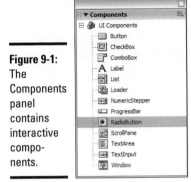

Figure 9-1:
The
Components
panel
contains
interactive
compo-
nents.

3. **With the component still selected, open the Properties panel, if it isn't open already, by choosing Window⇨Properties.**

   If the Properties panel is open but collapsed, click the Expand/Collapse arrow on its title bar.

4. **Click the Parameters tab.**

   The Properties panel with the Parameters tab displayed is shown in Figure 9-2.

Figure 9-2:
After you
place a
component
on the
Stage, you
set its
parameters
in the
Properties
panel. Here
you see the
Properties
panel when
a radio
button is
selected.

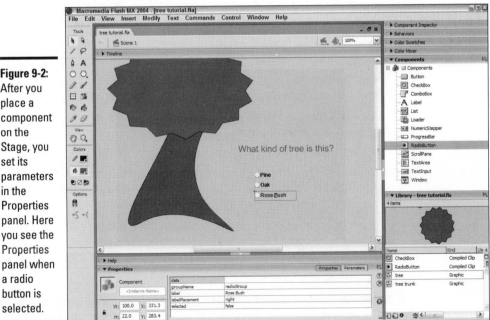

5. **In the Instance Name text field of the Properties panel, type an instance name.**

   Remember that an instance is a single iteration of a symbol. By naming each instance of the component, you can refer to it in your ActionScript.

6. **Set the parameters for the component in the Properties panel by clicking each parameter and entering the value in the field to its right.**

Repeat this procedure with all the components. The individual requirements of the components are listed in the next several sections.

Use the Align panel, which is accessed by choosing Window⇨Align, to line up and evenly distribute a series of components, such as radio buttons or check boxes.

You can resize components using the Free Transform tool, but they are not all infinitely flexible. For example, you can change the width of a check box, but not its height.

Check boxes

The CheckBox component allows users to select one or more choices from a list. Each item on the list has a small box next to it that has a check inside when the user clicks the box. The CheckBox component has the following parameters:

   ✦ **Label:** The Label parameter determines the text that is attached to the component.

   ✦ **LabelPlacement:** The LabelPlacement parameter places the text relative to the rest of the component. You can choose Left or Right.

   ✦ **Selected:** This parameter, when set to True, will show that your check box is already selected when the page is first viewed.

Radio buttons

Radio buttons are like check boxes, except that users can only select one at a time in any group of radio buttons. When a radio button is selected, it has a dot inside its circle. The RadioButton component has the following parameters:

   ✦ **Label:** The Label parameter determines the text that is attached to the component.

   ✦ **Selected:** The Initial State parameter determines if a radio button is initially selected.

✦ **Group Name:** Say that you want to poll your users to see if they like to swim and if they like to run. You want a Yes or a No for each. To create such independent groups of radio buttons, enter a Group Name parameter. Users can select one radio button in each group. For example, if you have four radio buttons, you can put two into a group named Swim and two into a group named Run. You can then label buttons Yes and No in each group and ask users "Do you like to swim?" for the buttons in the Swim group and "Do you like to run?" for the buttons in the Run group. Users can then answer Yes or No to each question.

✦ **Data:** Use the Data parameter to store data related to that button. For example, if you want to know if a user selected the radio button named Yes, you can put Yes in the Data field and use ActionScript to execute an action (perhaps go to a specific Web page) if a user selected the Yes radio button.

✦ **LabelPlacement:** The LabelPlacement parameter places the text relative to the rest of the component.

Push buttons

Push buttons are very similar to the buttons you create in Macromedia Flash. The main reason to use a push button component would be to create a consistent look with other components. However, the included parameters may make them quicker to use and require less code. They have a Label parameter that places text on the button and a click handler that uses a function you write to specify what happens when a user clicks the button.

Combo boxes

A combo box is a menu list of items with a scroll bar to its right. Users can scroll through the list of items and choose one, as shown in Figure 9-3.

Figure 9-3:
A combo box is a scrollable list.

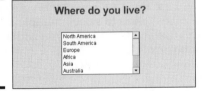

Where do you live?

Like radio buttons, combo boxes have Change Handler and Data parameters. You add the labels for the list items in the Values dialog box as follows:

1. **With the combo box selected, open the Properties panel, if it isn't open already, by choosing Window⇨Properties; or click the Expand/Collapse arrow on the Properties panel's title bar.**

2. **Click the Label row in the Parameter list, and then click the right side of the row to open the Values dialog box.**

   The Values dialog box is shown in Figure 9-4.

Figure 9-4: Use the Values dialog box to enter labels for a combo box.

3. **To add a new list item, click the plus (+) sign and type the label.**

   You can click any label to edit it.

4. **When you're done, click OK.**

The Editable parameter in the Parameter list specifies if the combo box is editable. If this parameter is set to `true`, users can enter text to search for a matching item. If it is set to `false`, users can only select an item.

The Row Count parameter in the Parameter list determines how many items must be in the combo box before the scroll bar is displayed. The default is eight items.

List boxes

A list box is like a combo box, except that (unlike a combo box) it can't be edited by the user, and you can allow users to select multiple items. To allow this, set the Select Multiple parameter to `true`. You add the labels as described in the section, "Combo boxes."

Scroll panes

Scroll panes are rather unusual. They allow you to put movie clips (and only movie clips) inside a scrollable pane. The advantage is to display large movies or images without taking up a lot of space, as shown in Figure 9-5. No programming is necessary. The movie clip must be in the Library, but it doesn't need to be on the Stage.

You can load JPG images into a scroll pane using ActionScript.

You also need to give the movie clip the Export for ActionScript option in the Linkage Properties dialog box:

1. **Open the Library by choosing Window⇨Library, and then right-click the movie clip and choose Linkage from the contextual menu.**

   The Linkage Properties dialog box opens.

2. **In the Identifier text field, enter a linkage name for the movie clip.**

   Usually, the linkage name is the name of the movie clip.

3. **Select the Export for ActionScript option. The Export in First Frame option should also be selected.**

4. **Click OK.**

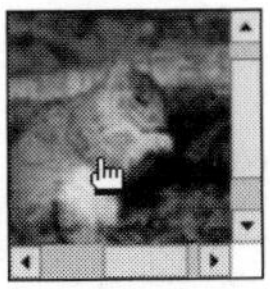

Figure 9-5:
A scroll pane allows you to display a movie clip in a very small space.

Select the scroll pane and display the Properties panel. The ScrollPane component has the following parameters:

✦ **Scroll Content:** In the contentpath area, enter the linkage name of the movie clip.

✦ **Horizontal Scroll:** Using the three available parameters — hlinescrollsize, hpagescrollsize, and hscrollpolicy — you can set the horizontal scroll options. Use hscrollpolicy to turn horizontal scrolling on and off and then use hlinescrollsize and hpagescrollsize to set the amount of movement for the horizontal line and for the pane overall.

✦ **Vertical Scroll:** Using the three available parameters — vlinescrollsize, vpagescrollsize, and vscrollpolicy — you can set the vertical scroll options. Use vscrollpolicy to turn vertical scrolling on and off and then use vlinescrollsize and vpagescrollsize to set the amount of movement for the vertical line and for the pane overall.

✦ **Drag Content:** Set the ScrollDrag parameter to `true` to allow users to drag the movie clip (pan it) to see the hidden portion without using the scroll bars. (The default is `false`.)

Label

The Label component is perhaps the simplest of the components, in that it is not dynamic in any way. It's is simply a label for another form element. That said, there are some settings that can be applied to a label. You can align the text within the label by selecting an autoSize option. You can also specify whether the label will be HTML text or not by selecting `true` or `false` from the HTML option.

Loader

The Loader component allows you to load an SWF movie or a JPEG within a Flash movie, effectively allowing you to play a movie within a movie. There are only a few options that you can specify for this component:

✦ Set autoload to `true` to let Flash load the movie for you in the keyframe the movie begins in.

✦ Provide a path to the SWF or JPEG file to be loaded using the contentPath field.

✦ Allow the movie to be scaled up or down by setting the scaleContent property to `true`.

When you render the movie, Flash renders not only your movie, but the one you've pointed to with the Loader component.

TextArea

The TextArea component creates, as you might expect, a text area on the screen. Four simple options apply to this component. To take advantage of this component, simply drag an instance of it from the Components panel onto the Stage. Here's what you can specify using parameters in the Properties panel:

✦ Make the text box editable (meaning you can type in it onscreen) by selecting `true` from the Editable property field.

✦ If you want the box to be in HTML format, select `true` from the HTML property field. For ease of use, you'll probably want to keep this set to `false`.

✦ If you want the field to be prefilled with text, input some text in the Text property field.

✦ Finally, if you want to use word wrap, be sure to select `true` in the wordWrap property field.

TextInput

Much like the TextArea component, the TextInput component allows viewers to input text on the screen. Again, you add it to your document by dragging an instance of it from the Components panel onto the Stage. In the Properties panel, you can set the following parameters:

✦ Make the text box editable (meaning you can type in it onscreen) by selecting `true` from the Editable property field.

✦ If you want the text field to be a password field, meaning only **** shows up instead of characters, select `true` from the Password property field. The default value is `true`.

✦ If you want the field to be prefilled with text, input some text in the Text property field.

NumericStepper

The NumericStepper can be a handy component when you have lists that have incremental numeric values in them. Essentially, this component creates a list that can be cycled either up or down by using arrows. To use a NumericStepper, simply drag it from the Components panel onto the Stage. There, you can specify the following through the Properties panel:

✦ To set the maximum value of the NumericStepper, input an integer in the Maximum property field.

✦ To set the minimum value of the NumericStepper, input an integer in the Minimum property field.

✦ The StepSize determines how big the increments are from step to step. Again, input an integer here.

✦ In the Value field property, input the initial value of the NumericStepper.

Window

Another interesting tool for adding some cool interactivity to your interface is the Window component. This component adds a window to your Flash movie. This can be useful if you're zooming in or loading a picture in your movie. You create a window by dragging it from the Components panel onto the Stage. Then, you can specify the following:

✦ If you want the window to be able to be closed, select `true` from the CloseButton property field.

✦ To load a picture into the window, provide a path to the image in the contentPath property field.

✦ If you'd like the window to have a text title, enter it in the Title property field.

Setting component properties

You can set the color and text properties of a component using Action-Script. You can also globally set properties of all the components in your movie. Finally, you can create *skins,* graphic elements that affect how components look. These methods are beyond the scope of this book. For more information, see Flash Help.

Creating Forms with Macromedia Flash

You can create forms that users can complete online. You can capture the information that users input into the forms and either use it elsewhere on your site or send it to a server and place it in a database. Forms are a great way to collect data about your users.

Collecting data within a Flash movie

You can collect data within a Flash movie to personalize the site. For example, if a user enters a name (Joe) and favorite book genre (science fiction), you can send the user to a page (or Flash frame) that incorporates the user's input, such as a page with the message shown in Figure 9-6.

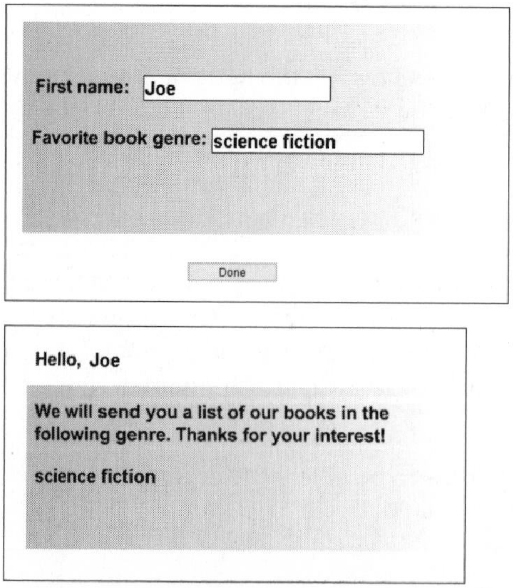

Figure 9-6:
This Flash form stored the user's name and interest and responds based on the results.

Creating this type of form requires some ActionScript. In general, advanced ActionScript is not covered in this book, but here we give you the Action-Script needed to accomplish this form.

To create this form, start a new movie and follow these steps:

1. **Use the Text tool to create the labels (such as First Name and Favorite Book Genre) on a separate layer, using the default static text.**

   You set the type of text in the Text Type drop-down list of the Properties panel.

2. **Next to each text label you just entered, create a new text field by dragging the TextInput component from the Component panel.**

3. **For each text field, choose an instance name and enter it in the Instance Name text field of the Properties panel.**

   We use the instance names `firstname` and `favorite`; these names are used later in the ActionScript.

4. **Use the Components panel to drag a push button onto the Stage.**

5. **In the Properties panel, type a label for the button, such as Done, and change the Click Handler to Done.**

   The Click Handler, Done, is used in the ActionScript as a function to tell Macromedia Flash what to do when the button is clicked. Your screen should be similar to the top image in Figure 9-6.

6. **Insert a new keyframe in Frame 2 of all the layers.**

7. **On the text layer of Frame 2, rearrange the text fields, as in the bottom image of Figure 9-6.**

   These text fields should have the same instance names as they did in Frame 1.

8. **Select each of the text fields with instance names and change their text type to Dynamic from the Text Type drop-down list of the Properties panel.**

   Dynamic text comes from another location and is dynamically placed into the SWF file when viewed. In this case, viewers input text in Frame 1 and the text they input is inserted into the dynamic text fields in Frame 2.

9. **Open the Actions panel by selecting Window⇨Development Panels⇨Actions or by simply pressing the F9 key.**

10. **Add a new layer and name it Actions.**

11. **Click Frame 1 of the Actions layer and type the following in the Script pane of the Actions panel:**

```
stop();
this.firstname.text = "";
this.favorite.text = "";
function done() {
    _global.myName = this.firstname.text;
    _global.myFave = this.favorite.text;
    gotoAndStop(2);

};
```

This ActionScript stops the animation on Frame 1 so that nothing happens until the viewer clicks Done. The next two lines reference the text fields on the current Timeline (using "this") to empty the two text fields in case they already contain text. The function, Done, creates two variables, `myName` and `myFave` and sets them equal to the text in the firstname and favorite input text fields. These variables are global so you can use them again in Frame 2. Finally, the ActionScript moves the playhead to Frame 2 and stops there.

12. **Click Frame 2 of the Actions layer and type the following in the Script pane of the Actions panel:**

```
stop();
this.firstname.text = myName;
this.favorite.text = myFave;
```

This code stops the animation and sets the two dynamic text fields in Frame 2 to the global variables you created in Frame 1. As a result, the text that viewers input in Frame 1 appears here in Frame 2.

13. **Choose Control⇨Test Movie to see how the form works.**

14. **Fill in the form and click the Done button.**

As you can see, although this form requires some ActionScript, it doesn't require very much. You can modify this ActionScript for your own needs.

The form created in this example is very simple. You can add many other features, such as a Thank You page and form validation.

Posting form data

In the example in Figure 9-6, you may have wondered how you would know to send the user the list of books. In order to accomplish this task, you need to post the data from the form to a Web server. You also post data when you want to collect visitors' names, e-mail addresses, and so on, in order to create a database of visitors.

Posting form data is complex because you need a script (often a CGI script, but there are several kinds) on the server to manage the data. The script sets the requirement for the format of the data you send.

As with HTML forms, you specify a method of sending the information (`get` or `post` are the only two options) and a URL. You can use the `loadVariables` function to load variables to a CGI script. Here is an example:

```
loadVariables("http://www.website.com/cgi-bin/scriptname.cgi", "", "POST")
```

For more information, choose Help➪ActionScript Dictionary and look up the `loadVariables` or `loadVars` functions.

Chapter 10: Integrating Macromedia Flash MX 2004 with Other Macromedia Products

In This Chapter

✔ Integrating Macromedia Flash with Fireworks

✔ Integrating Macromedia Flash with Dreamweaver

✔ Integrating Macromedia Flash with FreeHand

✔ Integrating Macromedia Flash with ColdFusion

All the Macromedia Studio MX 2004 products covered in this book are extremely useful for creating Web sites. If you are responsible for an entire site — content, art, interface, and server-side programming — you can bring the capabilities of the entire Macromedia Studio suite to bear on your site.

The integrated interface means that the programs look and work similarly. For example, the Properties panel basically serves the same purpose in Fireworks MX 2004, Dreamweaver MX 2004, FreeHand MX, and Macromedia Flash MX 2004.

In addition to similar interfaces, the programs also share common tool icons. When you look for the Pen tool in Macromedia Flash, it looks the same as the Pen tool in FreeHand and Fireworks. Nope, sorry, you won't find a Pen tool in Dreamweaver, it's only got WYSIWYG (What You See Is What You Get) tools for inserting graphic objects.

Integrating Macromedia Flash with Fireworks

Macromedia Fireworks is a full-featured Web graphics program. Its native format is PNG, which is a bitmap file format. Fireworks can also work with vector images. You can export Fireworks vector and bitmap images to Macromedia Flash's SWF movie format and then import them into Macromedia Flash.

You can also use the quick export feature to copy an object from Fireworks to the system Clipboard, and then paste it into Macromedia Flash, or you can export selected objects as SWF files. SWF files are generically referred to as Flash movies. You activate the Quick Export feature by clicking the Quick Export icon in the upper-right corner of the Fireworks Document window.

Importing a Fireworks PNG into Macromedia Flash

You can import both PNG files and the SWF files created in Fireworks into Macromedia Flash by choosing File⇨Import⇨Import to Stage. When you import a Fireworks PNG file into a Flash document, you have a tremendous amount of latitude. You can choose to import the file as a movie clip and retain layers, maintain paths as editable objects, and maintain text as editable. Additionally, you can decide to flatten the PNG file into a single bitmap.

If you import a graphic from Fireworks, you can start the editing process from within Macromedia Flash. Select the graphic and click Edit in the Properties panel (Window⇨Properties). Macromedia Flash opens Fireworks, where you can edit the image. In fact, there's even this spiffy Editing from Flash icon, in case you go on an extended break and when you return, you forget what you were doing.

If you import the PNG file into Macromedia Flash and flatten it to a single bitmap, when you edit the file from within Macromedia Flash, Fireworks opens the original PNG file, and you can then edit every object to your heart's content. When you're done editing, click the Done button and Fireworks updates the image in Macromedia Flash. It's known as *roundtrip editing*. Now is that cool or what? Figure 10-1 shows a PNG file being edited in Fireworks.

 Some software is horribly invasive. If you've installed other software after you installed the Macromedia Studio suite, this software may declare itself as the default editor for PNG files. If this happens, you may have to use your operating system to change the associated program for PNG files to Fireworks, or reinstall the Macromedia Studio suite. If this is not feasible, you'll have to choose the Edit With option in Macromedia Flash and navigate to the Fireworks.exe file.

As with other Macromedia products, the interface for Fireworks is very similar to the one you know in Macromedia Flash. So when you are roundtrip editing, it's not like you have to learn a new toolset or anything. You have similar tools, similar panels, and the familiar Properties panel, for example. The similar interface makes it easy to switch between programs without getting confused.

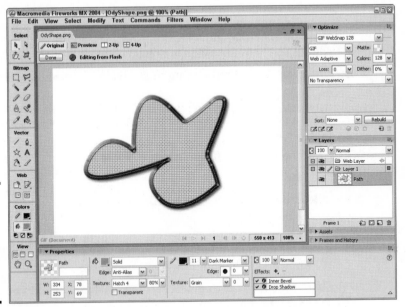

Figure 10-1:
Roundtrip
editing:
From Flash
to Fireworks
and back to
Flash.

Cutting and pasting between Macromedia Flash and Fireworks

Another option is to cut and paste between Macromedia Flash and Fireworks. If you're creating a graphic symbol in Macromedia Flash and it's just not working out, you can use the graphic tools in Fireworks to smooth out the lumps in your graphic by following these steps:

1. **Choose Edit⇨Cut.**

    Macromedia Flash cuts the object to your system Clipboard.

2. **Launch Fireworks.**

3. **Choose File⇨New.**

    Fireworks is so smart, it knows how big the object you cut from Macromedia Flash is, and the document is just the right size.

4. **Choose Edit⇨Paste.**

    Fireworks pastes the object into the new document.

5. **Edit the object in Fireworks.**

    You can use the Fireworks editing tools to modify the object you cut from Macromedia Flash, add objects, and even add layers. However, make sure you've got everything where you want it, because when you select everything in Fireworks and then cut it and paste it back into Macromedia Flash, the objects you added are flattened and cannot be edited. The better solution is to follow Step 6 onward.

6. **After you've finished editing in Fireworks, choose File⇨Save.**

The Save dialog box opens.

7. **Enter a name for the file and navigate to the folder where you want to save the file.**

Fireworks saves the file in its native PNG format.

8. **Exit Fireworks.**

9. **In Macromedia Flash, choose File⇨Import.**

The Import dialog box appears.

10. **Select the file you just saved in Fireworks and click the Open button.**

The Fireworks PNG Import Settings dialog box opens.

11. **Choose the settings that best suit the Flash document you're working on.**

If you want the ability to edit individual objects from the Fireworks file in Macromedia Flash, make sure you don't flatten the image. Import the file as a movie clip and retain layers. If you were editing a symbol when you cut the object from Macromedia Flash, select the Import into New Layer in Current Scene option, and Macromedia Flash imports the PNG file into the symbol you're editing and retains each object from the Fireworks PNG file as individual objects. You can now move individual objects as needed, or create additional layers for the objects.

Integrating Macromedia Flash with Dreamweaver

The Dreamweaver interface is also similar to the Macromedia Flash interface, with bunches of panels — including the ever-present Properties panel. You can use Dreamweaver to create HTML code that holds your SWF files. It's easy to insert SWF files into Dreamweaver Web pages — just click the Flash icon on the Common or Media categories of the Insert bar. You can also use Dreamweaver to generate Flash buttons for use in HTML and CFML pages.

You can open, create, edit, and optimize Macromedia Flash files directly from Dreamweaver. Finally, Dreamweaver now supports ActionScript editing. You can create server-side ActionScript in Dreamweaver and save a document as a Macromedia Flash AS (ActionScript), ASR (ActionScript Remote), or ASC (ActionScript Communication) file. The latter two options will only work if you're using Macromedia Flash MX Professional 2004.

When you have a Macromedia Flash file in a Dreamweaver document and it's not up to snuff, you don't have to exit Dreamweaver and reopen the original FLA file, edit it, and then publish the file again. That would be way too much work. In fact, we're exhausted from just typing the last few sentences. Fortunately, there's a much simpler way. When you're working on a Dreamweaver HTML file that has an SWF movie embedded within it, you can edit the Macromedia Flash file by following these steps:

1. **Select the Macromedia Flash file in the Dreamweaver HTML document.**

   It's the gray rectangle with an F emblazed on it. Note that you must be working in Design or Code and Design (Split) view to do this.

2. **Open the Properties panel.**

   For more information on the Dreamweaver Properties panel, see Book II, Chapter 1.

3. **Click the Edit button.**

   Dreamweaver launches Macromedia Flash, and the Locate Macromedia Flash Document File dialog box appears.

4. **Navigate to the folder where the native FLA file that you published the SWF movie from is stored.**

5. **Select the appropriate file and click the Open button.**

   The native FLA file that you published the Flash movie as opens in Macromedia Flash, and lo and behold, an icon that says Editing from Dreamweaver appears.

6. **Edit the file in Macromedia Flash as needed.**

7. **After editing the file, click the Done button.**

   This publishes the movie again and updates the file in Dreamweaver. Before exiting, you may want to choose Control⇨Test Movie to make sure all is in order.

That's roundtrip editing from Dreamweaver to Macromedia Flash. Too cool.

Integrating Macromedia Flash with FreeHand

Although at one time FreeHand was used mostly to create graphics for printed media, such as magazines, it now has many features that are very valuable for Web site use. FreeHand can create complex vector graphics beyond anything you can create with Macromedia Flash. You can easily import FreeHand graphics into Macromedia Flash by choosing File⇨Import.

When you import FreeHand graphics, you have a great deal of control over how graphics appear in Macromedia Flash. You can do the following:

✦ Assign pages of FreeHand documents to Macromedia Flash scenes or keyframes.

✦ Assign FreeHand layers to Macromedia Flash layers or keyframes, or choose to import the entire FreeHand graphic as one layer (flattened).

✦ Convert lens fills (for example, Magnify and Transparency) to Macromedia Flash equivalents.

✦ Import symbols from the FreeHand Library directly into your Macromedia Flash Library.

You can use the Flash Navigation panel in FreeHand to test SWF files before you export them to Macromedia Flash. FreeHand has an anti-alias display mode that uses Macromedia Flash's anti-alias feature to show you how your FreeHand artwork will look in Macromedia Flash. You can apply hyperlinks and Flash actions to graphics and text from within FreeHand.

FreeHand's animation feature means that you can create animations in FreeHand and use them in Macromedia Flash. This enables you to use the FreeHand vector drawing tools to create a character, bring it to life in FreeHand, and then export it as a Flash 4 or Flash 5 SWF file. After all, vector illustrations are FreeHand's claim to fame.

You can export FreeHand documents as SWF files. Furthermore, you can view FreeHand documents as temporary SWF files, a process similar to choosing Control⇨Test Movie in Macromedia Flash. FreeHand opens a Macromedia Flash Player window, and you can see how your FreeHand document will look as an SWF file.

When you create files in FreeHand with the intention of using them in Flash documents, make sure you use the RGB color model. (See Book IV, Chapter 6 for more about color management in FreeHand.) FreeHand files created with the CMYK color model are converted to RGB when you import them into Macromedia Flash. Macromedia Flash generally does a pretty good job of making the transformation, but if you're a stickler for detail and you want what you see in FreeHand to be what you get in Macromedia Flash, stick with the RGB color model when choosing colors for fills and strokes.

In spite of the fact that FreeHand and Macromedia Flash are distant cousins, if you try to copy an object from Macromedia Flash with the hope of pasting it into FreeHand for some hands-on editing, you can paste the file just fine, but all you can edit is the stroke of the object you created in Macromedia Flash. The fill acts just like a bitmap and refuses to yield to the FreeHand editing tools.

Integrating Macromedia Flash with ColdFusion

When you need to coordinate Flash applications with server-side ActionScript code, you use ColdFusion. ColdFusion supports server-side ActionScript that you can use to create your Macromedia Flash Remoting applications, making it easier to program both sides of the equation (server-side and client-side) in one programming language. *Server-side ActionScript* is a document stored in a directory at the Web server, as opposed to ActionScript in the Flash movie. These features are only available to Web developers who are using Macromedia Flash MX Professional 2004. Macromedia Studio, by default, does not include this version of Macromedia Flash.

Another plus when you use the Macromedia Studio suite is the fact that you can use ColdFusion as a testing server. When you start creating server-side ActionScript in Dreamweaver that dovetails with an application you're creating in Macromedia Flash, you don't have to upload everything to the Web server to test your application. You can use ColdFusion as a local server and test the Flash application (which, as you may remember, is embedded in an HTML file, the pearl in Dreamweaver's oyster), by testing the HTML document in Dreamweaver to make sure all is well.

You can also connect databases with Flash movies to provide personalized or continually updated information to viewers and add special features, such as text search and dynamic charting, to Flash movies.

Integrating Macromedia Flash with other Macromedia products

Macromedia also has two other Flash-related products that you should know about — Macromedia Flash Communication Server MX and Macromedia Flash Remoting MX. These products are for advanced users who want to build communications applications in Macromedia Flash and integrate Macromedia Flash with applications built in ColdFusion or other server-side systems.

Macromedia Flash Communication Server MX

Macromedia Flash Communication Server is a new Macromedia program that enables programmers to develop communications applications for Web sites. Some of the possibilities include the following:

- Video teleconferencing
- Video broadcasting for presentations
- Audio messaging
- Text messaging
- Live chat rooms
- Polling

(continued)

(continued)

- ✔ White boards

- ✔ Message boards (discussion groups)

To write the programming code, you can use Dreamweaver to create server-side Action-Script. A number of prebuilt components are available as downloads from Macromedia's Web site to make it easy to create communications application. For further information, go to the following URL:

```
www.macromedia.com/software/
    flashcom
```

If the previous paragraphs have piqued your interest, you may want to consider downloading the trial version of Macromedia Flash Communication Server. After you download the trial version and install it, you can peruse sample applications that Macromedia has already created for you. If you have a Web cam hooked up to your computer, you can test the video capabilities of Macromedia Flash Communication Server. The Macromedia Flash Player acts as the conduit between your Web camera and the Macromedia Flash Communication Server. You can download the trial version of Macromedia Flash Communication Server at this URL:

```
www.macromedia.com/software/
    flashcom/download/
    components/license.html
```

Macromedia has created some ready-built Macromedia Flash Communication Server components. The ActionScript in these babies is longer than most short stories, but don't fret, you don't have to write it; Macromedia Flash geeks have already done that for you. After you download the Macromedia Flash Communication Server components and install them, you have a new sub-group in the Components panel called Communications Components, as shown in the following figure. Instead of creating the graphics and ActionScript (which is very complicated),

you can just drag one of these components from the Components panel into your Flash application, and you're good to go. You can download the Macromedia Flash Communication Server MX components at this URL:

```
www.macromedia.com/software/
    flashcom/download/
    components/index.html
```

Macromedia Flash Remoting MX

Macromedia Flash Remoting offers tools for programmers to connect Macromedia Flash with a Web server application built with ColdFusion, .NET, or Java. You can integrate Macromedia Flash with databases and Web services by using special ActionScript commands. You can use your elegant Macromedia Flash artwork as the interface to display data from databases. For more information, go to the following URL:

```
www.macromedia.com/software/
    flashremoting
```

Macromedia Flash Remoting is an excellent tool you can use to create dynamic Flash applications. For example, if you want to create a Flash application that displays a slide show, you can use the Flash ListBox or ComboBox component and create a function to populate the ListBox or ComboBox with the titles and file names of the images you want to load. The down side is that if you need to change the images, you have to edit the Flash movie and enter new values in the ListBox or ComboBox. However, if you use Macromedia Flash Remoting, you can access a database that stores the titles and filenames of the images and load them into the Flash application through a ColdFusion component you created in Dreamweaver. The ColdFusion Component (or CFC as the ColdFusion geeks refer to them) is the conduit between your Flash application and the database. If you've dabbled in ColdFusion and feel comfortable with ActionScript, this is your ticket to creating dynamic Flash applications. A cool Flash interface with Macromedia Flash Remoting and the odd ColdFusion Component or four adds up to something very special.

Macromedia Flash Remoting can be accomplished with any server that has ColdFusion installed. If you're creating Macromedia Flash Remoting applications for a client that has a ColdFusion server, you can test the application on your local machine using the version of ColdFusion that ships with the Macromedia Studio MX 2004 application. But the first step is to download the Macromedia Flash Remoting MX Components you find at this URL:

```
www.macromedia.com/software/
    flashremoting/downloads/
    components
```

After you download and install the components, you may be a bit disappointed, because there are no new components installed in Macromedia Flash. That's true, but a whole lot of actions are added to the Actions panel that you find in the Remoting book, as shown in the following figure.

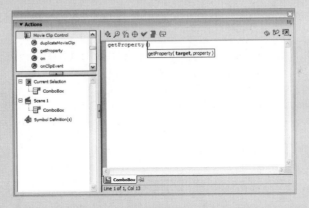

Book VI

ColdFusion MX 6.1 Developer Edition

The 5th Wave   By Rich Tennant

"Great goulash, Stan. That reminds me, are you still scripting your own Web page?"

Contents at a Glance

Chapter 1: Introduction to ColdFusion MX 6.1 Developer Edition

In This Chapter

✔ Defining dynamic Web sites

✔ Understanding the components of ColdFusion

✔ Beginning to work with the ColdFusion application server

✔ Working with databases

✔ Integrating ColdFusion with the rest of Macromedia Studio

ColdFusion MX 6.1 Developer Edition is a rapid development environment for creating dynamic — not to mention compelling — Internet applications. Three main components make up ColdFusion:

✦ An application server

✦ An administrative tool

✦ A custom scripting language

Together, these three components give you a diverse set of tools that make ColdFusion the quickest and easiest way to bring dynamic, interactive, database-driven content to your Web site. (A *database* is a program, such as Microsoft Access, that is used to collect information in tabular format: that is, rows and columns.) In this chapter, we give you a basic introduction to each of the three components as well as an overview of what makes a Web site dynamic.

Creating Dynamic Web Sites

Web pages are wonderful. After you create a page with HyperText Markup Language (HTML) and then upload it to a *Web server* (a program such as Microsoft Internet Information Server [IIS] or Apache that enables people to view your Web site), it's ready to be viewed by the world. If you know HTML, this approach is simple, but it can create problems when your Web site expands in size and complexity. When your Web site grows, you may find yourself wanting to do one or more of the following:

✦ Display Web pages for a variety of different products or services by maintaining the same *look and feel* (each page having the same banner, company logo, background image, and so on).

✦ Sort and display the same content in different ways. For example, you may want to highlight sports articles over news articles on a page if a user is more interested in sports than news.

✦ Customize content based on actions that a user takes at a site.

✦ Personalize content based on preferences that a user sets when visiting your site.

✦ Allow users to perform complex searches of documents and databases.

✦ Create shopping carts and user accounts that keep track of purchases and other shipping information.

If you've ever wanted to do any of these things, you're longing to create a *dynamic* Web site. Dynamic Web sites use a *Web application server,* such as ColdFusion, to extend the capabilities of a standard Web server by creating custom content for each browser request. A Web application server can also connect to a database to retrieve information used to build pages, or it can save information submitted by the user.

To demonstrate what we're talking about, take a look at the Web site for the California Healthcare Foundation, as shown in Figure 1-1. This foundation provides a diverse set of information — reports, studies, analyses — on a wide array of healthcare topics. From the figure, you can see that you can click on any of a number of relevant healthcare-related topics. Within each of these topics are literally hundreds of articles.

Instead of creating *static* (non-changing) pages for each of these topics and their subsequent articles, the foundation can instead use the ColdFusion application server and a database to drive its Web site, which allows the foundation to use a handful of ColdFusion pages to do the following:

✦ Look up the basic information about any number of reports and studies that the foundation funds.

✦ Insert data from a database into a specific topic or report template. A *template* is a bit of HTML and ColdFusion Markup Language (CFML) code that gets combined with data from a database to help construct a Web page. Several templates may make up one individual page.

✦ Display the topic or report page for an item that the user requests via a Web browser.

The idea behind creating a dynamic Web site is that you try to create the least number of templates to represent the largest number of pages on the site. That way, when you change something on the site, you don't have to make the change yourself on every single page.

Figure 1-2 shows a topic within the California HealthCare Foundation. If you compare Figure 1-2 with Figure 1-1, you can see that the topics are different, but the *architecture* (design) of the two pages is identical.

Book VI Chapter 1

Introduction to ColdFusion MX 6.1 Developer Edition

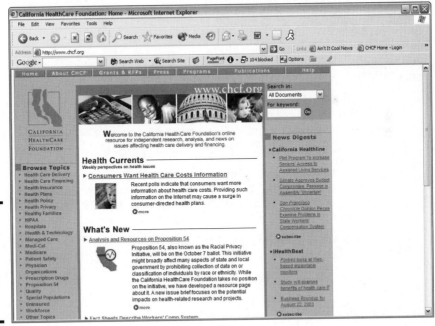

Figure 1-1: The California HealthCare Foundation: a dynamic Web site.

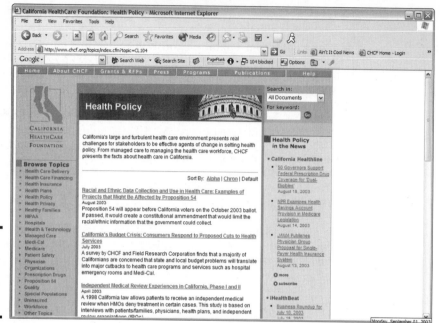

Figure 1-2:
Another
topic
within the
foundation.

Exploring the Components of ColdFusion

The workhorse of ColdFusion is the application server, which provides a fast, reliable platform for your Web applications. In order to make the most of this powerful application server, you need to be able to configure and control it, which you do by using the following:

✦ **ColdFusion Administrator:** The ColdFusion Administrator allows you to configure the server to meet your specific needs. (Read more about this in the upcoming section, "The ColdFusion Administrator," and in Book VI, Chapter 2.)

✦ **ColdFusion Markup Language (CFML):** ColdFusion Markup Language can be used to communicate instructions to the application server. (Read more about CFML in the upcoming section, "Investigating CFML," and in Book VI, Chapter 4.)

The ColdFusion Application Server is built on top of the Java 2 Platform, Enterprise Edition (J2EE). For more information on J2EE, where it came from, and who supports it, check out the Sun Microsystems Web site at `http://java.sun.com`.

Understanding the Role of the Web Application Server

An *application server* executes the business logic of your Web application. By *business logic,* we mean the way in which you want something to run for your business — in this case, how you want your Web site to display content. Your business logic may be as simple as verifying (that is, ensuring that users have entered all the required information) the data that the user enters in a form on your Web page and inserting it into a database. No matter what sort of task you need to accomplish, if it requires any sort of logical processing (conversion of CFML code to HTML), the application server is the component of ColdFusion that does the work.

The infrastructure of most Web applications can be divided into three parts, which are commonly referred to as a *three-tier architecture:*

+ **Display Tier:** A Web browser
+ **Application Tier:** ColdFusion
+ **Database Tier:** Any compatible database

The application server is responsible for managing the interactions between all three of these tiers. It accepts inputs from the Display Tier, interprets the CFML in the Application Tier, and brokers requests to databases at the Database Tier.

Investigating CFML

In a three-tier application, the application server executes all the business logic, as we discuss in the previous section. In ColdFusion, you use CFML to build that business logic.

CFML provides the instructions for each page while it is processed by the application server. Like HTML, CFML uses *tags,* which instruct the application server as to what kind of functions to perform. Built-in tags can handle many common tasks required by Web applications, including the following:

+ Page formatting
+ Form validation
+ Database access
+ Generating and sending e-mail
+ User security
+ Generating charts and graphs

In addition to tags, CFML also includes hundreds of built-in functions (best to think of them as tools built into ColdFusion) that you can use to test and manipulate your data. By adding CFML tags and functions to your pages, you build the instructions for the application server. We cover CFML in more detail in Book VI, Chapter 4.

The ColdFusion Administrator

ColdFusion Markup Language provides the application server with instructions for each page, but some information (such as database connectivity) is only configured once for the entire server — and thus, all the sites that use that server. The ColdFusion Administrator is used to control server-wide settings, such as the following:

✦ Database connections.

✦ Variable scopes. (Check out Book VI, Chapter 3 for more information on what variable scoping means in the context of ColdFusion.)

✦ Debugging options.

✦ Security settings.

✦ Application logging.

The ColdFusion Administrator is not only used to set up your server, but it's also a valuable maintenance tool for reporting on things going on in your Web site. We cover the ColdFusion Administrator, including how to use it to set up database connections, change your logging settings, set your debugging options, and optimize the speed of your Web site, in more detail in Book VI, Chapter 2.

Setting Up the ColdFusion Environment

To begin working with ColdFusion, you need access to a working server. You may want to find an Internet service provider (ISP) that already runs ColdFusion, or you can install your own server right on your desktop PC. Be aware that ColdFusion Server has traditionally been available for both the Unix and Windows environments, but Macromedia Studio is a Windows- and Macintosh-only product, and the Macintosh version of Macromedia Studio does not include ColdFusion.

Finding an ISP

If you need to get a site up and running as soon as possible, hosting your Web application via an ISP saves you the trouble of installing and configuring your own server. You generally have limited control over the server configuration with an ISP, but that drawback is usually outweighed by the other benefits of using an existing server.

A large number of ISPs have offered ColdFusion hosting for years, and many of these providers now support ColdFusion. You need to check the version of ColdFusion that the ISP supports before you sign up. Here are some of the more well-known ColdFusion ISPs:

✦ **CrystalTech:** www.crystaltech.com

✦ **CFDynamics:** www.cfdynamics.com

✦ **Definitive Web Solutions:** www.dwsgroup.com

✦ **Edge Web Hosting:** www.edgeWebhosting.net

Installing the application server

Installing your own application server on your personal computer is a great way to learn about ColdFusion. The Developer Edition is designed for a single user machine for personal development. You would want to install ColdFusion MX 6.1 Developer Edition on a Web server that is going to be put into production. (For more information on ColdFusion, check out the Macromedia ColdFusion site at www.macromedia.com/software/coldfusion.)

The setup wizard on the Macromedia Studio CD walks you through the application server installation process. To set up ColdFusion, just follow these steps:

1. **Insert the Macromedia Studio CD into your CD-ROM drive.**

The auto-run utility brings up an interactive menu from which you can install all the Macromedia Studio programs. If AutoPlay is disabled on your computer, browse to the root directory of your CD-ROM drive (usually the D: drive) and select Setup.exe from there.

2. **Click Install ColdFusion MX 6.1 Developer Edition.**

The Welcome screen appears.

3. **From the ColdFusion MX 6.1 installation screen, select your language and then click OK.**

4. **Click Next at the initial installation screen.**

5. **Select the I Accept the Terms in the License Agreement radio button on the Licensing Agreement screen and then click Next.**

6. **Enter the ColdFusion serial number in the Serial Number field, or select the 30-Day Trial (Enterprise Edition) or the Developer Edition (Single-IP Only) check box, and then click Next.**

If you already have an installation of ColdFusion MX on your system, the installer will preselect the Update ColdFusion MX to ColdFusion MX 6.1

radio button. Otherwise, it selects the Install New Version of ColdFusion MX 6.1 option.

7. **Select the Server Configuration radio button on the Install Configuration screen, and then click Next.**

8. **If you have a previous version of ColdFusion server running on your machine, select Next at the warning screen reminding you to shut down all ColdFusion services.**

It's always a good idea to have ColdFusion completely shut down when installing an upgrade.

9. **Choose a directory where you want to install the product.**

By default, ColdFusion installs the product in `C:\CFusionMX`, and the Web files in `C:\CFusionMX\wwwroot`. You can change this by clicking the Change button. Otherwise, you can just click the Next button to install into the default directories.

As a general rule, if you've got a partitioned drive (meaning a C: drive and a D: drive that are both hard drives), then it's a good idea to install your Web files on the D: drive. This makes it harder for potential hackers to find any other information on your computer, should you be attacked.

10. **Select a Web server you want to use with ColdFusion and click Next.**

For personal development on a single machine, we recommend selecting the Built-in Web Server option (as you may or may not have another Web server installed on your machine). For Microsoft IIS, you can configure the All IIS Websites option. If you choose the Configure Specific IIS Website or Another Web Server radio button, you must click Add and step through the wizard.

Choose the Web server you want to configure, as shown in Figure 1-3. If you choose IIS, then select the individual Web site in the IIS Web Site drop-down list. If you choose another Web server (for example, Apache), enter the path to the Web server's configuration directory (for example, `C:\Apache Group\Apache2\conf`).

If you chose the Built-in Web server option (such as IIS) in Step 10, continue on to Step 11b.

11a. **Enter the Web server's Web root path, and click Next. Continue to Step 11b.**

If you chose any Web server other than the Built-in Web server option (such as IIS) in Step 10, then the installer will prompt you to enter the Web root location for the ColdFusion Administrator, as shown in Figure 1-4. The installer will register this path in ColdFusion as the Web server root, and also create the ColdFusion Administrator directory (CFIDE) in this path.

11b. **Enter and Confirm your Administrator password, and then click Next.**

This password is required to enter into the ColdFusion Administrator.

12. **Review your installation settings and then click the Install button to install the product.**

Installation takes a few minutes, and the progress is shown as the installation is occurring.

13. **After the installation is complete, click the Done button to complete your installation.**

Leave the Launch the Configuration Wizard in the Default Browser radio button selected to go directly into the ColdFusion Administrator and finish configuring your server.

Book VI
Chapter 1

Introduction to
ColdFusion MX 6.1
Developer Edition

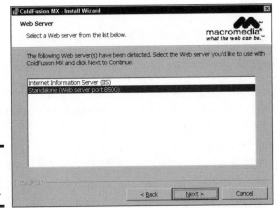

Figure 1-3:
Selecting a
Web server.

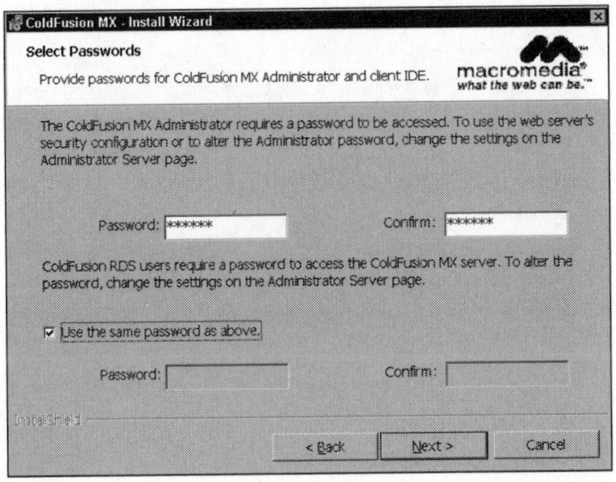

Figure 1-4:
Entering
passwords.

Configuring the application server

After the installation is complete, you can test and configure your application server by loading the ColdFusion Administrator:

1. **Load the ColdFusion Administrator.**

   Do this using the shortcut in the Start menu or navigating directly to `http://localhost:8500/CFIDE/administrator/index.cfm` (`http://127.0.0.1/CFIDE/administrator/index.cfm` **also works**) via your Web browser. (The administrator is a Web-based application.)

2. **Enter your password.**

   Use the username and password for the administrator (as opposed to the RDS; see Step 11b in the list in the preceding section) that you created during the installation process to log on to the administrator, as shown in Figure 1-5.

A number of administrative tasks, including setting up database connections, configuring e-mail, and setting your debugging options are covered in more detail in Book VI, Chapter 2.

If you're using another Web server, such as IIS or Apache, you also need to make sure that that application server is running properly and that it has its default directory as the same location where you installed ColdFusion.

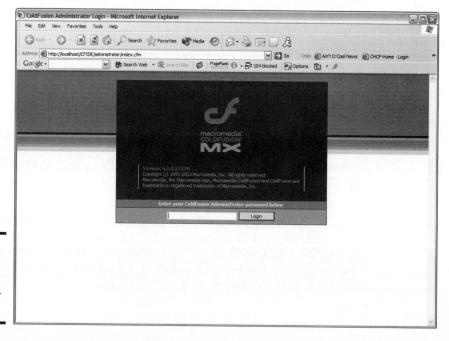

Figure 1-5:
The ColdFusion Administrator logon.

Introducing Databases

Databases are often an integral part of any dynamic site, and ColdFusion is no exception. A *database,* in very general terms, is simply a structured set of data. The power of a database is in the ability to organize data for easy retrieval when requested. If you've ever used a spreadsheet program, such as Microsoft Excel, you've probably created a structured collection of data that could, in fact, be a database.

Databases are generally made up of the following elements:

+ **Tables:** The containers for similar sets of data, made up of columns, rows, and cells. For example, a table might contain *records* (a collection of rows in a table) of all your products.

+ **Cells:** The individual blocks that make up the table. Cells contain only a single piece of data and are grouped by columns and rows.

+ **Columns:** The vertical block of cells that groups the data in the table into categories. Using our previous example of the product table, the data entered into columns in that table might include things like Name, Price, and Description.

+ **Rows:** The horizontal block of cells in a table that contains the information for each individual record, spanning all the columns. Using the example of the product table, a row contains all the information about a single product, such as `Silver Streak Bowling Ball`, `$200`, and `The finest pure silver bowling ball money can buy`.

Databases come in all shapes and sizes, from the simple to the complex. Following are the most common database types:

+ **Flat file:** A text file that contains a single set of columns and rows, with the data usually being separated by commas or tabs. A Comma Separated Values file (CSV) is an example of a flat file.

+ **Relational:** A collection of tables with common data elements (values in like-named columns) between them, providing expanded collection and reporting capabilities. These usually require a query language to retrieve information from the database.

When you become more comfortable with ColdFusion, you begin to see (and of course, we show you!) just where databases can be extremely useful. For now, you can whet your appetite by checking out Figure 1-6, which shows an example of a database table in Microsoft Access. Relational database design, which is central to harnessing the power of ColdFusion, is covered in more detail in Book VI, Chapter 6.

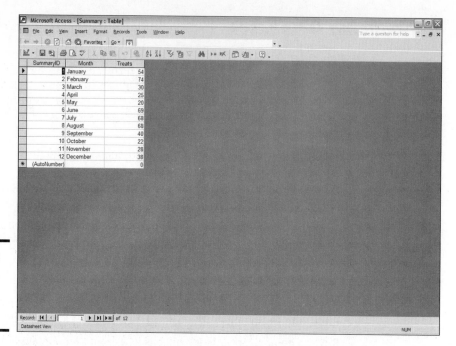

Figure 1-6:
A typical
Microsoft
Access
table.

Taking a Quick Tour of ColdFusion in Dreamweaver

Dreamweaver MX 2004 has been specially designed to make writing ColdFusion pages easier. The great thing about Dreamweaver is its ability to flip back and forth between Code view and Design view:

✦ **Design view:** Enables you to see a visual representation of your page, just like it would appear in a Web browser.

✦ **Code view:** Gives you direct control over the code. If you've used previous versions of ColdFusion Studio or HomeSite (the HTML editor that is part of previous versions of ColdFusion), you may notice that the Code view in Dreamweaver looks similar to those products.

✦ **Split Screen mode:** Displays both the code and the graphical representation on your screen, as shown in Figure 1-7.

When you're using Code view, many features are available to you that are made specifically for ColdFusion development:

✦ CFML toolbars

✦ CFML function auto-complete

✦ CFML validation

◆ Code view that works similarly to previous versions of HomeSite and ColdFusion Studio

◆ Debugging commands

◆ ColdFusion server connection

◆ Drag-and-drop components

◆ Database access

These features are covered in more detail in Book II, Chapter 6.

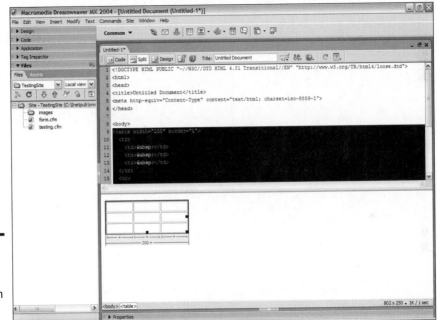

**Book VI
Chapter 1**

Introduction to
ColdFusion MX 6.1
Developer Edition

Figure 1-7:
Dream-
weaver in
Split Screen
mode.

Chapter 2: Working with the ColdFusion Administrator

In This Chapter

- ✔ **Understanding the ColdFusion Administrator**
- ✔ **Creating data sources**
- ✔ **Configuring an e-mail server**
- ✔ **Logging events on the Application Server**
- ✔ **Using debugging options**

*B*efore you begin writing code for your Web application, familiarize yourself with the ColdFusion server. If you're running your own server, you have the ability to set things up just the way you want. Even if you're using a preconfigured server at your Internet service provider (ISP), you want to know how the server is configured to aid in your development process.

This chapter walks you through a few important tasks that are accomplished in the ColdFusion Administrator.

Exploring the Functionality of the ColdFusion Administrator

The *ColdFusion Administrator* is a Web application that helps the human administrator manage the server by controlling a wide array of server settings. Although several of the server settings are aimed at giving the developer important information to assist in the writing of ColdFusion Markup Language (CFML) pages, the ColdFusion Administrator *does not create* CFML pages.

Many of the tasks in the ColdFusion Administrator are directly related to tasks that a ColdFusion developer carries out. For example, a developer cannot query a database if the database is not registered as an active data source through the Administrator. After a server is configured properly with the ColdFusion Administrator, the CFML developer can create a Web application that uses the many features of the application server.

Table 2-1 shows how the server settings correspond to actual CFML pages.

Table 2-1	How the ColdFusion Administrator Helps the Developer
ColdFusion Administrator's Function	*What the Developer Does with That Function*
Configures the e-mail server	Creates Web pages to send e-mail.
Sets up data sources (connections to databases)	Adds, edits, and deletes information in databases.
Sets up search collections	Uses CFML to perform searches on documents and databases.
Sets up debugging options	Outputs all the queries, variables, and processes at the bottom of the rendered ColdFusion page so that developers can monitor and fix their code.
Defines Web services	Creates Web services. A *Web service* is a bridge from your application server to another server with an application that you want to be able to access from within your application. This is a new feature to ColdFusion.

Logging On to the ColdFusion Administrator

Before you can work with any of the administrative tools in ColdFusion Administrator, you must first log on, which is a two-step process:

1. **Launch the ColdFusion Administrator.**

Because the Administrator is a Web application, you access it with your browser. The default URL of the logon page is `http://servername/cfide/Administrator/index.cfm`, where *servername* is the Internet Protocol (IP) number or fully qualified domain name of your server. If you're using the ColdFusion Web server, it uses port 8500, so the URL becomes `http://localhost:8500/cfide/Administrator/index.cfm`.

When you enter this URL, the logon screen appears, as shown in Figure 2-1.

2. **Enter your password.**

When you installed ColdFusion (See Book 6, Chapter 1 for more on installing ColdFusion MX 6.1 Developer Edition), you were asked to provide a password for the Administrator. Similarly, if you're using ColdFusion Administrator at your ISP, your ISP should have provided you with a password to log on to the ColdFusion Administrator. No username is required, and all administrative users use the same password.

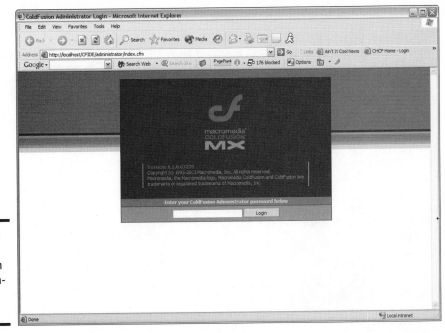

Book VI
Chapter 2

Working with
the ColdFusion
Administrator

Figure 2-1:
The
ColdFusion
Administra-
tor Login
screen.

If you're working in a secure development environment or using Remote
Development Services (RDS), you can choose to turn off the password protection by clicking the CF Admin Password hyperlink or the RDS Password
hyperlink under the Security section in the left navigation frame of the
ColdFusion Administrator. This just means that you'll have one less password to worry about!

Working with the ColdFusion Administrator

The ColdFusion Administrator tasks are divided into five sections. Each of
these sections, and their associated tasks, is listed as a series of text links
on the left-hand side of all Administrator pages. The sections, shown in
Figure 2-2, are as follows:

✦ **Server Settings:** The tasks in this section control how the ColdFusion
server behaves. The settings here affect overall server performance.

✦ **Data & Services:** These tasks control how the ColdFusion server connects to and exposes databases, Verity search indexes (collections
of data used to power ColdFusion's built-in search engine), and Web
services.

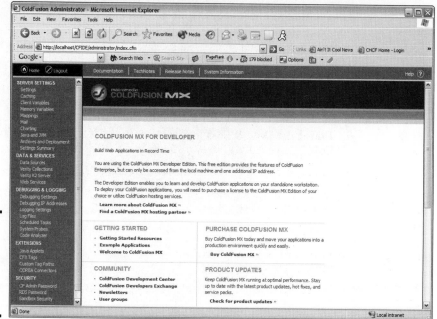

Figure 2-2:
The
ColdFusion
Administra-
tor home
page.

♦ **Debugging & Logging:** This section has tasks used to set debugging and logging options as well as tools to analyze your system and schedule tasks.

♦ **Extensions:** Tasks here allow you to install and remove components that extend the ColdFusion server's capabilities.

♦ **Security:** The security tasks include setting passwords and controlling access to resources.

Creating Data Sources

When you want to use information from a database in your Web application, you need to register the connection to the database with the ColdFusion Server. This registration process creates a *data source*. Each data source has a unique name that you use in your CFML to connect to the underlying database.

Many popular databases, such as Microsoft Access, Microsoft SQL, and MySQL, can be registered as data sources. After your data source has been set up, you can use the `<CFQUERY>` tag to access the data. We show you how to do this in more detail in Book VI, Chapter 4.

Setting up a data source

The exact procedure for setting up a data source varies, depending on the type of database that you're registering. We outline the process below for creating a connection between the ColdFusion server and Microsoft Access. Access is the most common database that is used with ColdFusion. If you are registering a different type of database, the process will be different after Step 4. Here's how you do it:

1. **Under the Data & Services section in the left navigation frame of the ColdFusion Administrator home page, click the <u>Data Sources</u> link.**

   This brings up the Data Sources main page, as shown in Figure 2-3.

2. **In the table titled Add New Data Source, enter a name for your data source in the Data Source Name text field.**

   As a general rule, this name should not include any spaces.

3. **From the Driver drop-down list, select the database driver that matches your database.**

   We use Microsoft Access for this example.

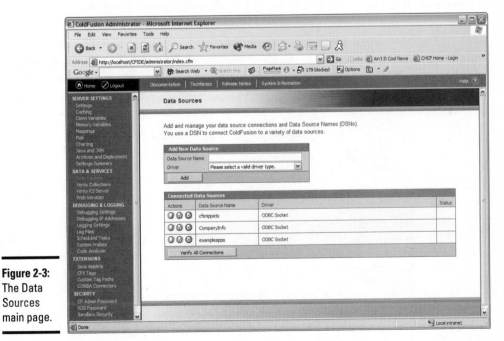

Figure 2-3:
The Data
Sources
main page.

4. **Click the Add button.**

   The Data Source Driver Information page, as shown in Figure 2-4, appears. On this page, you enter specific information about your database.

5. **Click the Browse Server button next to the Database File field to find the database file that you want to register.**

   In this case, the file is a Microsoft Access database, which has the file-name extension .mdb. You can also type the pathway directly in the Database File field.

6. **Leave the System Database File field blank.**

   From this field, you can choose to use Windows NT/Windows 2000 security by selecting a system database. (You click the Browser Server button to select a system database.) In reality, very few people use this feature, largely because of concerns about possible holes in Windows NT/ Windows 2000 security. If you do want to use it, though, the default location for this file is C:\winnt\system32\system.mdw.

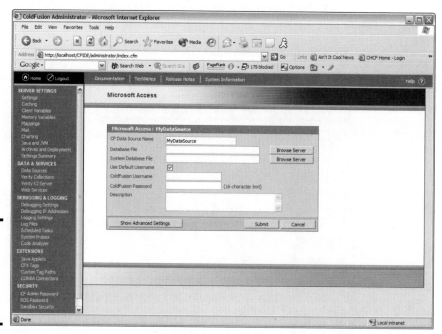

Figure 2-4:
The Data
Source
Driver
Information
page.

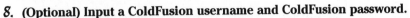

7. **Select the Use Default Username check box to use the Open Database Connectivity (ODBC) default if you do not want to pass a username and password from your** <CFQUERY> **tag.**

8. **(Optional) Input a ColdFusion username and ColdFusion password.**

   This is an optional setting, but you can specify a username and password to pass to the database if no username or password is specified through a ColdFusion <CFQUERY> tag.

9. **(Optional) Enter a descriptive note in the Description text field.**

10. **Click the Submit button.**

   Your new data source is verified automatically. Look for a confirmation message that says OK just below the data sources title in the main working area.

Your new data source will appear in the Connected Data Sources table at the bottom of the page. If the data source was created successfully, the data source name should be highlighted in green, and the status will be OK. If this is not the case, check the top of the page for an error message describing what went wrong.

To use a Microsoft Access database on Windows 98 or Windows Me, you must set up an Open Database Connectivity (ODBC) connection with Windows, and then use the Java Database Connectivity-Open Database Connectivity (JDBC-ODBC) driver from within ColdFusion. The Microsoft Access driver and the ODBC driver that come with ColdFusion will not work on Windows 98/ Me because these drivers require services that are not available under Windows 98/Me.

Other data source tasks

In addition to creating data sources, the Administrator is also used to edit, verify, and delete existing data sources. Each of these operations is represented by an icon in the Connected Data Sources table, which is shown in Figure 2-5.

The following list highlights what each of the data source operations does:

✦ **Edit:** Brings you to the data source settings page

✦ **Verify:** Verifies that the data source is operational and updates the Status column

✦ **Delete:** Begins the process of removing the data source

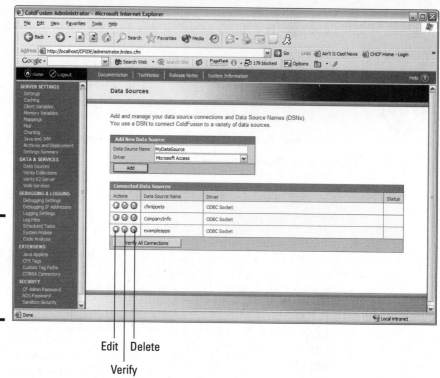

Figure 2-5:
The
Connected
Data
Sources
table.

Edit | Delete

Verify

Connecting to a Mail Server

Although ColdFusion is not a mail server, it can connect to an existing mail server to provide e-mail services to your Web application. This can be exceptionally useful if, for example, you want to send a confirmation e-mail to customers when they purchase a product or sign up for a newsletter. ColdFusion supports both sending and retrieving e-mail by using the Simple Mail Transport Protocol (SMTP) and POP3 protocols, respectively.

ColdFusion uses a spooled architecture to handle sending e-mails. You may be familiar with spooling because it is commonly used for network printers. E-mail spooling uses the same concept to manage the sending of e-mail in a timely manner. When ColdFusion encounters an e-mail request while building a Web page, it sends the request to the spool when it is received. As soon as the e-mail is successfully placed on the spool, ColdFusion continues to create the output page. The spool sends e-mail messages in the order that they were received without holding up the processing of your CFML. Using the spool allows ColdFusion to build pages quickly regardless of the speed of the e-mail server being used.

Use the following steps to set up a connection to an e-mail server:

1. **From the left navigation frame, click the <u>Mail</u> link under the Server Settings section.**

The Mail Server Settings page, as shown in Figure 2-6, appears.

2. **In the Mail Server text field, enter the IP address or the fully qualified domain name (usually `mail.yourdomain.com`, for example) of your mail server.**

3. **Enable the Verify Mail Server Connection option by selecting its check box.**

When this option is enabled, the Administrator attempts to connect to the mail server when you click the Submit Changes button. If a connection cannot be established, you receive an error at the top of the page. You also get a message if the verification succeeded.

4. **Enter the port that the mail server uses in the Server Port text field.**

Normally, mail servers use port 25, which is the default value.

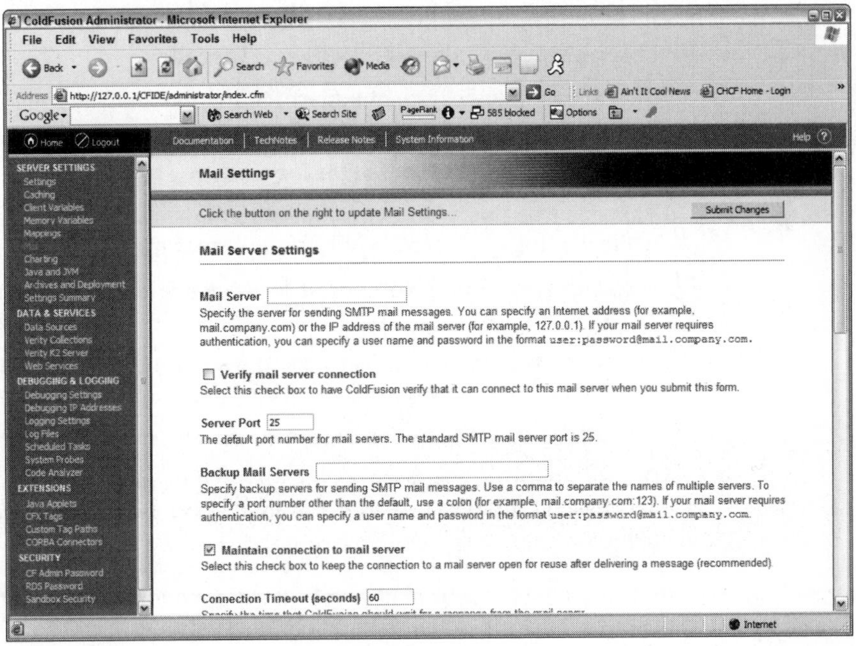

Figure 2-6:
The Mail
Server
Connection
Settings
page.

5. **Enter the IP addresses for any back-up mail servers that you may be using.**

   This is a new (and optional) feature in ColdFusion MX 6.1. In this field, you can specify other mail servers to be used in case your primary mail server fails. You can enter more than one simply by adding a comma between the IP addresses.

6. **Keep the Maintain Connection to Mail Server check box selected.**

7. **(Optional) Enter a new time in the Connection Timeout text field.**

   Connection timeout specifies the number of seconds that the ColdFusion server should wait for a response from the mail server before logging an error. The default value is 60 seconds.

   Leave this alone unless you know that you will be connecting to a slow mail server, meaning either a mail server that runs on an old machine or one that has a large amount of traffic.

8. **In the Spool Interval text field, enter a length of time in seconds.**

   The *spool interval* determines how often the messages on the spool will be sent to the mail server. The default value of 15 seconds (which can be left as-is) attempts to empty the spool four times a minute.

9. **Enter a value for the Mail Delivery Threads.**

   This value specifies the number of individual mail messages that are sent through the server at any one time.

10. **Keep the Spool Mail Messages for Delivery to Disk option selected.**

    This ensures that your e-mail messages are saved on your hard drive while waiting to be sent, saving your server memory space.

11. **Leave the Maximum Number of Messages Spooled to Memory setting alone.**

    Again, the way to go here is to use the spooling to disk setting, so this won't mean anything and you're free to keep on going!

12. **Click the Submit Changes button to set up your e-mail server.**

    Be sure that the gray bars enclosing the button turn green, signifying success. If they turn red, look for an error message at the top of the page.

Even if you validate your mail server, it's a good idea to send a test message from your Web application. A valid connection to the mail server does not guarantee that the Web application will send e-mail properly. If you try sending mail to yourself and it's not successful, you'll know because you never got the message.

Controlling Logging on Your Site

Basic logging is set up automatically when you install ColdFusion. The logs created by ColdFusion Server give the human administrator information about how well the server is handling its many tasks. Log entries are grouped together by type into separate log files.

Two tasks are related to log files: Logging Settings and Log Files. You see these two task items under the Debugging and Logging heading in the list along the left-hand side of the Administrator page. The Logging Settings task allows you to customize the following:

✦ Control where logs are stored

✦ Specify how big a log can get before it is archived

✦ Control how many archives should be kept

✦ Specify what sort of information is logged

To view the actual log entries, click the <u>Log Files</u> hyperlink in the left navigation frame. This will present a list of all of the logs on the server. Table 2-2 describes the most common log files.

Table 2-2	Common Log Files and Their Contents
Filename	*Description of Contents*
`application.log`	All errors that are reported to the end user
`mail.log`	Errors that are generated by the SMTP mail server
`server.log`	Internal server errors that are generated by ColdFusion

You can view any log by clicking the Action button with the magnifying glass or just by clicking its name. These buttons are in the Actions area of the Log Files page. The following four actions are available:

✦ **View:** Displays the contents of the log in the browser.

✦ **Download:** Downloads the raw log file.

✦ **Archive:** Creates a numbered copy of the log and clears the current log.

✦ **Delete:** Removes the log. A new one may be created by the server as needed.

When you create an archive with the archive button, the log file is renamed. The new name is just the old name with a digit at the end (1 if it is the first archive, 2 if it is the second, and so on). The important thing to note is that archive files do not show up in the Log Files page.

Debugging Options for Building Your Site

During the development of your Web application, you will most likely encounter errors. Some errors are quickly fixed, yet others require checking your CFML line by line to find the source. This process of hunting down and fixing errors is *debugging*.

ColdFusion can help you with the debugging process by including debugging data at the bottom of each page that it generates. Although there are a number of subtle options, here are the most important settings to consider:

✦ **Exceptions (Server Errors):** Errors that occurred when your ColdFusion page made a request to the server.

✦ **Execution times for each page template:** How long it takes all the code on a page to be read and then processed.

✦ **SQL Queries and Stored Procedures:** The actual queries that are made to the server. This shows you how many queries were made as well as what the specific queries were.

✦ **Page Variables:** Shows all the page variables that are active for a given page. You can select from the nine different variable types (cookies, application, and so on).

To enable debugging, simply select the Enable Debugging check box on the Debugging Settings page. The Debugging IP Address page allows you to select which desktop PCs, by IP number, are sent the debugging info. If you leave it blank, the information is sent to all PCs that view the pages.

If you're using Internet Explorer 4 (or above) or Netscape Navigator 6 (or above), check out the dockable debugging window. Just select `dockable.cfm` from the Select Debugging Output Format drop-down list on the Debugging Settings page. This option puts all the debugging info into a Dynamic HTML (DHTML) collapsible tree (much like the Windows Explorer), which can be displayed in a pop-up window or in a frame right alongside your CFML pages.

Chapter 3: ColdFusion MX 6.1 Developer Edition Basics

In This Chapter

✓ **Exploring ColdFusion architecture**

✓ **Working with the application server**

✓ **Understanding the power of CFML tags**

✓ **Calling functions**

✓ **Using variables**

✓ **Building expressions**

ColdFusion is an application development suite that helps you create Web applications quickly and easily. When you use ColdFusion, you're actually using several tools in concert:

+ **An application server:** This software processes requests from a ColdFusion file and returns HyperText Markup Language (HTML) to the end user's browser.

+ **An editing tool:** This tool allows you to create and edit your own sites by using the ColdFusion tag and scripting language. The scripting language is described in more detail in Book VI, Chapter 4.

+ **An administration tool:** This tool can be used to manage various elements of your application, including data sources, mail servers, and logs. You can read more about the ColdFusion Administrator in Book VI, Chapter 2.

Together, these three items provide developers with a power suite of tools to create custom HTML for every site visitor, based on user input and other data.

On its own, a Web server can only read files and deliver them to the browser. In order to rapidly build a robust Web application, the ColdFusion Application Server makes use of the ColdFusion Markup Language (CFML). CFML uses tags, which are very similar in structure to HTML tags (such as `<HTML>`, `<BODY>`, and `<TABLE>`), and functions to provide simple, yet powerful, tools to instruct the ColdFusion Application Server. The combination of CFML and the application server give you, the ColdFusion developer, the ability to provide the end user with a wide array of features:

✦ Database-driven pages

✦ E-commerce

✦ Advanced security

✦ Search engines on your site

This chapter focuses on the real magic behind ColdFusion — the ColdFusion Application Server and the scripting language used to drive it. Get comfy in that computer chair, grab a cup of coffee, and prepare to make your sites come alive!

Understanding the ColdFusion Application Server Model

The World Wide Web is built on a client-server architecture. Both client (browser) and server perform specialized tasks, and together they create what is known as *the Web*. The browser's job is to interface with the user and make requests of the server. The server needs to be able to handle the user's request — and possibly thousands of other simultaneous user requests — and return the proper response. The Web server may only need to read an HTML file to create the response, or it may pass the request on to the ColdFusion Application Server for advanced processing.

The ColdFusion Application Server works in conjunction with a standard Web server and can be installed alongside most of today's popular Web servers, including the following:

✦ Microsoft Internet Information Server (IIS)

✦ Netscape Enterprise Server

✦ iPlanet Enterprise Server

✦ Apache Web Server

✦ ColdFusion Internal Web Server

When the Web server receives a request for a ColdFusion page, which is identified by its .cfm or .cfml extension, the request is passed on to the ColdFusion Application Server. The application server interprets the CFML embedded in the page, processes the instructions, and returns the result to the Web server, which sends the final response to the end user's Web browser. Figure 3-1 shows how these transactions take place.

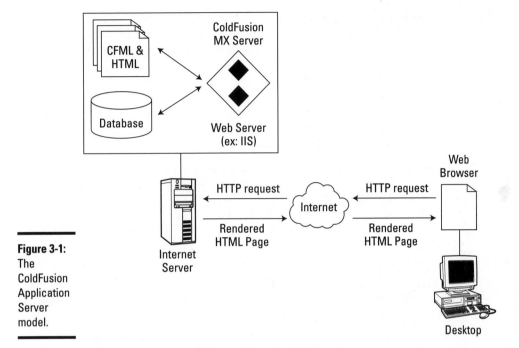

Figure 3-1:
The
ColdFusion
Application
Server
model.

ColdFusion Markup Language is the language that allows ColdFusion to create dynamic Web sites. Most ColdFusion pages contain a mix of CFML and HTML; each language has its own uses within the ColdFusion page. HTML is commonly used for the following tasks:

✦ Controlling overall page layout

✦ Building tables

✦ Displaying forms

✦ Setting colors and styles

✦ Implementing menus, rollovers, and other advanced browser features

You can use CFML to make a portion of your page customizable, based on user input, in the following ways:

✦ Retrieve and display data from a database

✦ Create dynamic forms

✦ Build complex navigation

✦ Control user sessions (a user's time visiting the site) and security

Getting Acquainted with CFML

ColdFusion Markup Language is a tag-based language that incorporates many of the features found in traditional programming languages, including the following:

✦ **Functions:** Tools in the language that perform specific operations

✦ **Variables:** Values that are used in areas of your site that can change, depending on condition

✦ **Expressions:** Collections of variables, functions, and operators (such as + and &) that are used to generate some specific desired action

In the following sections, you find a more detailed introduction to each of these concepts, plus some practical examples that you can use to dive right into using CFML.

Introducing CFML tags

CFML tags are very similar to HTML tags, only more powerful. CFML instructs the ColdFusion server how to handle the ColdFusion page, just like how HTML tags instruct the browser to display a Web page. In the end, though, the CFML is converted into HTML and won't be there when the page is displayed in a browser.

The format of CFML tags follows a few simple rules:

✦ CFML tags are enclosed in angle brackets (< and >).

✦ CFML tags begin with the letters cf.

✦ CFML tags can come in pairs, meaning that they have a closing tag that starts with a slash (/) in addition to their starting tag. Some tags, however, are fully self-contained, such as the <CFINLCUDE> and the <CFSET> tags.

✦ CFML tags may contain additional modifiers within the tag that allow you to specify more information about what the tag should do.

✦ CFML tags are case-insensitive, so <cfoutput> is the same as <CFOUTPUT>.

ColdFusion contains over 100 tags, which enable you to do everything from querying a database to making a form. We include the ten most common CFML tags in Table 3-1, with their respective functions.

Table 3-1	Common CFML Tags
CFML Tag	*Function*
`<CFINCLUDE>`	Grabs another file to be included in your page.
`<CFOUTPUT>`	Outputs content to the screen (both HTML and variables).
`<CFQUERY>`	Sets up and sends a query to a database.
`<CFLOOP>`	Loops through a dataset. (Generally, these are generated from a `<CFQUERY>`.)
`<CFSET>`	Allows you to create a variable and its value.
`<CFIF>`, `<CFELSE>`, `<CFELSEIF>`	The three tags in combination enable you to create conditional operations. (For example: *If this,* then do that; *if not,* then do this other thing.)
`<CFFORM>`	Creates a more feature-rich HTML `<FORM>`.
`<CFINSERT>`	Specifies the database, database table, and content to insert.
`<CFCASE>`, `<CFSWITCH>`	Evaluates an expression and then allows you to choose different responses based on the value of the expression.
`<CFPARAM>`	Allows you to test for a given parameter; and if it does not exist, assign a default value and data type for it.

When the ColdFusion Application Server processes the page, all the CFML tags are replaced with the results of the commands that are processed. The resulting HTML page should never contain any of your CFML tags. Figure 3-2 shows how this operation occurs.

Identifying the role of the pound sign (#)

The `<CFOUTPUT>` tag makes special use of the pound sign (#). When a text expression is included between two pound signs, it lets the ColdFusion Application Server know to look for a value that corresponds to the name of the variable within the pound signs. (See Book VI, Chapter 5 for more on variables.) For example, if you have a variable named `myname` and you want the value of that variable to be output to the screen, you could use the following bit of CFML code:

```
<CFOUTPUT> Hello, my name is #myname#. </CFOUTPUT>
```

The text enclosed by the `<CFOUTPUT>` tags is unchanged by the server unless pound signs surround it.

In addition to simply looking for variables, ColdFusion can evaluate expressions within the pound signs, as the example in the next section shows.

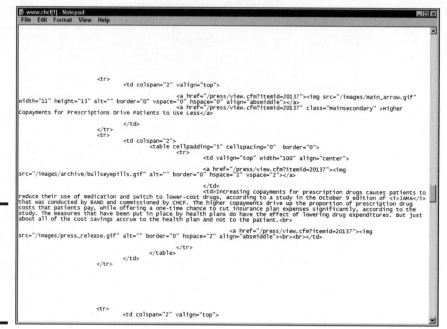

Figure 3-2:
CFML gets
parsed at
the server
and
rendered
as HTML.

If you want to display a pound sign within a `<CFOUTPUT>` tag, just put two pound signs together, and they will be displayed as one. For example, the following expression prints `Dial #0 for an Operator`:

```
<CFOUTPUT> Dial ##0 for an Operator</CFOUTPUT>
```

Putting a tag to work

Creating a ColdFusion page can be as simple as writing a few lines of code that answer the age old question, "What is two plus two?" We created a brief example that demonstrates how to answer the question as a ColdFusion page. Here's the code:

```
<HTML>
<HEAD>
    <TITLE>CFML Tags</TITLE>
</HEAD>
<BODY>
    <CFOUTPUT>two plus two equals #2+2#</CFOUTPUT>
</BODY>
</HTML>
```

The preceding sample looks a lot like HTML because most of it is HTML. The addition of the CFML tag (`<CFOUTPUT>`) and a `.cfm` extension to the filename of the page turns a simple HTML page into a ColdFusion page. Here are the steps to create your own `.cfm` page:

1. **Open your favorite HTML text editor.**

   Dreamweaver in Code view works well.

2. **Enter the text of the sample CFML page (from the preceding example).**

3. **Save your work as `four.cfm` in a directory running the ColdFusion Application Server.**

   On IIS in Windows, this is generally `C:/inetpub/wwwroot`. Check out Book VI, Chapter 2 for more information on setting up your ColdFusion Application Server.

4. **Load the page in your browser.**

   If you saved the page in the default location (like `wwwroot`), the URL should be `http://localhost/four.cfm`, as shown in Figure 3-3.

Book VI Chapter 3

ColdFusion MX 6.1 Developer Edition Basics

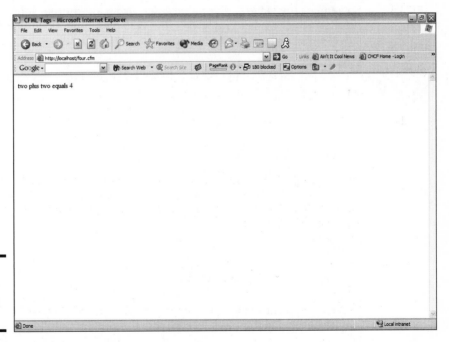

Figure 3-3:
Two plus two equals four!

Of course, the HTML that is sent to the browser is what's really important. If you view the source of your page while it's displayed in the browser, you see that the <CFOUTPUT> tags have been removed and that the simple addition (2+2) between the pound signs has been replaced by the sum. The HTML should look like this:

```
<HTML>
<HEAD>
    <TITLE>CFML Tags</TITLE>
</HEAD>
<BODY>
two plus two equals 4
</BODY>
</HTML>
```

Working with variables

When you are writing CFML, you may want to store information in memory for later use, which is exactly what a variable does. A *variable* is a named container used to temporarily store information.

Sometimes the value of a variable comes from an external source, such as a Web form; other times, you create the variables yourself. In ColdFusion, you can use the <CFSET> tag to create a variable. A <CFSET> tag looks like this:

```
<CFSET team_name="Pin Pals">
```

This tag sets the value of a variable called team_name to the text string "Pin Pals".

Naming variables

You can name your variables just about anything you want, but you should always follow a few rules:

✦ Variables must consist of letters, numbers, and underscores only.

✦ Variables should not start with a number.

✦ Variables should not contain spaces.

✦ Variables are case-insensitive. (LAST_NAME is the same as last_name.)

Usually, you want to choose a name that is clear and concise. The name should be long enough to fully describe the contents of the variable . . . but not so long that it takes too long to type. Table 3-2 summarizes some good and bad choices for variable names. ColdFusion also has a set of reserved words that can't be used for variables, such as anything starting with cf_, scope names such as session or form, or CFML script language names. For a complete listing of the reserved words, check out the Reserved Words section in the CFML Reference, which can be found by choosing Help⇨ Using ColdFusion.

Table 3-2	Variable Names	
Bad Name	*Good Name*	*Reason*
add	address	The name add is too short and could be confusing.
CustomerBillingAddressLine1	billAddress1	Long names are hard to type.
x	age	The name x does not describe the value.
First Name	FirstName or First_Name	Variables cannot have spaces in their names.

Understanding variable scope

Each variable used in your ColdFusion pages belongs to a particular *scope* (in what area the variable exists), as summarized in Table 3-3. The scope determines the following:

✦ How the variable was created

✦ How long the variable is available

✦ Where the variable can be used

Table 3-3	Common Scope Types
Scope	*Description*
Variables	The default Variables scope holds user-defined variables that are available only on the page where they are created.
Request	The Request scope holds variables that are available to any page used during a single HyperText Transfer Protocol (HTTP) request.
Form	Variables created in an HTML form are placed in the Form scope.
Cookie	End-user browser cookies are made available to ColdFusion in the Cookie scope.
Session	The Session scope holds variables that are available to each user during a single browser session.
Application	Variables in the Application scope are available to all users of the Web application.

All variables belong to one scope or another. If you don't explicitly declare the scope (you do this by adding the scope as a prefix to the variable name, so a form variable would look like this: `FORM.myvariable`), the default scope, `Variables`, is used. Two different scopes can contain variables of the same name without a problem. Each variable in a scope is held in a separate area of the computer's memory from variables in other scopes. A variable named `Form.username` (created by an HTML form) would not conflict with `Cookie.username`, which is a variable linked to the browser cookie.

Exploring data types

Variables can hold a variety of types of information. The type of information stored in a variable, which is its *data type,* determines how ColdFusion evaluates the variable. A number of variable types are available in ColdFusion, and variables can be generated and represented in a variety of ways. All variable types will fall into one of the following four categories. (These categories are explained further in Book VI, Chapter 4.)

✦ **Simple:** *Simple variables* hold a single value. You can read and write a value directly from a simple variable. Numbers, text strings, dates, and Boolean (true/false) values are stored in simple variables.

✦ **Complex:** *Complex variables* can hold more than one value. ColdFusion arrays and queries are complex variables. Complex variables often hold multiple simple variables. A database query, for example, might hold a list of names and numbers, each of which is a simple value by itself, but when they are combined into a single query, become a complex variable.

✦ **Binary:** The *binary data type* is used to hold information that is used directly by the computer, such as image files. Binary data is usually unreadable by humans and requires computer processing to become useful.

✦ **Objects:** *Objects* are variables that contain data, as well as methods to manipulate that data, all wrapped up into a single variable. ColdFusion supports several different types of objects, including COM objects, ColdFusion components, JavaBeans, and Web Services.

You don't need to declare a data type for a variable, but as a practice, it's a good idea to do so for more complex variables.

Using expressions

An *expression* is a grouping of variables, constants, operators, and/or function calls that can be evaluated by the ColdFusion Application Server to give a single value. Simple expressions can be created with a single variable, but others may involve several function calls. The result of an expression can be assigned to a variable or used to determine what action a CFML page must take.

The following <CFSET> tag assigns the result of the expression score+10 to the variable final_score:

```
<CFSET final_score=score+10>
```

The preceding expression consists of a variable (score), a constant (10), and the addition operator (+). Other expressions might make use of function calls. For example, the following expression between the # signs is used by the <CFOUTPUT> tag to display the formatted date. It consists of two function calls, Now() and DateFormat(), that are called in succession.

```
<CFOUTPUT>Today is #DateFormat( Now(), "d/m/yy" )#</CFOUTPUT>
```

Chapter 4: Understanding CFML Basics

You may be surprised by the types of complex Web applications that can be built by using basic ColdFusion concepts. You can use templates to break each page into smaller segments, which not only helps keep your code manageable but also allows you to make quick updates to your site. The benefits of your templates can be maximized by storing content in a database. The combination of templates and a database can help you build large, content-rich sites with just a few ColdFusion pages.

Setting Up Your Page Architecture

Just like how an architect creates blueprints of a building before it's constructed, a ColdFusion page can — and should — be planned out before it's built. To a Web designer, *page architecture* deals with how the elements of the page lay out graphically. As the Web developer, you need to consider how the CFML builds the page as well as the aesthetics of the final output.

Understanding template basics

The best way to think of a *template* is as a snippet of code that gets used over and over again for a specific purpose. For example, suppose that a site has several hundred products for sale. The product pages all generally look the same. Only the product content changes. Rather than make several hundred pages, all of which would look the same and contain 99 percent of the same content, you could more easily use one page over and over again to create each product page when that specific product is displayed. When you break up your site into templates, you do the following:

✦ Reduce the overall number of pages that you have to manage.

✦ Reduce your maintenance burden because you can make a change to one template and have it affect a large number of viewable pages on the site.

Today, most high-traffic sites that have tens of thousands of Web pages, such as www.cnn.com or www.yahoo.com, are driven by a surprisingly low number of templates.

Determining just how to break a single ColdFusion Markup Language (CFML) page into a series of templates can be more of an art than a science. One of the most common ways to break up a page is shown in Figure 4-1.

The page is broken into four sections, all of which will be different templates:

✦ **Header:** The area that appears at the very top of the page

✦ **Navigation:** The area that includes links to the other pages in the site, usually found on the left-hand side of the page

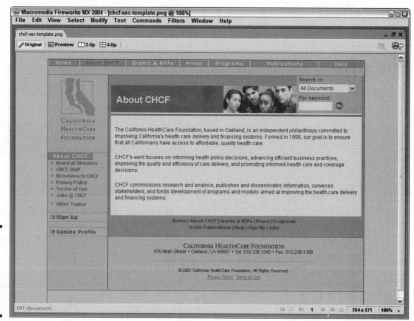

Figure 4-1:
Breaking a single page into multiple templates.

✦ **Content:** The area that includes most of the site content, generally appearing to the right of the navigation area

✦ **Footer:** The area that appears at the bottom of the page and usually includes links, privacy information, and copyright information

Each section becomes an individual ColdFusion file and contains a mix of HyperText Markup Language (HTML) and CFML. The most important thing to remember is that after the page templates are put together, they need to equal a properly formatted HTML page, with the correct number of `<HEAD>`, `<BODY>`, `<TABLE>`, `<TR>`, and `<TD>` tags.

It may not seem all that helpful to break one page into four smaller template pages, but the ability to reuse a piece of a page as a template gives you a lot of options. For example, the footer is usually the same on every page of a Web site. This makes it a great candidate to be extracted to a separate template file. After you isolate the footer text in its own template file, you can include it in as many pages as you like. Then, if you ever need to make a change to the footer, you only need to change the footer template file, and the footer will be automatically updated on all the pages that use the footer template.

**Book VI
Chapter 4**

**Understanding
CFML Basics**

Using <CFINCLUDE>

The easiest way to build a single HTML page from several templates is with the `<CFINCLUDE>` tag. You can use this tag in any ColdFusion page. Take a quick look back at Figure 4-1. To create this page, we might have a page called `index.cfm`, and within it, we'd use four `<CFINCLUDE>` tags to compose the page. The tag takes the following form:

```
<CFINCLUDE TEMPLATE="footer.cfm">
```

The `TEMPLATE` attribute specifies the name and location of the footer file on the ColdFusion server. The footer file, `footer.cfm` in this example, is also a ColdFusion page and can use all the ColdFusion tags, functions, and variables that are available in the main page (the page with the `<CFINCLUDE>` tag).

The contents of the file `footer.cfm` could look something like this (a standard copyright with a link to a copyright page):

```
<I>Copyright 2003, Your Fancy New Company.</I>
    <A href="copy_info.cfm">All rights reserved</A>
```

The text of `footer.cfm` is actually quite simple because it's used to print only a single line on each page. Because this file will be included as part of the larger page, it doesn't need to be a complete HTML page, so you don't need to include <HTML> or <BODY> tags because those are included in the file that originated the request for the template, which is as follows:

```
<HTML>
<BODY>
    <!--- body of HTML page here --->

<CFINCLUDE TEMPLATE="footer.cfm">
</BODY>
</HTML>
```

Building static include files can save you time when it comes to building and maintaining a site, but you can do a whole lot more with them! Each template that's included in the main page has access to all the variables, functions, and queries of the main page. This allows you to create a footer that uses CFML to generate dynamic output. For more information on how to use variables and functions, check out Book VI, Chapter 5.

Another common way to use the <CFINCLUDE> tag is to isolate database queries, user-defined functions, and other CFML templates. When a site is controlled by a database, it's very common to have each page use a *query* (a request to a data source) to retrieve necessary information from the database. (Queries are described in more detail later in this chapter.) Placing queries in included templates has several distinct advantages:

✦ **They're easier to work with during development.** If your queries are all in a common location and have descriptive terms in the filename (qry_getproducts.cfm, for example), finding the right query to build a page or edit becomes easier.

✦ **They're easier to find for maintenance.** A common development practice is to put your queries in a single location. This makes finding the right query to work on substantially easier.

✦ **They're easier to protect for security.** Again, putting queries in a single location external to your main ColdFusion pages makes them harder to find for anyone who may try to get access to your databases by stealing your queries.

Using Conditional Processing

Each ColdFusion Web application can receive information from a variety of sources:

✦ **User action:** A user clicks somewhere on a site.

✦ **User submitted forms:** A user submits a form from the site.

✦ **Database queries:** Data is retrieved from a database.

✦ **The Web application server:** ColdFusion keeps information resident in the server at all times and makes that information available to CFML.

✦ **E-mail servers:** Yes, ColdFusion can interact with an e-mail server!

✦ **COM objects, JavaBeans, and Web services:** These advanced services can all pass information to CFML. For more information on these advanced concepts, check out *ColdFusion MX For Dummies*, by John Paul Ashenfelter and Jon Kocen (published by Wiley Publishing, Inc.).

The information received from these sources can be of varying degrees of importance, and sometimes the information is not in a format that the end user can understand. CFML gives you several ways to control the flow of your page, based on the current set of information. Three of the most useful flow control tags are `<CFIF>`, `<CFELSE>`, and `<CFSWITCH>`.

Book VI Chapter 4

Understanding CFML Basics

Using <CFIF> and <CFELSE>

The `<CFIF>` tag, which is the most common way to control the flow of a page in CFML, is used in CFML in a way that's very similar to how the word *if* is used in English.

The `<CFIF>` tag is designed to test whether some condition is true or false. This is a *test expression*. Any HTML or CFML between the `<CFIF>` tag and the closing `</CFIF>` tag is to be evaluated if the test expression is TRUE. Often two values in the test expression are compared with each other, as you can see in the examples later in this section. Other times, the test expression is like those in Table 4-1, which shows some test expressions and their meanings.

Table 4-1	Test Expressions
Expression	*Meaning*
`Variables.first_name IS "Earl"`	The variable `first_name` has a value of `"Earl"`.
`Form.quantity GT 10`	The quantity field of the Web form is greater than 10.
`Day( Now() ) is 1`	The current day of the month is 1.

Book VI, Chapter 5 provides more details on how functions and variables — like those in Table 4-1 — work together.

If the expression is true, the code between the `<CFIF>` tags is processed. If it is false, the code is skipped. In the following example, if the quantity in the form element is greater than 10 — (GT) is code for *greater than* — the line `You qualify for the bulk discount.` is displayed on the page:

```
<CFIF Form.quantity GT 10>
You qualify for the bulk discount.
</CFIF>
```

So, what happens if the user inputs a quantity that isn't greater than 10? In this case, nothing is displayed. Suppose, however, that you want to send a different message if someone chooses fewer than ten items. In that case, you can use the <CFELSE> tag, which allows you to set the alternative condition to display if the <CFIF> condition isn't true.

Take a look at the following code snippet, which shows how you can construct a <CFELSE> element within your <CFIF> tag (the stuff in between the <!--- and the ---> are code comments to help you understand the flow of the code):

```
<CFIF Form.quantity GT 10>
    <!--- first option --->
    You qualify for the bulk discount.
<CFELSE>
    <!--- second option --->
    If you buy 10 items, you will qualify for the bulk discount.
</CFIF>
```

You might think of the <CFIF>-<CFELSE>-</CFIF> combination as, "*If* the test expression is true, do the first option, or *else* do the second option." Only one option can happen — the first *or* the second but never both.

Using *<CFELSEIF>*

If you need to test more than one condition, you can use <CFELSE> or <CFELSEIF> to extend the basic <CFIF> tag. Suppose that you have a Web form that asks for the user's age. The form passes the age information to the ColdFusion server processing in a variable, which can be tested before printing the proper response. The <CFELSEIF> tag allows you to insert more test expressions into the logic structure:

```
<CFIF Form.age LT 13>
    <!--- first option --->
    You are too young to place an order.
<CFELSEIF Form.age LT 18>
    <!--- second  option --->
    You must have parental permission before ordering.
<CFELSEIF Form.age GT 59>
    <!--- third option --->
    You qualify for the Senior Discount.
<CFELSE>
    <!--- last option --->
    Thank you for your order.
</CFIF>
```

Again, only a single option will be executed. If the user is under 13, the first option will be printed, and all the other tags will be skipped. If the user is not under 13, the next expression is checked. Each expression is checked, in order, until one evaluates to true. Only if none of the expressions are true will the <CFELSE> option be run. ***Note:*** When one test is met, the following conditions are not even checked: There is no need.

You don't need to have a <CFELSE> tag, but it's a good idea to include one every time that you use a <CFELSEIF> tag. Even if you don't think the <CFELSE> tag will ever be executed, it can be a useful error-tracking tool.

Using <CFSWITCH>

Sometimes you need to be able to handle a lot of different situations in a single page. The <CFSWITCH> tag compares a single test expression with a series of cases that are indicated by <CFCASE> tags and then executes the one that returns TRUE. Suppose that you need to apply special shipping and/or tax rates depending on the state from which an order originates. This is a good candidate for the <CFSWITCH> tag because one variable, #Form.State#, needs to be compared against a bunch of different state abbreviations.

Here's how the code could be represented for a selection of states:

```
<CFSWITCH EXPRESSION="#Form.State#">
    <CFCASE value="CA">
        8% tax for orders within California.
    </CFCASE>

    <CFCASE value="NY">
        6% tax for orders shipped to New York.
    </CFCASE>

    <CFCASE value="AK,HI">
        $10 additional shipping for orders shipped to Alaska and Hawaii.
    </CFCASE>

    <CFDEFAULTCASE>
        Standard shipping rules apply.
    </CFDEFAULTCASE>
</CFSWITCH>
```

Adding additional cases to the switch tag is as easy, and you can have as many as you want. The <CFDEFAULTCASE> tag is usually put at the end, and it occurs when none of the other cases are met. Note that you can have more than one value, separated by commas, which represents a specific case.

As your sites get more complex, you'll want to focus more on using <CFSWITCH> and <CFCASE>. ColdFusion processes these commands more quickly than <CFIF> and <CFELSE>, and as a result, using these will make your site run more quickly.

Using SQL Queries

Databases can be a powerful addition to your Web development toolbox. Whether you're storing customer information, Web site content, or document *metadata* (a description of some kind of data), a database gives you a way to store, retrieve, and modify your data. For more information on using databases with ColdFusion, check out Book VI, Chapter 6.

Many people are familiar with database concepts, even if they don't know it. The table structure of a spreadsheet is a lot like a table in a database. Each table in a database is given a unique name, and it has columns and rows that hold data. All the columns have the same type of information, and each row holds a set of information about a particular entity. Table 4-2 below shows a sample customer database table. Each row corresponds to a different customer, and each column holds a single kind of data.

Table 4-2		A Simple Customer Database Table	
CustomerID	*Name*	*Address*	*PostalCode*
1	Earl	1 Main St.	94110
2	Andrew	14 Evergreen Terrace	06810
3	Maggie	97 Rosemont Ave.	94110

The CustomerID column is an example of a *Identity Key*. Each time that a record is added to the database, the database automatically assigns a CustomerID to the new record. The new CustomerID will not be the same as any other CustomerID in the database. Having a unique identifier not only keeps your database running at optimal speed, but it also helps you manage the data. (If you don't know how to set up a unique key in your database, check with a database administrator or check your database documentation.)

Exploring SQL concepts

Asking a database to give you information is a *query*. Database queries use a Structured Query Language (SQL). Through queries, you can read, write, and modify data in your database. Consider the following SQL query:

```
SELECT firstname, lastname FROM Employees
WHERE lastname='Smith'
```

This query has several elements:

+ **SQL elements:** These items describe actions, conditions, restrictions, and locations. They include the SELECT, FROM, and WHERE clauses.

+ **Columns:** In this case, firstname and lastname are columns within a table. This is the data that you're interested in retrieving.

+ **Tables:** Here, Employees is a table that includes the columns firstname and lastname.

So, in sum, the query effectively states, "Select the firstname and lastname from the Employees table in the database, where the lastname is equal to Smith."

Table 4-3 shows some other basic SQL queries and what they do.

Table 4-3	Examples of SQL Statements
Statement	*Description*
SELECT Name, Address FROM Customers	Gets the name and address for all customers
SELECT * FROM Customers WHERE PostalCode = 94110	Gets all data for customers in the 94110 ZIP code
DELETE FROM Customer WHERE CustomerID = 3	Deletes the customer with a CustomerID equal to 3

Entire books are dedicated to SQL, and we can only begin to scratch the surface here. Macromedia has put a lot of effort into making SQL easy by adding query editors to Dreamweaver, so you can get the most out of your database without getting bogged down in SQL syntax. For the database tools of Dreamweaver to function properly, you need to be sure your database is set up properly in the ColdFusion Administrator. (See Book VI, Chapter 2 for more information on the ColdFusion Administrator. In addition, check out Book VI, Chapter 6 for more about using SQL.)

Wondering what that asterisk (*) is in that second SQL statement in Table 4-3? The asterisk (*) is a wildcard in SQL terminology. If you use a * following a SELECT statement, it will retrieve data from all the columns in the table that you specify in the FROM clause.

Pick up a copy of *SQL For Dummies*, 5th Edition, by Allen G. Taylor (published by Wiley Publishing, Inc.) for an easy-to-understand, comprehensive guide to the SQL language.

Using <CFQUERY>

ColdFusion has a special tag for running SQL queries: `<CFQUERY>`. The attributes that you specify in the `<CFQUERY>` tag tell ColdFusion what database to connect to and how to connect to it. The body of the `<CFQUERY>` tag contains the SQL that you want to run. Some of the important attributes of the `<CFQUERY>` tag are listed in Table 4-4. The basic format for `CFQUERY` is listed here:

```
<CFQUERY name="MyQuery" datasource="SomeDatasource">
INSERT YOUR SQL HERE
</CFQUERY>
```

Table 4-4	Common Attributes of the <CFQUERY> Tag
Attribute	*Description*
name	Required: The name you use to refer to this query in CFML.
datasource	Required: The name used to register the database in the ColdFusion Administrator.
username	Optional: Specifies the username used to log on to the data source.
password	Optional: Specifies the password used to log on to the data source.
maxRows	Optional: Limits the number of rows returned by the query.
timeout	Optional: Gives the time, in seconds, that the ColdFusion server should wait for a response from the data source before generating an error.

If all the attributes are set up correctly and the ColdFusion server can connect and communicate with the data source, the `<CFQUERY>` tag will provide you with a set of data from the data source. All this data will be available to you to use in your pages in the form of variables. Check out Book VI, Chapter 5 for more information on using variables from queries.

Using SQL commands

SQL provides you with a powerful way to get information out of a database. SQL is the predominant language for Web development, and although a complete primer on it is beyond the scope of this book, we want to give you an introduction to some of the critical SQL statements that will enable you to get data from a database.

Creating queries with SELECT

The `SELECT` keyword is used to retrieve rows of data from a database, and it is always the first word in a `SELECT` statement. Following the `SELECT` keyword is the list of columns that you want to retrieve data from. If you want data from all of the columns in a table, use an asterisk (*) instead of specific column names. The last required element of a SELECT statement is the name of the table FROM which the data is being retrieved.

Each of the following examples selects a different set of columns from each row of the Customers table:

✦ SELECT Name FROM Customers

✦ SELECT CustomerID, Name FROM Customers

✦ SELECT * FROM Customers

What if you don't want data from every row? The WHERE clause is used to filter rows from a query. The following examples use the WHERE clause to restrict the rows being returned:

✦ SELECT Name FROM Customers WHERE CustomerID = 2

✦ SELECT CustomerID, Name FROM Customers WHERE PostalCode > 94000

With the aid of the WHERE clause, you can build queries that retrieve only the information that you need to build your page. While looping through the query or outputting directly to the screen, each column can be accessed as a variable by using pound signs, such as #name# or #CustomerID#. The use of pound signs to output a variable is described in more detail in Book VI, Chapter 5.

If you find that you use <CFIF> to filter the data generated by <CFQUERY>, consider modifying the SQL to do the filtering for you. The database will probably be able to process the filter faster, plus you won't need to transfer useless information between servers.

Creating queries with DELETE

The DELETE keyword is extremely powerful because it can remove all the data from a table in one fell swoop. To delete all the rows from a table, simply issue the following query, where *tablename* is the name of the table:

DELETE *tablename*

Although the above statement will work in Microsoft SQL Server 2000 and MySQL, it won't work in Microsoft Access because Access doesn't support all SQL syntax. It uses a limited version of SQL called *Jet SQL*. For information on which SQL keywords are supported, check out the Microsoft Access Help files.

More often than not, you'll only want to delete a limited number of rows . . . or maybe only one row. You can filter the DELETE command by using the WHERE clause, as we describe in the previous section, "Creating queries with SELECT." The following examples use this technique:

✦ `DELETE Customers WHERE CustomerID = 2`

✦ `DELETE Customers WHERE PostalCode = 94110`

Your `DELETE` commands should always have a `WHERE` clause — this will keep you from accidentally deleting important data. Because it's so easy to delete data by mistake, some developers recommend never deleting data at all. By adding a status column, you can mark each record as *active* or *inactive* and then do periodic maintenance to remove inactive records by hand.

Creating queries with INSERT

Inserting data into a table is probably the toughest of the basic database operations. The elements of the command are similar to the `SELECT` statement. After the `INSERT` keyword, you give the table name, followed by a list of columns in parentheses. However, unlike a `SELECT` command, from which the database sends you data, now you need to send the data to the database. The information for the new row is placed at the end of the insert statement with the `VALUES` keyword, as in the following example:

```
INSERT INTO Customers( Name, Address, PostalCode ) VALUES
    ("Chris", "44 South St.", 06810 )
```

The order of the data after the `VALUES` keyword must match the order of the columns listed before the `VALUES` keyword.

If you have a column that is automatically generated, such as an ID column, you don't need to specify a value for that column.

Creating queries with UPDATE

Another powerful action is `UPDATE`. Without a `WHERE` clause, the `UPDATE` command updates every row in the data table, which is not usually what you want. The syntax of the `UPDATE` command starts off with the `UPDATE` keyword and the name of the data table, just like the `INSERT` command. However, rather than listing the columns and values separately, the value of each column is `SET` individually, as in the following example:

```
UPDATE Customers SET name='Margaret' WHERE CustomerID = 3
```

When the `UPDATE` command is running, the filter is applied first, and then the rows are modified. This means that you can modify a column that was used in the `WHERE` clause without affecting the results. The following SQL works just fine, changing customers' name from *Maggie* to *Margaret*.

```
UPDATE Customers SET Name='Margaret' WHERE Name = 'Maggie'
```

Outputting Content to the Screen

When you build a page in ColdFusion, you have data from Web forms, database queries, and other sources stored in variables. Some of these variables may hold data that you want to display to your users. The <CFOUTPUT> tag gives you the ability to put data from variables into HTML. The <CFOUTPUT> tag can print a single value, or it can be used to loop through the data in a query, displaying multiple rows of data with just one tag.

Using <CFOUTPUT>

Each <CFOUTPUT> tag must have a closing </CFOUTPUT> tag. Between the tags, you can place HTML or CFML. When you place a variable name between pound signs (#), <CFOUTPUT> displays the value of the variable and not the variable name.

**Book VI
Chapter 4**

**Understanding
CFML Basics**

```
<CFSET animal="badger">
<CFOUTPUT>
My <I>favorite</I> animal is the <B>#animal#.</B>
</CFOUTPUT>
```

This CFML snippet would print the text: "My *favorite* animal is the **badger**."

Exactly how you set up the tag is a matter of style. The following example prints the same text, but most developers find the nested tags to be less clear:

```
<CFSET animal="badger">
My <I>favorite</I> animal is the <B><CFOUTPUT>#animal#.</CFOUTPUT></B>
```

Looping

The <CFOUTPUT> tag can do a lot more than just print a single variable. When you specify a query in <CFOUTPUT>, the text between the opening and closing tags is repeated for each row of the query, as in the following example:

```
<CFQUERY name="CustomerData" datasource="CustomerDB">
SELECT * FROM Customers
<CFQUERY>
<CFOUTPUT query="CustomerData">
Customer #CustomerID# is named #name#.<BR>
</CFOUTPUT>
```

The columns from the query are available inside the <CFOUTPUT>, just like ordinary variables. However, every time the <CFOUTPUT> tag loops, a new row of data is used, so the values of each column change. If the query returned three rows of data, the <CFOUTPUT> tag would loop three times and print three lines of text.

Chapter 5: Variables, Functions, and Structured Data

In This Chapter

✔ **Working with variables and parameters**

✔ **Using CFML functions**

✔ **Putting data into arrays, lists, and structures**

After you've gotten your feet wet with the basics of ColdFusion MX 6.1 Developer Edition, it won't be long before you're itching to add even more functionality to your site. This chapter is designed to give you an introduction to some of the more advanced concepts in ColdFusion. In reality, working with variables, parameters, and data structures (collections of data in various forms) are concepts that are common to any technology platform. This just happens to be Macromedia's implementation, and as you'll soon find out, the folks at Macromedia tried to make it as easy as possible to pick up.

Working with Variables and Parameters

If you've ever logged on to a Web site by entering a username and password, you've probably seen a URL that looked something like this:

```
http://www.somesite.com/index.cfm?userID=123456
```

In that URL string, the `userID` is called the variable and `123456` is the value for that variable. Put simply, a *variable* is a value that can change, depending upon differing conditions within your site. In ColdFusion, a *parameter* can represent one of many different data types that are supported in the product, such as variables, queries, arrays, and even dates.

More often than not, variables are used by developers to change the way a Web page looks or responds to a user's input. In ColdFusion, variables can come from a variety of sources and appear in a variety of different formats. Variables can be created in ColdFusion in four different ways:

✦ By using `<CFSET>` or `<CFPARAM>` tags

✦ As a result of a database query using a `<CFQUERY>` tag

✦ Automatically by ColdFusion

✦ From within a `<CFSCRIPT>` tag

CFScript is scripting language that is similar to JavaScript and is available to developers from within CFML. Getting into detail about CFScript is beyond the scope of this book, but to find out more about it, check out *ColdFusion MX For Dummies*, by John Paul Ashenfelter and Jon Kocen (published by Wiley Publishing, Inc.).

The best reason to use variables in your site is that they expand your ability to deliver the right content for the right situation dynamically. In this section, we show you how you can begin to use variables to enhance the user experience on your site. For a review of variable type and scope, refer to Book VI, Chapter 3.

In addition to this tutorial and reference, you can also refer to the Using ColdFusion Help files, accessible from within Dreamweaver MX 2004 by pressing Ctrl+F1. The Help files are an exceptionally good reference tool to understanding both the type and scope of variables.

Creating Variables with <CFSET>

The most common way to create a variable in ColdFusion is by using a `<CFSET>` tag. With `<CFSET>`, you create the name of the variable, as well as the value (called an expression). The syntax for the `<CFSET>` tag is as follows:

```
<CFSET VariableName = "expression">
```

The following example shows you how you can use `<CFSET>` with the sample ColdFusion databases that come with Macromedia Studio MX 2004 to retrieve some information about an employee:

1. **In Dreamweaver, verify that you have a connection to the CompanyInfo database by opening the Application panel and selecting the Databases tab.**

   To open the Applications panel, select Window➪Databases. You should see the three default databases, as shown in Figure 5-1. If you can't see them, then you need to configure your database connections. For instructions on how to do this, check out Book VI, Chapter 2.

2. **Create a new ColdFusion file by choosing File➪New and selecting Dynamic Page and ColdFusion from the Category and Dynamic Page columns, respectively. Click Create to create the file.**

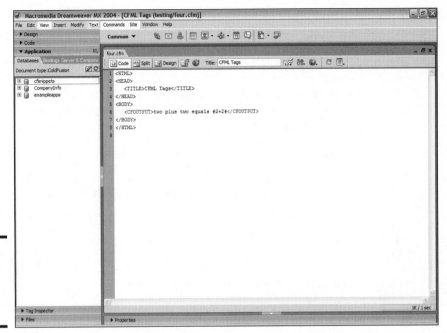

Figure 5-1:
You should
see three
active
databases.

3. Create a variable called EmployeeNumber and give it a value of 1.

Constants are the simplest form of variables because there's no real variation in them. In the Code view, your code should look as follows:

```
<CFSET EmployeeNumber = "1">
```

There are a number of rules for the naming of variables. The two most important rules are that variables should not start with a number and that they cannot contain spaces. For a complete set of variable naming rules, check out the Using ColdFusion Help files in Dream-weaver by choosing Help⇨Using ColdFusion, and then choosing Developing ColdFusion Applications⇨Using ColdFusion Variables⇨Creating Variables⇨Variable Naming Rules.

4. Expand the CompanyInfo database until you see the Employee table.

You can expand the database to the table level by clicking the plus box (+) next to the database and then next to the tables.

If you want to see the data in the Employee table, right-click the table name and choose View Data from the contextual menu.

5. Create a query in the Code view to the CompanyInfo database to get all information from the Employee table where emp_ID = EmployeeNumber.

Your query should look like this:

```
<CFQUERY datasource="CompanyInfo" name="GetEmployees">
SELECT * FROM employee
WHERE emp_ID=#EmployeeNumber#
</CFQUERY>
```

You'll notice something interesting is happening here. Within the query, we've included the `EmployeeNumber` variable. Because ColdFusion reads code from the top of the page to the bottom, the server first reads that there's a variable called `EmployeeNumber` and it has a value of 1. Then, when it reads this query, it swaps out `#EmployeeNumber#` with the value (1) that was previously set for the variable.

6. Output the data to the screen using a `<CFOUTPUT>` tag.

If you want to see what the query returns, you need to include a `<CFOUTPUT>` tag, as follows:

```
<CFOUTPUT query="GetEmployees">#firstname#
    #lastname#<BR>#startdate#<BR>#salary#</CFOUTPUT>
```

7. Press F12 to preview the page.

You should get a look at the personnel information of one Ben Frueh, as shown in Figure 5-2.

Figure 5-2:
Ben Frueh,
Employee
Number = 1.

Testing the existence of variables with <CFPARAM>

The `<CFPARAM>` tag is an interesting ColdFusion tag because it checks for the existence and type of a local variable on a page. Depending upon whether that variable exists and what type of variable it is, ColdFusion either creates a new variable, gives it a default value, or generates an error. The `<CFPARAM>` tag has three elements:

✦ `name`: The name of the variable

✦ `type`: The data type of the variable, such as a number, string, array, query, and so on

✦ `default`: The default value for a variable

The structure for the tag is as follows:

```
<CFPARAM name="SomeName" type="DataType" default="Value">
```

The only value that's required for the `<CFPARAM>` tag is `name`. If you use only the name, the tag tests for the existence of a variable with that name. If it does not exist, ColdFusion returns an error message, as shown in Figure 5-3, and stops processing. If you include `type` with the name in the tag, then ColdFusion requires both the name and the corresponding data type for the variable to exist, or it generates an error. Finally, you can choose to include just the `name` and the `default` values. In this case, if no variable exists when the page is processed, ColdFusion creates the variable with the default value.

Suppose that you've got a product page on your corporate site. On this product page, you want to be able to show products specific to your various target audiences: consumers, educators, and the government. To accomplish this, you include a form on the product page that asks users to select whether they want to view education or government products.

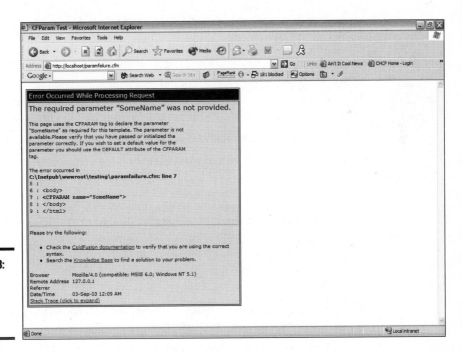

Figure 5-3:
This variable does not exist.

Because a user won't be choosing a product type until they reach the product page, you can use `<CFPARAM>` to evaluate whether or not a variable exists to show specific product information based on a form input. Here's a simple way to do it:

1. **In Dreamweaver, create a new page called** `param.cfm` **and save it locally or on a remote testing server (wherever you have the ColdFusion server running).**

2. **Create a** `<CFPARAM>` **called** `type` **and give it an empty default value, as follows:**

   ```
   <CFPARAM name="type" default="">
   ```

   While it's not required, it's always a good idea to scope your variables. That way, you're less likely to run into any errors as ColdFusion looks for the right scope for the variable you're testing. Scoping is also covered in more detail in Book VI, Chapter 3. So in the previous example, if you scoped the variable, it would look as follows:

   ```
   <CFPARAM name="FORM.type" default="">
   ```

   Adding this tag first is critical, because farther down the page, you need to look for the variable `type`. This tag ensures that the variable exists, whether or not someone has selected a product type from the drop-down list.

   When this exercise is complete, try removing this line to see what happens when the variable isn't defined. ColdFusion will generate an error and tell you that the variable isn't defined when you first load the page.

3. **Create a drop-down list that allows a user to select a product type.**

   Here's a simple version of what that form element looks like:

   ```
   <FORM action="param.cfm" method="post">
   <SELECT name="type">
     <OPTION value="">Select One</OPTION>
     <OPTION value="consumer">Consumer</OPTION>
     <OPTION value="education">Education</OPTION>
     <OPTION value="government">Government</OPTION>
   </SELECT>
   <INPUT type="submit" value="Go">
   </FORM>
   ```

4. **Evaluate whether the variable type exists and show the product information based on the variable value.**

   The most straightforward way to do this is to use `<CFIF>` and `<CFELSEIF>`, as shown here:

   ```
   <CFIF type is "consumer">
   <UL>
   <LI>Consumer Product One</LI>
   <LI>Consumer Product Two</LI>
   ```

```
</UL>
<CFELSEIF type is "education">
<UL>
<LI>Education Product One</LI>
<LI>Education Product Two</LI>
</UL>
<CFELSEIF type is "government">
<UL>
<LI>Government Product One</LI>
<LI>Government Product Two</LI>
</UL>
</CFIF>
```

Refer to Book VI, Chapter 4 on the variety of ways you can use <CFIF> and <CFELSEIF> to evaluate conditional statements.

You can also use <CFSWITCH> and <CFCASE> for this very same example. Indeed, as your applications become more complex, you'll want to use <CFSWITCH> and <CFCASE>, because they process faster, even if <CFIF> and <CFELSE> are easier concepts to understand. <CFSWITCH> is covered in Book VI, Chapter 4.

Getting access to variables through <CFQUERY>

Consider the query that we use in the variable example in the section, "Creating variables with <CFSET>":

```
<CFQUERY datasource="CompanyInfo" name="GetEmployees">
SELECT * FROM employee
WHERE emp_ID=#EmployeeNumber#
</CFQUERY>
```

This query returns information from all the columns in the employee table, namely

- FirstName
- LastName
- Dept_ID
- StartDate
- Salary
- Contract
- emp_ID

Each of these columns becomes a variable that can be output to the screen using a <CFOUTPUT> tag. To use them, surround the column name with pound signs (#). So, for example, to output FirstName, you would use #FirstName#.

Using variables generated by ColdFusion

ColdFusion generates a variety of variables that you can use in your applications. These variables work just like variables that you create, and they're called in a similar fashion. For example, if you want to show the operating system of the server that ColdFusion is running on, you can use the following *resident variable* (meaning it's active in ColdFusion at all times):

```
<CFOUTPUT>#Server.OS.Name#</CFOUTPUT>
```

For a complete listing of these resident variables that ColdFusion generates, check out the CFML reference guide in the Using ColdFusion Help files, accessible by pressing Ctrl+F1 within Dreamweaver.

Using CFML Functions

Hundreds of different functions are available to ColdFusion developers, and they do everything from creating a date to generating random numbers. Although there are numerous ColdFusion functions, nearly all of them do one of the following four things:

✦ Create new data and data structures

✦ Evaluate some type of data to determine its existence or format

✦ Evaluate some type of data to produce some new type of data

✦ Change the composition of some type of data

To give you some idea of the breadth of functions that are available, Macromedia puts them into 17 different categories (plus an Other category), with many functions being represented in more than one category. We list all these categories in Table 5-1, as well as provide a brief description of the kinds of functions found in each group.

Table 5-1	Categories of Functions in ColdFusion
Function Category	*What They're For*
Array functions	Creating, evaluating, and manipulating arrays
Authentication functions	Authenticating a user
Conversion functions	Converting array, list, XML, and URL information into other formats
Date and time functions	Creating and formatting dates and times
Decision functions	Checking whether various objects are defined or meet various criteria

Function Category	What They're For
Display and formatting functions	Formatting different kinds of data, such as currency, decimal formats, and number formats
Dynamic evaluation functions	Evaluating different kinds of dynamic data, such as Boolean searches or string expressions
Extensibility functions	Extending the functionality of ColdFusion to other data types, such as XML
Full-text search functions	Performing searches in conjunction with ColdFusion's built-in searching tools
International functions	Setting, converting, and evaluating currency, time, and location for other countries
List functions	Testing length, sorting, converting to arrays, and appending lists
Mathematical functions	Performing advanced calculations on data
Other functions	Other functions that don't fall into any of these categories
Query functions	Manipulating and evaluating ColdFusion queries
String functions	Containing or manipulating string data
Structure functions	Creating, manipulating, and evaluating ColdFusion structures
System functions	Interacting with or getting information from the server
XML functions	Reading and transformation of XML documents

Functions can be called in a few different ways:

✦ **As part of a CFML tag:** An example of this kind of function is `IsDefined`, which checks to see if a variable is defined. The `IsDefined` function looks like this:

```
<CFIF IsDefined("SomeVariable")>
```

✦ **As part of defining a variable:** An example of this kind of function is `arrayNew(n)`, which creates an *array* (a collection of data) in *n* dimensions. The `arrayNew` function is called from within a `<CFSET>` tag, as follows:

```
<CFSET MyArray = arrayNew(1)>
```

✦ **When outputting a variable:** An example of this kind of function is `DateFormat`, which enables you to change the way the date looks. `DateFormat` can be called as follows, where date is a variable that represents a date:

```
#DateFormat(date, "mm-dd-yyyy")#
```

✦ **From within another function:** It's not uncommon that functions support calling other functions to provide some value. Take the following example:

```
<CFSET discountprice = DollarFormat(Evaluate(price -
    (price * discount))) >
```

In this case, we are setting a variable `discountprice`, using the `DollarFormat` function, and within that function, using the `Evaluate` function to perform some basic arithmetic functions.

Going through each of the ColdFusion functions is beyond the scope of this book, but the following sections show you how to get started with the five most useful ColdFusion functions for beginners.

Using the arrayNew function

The `arrayNew` function, as you might expect from the name, creates a new array. Arrays, which are collections of data, are a great way to capture information and then redisplay it or manipulate it before committing it to a database.

The syntax for `arrayNew` is as follows:

```
<CFSET AnArray = arrayNew(n)>
```

Using `<CFSET>` is the most common way to create an array. `AnArray` is the variable that represents the elements of the array. `arrayNew` creates the array and `(n)` represents the number of dimensions (*dimensions* specify the structure of the data) of the array. ColdFusion supports up to three-dimensional arrays. Figure 5-4 shows a graphical representation of an array in ColdFusion.

Figure 5-4:
The arrayNew function creates an array for you.

Building arrays is covered in more detail in the section, "Casting Data into Arrays, Lists, and Structures," later in this chapter.

Using the isDefined function

The isDefined function is one of the most popular ColdFusion functions because it works so nicely in conditional statements, especially the `<CFIF>` tag. The syntax for the function looks like this:

```
<CFIF isDefined("someVariable")>
```

This function returns a value of TRUE or FALSE, depending upon whether the variable is defined when the page is being processed. In the example code above, if the value returned is TRUE, then whatever immediately follows that `<CFIF>` will be executed. If it returns a FALSE value, then the code immediately following the `<CFIF>` will be not be executed.

TIP

It's quite common to use this function for validating and processing forms. After the user submits the form, you can use isDefined to ensure that all required fields have been filled out. Alternatively, isDefined can be used to instigate some action — updating a database, for example — if a value exists for the form field submitted.

Using the len function

Developers love to use the len (length) function. len is an incredibly simple function, in that all it does is return the length of a string. Much like isDefined, this function becomes exceptionally valuable when doing error handling and processing because if you're looking for a variable that should be of at least some length and len returns a value of zero, you immediately know that the user hasn't filled in the field or made a selection from a menu. Used as part of a `<CFIF>` statement, the syntax for len is as follows:

```
<CFIF len(string) is not 0>
```

Using the DateFormat function

Everybody likes to use dates in their Web sites. The DateFormat function in ColdFusion allows you to take a date and format it in a variety of ways. To output today's date in mm-dd-yyyy format, you'd use the following:

```
<CFOUTPUT>#dateformat(Now(), "mm-dd-yyyy")#</CFOUTPUT>
```

Incidentally, Now() is a related function that provides you with the server's current date and time. You can format the date in a number of different ways using month, date, and year. Here are the basics:

♦ d: Day of the month, but single digit days aren't preceded by a zero (1, 2, and 13, for example).

♦ dd: Day of the month, and single digit days are preceded by a zero (01, 06, and 23, for example).

✦ `ddd`: A three-letter abbreviation for day of the week (such as Mon, Tue, and Wed).

✦ `dddd`: The full name of the day of the week.

✦ `m`: Month of the year, but single digit months aren't preceded by a zero (such as 1, 6, and 11).

✦ `mm`: Month of the year, and single digit months are preceded by a zero (01, 04, and 10, for example).

✦ `mmm`: The month as a three-letter abbreviation (such as Jan, Mar, and Oct).

✦ `mmmm`: The full name of the month.

✦ `y`: The year as last two digits, but only one digit for years ending lower than 10 (1, 5, and 23, for example).

✦ `yy`: The year as last two digits (such as 01, 08, and 98).

✦ `yyyy`: The year represented by four digits (1998, 2002, and 2014, for example).

Some similar functions to `DateFormat` are worth checking out in the CFML Reference, which you can get to by pressing Ctrl+F1 in Dreamweaver. They include `TimeFormat`, `CreateDate`, `Now`, and `NumberFormat`.

Using the Trim function

`Trim` is another exceptionally simple, but often used and valuable function. `Trim` removes any leading spaces from either side of data in a string. This is most useful, for example, when processing searches from text form fields, because you can strip out the spaces in a text field entry like "new homes" to create a search string that could look like "newhomes." Here's how the function looks when used to set a variable that comes from a form:

```
<CFSET HomeSearch = trim(form.HomeType)>
```

In the preceding example, the `HomeType` form input will have any leading or trailing spaces removed, and the resulting input will be assigned to the variable `HomeSearch`.

In addition to `Trim`, there are also two related functions, `Ltrim` and `Rtrim`. These functions, as you might expect, remove spacing from the left or the right of a string value.

Casting Data into Arrays, Lists, and Structures

In the course of building a dynamic Web site, you will oftentimes find yourself looking for different ways to use *structured datasets* — collections of data that fit a predefined structure. These datasets can be used for a variety of activities, such as populating form elements, creating name/value pairs for things like link-text navigation, or even creating altogether new data structures. To help facilitate the use of structured datasets, ColdFusion has three different kinds of tools available to developers:

✦ **Lists:** Lists are simple collections of a number of items.

✦ **Arrays:** Arrays are sets of structured data that can be like a structured list, like a spreadsheet (with rows and columns), or an even more complex configuration.

✦ **Structures:** Structures are collections of related data that are put together in a virtual container of sorts to make them easier to use.

This section covers when and how you can add each of these different elements to your dynamic Web site.

All these data structures support the use of queries to populate them. For more information on how to query a database, check out Book VI, Chapter 3.

Creating lists

Lists allow you to take single sets of structured data and output them to a Web page. You can create a list in ColdFusion in two ways:

✦ Using a `<CFLOOP>` tag

✦ Using the `ListAppend` function

Creating a list with `<CFLOOP>` is the more common method, but we cover both techniques.

Using <CFLOOP> to run through a list

To create a simple list using `<CFLOOP>`, just follow these steps:

1. **Create a `<CFLOOP>` tag in Code view of your ColdFusion document.**

The tag should look like this: `<CFLOOP></CFLOOP>`.

2. **Within the `<CFLOOP>` tag, create a variable using the `index` parameter.**

Call this variable `MyList`, which would make the open tag look like `<CFLOOP index="MyList">`.

3. **Create your list using the `list` parameter.**

The list has to be a separated group of values. You use the `list` parameter to specify the list. The default item delimiter is a comma. Creating a list of some of the contributing authors of this book would look like this:

```
<CFLOOP index="ListElement" list="Damon Dean,Andy
    Cowitt,Ellen Finkelstein">
```

The default delimiter is a comma, but you can use the delimiters parameter to specify different delimiters, such as the colon. To create the same list as in Step 3 with a colon (:) as a delimiter, just use this code:

```
<CFLOOP index="ListElement" delimiters=":" list="Damon
     Dean:Andy Cowitt: Ellen Finkelstein">
```

4. **To view the list, add a `<CFOUTPUT>` tag within the `<CFLOOP>` tags and call the variable.**

   Figure 5-5 shows the resulting output, and here's the code:

```
<CFLOOP index="MyList" list="Damon Dean, Andy Cowitt,
     Ellen Finkelstein">
<CFOUTPUT>#MyList#<BR></CFOUTPUT></CFLOOP>
```

Figure 5-5:
Three of the authors of this book!

5. **Press F12 to view your list.**

You can also use the results of a query to populate a list using `<CFLOOP>`. Consider the following query of the sample CompanyInfo database:

```
<CFQUERY datasource="CompanyInfo" name="GetEmployees">
SELECT firstname FROM employee</CFQUERY>
```

Now, if your `<CFLOOP>` tag looks as follows, you can generate a list of the first names of all the company's employees as a loop:

```
<CFLOOP query="GetEmployees">
<CFOUTPUT>#firstname#<BR></CFOUTPUT>
</CFLOOP>
```

Using ListAppend to create a list

Creating a list with the `ListAppend` function is a more advanced and dynamic way of creating a list. This quick example shows you how to do it:

1. **Create a variable using `<CFSET>` and give it the first value of your list.**

   You can use the same variables and lists from the previous example:

```
<CFSET MyList = "Damon Dean">
```

2. **Append the list by using** `ListAppend` **and** `<CFSET>`.

   `ListAppend` asks you to specify the list, and then add the new value. So the code would look as follows:

   ```
   <CFSET MyList = ListAppend(Mylist, "Andy Cowitt")
   ```

3. **To output the new list, create an output tag and call the new** `MyList` **variable.**

   Your code should look similar to this:

   ```
   <CFOUTPUT>#Mylist#</CFOUPUT>
   ```

4. **Press F12 in Dreamweaver to preview your work.**

   You should see the names Damon Dean, Andy Cowitt, and Ellen Finkelstein, in your Web browser.

Creating arrays

Arrays are, very simply, structured datasets. These datasets can exist in *n* number of dimensions. A one-dimensional array looks surprisingly similar to a list. A two-dimensional array is akin to a spreadsheet. A three-dimensional array is, well, complicated, but if you can imagine data with height, width and depth, then you'd pretty much have the concept. While they're possible, don't even ask about four-dimensional arrays, in part because they're really tough to conceptualize, and because ColdFusion only supports up to three-dimensional arrays.

Creating an array

Creating basic arrays is a fairly straightforward proposition. If you want to create an array with some of the jobs related to the creation of this book, here's how you could do it:

1. **Use the** `ArrayNew` **function to create an array and give it a dimension.**

   To keep things simple, use a one-dimensional array, so the code looks like this:

   ```
   <CFSET BookJobs= ArrayNew(1)>
   ```

2. **Add items to the array using** `<CFSET>`.

   When adding items to the new array, you use the `<CFSET>` and then the array name to first specify the array, and then integers enclosed in brackets to specify to which element in the array you're going to be assigning a value.

If the value is a string, you also need to make sure that the array value is enclosed in quotes. If it's another variable, the quotes aren't needed. For this example, you are using strings, so the code looks like this:

```
<CFSET BookJobs[1] = "Writer">
```

3. **Fill out the remaining items in your array.**

Add a few more jobs to complete the array. Here's the remainder of the list:

```
<CFSET BookJobs[2] = "Editor">
<CFSET BookJobs[3] = "Production Manager">
<CFSET BookJobs[4] = "Copywriter">
<CFSET BookJobs[5] = "Illustrator">
```

4. **Add a `<CFDUMP>` tag to the bottom of the array and output the array to the screen by pressing F12.**

The `<CFDUMP>` tag outputs variables to the screen. It's exceptionally handy for debugging your code. When you add the `<CFDUMP>` tag, you need to specify the variable you want to dump. So in this case, the code would look as follows:

```
<CFDUMP var="#BookJobs#">
```

5. **Press F12, and you should get a screen that looks a lot like Figure 5-6.**

Be sure to remove the `<CFDUMP>` tag when you're finalizing your code, otherwise you'll have that lingering output of your array structure.

Figure 5-6:
Hooray for
your first
array!

array	
1	Writer
2	Editor
3	Production Manager
4	Copywriter
5	Illustrator

If you want to see an individual item in an array, such as the Copywriter position, you would use the following syntax:

```
<CFOUTPUT>I was the #BookJobs[4]# for Macromedia Studio MX
    2004 All-in-One Desk Reference For Dummies</CFOUTPUT>
```

Using an array

Now that you've created an array, you can do something more with it than just dump it to the screen. A common use for one-dimensional arrays is to populate lists in form elements. In the following example, you create a drop-down list using the elements from an array:

1. **Create a new file entitled** `inc_array.cfm` **and include the array information from the previous example in it.**

Figure 5-7 shows what the code and filename should look like on your screen in Dreamweaver. We put this in a separate file so that it can be made available to other forms on the site that might need the same list, and so that, if we ever need to update that array, we would only need to do it in one location.

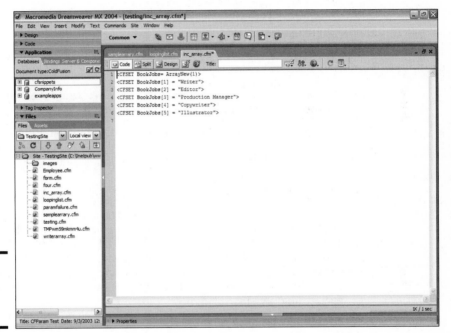

**Book VI
Chapter 5**

Variable, Functions, and Structured Data

Figure 5-7:
Your
inc_array
file.

2. **In a new document, create an include tag to include the array.**

A CFML tag for this very purpose is called `<CFINCLUDE>`. With the `<CFINCLUDE>` tag, you specify a file that will have its contents swapped in for the tag when the page is processed by the ColdFusion server. In this case, we call a template, which is just a reference to another file. Here's what it looks like:

```
<CFINCLUDE template="inc_array.cfm">
```

3. **Convert the array to a list.**

At present, the array is still just a single comma-separated collection of information. Before it can be output to the screen, it needs to be broken down into its individual elements. To do this, use a function called `ArraytoList`. With `ArraytoList`, you can specify an array and a delimiter (optional), and the function creates a new variable as a list. Here's the code:

```
<CFSET JobsList = ArraytoList (BookJobs, ",")>
```

4. **Create a form element.**

   Now that you've got the list settled, you can go about creating the form. Here's some basic code that creates a form element. For the time being, leave all the `<OPTION>` tags out:

```
<FORM action="param.cfm" method="post">
<SELECT name="job">
</SELECT>
<INPUT type="submit" value="Go">
</FORM>
```

5. **Within the `<SELECT>` tags, create a `<CFLOOP>` that takes the list and uses the values in option tags for the drop-down list.**

   Here is the resulting code first, followed by an explanation:

```
<CFLOOP index="FormOptions" list="#JobsList#">
   <CFOUTPUT><OPTION value="#FormOptions#"
   >#FormOptions#
   </OPTION></CFOUTPUT>
</CFLOOP>
```

   To make this work is a tad bit tricky. First you need to create a `<CFLOOP>` and give the `index` a name. In this case, call it `FormOptions`. Then, you call the new `#JobsList#` variable using a `<CFOUTPUT>` tag to get the list elements. Finally, you create a single option tag and use the `#FormOptions#` index value to output the values and names for each drop-down list.

6. **To preview your page, press F12.**

   Figure 5-8 shows the resulting output.

Figure 5-8: Congratulations, you've used your first array!

Working with a two-dimensional array

Two-dimensional arrays give you even more options for adding complex datasets to your site without necessarily using a database. To show you what we mean, we walk you through how to create a dynamically generated text navigation by using a two-dimensional array.

First, take a look at this array:

```
<CFSET MyTwoDArray = ArrayNew(2)>
<CFSET MyTwoDArray[1][1] = "Home">
<CFSET MyTwoDArray[1][2] = "index.cfm">
<CFSET MyTwoDArray[2][1] = "Products">
<CFSET MyTwoDArray[2][2] = "products.cfm">
<CFSET MyTwoDArray[3][1] = "About Us">
<CFSET MyTwoDArray[3][2] = "about.cfm">
```

A couple of things jump out immediately as being different from the previous arrays in this chapter:

+ We designated this array as a two-dimensional array by adding a 2 in the parentheses following the `ArrayNew` function.

+ Two sets of numbers are in brackets next to the variable when you're setting the values. Because this is a two-dimensional array, two number pairs specify which row things are in (the first number), and which column they're in (the second number). In this case, we've made all the row to column combinations equal, but they don't need to be that way.

After you have created this two-dimensional array, you can turn it into a navigation bar. And here's some good news: It's actually easy to do! Just follow these steps:

1. **Make sure that you've included the previous array in your document.**

2. **Create a `<CFLOOP>` tag with an** `index` **of** `count` **that starts at one and goes to three, and be sure that the `<CFLOOP>` is enclosed within a `<CFOUTPUT>` tag.**

The code would look like this:

```
<CFOUTPUT>
<CFLOOP index="count" from="1" to="3"></CFLOOP>
</CFOUTPUT>
```

3. **Within the `<CFLOOP>` tags, create a link that references the array files within the `href` and the array names within the link.**

In this step, you're adding the code that will output both the name of the link and the corresponding linked file as the loop is being processed. To accomplish this, use the `index="count"` to pull the appropriate name or page by checking the stage of the loop. Note that all the names are in the 1 column and all the files are in the 2 column. Here's the code you would need to do it:

```
<A href="#MyTwoDArray[count][2]#">#MyTwoDArray[count][1]#</A><BR>
```

4. **Press the F12 key to preview your new page.**

   And voilà! You should have three links, as shown in Figure 5-9.

Figure 5-9:
Nav bar based on an array.

Home
Products
About Us

Using structures

Structures are an interesting alternative to arrays because they can contain any number of different kinds of data. Structures contain discreet elements, but they are accessed through names given to the structure. Structures are both powerful containers for data and easier to think about than arrays. Here's a simple example that shows how you can create a structure for employee information:

1. **Create the structure with a <CFSET> tag.**

   Like an array, there's a ColdFusion function, called structnew, that you use to cast a variable as a structure. The following code creates a new structure for employees:

   ```
   <CFSET employee= structnew()>
   ```

2. **Add some data to the structure.**

   For this employee structure, add first name, last name, e-mail address, department, and salary, which requires the following code:

   ```
   <CFSET employee.firstname = "Bob">
   <CFSET employee.lastname = "Smith">
   <CFSET employee.email = "bobsmith@somecompany.com">
   <CFSET employee.department = "IT">
   <CFSET employee.salary= "100000">
   ```

   In a structure, the word to the right of the dot (firstname in employee. firstname, for example) is called a *key*, and the combination of this key and it's corresponding value is called a key/value pair. New structure items are added to the employee variable, separated by a dot (the same basic syntax that you'd see with form variables, such as #FORM. firstname#).

3. **To call the values in a structure, use a** `<CFOUTPUT>` **tag and specify the value using its key.**

   To output this information to the screen, you can use the following code:

   ```
   <CFOUTPUT>
   Name: #employee.firstname# #employee.lastname# <BR>
   Email: #employee.email# <BR>
   Department: #employee.department# <BR>
   Salary: #employee.salary# <BR>
   </CFOUTPUT>
   ```

4. **Press F12 to preview the page.**

   As shown in Figure 5-10, you should see the information about an employee, Mr. Bob Smith.

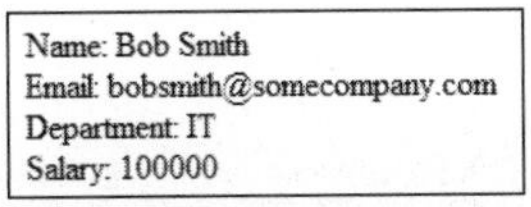

**Book VI
Chapter 5**

Variable, Functions, and Structured Data

Figure 5-10:
All about
Mr. Smith.

```
Name: Bob Smith
Email: bobsmith@somecompany.com
Department: IT
Salary: 100000
```

You can also cast data from a query into a structure. Imagine that a user logged on to your corporate intranet. After the user was authenticated, the intranet might make a query like the one we used earlier in this chapter:

```
<CFQUERY datasource="CompanyInfo" name="GetEmployeeInfo">
SELECT * FROM employee
WHERE emp_ID=#EmployeeNumber#
</CFQUERY>
```

This would make all the data from the query available as variables that can be copied into a structure.

So, as you can see, structures offer a tremendous amount of flexibility to the developer. There are also a number of functions that can allow you to manipulate the data in a structure. Table 5-2 includes some of these other structure-related functions and what they do.

Table 5-2	Common Structure Functions
Function	*What It Does*
StructNew	Creates a new structure
IsStruct	Tests to make sure a variable is in fact a structure

(continued)

Table 5-2 *(continued)*

Function	What It Does
StructAppend	Appends one structure to another
StructDelete	Removes an item from a structure
StructCount	Counts the number of items in a structure
StructFind	Enables you to find values in a structure
StructKeyList	Provides a list of all the keys in a structure
StructSort	Sorts elements within a structure

Chapter 6: Using Databases with ColdFusion MX 6.1 Developer Edition

In This Chapter

✔ **Investigating relational databases**

✔ **Understanding Open Database Connectivity**

✔ **Understanding Object Linking and Embedding**

✔ **Creating queries in ColdFusion**

*B*ook VI, Chapter 4 gives you a brief introduction to some of the basic database concepts in ColdFusion. This chapter gives a more in-depth look at what it means to build a database-driven Web site, both conceptually and practically. This chapter also gives you a more detailed description of how you can build a database and add, update, and delete data from that database.

ColdFusion comes with some sample databases, but it isn't a program that you can use to build and maintain a database. To create a database, you need a product such as Microsoft Access, Microsoft SQL Server, MySQL, or Oracle.

A number of other interesting tips and tricks are covered in Book VI, Chapter 4, such as how to use the WHERE clauses to filter data. Similarly, we also show you how to use the SQL functions of INSERT, UPDATE, and DELETE in Book VI, Chapter 4.

Understanding Relational Databases

A traditional database is similar to a spreadsheet, where a collection of worksheets make up the entire spreadsheet, usually called a *workbook*. These worksheets, however, don't have any real connection to one another, except for the fact that they're all part of the same workbook. A traditional database is made up of rows and columns, as shown in Table 6-1, and functions in much the same fashion as these spreadsheets. Traditional databases all have a one-to-one relationship between the table and its data, which means that each table has its own set of data, and that data in one table is not connected to the data in any other table.

Table 6-1		A Traditional Database Table
FirstName	*LastName*	*EmailAddress*
Bob	Smith	bsmith@somecompany.com
Robert	Williams	rwilliams@somecompany.com
Sarah	Kahn	skahn@somecompany.com
Jane	Gasteyer	jgasteyer@somecompany.com

Relational databases have been around since 1970, when E. F. Codd invented them at IBM. In a *relational database*, multiple tables are linked together through the use of data that exists in more than one table (this is usually referred to as cross-referencing).

In contrast to a traditional database, a relational database makes a direct connection between items in one table and items in another table through the use of unique identifiers, or *keys*. This simple concept opens up a wide array of possibilities in database design.

Here's a simple example. Table 6-1 shows four people that all work at the same company, Some Company. Say that the data sits in the Contacts table. You might have another table specifically for addresses of all the companies you do business with, called Companies. These two tables, in the relational style, are shown in Tables 6-2 and 6-3, respectively.

Table 6-2			The Contacts Table
ContactID	*FirstName*	*LastName*	*EmailAddress*
1	Bob	Smith	bsmith@somecompany.com
2	Robert	Williams	rwilliams@somecompany.com
3	Sarah	Kahn	skahn@somecompany.com
4	Jane	Gasteyer	jgasteyer@somecompany.com

Table 6-3			The Companies Table		
CompanyID	*Organization*	*Address*	*City*	*State*	*Zip*
10	Some Company	1234 Main Street	Some City	CA	94101
11	Another Company	22 Minor Way	Another City	NE	10110

To connect the Contacts table to the Companies table, you need to cross-reference them somehow. To do this, you can use another table. We call that table ContactToCompany, and it includes the data shown in Table 6-4.

Table 6-4	The ContactToCompany Table
ContactID	*CompanyID*
1	10
2	10
3	10
4	10

**Book VI
Chapter 6**

**Using
Databases with
ColdFusion MX 6.1
Developer Edition**

If you look closely at Tables 6-2 and 6-3, you see that Table 6-4 shows that all the employees in the Contacts table are now being associated with the same address for Some Company through this intermediary table.

Designing your database using cross-reference tables provides many advantages, including the following:

✦ You can represent complex, many-to-many relationships, rather than simple one-to-one relationships.

✦ Updating an individual data element can impact a large number of related records, as in the case of the address. Updating the address automatically updates four other records in the database.

✦ Your databases are more scalable. Relational databases are capable of handling data that is more complex, and therefore can be used for a greater variety of applications.

The net result of using relational databases is that Web developers have been able to build increasingly complex applications based on more advanced database designs. But the great part about relational databases is that they're just as applicable to smaller dynamic sites as well. It's more about the way you think about representing data in a database, rather than the content itself. So as you begin to think of your first dynamic Web site, challenge yourself to start thinking about how you want to collect data about your products, and see if the relational database model makes sense for you.

It wouldn't make sense to walk you through the process of building a relational database because ColdFusion is designed to use relational databases, not to build them. However, ColdFusion supports the following products that you can use to generate your databases:

✦ Microsoft Access (Windows)

✦ Microsoft SQL Server (Windows)

✦ MySQL (Windows, Mac, Linux, Unix), an OpenSource database server

✦ Oracle (Unix, Windows)

At last check, `www.dummies.com` has more than 50 books related to database development. If you plan to use databases heavily for your Web site, you should point your browser to `www.dummies.com` and check some of them out! Our favorite is *Microsoft SQL Server 2000 For Dummies*, by Anthony T. Mann (published by Wiley Publishing, Inc.).

Understanding ODBC and OLE

Truthfully, you don't really need to know much about Open Database Connectivity (ODBC) or Object Linking and Embedding (OLE) to begin using ColdFusion. However, in the interest of clarity, we want you to know what they are. Simply put, ODBC and OLE are different protocols that enable the Web server to communicate with a database. Specifically, here's what they mean:

✦ **ODBC (Open Database Connectivity):** ODBC is the workhorse application programming interface (the method for interfacing between your application and a data source) for accessing a database. We call it a workhorse because over the past decade, this has become the method of choice for interacting with Structured Query Language (SQL) databases.

✦ **OLE (Object Linking and Embedding):** OLE is the future of desktop communication. OLE can talk to a database, much like ODBC, but OLE is designed to provide greater integration between your desktop and a host of interactive applications that utilize technologies like Microsoft's ActiveX.

In practical terms, it doesn't make a whole lot of difference which method you use to connect to a database. That being said, most people will agree that OLE does provide a faster connection. However, despite the big push by Microsoft, most people are still using ODBC as their connection method of choice within ColdFusion, simply because of its stability and market acceptance. Figure 6-1 shows the ColdFusion Administrator, where you can choose your method of database connection.

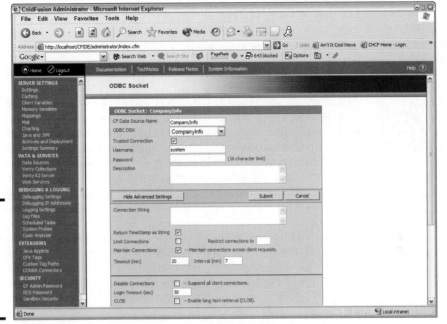

Book VI Chapter 6

Using Databases with ColdFusion MX 6.1 Developer Edition

Figure 6-1: Choose to use OLE or ODBC to connect to your database.

Creating Queries in ColdFusion

Querying a database in ColdFusion is done through different CFML tags, depending upon the situation. You use three basic tags to perform database operations (there are others, too, but they're more specialized):

✦ `<CFQUERY>`: This is the most common query tag, and the one with which you will no doubt become exceptionally familiar. `<CFQUERY>` supports the use of SQL (Structured Query Language), and allows you to perform a host of SQL database operations, including `SELECT`, `INSERT`, `UPDATE`, and `DELETE`.

✦ `<CFINSERT>`: CFML includes its only `INSERT` function through the `<CFINSERT>` tag. You can use either `<CFQUERY>` or `<CFINSERT>` to insert data into a database.

✦ `<CFUPDATE>`: Similar to `<CFINSERT>`, this tag allows you to update records in a database.

The details about using each of these tags are covered in the following sections.

Using <CFQUERY>

<CFQUERY> is the workhorse tag in ColdFusion. You use it when you want to perform any kind of database operation. The structure of <CFQUERY> is as follows:

```
<CFQUERY name="somename" datasource="somedatabase"> Insert
    your SQL statement here</CFQUERY>
```

Within this code, name is the name you assign to the query, and datasource is a mapped database in ColdFusion and SQL. The SQL within the tags is passed directly to the database for execution; the resulting dataset is resident in memory while the page is active, and then is made available as a series of variables that correspond to the columns requested from the database.

Book VI, Chapter 4 covers <CFQUERY> in more detail, including examples on usage and how to output data from queries to the screen. Also check out Book VI, Chapter 5 for more information on how to use the variables generated from a <CFQUERY>.

Using <CFINSERT>

<CFINSERT>, to some degree, takes the place of the INSERT SQL function. In fact, when you use this tag, all ColdFusion is doing is taking the parameters you specify in the tag and turning it into SQL to be executed at the database. The basic structure of the <CFINSERT> tag is as follows:

```
<CFINSERT datasource="SomeDatabase " tablename="SomeTable"
    formfields="FormVariable1, FormVariable2, etc. ">
```

<CFINSERT> is only valuable when you're doing simple inserts to a database. If the queries are more complex and require inputting into more than one table, for example, you'll have to use <CFQUERY> and include your SQL there.

Here's an example that you can try with the databases that come with ColdFusion to show how <CFINSERT> works:

1. **Create a ColdFusion page by pressing Ctrl+N in Dreamweaver, and then save the page to your local testing area on your hard drive.**

2. **Create two form variables using** <CFSET>.

    Usually, these variables would be passed from a form to the page, but for this demo, we're just going to create them here in the page. Here's what the code for these two variables looks like:

```
<CFSET form.dept_name = "Web Development">
<CFSET form.location = "San Francisco">
```

3. **Create a <CFINSERT> tag to put this data into the Departmt table in the CompanyInfo database as follows:**

```
<CFINSERT datasource="CompanyInfo" tablename="Departmt"
    formfields="dept_name, location">
```

The CompanyInfo database comes with ColdFusion and is already mapped as a datasource (as shown in Figure 6-2), so you don't have to worry about that step. This database also doesn't need a password, so you won't need to include that parameter in your <CFINSERT> tag.

Now, we're sure a couple things immediately popped into your head when you saw this code snippet. One is that the variables are the same name as the columns in the database. To use this tag, you need to map the variable name to the table column. For example, if in your form, you were capturing department as simply dept, then you could use a <CFSET> tag to convert dept to dept_name as follows:

```
<CFSET dept_name = form.dept>
```

**Book VI
Chapter 6**

**Using
Databases with
ColdFusion MX 6.1
Developer Edition**

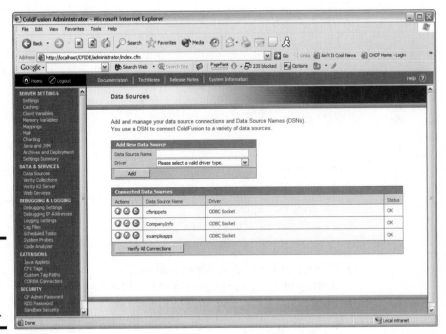

Figure 6-2:
Company-
Info comes
with
ColdFusion.

4. **Create an output to see if your update worked.**

   You want to check to make sure your update worked, so you should create a `<CFQUERY>` that checks the database to see if the record is there. Then, of course, you need to output it to the screen with a `<CFOUTPUT>` tag. Here's the resulting code:

   ```
   <CFQUERY datasource="CompanyInfo" name="CheckUpdate">
   SELECT Dept_ID, Dept_Name, location FROM Departmt WHERE
       dept_name ='#dept_name#'
   </CFQUERY>

   <CFOUTPUT query="CheckUpdate">#Dept_ID#, #dept_name#,
       #location#</CFOUTPUT>
   ```

5. **Press F12 to preview your work.**

Using *<CFUPDATE>*

`<CFUPDATE>` is similar in design to the `<CFINSERT>` tag. The difference is that `<CFUPDATE>` is used to update information in an existing row, rather than create a new row in a table. It also shares a similar structure, as follows:

```
<CFUPDATE datasource="SomeDatabase"
    tablename="SomeTable"
    formfields="UniqueID, UpdateVariable, UpdateVariable">
```

The slight difference here is that you need to select the record that you want to update. Take the case of the change we just made to the CompanyInfo table. The output query returned a value of 7 as the `Dept_ID`. So if we wanted to update that record to reflect that Los Angeles was now where the Web Development department was located, we'd have to do the following:

1. **Set `location` equal to Los Angeles and `Dept_ID` equal to 7.**

   You'll find it best if you do this in a new ColdFusion page. Here's what the code would look like:

   ```
   <CFSET form.Dept_ID = 7>
   <CFSET form.location = "Los Angeles">
   ```

2. **Create the `<CFUPDATE>` tag.**

   In this case, we specified `Dept_ID` so that ColdFusion knows which record it's looking for. We also need to specify the other field to update, as well as the database and appropriate table. Here's the code to update the two columns:

```
<CFUPDATE datasource="CompanyInfo"
     tablename="Departmt"
     formfields="Dept_ID,location">
```

3. Press F12 to update the database.

After you've done this, you can also then run the output query from the previous example to see the change.

<CFUPDATE> is really only good for the most basic of updates to a database. If you need to update more than one record at a time, you're better off using <CFQUERY>.

Book VI
Chapter 6

Using
Databases with
ColdFusion MX 6.1
Developer Edition

Chapter 7: Advanced Features in ColdFusion MX 6.1 Developer Edition

In This Chapter

✔ **Using** `<CFFORM>`

✔ **Working with sessions and cookies**

✔ **Sending e-mail**

✔ **Creating dynamic graphs**

✔ **Creating custom tags**

*W*hen you've got the basics of your site running smoothly, you can start taking a closer look at some of the more advanced features in ColdFusion. In this chapter, we show you how you can extend the functionality of forms on your site, as well as how to keep information available throughout the duration of a user's visit. We also walk you through how to send e-mail and make charts, and finally, provide you with all the information you need to create your own CFML tags.

Using `<CFFORM>`

You may be familiar with HTML forms from Dreamweaver MX 2004. But did you know that you can use ColdFusion to check form fields for values? You can do precisely that using `<CFFORM>` and `<CFINPUT>` tags. Although `<CFFORM>` and `<CFINPUT>` initially look similar to plain old HTML forms, you can set a number of different parameters with ColdFusion forms. These parameters, when read by a ColdFusion server, are converted to JavaScript to provide the desired functionality.

Take a look at this brief code snippet:

```
<CFFORM action="form.cfm" method="post" name="MyForm">
<CFINPUT type="text" name="FirstName" required="yes"
    message="This is a required field">
<INPUT type="submit" value="Go">
</CFFORM>
```

This is a simple form that looks almost like any other form you'd see in an HTML page, except for the addition of `required ="yes"` and `message="This is a required field"`. If you saved this code in a page entitled `form.cfm`, loaded the page on a ColdFusion-enabled server, and clicked the Go button without including a value for the field, you'd get an error message, just like the one you see in Figure 7-1.

Figure 7-1:
An error
message.

If you think the dialog box in Figure 7-1 looks a lot like something you'd see coming from JavaScript, well, you're correct: It is JavaScript! If you view the source of the resulting page, you can see what happened. First, the following code was added to the head of the document:

```
<SCRIPT LANGUAGE="JavaScript" TYPE="text/javascript">
<!--

function  _CF_checkMyForm(_CF_this)
{
        if  (!_CF_hasValue(_CF_this.FirstName, "TEXT" ))
        {
               if  (!_CF_onError(_CF_this,
    _CF_this.FirstName, _CF_this.FirstName.value, "This is a
    required field"))
               {
                      return false;
               }
        }

        return true;
}

//-->
</SCRIPT>
```

All this JavaScript does is check to see if the text field has a value in it. If it does, great, nothing happens. If it doesn't, then the JavaScript code creates a pop-up warning saying, "This is a required field."

The form itself was also changed, as follows:

```
<FORM NAME="MyForm" ACTION="form.cfm" METHOD="POST"
   onSubmit="return _CF_checkMyForm(this)">
<INPUT TYPE="text" NAME="FirstName">
<INPUT type="submit" value="Go">
</FORM>
```

When `<CFFORM>` was read by the ColdFusion server, it collected all the requirements of all the `<CFINPUT>` tags and then generated all the JavaScript needed for the form validation. Then, it converted the `<CFFORM>` and `<CFINPUT>` tags to regular HTML form elements. Finally, it added `onSubmit="return _CF_checkMyForm(this)"`, which calls the JavaScript that is doing the validation.

This feature provides you with an easy and fast way to validate your forms on the browser, before any data is ever submitted, and there are several parameters that you can set. All of these parameters are set in the `<CFINPUT>` tag, and the most common ones for `<CFFORM>`, `<CFINPUT>`, and `<CFSELECT>` are listed in Table 7-1.

Because this type of form validation uses JavaScript that is read by a user's browser, if a user chooses to turn off JavaScript in his or her browser, this type of validation won't work.

Form validation done in the manner discussed here is called *client-side validation*. You can also validate forms after the data has been sent to the server, called *server-side validation*. To learn more about server-side validation, check out *ColdFusion MX For Dummies*, by John Paul Ashenfelter and Jon Kocen (published by Wiley Publishing, Inc.).

In addition to `<CFINPUT>`, `<CFSELECT>` can also be used to create drop-down lists. Check out `<CFSELECT>` in the CFML Reference in the ColdFusion documentation for a good example of how to use `<CFSELECT>` with a database query to populate a drop-down list.

**Book VI
Chapter 7**

**Advanced
Features in
ColdFusion MX 6.1
Developer Edition**

Table 7-1   Common Parameters for <CFFORM>, <CFINPUT>, and <CFSELECT>

Tag	Parameter	Description
`<CFFORM>`, `<CFINPUT>`, `<CFSELECT>`	Name	Describes the name of the element.
`<CFFORM>`	Action	Gives the page to execute when the form is submitted.
`<CFFORM>`, `<CFSELECT>`, `<CFINPUT>`	passThrough	Allows you to pass HTML code that isn't supported by `<CFFORM>` through to the resulting HTML form.

(continued)

Table 7-1 *(continued)*

Tag	Parameter	Description
`<CFINPUT>, <CFSELECT>`	`Required`	Determines whether a value for the field is required or not.
`<CFINPUT>`	`Validate`	Verifies the format of a given value. There are several formats to choose from, including `date`, `eurodate`, `time`, `float`, `integer`, `telephone`, `zipcode`, `creditcard`, and `social_security_number`.
`<CFINPUT>, <CFSELECT>`	`Message`	Gives a message to display if validation is unsuccessful.
`<CFSELECT>`	`Query`	Specifies a query to be used to populate the list.

Working with Sessions and Cookies

Before getting into the "how" of sessions and cookies, it would be good to review what both sessions and cookies are and why they can be exceptionally useful in Web development. ColdFusion uses two different types of variables:

+ **Persistent:** Session variables and cookies are examples of persistent variables. These variables are present throughout the user's time on the site and perhaps longer. Session variables are kept in memory, and cookies can be kept in a text file or in memory on the user's computer.

+ **Non-persistent:** These variables are present only in a single ColdFusion page. By default, all variables are non-persistent variables. Unless they are actively passed from page to page — through a URL string like `page.cfm?itemID=10000`, for example — these variables will be resident only for that single page.

Persistent variables are great because after they've been set, they're always available, and you don't have to worry about passing them from page to page. For things like user IDs, user preferences, contact information, e-mail addresses, and other custom information about a user, persistent variables are a perfect way to store that information. The following sections walk you through how to generate cookies and use session variables, and point out the advantages to each method.

Using session variables

Session variables, variables which are resident throughout a users time on a site, are best used when you have information that you only want to keep available while the user's browser is open and while the user is on your site. For example, you may want to use a session variable for things like a user ID or user preferences. These are global items, in the sense that they're needed throughout the user's time on the site, as opposed to just one section or function of the site.

Follow these steps to create a session variable:

1. **In the ColdFusion Administrator, make sure that session variables are enabled.**

By default, they should be enabled, but it's always a good idea to check. In the ColdFusion Administrator, which is shown in Figure 7-2, you can find session variables by selecting Memory Variables from the left navigation bar under Server Settings.

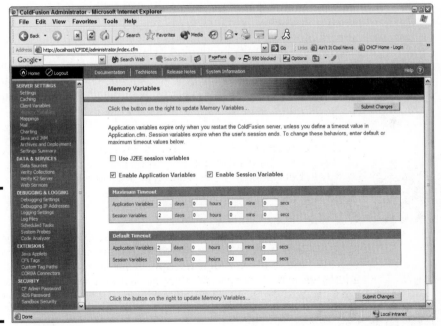

Figure 7-2: Enabling session variables in the ColdFusion Administrator.

2. In your `Application.cfm` **file, turn on session management.**

You turn on session management by adding a `<CFAPPLICATION>` tag to your `application.cfm` file. You enable it by setting `sessionmanagement="yes"`. You can also specify the timeout (how long the cookie is valid for) here by using the `sessiontimeout` parameter. The code is as follows:

```
<CFAPPLICATION NAME="Name of Application"
    SESSIONMANAGEMENT="Yes"
  SESSIONTIMEOUT="#CreateTimeSpan(days, hours, minutes,
    seconds)#">
```

The values that you choose for *days*, *hours*, *minutes*, and *seconds* are all integers.

3. Create your session variable.

Creating a session variable has two components:

- **Set the variable:** Setting the variable looks like setting any other type of variable, except that the variable name must be preceded by the session scope (this is the same scope that we discuss in Book VI, Chapter 3) followed by a period, as follows:

```
<CFSET session.MySessionVariable = SomeValue>
```

- **Lock the code:** In addition to setting the variable, you also need to lock the code. Locking the code simply means that you're going to make sure that the server keeps your request separate from any others that may be occurring at the same time. To do this, you use a `<CFLOCK>` tag that encompasses the `<CFSET>` tag, as follows:

```
<CFLOCK scope="SESSION" timeout="20" type="EXCLUSIVE">
<CFSET session.MySessionVariable = SomeValue>
</CFLOCK>
```

In this code, `scope` is where you want the lock to occur, `timeout` is how long you want the session to remain locked, and `type` is the kind of lock you want to perform. Exclusive locks allow one server request at a time to read or write shared data, where as read-only locks allow more than one request to read shared data. For more information on where you should use exclusive or read-only locks, check out the ColdFusion documentation by pressing Ctrl+F1 in Dreamweaver.

4. Include the session scope so that you can call the variable in your code when it's set.

All session variables need to include the "`session.`" precursor when calling the variable in a `<CFOUTPUT>` tag, as follows:

```
<CFOUTPUT>#session.MySessionVariable#</CFOUTPUT>
```

Setting and retrieving cookies

Cookies are a great way to keep information about a user around for an extended period of time so that you can use it when they visit your site a multitude of times. Unlike a session, which expires after a given period of time, a cookie actually is a text file that resides on a user's computer. This text file usually contains some kind of persistent information about the user, such as an e-mail address, site preferences, or perhaps a log of when he or she last was on the site. As a developer, the value in being able to retrieve this information is to deliver a more targeted, user-friendly application.

Not everyone likes cookies. Some people view them as intrusive or even dangerous because they're allowing an outside site the ability to write a file to their computer. Some people even block cookies. Good net etiquette requires that you must always be judicious when using cookies, and be sure to explicitly state in your site's privacy policy just what you're using those cookies to accomplish.

Here's how you can use ColdFusion to add a cookie:

1. **Enable cookies in your application.**

   Much like sessions, before you can create a cookie, you first have to set up your application to support cookies. This can be done in the `application.cfm` file, using the same `<CFAPPLICATION>` tag that you would use to set up sessions. You need the following three tag values to be set:

   - `CLIENTMANAGEMENT="Yes"`
   - `CLIENTSTORAGE="Cookie"`
   - `SETCLIENTCOOKIES="Yes"`

   After these are set, you can get about the business of generating cookies.

2. **On the page you want to set a cookie, create a `<CFCOOKIE>` tag and give it a name.**

   ColdFusion includes a tag specifically for the writing of cookies. While you can use dots (.) in cookie names, be sure to avoid spaces and vague names. Here's an example of a well-named and well-formed cookie:

   ```
   <CFCOOKIE name="EmailAddress">
   ```

3. **Assign the cookie a value.**

   A cookie value can be just about any kind of string, constant, or variable. It cannot, however, include complex values like arrays or structures. For example, if your site has a newsletter that requires a user's e-mail

Book VI
Chapter 7

Advanced
Features in
ColdFusion MX 6.1
Developer Edition

address, you could include a check box at sign-up that says "Remember my e-mail address." If you set the cookie value to #email#, then you could retrieve that value when the user returns to the site. The syntax for setting this value would be as follows:

```
<CFCOOKIE name="EmailAddress" value="#email#">
```

4. Set an expiration date for the cookie.

Setting the expiration date lets the computer know when to remove the cookie from the user's machine. You can give the expires parameter several possible types of values:

- A specific date (in mm/dd/yy format)
- A specific number of days into the future (1, 2, 30, and so on)
- now, which deletes the cookie
- never, which writes the cookie and never removes it

If you don't want this cookie to expire, the syntax for the cookie would now look as follows:

```
<CFCOOKIE name="EmailAddress" value="#email#"
    expires="never">
```

5. Add additional parameters to the cookie tag.

You can choose to specify three other pieces of information through this tag (check out the CFML reference in Dreamweaver for more detailed information on these parameters):

- **Domain:** This parameter sets the Internet Domain for which the cookie's content is valid. The domain name must start with a period (.), and is a required tag if you use the path parameter. The syntax is as follows: domain =".mydomain.com"

- **Path:** This parameter limits the validity of a cookie to a specific path within a domain. If you use this parameter, then the domain parameter is also required. The syntax is as follows: path="/newsletters"

- **Secure:** This is a simple yes or no flag for the parameter. If yes is selected, then the cookie will only be set if the site is using Secure Socket Layers (SSL). The syntax is as follows: secure="no"

When the page is processed, the cookie will be set. To check to see if your cookie worked locally while you're testing, check out the local cookies directory on your computer, as shown in Figure 7-3.

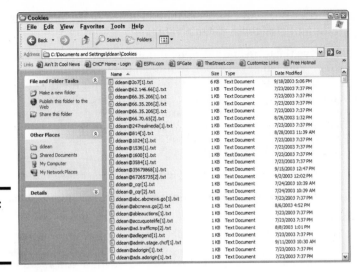

Figure 7-3:
The local
cookies
directory.

Sending Mail

If you want to have users sign up for something on your site — a mailing list for example — then you're probably going to want to take advantage of ColdFusion's mail tools. Before we describe how to do it, though, be warned: You're going to need to have access to an e-mail server (SMTP) to take advantage of this tag, so be sure to check with your Internet service provider and make sure that you have this kind of service.

**Book VI
Chapter 7**

**Advanced
Features in
ColdFusion MX 6.1
Developer Edition**

After you've got that squared away, sending mail is a breeze. Check out the code snippet in the following example. In it, we create a very simple little form that includes first name, last name, and e-mail address, and then with the Steps list, we walk you through sending an e-mail. All of this code goes in the same file, called `mail.cfm`.

Here's the initial FORM code:

```
<FORM method="post" action="mail.cfm">
First Name:  <INPUT name="first" type="text" maxlength="60"><BR>
Last Name:  <INPUT name="last" type="text" maxlength="60"><BR>
Email:  <INPUT name="email" type="text" maxlength="60"><BR>
<INPUT type="submit" value="Send Mail">
</FORM>
```

To make things simple, we post the request to the same page as the form, as indicated by the `method="post"` and `action="mail.cfm"` parameters. Certainly you could have your send-mail page separate. To create the mail, follow these steps:

1. **Use** `<CFPARAM>` **to check for the existence of the three variables in the form and give them default values.**

   Because the form and the logic required to send the mail are on the same ColdFusion page, you first need to make sure that the variables exist. If they don't, ColdFusion returns an error for the code in the next step. This code, placed above the `<FORM>` tag, checks for the existence of the three variables in the form, and if they don't exist, creates them and gives them an empty value. Here's the code:

   ```
   <CFPARAM name="email" default="">
   <CFPARAM name="first" default="">
   <CFPARAM name="last" default="">
   ```

2. **Create a conditional statement that checks for the existence of the variable** `email`.

   You really only need the e-mail address to make this work, so we want to make sure that it has a value associated with it. To do this, you can use a simple `<CFIF>` tag to test for the length of the variable `email`, as shown here:

   ```
   <CFIF len(first) is NOT 0>
   ```

   Place this `<CFIF>` after the `FORM` element in your page. If the length of the variable `email` is not 0, then you know it must have a value and then you can send a message.

   Even though you've tested for the existence of the variable, you haven't tested to see whether or not that e-mail address is "well-formed," meaning it has an at symbol (@) and a dot (.). As it's currently structured, if we put the word "boo" in the e-mail field, it would try to send mail to "boo," which, of course, is not a valid e-mail address.

3. **Create a** `<CFMAIL>` **tag within the** `<CFIF>` **tag.**

   With `<CFMAIL>`, you can specify a number of options. (You can press Ctrl+F1 to access the ColdFusion reference within Dreamweaver to find out more about all the options.) For this message, you only need to be concerned about the following set of parameters:

   - **to:** The address the message is being sent to

   - **from:** The address you want the message to be shown as coming from

   - **subject:** The subject of the message

   - **server:** The mail server that's going to send the message

   For the `<CFMAIL>` parameters, you can use static values and variables, as well as putting the body of the message in between the opening and closing tags.

For an example message, we use #email# to specify the destination address, and then we use #first# and #last# to personalize the message by addressing it to the recipient. Finally, we include a small note to let the user know the message was sent. Again, this will be part of the <CFIF> tag, following the FORM element. The resulting code looks like this:

```
<CFMAIL to="#email#" from="damon@loungeboy.com"
    subject="Here's Your Message, #first#"
    server="mail.loungeboy.com">Dear #first# #last#,
Isn't this mailer the coolest thing!
</CFMAIL>
<P style="color: green">Thank you. Your message has
    been sent to <CFOUTPUT>#email#</CFOUTPUT></P>
```

4. **Move the message to your testing server and try it out by sending yourself an e-mail.**

   Figure 7-4 shows the e-mail you get in your Inbox.

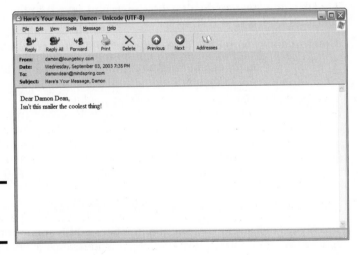

Figure 7-4: You've got mail!

Book VI Chapter 7

Advanced Features in ColdFusion MX 6.1 Developer Edition

Creating Graphs

Imagine for a moment that you're a world-renowned scientist who's been tracking doggie treat consumption for the year 2003. Table 7-2 includes some very important information that any dog would be inter-ested in knowing.

Table 7-2		Average Doggie Treat Allocation by Month for 2003	
Month	*Treats*	*Month*	*Treats*
January	54	July	68
February	74	August	68
March	30	September	40
April	25	October	22
May	20	November	28
June	69	December	38

This data is collected from hundreds of different interviews with dog owners and has been saved as a table called Summary in a Microsoft Access database. Now, you want to make this information available on the Internet as part of your ongoing search for funding sources. With ColdFusion, you can easily generate charts of this information dynamically:

1. **Create a new page to display the charts and save it to the local machine where your testing server is located.**

2. **Create a query to get the data you want to display graphically.**

The following query can be used to get the doggie treat data:

```
<CFQUERY name="TreatSummary" datasource="DoggieTreats">
SELECT Month, Treats, SummaryID FROM Summary
ORDER BY SummaryID
</CFQUERY>
```

Before you can make this query, you need to have a data source set up in ColdFusion Administrator. For details on how to do this, refer to Book VI, Chapter 2.

3. **Set up the parameters of the chart using** `<CFCHART>`.

Much like `<CFMAIL>`, you can set a number of different options to customize the labels, size, color, and overall appearance of your graphs. The following code snippet only uses a handful of them. Refer to the CFML Reference Guide (press Ctrl+F1 in Dreamweaver) for a complete listing of the parameters you can set. Here's one way to configure your chart:

```
<CFCHART chartheight="500" chartwidth="500"
    format="jpg" font="Arial" fontsize="10"
    labelformat="number" show3d="yes">
```

In this snippet, we set the chart to be 500 pixels wide by 500 pixels high, set the graph file format to be a JPEG, set the font to Arial, and set the font size to 10 pixels. Lastly, we set the label format to a number, and we make the graph 3D.

4. **Specify the type of chart you want using** `<CFCHARTSERIES>`.

   The `<CFCHARTSERIES>` tag allows you to define the kind of chart you want to display. Again, you can specify a number of different parameters. If you're only interested in making this a simple bar chart, your code would look as follows:

   ```
   <CFCHARTSERIES type="bar">
   ```

5. **Create a** `<CFLOOP>` **to create all the** `<CFCHARTDATA>` **entries that represent the data for the graph.**

   The `<CFCHARTDATA>` tag is used to specify the item/value pairs for the data in the graph. (In this example, January is an item and 54 is a value.) To create these tags, use a `<CFLOOP>` to get all the month and treat pairs into individual `<CFCHARTDATA>` tags. Here's how it looks:

   ```
   <CFLOOP query="TreatSummary" startrow="1" endrow="12">
   <CFCHARTDATA item="#Month#" value="#Treats#"></CFLOOP>
   ```

6. **Make sure that all your code is closed out by including close tags for all the chart functions.**

   The `<CFCHART>`, `<CFCHARTSERIES>`, and `<CFCHARTDATA>` tags require closing tags. So all the chart code together should look as follows:

   ```
   <CFCHART chartheight="500" chartwidth="500"
       format="jpg" font="Arial" fontsize="10"
       labelformat="number" show3d="yes">
   <CFCHARTSERIES type="bar">
   <CFLOOP query="TreatSummary" startrow="1" endrow="12">
   <CFCHARTDATA item="#Month#" value="#Treats#"></CFLOOP>
   </CFCHARTSERIES>
   </CFCHART>
   ```

7. **Press F12 to see the new graph.**

   Figure 7-5 shows the rather unglamorous but nonetheless effective graph that is generated.

Although these specific charting tags are a great feature for ColdFusion, creating dynamic graphs is definitely slow and a processor hog. You should consider carefully whether or not you can live with slow-loading pages to have dynamic graphs.

**Book VI
Chapter 7**

**Advanced
Features in
ColdFusion MX 6.1
Developer Edition**

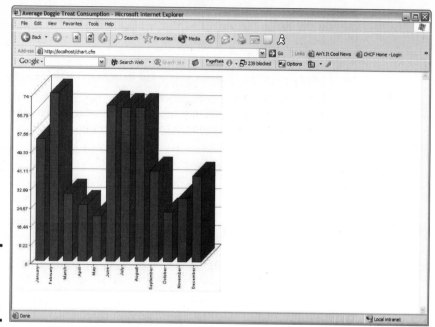

Figure 7-5:
It's not
glamorous,
but it works.

Building Custom Tags

As diverse as ColdFusion is, you may find at times that the base set of functions and tags can't do exactly what you'd like it to do. In those instances, you might consider taking advantage of ColdFusion's custom tags. In ColdFusion, you can create your own CFML tags that are read by the server just like any other ColdFusion tag. ColdFusion custom tags can be made up of CFML code or a scripting language, such as JavaScript or ColdFusion Script.

Here's a good example of a handy custom tag to have around your online store that also shows how custom tags work. This tag, called `<CF_makediscount>`, takes a price and a discount and returns to the page the discounted price.

Here's how you would create the tag if you were doing it from scratch:

1. **Create a structure for the custom tag.**

   Before you begin anything, you have to decide how you want the information to be passed to the custom tag. Your tag should follow the following conventions:

- The tag is enclosed by brackets ($<$ and $>$).

- The tag begins with a `CF_` so that ColdFusion recognizes it as a custom tag and looks for it in the custom tag directory (usually `C:\cfusionMX\customtags` on the server).

- The rest of the name of the tag corresponds to the filename that includes the code for the custom tag. So if your tag is `<CF_somename>`, then there should be a file called `somename. cfm` in the ColdFusion custom tag directory.

- Any parameters within the tag are passed as variables to the file that contains the tag's code. Accordingly, `<CF_somename name="foo">` will pass the value `foo` to the file `somename.cfm`.

In the `<CF_makediscount>` example, the tag follows this structure:

```
<CF_makediscount price='someprice'
    discount='somediscount'>
```

`somediscount`, by the way, is a decimal value, not a dollar amount.

2. **Create a new ColdFusion file called** `makediscount.cfm`.

    This file contains the code that evaluates the price and the discount, and then returns the resulting discounted price back to the page that's asking for it.

3. **Within the** `makediscount.cfm` **file, create the code needed to return the discounted price.**

    Here's the code required to perform the entire operation:

    ```
    <CFIF len(attributes.price) gt 1>
        <CFSET caller.newprice = DollarFormat
      (Evaluate(price - (price * discount))) >
    <CFELSE>
        <CFSET caller.newprice = ''>
    </CFIF>
    ```

    Here's what's going on this code:

    - First, it checks to make sure that, in fact, the tag has passed a value by saying that if the length of the variable is greater than 1 — in which case something must be there — then the code assumes it's a valid value. If no value exists, then the code sets the variable `caller. newprice` equal to a null value (a *null value* is an empty value) and passes that empty value back to the page that made the request to the tag.

    - When these variables have been passed to the page, the simple equation of `discount price = price - (price * discount)` is performed.

**Book VI
Chapter 7**

Advanced
Features in
ColdFusion MX 6.1
Developer Edition

• Performing this equation is also part of setting a new variable, `caller.newprice`, which is sent back to the page that made the call to the custom tag originally.

You may not be familiar with two scopes in the preceding code. The *attribute scope* is used in custom tags to denote the value being passed to the custom tag by the calling page. The *caller scope* sends the value from the custom tag back to the original calling page.

4. **Test the tag by giving it values and outputting the return value to the screen using** `<CFOUTPUT>`.

Figure 7-6 shows how this tag works on a Web page. In the page, you see places for price, discount, and the resulting discounted price.

Figure 7-6:
Discount
pricing!

After you've tried this and it's successful, you've built your very first custom tag, and you're well on your way to building new tags for all those complex functions on your site!

Chapter 8: Integrating ColdFusion MX 6.1 Developer Edition with Other Macromedia Products

In This Chapter

✔ **Integrating ColdFusion with Dreamweaver**

✔ **Integrating ColdFusion with Fireworks**

✔ **Integrating ColdFusion with Macromedia Flash**

C oldFusion can add a tremendous amount of dynamic power to your Web applications. As a member of Macromedia Studio MX 2004, ColdFusion has also become more integrated with other Macromedia products. In this chapter, we provide a brief overview of how Macromedia has chosen to integrate ColdFusion 6.1 Developer Edition with Dreamweaver MX 2004, Fireworks MX 2004, and Macromedia Flash MX 2004. ColdFusion and FreeHand MX don't overlap or integrate, feature-wise.

Integrating ColdFusion with Dreamweaver

Nowhere is the integration effort more apparent than within Dreamweaver. ColdFusion Studio, previously its own stand-alone application, has been fully integrated into Dreamweaver. This melding of the products provides developers with the best of both worlds: The easy to use, graphical orientation of Dreamweaver has been combined with the dynamic development platform of ColdFusion. You can now find ColdFusion tools throughout Dreamweaver:

✦ **The Insert bar:** The Insert bar has three categories that include a wide array of ColdFusion tags, functions, and wizard-like tools. These tools are covered in more detail in Book II, Chapter 6.

✦ **The Application panel:** The Application panel allows you to view data in databases, generate queries, and even build ColdFusion components (bits of code that are encapsulated and made available to all the parts of your application). The Applications panel is discussed in depth in Book II, Chapter 6.

✦ **The Code view:** The Code view, which is shown in Figure 8-1, is the development interface that users had grown accustomed to using in previous versions of HomeSite and ColdFusion Studio. Now, this same interface is available directly in Dreamweaver.

✦ **The Code panel:** The Code panel includes documentation and tools that were previously available in ColdFusion Studio and have simply been ported to this new interface.

With all these areas of Dreamweaver that include ColdFusion components, you also have access to many ColdFusion features. The following ColdFusion features are now fully integrated into Dreamweaver:

✦ **Insert variables, functions, and queries:** You can insert variables, functions, and queries through wizards and dialog boxes. You can find the tools to insert these objects on the Insert bar. For example, if you select the CFML category and click the database icon, you can fill in the blanks and create a `<CFQUERY>` tag to retrieve content from a database.

✦ **Work with databases:** You can select databases and collect record sets from them. To do this, select the Databases tab in the Application panel. If you don't have a site set up, you'll need to configure your Data Sources. Don't worry, Dreamweaver provides a checklist for you to follow to do this! You also find more information on how to retrieve data from a database in Book II, Chapter 6.

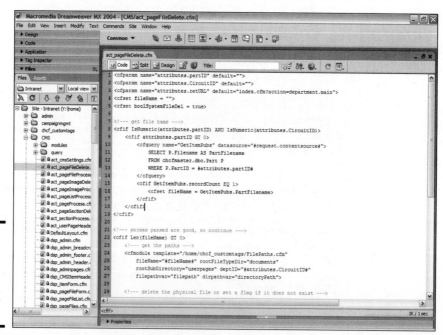

Figure 8-1: The Code view in Dreamweaver MX 2004.

✦ **Generate dynamic content:** You can generate dynamic content by accessing different sources through the Bindings tab on the Application panel. You can also set up variables, give them names, and then just drag them right onto your workspace. For more information on how to use variables in ColdFusion, check out Book VI, Chapter 5.

✦ **Specify server-side actions:** You can specify a variety of server-side actions through the Server Behavior tab in the Application panel.

✦ **Set connections to remote servers:** You can set connections to remote servers using ColdFusion's RDS (Remote Development Services). To use this feature, create a site and specify the RDS connection in the Remote Info category of the Site Definition dialog box, as shown in Figure 8-2. To bring up the Site Definition dialog box, choose Site➪Edit Sites, and then from the Edit Sites dialog box, select your Web site's name and click the Edit button.

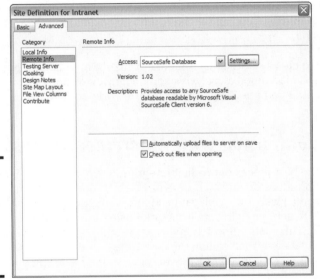

Figure 8-2:
Here's where you can set a connection to a remote server.

✦ **Create and add ColdFusion components to your application:** Using components is beyond the scope of this book. However, *ColdFusion MX For Dummies*, by John Paul Ashenfelter and Jon Kocen (published by Wiley Publishing, Inc.), includes hands-on tutorials of how to use components in ColdFusion.

✦ **Link directly to the ColdFusion Administrator:** You can link directly from Dreamweaver to the ColdFusion Administrator by selecting Modify Data Sources in the Database tab of the Application panel.

✦ **Change the Dreamweaver interface:** You can change the product interface to look just like ColdFusion Studio or HomeSite. This procedure is covered in detail in Book II, Chapter 1.

For a more detailed analysis of Macromedia's integration of Dreamweaver and ColdFusion, check out Book II, Chapter 6.

Integrating ColdFusion with Fireworks

The integration between Fireworks and Dreamweaver is both extensive and well-thought-out. ColdFusion, however, doesn't play much of a role at all in that integration. In fact, the only place in Fireworks where ColdFusion is mentioned at all is in the Export feature. In Fireworks, if you choose File⇨ Export⇨Options, you can set the export extension to a `.cfm` file for ColdFusion.

Be sure to check out the Macromedia Exchange at `www.macromedia.com/exchange`. Macromedia is always adding new extensions for products, and it's here that you are likely to find any Fireworks-to-ColdFusion tools.

Integrating ColdFusion with Macromedia Flash

One of the best pieces of product integration in Macromedia Studio is between ColdFusion and Macromedia Flash. In the recent versions of Macromedia Flash and ColdFusion, Macromedia provided developers with a new way to get dynamic data from ColdFusion into the Macromedia Flash interface. This method, which involved creating XML in ColdFusion with the dynamic data and then calling the file through ActionScript, was a good first step, but it was a convoluted way to query a database, and it slowed down your Flash movies.

With the introduction of ColdFusion MX, Macromedia significantly expanded its integration efforts in an effort to define Macromedia Flash as an interactive, Web-compatible display layer that can easily and efficiently communicate with the business logic through ColdFusion. In other words, Macromedia is betting the proverbial farm that developers really want to create dynamic sites using Macromedia Flash for the display side and ColdFusion for the database side.

The information that follows is specific to Macromedia Flash MX Professional 2004. Macromedia Flash MX 2004 (no Professional) is currently bundled with Macromedia Studio. So, while these features do exist, you'll need to upgrade to the Professional version of Macromedia Flash to take advantage of them.

The result of all this development work can be boiled down to two features:

✦ **The Macromedia Flash Remoting service:** This service allows you to connect directly to an application server, such as ColdFusion, and execute server-side ActionScript.

✦ **New query support for ActionScript:** Now, with server-side ActionScript, you can access data in ColdFusion directly using two new functions, called `CF.query` and `CF.http`, that are functionally akin to the `<CFQUERY>` and `<CFHTTP>` CFML tags.

In addition to the Macromedia Flash Remoting service, Macromedia also provides another communication server product, the Macromedia Flash Communication Server. With this product, Macromedia Flash talks to a communication server using ActionScript, and the server in turn can communicate with a ColdFusion server. For more information on these tools, check out the *Macromedia Flash MX ActionScript Bible*, by Robert Reinhardt and Joey Lott (published by Wiley Publishing, Inc.).

Advanced Macromedia Flash and ColdFusion integration just isn't easy, and it really goes beyond the scope of this book. If you're looking for a good hands-on guide to these new features, check out *ColdFusion MX For Dummies*, by John Paul Ashenfelter and Jon Kocen (also published by Wiley Publishing, Inc.).

Macromedia provides developers with the Designer & Developer Center, a fine resource for discovering more about Macromedia products and how to use them. You can find the Designer & Developer Center at `www.macromedia.com/desdev`.

Using the Macromedia Flash Remoting service

The Macromedia Flash Remoting service enables you to use Macromedia Flash to connect directly to an application server, such as ColdFusion, and it also offers developers greater access to dynamic content and more advanced scripting tools. The basic way in which this interaction takes place between the Flash client and the server is shown in Figure 8-3.

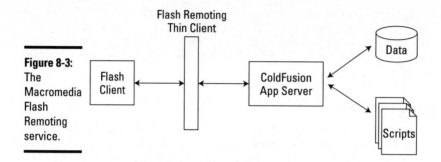

Figure 8-3:
The
Macromedia
Flash
Remoting
service.

The following steps outline the process of making the connection to the Macromedia Flash Remoting service, both on the ColdFusion and on the Macromedia Flash sides:

1. **Make sure that the remoting service is installed and that you have a copy of Macromedia Flash MX Professional 2004 installed.**

   You can find the installer for the remoting service in the folder `D:\Flash MX\Extending Flash MX`, assuming that `D:\` is your CD-ROM drive with the Macromedia Studio installation disc in it.

2. **To be able to use the service, you need to include the files `NetSevices.as` and `NetDebug.as` in your Macromedia Flash ActionScript.**

   These two files tell Macromedia Flash how to manage the remote connection after it's been made and to provide the debugging output for the service. `NetDebug` is optional, and really should only be used when you're testing your application. Your ActionScript should look as follows:

   ```
   #include "NetServices.as"
   #include "NetDebug.as"
   ```

3. **Specify the location for the remote service.**

   Basically, this just means that you need to tell Macromedia Flash where to look to find the ColdFusion application server on the machine where your server-side ActionScript resides. Usually, your ColdFusion server (and therefore, the Remoting Gateway) is located at `http://localhost`, or `http://localhost:8500`. The code in your Macromedia Flash ActionScript should look like the following:

   ```
   NetServices.setDefaultGatewayURL("http://localhost/
       flashservices/gateway ")
   ```

   The `/flashservices/gateway` part is a built-in virtual directory that uses ActionScript to connect to the remoting service.

4. Set the connection.

When you're ready, in your ActionScript you need to say, "Open, gateway," which can be done with the following ActionScript:

```
gatewayConnection =
    NetServices.createGatewayConnection()
```

5. Go get your content!

This is where the approaches to getting content diverge. At this point, you can choose to either call a ColdFusion component or a server-side ActionScript file. For every service you call, though, you need the following bit of ActionScript:

```
Service = gatewayConnnection.getService("Filename",
    this);
```

Where `service` is the name of the instance you are invoking, `gatewayConnection.getService` is the function that gets the server-side ActionScript file, `filename` is the name of the ActionScript file without the extension, and `this` represents the current instance of the service.

The Macromedia Web site has a great paper written by Stephen Gilson that walks you through a lot of this in more detail. The paper is entitled "Using Macromedia Flash Remoting with Macromedia ColdFusion," and you can find it by going to the Designer & Developer Center and selecting Flash Remoting from the Development Centers drop-down list. You can also find this paper in the ColdFusion support documentation area of the Macromedia Web site.

Working with CF.query and CF.http

As part of the new server-side ActionScript element of the Macromedia Flash Remoting service, Macromedia has developed two new functions that you can use to interact with the ColdFusion server without having to learn CFML:

✦ `CF.query`: `CF.query` is a server-side ActionScript function that allows you to execute ColdFusion queries from within a Flash movie. This functionality allows developers to execute database-driven applications directly from Macromedia Flash through server-side ActionScripts. The following syntax shows the arguments that `CF.query` supports in this version:

```
CF.query
    ({
        datasource:"data source name",
        sql:"SQL stmts",
        username:"username",
        password:"password",
```

```
        maxrows:number,
        timeout:milliseconds
    })
```

There are actually two different ways you can express the `CF.query` and `CF.http` functions. Both are acceptable, and here's what the other method looks like:

```
CF.query(datasource, sql);
CF.query(datasource, sql, maxrows);
CF.query(datasource, sql, username, password);
CF.query(datasource, sql, username, password, maxrows);
```

✦ `CF.http`: `CF.http` is an ActionScript function that allows `HTTP POST` and `GET` methods to be executed from within a Flash movie. `CF.http` provides a gateway through which information can be passed back and forth to the ColdFusion server. The following syntax shows the arguments that `CF.http` supports in this version:

```
CF.http
    ({
        method:"get or post",
        url:"URL",
        username:"username",
        password:"password",
        resolveurl:"yes or no",
        params:arrayvar,
        path:"path",
        file:"filename"
    })
```

Within Dreamweaver, check out the ColdFusion Help (Using ColdFusion in Dreamweaver) for a complete description of how to set up Macromedia Flash Remoting and invoking `CF.query` and `CF.http`. You can access Using ColdFusion in Dreamweaver by pressing Ctrl+F1.

Understanding the Macromedia Flash Communication Server

The Macromedia Flash Communication Server provides a similar functionality as Macromedia Flash Remoting; the primary difference between the two is in the design. In the Macromedia Flash Communication Server design, rather than talking directly to an application server, the Macromedia Flash client talks to the Macromedia Flash Communication Server, which in turn talks to the ColdFusion server. You can find out more about the Macromedia Flash Communication Server in Book V, Chapter 10.

If you're interested in finding out more about how and when to use the Macromedia Flash Communication Server, you should check out

"Macromedia Flash Communication Server: Use Cases and Feature Overview for RichMedia, Messaging, and Collaboration," a white paper written by Jonathan Gay and Sarah Allen, the engineers who built the product. You can find this paper in the ColdFusion support documentation area of the Macromedia Web site at `www.macromedia.com/desdev/mx/flashcom`.

Charting

The other integration point between ColdFusion and Macromedia Flash is in ColdFusion's charting tools. The default file type for charts generated using the `<CFCHART>` tag is `.fla`. You can also choose to have the files generated as JPEG and PNG files. At present, if you select Macromedia Flash as the format, ColdFusion does not animate or otherwise take advantage of Flash animation in the generated chart.

Book VII

Contribute 2

The 5th Wave   By Rich Tennant

"What do you mean you're updating our home page?"

Contents at a Glance

Chapter 1: Introduction to Contribute 2

In This Chapter

✔ Deciding when to use Contribute

✔ Checking out the Contribute interface

✔ Setting your preferences

For many big Internet and intranet sites these days, Web development experts are the ones who author the site (that is, they design it and build it from scratch, or at least set up its basic framework). After a site is established, it may then need to grow and change — which in the past meant calling in that handy Web development expert again to update a Web site. Now, however, people more familiar with the content that needs to go on the site than with the vagaries of Web development are being asked to take on the responsibility of updating the original pages or adding new pages based on existing designs.

The original version of Dreamweaver was built to enable people to create and modify Web pages without having to learn the boring ins and outs of HTML. The funny thing is, the "new-and-improved" Dreamweaver MX 2004 has become so powerful as an authoring tool that it's too complex and intimidating (and expensive!) for non-experts who simply want to maintain an existing site.

So what's a non-expert to do? Read on to discover the answer.

Why Contribute?

When Dreamweaver is too much, Contribute is just right. Contribute is designed especially for people who must contribute to an existing site but don't need or want to know how to develop a site from scratch.

Contribute is streamlined to make Web page production as simple as possible, which means there are many things the application can't do, such as editing the HTML making up the page. For those kinds of tasks, you definitely still need Dreamweaver. Table 1-1 offers a list of some common Web page tasks that each application can be used for.

Table 1-1	Comparing the Capabilities of Dreamweaver and Contribute		
Task		*Dreamweaver*	*Contribute*
Creating a new page from scratch		x	x
Creating a new page from a Dreamweaver template		x	x
Creating a Dreamweaver template		x	
Viewing and editing the underlying HTML code directly		x	
Adding, deleting, and modifying text and tables		x	x
Adding and deleting images		x	x
Creating DHTML navigation bars		x	
Adding, modifying, and deleting behaviors (such as JavaScript button rollovers)		x	
Creating and modifying framesets		x	
Modifying content (such as text and images) within frames		x	x
Creating forms		x	
Creating and editing Cascading Style Sheets (CSS)		x	
Applying CSS styles to text		x	x
Uploading and downloading Web Pages to/from a remote server		x	x

As you can see, there's quite a bit of overlap in the capabilities of the two applications, but the more complicated tasks are best accomplished using Dreamweaver.

Exploring the Contribute Interface

The Contribute interface is as streamlined as its functionality, as you can see in Figure 1-1. Two panels are at the left, with a big work area — known as the Browser — at the right.

Panel basics

While other applications in the Macromedia Studio MX 2004 suite have many customizable panels, Contribute has just two basic panels, the Pages panel and the How Do I panel, as shown in Figure 1-1. Unlike the panels in other Macromedia Studio applications, you can't move, group, or delete the panels in Contribute.

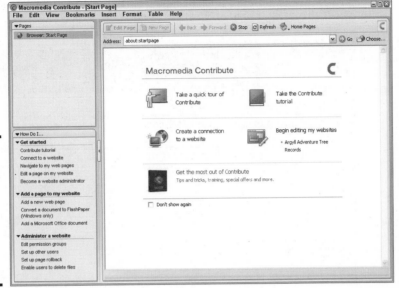

Figure 1-1:
Contribute's
streamlined
interface
includes
two panels
(at left)
and the
Browser.

You can, however, collapse and expand the panels by clicking the arrow at the top left of the panel or by clicking the panel name. If the panel was expanded before you clicked, it collapses. If it was collapsed originally, it expands.

You can hide (or show) both panels by using the keyboard shortcut F4.

The Pages panel

The Pages panel displays the name of the most recent page you browsed to, any unpublished drafts you have (that is, any pages you have downloaded and edited but not uploaded back to the server), and the page on which you're currently working. Figure 1-2 shows that we're currently working on the page titled "AAT : Treets," and that we have a draft of the "AAT : Artists" page that has been edited but not yet uploaded.

To navigate to any page listed in the Pages panel, click the title or the icon to the left of the title of the page you want to display in the Browser.

If you click on the page at the top of the list, the Browser automatically switches to Browse mode. If you're already in Browse mode and you click a Draft, the Browser automatically switches to Edit mode and displays your page, ready to edit.

Figure 1-2:
The title of
the page
currently
being
edited is
highlighted
in the Pages
panel; the
page itself
is available
for editing
in the
Browser.

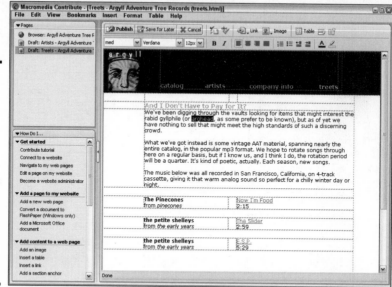

The Browser is always at the top of the list in the Pages panel. See "The Browser/Editor" section, later in this chapter, for more information on the Browser itself.

The How Do I panel

The How Do I panel has three sections when you open Contribute for the first time (refer to Figure 1-1 to see the panel in its basic state):

✦ **Get Started**

✦ **Add a New Page to My Website**

✦ **Administer a Website**

By default, all sections are expanded. It's easy to collapse or expand a section; just click the arrow at the left of the section name, or click on the section name itself. If the section is expanded when you clicked, it collapses. If the section is collapsed when you click, it expands.

Each section has a list of actions you might want to perform. The list is in the form of text links, just like on a Web page. The list of links changes, based on what you're currently working on. We collapsed the first two sections in Figure 1-2 so that you can see some of the other sections that show up automatically in the How Do I panel when you're editing a page.

When you click a link, the How Do I panel updates, as shown in Figure 1-3. To return to the previous page of information in the panel, click on the Back button at the top left of the How Do I panel. To go back to the original list of links, click the Topics icon at the top right of the panel.

Figure 1-3:
The
How Do I
panel fits
a lot of
information
in a small
space by
using links.

> ▼ How Do I...
> ⇦ Back   🗐 Topics
>
> **Connect to a website**
>
> Contribute provides two ways for you to connect to your website:
>
> • **Import a connection key** created by your website administrator. The connection key contains the necessary settings for connecting to a website.
>
> • **Enter the connection information** in the Connection Wizard (Windows) or Connection Assistant (Macintosh). The wizard prompts you for all the necessary connection information.

The Browser/Editor

The main work area is called the Browser/Editor (we call it the Browser to save space). The Browser has two modes, Browse and Edit, and you can only be in one mode at a time. The appearance and functionality of the Browser depend on which mode you're in.

When you're in Browse mode in the Browser, you can navigate anywhere a regular Web browser, such as Internet Explorer or Netscape Navigator, could take you. When you're in Edit mode, you can make changes to a Web page.

Browse mode

In order to browse to a page you want to update, you must use the Browser in its Browse mode. You can tell when the Browser is in Browse mode by looking at the buttons at the top. The following buttons (as shown in Figure 1-4) allow you to navigate as you would using any browser, like IE or Navigator:

✦ **Back:** Click this button to view the previous page you were viewing in the Browser. You can step back one at a time through each of the pages you viewed since you opened the browser. The Back option in the View menu performs the same function.

✦ **Forward:** Click Forward to go one page at a time from pages you viewed earlier to pages you viewed most recently.

✦ **Stop:** Pages with lots of big images or complex Flash movies sometimes take awhile to load in the Browser. Click this button to stop a page from loading further in the Browser.

✦ **Refresh:** As with your regular Web browser's Refresh button, this button reloads the current Web page in the Contribute Browser.

The rest of the buttons are specific to the Contribute Browser:

✦ **Edit Page:** Click this button to edit the page you have browsed to. When you click Edit, Contribute downloads the page and automatically sets the Browser to Edit mode. This option is not available if you don't have what Contribute calls a *connection* — that is, permission to edit the page.

✦ **New Page:** Click this button to create a new page on the current Web site. You will be prompted to name the page and, if you desire, to choose a page or template to use as a basis for the new page. See Book VII, Chapter 2 for more details.

✦ **Home pages:** Use this button to navigate quickly to the home pages of the sites to which you have Contribute connections. Click and hold to see a drop-down list of eligible home pages.

✦ **Go:** This button works in conjunction with the Address text input field. See the following instructions for browsing to a page on the Internet.

✦ **Choose:** Click this button to open a dialog box in which you can navigate quickly to any page on the Web site you're currently updating.

Figure 1-4:
The
Browser
toolbar in
Browse
mode.

To browse to a page on the Internet, just follow these simple steps:

1. **Type or paste a URL (such as** www.earlsbowlateria.com**) into the Address field at the top of the Browser.**

2. **Click the Go button at the right of the address input field or press Enter.**

The requested Web page opens in the Browser.

When you browse to a site you have been set up to edit with Contribute, the top left of the Browser toolbar has two buttons: Edit Page and New Page.

(Refer to Figure 1-4). When you browse to a page you are not set up to edit with Contribute, the Edit Page and New Page buttons are replaced by the Create Connection button (see the section on connecting to a site in Book VII, Chapter 2 for more information on creating connections).

Edit mode

The Edit mode is what Contribute is all about: It's the mode that you use to make changes to Web pages. To get into Edit mode after you've browsed to an editable page, do one of the following:

✦ **Click the Edit Page button at the top left of the Browser**

or

✦ **Choose File➪Edit Page or use the keyboard shortcut Ctrl+Shift+E**

To get into Edit mode if you haven't yet browsed to a page you have permission to edit, click the name of an existing Draft in the Pages panel (or click the icon next to the name). The Draft opens in the Browser, and the Browser automatically switches to Edit mode.

Most of Book VII, Chapter 2 is about the things you can do in Edit mode, so if you're anxious to get to work on a site, skip ahead to the next chapter.

Menus

The Contribute menu bar sports eight menus, each of which includes several choices. (Many of the choices are also available from buttons at the top of the Browser.) We give you some details about the first three menus, as well as brief descriptions of what the other five offer:

✦ **File:** Every computer program has a File menu, with options like Open, Save, and the like. The Contribute File menu offers the following:

- **New Page:** Select this option to create a new Web page. You can create a new page from scratch, from an existing page, or from a Dreamweaver MX 2004 template. See Book VII, Chapter 2 for details.

- **Edit Page:** This option is only available when the Browser is in Browse mode and is currently displaying a page you have permission to edit. When you select File➪Edit Page, Contribute downloads the page to your computer and makes it available for modification. Clicking the Edit Page button in the Browser does the same thing.

- **Publish:** Select this option to upload an edited page to the server.

- **Publish as New Page:** Select this option to upload a page to the server with a new filename (such as `aboutus.htm`). You're prompted to type or paste in the new filename. See Book VII, Chapter 2 for details.

**Book VII
Chapter 1**

Introduction to
Contribute 2

- **Save:** Select this option to save the work you have done on a draft without publishing the edited page. After you have saved, you may continue work on the draft.

- **Save for Later:** Select this option to save the work you have done on a draft without publishing the edited page; the Browser will automatically change from Edit mode to Browse mode and load the last page you were looking at in Browse mode.

- **Cancel Draft:** Select this to delete the draft you're currently working on from your computer. *Note:* Selecting Cancel Draft will not delete the page from your Web site.

- **Preview in Browser:** Select this to see what your draft looks like in your regular browser (IE, Navigator, Opera, Safari, and so on).

- **E-mail Review:** Select this to upload a temporary version of your page to the server and send an e-mail to a coworker with a link to the temporary page. If you need someone's approval before you publish a page (make it live on the site so users can see it), E-mail Review is a handy automated way to show your work to the person who can approve it.

- **Export:** Select Export to save a copy of the page you're working on to your local hard drive (or to a removable disk or remote hard drive).

- **Page Setup:** Select this option to open a dialog box that allows you to customize how your printer deals with your page (paper size, orientation, and so on).

- **Print:** As you might expect, you can print your Web page by selecting Print from the File menu.

- **Print Preview:** Select Print Preview to see on your computer screen a representation of how your Web page will appear on paper when you print it.

- **Roll Back to Previous Version:** If you find you've published a page that has a mistake on it, select Roll Back to Previous Version to restore the previously published version of the page. See Book VII, Chapter 3 for more information on this feature, which must be set up by an administrator.

- **Delete Page:** Select Delete Page to remove a page from your Web site. This option is available only when the Browser is in Browse mode.

- **Work Offline:** Select this option if you don't need to upload or download any unpublished drafts you're editing, or if you're temporarily unable to connect with your network or the Internet.

- **Drafts:** Use this option to open an unpublished draft of a page.

- **Recently Published Pages:** Use this option to view in the Browser a page you recently published.

- **Exit:** Select this option to close Contribute. You can also close Contribute by pressing Ctrl+Q or Alt+F4 on your keyboard.

✦ **Edit:** The options under the Edit menu include such perennial favorites as Cut and Paste, as well as a few Contribute-specific options. Which options are "live" (not grayed out) at any given time depends on your most recent action. (Figure 1-5 shows the Edit menu after some text has been cut from the current draft.)

Figure 1-5:
The Edit menu as it appears after some text has been cut.

- **Undo:** Select this option to undo your most recent actions in a draft, one at a time. You can't use Undo to alter a published page; for that, you need to choose File⇨Roll Back. The keyboard shortcut for Undo is Ctrl+Z.

- **Redo:** Redo is sort of an undo of an undo. Select this option to redo the last actions you undid in your draft, one at a time, or use the keyboard shortcut Ctrl+Y.

- **Cut:** Select this option to remove highlighted text or objects from your draft. You can then paste the text or objects into the same page, a different page, or even a different kind of document (for example, a Word document). The keyboard shortcut to cut highlighted objects is Ctrl+X.

- **Paste:** After you've selected some text and/or objects (like images, for example), select this option to paste the text and/or objects into your draft, or use the keyboard shortcut Ctrl+V.

- **Paste Text Only:** After selecting a block of text that also includes images or other objects, you can use this option to paste only the text from your selection. You can also use the keyboard shortcut Ctrl+Shift+V.

- **Clear:** Use this option to remove selected text or objects from your Web page. Unlike Cut, this option does not allow you to paste the removed text or objects elsewhere.

**Book VII
Chapter 1**

Introduction to
Contribute 2

- **Select All:** Use this option to select everything in a draft. You can then cut, paste, or clear everything at once. The keyboard shortcut for select all is Ctrl+A.

- **Preferences:** Select this option to open a dialog box that allows you to customize the way Contribute works. See the "Setting Preferences" section, later in this chapter, for details.

- **My Connections:** Use this option to view, edit, and delete the connections you have to the sites you maintain.

- **Administer Websites:** If you have Administrator privileges on any sites to which you have connections, use this option to open the Administration dialog box and change any settings for the selected site. See Book VII, Chapter 3 for information on sitewide settings, permission groups, and setting up users.

✦ **View:** The View menu offers options related to what you see on-screen in Contribute.

- **Sidebar:** Select this option to show or hide the sidebar, which contains the Pages and How Do I panels.

- **Browser:** Select this option to switch to the Browse mode of the Browser. The last page you looked at in that mode appears in the Browser. You can use the keyboard shortcut Ctrl+Shift+B or click the top line in the Pages panel to do the same thing.

- **Go to Web Address:** If you select this option, a dialog box opens in which you can type or paste a URL to open a particular Web page in the Browser. When you click OK, the Browser switches to Browse mode — if it wasn't already in Browse mode — and loads the page you requested. You can also use the keyboard shortcut Ctrl+O to open the Go to Web Address dialog box.

- **Choose File on Website:** This option allows you to navigate directly to an editable page from a window that displays all the sites to which you have a Contribute connection.

  The Back, Forward, Stop, Refresh, and Home Pages options function just like their corresponding buttons in the Browser. See the "Browse mode" section, earlier in this chapter, for the skinny on them.

✦ **Bookmarks:** A bookmark is a link to a Web page. Options here allow you to add and delete bookmarks to Web pages you visit often. If your main Web browser is IE, you see all your IE bookmarks listed under the Other Bookmarks option.

✦ **Insert:** Select an option in this menu to insert an item into a draft. The Insert menu allows you to insert the following items into a draft:

- Image
- Table
- Link
- Date
- Section Anchor
- Horizontal Rule

- Line Break
- Special Characters
- Microsoft Office Document
- Other Document
- Flash Movie

✦ **Format:** You can use the options in this menu to format selected text in a draft. You can apply CSS styles, as well as more traditional HTML text treatments like bold and italic. See Book VII, Chapter 2 for details on text formatting in Contribute. The Format menu also gives you access to the Contribute Spell Check (keyboard shortcut: F7) and to edit Page Properties, such as title and background color (keyboard shortcut: Ctrl+J).

✦ **Table:** This menu offers commands that allow you to insert and edit tables in your draft.

✦ **Help:** The Help menu gives you a choice of several kinds of help:

- **Macromedia Contribute Help:** Select this option to view standard help files, with step-by-step instructions.

- **Quick Start Guide:** Select this option to see instructions on the basics of Contribute to help get you up and running quickly.

- **Contribute Support Center:** When you select this option, your regular Web browser opens to the Contribute Support home page on Macromedia's Web site.

- **Contribute Tutorial:** Select this option to access a set of guided lessons on basic tasks you can perform with Contribute.

  The Help menu also allows you to open the Contribute Welcome page in the Browser, print your Contribute registration form or submit your registration online, and see the About Contribute window, which shows information about the version of Contribute you're running.

The Insert, Format, and Table menus give you ways to perform tasks we discuss in more detail in Book VII, Chapter 2.

Setting Preferences

For most users, the default Preferences should suffice, but you may wish to (or need to) make a few changes in order to use Contribute most efficiently. To open the Preferences dialog box, choose Edit➪Preferences.

**Book VII
Chapter 1**

Introduction to
Contribute 2

The Preferences dialog box includes five "screens"; you access the different screens by selecting one of the items in the list on the left side of the dialog box (see Figure 1-6). A brief overview of each page follows.

Setting general preferences

The General screen of the Preferences dialog box has two sections:

✦ **Editing Options**

- **Faster Table Editing (Deferred Update):** This check box is selected by default. Deselect this check box if you want Contribute to update the way tables appear on-screen as you edit them, which may slow down other Contribute operations.

- **Enable ScreenReader Support:** Select this check box if you have a visual impairment that hinders your ability to work with Contribute.

- **Spelling Dictionary:** Choose a dictionary language from the drop-down list. Contribute uses the dictionary to spell-check Web page drafts.

✦ **Microsoft Office Documents:** You can choose one of the following options for the way Contribute treats a Word document or Excel spreadsheet when you insert it into a draft.

- **Insert the Contents of the Document into the Current Web Page:** Choose this option if you want Contribute to convert the contents of the document into HTML.

- **Insert a FlashPaper Viewer for the Document into the Page:** Use this option if you want to use Contribute's new FlashPaper technology to convert the document. See Book VII, Chapter 4 for details.

- **Create a Link to the Document (Recommended for Large Documents):** Use this option if you want Contribute to upload the Office document to your Web site and put a link to the document in the draft you're currently editing.

- **Ask Whenever I Insert a Microsoft Office File into Contribute:** Use this option if you need to handle inserting Office documents into your Web pages on a case-by-case basis. This option is selected by default.

Setting file editor preferences

You can tell Contribute what application you want it to use to open various types of files when you double-click the files in the Browser in Edit mode. To set Contribute to open a particular type of file with a particular application, just follow these steps:

1. **Select File Editors from the list on the left side of the Preferences dialog box.**

The File Editors options appear, as shown in Figure 1-7.

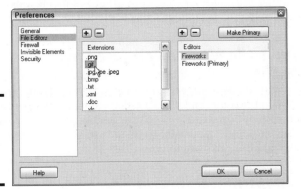

**Book VII
Chapter 1**

Introduction to
Contribute 2

Figure 1-7:
Setting the
File Editor
Preference
for GIFs.

2. **If the extension is not already listed in the Extensions list box, click the + button above the Extensions box (if the extension is already listed in the Extensions box, skip to Step 4).**

A cursor blinks at the bottom of the list.

3. **Type the name of the extension, including the dot (for example, type .wav for a WAV audio file) and press Enter.**

The extension you typed in remains highlighted.

4. **If the application is not already listed, click the + button above the Editors box (if the application is listed, click its name to select it and skip to Step 6).**

The Select External Editor dialog box pops up.

5. **Navigate to the application and double-click its icon, or type the path-name (including the application name) into the File Name text field.**

   The application name appears in the Editors box.

6. **Set any other file editor preferences and click OK when you've finished.**

Contribute comes with quite a few defaults (naturally, Macromedia Studio MX 2004 applications feature prominently), so you may never need to touch the File Editors preferences. You can assign more than one application to edit a particular file type. If you do that, you need to designate one of the programs as the primary application by selecting it in the File Editors screen of the Preferences dialog box and clicking the Make Primary button.

Setting firewall preferences

If your computer is separated by a firewall from the server that houses your site (or sites), use the Firewall screen of the Preferences dialog box to input the host name and port number that allow you to tunnel through the firewall. If you're not sure what all that means, ask someone in your IT department.

Setting invisible element preferences

When you link some text or an image to a particular line on a Web page, you need to place an invisible target (an anchor) at that line. Select Invisible Elements in the list box on the left of the Preferences dialog box to see the Invisible Elements options. Leave the Show Section Anchors When Editing a Page check box selected if you want to be able to see icons that identify where invisible anchor links are in your draft.

Setting security preferences

If you share a computer with other people and don't want them to have access to Contribute (and therefore to the sites you maintain), open up the Security options on the Preferences dialog box and select the Require Contribute Startup Password check box. Then follow these steps:

1. **Click in the Password text field, type a password, and press the Tab key.**

   The cursor moves to the Confirm Password text field.

2. **Retype your password in the Confirm Password text field exactly as you typed it in the Password text field above. Press Enter or click OK.**

   Contribute will ask for a password when you launch the application.

You can change your preferences at any time by choosing Edit⇨Preferences.

Chapter 2: Basics for Contributors

In This Chapter

✔ Connecting to a site

✔ Opening an existing page for editing

✔ Creating a new page

✔ Working with text and tables

✔ Adding images, links, and more

✔ Previewing your work

✔ Uploading (publishing) a page

✔ Collaborating

The new and improved Macromedia Contribute, bearing the daringly original title "Contribute 2," is a remarkably easy-to-use tool for editing existing Web pages on — or adding new pages to — a Web site. As with the original version of Contribute, many of the things you need to do to add or replace content on a page (or build a page based on an existing design) take little more than a click. And you don't have to know a thing about HTML.

With Contribute 2, Macromedia has improved upon the original version of the application while keeping it simple enough for nontechnical users — no small task. This chapter is all about how using the Contribute 2 tools can make modifying or creating a basic Web page easier. If you need to know about things like setting yourself up as a site administrator or sending a connection key to a fellow site contributor, see Book VII, Chapter 3.

Connecting to a Site

In order to put Contribute 2 to use when working on a Web site, you must be connected to that site. Being *connected* means establishing an FTP (File Transfer Protocol) connection between your computer and the remote server that your site lives on. If that sounds complicated, don't worry. It's actually pretty simple.

You can connect in two ways:

✦ By using a connection key that the site administrator has e-mailed to you

✦ By entering information in the Connection Wizard

Both ways are pretty simple, but you'll need some information about your Web server to employ the latter method. If you've been sent a connection key, read the next section to find out how to use it. If you need to connect to a site but don't have a key, skip ahead to the "Connecting to a site with the Connection Wizard" section.

Connecting to a site with the connection key

A *connection key* is an encrypted file that contains nearly all the information Contribute needs to connect your copy of Contribute to the Web site you'll be updating. (You also need to get a password from your administrator.) You might receive a connection key

✦ Via e-mail sent to you by the site administrator

✦ By downloading it from your local network

Most likely, you'll get your connection key via e-mail, but it works the same either way (just skip Step 2 below). To open a connection to the Web site you'll be working on, just follow these simple steps:

1. **Open the e-mail from your site administrator that contains the connection key.**

    The connection key shows up as an attachment (see Figure 2-1). The body of the e-mail contains instructions on using the key. The name of the connection key is based on the name the site administrator has given the site connection in Contribute.

2. **Double-click the connection key.**

    Contribute starts up (if it's not already open), and the Import Connection Key dialog box opens.

3. **If your name is not already there, click in the What Is Your Name? text field and type your name. Press Tab or click in the E-mail text field.**

4. **If your e-mail address is not already there, type your e-mail address in the next field. Press Tab or click in the next text field.**

    If you already have a connection to another Web site, your e-mail address may already be entered in the field.

5. **In the What Is the Connection Key Password? text field, type the password given to you by the site administrator.**

    The password may have been sent in a separate e-mail or told to you on the phone. If you don't yet know the password, check with the site administrator.

6. **Click OK.**

The Contribute Browser loads the site's home page.

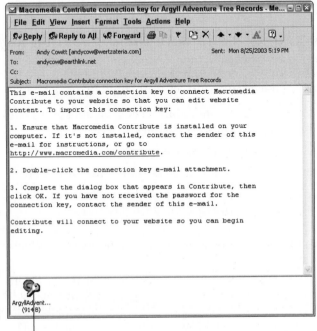

Connection key

The connection key should have all the FTP information that allows you to connect to your Web server. In some cases, you may have to input the FTP information manually. The next section tells you how.

Connecting to a site with the Connection Wizard

Contribute saves you the trouble of having to use an FTP client to move Web pages back and forth between your computer and the server that hosts your Web site. When you click the Edit button in the Browser, Contribute automatically gets (downloads) the page for editing. When you click the Publish button, Contribute puts (uploads) the page to the Web server. After you've set up a connection, Contribute handles all the getting and putting of files seamlessly.

The Connection Wizard makes connecting to a remote Web server a snap, if you have the login information at hand. Just follow these steps to set up a connection, after you have opened Contribute:

1. **Type or paste the URL for your site (for example,** `http://www.mysite.com`**) into the Address field of the Contribute Browser and either press Enter or click the Go button.**

   The Contribute Browser takes you right to your site.

   You can use the Contribute Browser to view any site on the Web, but you can only set up a connection to a site if you have FTP information for that site.

2. **Click the Create Connection button at the top left of the Browser.**

   The Connection Wizard opens to its Welcome screen.

3. **We're assuming you don't have a connection key, so click the Next button at the bottom of the wizard.**

   The User Information screen appears.

4. **Enter your name in the What Is Your Name? text field.**

   Your name may already appear. The name in this field will identify you to other contributors to your site, if there are any.

5. **If it's not already there, enter your e-mail address in the What Is Your E-mail Address? text field, and then click Next.**

   The Website Home Page screen appears.

6. **Enter the URL (**`http://www.mysite.com`**, for example) for the Web site you'll be editing into the text field, and then click Next.**

   You can also click the Browse button, which will open a browser window you can use to navigate to the site.

   When you click Next, the Connection Information screen appears in the wizard.

7. **Select a connection method from the drop-down list.**

   You have the following options: FTP, Secure FTP (SFTP), and Local/Network. If you're not sure what to select, check with your IT person or site administrator. Depending on what you choose, different text fields appear below the drop-down list. As you can see in Figure 2-2, we've entered FTP.

8a. **If you selected FTP or SFTP, enter the FTP server name (for example,** `ftp.earlsbowlateria.com`**), the FTP login (sometimes called the username), and the FTP password in the respective text fields. Click Next.**

   If the site already has an administrator, the Group Information screen appears (go to Step 9a). If the site doesn't yet have an administrator, the Administrator Information screen appears (go to Step 9b).

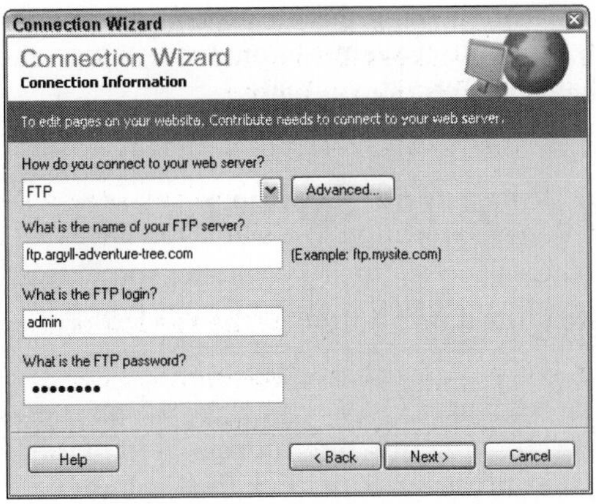

Figure 2-2:
FTP
information
entered
in the
Connection
Information
screen.

8b. **If you selected Local/Network, enter the network path (for example, `\\mynetwork\mydepartment\site`) by typing or pasting it in, or by clicking the Choose Folder button and browsing in your network to the folder that contains your site. Click Next.**

If the site already has an administrator, the Group Information screen appears (go to Step 9a). If the site doesn't yet have an administrator, the Administrator Information screen appears (go to Step 9b).

9a. **If you plan to be the site administrator, click Administrator. Otherwise, click User. If your administrator has given you a different group name to use, it should appear in the list on the left, where you should click it. Then click Next.**

Contribute has two default categories for contributors: Users, who can perform basic page editing tasks, and Administrators, who can do everything Users can do *and* also perform additional tasks (like deciding whether other contributors are Users or Administrators). If you are going to be an administrator, go to step 9b.

9b. **Enter a password in the top text field on the Administrator Information screen. Then re-enter the password in the text field below, exactly as you typed it above. Click Next.**

You can use any combination of numbers and letters for your password. The password is case-sensitive (so as far as the password is concerned, a big "S" and a small "s" are different characters). Only contributors who know that password will be able to perform administrator functions on the site. For more information on Administrator functions, see Book VII, Chapter 3.

10. **Congratulations! You've made it to the Summary screen. Make sure the information is correct. If it isn't, use the Back button to go to the screen with incorrect info and fix the mistake; then use the Next button to return to the Summary screen. Click Done.**

Unless any of the information you put in the Connection Wizard changes, you never have to think about it again — from here on in, you can just get straight to work making changes to your site.

Opening an Existing Page for Editing

After you've established a connection to your site, you're ready to start making changes to existing pages and even creating new ones. Downloading a page to edit is extremely easy — just follow these steps:

1. **Type or paste the URL of the page you want to edit (for example,** `http://www.mysite.com`**) into the Address field of the Contribute Browser and either press Enter or click the Go button.**

The Browser loads your page, and the Edit Page and New Page buttons appear at the top left of the Browser. If the page is not available for editing, the warning `You are viewing a page on a Web site that you haven't created a connection to` appears under the Address field in the Browser.

2. **Click the Edit Page button.**

The Browser switches to Edit mode, and the page appears as a draft in the Browser. The Browser's toolbar at the top changes to show buttons for inserting links, images, tables, and text, as shown in Figure 2-3.

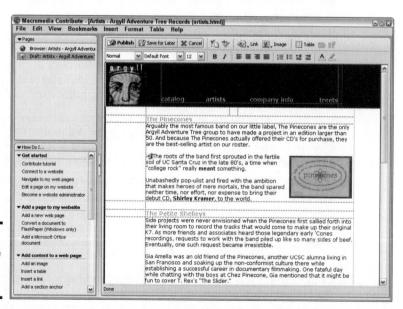

Figure 2-3: A Web page ready for editing.

Creating a New Page

If opening a page for editing is a snap, creating a new page is maybe three snaps. To create a new page for your site, follow these simple steps:

1. **If you have connections to more than one Web site, use the Contribute Browser to browse to the site to which you want to add a page. Otherwise, skip to Step 2.**

The Browser loads your page, and the Edit Page and New Page buttons appear at the top left of the Browser. If the site is not available for editing, the warning `You are viewing a page on a Web site that you haven't created a connection to` appears under the Address field in the Browser.

2. **Click the New Page button, or choose File⇨New Page.**

The New Page dialog box appears.

3a. **If you want the new page to have the same basic appearance and structure (for example, to have the same navigation items and basic layout) as the page currently showing in your browser, click the Copy of Current Page option in the Create New Page From pane of the New Page dialog box.**

3b. **If you want to create a page from a Dreamweaver MX 2004 template, click the template name in the Create New Page From pane.**

If the templates are in a folder and you don't see them, click the plus (+) sign next to the folder that holds the templates; the contents of the folder will appear. A preview of the template appears in the Preview pane, as shown in Figure 2-4.

3c. **If you want to start the page from scratch, skip to Step 4. (Blank Web Page is selected by default.)**

The Blank Web Page option may not be available to you, depending on how the administrator has set up your connection.

4. **Type or paste a page title in the Page Title text field. Click OK.**

Your new page opens in the Browser, as a draft ready for editing.

The page title will appear at the top of the Web browser's window when people view your Web site.

You can also create a new page by using the keyboard shortcut Ctrl+N.

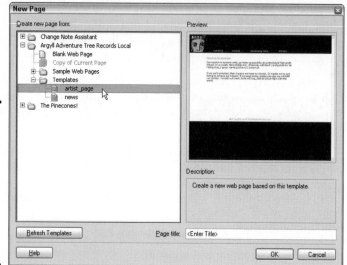

Figure 2-4:
The New Page dialog box allows you to select a template on which to base your new page.

Working with Text

Text is often the most abundant element on a Web site. Contribute makes adding, formatting, and deleting text a piece of cake.

Adding text

To add text to a draft (that is, to a page that's ready for editing; see the previous sections, "Opening an Existing Page for Editing" or "Creating a New Page"), just follow these easy steps:

1. **Click the place in the draft where you want to insert text.**

A cursor blinks in the spot you selected.

2. **Type or paste the text.**

You may need to format the text. See the "Formatting Text" section for the low-down.

Formatting text

Text formatting entails everything from setting a font face and font size to emphasizing words or phrases by making them bold or italic, to creating numbered or bulleted lists. It's all as easy as clicking a button in Contribute.

You can format text either before or after you insert it on a page. If you're working from a template, text areas may be preformatted for things like font size, color, and font face. If not, the text you insert will conform to the settings in the text toolbar (the second row of the Browser).

Setting a text style

To set the font style, choose a style from the Style drop-down list at the top left. If you have CSS styles attached to your page, they will appear in the menu; otherwise, your choices are Normal and Heading 1 (largest) through Heading 6 (smallest).

Setting a text face

To set a face for your font (for example, Arial, Verdana, and so on), choose one from the Font drop-down list to the right of the Style list. If you leave the setting at "Default," the text's appearance will be determined by the browser settings of a visitor to your site.

Setting a text size

Choose a text size from the Size drop-down list. The smallest is 8 (too small for anything but the proverbial "fine print"), and the largest is 36. If you select "Default," the text's size will be determined by the browser settings of a visitor to your site. Figure 2-5 shows just some of the ways you can format text.

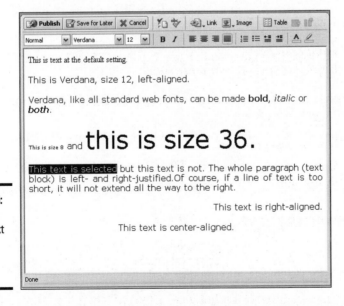

Figure 2-5: You can format text in many different ways.

Selecting text

To select text, click and drag over the text you want to select. The selected text is highlighted. If you change the text style, font face, size, color, or background color settings while text in your draft is selected, the selected text (and only the selected text) will change to reflect the new settings.

Aligning text

Contribute allows you to align text to the left, center, or right, or to justify the text at the left and right (though the latter is extremely rare on the Web). To align text, place the cursor anywhere in the block of text you want to align (or select a block of text by clicking and dragging) and click an Align button (from left to right, the Align buttons are Align Left, Align Center, Align Right, and Justify).

Adding boldness to your text

To make some text bold, follow these steps:

1. **Select the text by clicking and dragging until all the text you want bold is highlighted.**

2. **Click the Bold button or use the keyboard shortcut Ctrl+B.**

   The selected text becomes bold.

You can remove the bold formatting from text by following the same steps.

Italicizing your text

To italicize some text, follow these steps:

1. **Select the text by clicking and dragging until all the text you want changed is highlighted.**

2. **Click the Italic button or use the keyboard shortcut Ctrl+I.**

   The selected text becomes italicized.

You can remove the italic formatting from text by following the same steps.

Changing the text color

Web text is typically black by default but can be set to default to other colors. If you're working with CSS styles or Dreamweaver templates, default text colors may be set for you already.

To change the color of a specific block of text, follow these steps:

1. **Select the text by clicking and dragging until all the text you want changed is highlighted.**

2. **Click the Text Color button in the Browser's Text toolbar.**

   The Text Color button is the one on the second row toward the right with a capital A on it. When you click it, the Color Picker pops up.

3. **Click on a cube of color with the eyedropper to make the selected text that color.**

   For details on how to use the advanced features of the Color Picker, see the section on adding color in Book III, Chapter 3.

Changing the text background color

When you change the text background color, you're changing just that: the background of each chunk of text, be it letters or numbers.

To change the text background color of some text, follow these simple steps:

1. **Select the text by clicking and dragging until all the text you want changed is highlighted.**

2. **Click the Highlight Color button in the Browser's Text toolbar, as shown in Figure 2-6.**

   The Highlight Color button is the one with the highlighter marker; it's just to the right of the Text Color button. When you click on the Highlight Color button, the Color Picker pops up.

3. **Click on a cube of color with the eyedropper to make the background of selected text that color.**

   For details on how to use the advanced features of the Color Picker, see the section on adding color in Book III, Chapter 3.

**Book VII
Chapter 2**

**Basics for
Contributors**

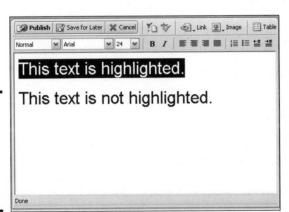

Figure 2-6:
The text
background
color acts
like a
highlighter
marker.

Creating a numbered list

You can create a numbered list the fancy way, with complicated tables and such, or you can do it the easy way, using the numbered list convention built into HTML. Contribute makes the easy way even easier. To create a numbered list, just follow these steps:

1. **Click the Numbered List button in the Browser's toolbar, as shown in Figure 2-7.**

   The indented number 1 appears, followed by a period, a space and a blinking cursor.

2. **Type the first item in your numbered list. Press Enter when you're finished.**

   The number 2 automatically appears on the next line, followed by a period, a space, and a blinking cursor.

3. **Type the second item in your numbered list, press Enter, and continue to enter items until you have completed your list.**

   Leave the extra number you don't have an item for.

4. **Click the Numbered List button to deactivate the numbering.**

   The last (extra) number disappears, and the cursor goes to its non-indented position below the list.

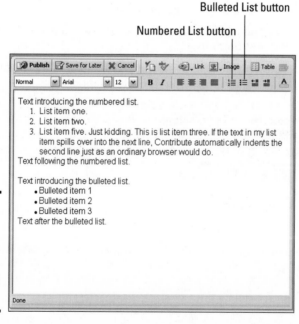

Figure 2-7: Contribute allows you to create numbered and bulleted lists easily.

Creating a bulleted list

HTML has a specification for bulleted lists just as it does for numbered lists. Contribute knows the specification so you don't have to.

To create a bulleted list, simply follow these steps:

1. Click the Bulleted List button in the Browser's toolbar.

An indented bullet appears, followed by a little space and a blinking cursor.

2. Type the first bullet item and press the Enter key.

A bullet appears on the next line, followed by a little space and a blinking cursor.

3. Type the second bullet item, press the Enter key, and repeat the process until you have completed your list.

An extra bullet remains temporarily at the bottom of your list.

4. Click the Bulleted List button to deactivate the bulleting.

The last (extra) bullet disappears, and the cursor goes to its non-indented position below the list.

Working with Tables

You might use tables on a Web page in two basic ways:

✦ To display tabular information, such as a spreadsheet

✦ To control page layout

No matter which function you want the table to have, you can add, modify, and delete the table using the same simple methods. Tables are made up of cells, arranged in rows and columns. Picture a basic tic-tac-toe game. It's played on a kind of table, with nine cells arranged in three rows and three columns. If you can draw a tic-tac-toe game, you can make a table on a Web page.

Inserting a table

To insert a table into your page, just follow these steps:

1. Click the spot in your draft where you want the top-left corner of the table to go.

A blinking cursor marks the spot.

2. **Click the Insert Table button in the top row of the Browser toolbar.**

   The Insert Table dialog box appears, as shown in Figure 2-8.

3. **Enter the number of rows you want the table to have into the Number of Rows field.**

   You can always add more rows or delete extra rows later, if you need to.

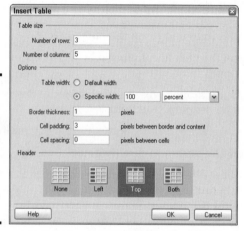

Figure 2-8:
The Insert Table dialog box asks for enough information to create a basic HTML table.

4. **In the Number of Columns field, enter the number of columns you want the table to have.**

   You can always add more columns or delete extra columns later.

5a. **If it doesn't matter how wide the table is, leave the Default Width setting as is and skip to Step 6.**

5b. **If you have a particular width you want the table to be, select the Specific Width radio button, enter a number for the width of your table, and then choose either Pixels or Percent from the drop-down list to the right.**

   If you choose Pixels, the table will be the number of pixels wide that you specified. If you choose Percent, you must choose a numeral between 1 and 100; the table's width will vary according to the overall page layout, and it may vary according to the width of the browser window of a visitor to your site.

6. **In the Border Thickness field, enter a number for how many pixels thick you want the border of your table to be.**

   If you don't want the table border to show (which you probably don't if you're using the table for page layout purposes), enter 0 (zero).

7. In the Cell Padding field, enter a number for the amount of pixels you want between the border of the cell and the text or object inside the cell.

The cell padding applies to the top, bottom, left, and right of the inside of each and every cell.

8. In the Cell Spacing field, enter a number for the amount of pixels you want between the cells.

The cell spacing applies to the whole table; you can't have different cell spacing for individual rows or columns.

9. If your table has a header row or header column (or both), click the icon that represents the header structure of your table.

Figure 2-9 shows a table with a single header row. The text in that row is automatically bold and center-aligned in the cells.

10. Click OK.

The Insert Table dialog box closes, and an empty table appears in your draft, built to your specifications and ready to be filled with content.

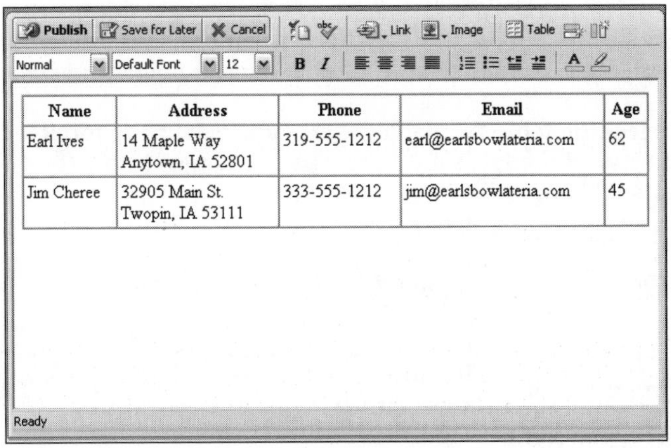

**Book VII
Chapter 2**

**Basics for
Contributors**

Figure 2-9:
A small table, built according to the specifica-tions shown in Figure 2-8.

Publish	Save for Later	Cancel			Link	Image	Table	
Normal	Default Font	12	**B** *I*					

Name	Address	Phone	Email	Age
Earl Ives	14 Maple Way Anytown, IA 52801	319-555-1212	earl@earlsbowlateria.com	62
Jim Cheree	32905 Main St. Twopin, IA 53111	333-555-1212	jim@earlsbowlateria.com	45

Ready

Adding information to a table

Adding text and images to a table is pretty much the same as adding them anywhere else on a draft. To add text to a table, follow these steps:

1. Click in the cell where you want to put the text.

A cursor blinks in the cell.

2. **Type or paste in the text.**

   The cell expands downwards. In some cases, the cell also expands to the right, depending on the width of the cell and the nature of the text. For example, a long e-mail address, which is made of many characters strung together without a space, can stretch a cell. (Refer to Figure 2-9.) The other cells may become narrower to compensate.

3. **Click in another cell or outside the table if you want to add more information to the table or elsewhere on the draft.**

To add an image or other object to a cell, click in the cell and then follow the directions in the "Adding Images, Links, and More" section, later in this chapter.

Modifying a table

You can modify many properties of an existing table quickly and easily. In some cases, you can make the changes by clicking and dragging table or cell borders; in other cases, you can enter new settings in the Table Properties dialog box.

Changing the whole table using the Table Properties dialog box

To make changes to the entire table at once, follow these steps:

1. **Select the table by placing your cursor over the top-left or bottom-left corner of the table until the cursor changes into a four-pointed arrow and clicking.**

   The border of the table highlights.

2. **Click the Table button on the Browser toolbar.**

   Yes, it's the same button you click to insert a table, but when you've selected a table that's already there, the button opens the Table Properties dialog box. The dialog box has two tabs: the Table tab and the Row and Column tab. (The default view opens to the Table tab, as shown in Figure 2-10.)

3. **Select an alignment for the table from the Table Alignment drop-down list.**

   A table can be justified left, center, or right.

4. **Change the table width, border thickness, cell padding, and cell spacing as needed.**

   For more information on those table properties, see the "Inserting a table" section, earlier in this chapter.

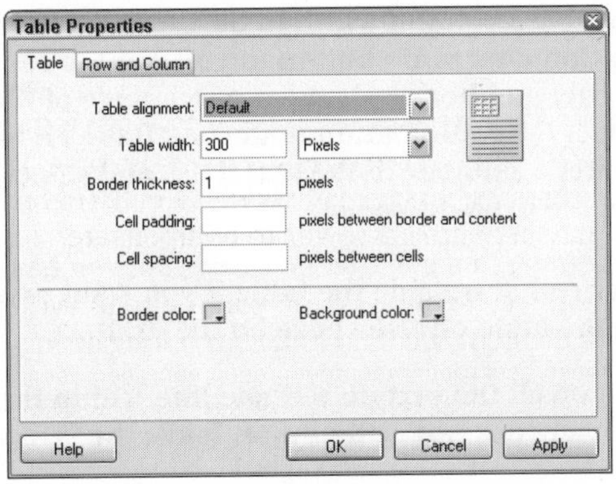

Figure 2-10:
Change
the table's
alignment,
width, and
other
properties
in the Table
Properties
dialog box.

5. **To change the color of the table border, click the Border Color icon and use the Color Picker to choose a color.**

   For details on how to use the advanced features of the Color Picker, see the section on adding color in Book III, Chapter 3.

6. **To change the color of the table's background, click the Background Color icon and use the Color Picker to choose a color.**

   Book III, Chapter 3 gives details on how to use the advanced features of the Color Picker.

7. **To change other properties of the table, click the Row and Column tab at the top of the dialog box.**

   The Row and Column options appear. If you have selected only a row and not the whole table, the tab will say only Row. Likewise, if you have selected only a column and not the whole table, the tab will read Column.

8. **To change the horizontal alignment of the elements in each cell, select an option from the Horizontal Alignment drop-down list.**

   Your options are Default, Left, Center, and Right. Choosing Default allows the visitor's browser to set how the elements in the cells are aligned.

9. **To change the vertical alignment of elements in each cell, select an option from the Vertical Alignment drop-down list.**

   Your options are Default, Top, Middle, and Bottom. Choosing Default allows the visitor's browser to set how the elements in the cells are aligned.

10. **To change the background color for the cells in the table, click the Background Color icon and use the Color Picker to choose a color.**

    See Book III, Chapter 3 for details on how to use the Color Picker.

11. **If you want the table's column width to be allotted automatically, select the Fit to Contents radio button. If you want to set the column widths to a specific number of pixels or percentage of the overall table width, select the radio button underneath the Fit to Contents radio button, enter a number in the text field, and select either Pixels or Percent from the drop-down list.**

If you insert something in a cell that is wider than you have set the column to handle, the cell will override your column width setting to accommodate the element, be it an image or a long string of text.

12. **If you want to keep all the text on a single line within the cells, deselect the Wrap Text check box. Otherwise, leave the Wrap Text check box selected.**

If all the text in a cell won't fit on a single line and the Wrap Text box is checked, the text will be split into as many lines as are necessary, given the width of the cell. The line breaks come at spaces, dashes, and carriage returns. Deselecting the Wrap Text option may increase the width of your table.

13. **If you've selected the entire table, leave the Header Row check box alone.**

If you've selected a row, you can make it a header row by selecting the Header Row check box, or removing its header row formatting by deselecting the Header Row check box.

14. **If you want the row heights in your table to be determined by the content in the rows (each row is only as large as the biggest cell in that row), select the Fit to Contents radio button next to the Row Height section. If you want to set a row height in pixels, select the radio button below the Fit to Contents radio button and enter a number for the height you want the row to be in pixels.**

15. **When you've made all the changes you want, click OK.**

At any time while you are changing settings, you can click the Apply button to see the effect of the changes before moving on to the next property.

Changing rows, columns, or individual cells using the Table Properties dialog box

There may be times when you want to change the text alignment in some cells but not others, or you want to perform some other task that applies only to a particular row or column. In those circumstances, you need to select only the cells you want to affect; then you can make the changes using the Table Properties dialog box.

Selecting a row

To select a row, place your cursor on the table border at the left of the row you want to select and click when the cursor becomes a bold right-pointing arrow, as shown on the top in Figure 2-11. The row will highlight.

Selecting a column

To select a column, place your cursor on the table border at the top of the column you want to select and click when the cursor becomes a bold down-pointing arrow, a shown in the middle in Figure 2-11. The column will highlight.

Selecting an individual cell or group of cells

To select an individual cell, triple-click the cell. The cell will highlight. To select multiple cells, click in one cell, hold the Shift key, and click three times in another cell. The two cells you clicked in and every cell between highlights.

After you've made your selection, click the Table button to open the Table Properties dialog box and make the changes just as outlined in the "Changing the whole table using the Table Properties dialog box" section, earlier in this chapter. If you have selected a row, the Rows and Columns tab will say only Row, and if you have selected a column, the Rows and Columns tab will reflect that by saying only Column.

**Book VII
Chapter 2**

**Basics for
Contributors**

Name	Address	Phone	Email	Age
Earl Ives	14 Maple Way Anytown, IA 52801	319-555-1212	earl@earlsbowlateria.com	62
Jim Cheree	32905 Main St. Twopin, IA 53111	333-555-1212	jim@earlsbowlateria.com	45

Name	Address	Phone	Email	Age
Earl Ives	14 Maple Way Anytown, IA 52801	319-555-1212	earl@earlsbowlateria.com	62
Jim Cheree	32905 Main St. Twopin, IA 53111	333-555-1212	jim@earlsbowlateria.com	45

Name	Address	Phone	Email	Age
Earl Ives	14 Maple Way Anytown, IA 52801	319-555-1212	earl@earlsbowlateria.com	62
Jim Cheree	32905 Main St. Twopin, IA 53111	333-555-1212	jim@earlsbowlateria.com	45

Figure 2-11:
Selecting a row (top), a column (middle), and a group of adjacent cells (bottom).

Adding Images, Links, and More

Adding images to a page is a snap with Contribute. In a way, it's easier than adding a table, because there are fewer properties you need to set. Same goes for adding Flash movies to a page.

Inserting an image

If the image you want to insert in your page is on your computer's hard drive, just follow these steps to insert it:

1. **Place your cursor in the draft and click where you want to add the image.**

   The cursor blinks where the top-left corner of your image will appear on the page. You can insert an image in a table cell or anywhere else on the page.

2. **Choose Insert⇨Image⇨From My Computer or use the keyboard short-cut Ctrl+Alt+I.**

   The Select Image dialog box appears.

3. **Navigate to the folder the image is in, and then either double-click the image's file name, or click the filename and click Select.**

   The image is placed in your draft. When you publish the page, Contribute automatically uploads the image. Your site administrator can set a maximum file size for any image uploaded to your site. If you get an error message saying your image is too big, see your site administrator or re-export the image from Fireworks at a smaller file size.

Inserting a Flash movie

Adding a Flash movie to your page from your computer's hard drive is easy. Just follow these steps:

1. **Place your cursor in the draft and click where you want to add the Flash movie.**

   The cursor blinks where the top left of your movie will appear on the page. You can insert movie in a table cell or anywhere else on the page.

2. **Select Insert⇨Flash Movie⇨From My Computer.**

   The Open dialog box appears.

3. **Navigate to the folder the movie is in, and then either double-click the Flash movie's file name, or click the filename and click Open.**

   The Flash movie is placed in your draft. When you publish the page, Contribute automatically uploads the `.swf` file.

Flash movies have parameters that can be set on a Web page that will affect how the movies appear and function, but Contribute only gives you access to a couple of them. To make these (limited) changes, select the movie by clicking it and then select Format⇨Flash Movie Properties to open the Flash Movie Properties dialog box and set the Play on Page Load and Loop properties.

Inserting a link

Links (short for hyperlinks) are what the Web is all about, so naturally Contribute allows you to add links to your pages. You can link *from* both text and images, and you can link *to* other pages on your site, other pages on the Web, e-mail addresses, and things like PDF files.

Linking to a Web page

To add a link from text or an image to a page on your Web site or any other Web site, just follow these steps:

1. **Click an image or click and drag to select some text that you want to link to another page on the Web.**

   The image or text highlights.

2. **Select Insert⇨Link⇨Browse to Web Page.**

   The Insert Link dialog box opens, with Browse to Web Page selected at the top, as shown in Figure 2-12.

**Book VII
Chapter 2**

**Basics for
Contributors**

Figure 2-12:
The Insert Link dialog box varies slightly in appearance, depending on what type of link you're creating.

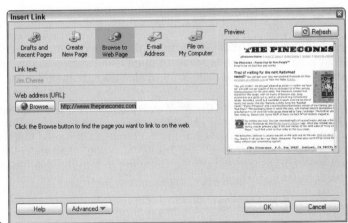

3. **Enter a URL (for example,** `http://www.mysite.com/contactus.htm`**) in the Web Address text field, or click the Browse button to browse to the page you want to link to.**

Browsing to the page is often the best way to ensure that you link to the correct page. The page you browsed to appears in the Preview area on the right.

4. **Click OK.**

You've just created a hyperlink.

Linking to an e-mail address

When you link to an e-mail address, the link on your Web page opens up a new e-mail message in your visitor's e-mail program. The e-mail is automatically addressed to the e-mail address you specify in the link.

To add an e-mail link to some text or an image:

1. **Click and drag to select some text or click on an image that you want to link to an e-mail address.**

The image or text highlights.

2. **Select Insert⇨Link⇨E-mail Address.**

The Insert Link dialog box opens, with E-mail Address selected at the top.

3. **Enter the e-mail address in the E-mail Address text field.**

4. **Click OK.**

The selected text or image links to the e-mail address.

Linking to an e-mail address will open the visitor's e-mail program only if the visitor's e-mail program is set up to open when such a link is clicked. Most current e-mail programs are set up by default to handle an e-mail link.

You can also link to other drafts, to new pages, and to files on your computer (like Word documents and PDF files). See Contribute's Help files for details on how to perform those tasks, or check out *Macromedia Contribute For Dummies*, by Janine Warner and Frank Vera (published by Wiley Publishing, Inc.), which has many details that we can't fit into this minibook.

Inserting a Document as FlashPaper

Contribute 2 owners with Windows 2000 or Windows XP operating systems have access to a special utility: the FlashPaper Printer. No, it doesn't print Flash movies. What it does is convert your Office documents (Word files,

Excel spreadsheets, even PowerPoint presentations) into compact .swf files (Flash movies) that can be displayed on your Web page and viewed by anyone with the Flash plug-in in their browser (which is almost everyone!).

To insert an Office document into your draft as a Flash movie, just follow these steps:

1. Place your cursor in the draft and click where you want to add the document.

The cursor blinks where the top left of your image will appear on the page. You can insert an image in a table cell or anywhere else on the page.

2. Choose Insert⇨Document as FlashPaper.

The Open dialog box appears.

3. Navigate to the folder the document is in, and then either double-click the document's file name, or click the filename once and click Open.

The FlashPaper Options dialog box appears, as shown in Figure 2-13.

Figure 2-13:
The FlashPaper Options dialog box includes a couple of very basic display options.

4. Choose either Portrait (vertical) or Landscape (horizontal) for the Page orientation, and then either select a standard printed document size from the Standard drop-down list or select the Custom radio button and enter a custom size (width, height, and, from the drop-down list, either inches or millimeters).

The Converting to FlashPaper dialog box appears while the conversion takes place. Then the Flash SWF movie is placed in your draft. When you publish the page, Contribute automatically uploads the .swf file.

You can also use the standalone FlashPaper Printer outside of Contribute if you want. See the Help files in Contribute for details.

You can't edit a FlashPaper movie. If you want to change a FlashPaper movie, you must go back and change the document it was made from and convert the updated document.

Previewing Your Work

If you make minor text changes to a page, you may not need to see it in a browser like Internet Explorer or Opera before you put it on your Web site for the whole world to see. But if you make extensive changes, or if you've created a new page, you may wish to check out how it looks in your regular Web browser before you publish it to your site.

To preview a draft in your regular Web browser, select File⇨Preview or use the keyboard shortcut F12. Your regular Web browser (such as Internet Explorer) opens and displays the page you're editing.

Uploading (Publishing) a Page

When you've finished editing a page or creating a new one, you'll want to put it on your Web site where people can browse to it — that is, if you don't want to preview the page (see the preceding section, "Previewing Your Work") and you don't need approval to post the page (see "Collaborating," the next section in this chapter). In Contribute, uploading the page to your Web server, where it can be seen by any visitor who goes to the right URL, is known as *publishing a draft*.

Publishing a draft is incredibly simple: Just click the Publish button at the top left of Contribute's Browser. The page and any images or Flash movies you've added to it are uploaded to the server, and Contribute's Browser automatically switches to Browse mode to display the uploaded page as it will appear to visitors to your site.

Collaborating

Contribute has several features that make collaborating on a site easy. For example, when you edit a page, Contribute prevents anyone else from editing the page at the same time. That way, you'll never accidentally overwrite someone else's changes — and they'll never overwrite yours!

Contribute also has a special feature that comes in very handy if someone else needs to check your work before you publish it to your site: E-mail Review.

To make a preview of your draft and send an e-mail to a colleague with a link to the preview, just follow these steps:

1. **While you're in Edit mode on the page you want to show to your colleague, select File⇨E-mail Review.**

   An informational Contribute window appears, unless you selected the "Don't show this window again" check box earlier. If the window appears, click OK. Then an e-mail opens with a link to the page and a brief request for review.

2. **Edit the e-mail if necessary and send it.**

3. **If you think you may have to wait awhile for approval, save the draft by clicking the Save for Later button at the top of the Browser.**

   The draft will appear in the Pages panel.

4. **When you have approval, click the draft's name in the Pages panel.**

   The Browser switches to Edit mode and loads the draft in the Browser.

5. **Click Publish.**

   The Browser switches to Browse mode and displays the published page as it appears on your Web site.

Chapter 3: Contribute 2 Administration

In This Chapter

✔ **Making yourself a site administrator**

✔ **Creating sitewide settings, including rollbacks**

✔ **Working with groups**

✔ **Granting group access**

✔ **Creating connection keys**

*I*f you're set up to be a Contribute 2 site administrator, you can do everything a regular user can do — edit existing pages and make new ones — but you can also control who the regular users are, what access they have to a site, and more.

A site may have multiple administrators as well as multiple users. All administrators have the same privileges, including the privilege to set up groups of users with distinct privileges. If reading that last sentence makes you feel like you've just stumbled into a hall of mirrors, don't worry. Read on, and you'll be a site administrator in no time.

Setting Yourself Up as Site Administrator

You can set yourself up as an administrator, or you can set someone else up as an administrator. But first things first: If you want to make site administrators of your colleagues, you have to make yourself a site administrator first. By the way, if you want to be an administrator on a site that already has one, you'll need that site's administrator to set you up with administrator privileges.

Though you may be able to set yourself up as site administrator at any time by editing your settings, we assume for the purposes of this book that you are setting yourself up as an administrator at the same time you are making your first connection to the site in Contribute, and that nobody else has yet done so. To set yourself up as an administrator, just follow these steps:

1. **Browse to the site to which you want to connect via Contribute's Browser by typing or pasting a URL (for example, `http://www.mysite.com`) into the Address text field and pressing Enter or clicking the Go button.**

You can use Contribute's Browser to view any site on the Web, but you can only set up a connection to a site if you have FTP information for that site.

2. **Click the Create Connection button at the top left of the Browser, as shown in Figure 3-1.**

The Connection Wizard opens to its Welcome screen.

Figure 3-1:
Getting
ready to
connect to
a Web site.

3. **We're assuming you don't have a connection key, so click the Next button at the bottom of the wizard.**

The User Information screen appears. For more information about connection keys, see the "Creating Connection Keys to Provide Access to Contributors" section, later in this chapter.

4. **Enter your name in the What Is Your Name? text field.**

Your name may already appear. The name in this field will identify you to other contributors to your site, if there are any.

5. **If it's not already there, enter your e-mail address in the What Is Your E-mail Address? text field and click Next.**

The Website Home Page screen appears.

6. **If necessary, enter the URL (**`http://www.mysite.com`**, for example) for the Web site you'll be editing by typing it or pasting it into the text field. Click Next.**

The URL should be there already, because you browsed to the site to start the connection process. When you click Next, the Connection Information screen appears in the wizard.

7. **Select a connection method from the drop-down list.**

You have the following options: FTP, Secure FTP (SFTP), and Local/Network. Depending on what you choose, different text fields appear below the drop-down list. As you can see in Figure 3-2, we entered SFTP.

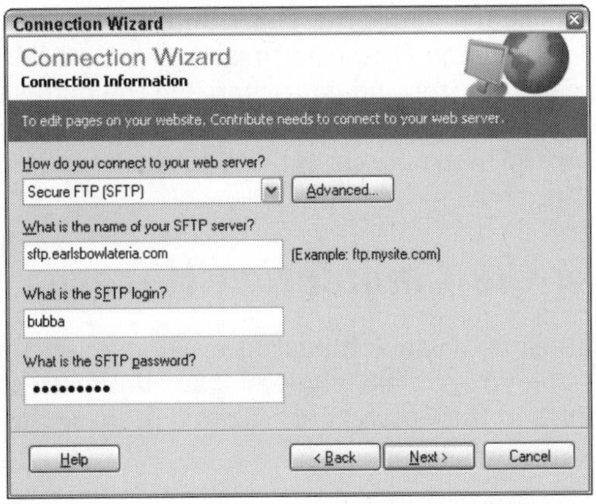

Figure 3-2:
FTP
information
entered
in the
Connection
Information
screen.

8a. **If you selected FTP or SFTP, enter the FTP server name (such as** `sftp.earlsbowlateria.com`**), the ftp login (sometimes called the username), and the ftp password in the respective text fields. Click Next.**

When you click Next, the Administrator Information screen appears (go to Step 9).

8b. **If you selected Local/Network, enter the network path (for example,** `\\mynetwork\mydepartment\site`**) by typing or pasting it in, or by clicking the Choose Folder button and browsing in your network to the folder that contains your site. Click Next.**

When you click Next, the Administrator Information screen appears.

9. **Select the Yes, I Want to Be the Administrator option.**

Two password text fields appear on the screen.

10. **Enter a password in the top text field on the Administrator Information screen. Then re-enter the password in the text field below, exactly as you typed it above. Click Next.**

You can use any combination of numbers and letters for your password. The password is case-sensitive (so as far as the password is concerned, a big "S" and a small "s" are different characters). Only contributors who know that password will be able to perform administrator functions on the site. When you click Next, the Summary screen appears.

11. **Make sure the information is correct. If it isn't, use the Back button to go to the screen with incorrect info and fix the mistake; then use the Next button to return to the Summary screen. Click Done.**

Your connection is set. When you click Done, a dialog box pops up that says, "Would you like to change the Contribute administration settings for this Web site? To change these settings later, select Edit⇨Administer Websites." You can click Yes and go to Step 2 in the following section, "Changing Settings in the Connection Wizard," or you can click No and proceed to follow the instructions in that section from Step 1.

Changing Settings in the Connection Wizard

If you didn't set yourself up as an administrator when you made your original connection to a site, you can make yourself an administrator later by changing some settings in the Connection Wizard. To do so, just follow these steps:

1. **Choose Edit⇨My Connections.**

The My Connections dialog box appears, as shown in Figure 3-3.

2. **Double-click the line that shows the name of the site you want to administer.**

The Connection Wizard appears.

3. **Click the Next button a few times until you see the Administrator Information screen.**

4. **Select the Yes, I Want to Be an Administrator option.**

Text fields for a password appear.

5. **Enter a password in the top text field. Then re-enter the password in the text field below, exactly as you typed it above. Click Next.**

You can use any combination of numbers and letters for your password. Again, the password is case-sensitive. Only contributors who know that password will be able to perform administrator functions on the site. When you click Next, the Summary screen appears.

6. **Make sure the information is correct. If it isn't, use the Back button to go to the screen with incorrect info and fix the mistake; then use the Next button to return to the Summary screen. Click Done.**

Your connection is set. When you click Done, a dialog box pops up that says, "Would you like to change the Contribute administration settings for this Web site? To change these settings later, select Edit⇨Administer Websites."

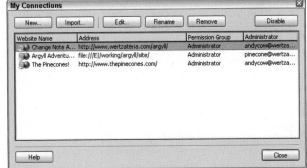

Figure 3-3:
The My
Connections
dialog box
allows you
to pick one
from all
of your
connections.

Creating Sitewide Settings

Sitewide settings apply to all contributors to the site, regardless of any group settings you may make. Using the Sitewide Settings dialog box, shown in Figure 3-4, you can

+ Change the administrator's e-mail address

+ Change the administrator's password

+ Enable rollbacks and customize rollback settings

+ Set up index and URL mapping

+ Delete all permissions and settings at once

We discuss each of those settings in the following subsections.

Changing the administrator's e-mail address

To change the administrator's e-mail address, just follow these steps:

1. **Choose Edit⇨Administer Websites⇨*Name of Site*, where *Name of Site* is the name of the site you want to administer.**

The Administrator Password dialog box appears.

Book VII
Chapter 3

Contribute 2
Administration

2. **Enter your password and click OK or press Enter.**

   The Administer Website dialog box appears.

3. **Click the Sitewide Settings button in the Sitewide Settings section at the top of the Administer Website dialog box.**

   The Sitewide Settings dialog box appears.

4. **The existing administrator e-mail address should be highlighted. If it isn't, select it by clicking and dragging until the address is highlighted.**

5. **Enter a new address by pasting or typing it into the Administrator Contact E-mail text field.**

6. **Click OK.**

   The Sitewide Settings dialog box disappears, and the new e-mail address is set.

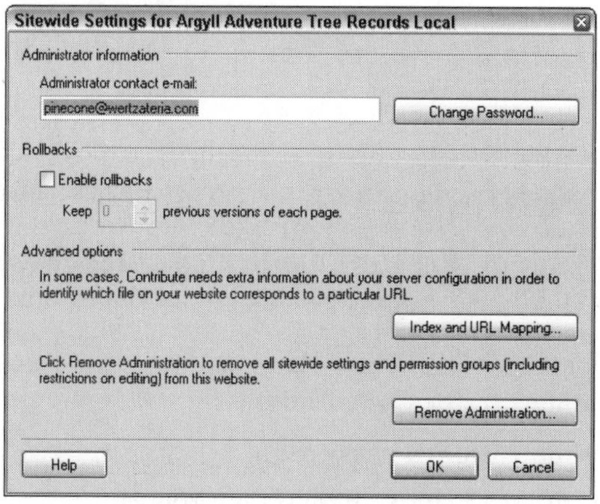

Figure 3-4:
The Sitewide Settings dialog box shows we're not using the rollback feature for the Argyll Adventure Tree site.

Changing the Administrator password

To change the Administrator password, follow Steps 1 through 3 in the previous section, and then do the following:

1. **Click the Change Password button.**

   The Change Password dialog box appears.

2. **In the first (top) field, enter your current Administrator password. Press the Tab key or click in the second field and enter the new password you would like to use. Press the Tab key or click in the third field and re-enter the new password exactly as you entered it in the second field.**

3. **Click OK.**

The Change Administrator Password dialog box closes. If you wish to make changes to other Sitewide Settings, do so. Otherwise, click OK to close the Sitewide Settings dialog box and OK to close the Administer Website dialog box and save your changes.

Using the Rollback feature to save file backups

Contribute's Rollback feature allows contributors to "roll back" to a previously published version of a page — sometimes reverting back to a prior state of things is the best way out of a jam. In order to make it possible to roll back, Contribute keeps backup copies of edited pages on the Web server. Administrators can specify how many versions Contribute backs up. Administrators can also disable the Rollback feature.

The main advantage to the rollback feature is pretty obvious: Backups can help you recover quickly if a newly published version of a page has multiple errors. Rather than having to scramble to fix the errors while the faulty page is up on your site for the world to see, you can just roll back almost instantaneously to the previously published version of the page.

The major disadvantage of the rollback feature, particularly for large sites, is that backups take up space on the Web server. If you have Contribute set to save three versions of each page, by the time your colleagues have published changes to a hundred pages three times each, three hundred backup pages have been created and stored in the _baks directory Contribute has placed on the Web server that contains your site.

To activate and customize the Rollback feature for a site, just follow these steps:

1. **Choose Edit➪Administer Websites➪*Name of Site* where *Name of Site* is the name of the site you want to administer.**

The Administrator Password dialog box appears.

2. **Enter your password and click OK or press Enter.**

The Administer Website dialog box appears.

3. **Click the Sitewide Settings button in the Sitewide Settings section at the top of the Administer Website dialog box.**

The Sitewide Settings dialog box appears.

4. **Click the Enable Rollbacks check box.**

A check appears in the check box, and the text field below is no longer grayed out.

5. **Use the toggle buttons at the right of the text field to increase the number of backups from 0, or double-click the 0 and enter a whole number between 1 and 99.**

    Though you may elect to keep up to 99 versions of each page, you're probably better off limiting the number to 2 or 3 to conserve space on your Web server.

6. **Click OK to close the Sitewide Settings dialog box, or make any other changes you wish to make to Sitewide Settings, and click OK in the Administer Website dialog box.**

To disable rollbacks, follow Steps 1 through 4 above, and then skip to Step 6. Disabling rollbacks will not remove existing backups. To remove existing backups, disable rollbacks, and then use Dreamweaver or your favorite FTP client to delete the files. Do not delete the _baks folder.

Setting up index and URL mapping

In some cases, the way your Web server is configured to retrieve index pages may require you to adjust some settings in Contribute to get your connections between Contribute and the server working properly. The Advanced Options section of the Sitewide Settings dialog box includes the Index and URL Mapping button, which allows you to open a dialog box in which you can customize index page and URL mapping.

Mapping to index files

If your server is configured to default to home pages in a non-standard way (if, for example, the server first checks a directory for start.cfm and then looks for index.htm if it doesn't find start.cfm), you can set up Contribute to mirror that configuration.

Contribute has 30 possible index page file names listed (index and default, for each of 15 extensions). If your server is configured to look for a page with a different filename (such as start.cfm or main.html), you need to add that filename to the list.

To add a filename to the list, just follow these steps:

1. **Choose Edit⇨Administer Websites⇨*Name of Site*, where *Name of Site* is the name of the site you want to administer.**

    The Administrator Password dialog box appears.

2. **Enter your password and click OK or press Enter.**

    The Administer Website dialog box appears.

3. **Click the Sitewide Settings button in the Sitewide Settings section at the top of the Administer Websites dialog box.**

   The Sitewide Settings dialog box appears.

4. **Select the Index and URL Mapping button in the Advanced options section.**

   The Index and URL Mapping dialog box appears.

5. **Click the Add button in the Index Files section.**

   The Add or Edit Index Filename dialog box appears.

6. **Enter the filename in the Index Filename text field.**

7. **Click OK.**

   The Add or Edit Index Filename dialog box disappears, and the new file-name appears at the bottom of the list in the Index and URL Mapping dialog box.

8. **Use the arrow buttons at the right to move the new filename to the spot in the list that reflects the order the server uses.**

   For example, if the server checks index.cfm first, that filename should be at the top of the list (as it appears in Figure 3-5). Each time you click the up-arrow button, the selected name moves up one spot in the list.

9. **Make any other changes to the Index and URL Mapping settings, if necessary, and click OK. Then click OK in the Administer Website dialog box to save your settings.**

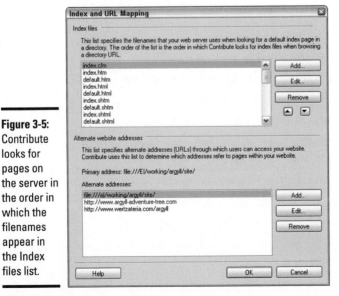

Figure 3-5:
Contribute
looks for
pages on
the server in
the order in
which the
filenames
appear in
the Index
files list.

To edit or remove a filename from the list, just follow these steps:

1. **Open the Index and URL Mapping dialog box, as shown in Steps 1 through 4 in the previous list.**

2. **Click the filename you want to edit or remove.**

   The filename is highlighted.

   - **To edit the filename, click the Edit button.** The Add or Edit Filename dialog box appears, with the current filename highlighted. Type a new filename and click OK. The Add or Edit Index Filename dialog box closes, and the edited filename appears in the list.

   - **To remove the filename from the list, click the Remove button.** The filename disappears from the list.

3. **Make any other changes to the Index and URL Mapping settings, if necessary, and click OK. Then click OK in the Administer Website dialog box to save your settings.**

Mapping to alternate Web site addresses

If you have multiple DNS entries pointing toward a single IP address (if `http://www.earlsbowlateria.com` and `http://www.earls-bowlateria.com`, for example, both point to the same Web server), or if your contributors will be accessing your Web server using different addresses (from the Web and from your internal network, for example), you need to set up Contribute to recognize the additional addresses. Luckily, doing so is simple.

To map Contribute to an alternate Web site address, just follow these steps:

1. **Choose Edit⇨Administer Websites⇨*Name of Site*, where *Name of Site* is the name of the site you want to administer.**

   The Administrator Password dialog box appears.

2. **Enter your password and click OK or press Enter.**

   The Administer Website dialog box appears.

3. **Click the Sitewide Settings button in the Sitewide Settings section at the top of the Administer Websites dialog box.**

   The Sitewide Settings dialog box appears.

4. **Select the Index and URL Mapping button in the Advanced options section.**

   The Index and URL Mapping dialog box appears.

5. **Click the Add button in the Alternate Website Addresses section.**

   The Add or Edit Alternate Address dialog box appears.

6. **Enter the URL in the Alternate Website Address text field.**

7. **Click OK.**

   The Add or Edit Alternate Address dialog box disappears, and the additional address appears at the bottom of the list, highlighted (refer to Figure 3-5, in which the address `http://www.argyll-adventure-tree.com` has been added).

8. **Make any other changes to the Index and URL Mapping settings, if necessary, and click OK. Then click OK in the Administer Website dialog box to save your settings.**

To edit or delete an alternate Web site address, do the following:

1. **Follow Steps 1 through 4 in the previous list to open the Index and URL Mapping dialog box.**

2. **Click the address you want to edit or delete.**

   The address is highlighted.

   - **To edit the address, click the Edit button.** The Add or Edit Alternate Address dialog box appears, with the address highlighted. Edit the address (URL) in the Alternate Website Address text field and click OK to close the Add or Edit Alternate Address dialog box.

   - **To delete the address, click the Remove button.** The address disappears from the dialog box.

3. **Make any other changes to the Index and URL Mapping settings, if necessary, and click OK. Then click OK in the Administer Website dialog box to save your settings.**

Deleting all permissions and settings at once

The Sitewide Settings dialog box includes a button that allows you to delete all your custom sitewide settings and permission groups with a single click. You might find it efficient to delete all the settings at once if your company or your Web site has just gone through a massive reorganization.

If you click this button, then you nullify all restrictions you may have placed on any of your contributors. This means that all contributors will have standard user access to all files on your site. It also means if you have an elaborate array of restrictions and permission groups and you change your mind the next day, you'll have to recreate all those settings from scratch.

To delete all your sitewide settings and permission groups, simply click the Remove Administration button in the Advanced Options section of the Sitewide Settings dialog box. A Warning dialog box appears to give you a chance to back out. If you're sure you want to delete the settings, click Yes. Then click OK in the Sitewide Settings dialog box and click OK in the Administer Website dialog box.

Setting Up Groups

After you have designated yourself an administrator, you have access to the Administer Website dialog box, in which you can do things like configure sitewide settings, send connection keys, and more.

When you set up a connection, Contribute automatically creates two default groups of contributors: Administrators and Users. You can set up as many additional groups as you like; each group might have different new page creation permissions or access to different directories on the site, or other different settings and permissions.

Opening the Administer Website dialog box

To open the Administer Website dialog box for a site to which you have administrator access, simply do the following:

1. **Choose Edit⇨Administer Websites⇨*Name of Site*, where *Name of Site* is the name of the site you want to administer.**

   The Administrator Password dialog box appears.

2. **Enter your password and click OK or press Enter.**

   The Administer Website dialog box appears.

Setting up a new group

If you don't need more than one group of users and one group of administrators, you can skip this section. If you want to create a new group, you can do it one of two ways:

✦ By creating a new group from scratch

✦ By duplicating an existing group and modifying the duplicated group's settings

To create a new group from scratch, just follow these steps:

1. **Open the Administer Website dialog box by following the steps described in the previous section, "Opening the Administer Website dialog box."**

2. **Click the New button in the Permission Groups section of the Administer Website dialog box.**

The Permission Group Name dialog box appears.

3. **Enter a name for the new group in the New Permission Group Name field and click OK or press Enter.**

The Permission Group Name dialog box closes. The new group's name is highlighted in the Administer Website dialog box, as shown in Figure 3-6, where we added a group called, "Communications Dept."

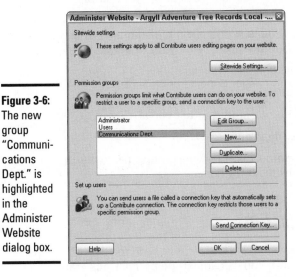

Figure 3-6: The new group "Communications Dept." is highlighted in the Administer Website dialog box.

If you're creating a new group whose settings largely overlap with an existing group's, you can duplicate the existing group, and then edit the duplicated group's settings as necessary. To create a new group by duplicating an existing group, just follow these steps:

1. **Open the Administer Website dialog box by following the steps described in the earlier section, "Opening the Administer Website dialog box."**

2. **Click the Duplicate button in the Permission Groups section of the Administer Website dialog box.**

The Permission Group Name dialog box appears.

3. **Enter a name for the new group in the New Permission Group Name field and click OK or press Enter.**

   The Permission Group Name dialog box closes. The new group's name is highlighted in the Administer Website dialog box. If you want to edit that group's settings, just click the Edit Group button. The "Granting Group Permissions" section, later in this chapter, details the settings you can make.

Deleting groups

Deleting a group is easy. Simply follow these steps:

1. **Open the Administer Website dialog box by following the steps described in the earlier section, "Opening the Administer Website dialog box."**

2. **In the Permission Groups section of the Administer Website dialog box, click the name of the group you want to delete.**

   The group name highlights.

3. **Click the Delete button.**

   A dialog box pops up, warning you that you are about to delete a group.

4. **Click Yes to delete the group.**

   The Warning dialog box closes and the group's name disappears from the Administer Website dialog box.

Granting Group Permissions

After you've created a group (or decided to go with the default groups, Administrators and Users), you can adjust the permissions granted to the group. Permissions may be wholesale (contributors in the Users group may upload any images) or conditional (Users may upload images, but only if the image's file sizes are smaller than 32 kilobytes, for example).

Unlike sitewide settings, group permissions apply only to individual groups, not to all groups. Each group may have its own permissions or settings in the following areas:

+ General
+ Folder/File Access
+ Editing
+ Styles and Fonts

✦ New Pages

✦ New Images

We discuss each of the areas in detail in the following subsections.

Making general settings

When you open the Permission Group dialog box, you see the General screen by default. The General options allow you to make two settings for a group:

✦ **Group Description:** A sentence or two that describes the group. The Group Description is what people will see when they click the group name in the Connection Wizard.

✦ **Group Home Page:** The page that will load when members of the group connect to the Web site in Contribute.

To create a group description, follow these simple steps:

1. **Choose Edit➪Administer Websites➪*Name of Site*, where *Name of Site* is the name of the site you want to administer.**

   The Administrator Password dialog box appears.

2. **Enter your password and click OK or press Enter.**

   The Administer Website dialog box appears.

3. **In the Permission Groups section of the Administer Website dialog box, click the name of the group whose settings you want to edit and click the Edit button on the right, or double-click the group name.**

   The Permission Group dialog box appears, opened to the General screen, with the text in the Group Description field highlighted, as shown in Figure 3-7.

4. **Enter a group description by typing or pasting it into the Group Description text field.**

5. **Click OK to save your changes and close the dialog box, or make other changes to the group's permissions as needed before you click OK.**

If your Web site has several directories, each of which is maintained by a different department, you can make a group for each department and set a default home page for each group. For example, members of the Communications Department, who are responsible only for updating press releases, might have `http://www.mycompany.com/news/index.htm` as their home page.

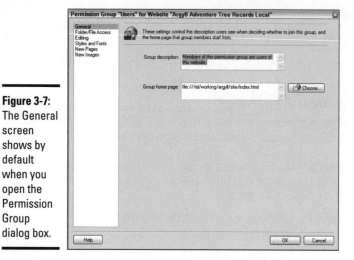

Figure 3-7:
The General
screen
shows by
default
when you
open the
Permission
Group
dialog box.

To specify a special home page for a group, follow these steps:

1. **Open the Permission Group dialog box by following Steps 1 through 3 in the previous list.**

The Group Home Page field includes the name of the site's default home page.

2. **Click and drag to select the current group home page and enter a new URL by typing or pasting the URL into the Group Home Page text field. Alternatively, you can click the Choose button at the right and navigate to the page in the Choose File on Website dialog box.**

One advantage of navigating via the Choose File on Website dialog box is that you avoid the possibility of misspelling the URL.

3. **Click OK to save your changes and close the dialog box, or make other changes to the group's permissions as needed before clicking OK.**

Figure 3-8 shows a detail of the General screen with customized description and home page for a group called "Communications Dept." The description is not fully visible in Figure 3-8; the full text reads, "This group has access to the News directory only, and may create new pages only from the News template."

Granting access to folders and files

You may wish to restrict certain groups of contributors from editing particular files on your site. For example, you may want the members of your

Communications Department to be able to update the News section of your site but not have access to the Products section. Contribute allows you to specify which folders (directories) a group may access to edit the files within.

Figure 3-8:
The
Communica-
tions Dept.
group's
General
Permissions
settings.

To grant a group access to the files in a particular folder that already exists on your site, just follow these steps:

1. **If you have the Permissions Group dialog box open already, skip to Step 5. Otherwise, continue with Step 2.**

2. **Choose Edit⇨Administer Websites⇨*Name of Site*, where *Name of Site* is the name of the site you want to administer.**

    The Administrator Password dialog box appears.

3. **Enter your password and click OK or press Enter.**

    The Administer Website dialog box appears.

4. **In the Permission Groups section of the Administer Website dialog box, click the name of the group whose settings you want to edit and click the Edit button on the right, or double-click the group name.**

    The Permission Group dialog box appears, showing the General options, with the text in the Group Description field highlighted (refer to Figure 3-7).

5. **Click Folder/File Access in the list on the left.**

    The Folder/File Access screen appears, replacing the General screen.

6. **Select the Only Allow Editing within These Folders option.**

   The text field below becomes editable.

7. **Click the Add Folder button.**

   The Choose Folder dialog box appears, with your site's directory structure represented on the left, as shown in Figure 3-9.

8. **Double-click the folder you want the group to be able to edit, and then click Select *folder name* where *folder name* is the name of the folder.**

   The Choose Folder dialog box disappears, and the URL for the folder you selected appears in the Folder access text field, highlighted.

9. **Click OK to save your changes and close the dialog box, or make other changes to the group's permissions as needed before clicking OK.**

Figure 3-9:
Restricting a group's permissions to editing files only in a specified folder.

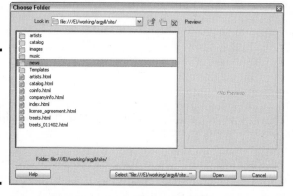

Extending file deletion privileges

The Folder/File Access screen in the Permission Group dialog box also allows you to choose whether or not a group will be permitted to delete files from the site. Members of the group may only delete files that they have permission to edit.

To allow users to delete files from a site, follow these simple steps:

1. **If the Folder/File Access screen in the Permission Group dialog box is not already showing, open it by following Steps 2 through 5 in the previous list. Otherwise, skip to Step 2.**

2. **Select the Allow Users to Delete Files They Have Permission to Edit check box at the top of the File Deletion section of the dialog box.**

   The Remove Rollback Versions on Delete check box becomes available.

3. **(Optional) If you want rollback files for a page to be deleted when that page is deleted, select the Remove Rollback Versions on Delete check box.**

4. **Click OK to save your changes and close the dialog box, or make other changes to the group's permissions as needed before clicking OK.**

Customizing editing settings

The Editing options in the Permission Group dialog box, shown in Figure 3-10, allow you to set what aspects of a page's underlying HTML code can be edited by a group member. It also allows you to specify how Contribute will write some basic HTML formatting code.

**Book VII
Chapter 3**

Contribute 2
Administration

Figure 3-10:
The Editing options make it easy to customize editing settings.

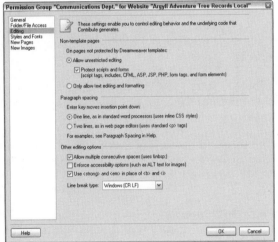

Setting non-template page editing options

Dreamweaver templates "lock" certain chunks of code so that people editing pages based on those templates cannot change certain aspects of the way the page is built to preserve the structure and look of the page. (For details on creating Dreamweaver templates, see Book II, Chapter 7).

If you're not using Dreamweaver templates but you still want to protect any specialized code (ColdFusion markup, for example) from being edited, select the Protect Scripts and Forms check box in the Non-Template Pages section. (The Allow Unrestricted Editing option is selected by default; if you want to allow everything on the page to be edited except scripts and forms, the Allow Unrestricted Editing option must be selected before the Protect Scripts and Forms check box can be selected).

If you want members of a group to be able to edit and format text only, select the Only Allow Text Editing and Formatting option.

Setting the Paragraph Spacing option

When you're writing text in a regular word processing program (such as Microsoft Word) and you press the Enter key on your keyboard, your cursor goes to the next line, just as a carriage return works on a typewriter. When you press Enter to go to a new line in a WYSIWYG HTML editor like Dreamweaver, a blank line is inserted between the previous line you were on and the new line. You can set up Contribute to function either like a word processor or like Dreamweaver when a contributor presses the Enter key.

It's not just Contribute's behavior that changes when you change this setting, it's also the underlying HTML code Contribute generates. When you select the One Line option in the Paragraph Spacing section, Contribute generates an inline CSS style to create the line break. When you select the Two Lines option, Contribute uses the standard HTML paragraph tag <P> to create the line break.

To set up Contribute to start a new line of text directly under the old one when a contributor presses the Enter key, select the One Line, As in Standard Word Processors (Uses Inline CSS Styles) option.

To set Contribute to start a new line of text two lines down from the old line, leaving a space in between, select the Two Lines, As in Web Page Editors (Uses Standard <P> Tags) option.

Setting other editing options

In the Other Editing Options section of the Editing screen, the Allow Multiple Consecutive Spaces (Uses) option is selected by default. Deselect this option only if you want to prevent contributors from creating vertical space in a page by inserting multiple spaces.

Select the Enforce Accessibility Options (Such As ALT Text for Images) option if you want Contribute to prompt contributors to include information that makes the page more accessible to visitors to your site who might have disabilities.

Leave the Use <STRONG> and <EM> in Place of <B> and <I> option selected if you want Contribute to use the latest HTML tags for bold and italic formatted text.

To choose a line break type for the underlying code (not the text as it appears in a browser), select one from the Line Break Type drop-down list. In most cases, you may leave this at its default setting; if the people working directly on the HTML use a particular type of computer, you may wish to select the line break type accordingly. "CR" stands for "Carriage Return," and "LF" is short for "Line Feed." Contribute offers the following line break types:

✦ Windows (CR LF)

✦ Mac (CR)

✦ Unix (LF)

Granting styles and fonts permissions

To change the permissions for a group's ability to format text on Web pages, click Styles and Fonts in the list on the left side of the Permission Group dialog box (see Figure 3-11). Formatting text is usually one of the main responsibilities of anybody maintaining a Web site. Contribute makes formatting text easy as it is; setting styles and fonts permissions can make formatting text even easier for contributors by taking away options that might lead to incorrect formatting.

**Book VII
Chapter 3**

**Contribute 2
Administration**

Figure 3-11:
The Styles and Fonts screen of the Permissions Group dialog box allows you to limit text formatting options by removing menus from Contribute's browser.

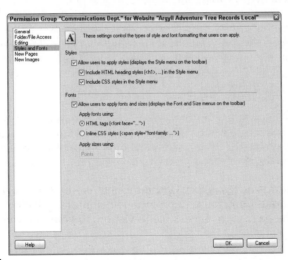

Setting styles options

By default, contributors are permitted to apply CSS styles and HTML paragraph and heading styles to text on pages they have permission to edit. By deselecting the Allow Users to Apply Styles (Displays the Style Menu on the Toolbar) check box, you can prevent users from being able to apply HTML and CSS styles by removing the Style menu from the Contribute Browser's toolbar. If you deselect that check box, the other two boxes in the Styles section become grayed out, because if there's no Styles menu on the toolbar, there's no way to apply HTML or CSS styles.

If you don't want contributors to be able to apply CSS styles but you *do* want them to be able to apply styles to <P> tags and to insert header tags (<H1>, <H2>, and so on), deselect the Include CSS Styles in the Style Menu check box, but leave the other two check boxes selected.

If, on the other hand, you have set up a thorough CSS style sheet and don't want contributors using generic HTML paragraph and heading styles to format text, deselect the Include HTML Paragraph and Heading Styles (<P>, <H1>, . . .) in the Style Menu check box, but leave the other two check boxes selected.

Setting fonts options

When the Allow Users to Apply Fonts and Sizes (Displays the Font and Size Menus on the Toolbar) check box is selected, as it is by default, contributors can format text by choosing a font face and font size from drop-down lists on the Contribute Browser's toolbar.

If you're using a CSS style sheet that includes font face, size, color, and other attributes for all text on your site, deselect the Allow Users to Apply Fonts and Sizes check box and make sure the Include CSS Styles in the Style Menu check box is selected above.

If you want to allow contributors to apply text formatting, and you want Contribute to generate basic HTML <FONT> tags, just follow these steps (assuming you have the Styles and Fonts options of the Permission Group dialog box showing):

1. **Select the Allow Users to Apply Fonts and Sizes check box, if it isn't already selected.**

   This box is selected by default.

2. **Select the HTML Tags option under the Apply Fonts Using heading.**

3. **Click OK to save your changes and close the dialog box, or make other changes to the group's permissions as needed before clicking OK.**

If you want to allow contributors to apply text formatting, but you want Contribute to generate CSS style code instead of HTML <FONT> tags, just follow these steps (assuming you have the Styles and Fonts options of the Permission Group dialog box showing):

1. **Select the Allow Users to Apply Fonts and Sizes check box, if it isn't already selected.**

   This box is selected by default.

2. **Under the Apply Fonts Using heading, select the Inline CSS Styles option.**

   The Apply Sizes Using drop-down list becomes active.

3. **Select a unit of font measurement from the Apply Sizes Using drop-down list.**

   The choices are Pixels, Points, or Ems. Whichever you choose will be available from a drop-down list in the Contribute Browser.

   For information about the relative advantages and disadvantages of using each of the units of font measurement, browse to Mulder's style sheet tutorial at the Webmonkey Web site (hotwired.lycos.com/ webmonkey/98/35/index2a.html?tw=authoring).

4. **Click OK to save your changes and close the dialog box, or make other changes to the group's permissions as needed before clicking OK.**

Granting permission to create new pages

Chances are, your contributors are going to need to create new pages for your Web site. If your company paid good money to have the site professionally designed, however, you probably don't want the people maintaining your site to fashion pages that diverge from the approved design.

Contribute gives Administrators a way to force contributors to use Dreamweaver templates (the safest bet) or to use existing pages to create new ones. That helps keep the site design uniform and saves time for the people maintaining the site, as well.

To control the types of Web pages contributors can create, just follow these steps:

1. **If you don't already have the Permission Group dialog box open, choose Edit⇨Administer Websites⇨*Name of Site*, where *Name of Site* is the name of the site you want to administer.**

   The Administrator Password dialog box appears.

2. **Enter your password and click OK or press Enter.**

   The Administer Website dialog box appears.

3. **In the Permission Groups section of the Administer Website dialog box, click the name of the group whose settings you want to edit and click the Edit button on the right, or double-click the group name.**

   The Permission Group dialog box appears, opened to show the General screen, with the text in the Group Description field highlighted (refer to Figure 3-7).

4. **Click New Pages in the list on the left.**

   The New Pages screen replaces the General screen, as shown in Figure 3-12.

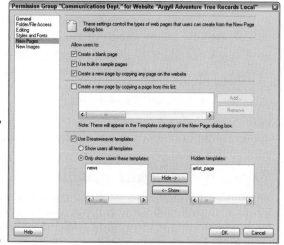

Figure 3-12: Setting the permissions for a group's ability to create new Web pages.

5. **If you want group members to have the option of creating a page from scratch, select the Create a Blank Page check box. (This check box is selected by default.)**

   If you don't want users to be able to create a page from scratch, deselect the check box.

6. **If you want group members to be able to create new pages based on Contribute's sample pages, select the Use Built-In Sample Pages box (This check box is selected by default.)**

   If you don't want group members to be able to create a page from one of Contribute's sample pages, deselect the check box.

7. **If you want group members to be able to use any page on your Web site as a basis for a new page, select the Create a New Page by Copying Any Page on the Website check box — this check box is selected by**

default — and skip to Step 9a. If you want contributors to be able to use only specific existing pages on the site to create new ones, make sure this check box is deselected and proceed to Step 8a.

If you don't want group members to be able to base a new page on any page on your site, deselect the Create a New Page by Copying Any Page on the Website check box.

8a. **If you want group members to be able to create a new page based on a specific page (or set of pages) on your site, select the Create a New Page by Copying a Page from This List check box. (If you do not want group members to be able to create a new page based on a specific page, skip to Step 9a.)**

The Add and Remove buttons become active.

8b. **Click the Add button.**

The Choose File dialog box appears, with the directory structure of your site on the left.

8c. **Click the page you want contributors to be able to model a new page on. If the page is in a folder, double-click the folder to open it in the dialog box, and then click the page.**

The preview section on the right displays the page you selected.

8d. **Click OK.**

The Choose File dialog box disappears, and the selected page appears in the list. Repeat Steps 8a through 8d if you want to add more pages. These pages will appear as choices when the group member tries to create a new page.

9a. **If you want group members to work from a Dreamweaver template when creating a new page, select the Use Dreamweaver Templates check box and continue with Step 9b. Otherwise, skip to Step 10.**

When the Use Dreamweaver Templates box is selected, the Use Dreamweaver Templates section of the dialog box becomes active.

9b. **If you want group members to be able to base a new page on any Dreamweaver template on your site, select the Show Users All Templates option and proceed to Step 10. If you want group members to be able to base a new page only on a specific template (or set of templates), select the Only Show Users These Templates option and proceed to Step 9c.**

9c. **Double-click the name of the template (or names of the templates) in the Hidden Templates field, or click the name of the template, and then click the Show button.**

The name of any template that group members will see when they try to create a new page is listed in the Only Show Users These Templates field on the left. Figure 3-12 shows that we only want the Communications Dept. group to be able to create new pages from the News template.

10. **Click OK to save your changes and close the dialog box, or make other changes to the group's permissions as needed before clicking OK. Then click OK in the Administer Website dialog box to save the changes.**

Customizing options for adding new images

As an administrator, you can set a file size limit for images; Contribute won't allow a group member to add an image with a file size greater than the maximum you set. By default, there's no limit.

If you want to set a maximum image file size, just follow these steps:

1. **If you don't already have the Permission Group dialog box open, choose Edit⇨Administer Websites⇨*Name of Site*, where *Name of Site* is the name of the site you want to administer.**

The Administrator Password dialog box appears.

2. **Enter your password and click OK or press Enter.**

The Administer Website dialog box appears.

3. **In the Permission Groups section of the Administer Website dialog box, click the name of the group whose settings you want to edit and click the Edit button on the right, or double-click the group name.**

The Permission Group dialog box appears, opened to show the General options, with the text in the Group Description field highlighted (refer to Figure 3-7).

4. **Click New Images in the list on the left.**

The New Images options in the Permission Group dialog box, as shown in Figure 3-13, replaces the General options.

5. **Select the Limited to Kilobytes option.**

The Limited to Kilobytes text field, with its default value of 64, becomes editable.

6. **Double-click or click and drag to highlight the default value and enter a new number.**

If you want the maximum file size to be 64 kilobytes, you can skip this step, of course.

7. **Click OK to save your changes and close the dialog box, or make other changes to the group's permissions as needed before clicking OK.**

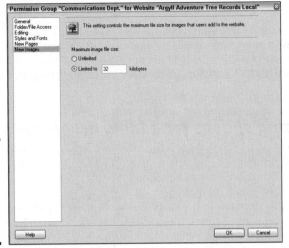

Figure 3-13:
The New
Images
screen
offers only
two options.

Creating Connection Keys to Provide Access to Contributors

Connection keys are password-protected, encrypted text files that contain the data Contribute needs to establish a connection with a Web site. When you send a connection key to a group member, all the member needs to do to establish a connection is double-click the key (and enter a password). That can be pretty handy if you have several people in a group, since you can e-mail the same key to all of them, or post the key on your internal network.

You don't have to go to each member's machine to set up the connection, nor do you have to worry about providing tech support if you've decided to let people establish their own connections. Best of all, connection keys are specific to groups, so you don't have to worry that a contributor will choose to be in the wrong group.

To create a connection key, follow these steps:

1. **Choose Edit⇨Administer Websites⇨*Name of Site*, where *Name of Site* is the name of the site you want to administer.**

The Administrator Password dialog box appears.

2. **Enter your password and click OK or press Enter.**

The Administer Website dialog box appears.

3. **Click the Send Connection Key button.**

   The Export Wizard's Welcome screen appears, as shown in Figure 3-14.

Figure 3-14:
The Export
Wizard's
Welcome
screen
starts you
off with a
basic Yes or
No question.

4a. **If the group members will connect to your Web server in the same way as you do, leave the Yes option selected under the question, Would You Like to Send Your Current Connection Settings? If not, skip to Step 4c.**

   Proceed to Step 4b.

4b. **If you want to include FTP or SFTP login information in the connection key, make sure that the Include My FTP Login and Password check box is selected (if your connection to the site is Local/Network, the box will be grayed out). Click Next and skip to Step 6.**

   When you click Next, the Group Information screen appears.

4c. **If group members will be connecting to the site in a different way than you do, select the No, I Would Like to Customize the Connection Settings for Other Users option. Then click Next and go to Step 5.**

   If group members will be connecting via the Web while you connect via your network, you'll need to customize the connection settings for the group members. When you click Next, the Connection Information screen appears.

5. **Enter the information to set up a connection and click Next.**

   For information about the Connection Information screen, see the section on connecting to a site with the Connection Wizard in Book VII, Chapter 2. When you click Next, the Group Information screen appears.

6. **In the Select a Group area, click the name of the group of users who will use the connection key you're creating. Click Next.**

   When you click the group name, the group's description appears at the right, as shown in Figure 3-15. When you click Next, the Connection Key Information screen appears.

Figure 3-15: When a group is selected, the group's description appears at the right.

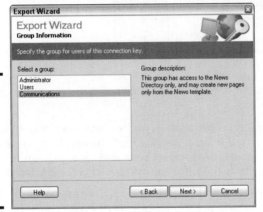

7. **To answer the question, How Would You Like to Export the Connection Key File? select either the Send in E-mail or the Save to Local Machine option.**

   Macromedia recommends you not send the key via Web-based e-mail (like Hotmail or Yahoo!) because, even though the key is encrypted, it contains sensitive information that should never be sent via inherently less secure Web-based e-mail.

8. **In the top text field, enter a password that will enable group members to use the key. Press the Tab key or click in the bottom text field.**

   A contributor must have the password in order to use the key. The password may contain spaces, numbers, and letters and be up to thirty characters long; the password is case-sensitive. If you send the key in an e-mail, it's safest not to include the password in the same e-mail. Instead, send the password in a separate e-mail or, better yet, reveal the password verbally to group members.

9. **Re-enter the password exactly as you entered it in the above text field and click Next.**

   The Summary screen appears, as shown in Figure 3-16.

**Book VII
Chapter 3**

**Contribute 2
Administration**

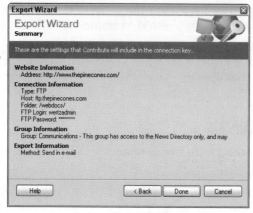

Figure 3-16:
The Export
Wizard's
summary
screen
shows the
connection
key settings
at a glance.

10. **Carefully check the information on the Summary screen to make sure it is correct. If it isn't, use the Back button to go back and correct any information on previous screens and click Next to return to the Summary screen. If the information is correct, click Done.**

If you selected the Send in E-mail option, a new e-mail with the connection key attached will open automatically in your e-mail program. Customize the e-mail as necessary, add a recipient or recipients, and send the message. If you selected the Save to Local Machine option, the Export Connection Key dialog box opens. Navigate to the folder on the local machine or on your network where you want to place the key and click Save.

Chapter 4: Contribute 2 and Other Macromedia Products

In This Chapter

✔ **Introducing FlashPaper**

✔ **Teaming Contribute 2 with Dreamweaver**

✔ **Using the PayPal extension**

Contribute 2 isn't really integrated into the Macromedia Studio MX 2004 suite. It's very much a standalone product created for people who need to maintain Web sites but not build them. Contribute 2 for Windows comes with its own standalone product: FlashPaper.

Introducing FlashPaper

FlashPaper converts any printable file (word processing document, spreadsheet, slide show) into an SWF file that can be viewed by anyone with the latest version of the standalone Macromedia Flash Player or a browser with the latest version of the Flash plug-in.

Unless you specified otherwise, when you installed Contribute, you installed FlashPaper also, and the FlashPaper icon was placed automatically on your desktop, as shown in Figure 4-1.

Figure 4-1:
The
FlashPaper
icon.

FlashPaper can be accessed from within Contribute (see the section on adding images, links, and more in Book VII, Chapter 2 for details). That means when you insert a document as FlashPaper into a draft, you might not even realize you're using another application. But FlashPaper can run quite independently of Contribute.

You can use FlashPaper as a standalone application to in two ways:

✦ By dragging a printable document onto the FlashPaper desktop icon.

✦ By selecting the FlashPaper printer when you print from within an application like Word or Excel. Figure 4-2 shows FlashPaper selected in two different applications; the Print dialog box on the top is from Word and the Print dialog box on the bottom is from Internet Explorer.

Whichever method you choose, your printable document is cloned as an SWF file.

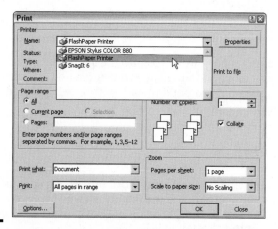

Figure 4-2: To "print" to an SWF, you can select the FlashPaper printer when you print from many applications, including Word (top) and IE (bottom).

While you could theoretically "print" an image as an SWF, there's no compelling reason to do so, because image formats like GIF and JPEG are nearly universally compatible with image display and editing programs as well as browsers.

There is one catch: SWF files generated by FlashPaper cannot be edited with Macromedia Flash MX 2004. If you need to change a file you've converted with FlashPaper, you have to change the original file, and then make a new FlashPaper document from it.

As of this writing, FlashPaper is available only for Windows versions after Windows 95; presumably Macromedia is at work on a Mac version. (Contribute was originally available only for Windows, but with version 2, it is now available for Mac users.)

Teaming Contribute with Dreamweaver

For Web developers who plan to hand off the maintenance of the sites they've built to people who don't know anything about HTML, FTP, or CSS, Contribute represents a certain amount of peace of mind. Especially when combined with Dreamweaver templates, Contribute can make creating new pages with a consistent design faster and simpler for nontechnical people doing site maintenance.

Understanding Dreamweaver Templates

A Dreamweaver template is a special type of file (it uses the extension .dwt) that may contain HTML, CFML, and other typical Web page code, and that also contains hidden instructions that tell Dreamweaver and Contribute to "lock" certain portions of the code — basically making those chunks of code unavailable for editing.

Figure 4-3 shows a new page based on a simple Dreamweaver template. The template has three editable areas: the top navigation, the page header, and the main text area. When the cursor is over any other area on the draft, it becomes a circle-slash, signifying that edits to the area are not permitted.

The page title, which you can see highlighted in the Pages panel as well as prominently displayed in the Contribute title bar in Figure 4-3, has been entered in the New Page dialog box that appears when a contributor creates a new page. (See Book VII, Chapter 2 for details on creating a new page based on a Dreamweaver template.)

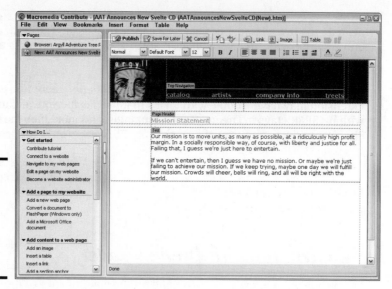

Figure 4-3:
Creating a
new page
from a
Dream-
weaver
template.

For details about creating Dreamweaver templates, see Book II, Chapter 7. For details about how to ensure that contributors use particular templates to create new pages on your site, see the section on granting group permissions in Book VII, Chapter 3.

Working with PayPal

Contribute 2 includes an extension similar to the one available for Dreamweaver that makes adding PayPal buttons to your page a snap. (**Note:** You must have a PayPal Business or Premier account to insert the PayPal buttons into your page, and your site must already have the code for the shopping cart.) In order to use the extension, you have to select it when you install Contribute, as shown in Figure 4-4.

If you have the PayPal extension installed, you see an extra button at the right side of the browser toolbar when you're editing a page. When you click and hold that button, you can select the following options from the pop-up menu:

✦ Buy Now Button

✦ Add to Cart Button

✦ View Cart Button

✦ Subscription Button

Those same options are also available when you choose Insert⇨PayPal. A wizard guides you through the steps necessary to insert the buttons on your page — be sure to have your PayPal account information at hand.

Make sure that any contributor working on a page with PayPal buttons has the PayPal extension installed. Also, be aware that Contribute's PayPal extension may have trouble with forms that use JavaScript validation, forms within `<SPAN>` tags in Dreamweaver templates, and more. See the Contribute TechNote at `www.macromedia.com/support/contribute/ts/documents/paypal.htm` for details on workarounds.

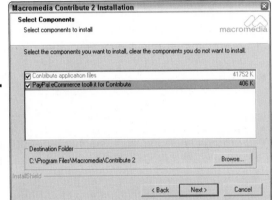

Figure 4-4:
Select the
PayPal
eCommerce
toolkit when
you install
Contribute.

**Book VII
Chapter 4**

**Contribute 2 and
Other Macromedia
Products**

Index

A

actions
  ActionScripts,
    Macromedia Flash,
    562–563, 585–594
  Browser/Network,
    Macromedia Flash,
    588
  buttons, ActionScripts,
    592–594
  forms, Dreamweaver, 97
  frames, ActionScripts,
    590–592
  Movie Clip Control,
    Macromedia Flash,
    588–589
  Timeline Control,
    Macromedia Flash,
    587–588
Actions panel
  Browser/Network
    actions, 588
  task types, Macromedia
    Flash, 586–587
  Timeline Control actions,
    587–588
ActionScripts,
    Macromedia Flash
  Actions panel tasks, 587
  Browser/Network
    actions, 588
  built-in methods, 589
  button actions, 592–594
  comments, 589
  form data collection,
    605–606
  form data posting,
    606–607

frame actions, 590–592
FreeHand MX
    integration, 474–475
Help system, 586
interactive animations,
    562–563
Movie Clip Control
    actions, 588–589
operators, 589
preference settings, 504
task types, 585–586
Timeline Control actions,
    587–588
tutorials, 586
variables, 589
active links, page
    properties,
    Dreamweaver, 59
ActiveX, Dreamweaver
    insertion, 149–150
Add Pages dialog box,
    FreeHand, 360–361
administrative tools,
    ColdFusion MX 6.1
    Developer Edition, 29
Administrator Website
    dialog box, Contribute
    2, 784
administrator. *See* site
    administrator
Adobe Acrobat, content
    creation tool, 21
Align and Transform
    panel, FreeHand,
    428–436
Align panel
  FreeHand, 355
  object alignments
    FreeHand, 421–422
    Macromedia Flash, 526

alignments
  layers, Dreamweaver,
    111, 113–114
  objects, Macromedia
    Flash, 525–526
  text to a path, FreeHand,
    402–405
  text, FreeHand, 393
alpha transparencies,
    Macromedia Flash
    support, 333
anchor points, tangent
    lines, 519
animated GIFs
  exporting, Fireworks, 310
  Fireworks, 284–287
  frame rates, Fireworks,
    285–286
  loops, Fireworks,
    286–287
animations
  button symbols,
    Macromedia Flash,
    540
  creating, FreeHand,
    472–474
  frame rates, 552
  frame-by-frame,
    Macromedia Flash,
    555–556
  interactivity,
    Macromedia Flash,
    562–563
  Macromedia Flash MX
    2004 capability, 28
  motion tweens,
    Macromedia Flash,
    558–560

Notes

Notes